Communications
in Computer and Information Science   89

Natarajan Meghanathan   Selma Boumerdassi
Nabendu Chaki   Dhinaharan Nagamalai (Eds.)

Recent Trends
in Network Security
and Applications

Third International Conference, CNSA 2010
Chennai, India, July 23-25, 2010
Proceedings

 Springer

Volume Editors

Natarajan Meghanathan
Jackson State University, Jackson, MS, USA
E-mail: nmeghanathan@jsums.edu

Selma Boumerdassi
CNAM / CEDRIC, Paris, France
E-mail: selma.boumerdassi@cedric.fr

Nabendu Chaki
University of Calcutta, India
E-mail: nchaki@gmail.com

Dhinaharan Nagamalai
Wireilla Net Solutions PTY Ltd, Australia
E-mail: dhinthia@yahoo.com

Library of Congress Control Number: 2010930428

CR Subject Classification (1998): C.2, K.6.5, D.4.6, E.3, H.4, D.2

ISSN   1865-0929
ISBN-10   3-642-14477-2 Springer Berlin Heidelberg New York
ISBN-13   978-3-642-14477-6 Springer Berlin Heidelberg New York

springer.com

© Springer-Verlag Berlin Heidelberg 2010
Printed in Germany

Typesetting: Camera-ready by author, data conversion by Scientific Publishing Services, Chennai, India
Printed on acid-free paper   06/3180   5 4 3 2 1 0

Preface

The Third International Conference on Network Security and Applications (CNSA-2010) focused on all technical and practical aspects of security and its applications for wired and wireless networks. The goal of this conference is to bring together researchers and practitioners from academia and industry to focus on understanding modern security threats and countermeasures, and establishing new collaborations in these areas. Authors are invited to contribute to the conference by submitting articles that illustrate research results, projects, survey work and industrial experiences describing significant advances in the areas of security and its applications, including:

- Network and Wireless Network Security
- Mobile, Ad Hoc and Sensor Network Security
- Peer-to-Peer Network Security
- Database and System Security
- Intrusion Detection and Prevention
- Internet Security, and Applications Security and Network Management
- E-mail Security, Spam, Phishing, E-mail Fraud
- Virus, Worms, Trojon Protection
- Security Threats and Countermeasures (DDoS, MiM, Session Hijacking, Replay attack etc.)
- Ubiquitous Computing Security
- Web 2.0 Security
- Cryptographic Protocols
- Performance Evaluations of Protocols and Security Application

There were 182 submissions to the conference and the Program Committee selected 63 papers for publication. The book is organized as a collection of papers from the First International Workshop on Trust Management in P2P Systems (IWTMP2PS 2010), the First International Workshop on Database Management Systems (DMS-2010), and the First International Workshop on Mobile, Wireless and Networks Security (MWNS-2010). Finally, we would like to thank the General Chairs, local organizing team and Program Committee members and reviewers for arranging and organizing this conference.

Natarajan Meghanathan
Selma Boumerdassi
Nabendu Chaki
Dhinaharan Nagamalai

Organization

General Chairs

S.K. Ghosh   Indian Institute of Technology, Kharagpur, India
David C. Wyld   Southeastern Louisiana University, USA
Selwyn Piramuthu   University of Florida, USA

Steering Committee

Selma Boumerdassi   CNAM/CEDRIC, France
Chih-Lin Hu   National Central University, Taiwan
Dhinaharan Nagamalai   Wireilla Net Solutions PTY LTD, Australia
Krzysztof Walkowiak   Wroclaw University of Technology, Poland
Abdul Kadhir Ozcan   The American University, Cyprus
Robert C. Hsu   Chung Hua University, Taiwan
Sajid Hussain   Acadia University, Canada

Program Committee Members

Sajid Hussain   Acadia University, Canada
Seungmin Rho   Carnegie Mellon University, USA
Emmanuel Bouix   iKlax Media, France
Charalampos Z. Patrikakis   National Technical University of Athens, Greece
Chin-Chih Chang   Chung Hua University, Taiwan
Yung-Fa Huang   Chaoyang University of Technology, Taiwan
Jeong-Hyun Park   Electronics Telecommunication Research
                               Institute, South Korea
A. Arokiasamy   Eastern Mediterranean University, Cyprus
Abdul Kadir Ozcan   The American University, Cyprus
Al-Sakib Khan Pathan   Kyung Hee University, South Korea
Andy Seddon   Asia Pacific Institute of Information Technology,
                               Malaysia
Athanasios Vasilakos   University of Western Macedonia, Greece
Atilla Elci   Eastern Mediterranean University, Cyprus
B Srinivasan   Monash University, Australia
Balasubramanian K.   Lefke European University , Cyprus
Balasubramanian Karuppiah   MGR University, India
Bong-Han, Kim   Chongju University, South Korea
Boo-Hyung Lee   KongJu National University, South Korea
Chih-Lin Hu   National Central University, Taiwan
Cho Han Jin   Far East University, South Korea
Cynthia Dhinakaran   Hannam University, South Korea

Organized By

ACADEMY & INDUSTRY RESEARCH COLLABORATION CENTER (AIRCC)

Workshop Preface

The *First International Workshop on Trust Management in Peer-to-Peer (P2P) Systems* (IWTMP2PS 2010), held in Chennai, India, during July 23–25, 2010, was co-located with the Third International Conference on Network Security and Applications (CNSA 2010). It attracted many local and international delegates, presenting a balanced mixture of intellects from the East and from the West.

A distributed system involves numerous entities, many of which have not yet previously interacted with each other. Thus, there is a need for a flexible and general-purpose trust management system which can maintain information that is current, secured and consistent for these different entities in the distributed system. Hence, P2P computing has emerged as a new distributed computing paradigm for sharing distributed resources that are available on the Internet. Currently, more complex P2P systems require more management solutions especially in the areas of security and trust. The open and anonymous nature of a P2P network makes it an ideal medium for attackers to spread malicious content. Hence, the IWTMP2PS 2010 workshop was aimed at establishing a state of the art for security and trust in P2P systems, and to provide a forum for the exchange of ideas between P2P researchers working on trust and security issues. The areas of interest included topics such as advances in theoretical, managerial and/or performance analysis of security and trust issues in P2P frameworks and applications.

The IWTMP2PS 2010 Workshop Committee rigorously invited submissions for many months from researchers, scientists, engineers, students and practitioners related to the relevant themes and tracks of the workshop. This effort guaranteed submissions from an unparalleled number of internationally recognized top P2P trust and security experts. All the submissions underwent a strenuous peer-review process which comprised expert reviewers. These reviewers were selected from a talented pool of Technical Committee members and external reviewers on the basis of their expertise. The papers were then reviewed based on their contributions, technical content, originality and clarity. The entire process, which includes the submission, review and acceptance processes, was done electronically. All these efforts undertaken by the Organizing and Technical Committees led to an exciting, rich and a high-quality technical workshop program, which featured high-impact presentations, for all attendees to enjoy, appreciate and expand their expertise in the latest developments in P2P trust and security research.

In closing, IWTMP2PS 2010 brought together researchers, scientists, engineers, students and practitioners to exchange and share their experiences, new ideas and research results in all aspects of the main workshop themes and tracks, and to discuss the practical challenges encountered and the solutions adopted. We would like to thank the General and Program Chairs, organization staff, the members of the Technical Program Committees and external reviewers for their excellent and tireless work. We also want to thank Springer for the strong support and the authors who contributed to the success of the workshop. We also sincerely wish that all attendees benefited scientifically from the workshop and wish them every success in their research.

It is the humble wish of the workshop organizers that the professional dialogue among the researchers, scientists, engineers, students and educators continues beyond the workshop and that the friendships and collaborations forged will linger and prosper for many years to come.

Antonio Coronato
K. Chandra Sekaran
Sajid Hussain
Jiankun Hu
Sabu M. Thampi
Victor Govindaswamy

Workshop Organization

Workshop General Chairs

Antonio Coronato — Institute for High Performance Computing and Networking, Italy

K. Chandra Sekaran — Indian Institute of Technology Madras, India

Sajid Hussain — Fisk University, USA

Program Chairs

Jiankun Hu — RMIT University, Australia

Sabu M. Thampi — Rajagiri School of Engineering and Technology, Kerala, India

Victor Govindaswamy — Texas A&M University, USA

TPC Members

Andreas Riener — Johannes Kepler University Linz, Austria

Aneel Rahim — King Saud University, Saudi Arabia

Ankur Gupta — Model Institute of Engineering and Technology, Jammu, India

Chang Wu Yu (James) — Chung Hua University, P.R. China

Claudio E. Palazzi — University of Padua, Italy

Danda B Rawat — Old Dominion University, USA

Deepak Garg — Thappar University, India

Demin Wang — Microsoft, USA

Elvira Popescu — University of Craiova, Romania

Fangyang Shen — Northern New Mexico College, USA

Farag Azzedin — King Fahd University of Petroleum and Minerals, Saudi Arabia

Fatos Xhafa — Universitat Politecnica de Catalunya, Spain

Felix Gomez Marmol — Universidad de Murcia, Spain

Francesco Quaglia — Sapienza Università di Roma, Italy

Ghulam Kassem — NWFP University of Engineering and Technology, Pakistan

Gregorio Martinez — University of Murcia (UMU), Spain

Guangzhi Qu — Oakland University, USA

Hamed Saghaei — Shahed University, Iran

Helge Janicke — De Montfort University, UK

Houcine Hassan — Universidad Politecnica de Valencia, Spain

Ioannis E. Anagnostopoulos — University of the Aegean, Greece

Jack Hu — Microsoft, USA

Jaime Lloret Mauri	Polytechnic University of Valencia, Spain
Jerzy Doma	AGH University of Science and Technology, Poland
Jianguo Ding	Norwegian University of Science and Technology (NTNU), Norway
Jiping Xiong	Zhejiang Normal University of China, P.R. China
John Mathew	Rajagiri School of Engineering and Technology, India
John Strassner	Pohang University of Science and Technology, Republic of Korea
Jonathan Loo	Brunel University, UK
Juan Carlos Cano	Universidad Politecnica de Valencia, Spain
Lourdes Penalver	Universidad Politecnica de Valencia, Spain
Madhukumar S.D.	National Institute of Technology Calicut, India
Marjan Naderan Tahan	Amirkabir University of Technology, Iran
Markus Fiedler	Blekinge Institute of Technology, Sweden
Michael Hempel	University of Nebraska, USA
Mohamed Ali Kaafar	INRIA Rhone-Alpes, France
Mohsen Sharifi	Iran University of Science and Technology, Iran
Niloy Ganguly	Indian Institute of Technology, Kharagpur, India
Nouha Oualha,	Telecom ParisTech, France
Paulo Gondim	Universidade de Brasilia, Brazil
Phan Cong-Vinh	London South Bank University, UK
Ramakant Komali	RWTH Aachen University, Germany
Renjie huang	Sensorweb Research Laboratory, Washington State University, USA
Roksana Boreli	University of NSW, Australia
Salman Abdul Moiz	Centre for Development of Advanced Computing, Bangalore, India
Samir Saklikar	RSA, Bangalore, India
Sathish Rajasekhar	RMIT University, Australia
Shajee Mohan B.S	Govt. Engineering College, Calicut University, India
Shan Cang Li	Swansea University, UK
Stephan Sigg	Technische Universität Braunschweig, Germany
Steven Gordon	Thammasat University, Thailand
Subir Saha	Nokia Siemens Networks, India
T.S.B Sudarshan	Amrita Vishwa Vidya Peetham University, Bangalore, India
Thomas C. Schmidt	Hamburg University of Applied Science, Germany
Thorsten Strufe	Technische Universität Darmstadt, Germany
Velmurugan Ayyadurai	University of Surrey, UK
Waleed W. Smari	University of Dayton, USA
Wang Wei	Zhejiang University, P.R. China
Yann Busnel	University of Nantes, France
Yonglin Ren	University of Ottawa, Canada
Zeeshan Shafi Khan	King Saud University, Saudi Arabia
Zhihua Cui	Taiyuan University of Science and Technology, P.R. China

Table of Contents

The Third International Conference on Network Security and Applications (CNSA 2010)

First International Workshop on Trust Management in P2P Systems (IWTMP2PS 2010) P2P

First International Workshop on Database Management Systems (DMS 2010) and MWNS 2010

Secure Framework for Data Centric Heterogeneous Wireless Sensor Networks

M.K. Sandhya[1] and K. Murugan[2]

[1] Research Scholar, Anna University Chennai, Chennai-25
mksans@gmail.com
[2] Assistant Professor, Ramanujan Computing Centre, Anna University Chennai , Chennai-25
murugan@annauniv.edu

Abstract. Data aggregation is an important task in data centric heterogeneous wireless sensor networks because of its varying power and computational capabilities. Due to the deployment of sensor nodes in large numbers for different applications, a single node is not sufficient for performing data aggregation. Hence multiple nodes are required to summarize the relevant information from huge data sets. The process of data aggregation is vulnerable to many threats like loss of cryptographic keys, false data injection etc. To address these issues, we present the Secure Data Aggregation with Key Management (SDAKM) scheme. It provides a secure framework for the data centric heterogeneous wireless sensor networks using additive privacy homomorphism. It uses the heterogeneity of the sensor nodes for performing encrypted data processing and also provides an efficient key management scheme for data communication among sensor nodes in the network. This scheme offers higher security and has less computing overhead as it uses additive privacy homomorphism.

Keywords: Data Centric Heterogeneous Wireless Sensor Networks, Data Aggregation, Security, Key Management, Privacy Homomorphism.

1 Introduction

Heterogeneous Wireless Sensor Networks comprises of numerous wireless sensor nodes having different physical capabilities in terms of energy, computing power, or network bandwidth. Generally they are useful for a wide spectrum of applications, such as military applications, remote surveillance, target tracking. Fig 1 shows the heterogeneous wireless sensor networks. Typically, there are different types of nodes in heterogeneous wireless sensor networks such as the normal sensor nodes and the aggregator nodes. The aggregator nodes have higher computing capabilities than the normal nodes. These aggregator nodes collect data from a subset of the network, aggregate the data using a suitable aggregation function and then transmit the aggregated result to the next aggregator. A few nodes called the querying nodes process the received sensor data and derive meaningful information reflecting the events in the target field. The base station interacts with the network to get the aggregated information. In this process of data aggregation, security is a serious issue as it is vulnerable to many threats.

N. Meghanathan et al. (Eds.): CNSA 2010, CCIS 89, pp. 1–10, 2010.

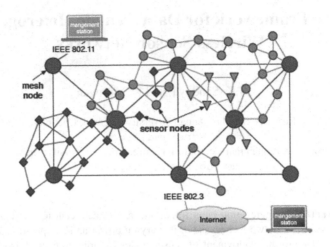

Fig. 1. Heterogeneous Wireless Sensor Networks

2 Preliminaries

Privacy homomorphism or homomorphic encryption is a special class of encryption functions which allow the encrypted data to be operated on directly without requiring any knowledge about the decryption function. The definition of a privacy homomorphism is as follows:

Definition 1: Suppose E_K $(\cdot)$ is an encryption function with key K and D_K $(\cdot)$ is the corresponding decryption function. Then E_K $(\cdot)$ is homomorphic with the operator $\circ$, if there is an efficient algorithm Alg such that: Alg $(E_K(x), E_K(y)) = E_K(x \circ y)$

For example, RSA algorithm is a multiplicative homomorphic encryption, that is, $\circ$ is multiplication. Although RSA gives a good demonstration for privacy homomorphism, it cannot support addition which is the most frequently used operation. For use in most applications, a practical homomorphic encryption scheme needs to support two basic types of encrypted data processing, namely addition and scalar multiplication.

Addition: Given $E_K(x)$ and $E_K(y)$, there exists a computationally efficient algorithm Add such that: $E_K(x + y) = $ Add $(E_K(x), E_K(y))$. That is, $E_K(x + y)$ can be found easily from $E_K(x)$ and $E_K(y)$ without needing to know what x or y is.

Scalar Multiplication: Given $E_K(x)$ and t, there exists a computationally efficient algorithm sMulti such that: $E_K(t \cdot x) = $ sMulti$(E_K(x), t)$. That is, E_K $(t \cdot x)$ can be found easily from t and $E_K(x)$ without needing to know what x is. When a scheme supports addition, it would also support scalar multiplication because E_K $(t \cdot x)$ can be achieved by summing $E_K(x)$ successively t times.

3 Related Work

In this section we review the existing key management and various security schemes for data aggregation in wireless sensor networks.

3.1 Key Pre-distribution Schemes

Eschenauer-Gligor [1] (E-G) proposed a random key pre- distribution scheme Based on the E-G Scheme, Chan et al. [2] proposed a q-Composite random key pre-distribution scheme. The major difference between this scheme and the E-G Scheme is that q Common Keys (q >=1), are needed to establish secure communications between a pair of nodes. Du et al. proposed a new key pre-distribution scheme [3], which substantially improved the resilience of the network compared to the existing schemes. Liu and Ning [4, 5] independently developed a scheme using pre-deployment knowledge. However, this introduces a novel group-based deployment model. This group-based deployment model is further explored by Huang et al [6, 7]. Perrig et al. proposed SPINS [8], a security architecture specifically designed for sensor networks. In SPINS, each sensor node shares a secret key with the base station. Two sensor nodes cannot directly establish a secret key. However, they can use the base station as trusted third party to set up the secret key. Chan and Perrig [9] proposed PIKE, a class of key-establishment protocols that involves one or more sensor nodes as a trusted intermediary to facilitate key establishment.

3.2 Revocation of Keys

Key revocation for captured sensor nodes poses new design challenges that do not arise in key pre-distribution. Key revocation protocols are carried out in the presence of active adversaries. These adversaries can monitor and modify network messages and also pretend to be legitimate participants [10]. Recent research on key revocation in sensor networks illustrates two different approaches with orthogonal properties; i.e., a centralized approach and distributed approach. In the centralized approach, upon detection of a compromised node, the base station broadcasts a revocation message to all sensor nodes in order to remove the copies of keys from the compromised node. In distributed revocation, decisions are made by the neighbors of a compromised node.

3.3 Secure Data Aggregation Schemes

In wireless sensor network domain, secure data aggregation is a serious issue. In [11], random sampling mechanisms and interactive proofs are used to check the correctness of the aggregated data at the base station. In [12], witness nodes aggregate data and compute MAC to verify the correctness of the aggregators' data at base station. Because the data validation is performed at base station, the transmission of false data and MAC up to base station adversely affects the utilization of sensor network resources. In [13], sensor nodes use the cryptographic algorithms only when a cheating activity is detected. Topological constraints are introduced to build a Secure Aggregation Tree (SAT) that facilitates the monitoring of data aggregators. In [14], a Secure hop-by-hop Data Aggregation Protocol (SDAP) is proposed. In this protocol more trust is placed on the high-level nodes (i.e., nodes closer to the root) compared to low level sensor nodes, during aggregation process. Privacy homomorphism is introduced by Rivest et al. [15]. For example, Rivest's asymmetric key algorithm RSA is multiplicatively homomorphic. Due to their high computational overhead it is not feasible for sensor node. The privacy homomorphic encryption algorithm introduced by Domingo-Ferrer [16] is symmetric key based scheme.

4 SDAKM Scheme

In this section we propose the Secure Data Aggregation with Key Management (SDAKM) scheme for data centric heterogeneous wireless sensor networks.

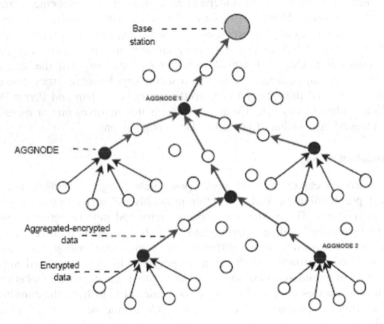

Fig 2. Network Model for Data Aggregation

Due to large scale deployment, multiple aggregator nodes are required to perform data aggregation. The aggregator nodes have higher computing capabilities than the normal sensor nodes and they aggregate the relevant information from the sensor nodes. The sensor nodes transmit encrypted data to the aggregators. Hence the aggregators must be capable of performing encrypted data processing. To provide additional security there must be an efficient key management scheme for data communication among the sensor nodes. In SDAKM scheme, we perform Secure Data Aggregation using Iterated Hill Cipher (IHC) technique. It is an additive privacy homomorphism scheme for aggregator to aggregator communication. An efficient Key Management scheme is presented for the sensor node to sensor node communication in the network. This key management scheme involves key predistribution and revocation scheme. This scheme relies on decentralized approach for key management. It exploits the heterogeneity of the sensor nodes with respect to computing capabilities. The problem of key revocation in compromised nodes is addressed by means of a distributed approach.

4.1 Secure Data Aggregation Scheme

The encryption and decryption of an Iterated Hill Cipher (IHC) with k iterations is described below:

Encryption: The encryption function is of the form E $(\cdot)$: $V_l \to V_l \times V_l$ and the encryption process is given below:
• Randomly choose a key matrix $A \in M_{lxl}$ and an initialization vector $u \in V_l$.
• Set $x_{-1} = u$ and $x_0 = m$, where $m \in V_l$ is the plaintext vector.
• For $0 \leq i < k$, compute $x_{i+1} = Ax_i - x_{i-1}$ (For example, $x_1 = Ax_0 - x_{-1}$.)
• Cipher text $c = (x_k, x_{k-1})$.

Decryption: With $c = (x_k, x_{k-1})$ as the initial condition, iterate the following k times to get back x_0 which is the plaintext: $x_{i-1} = Ax_i - x_{i+1}$

The major advantage of this iterative algorithm is that there is no restriction on the choice of A. Addition and scalar multiplication of the plaintexts can be done by component-wise vector addition and scalar multiplication of the cipher texts.

4.2 Efficient Key Management Scheme

Here, we also propose a scheme for efficient key management in heterogeneous wireless sensor networks. This scheme relies on decentralized approach for key predistribution as well as revocation. The algorithm for key predistribution and revocation comprises of the following:
a) Key Predistribution Phase: In this step the keys are predistributed from the key pools. Fig 3 indicates the key predistribution from the given pools.

Node	Key 1	Key 2 . . .
1	0001001011	0101111001
2	1000011000	0001001011
-	-	-

Fig. 3. Key Pool

b) Shared-Key Discovery Phase: Here the common key is identified between the neighboring nodes from the predistributed keys (refer Fig 4).

Node	Shared Key 1	Shared Key 2
2	1010101111	1000111100
3	1000101010	-

Neighbors for Node 1

Fig. 4. Sharing of keys

c) Path-Key Establishment Phase: After secret key discovery, the secure path for data communication is established. It includes encryption and decryption (refer Fig 5).

Path 1-3			
Encryption	Plain Text 01000111	Key 0000011000	Cipher Text 00000010
Decryption	Cipher Text 00000010	Key 0000011000	Plain Text 01000111

Fig. 5. Encryption & Decryption Process

d) Key Revocation phase: If a node is either compromised or captured by an adversary then the keys shared between the nodes are revoked. This is done by voting scheme. The compromised nodes are identified by their behavior and such nodes are isolated.

5   Performance Evaluation

In this section we evaluate the performance of the SDAKM scheme by analyzing the security aspects of the IHC technique and then the key management scheme in the context of data centric heterogeneous wireless sensor networks.

5.1   Security Analysis of IHC

For decrypting a cipher text of IHC, both A (the secret key matrix) and k (the number of iteration steps) should be known. Even if an adversary knew the key matrix A, without the knowledge of k, he would not be unable to decrypt any given cipher text. Therefore, if the number of iterations k is kept secret as a part of the private key, the security of IHC is increased. Moreover, if a different u is used for encrypting each plaintext vector, the security of IHC could be significantly improved. The result is summarized by the following lemma.

Lemma 1: If each plaintext vector is encrypted with a different initialization vector while the same key matrix is used, IHC is secure to both cipher text-only and known-plaintext attacks.

This homomorphic encryption scheme has the following properties suitable for our network model:

a) **Secure to Cipher text-only Attacks**: Given only the cipher text $E_K(x)$, it is hard for an adversary to find the encryption key K or the corresponding plaintext x. IHC could even be secure to known plaintext attacks if different initialization vectors are used for each plaintext.

b) **Additive**: $E_K(x+y)$ can be found easily from $E_K(x)$ and $E_K(y)$ without needing to know what x or y is.

c) **Scalar Multiplicative**: $E_K(t \cdot x)$ can be found easily from t and $E_K(x)$ without needing to know what x is.

d) **Randomized Zero Encryption**: Suppose $x_1 + y_1 = 0$ and $x_2 + y_2 = 0$ (usually in modular arithmetic, say in Z_N), then

- $Add(E_K(x_1), E_K(y_1)) = Add(E_K(x_2), E_K(y_2))$ if and only if $x_1 = x_2$, $y_1 = y_2$.
- $D_K(Add(E_K(x_1), E_K(y_1))) = D_K(Add(E_K(x_2), E_K(y_2))) = 0$.

5.2 Security Analysis of Key Management Scheme

First, scalability is analyzed i.e., the number of nodes with respect to the number of keys. It is identified from Fig 6 that by using a trusted third party (KDC), the number of keys required is lesser than that of the random key pre-distribution scheme. In KDC method the number of keys is (n-1) and for the SDAKM scheme it is n*(3/2). Here n, is the number of nodes in the network. But this increase in number of keys does not pose a threat to the memory and storage requirements of heterogeneous wireless sensor networks due to decentralized approach of our scheme.

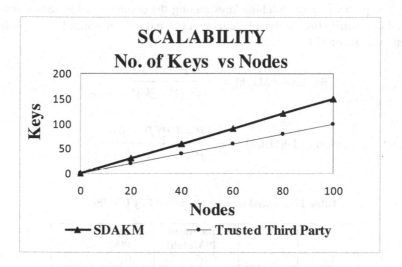

Fig. 6. Scalability- Keys versus Nodes

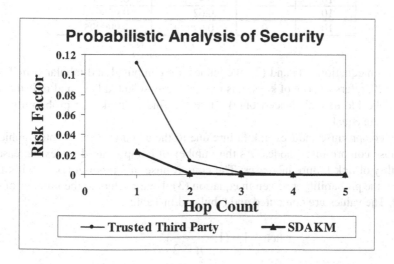

Fig. 7. Probabilistic Analysis of Security- Risk Factor versus Hop Count

Next, the probabilistic analysis of security is evaluated. In this, the risk factor is compared with the hop count. It is noted from Fig 7 that the risk factor reduces as the hop count increases in the proposed scheme as compared to using a KDC. It is because of the fact that as the number of trustworthy nodes increases as the number of intermediate nodes (hop count) increases and hence the risk factor reduces. Moreover, for single hop networks or for networks having lesser intermediate nodes i.e., hop count <=2, the proposed scheme offers very high security compared to KDC scheme.

Next we analyze the probability of keys matching among the sensor nodes for data communication. There is a comparison between balanced and unbalanced key distribution. The probability of matching keys among the communicating sensor nodes in balanced key distribution is given by equation (1) and for unbalanced key distribution is given by equation (2).

$$\text{Balanced P[Match]} = 1 - \frac{((P - k)!)^2}{P!(P - 2k)!} \tag{1}$$

$$\text{Unbalanced P[Match]} = 1 - \frac{(P - k)!(P - m)!}{P!(P - m - k)!} \tag{2}$$

Table 1. Balanced verses Unbalanced Key Distribution

m	k	Balanced P[Match]	Unbalanced P[Match]
10	1	0.05	0.5
10	2	0.19	0.763
10	3	0.4	0.89
10	4	0.62	0.9566
10	10	0.999995	0.999995

Based on equations (1) and (2), the values are computed and tabulated in Table 1. Here P =20, refers to pool of keys, k is the randomly selected keys and m is the subset of P (applicable to Unbalanced only). Here we find as m=k, the probability of key matching are equal.

Node compromise induces link failure due to the capture of the cryptographic keys from those compromised nodes. As the number of compromised nodes increases the probability of link failure increases. The compromise of s random nodes will affect a link with the probability as given in equation (3). Here r refers to the number of nodes per key. The values are computed and tabulated in Table 2.

$$\text{fail(s)} \approx 1 - (1 - \frac{r - 2}{n - 2})^s \tag{3}$$

Table 2. Link Failure probability versus Compromised nodes

Compromised nodes	Probability of link failure r = Number of nodes per key	
s	r=20	r=30
10	0.16	0.24
20	0.31	0.43
50	0.42	0.76
100	0.83	0.94
200	0.97	0.996
300	0.995	0.9998
400	0.9993	0.99998
500	0.9998	0.999999

6 Conclusion

SDAKM offers better security to the data centric heterogeneous wireless sensor networks in spite of its varied computing capabilities of the sensor nodes by providing a secure framework through encrypted data processing for data aggregation and an efficient decentralized key management. It helps in achieving better efficiency compared to using trusted third party or by applying asymmetric cryptography (Public Key Infrastructures). This is evident from the analysis of security. This scheme does not involve much computing overhead as it uses homomorphic encryption and symmetric key processing.

References

1. Eschenauer, L., Gligor, V.D.: A Key Management scheme for distributed sensor networks. In: Proceedings of the 9th ACM Conference on Computer and Communication Security, Washington DC, USA (2002)
2. Chan, H., Perrig, A., Song, D.: Random Key Predistribution Schemes for Sensor Networks. In: IEEE Symposium on Security and Privacy, p. 197 (2003)
3. Du, W., Deng, J., Han, Y.S., Varshney, P.K.: A Key Predistribution Scheme for Sensor Networks using Deployment Knowledge. IEEE Transactions on Dependable and Secure Computing 3(1), 62–77 (2008)
4. Liu, D., Ning, P.: Establishing Pairwise Keys in Distributed Sensor Networks. In: Proc. 10th ACM Conf. Computer and Comm. Security (CCS), pp. 52–61 (2003)
5. Liu, D., Ning, P.: Location-Based Paiwise Key Establishments for Relatively Static Sensor Networks. In: Proc. ACM Workshop Security of Ad Hoc and Sensor Networks (2003)
6. Huang, D., Mehta, M., van de Liefvoort, A., Medhi, M.: Modeling Pairwise Key Establishment for Random Key Predistribution in Large Scale Sensor Networks. IEEE/ACM Transactions on Networking 15(5), 1204–1215 (2007)
7. Huang, D., Mehta, M., Medhi, D., Harn, L.: Location-Aware Key Management Scheme for Wireless Sensor Networks. In: Proc. ACM Workshop Security of Ad Hoc ang Sensor Networks (2004)

 8. Perrig, A., Szewczyk, R., Tygar, J.D., Wen, V., Culler, D.E.: SPINS: security protocols for sensor networks. Wireless Networks 8(5), 521–534 (2002)
 9. Chan, H., Perrig, A.: PIKE: Peer Intermediaries for Key Establishment in Sensor Networks. In: Proc. IEEE INFOCOM (2005)
10. Chan, H., Gligor, V.D., Perrig, A., Muralidharan, G.: On the Distribution and Revocation of Cryptography Keys in Sensor Networks. IEEE Transactions on Dependable and Secure Computing 2(3), 233–247 (2005)
11. Przydatek, B., Song, D., Perrig, A.: SIA: Secure information aggregation in sensor networks. In: Proc. of SenSys 2003, pp. 255–265 (2003)
12. Du, W., Deng, J., Han, Y.S., Varshney, P.K.: A Witness-Based Approach for Data Fusion Assurance in Wireless Sensor Networks. In: Proc. GLOBECOM 2003, pp. 1435–1439 (2003)
13. Wu, K., Dreef, D., Sun, B., Xiao, Y.: Secure data aggregation without persistent cryptographic operations in wireless sensor networks. Ad Hoc Networks 5(1), 100–111 (2007)
14. Yang, Y., Wang, X., Zhu, S., Cao, G.: SDAP: A Secure Hop-by-Hop Data Aggregation Protocol for Sensor Networks. In: Proc. of ACM MOBIHOC 2006 (2006)
15. Rivest, R.L., Adleman, L., Dertouzos, M.L.: On Data Banks and Privacy Homomorphisms. Foundations of Secure Computation, 169–179 (1978)
16. Domingo-Ferrer, J.: A provably secure additive and multiplicative privacy homomorphism. In: Chan, A.H., Gligor, V.D. (eds.) ISC 2002. LNCS, vol. 2433, pp. 471–483. Springer, Heidelberg (2002)

Data Security in Local Area Network Based on Fast Encryption Algorithm

Prof. G. Ramesh[1] and Dr. R. Umarani[2]

[1] Dept of MCA, Thiruvalluvar College of Engineering & Technology, Tamilnadu
mgrameshmca@yahoo.com
[2] Reader in Computer Science, Sri Sarada college for women, Salem -16
umainweb@gmail.com

Abstract. Hacking is one of the greatest problems in the wireless local area networks. Many algorithms have been used to prevent the outside attacks to eavesdrop or prevent the data to be transferred to the end-user safely and correctly. In this paper, a new symmetrical encryption algorithm is proposed that prevents the outside attacks. The new algorithm avoids key exchange between users and reduces the time taken for the encryption and decryption. It operates at high data rate in comparison with The Data Encryption Standard (DES), Triple DES (TDES), Advanced Encryption Standard (AES-256), and RC6 algorithms. The new algorithm is applied successfully on both text file and voice message.

Keywords: Plaintext; Encryption; Decryption; S-Box; Key-updating; Outside attack.

1 Introduction

Wireless Local Area Network (WLAN) is one of the fastest-growing technologies. The demand for connecting devices without the use of cables is increasing everywhere. WLAN is found in the office buildings, and in many other public areas [1]. The security in WLAN is based on cryptography, the science and art of transforming messages to make them secure and immune to attacks by authenticating the sender to receiver within the WLAN. The cryptography algorithms are divided into two groups: symmetric-encryption algorithms and asymmetric-encryption algorithms. There are a lot of symmetric-encryption algorithms used in WLAN, such as DES [2], TDES [3], AES [4], and RC6 [5]. In all these algorithms, both sender and receiver have used the same key for encryption and decryption processes respectively. The outside attackers use the fixed plaintext (such as: the company-title which is sent in the first packets of the message) and encrypted text to obtain the key used in the WLAN. A new symmetrical encryption algorithm is proposed in this paper. The new algorithm avoids fixed-key exchange between sender and receiver with each authentication process in WLAN. The paper is organized as follows. Section 2 gives a short review of the symmetrical-encryption algorithms. Section 3 presents the proposed algorithm. Section 4 shows the results. Finally, conclusions are presented in section 5.

N. Meghanathan et al. (Eds.): CNSA 2010, CCIS 89, pp. 11–26, 2010.

2 Review on the Symmetrical-Encryption Algorithms

There is a lot of the symmetrical-encryption algorithms used in WLAN. DES [2], known as Data Encryption Algorithm (DEA) by the ANSI [6] and the DEA-1 by the ISO [6] remained a worldwide standard for very long time and was replaced by AES on October 2000. DES provides a basis for the comparison of new algorithms. It is a block cipher symmetric algorithm that uses the same key for both encryption and decryption. The basic building block (a substitution followed by a permutation) is called a round and is repeated for 16 times [2]. The substitutions process depends on the S-Box. S-Box is a matrix of 4 rows and 16 columns. DES has 8 different S-Boxes in each round. S-Box is used to map the input code to another code to the output. The input code specifies the output code position in this S-Box. The first and last bits specify the row number, and the rest bits specify the column number. The permutation tables are used for changing the bit-orders in the packet. For each DES round, a sub-key is derived from the original key using an algorithm called key schedule which is the same for encryption and decryption except for the minor difference in the order (reverse) of the sub-keys for decryption. In the encryption process, DES encrypts the data in 64-bit blocks using a 64-bit key (although its effective key length in reality is only 56-bit).

TDES is a block cipher formed from the DES cipher by using it three times. When it was found that a 56-bit key of DES is not enough to guard against brute force attacks, TDES was chosen as a simple way to enlarge the key space without the need to switch to a new algorithm. The simplest variant of TDES encryption operates as follows: DES(k3;DES-1(k2;DES(k1;M))), where M is the message block to be encrypted , k1, k2, and k3 are DES keys, and DES and DES-1 refer to the encryption and decryption modes respectively. While the TDES decryption operates as follows: DES-1(k1; DES(k2;DES-1(k3;C))) , where C is the cipher text block.

AES algorithm is a symmetric block. It is used to encrypt and decrypt the plaintext and cipher text of 128-bits respectively by using cryptographic keys of 128-bits (AES-128), 192-bits (AES-192), or 256-bits (AES-256). The number of rounds in the encryption or decryption processes depends on the key size.

RC6 is more accurately specified as RC6-w/r/b where the word size is w bits, encryption consists of a nonnegative number of rounds r, and b denotes the length of the encryption key in bytes. Since the AES submission is targeted at w = 32 and r = 20, RC6 shall be used as shorthand to refer to such versions. When any other value of w or r is intended in the text, the parameter values is specified as RC6-w/r. Of particular relevance to the AES effort is the versions of RC6 with 16-, 24-, and 32-byte keys.

The complexity of the algorithm and the key size enhance the data security in WLAN, and they increase the difficulty to the attackers to discover the original message.

The new algorithm adds some difficulties to the attackers to discover the key. These difficulties are

- The longer key size, 512-bits, compared with DES, TDES, AES-256, and RC6.
- The key-updating with each packet.

The new symmetrical algorithm is applied on a text message and voice message. The comparison between the plain text and the decrypted text is easier than voice message. The two approaches used for measuring speech quality are the subjective and the objective approaches [8]. Subjective measures assess speech quality based on the perceptual ratings by a group of listeners [9]. Objective measures assess speech quality using the physical parameters [10]. The physical parameters are calculated from equations (1, 2, 3, and 4).

$$SNR = 10 Log_{10} \frac{\sum_{i=1}^{N} x^2(i)}{\sum_{i=1}^{N} (x(i) - y(i))^2} \tag{1}$$

$$SNRseg = \frac{10}{M} \sum_{m=0}^{M-1} Log_{10} \sum_{i=Nm}^{Nm+N-1} \left(\frac{x^2(i)}{(x(i) - y(i))} \right)^2 \tag{2}$$

$$LLR = \left| Log \left(\frac{\overrightarrow{ax} \overrightarrow{Ry} \overrightarrow{ax}^T}{\overrightarrow{ay} \overrightarrow{Ry} \overrightarrow{ay}^T} \right) \right| \tag{3}$$

$$SD = \frac{1}{M} \sum_{m=0}^{M-1} \sum_{i=Nm}^{Nm+N-1} |Vx(i) - Vy(i)| \tag{4}$$

Where: SNR is the signal-to-noise ratio [10], x(i) and y(i) are the original and decrypted speech respectively, N is the total number of samples in both encrypted and decrypted speech signals, M is the number of segments in the speech signals, LLR is the Likelihood Ratio [10], $\overrightarrow{ax}$ and $\overrightarrow{ay}$ are the Linear Predictive Coding (LPC) for the original and decrypted speech signals respectively, $\overrightarrow{Ry}$ is the autocorrelation matrix for the decrypted speech signal, SD [10] is Spectral Distortion, and Vx(i) and Vy(i) are the spectrum of the original and the decrypted speech signals respectively in dB for a certain segment in time domain.

Correlation [11] is a measure of the relationship between two variables. If the two variables are

- In perfect correlation, then the correlation coefficient (C.C) equals one.
- Highly dependent (identical), In this case the encrypted data is the same as the original data and the encryption process failed in hiding the details of the original data.
- If the C.C equals zero, then the original data and its encryption are totally different, i.e., the encrypted data has no features and highly independent on the original data.

- If C.C equals (-1), this means the encrypted data is the negative of the original data.

So, the success of the encryption process means smaller values of the C.C. The C.C is measured by the following equation:

$$C.C = \frac{\sum_{i=1}^{N}(x_i - E(x))(y_i - E(y))}{\sqrt{\sum_{i=1}^{N}(x_i - E(x))^2}\sqrt{\sum_{i=1}^{N}(y_i - E(y))^2}} \tag{5}$$

Where: $E(x) = \frac{1}{N}\sum_{i=1}^{N}x_i$, and x and y are values of the original and encrypted data.

3   The New Symmetrical Algorithm

The new algorithm uses a key size of 512-bits to encrypt a plaintext of 512-bits during the 16-rounds. In this Algorithm, a series of transformations have been used depending on S-BOX, different shift processes, XOR-Gate, and AND-Gate. The S-Box is used to map the input code to another code at the output. It is a matrix of $16\times16\times16$. The S-Box consists of 16-slides, and each slide having 2-D of 16×16. The numbers from 0 to 255 are arranged in random positions in each slide. The S-Box is generated according to the flowchart of figure (1). Each slide in the S-Box is described by the following equation:

$$S^i \mid_{X\times Y} = S \mid_{X\times Y\times i} \tag{6}$$

Where i=1,2,...,16, and i is defined as the round number used in the key-generation, encryption, and the decryption processes. So, the first round operates on the first slide, $S^1 \mid_{X\times Y} = S \mid_{X\times Y\times 1}$, and the second round operates on the second slide, $S^2 \mid_{X\times Y} = S \mid_{X\times Y\times 2}$, and so on. For example, if the input 5A, in the hexadecimal form, is applied on the S-Box in round number 12, then $S^i \mid_{X\times Y} = S^{12} \mid_{X\times Y} = S \mid_{X\times Y\times 12}$. Let $S \mid_{X\times Y\times 12}$ have the contents of table (1). The output code takes the row number 5 and column number A, or the output code is ED.

3.1   Key Generation

The key generation generates 16-keys during 16-rounds. One key of them is used in one round of the encryption or decryption process. In the first time, the initial key is divided into four parts a, b, c, and d, 128-bits each. In each round of the key generation, there are series of the transformation used to generate the round-key. The round-key consists of four parts a*, b*, c*, and d*, and it is used in the same round – order to encrypt to the data, see figure (2).

The procedures of the key-generation are as the following:

Step 1: divide the initial key into four parts a, b, c, and d, 128-bits each.

For example, Let the initial key be

BC107FE3F95071555D8DB639D0782BD62F5D35EBCEA7627C7334D3A03
41F0D61CEEDB8AB2A8DE37195F350F5B4DF06BC54DB4585EE4538A331
8792CFCF4E112F

Thus,

a= BC107FE3F95071555D8DB639D0782BD6
b= 2F5D35EBCEA7627C7334D3A0341F0D61
c= CEEDB8AB2A8DE37195F350F5B4DF06BC
d= 54DB4585EE4538A3318792CFCF4E112F

Step 2: $a^* = a \oplus b$

a*=934D4A0837F713292EB96599E46726B7

Step 3: Horizontal Left-Shift (Circular Shift)

The c-part is rearranged to a matrix form of 4*4, and each element of the matrix appears as two hexadecimal numbers. No shift in the first row. The second, third, and forth row is left-shifted by one, two, three elements (circular shift) respectively.

$$C= \begin{array}{|c|c|c|c|} \hline CE & 2A & 95 & B4 \\ \hline ED & 8D & F3 & DF \\ \hline B8 & E3 & 50 & 06 \\ \hline AB & 71 & F5 & BC \\ \hline \end{array} \rightarrow h= \begin{array}{|c|c|c|c|} \hline CE & 2A & 95 & B4 \\ \hline 8D & F3 & DF & ED \\ \hline 50 & 06 & B8 & E3 \\ \hline BC & AB & 71 & F5 \\ \hline \end{array}$$

Step 4: $b^*=m= S^i \mid_{X \times Y} (h)$

h is mapped into another code by applying S-Box on h to have m at the output. Each round uses one slide from S-Box according to the round number i, where i=1,2,...,16, as discussed later. Let $S \mid_{X \times Y \times 12}$ have contents of table (1), thus b* is obtained as the following:

$$\begin{array}{|c|c|c|c|} \hline 57 & F2 & E9 & 94 \\ \hline 82 & 42 & 02 & D1 \\ \hline 85 & C8 & 3C & 6A \\ \hline 25 & 91 & 8A & 15 \\ \hline \end{array}$$

b*=57828525F242C891E9023C8A94D16A15

Step 5: Vertical Upper-Shift (Circular Shift)

The d-part is rearranged to a matrix form of 4*4, and each element of the matrix appears as two hexadecimal numbers. No shift in the first column. The second, third, and forth column is upper-shifted by one, two, three elements (circular shift) respectively.

$$d= \begin{array}{|c|c|c|c|} \hline 54 & EE & 31 & CF \\ \hline DB & 45 & 87 & 4E \\ \hline 45 & 38 & 92 & 11 \\ \hline 85 & A3 & CF & 2F \\ \hline \end{array} \rightarrow w= \begin{array}{|c|c|c|c|} \hline 54 & 45 & 92 & 2F \\ \hline DB & 38 & CF & CF \\ \hline 45 & A3 & 31 & 4E \\ \hline 85 & EE & 87 & 11 \\ \hline \end{array}$$

Step 6: $c^* = m \oplus w$

    c*=359C0A0B77A6B7F7BCD0D0DBB1E2404

Step 7: d*=a

    d*=BC107FE3F95071555D8DB639D0782BD6

       Thus, the round key consists of four parts a*, b*, c*, and d*, or Ki=934D4A0837F713292EB96599E46726B757828525F242C891E9023C8A9 4D16A15359C0A0B77A6B7F7BCD0D0DBB1E2404BC107FE3F95071555D 8DB639D0782BD6

Step 8: repeat the previous steps 15-times to obtain the 16-keys used to encrypt or decrypt the data.

3.2 Encryption

The Encryption process in the new algorithm is used to encrypt the plaintext of size of 512-bits by a key of size of 512-bits in each round during 16-rounds. Series of transformations are applied on the plaintext in each round as shown in figure (3) to obtain a cipher text finally.

Table 1. The contents of S-Box at round 12, $S^{12}|_{X*Y}$

	0	1	2	3	4	5	6	7	8	9	A	B	C	D	E	F
0	6E	C7	0B	F8	FF	75	C8	B9	07	49	5C	72	67	FC	0F	C3
1	DF	5B	2D	45	E3	FD	58	D2	CC	FE	AE	6F	A8	B4	70	80
2	42	B0	13	BC	5D	7B	F6	5A	65	2F	F2	44	73	EB	D6	CF
3	D0	3F	2B	A7	04	EC	18	B2	39	EA	8B	76	EA	D8	DA	90
4	D3	8E	3B	D1	F4	F9	33	3A	C2	DC	9A	4D	9D	9C	DE	4B
5	85	35	42	B5	F1	23	D4	81	14	79	ED	32	A6	EF	63	7E
6	8D	0A	17	7C	6C	1D	4A	21	E6	E8	B6	2C	88	9E	E5	B1
7	E7	8A	36	69	22	A5	87	E1	26	0D	89	29	A9	55	1B	97
8	95	F3	74	C6	EE	D5	68	4F	40	CE	30	6B	43	82	78	37
9	B3	64	E4	F7	1E	E9	1F	D9	28	52	48	F5	19	A4	10	1C
A	5F	A3	A0	15	C9	92	56	C1	0E	AC	F0	91	A2	7F	60	84
B	CD	A1	77	CA	94	53	09	0C	3C	8F	3D	93	25	50	31	71
C	E2	DB	41	AB	AA	24	1A	00	54	08	66	E0	06	9B	57	AD
D	C5	16	FA	7A	3E	CB	BE	BB	C0	D7	8C	61	6D	4E	27	02
E	FB	11	9F	6A	51	B7	86	20	2A	47	BA	01	12	D1	4F	26
F	AC	E5	72	42	C0	15	43	D0	95	56	7B	00	01	76	EF	D1

       The encryption procedures are as the following:

Step 1: $Kp = Kv \oplus Ki$

Where:

-    Ki is the round-key that generated by the key-generation process.
-    i is the round number, and i=1,2,…,16.
-    Kv is the value of the feedback, as shown in the figure (3), and its value in the first time is zeroes in all its 512-bits.

Step 2: $Kpi = S^i |_{X \times Y} (Kp)$

Kp is rearranged into a matrix format of 8×8, and each element has two hexadecimal numbers, as descript in the key-generation procedures. Then, Kp is applied on one slide of the S-Box according to the round number to produce Kpi. Kpi is a 512-bits key. It is used to update the total key used to encrypt the data with each packet depending on the feedback as shown in figure (3). Kpi value is backed to AND with Rv to obtain Kv, see equation (7).

$$Kv = Kpi \bullet Rv \tag{7}$$

Where, Rv is a 512-bits key, and all bits are one. It is used to reset the system if the synchronization is lost during the encryption and decryption processes due to the total key-updating with each packet in each round.

Step 3: $Mn = S^i \mid_{X \times Y} (M)$

Step 4: $Ms = R(Mn)$

R(Mn) is a series of different shifting direction followed by XOR with Ki, see figure (4). The steps of R(Mn) as the following:

First, Horizontal Left-Shift (circular shift), as descript in key-generation process. But, the matrix becomes 8×8 instead of 4×4.

Second, Vertical Upper-Shift (circular shift), as descript in key-generation process. But, the matrix becomes 8×8 instead of 4×4.

Third, the result of shift processes is XORed with ki.

Step 5: $Mp = Ms \oplus Kpi$

Step 6: $M* = S^i \mid_{X \times Y} (Mp)$

Step 7: Repeat the previous steps 15-times to obtain the cipher text of size of 512-bits.

3.3 Decryption

The decryption of the new algorithm is the same as the encryption except:
- The direction of the encryption process is reversed, see figure (5).
- The direction of R(Mn) is reversed, see figure (6).
- The shift direction is reversed
  - Horizontal right-shift instead of left-shift
  - Vertical down-shift instead of upper-shift.

3.4 Applications

Text and voice messages are used as applications to prove the success of the new encryption algorithm to encrypt and decrypt the different messages. The application is run inside the WLAN environment, see figure (7). The voice message is also applied inside the Wired LAN environment using the point-to-point connection, see figure (8). The proposed algorithm uses the following:

i. Software
- Microsoft Visual C# dot net program.
- MATLAB v7.

ii. Hardware
- Desktop: Intel® Pentium® 4 CPU 2.8GHz 1GB of RAM
- LAPTOP Acer: Intel® Atom™ CPU N270 @ 1.60GHz 1GB of RAM
- A 54M Wireless Access Point of TP-Link (TL-WA501G)
- A 54M Wireless USB Adapter of TP-Link (TL-WN322G).
- 1.5 m Ethernet cable.

Figure (9.a) gives a plain text, and its decrypted version and the encrypted version are shown in figure (9.b and c). Figure (9.d) shows the other encrypted version for the same plain text. The difference between the two encrypted texts is cleared in figure (9.c and d) which proves the principle of the key-updating.

The voice encryption and decryption processes are applied between two computers using wired or wireless connection. The voice transmission is applied using a microphone at one side, and a speaker at the other computer. The distance between them is about 1.5m to minimize the errors and the noise even if using the wired or wireless connection. In the wireless connection, the original voice and the decrypted voice are shown in figure (10.a), and their spectrograms are shown in figure (10.b), and the encrypted voice and its spectrogram are shown in figure (10.c). In the wired connection, the original voice and the decrypted voice are shown in figure (11.a), and their spectrogram are shown in figure (11.b), and the encrypted voice and its spectrogram are shown in figure (11.c).

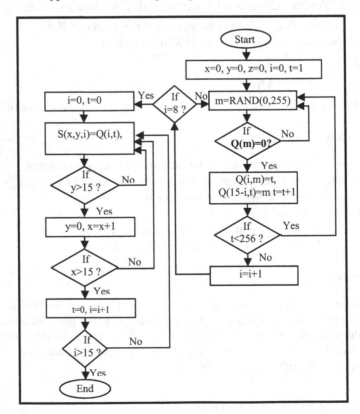

Fig. 1. Flowchart of the S-Box Generation $S|_{X \times Y \times i}$ $(16 \times 16 \times 16)$

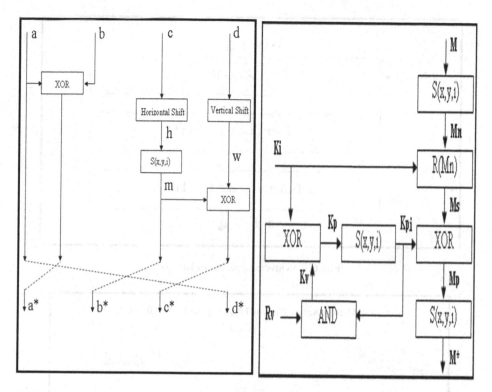

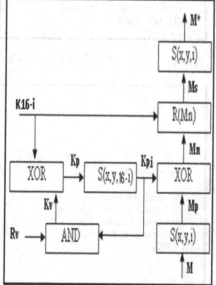

Fig. 2. Key-Generation procedures in one round   **Fig. 3.** The Encryption Process in each round

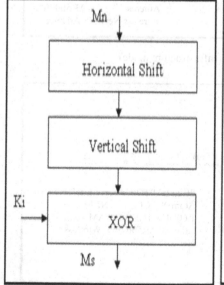

   **Fig. 4.** R(Mn) Steps   **Fig. 5.** The decryption Process in each round

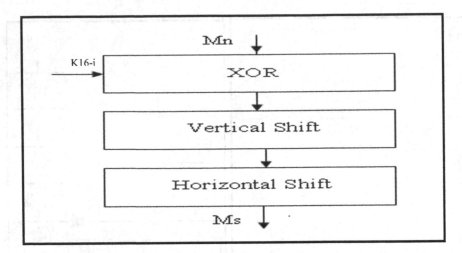

Fig. 6. The inverse process of R(Mn)

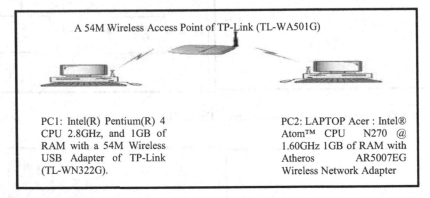

Fig. 7. Wireless LAN (Infrastructure mode)

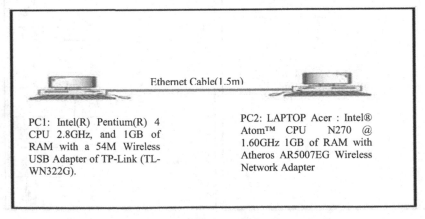

Fig. 8. Wired LAN (Point-to-Point Connection)

Wireless local area network (WLAN) is one of the fastest-growing technologies. The demand for connecting devices without use of cables is increasing everywhere. WLAN can be found on collage campus, in office buildings, and in many public areas [1]. The security in WLAN is based on cryptography, the science and art of transforming messages to make them secure and immune to attack. Cryptography can be used to authenticate the sender and receiver of the message to each other within WLAN. The cryptography algorithms can be divided into two groups: symmetric-encryption algorithms and asymmetric-encryption algorithms.

Wireless local area network (WLAN) is one of the fastest-growing technologies. The demand for connecting devices without use of cables is increasing everywhere. WLAN can be found on collage campus, in office buildings, and in many public areas [1]. The security in WLAN is based on cryptography, the science and art of transforming messages to make them secure and immune to attack. Cryptography can be used to authenticate the sender and receiver of the message to each other within WLAN. The cryptography algorithms can be divided into two groups: symmetric-encryption algorithms and asymmetric-encryption algorithms.

Fig. 9.a. The Plain Text

Fig. 9.b. The Decrypted Text

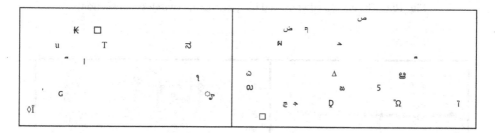

Fig. 9.c. The Cipher Text

Fig. 9.d. The other Cipher Text for the same Plain Text

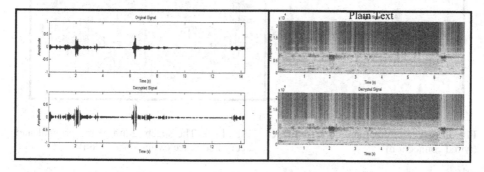

Fig. 10.a. The original and decrypted voice (wireless connection)

Fig. 10.b. The spectrogram of the original and decrypted voice (wireless connection)

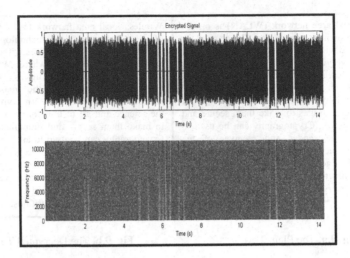

Fig. 10.c. The encrypted voice and its spectrogram (wireless connection)

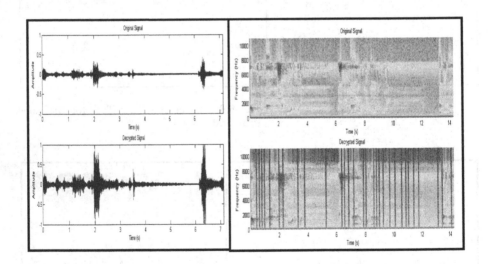

Fig. 11.a. The original and decrypted voice (wired connection)

Fig. 11.b. The spectrogram of the original and decrypted voice (wired connection)

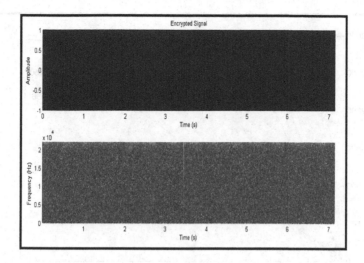

Fig. 11.c. The encrypted voice and its spectrogram (wired connection)

4 The Results

The data rate of the new algorithm is compared with DES, TDES, AES-256, and RC6
using different messages with different sizes, from 50KB until 3MB, see figure (12).
The delay time taken for encryption process of the different algorithms is measured
inside their programs by using the DESKTOP device for the comparison purpose, see
figure (12). The Average data rate of the different algorithms is calculated from equation (8), and the measured values of the average data rate for different algorithms are
shown in table (2).

$$Bravg = \frac{1}{Nb} \sum_{i=1}^{Nb} \frac{Mi}{ti} \text{(KB/s)} \qquad (8)$$

Where:
- Bravg is the average data rate (KB/s).
- Nb is Number of messages with different sizes, from 50KB until 3MB.
- M_i is the message size (KB).
- t_i is the time taken to encrypt the message M_i .

Table 2. Average data rates comparison

	AES-256	TDES	New	RC6	DES
Average Data Rate (KB/s)	120.73	31.32	**146.73**	**271.56**	93.98

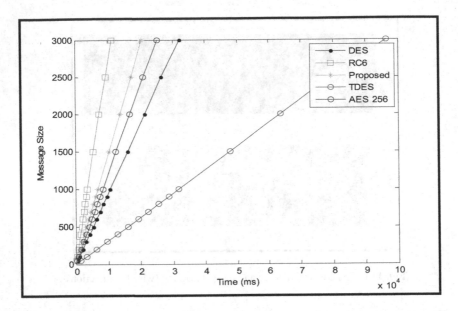

Fig. 12. The Encryption delay time for the proposed, DES, TDES, AES-256, and RC6 algorithms

Table (2) shows that, the new algorithm has higher average data rate than DES, TDES, and AES-256, but the RC6 has the higher value than the proposed algorithm. In addition, the new algorithm adds some difficulties to the attackers to discover the key. These difficulties are

- The longer key size, 512-bits, compared with DES, TDES, AES-256, and RC6.
- The key-updating with each packet.

Table (3) shows the calculated correlation factor of the speech signal between the plain wave and the encrypted wave in the case of wired and wireless connection.

Table 3. The Correlation factor in the case of the wired and wireless connection (Speech Signal)

	Plain and encrypted waves
Wired Connection	0.0013
Wireless Connection	-0.0021

The success of the encryption process means smaller values of the correlation coefficient, and if the correlation coefficient equals zero, then the original data and its encryption are totally different, i.e., the encrypted data has no features and highly independent on the original data. All values of table (3).

The parameters of equations (1, 2, 3, and 4) are measured for new algorithm environment in the case of wireless connection and wired connection, see table (4).

Thus, the system is more secure because of the following reasons.

1. The new algorithm adds some difficulties to the attackers to discover the key. These difficulties are
- The longer key size, 512-bits, compared with DES, TDES, AES-256, and RC6.
- The key-updating with each packet.

2. The outside attacks cannot obtain the key or any information about the algorithm even if he had the plaintext, the company title, S-Box, and the encrypted message because they lose the synchronization or the initial key of each round where they are independent.

In addition, the proposed algorithm has the following advantages:
- The delay time taken for the encryption and the decryption processes by the proposed algorithm is less than the time taken DES, TDES, and AES-256 algorithms.
- Higher data rate than DES, 3DES, AES, and AES-256 algorithms.
- The updating of the round-key with each packet.
- The updating of the round-key prevents any change in the transmitted message because it is known to the sender and the receiver because of losing the synchronization between the encryption and the decryption. So it prevents the attackers such as, man-in-the middle attacks to analysis the traffic or to decrypt the encrypted message.

Table 4. The measured parameters in the case of wireless connection and wired connection

	Wireless Connection	Wired Connection
SNR	-3.5779	-3.5093
SNRseg	-3.6484	-3.5134
LLR	0.555	0.4667
SD	14.5672	14.1494

5 Conclusion

The key-updating is a new approach to increase the difficulty to discover the key. The text and speech signals used to prove the success of the proposed algorithm. The proposed algorithm has higher data rate than DES, TDES, and AES-256 algorithms. The voice encryption and decryption is applied using wired and wireless connection. It is efficient and useable for the security in the WLAN systems.

References

[1] Stallings, W.: Network Security Essentials (Applications and Standards). Pearson Education, London (2004)

[2] Paul, A.J., Paul, V., Mythili, P.: A Fast And Secure Encryption Algorithm For Message Communication. In: IET-UK International Conference on Information and Communication Technology in Electrical Sciences (ICTES 2007), December 20-22, pp. 629–634. Dr. M.G.R. University, Chennai (2007)

[3] Amador, J.J., Green, R.W.: Symmetric-Key Block Ciphers for Image and Text Cryptography. International Journal of Imaging System Technology (2005)

[4] Daemen, J., Rijmen, V.: Rijndael: The Advanced Encryption Standard. Dr. Dobb's Journal (March 2001)

[5] El-Fishawy, N.A., El-Danaf, T.E., Zaid, O.M.A.: A Modification Of Rc6 Block Cipher Algorithm For Data Security (MRC6). International Journal of Network Security, IJNS (2007)

[6] ANSI3.106, American National Standard for Information Systems—Data Encryption Algorithm—Modes of Operation. American National Standards Institute (1983)

[7] Schneider, B.: Applied Cryptography, 2nd edn. John Wiley & Sons, Inc., New York (1996)

[8] O'Shaughnessy, D.: Speech Communication: human and machine. The Institute of Electrical and Electronics Engineers, Inc., New York (2000)

[9] ITU, Methods for Subjective Determination of Transmission Quality, ITU-T, pp. 800 (1996)

[10] Falk, T., Chan, W.-Y.: Single Ended Method for Objective Speech Quality Assessment in Narrowband Telephony Applications, ITU-T, pp. 563 (2004)

[11] El-Fishawy, N., Zaid, O.M.A.: Quality of Encryption Measurement of Bitmap Images with RC6, MRC6, and Rijndael Block Cipher Algorithms. International Journal of Network Security, IJNS (2007)

Fuzzy Rule-Base Based Intrusion Detection System on Application Layer

S. Sangeetha, S. Haripriya, S.G. Mohana Priya, Dr.V. Vaidehi, and Dr.N. Srinivasan

Department of CSE, Angel College of Engineering and Technology, Tirupur
visual.sangi@gmail.com

Abstract. The objective of this paper is to develop a Fuzzy Rule-Base Based Intrusion Detection System on Application Layer which works in the application layer of the network stack. FASIDS consist of semantic IDS and Fuzzy based IDS. Rule based IDS looks for the specific pattern which is defined as malicious. A non-intrusive regular pattern can be malicious if it occurs several times with a short time interval. At application layer, HTTP traffic's header and payload are analyzed for possible intrusion. In the proposed misuse detection module, the semantic intrusion detection system works on the basis of rules that define various application layer misuses that are found in the network. An attack identified by the IDS is based on a corresponding rule in the rule-base. An event that doesn't make a 'hit' on the rule-base is given to a Fuzzy Intrusion Detection System (FIDS) for further analysis.

In a Rule-based intrusion detection system, an attack can either be detected if a rule is found in the rule base or goes undetected if not found. If this is combined with FIDS, the intrusions went undetected by RIDS can further be detected. These non-intrusive patterns are checked by the fuzzy IDS for a possible attack. The non-intrusive patterns are normalized and converted as linguistic variable in fuzzy sets. These values are given to Fuzzy Cognitive Mapping (FCM). If there is any suspicious event, then it generates an alarm to the client/server. Results show better performance in terms of the detection rate and the time taken to detect. The detection rate is increased with reduction in false positive rate for a specific attack.

Keywords: Semantic Intrusion detection, Application Layer misuse detector, Fuzzy Intrusion detection, Fuzzy Cognitive Mapping, HTTP intrusion detection.

1 Introduction

Most of the commercially available intrusion detection systems work in the network layer of the network stack and this paves way for the hackers to intrude at various other layers, especially in the application layer. Misuse detection uses rule based IDSs that follow a signature-match approach where attacks are identified by matching each input text or pattern against predefined signatures that model malicious activity. The pattern matching process is time consuming. Now a day's hackers are continuously creating new types of attacks. Because of the continuously changing nature of attacks,

N. Meghanathan et al. (Eds.): CNSA 2010, CCIS 89, pp. 27–36, 2010.

signature should be updated periodically when a new threat is discovered. Rule based Intrusion Detection System looks for the specific pattern which is defined as malicious [5]. A non-intrusive regular pattern can be malicious if it occurs several times with a short time interval. The non-intrusive patterns are checked by the fuzzy IDS for a possible attack. The detection rate increases by checking the non-intrusive patterns using fuzzy IDS.

2 Architecture of the Fasids

The architecture of the system is as shown in Fig. 1. The block diagram shows the order in which the different modules process the incoming payload. The HTTP data capture block collects the application-layer traffic from the network. Captured data is then separated into the header and payload parts and are forwarded to separate buffers.

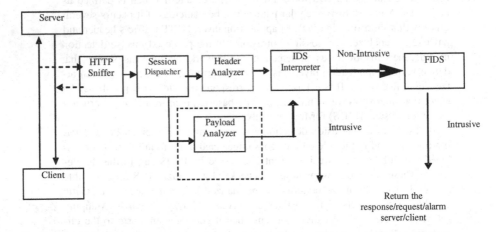

Fig. 1. Block diagram view of integrated FASIDS

The Header parser [6] module reads the header and prepares a list of the objects in the HTTP packets. Each object represents a field of the HTTP protocol [1] and is a five tuple *<message-line, section, feature, operator, content>*. This sequence of objects is given to the IDS interpreter that refers to the rule-base and correlates the different objects to trigger one or more of the rules. Simultaneously the HTML parser parses the HTML data and searches for misappropriate usage of tags and attributes and also observes for the javascript based attacks injected in the HTTP [7]. The state transition analysis is done by defining states for every match. The incoming pattern is semantically looked-up only in specified states, and this increases the efficiency of the IDS pattern-matching algorithm [8]. If the pattern matches with some predefined pattern then it generates intrusion alert to client/server. If non-Intrusive, the output of the rule-based IDS goes to the Fuzzy IDS for further analysis [9]. Fuzzy Cognitive Mapping captures different types of intrusive behavior as suspicious events and generates an alert to the server/client, if there are any attacks.

3 Fuzzy Component for Non-intrusive Traffic

Parts of traffic that get past the rule-based intrusion detection system with no matches of intrusion are fed into the fuzzy component for further analysis. A functional block diagram of the fuzzy component is shown in Fig. 2.

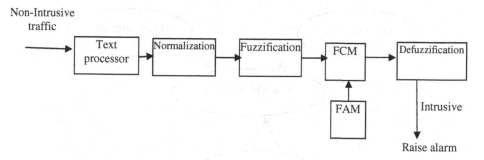

Fig. 2. Functional blocks of FIDS

The traffic is first given to a text processor such as *awk*, which helps in finding the number of occurrences of a specific pattern in it. These nos. are later normalized to keep the obtained values in a specific range to aid relative comparison. The normalized values are fuzzified into linguistic terms of fuzzy sets before feeding to the Fuzzy Cognitive Mapper (FCM) [4]. The output of the text processor for Denial of Service attack. The output of this is normalized between 0.0 and 1.0 which then goes for fuzzification. Fuzzification converts a normalized value into linguistic terms of fuzzy sets. The output of the fuzzification is given for Fuzzy Cognitive Memory [2,3] which makes use of Fuzzy Associative Memory (FAM).

3.1 Working of Fuzzy Cognitive Mapper in Ids

Fuzzy rules are constructed based on a map of multiple inputs to a single output. For eg., No. of login failures, time interval between any two login failures, time duration of a login session, etc. Malicious activities that are defined by one or more fuzzy rules are mapped using the FCM. The FCM uses a Fuzzy Associative Map (FAM) to evaluate the fuzzy rules to generate an alert that could fall under either of *very high, high, medium, low* or *very low* categories, based on the severity of the attack.

The following example demonstrates the sequence of events in the fuzzy component identifies a brute-force attack, where an intruder tries to login with several users' passwords and fails. This attack can be identified by observing the number of login failures and the time interval between each failure.

FCM for *login_failure* is shown in Fig. 3, which shows that if *login_failure* is very high for small *interval* of time and for *same machine*, then there is a suspicious event. ++, +, ∈, - & -- represents *very high, high, medium, low* & *very low* respectively. In

Fig. 3, the *time interval* for login failure is *small* which is represented by '-' and no. of login failure is *high* which is represented by '+'.

 Fuzzy rule: no. of *login_failure* is *very high* AND *time interval* is *small* is triggered which identifies that the specific scenario may be due to a brute-force attack. FAM table for a brute force attack as shown in Table 1 is used to evaluate this rule.

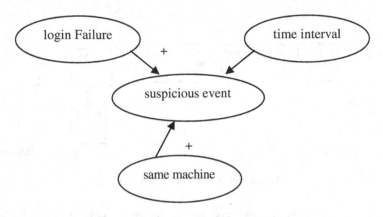

Fig. 3. FCM for login_failure

3.2 Fuzzy Associative Memory by Fuzzy Rules

Fuzzy Associate Memory(FAM) is used to map fuzzy rules in the form of a matrix. These rules take two variables as input and map them into a two dimensional matrix. The rules in the FAM follow a simple *if-then-else* format. Fuzzy Associative Memory facilitates the conclusion of the rate of false negatives for few attacks such as Denial of Service (DoS) and brute force attacks.

Table 1. Fuzzy Associative Memory for a Brute force attack

t \ x	VS	S	έ	H	VH
VS	VS	VS	S	έ	έ
S	VS	έ	S	S	έ
έ	H	H	έ	έ	S
H	VH	H	H	έ	VS
VH	VH	VH	H	VS	VS

 Table 1 shows that the FAM table for a Brute force attacks in a matrix format. Rows in this table represent the rate of *no. of login failure* and the columns represent the rate of *time interval* between each failure. A linguistic representation of the same is as shown below in Fig. 4.

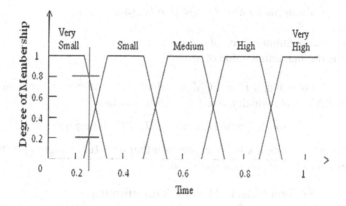

Fig. 4. Linguistic representation of time interval during Brute force attack

The *time interval* between each login failure is taken in X axis as a normalized value. The degree of membership is taken in Y axis. The min-max normalization scheme is used to normalize the time interval for login failure to a common range i.e., between 0 and 1. Fig. 5 shows the time values assigned to the linguistic variables (very small, small, medium, high and very high). Fig.5 shows the *login_failure* values assigned to the linguistic variables.

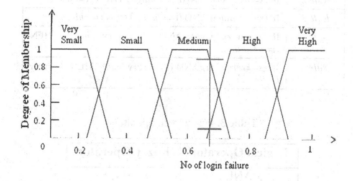

Fig. 5. Linguistic representation of no. of login failures during Brute force attack

Consider a scenario in which the *time interval* between login failures is *very small* and *no. of login failures* is *very high*. From Table 1, we can conclude that the possibility of such a scenario being detected as an intrusion is *very high*.

3.3 Algorithm for Fuzzy Intrusion Detection System

The following algorithm presents the step in Fuzzy Intrusion Detection System.

Step 1:   Let x = *set of number of login failures*
               t = *time interval*

Step 2: x = normalization of (x)= $(x\text{-}min)/(max\text{-}min)$
    where,
      min is the minimum value of x
      max is the maximum value of x

Step 3:   Give x and t to FCM to select the appropriate fuzzy rules (Refer Table 2) from FAM table which has the following format:

IF condition AND condition THEN consequent

where, *condition* is a complex fuzzy expression that uses fuzzy logic operators (Refer Table 3), *consequent* is an atomic expression.

Step 4:   Perform Mean of Maxima defuzzification

$$(D_{MM}) = \text{sum } \Sigma x_i / |X|$$

where, x_i belongs to X

Table 2. Fuzzy rules for detecting intrusions

Rule No.	Rules
Rule 1	If (x==*very small*) AND (t ==*very small*) THEN (I==*very small*);
Rule 2	IF (x==*very small*) AND (t ==*high*) THEN (I==*small*);
Rule 3	IF (x==*medium*) AND (t ==*high*) THEN (I==*high*);
Rule 4	IF (x==*very high*) AND (t ==*very small*) THEN (I==*medium*);
Rule 5	IF (x==*very high*) AND (t == *very high*) THEN (I==*very high*);

Table 3. Fuzzy logic operators

Logical Operator	Fuzzy Operator
x AND t	$min\{x, t\}$
x OR t	$max\{x, t\}$
NOT x	$1.0 - x$

Several methods are available in the literature for defuzzification. Some of the widely used methods are centroid method, centre of sums, and mean of maxima. In mean of maxima defuzzification method, one of the variable value for which the fuzzy subset has its maximum value is chosen as crisp value. According to the FAM table, the defuzzification graph is obtained and is shown in Fig. 6.

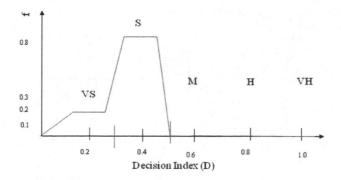

Fig. 6. Defuzzification

$$Defuzzification = \frac{\sum_{x_i \in M} x_i}{|M|} = \frac{(0.3 + 0.5)}{0.2} * 100$$

$$= 40\%$$

The defuzzification value thus calculated for Brute Force attack is 40%.

In many situations, for a system whose output is fuzzy, it is easier to take a crisp decision if the output is represented as a single scalar quantity. For this reason, defuzzification value is calculated. Based on the defuzzification value, decision is taken if the traffic contains intrusive pattern or not.

The output of the rule-based intrusion detection module is non-intrusive for few attacks such as DoS, login failures. In DoS attack, instead of having infinite loop, the intruder will execute the loop for larger number of times. There is a bigger class of attacks which doesn't have a clear rule entry in the rule base can also be detected. These patterns are checked by the fuzzy IDS for a possible attack. Fuzzy Cognitive Mapping is used to capture different types of intrusive behavior as suspicious events.

4 Results and Analysis

The objects in each of the protocol field that are to be searched is plotted in Fig. 7. It is observed that if the number of objects to be matched in each protocol field is increasing the Response time increases linearly. But the response time tends to saturate after a specific number of rules. This is because it is expected that the rules contain some common objects which are to be checked once thus improving the response time. Fig.8 shows the detection rate with various components of IDS. From the Fig. 6.8, the detection rate increases by combining HTTP header and payload (HTML and Scripts).

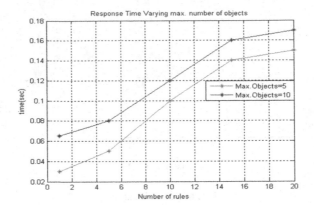

Fig. 7. Response time vs. Rules with different number of maximum objects for each protocol field

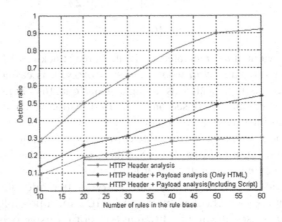

Fig. 8. Detection Ratio with various component of IDS

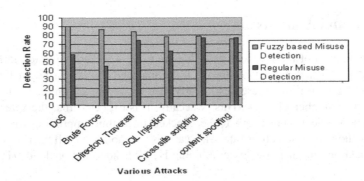

Fig. 9. Comparison of Fuzzy based Misuse Detection and Regular Misuse Detection

Fig.9 shows the comparison of Fuzzy based Misuse Detection and Regular Misuse Detection for various attacks. Fig. 6.9 shows the detection rate of fuzzy based misuse detection is high when compared to the regular misuse detection for some attacks such as Dos, brute force, Directory Traversal attacks.

5 Conclusion

The rule-based semantic intrusion detection system proposed in this thesis has an efficient memory usage since the amount of memory needed for working of the IDS depends on the rule table size. A fuzzy component that is added to this rule based semantic IDS as proposed in this thesis uses Fuzzy Cognitive Mapping (FCM) in order to have an accurate prediction. Thus, the system proposed in this thesis namely Fuzzy aided Application layer Semantic Intrusion Detection System draws advantages from two different concepts. The semantic rule base keeps the rules updated for detecting newer intrusions by semantically matching the patterns. The Fuzzy component contributed to improving the detection rate by scanning through the traffic for attacks which goes undetected by a typical rule based IDS. The results show better performance in terms of the detection rate and the time taken to detect an intrusion. The semantic rule base can be appended with more number of semantic parameters by way which improving the accuracy of attack detection of the system is possible. Also that, more number of application layer protocols like FTP, SMTP, etc can be considered for implementation and the performance of the concept of application layer semantic intrusion detection can be validated with these protocols.

References

1. Abbes, T., Bouhoula, A., Rusinowitch, M.: Protocol Analysis in Intrusion Detection Using Decision Tree. In: The Proceedings of International Conference on Information Technology: Coding and Computing (ITCC 2004). IEEE, Los Alamitos (2004)
2. Siraj, A., Bridges, S.M., Vaughn, R.B.: Fuzzy Cognitive Maps For Decision Support in an Intelligent Intrusion Detection System. In: The Proceedings of 20th International Conference of North American Fuzzy Information (NAFIPS), vol. 4, pp. 2165–2170 (2001)
3. Brubaker, D.: Fuzzy cognitive maps, EDN access (1996)
4. Carvalho, J.P., Tome, J.A.B.: Rule-based fuzzy cognitive maps and fuzzy cognitive maps – a comparative study. In: The Proceedings of the 18th International Conference of the North American Fuzzy Information (NAFIPS), pp. 115–119 (1999)
5. Sangeetha, S., Vaidehi, V., Srinivasan, N.: Implementation of Application Layer Intrusion Detection System using Protocol Analysis. In: Proceedings of International Conference on Signal Processing, Networking and Communications, ICSCN 2008, pp. 279–284 (2008)
6. Bellamy Jr., W.: TCP Port 80 - HyperText Transfer Protocol (HTTP) Header Exploitation (2002), http://Cgisecurity.com
7. Hallaraker, O., Vigna, G.: Detecting malicious JavaScript code in Mozilla. In: The Proceedings of the 10th International Conference on Engineering of Complex Computer Systems (ICECCS 2005), pp. 85–94 (2005)

8. Krugel, C., Toth, T.: Using decision trees to improve signature-based intrusion detection. In: Vigna, G., Krügel, C., Jonsson, E. (eds.) RAID 2003. LNCS, vol. 2820, pp. 173–191. Springer, Heidelberg (2003)

9. Bridges, S.M., Vaughn, R.B., Siraj, A.: AI Techniques Applied to High Performance Computing Intrusion Detection. In: Proceeding of the Tenth International Conference on Telecommunication Systems, Modeling and Analysis, Monterey CA, vol. 2, pp. 100–114 (2002)

Trust Models in Wireless Sensor Networks: A Survey

Mohammad Momani

Faculty of Engineering and Information Technology, School of Computing and
Communications, University of Technology, Sydney, Australia
Mohammad.Momani@uts.edu.au

Abstract. This paper introduces the security and trust concepts in wireless sensor networks and explains the difference between them, stating that even though both terms are used interchangeably when defining a secure system, they are not the same. The difference between reputation and trust is also explained, highlighting that reputation partially affects trust. The methodologies used to model trust and their references are presented. The factors affecting trust updating are summarised and some examples of the systems in which these factors have been implemented are given. The survey states that, even though researchers have started to explore the issue of trust in wireless sensor networks, they are still examining the trust associated with routing messages between nodes (binary events). However, wireless sensor networks are mainly deployed to monitor events and report data, both continuous and discrete. This leads to the development of new trust models addressing the continuous data issue and also to combine the data trust and the communication trust to infer the total trust.

Keywords: Trust, model, wireless, sensor, networks, survey.

1 Introduction

Wireless sensor networks (WSNs) in recent years, have shown an unprecedented ability to observe and manipulate the physical world, however, as with almost every technology, the benefits of WSNs are accompanied by a significant risk factors and potential for abuse. So, someone might ask, how can a user trust the information provided by the sensor network?

Sensor nodes are small in size and able to sense events, process data, and communicate with each other to transfer information to the interested users. Typically, a sensor node consists of four sub-systems [1, 2].

- Computing sub-system (processor and memory): responsible for the control of the sensors and the execution of communication protocols.
- Communication sub-system (transceiver): used to communicate with neighbouring nodes and the outside world.
- Sensing sub-system (sensor): link the node to the outside world.
- Power supply sub-system (battery): supplies power to the node.

WSNs are a collection of self-organised sensor nodes that form a temporary network. Neither pre-defined network infrastructure nor centralised network administration

N. Meghanathan et al. (Eds.): CNSA 2010, CCIS 89, pp. 37–46, 2010.
© Springer-Verlag Berlin Heidelberg 2010

exists. Wireless nodes communicate with each other via radio links and since they have a limited transmission range, nodes wishing to communicate with other nodes employ a multi-hop strategy for communicating and each node simultaneously acts as a router and as a host.

It should be noted that bandwidth available between communicating wireless nodes is restricted. This is because wireless networks have a significantly lower data transmission capacity compared to fixed-line data networks. Furthermore, wireless nodes only have a limited power supply available, as power supplied by batteries is easily exhausted. Lastly, wireless nodes may join or leave a network at any given time and frequently change their location in a network; this results in a highly dynamic network topology.

Due to impressive technological innovations in electronics and communications, small low-cost sensor nodes are available, which can collect and relay environmental data [3, 4]. These nodes have sensing, computing and short-range communication abilities and can be deployed in many environments. Such deployment can be in controlled environments, such as sensing the atmosphere in buildings and factories, where the mobility of the nodes is of interest. Or they can be spread in hazardous and hostile environments and left unattended. Originally motivated by surveillance in battlefields for the military, interest in WSNs spread over a wide range of applications, from scientific exploration and monitoring, for example, the deployment of a WSN on an active volcano [5, 6], to monitoring the microclimate throughout the volume of redwood trees [7], to building and bridge monitoring [8, 9], to health-care monitoring [10] and a number of other applications presented in [2, 3, 11, 12].

The rest of the paper is organised as follows: Section 2 discusses security in WSNs and section 3 introduces the notion of trust. Trust and reputation models in WSNs are presented in section 4 and section 5 concludes the paper.

2 Security in WSNs

In general, the key security goals of any network are to protect the network against all sorts of attacks, such as eavesdropping, fabrication, injection and modification of packets, impersonation; node capturing and many others, and to address other issues, like privacy, availability, accountability, data authentication, data integrity and data freshness. All these issues apply to traditional and wireless networks, but can have different consequences in WSNs, due to the open transmission medium, the resource constraints and the mass unattended deployment, especially in difficult and dangerous environments.

Research continues to be conducted into the design and optimisation of WSNs, as the use of these networks is still in its infancy phase. The security issue has been raised by many researchers [13-23], and, due to the deployment of WSN nodes in hazardous and/or hostile areas in large numbers, such deployment forces the nodes to be of low cost and therefore less reliable or more prone to overtaking by an adversary force. Some methods used, such as cryptographic authentication and other mechanisms [24-31], do not entirely solve the problem. For example, adversarial nodes can have access to valid cryptographic keys to access other nodes in the network. The reliability issue is certainly not addressed when sensor nodes are subject to system faults. These two sources of problems, system faults and erroneous data or bad routing by malicious nodes, can result in the total breakdown of a network and cryptography by itself is insufficient to solve these problems. So new tools from different domains – social sciences, statistics, e-commerce and others – should be integrated with cryptography to completely solve the unique security attacks in WSNs, such as node capturing, Sybil attacks, denial of service attacks, etc.

3 Notion of Trust

Due to the nature of WSN deployment being prone to the surrounding environment and suffering from other types of attacks in addition to the attacks found in traditional networks, other security measurements different from the traditional approaches must be in place to improve the security of the network. The trust establishment between nodes is a must to evaluate the trustworthiness of other nodes, as the survival of a WSN is dependent upon the cooperative and trusting nature of its nodes.

Security and trust are two tightly interdependent concepts and because of this interdependence, these terms are used interchangeably when defining a secure system [32]. However, security is different from trust and the key difference is that, it is more complex and the overhead is high.

Trust has been the focus of researchers for a long time [33], from the social sciences, where trust between humans has been studied to the effects of trust in economic transactions [34-36]. Although intuitively easy to comprehend, the notion of trust has not been formally defined. Unlike, for example, reliability, which was originally a measure of how long a machine can be trustworthy, and came to be rigorously defined as a probability, trust is yet to adopt a formal definition.

Along with the notion of trust, comes that of reputation [37], which is occasionally treated by some authors as trust. Reputation is not to be confused with trust: the former only partially affects the latter. Reputation is the opinion of one person about the other, of one internet buyer about an internet seller, and by construct, of one sensor node about another. Trust is a derivation of the reputation of an entity. Based on the reputation, a level of trust is bestowed upon an entity. The reputation itself has been built over time based on that entity's history of behaviour, and may be reflecting a positive or negative assessment. It is these quantities that researchers try to model and apply to security problems in WSNs.

Among the motivating fields for the development of trust models is e-commerce, which necessitated the notion of judging how trusted an internet seller can be [37, 38]. This was the case for peer-to-peer networks and other internet forums where users deal with each other in a decentralised fashion [39-43]. Recently, attention has been given to the concept of trust to increase security and reliability in ad-hoc [32, 44-51] and sensor networks [52-54]. WSNs are open to unique problems, due to their deployment and application nature. The low cost of the sensor nodes of a WSN prohibits sophisticated measures to ensure data authentication. Some methods used, such as cryptographic, authentication and other mechanisms [24-28, 30], do not entirely solve the problem. In the following section a brief survey, introducing only the methodology used to formulate trust and how is it being updated, of existing research on trust in WSNs is presented in order to easily understand the concept of trust.

4 Trust in Sensor Networks

Trust in WSN networks plays an important role in constructing the network and making the addition and/or deletion of sensor nodes from a network, due to the growth of the network, or the replacement of failing and unreliable nodes very smooth and transparent. The creation, operation, management and survival of a WSN are dependent upon the cooperative and trusting nature of its nodes, therefore the trust establishment between nodes is a must. However, using the traditional tools such as cryptographic tools to generate trust evidence and establish trust and traditional protocols to exchange and distribute keys is not possible in a WSN, due to the resource limitations of sensor nodes [44]. Therefore, new innovative methods to secure communication and distribution of trust values between nodes are needed. Trust in WSNs, has been studied lightly by current researchers and is still an open and challenging field.

Reputation and trust systems in the context of sensor networks prior to this research have received little attention from researchers, however, recently researchers have started to make efforts on the trust topic, as sensor networks are becoming more popular. Ganeriwal and Srivastava were the first to introduce a reputation model specific to sensor networks in [52]; the RFSN (Reputation-based Framework for High Integrity Sensor Networks) model uses the Beta distribution, as a mathematical tool to represent and continuously update trust and reputation. The model classifies the actions as cooperative and non-cooperative (binary) and uses direct and indirect (second-hand) information to calculate the reputation. The second-hand information is weighted by giving more weight to the information coming from very reliable nodes. Trust is calculated as an expected value of the reputation and the behaviour of the node is decided upon a global threshold; if the trust value is below a threshold, the node is uncooperative, otherwise it is cooperative. The system propagates only the positive reputation information about other nodes [52], and by doing so, it eliminates the bad-mouthing attack, but at the same time it will affect the system's efficiency, as nodes will not be able to exchange their bad experience with malicious nodes. The aging factor is also introduced to differently weight the old and new interactions; more weight is given to recent interactions.

The DRBTS (Distributed Reputation-based Beacon Trust System) presented in [53] is an extension to the system introduced in [55], which presented a suite of techniques that detect and revoke malicious beacon nodes that provide misleading location information. It is a distributed security protocol designed to provide a method in which beacon nodes can monitor each other and provide information so that sensor nodes can choose to trust, using a voting approach. Every beacon node monitors its one hope neighbourhood for misbehaving beacon nodes and accordingly updates the reputation of the corresponding beacon node in the neighbour-reputation table. Beacon nodes use second-hand information for updating the reputation of their neighbours after the second-hand information passes a deviation test. A sensor node uses the neighbour-reputation table to determine whether or not to use a given beacon's location information based on a simple majority voting scheme. The DRBTS models the network as an undirected graph, uses first-hand and second-hand information to build trust.

Garth et al., [56] proposed a distributed trust-based framework and a mechanism for the election of trustworthy cluster heads in a cluster-based WSN. The model uses direct and indirect information coming from trusted nodes. Trust is modelled using the traditional weighting mechanism of the parameters: packet drop rate, data packets and control packets. Each node stores a trust table for all the surrounding nodes and these values are reported to the cluster head only and upon request. This approach is not based on second-hand information, so it reduces the effect of bad-mouthing. Hur et al., proposed a trust model in [57], to identify the trustworthiness of sensor nodes and to filter out (remove) the data received from malicious nodes. In their model, they assume that each sensor node has knowledge of its own location, time is synchronised and nodes are densely deployed. They computed trust in a traditional way, weighting the trust factors (depending on the application) and there is no update of trust.

The proposed reputation-based trust model in WSNs by Chen et al., in [58], borrows tools from probability, statistics and mathematical analysis. They argued that the positive and/or negative outcomes for a certain event are not enough to make a decision in a WSN. They built up a reputation space and trust space in WSNs, and defined a transformation from the reputation space to the trust space [58]. The same approach presented in RFSN [52] is followed; a watchdog mechanism to monitor the other nodes and to calculate the reputation and eventually to calculate trust, and Bayes' theorem is used to describe the binary events, successful and unsuccessful transactions, with the introduction of uncertainty. Initially, the trust between strangers is set to (0) and the uncertainty is set to (1). The model does not use second-hand information, and how to refresh the reputation value is an issue. Xiao et al., in [59] developed a mechanism called SensorRank for rating sensors in terms of correlation by exploring Markov Chains in the network. A network voting algorithm called TrustVoting was also proposed to determine faulty sensor readings. The TrustVoting algorithm consists of two phases: self diagnose (direct reading) and neighbour diagnose (indirect reading), and if the reading is faulty then the node will not participate in the voting.

Crosby and Pissinou, in [60], proposed a secure cluster formation algorithm to facilitate the establishment of trusted clusters via pre-distributed keys and to prevent the election of compromised or malicious nodes as cluster heads. They used Beta distribution to model trust, based on successful and unsuccessful interactions. The updating occurs through incorporating the successful/unsuccessful interactions at time $t+1$ with those of time t. Their trust framework is designed in the context of a cluster-based network model with nodes that have unique local IDs. The authors of [61] proposed the TIBFIT protocol to diagnose and mask arbitrary node failures in an event-driven wireless sensor network. The TIBFIT protocol is designed to determine whether an event has occurred or not through analysing the binary reports from the event neighbours. The protocol outperforms the standard voting scheme for event detection.

A few other systems related to trust in WSNs, have been proposed in the literature such as [62-68], which use one or more of the techniques mentioned before to calculate trust. The proposed model in [62] uses a single trust value for a whole group (cluster), assuming that sensor nodes mostly fulfil their responsibilities in a cooperative manner rather than individually. In [63], the model is based on a distributed trust model to produce a trust relationship for sensor networks and uses the weighting approach to combine trust from different sources. In [64], a trust-based routing scheme is presented, which finds a forwarding path based on packet trust requirements, also using the weighting approach. In [65], a stochastic process formulation based on a number of assumptions is proposed to investigate the impact of liars on their peers' reputation about a subject. In [66], the authors proposed a new fault-intrusion tolerant routing mechanism called MVMP (multi-version multi-path) for WSNs to provide both fault tolerance and intrusion tolerance at the same time.

The proposed model in [67] is an application-independent framework, built on the alert-based detection mechanisms provided by applications, to identify the malicious (compromised) nodes in WSNs. In [68], a parameterised and localised trust management scheme for sensor networks security (PLUS) is presented, whereby each sensor node rates the trustworthiness of its interested neighbours, identifies the malicious nodes and shares the opinion locally.

It is also worth mentioning that almost all the work undertaken on trust is based on successful and unsuccessful (binary) transactions between entities, that is, trust has been modelled in networks in general from a communication point of view, with no exception for WSNs, which is characterised by a unique feature: sensing events and reporting data. This unique characteristic is the basis of our research, which is focusing on modelling and calculating trust between nodes in WSNs based on continuous data (sensed events) and will eventually introduce the communication as a second factor of trust. Accordingly, a trust classification for WSNs has been introduced in [69] and in [70, 71] a new framework to calculate trust in WSNs has been introduced, using the traditional weighting approach to combine direct and indirect trust. In [72], the sensed data was introduced as the decisive factor of trust, that is, trust in WSNs was modelled from the sensor reliability perspective. The RBATMWSN model introduced in [73], represents a new trust model and a reputation system for WSNs, based on sensed continuous data. The trust model establishes the continuous version of the Beta reputation system applied to binary events and presents a new Gaussian Trust and Reputation System for Sensor Networks (GTRSSN), as introduced in [74], which introduces a theoretically sound Bayesian probabilistic approach for mixing second-hand information from neighbouring nodes with directly observed information to calculate trust between nodes in WSNs, and finally a Bayesian fusion approach was introduced in [75], to combine continuous data trust based on sensed events and binary communication trust based on successful and unsuccessful transactions between nodes.

References

1. Bharathidasan, A., Ponduru, V.A.S.: Sensor Networks: An Overview, Technical Report, Dept. of Computer Science, University of California at Davis (2002)
2. Tubaishat, M., Madria, S.: Sensor networks: an overview. IEEE Potentials 22, 20–23 (2003)
3. Akyildiz, I.F., Su, W., Sankarasubramaniam, Y., Cayirci, E.: Wireless Sensor Networks: a Survey. Computer Networks 38, 393–422 (2002)
4. Rajaravivarma, V., Yang, Y., Yang, T.: An Overview of Wireless Sensor Network and Applications. In: The 35th Southeastern Symposium on System Theory (2003)
5. Werner-Allen, G., Lorincz, K., Ruiz, M., Marcillo, O., Johnson, J., Lees, J., Welsh, M.: Deploying a Wireless Sensor Network on an Active Volcano. IEEE Internet Computing (2005)
6. Werner-Allen, G., Johnson, J., Ruiz, M., Lees, J., Welsh, M.: Monitoring Volcanic Eruptions with a Wireless Sensor Network. In: Second European Workshop on Wireless Sensor Networks (EWSN 2005), Istanbul, Turkey (2005)

7. Culler, D., Estrin, D., Srivastava, M.: Overview of Sensor Networks. IEEE Computer Journal 37, 41–49 (2004)
8. Glaser, S.D.: Some Real-world Applications of Wireless Sensor Nodes. In: Proceedings of the SPIE Symposium on Smart Structures and Materials NDE, San Diego, CA, USA (2004)
9. Paek, J., Gnawali, O., Jang, K.-Y., Nishimura, D., Govindan, R., Caffrey, J., Wahbeh, M., Masri, S.: A Programmable Wireless Sensing System for Structural Monitoring. In: The 4th World Conference on Structural Control and Monitoring (4WCSCM), San Diego, CA (2006)
10. Gao, T., Greenspan, D., Welsh, M., Juang, R., Alm, A.: Vital Signs Monitoring and Patient Tracking over a Wireless Network. In: The 27th Annual International Conference of the Engineering in Medicine and Biology Society, IEEE-EMBS 2005 (2005)
11. Yoneki, E., Bacon, J.: A Survey of Wireless Sensor Network Technologies: Research Trends and Middlewares Role, Computer Laboratory. University of Cambridge, Cambridge (2005)
12. Callaway, E.H.: Wireless sensor networks: architectures and protocols. CRC Press LLC, Boca Raton (2004)
13. Wang, Y., Attebury, G., Ramamurthy, B.: A Survey of Security Issues in Wireless Sensor Networks. IEEE Communications Surveys and Tutorials 8, 2–23 (2006)
14. Stajano, F., Anderson, R.: The Resurrecting Duckling: Security Issues for Ad-hoc Wireless Networks. In: Malcolm, J.A., Christianson, B., Crispo, B., Roe, M. (eds.) Security Protocols 1999. LNCS, vol. 1796, pp. 172–182. Springer, Heidelberg (2000)
15. Perrig, A., Stankovic, J., Wagner, D.: Security in Wireless Sensor Networks. Communications of the ACM 47, 53–57 (2004)
16. Chan, H., Perrig, A.: Security and Privacy in Sensor Networks. IEEE Computer Journal 36, 103–105 (2003)
17. Zia, T., Zomaya, A.: Security Issues in Wireless Sensor Networks. In: International Conference on Systems and Networks Communication (ICSNC 2006), Tahiti, French Polynesia (2006)
18. Newsome, J., Shi, E., Song, D., Perrig, A.: The Sybil Attack in Sensor Networks: Analysis & Defenses. In: The 3rd International Symposium on Information Processing in Sensor Networks, New York (2004)
19. Walters, J.P., Liang, Z., Shi, W., Chaudhary, V.: Wireless Sensor Network Security: A Survey. In: Xiao, Y. (ed.) Security in Distributed, Grid, and Pervasive Computing. Auerbach Publications/CRC Press (2006)
20. Zhou, D.: Security Issues in Ad-hoc Networks. In: The Handbook of Ad-hoc Wireless Networks, pp. 569–582. CRC Press, Inc., Boca Raton (2003)
21. Papadimitratos, P., Haas, Z.J.: Securing Mobile Ad-hoc Networks. In: The Handbook of Ad-hoc Wireless Networks. CRC Press LLC, Boca Raton (2003)
22. Zhou, L., Haas, Z.J.: Securing Ad-hoc Networks. IEEE Network Magazine (1999)
23. Przydatek, B., Song, D., Perrig, A.: SIA: Secure Information Aggregation in Sensor Networks. In: The 1st International Conference on Embedded Networked Sensor Systems Los Angeles, California, USA (2003)
24. Karlof, C., Wagner, D.: Secure Routing in Sensor Networks: Attacks and Countermeasures. In: First IEEE International Workshop on Sensor Network Protocols and Applications (2003)
25. Bohge, M., Trappe, W.: An Authentication Framework for Hierarchical Ad-hoc Sensor Networks. In: 2003 ACM Workshop Wireless security (WiSe 2003), San Diego, CA, USA (2003)

26. Karlof, C., Sastry, N., Wagner, D.: TinySec: A Link Layer Security Architecture for Wireless Sensor Network. In: Proceedings of the 2nd International Conference on Embedded Networked Sensor Systems, Baltimore, MD, USA (2004)
27. Perrig, A., Zewczyk, R., Wen, V., Culler, D., Tygar, D.: SPINS: Security Protocols for Sensor Networks. Wireless Networks 8, 521–534 (2002)
28. Ye, F., Luoa, H., Lu, S., Zhang, L.: Statistical En-route Filtering of Injected False Data in Sensor Networks. Selected Areas in Communications of the ACM 23 (2005)
29. Zhu, S., Setia, S., Jajodia, S.: LEAP: Efficient Security Mechanisms for Large-Scale Distributed Sensor Networks. In: The 10th ACM Conference on Computer and Communications Security, Washington D.C., USA (2003)
30. Zhang, Y., Liu, W., Lou, W., Fang, Y.: Location-based Compromise Tolerant Security Mechanisms for Wireless Sensor Networks. IEEE Journal on Selected Areas in Communications 24, 247–260 (2006)
31. Zhang, W., Cao, G.: Group Rekeying for Filtering False Data in Sensor Networks: A Predistribution and Local Collaboration-based Approach. In: The 24th Annual Joint Conference of the IEEE Computer and Communications Societies (INFOCOM 2005), Miami, USA (2005)
32. Pirzada, A.A., McDonald, C.: Establishing Trust in Pure Ad-hoc Networks. In: The 27th Australasian Conference on Computer Science, Dunedin, New Zealand (2004)
33. McKnight, D.H., Chervany, N.L.: The Meanings of Trust: MIS Research Center, Carlson School of Management. University of Minnesota (1996)
34. Ba, S., Pavlou, P.A.: Evidence of the Effect of Trust Building Technology in Electronic Markets: Price Premiums and Buyer Behavior. MIS Quarterly 26, 243–268 (2002)
35. Dasgupta, P.: Trust as a Commodity. In: Ingram, D. (ed.) Trust: Making and Breaking Cooperative Relations, electronic edn., pp. 49–72. Department of Sociology, University of Oxford (2000)
36. McKnight, D.H., Cummings, L.L., Chervany, N.L.: Trust Formation in new Organaizational Relationships: MIS Research Center, Carlson School of Management. University of Minnesota (1996)
37. Resnick, P., Kuwabara, K., Zeckhauser, R., Friedman, E.: Reputation systems. Communications of the ACM 43, 45–48 (2000)
38. McKnight, D.H., Chervany, N.L.: Conceptualizing Trust: A Typology and E-Commerce Customer Relationships Model. In: The 34th Hawaii International Conference on System Sciences (2001)
39. Aberer, K., Despotovic, Z.: Managing Trust in a Peer-2-Peer Information System. In: The Tenth International Conference in Information and Knowledge Management, Atlanta, Georgia, USA (2001)
40. Blaze, M., Feigenbaum, J., Ioannidis, J., Keromytis, A.: The KeyNote Trust Management System. University of Pennsylvania, Philadelphia (1999)
41. Xiong, L., Liu, L.: A Reputation-based Trust Model for Peer-to-Peer E-Commerce Communities. In: IEEE International Conference on E-Commerce Technology (CEC 2003), pp. 275–284 (2003)
42. Blaze, M., Feigenbaum, J., Lacy, J.: Decentralized Trust Managament. In: IEEE Symposium on Security and Privacy (1996)
43. Chen, R., Yeager, W.: Poblano: A Distributed Trust Model for Peer-to-Peer Networks. Sun Microsystems (2001)
44. Eschenauer, L.: On Trust Establishment in Mobile Ad-hoc Networks. In: Department of Electrical and Computer Engineering, vol. Master of Science, p. 45. University of Maryland, College Park (2002)

45. Baras, J.S., Jiang, T.: Dynamic and Distributed Trust for Mobile Ad-hoc Networks. University of Maryland, Orlando (2004)
46. Liu, Z., Joy, A.W., Thompson, R.A.: A Dynamic Trust Model for Mobile Ad-hoc Networks. In: The 10th IEEE International Workshop on Future Trends of Distributed Computing Systems, FTDCS 2004 (2004)
47. Davis, C.R.: A Localized Trust Management Scheme for Ad-hoc Networks. In: The 3rd International Conference on Networking, ICN 2004 (2004)
48. Buchegger, S., Boudec, J.Y.L.: Performance analysis of the CONFIDANT protocol (Co-operation of Nodes- Fairness in Dynamic Ad-hoc NeTworks). In: The 3rd ACM Internationa Symposium Mobile Ad-hoc Networking & Computing (MobiHoc 2002), Lausanne, CH (2002)
49. Michiardi, P., Molva, R.: CORE: A Collaborative Reputation Mechanism to Enforce Node Cooperation in Mobile Ad-hoc Networks. In: The IFIP TC6/TC11 Sixth Joint Working Conference on Communications and Multimedia Security: Advanced Communications and Multimedia Security Portoroz, Slovenia (2002)
50. Capra, L.: Towards a Human Trust Model for Mobile Ad-hoc Networks. In: The 2nd UK-UbiNet Workshop. Cambridge University, Cambridge (2004)
51. Serugendo, G.D.M.: Trust as an Interaction Mechanism for Self-Organising Systems. In: International Conference on Complex Systems (ICCS 2004). Marriott Boston Quincy, Boston (2004)
52. Ganeriwal, S., Srivastava, M.B.: Reputation-based Framework for High Integrity Sensor Networks. In: The 2nd ACM Workshop on Security of Ad-hoc and Sensor Networks, Washington, DC, USA (2004)
53. Srinivasan, A., Teitelbaum, J., Wu, J.: DRBTS: Distributed Reputation-based Beacon Trust System. In: The 2nd IEEE International Symposium on Dependable, Autonomic and Secure Computing, DASC 2006 (2006)
54. Ganeriwal, S., Balzano, L.K., Srivastava, M.B.: Reputation-based Framework for High Integrity Sensor Networks. ACM Transactions on Sensor Networks v (2007)
55. Liu, D., Ning, P., Du, W.: Detecting Malicious Beacon Nodes for Secure Location Discovery in Wireless Sensor Networks. In: The 25th IEEE International Conference on Distributed Computing Systems, ICDCS 2005 (2005)
56. Crosby, G.V., Pissinou, N., Gadze, J.: A Framework for Trust-based Cluster Head Election in Wireless Sensor Networks. In: The Second IEEE Workshop on Dependability and Security in Sensor Networks and Systems (DSSNS 2006), Columbia, Maryland (2006)
57. Hur, J., Lee, Y., Yoon, H., Choi, D., Jin, S.: Trust Evaluation Model for Wireless Sensor Networks. In: The 7th International Conference on Advanced Communication Technology (ICACT 2005), Gangwon-Do, Korea (2005)
58. Chen, H., Wu, H., Zhou, X., Gao, C.: Reputation-based Trust in Wireless Sensor Networks. In: International Conference on Multimedia and Ubiquitous Engineering (MUE 2007), Seoul, Korea (2007)
59. Xiao, X.-Y., Peng, W.-C., Hung, C.-C., Lee, W.-C.: Using SensorRanks for In-Network Detection of Faulty Readings in Wireless Sensor Networks. In: The 6th ACM International Workshop on Data Engineering for Wireless and Mobile Access Beijing, China (2007)
60. Crosby, G.V., Pissinou, N.: Cluster-based Reputation and Trust for Wireless Sensor Networks. In: The 4th IEEE Consumer Communications and Networking Conference (CCNC 2007), Las Vegas, Nivada (2007)
61. Krasniewski, M., Varadharajan, P., Rabeler, B., Bagchi, S.: TIBFIT: Trust Index Based Fault Tolerance for Arbitrary Data Faults in Sensor Networks. In: The 2005 International Conference on Dependable Systems and Networks, Yokohama, Japan (2005)

62. Shaikh, R.A., Jameel, H., Lee, S., Rajput, S., Song, Y.J.: Trust Management Problem in Distributed Wireless Sensor Networks. In: The 12th IEEE International Conference on Embedded and Real-Time Computing Systems and Applications (RTCSA 2006), Sydney, Australia (2006)
63. Yao, Z., Kim, D., Lee, I., Kim, K., Jang, J.: A Security Framework with Trust Management for Sensor Networks. In: The 1st International Conference on Security and Privacy for Emerging Areas in Communication Networks (2005)
64. Hung, K.-S., Lui, K.-S., Kwok, Y.-K.: A Trust-Based Geographical Routing Scheme in Sensor Networks. In: The IEEE Wireless Communications and Networking Conference (WCNC 2007), Hong Kong (2007)
65. Mundinger, J., Boudec, J.-Y.L.: Reputation in Self-Organized Communication Systems and Beyond. In: The 2006 Workshop on Interdisciplinary Systems Approach in Performance Evaluation and Design of Computer & Communications Sytems, Pisa, Italy (2006)
66. Ma, R., Xing, L., Michel, H.E.: Fault-Intrusion Tolerant Techniques in Wireless Sensor Networks. In: The 2nd IEEE International Symposium on Dependable, Autonomic and Secure Computing (2006)
67. Zhang, Q., Yu, T., Ning, P.: A Framework for Identifying Compromised Nodes in Sensor Networks. ACM Transactions on Information and System Security (TISSEC) 11 (2008)
68. Yao, Z., Kim, D., Doh, Y.: PLUS: Parameterized and Localized trUst Management Scheme for Sensor Networks Security. In: The Third IEEE International Conference on Mobile Ad-hoc and Sensor Systems (MASS). IEEE, Vancouver (2006)
69. Momani, M., Agbinya, J., Navarrete, G.P., Akache, M.: Trust Classification in Wireless Sensor Networks. In: The 8th International Symposium on DSP and Communication Systems (DSPCS 2005), Noosa Heads, Queensland, Australia (2005)
70. Momani, M., Agbinya, J., Navarrete, G.P., Akache, M.: A New Algorithm of Trust Formation in Wireless Sensor Networks. In: The 1st IEEE International Conference on Wireless Broadband and Ultra Wideband Communications (AusWireless 2006), Sydney, Australia (2006)
71. Momani, M., Agbinya, J., Alhmouz, R., Navarrete, G.P., Akache, M.: A New Framework of Establishing Trust in Wireless Sensor Networks. In: International Conference on Computer & Communication Engineering (ICCCE 2006), Kuala Lumpur, Malaysia (2006)
72. Momani, M., Challa, S., Aboura, K.: Modelling Trust in Wireless Sensor Networks from the Sensor Reliability Prospective. In: Sobh, T., Elleithy, K., Mahmood, A., Karim, M. (eds.) Innovative Algorithms and Techniques in Automation, Industrial Electronics and Telecommunications. Springer, Netherlands (2007)
73. Momani, M., Aboura, K., Challa, S.: RBATMWSN: Recursive Bayesian Approach to Trust Management in Wireless Sensor Networks. In: The Third International Conference on Intelligent Sensors, Sensor Networks and Information, Melbourne, Australia (2007)
74. Momani, M., Challa, S.: GTRSSN: Gaussian Trust and Reputation System for Sensor Networks. In: International Joint Conferences on Computer, Information, and Systems Sciences, and Engineering (CISSE 2007). University of Bridgeport (2007)
75. Momani, M., Challa, S., Alhmouz, R.: Can we Trust Trusted Nodes in Wireless Sensor Networks? In: The International Conference on Computer and Communication Engineering (ICCCE 2008), Kuala Lumpur, Malaysia (2008)

Load Balancing in Distributed Web Caching

Tiwari Rajeev[1] and Khan Gulista[2]

[1] Lecturer, Department of Computer Science and Engineering ,HEC, Jagadhri, India
[2] Department of Computer Science Engineering,MMEC,Mullana,India
{errajeev.tiwari,gulista.khan}@gmail.com
http://www.hec.ac.in

Abstract. The World Wide Web suffers from scaling and reliability problems due to overloaded and congested proxy servers. Caching at local proxy serves help, but cannot satisfy more than a third to half of requests; more requests are still sent to original remote servers. In this paper we have developed an algorithm for Distributed Web Cache, which incorporates cooperation among proxy servers of one cluster. This algorithm uses Distributed Web Cache concepts along with static hierarchies with geographical based clusters of level one proxy server with dynamic mechanism of proxy server during the congestion of one cluster. Congestion and scalability problems are being dealt by clustering concept used in our approach. This results in higher ratio of caches, with lesser latency delay for requested pages. This algorithm alsi guarantees data consistency between the original server objects and the proxy cache objects.

Keywords: Distributed Web Caching, Clustering, Proxy Server, Latency, Hit Ratio.

1 Introduction

The Web is a highly distributed system with documents scattered in various hosts around the world. What an end user requests by a click triggers a chain of events and could result in the document travelling through numerous international, national, local gateways and routers before it reaches higher desktop. This chain of events could result in the end user experiencing considerable latency. When many end-users request for the same document, the document will be transmitted from the origin server to all the end users for each request. This result in many transmissions of the same document from the origin, increasing the response latency, as each transmission takes up network bandwidth. With more users getting connected to the Internet every day and the global move towards attractive and flashy multimedia oriented websites, thereby resulting in a huge growth in the size of objects assessed, methods to more effective delivery of information are becoming very important. Caching objects at a location nearer to potential requesting computer nodes is one such method. By caching recently used documents at a location closer to the end user, the latency for subsequent requests of a document within the locality of the first request is reduced. The most common form of cache today is that provided within the computer of the user.

N. Meghanathan et al. (Eds.): CNSA 2010, CCIS 89, pp. 47–54, 2010.
© Springer-Verlag Berlin Heidelberg 2010

Most modem web browsers allow pages recently accessed by the user of a computer to be stored as temporary files in the disks of the computer. These pages are then quickly displayed should the user needs to revisit the pages.

In other cases dedicated computers within a local area network are set up to cache documents normally or recently accessed by users within the network. Therefore in situations where clients in the same locality are likely to access similar documents, these caches are effective in improving the performance of the delivery system. Consequently the bandwidth usage and workload on the origin server are also reduced. A question is how to organize and manage the cache such that maximum benefit can be derived.

1.1 Issues

The various issues associated with web cache are summarized as follows:

1.1.1 Cache Size
The documents requested by any user in a typical session can run into many megabytes. Multiplies this by the number of users and then factors in the desired period the documents have to remain in cache, the number is huge. Ideally to maximize cache hits, as many documents as possible should be cached for as long a period as possible. In the event that the storage capacity is not sufficient, replacement algorithms are used to determine the documents to be replaced.

1.1.2 Congestion
A one-to-multipoint cache system, where one cache server serves many clients may lead to a major congestion set back. This is especially so for cache server that has a big disk capacity. Since the disk capacity is huge, the probability of cache hits is high. All the requests and responses thus concentrate at the cache server node, leading to a high peak bandwidth demand at the cache server and the attached communication link. When designing a cache system, it is important to factor in the requirement for this peak bandwidth demand at the server node, so as to maintain a certain minimum quality of service, or at least to ensure a non-blocking system. The larger the number of documents a cache server caches, and the larger the number of clients a cache server serves would translate into a higher peak bandwidth required at the server node. To fulfill this peak bandwidth, would mean an excess of resources during off-peak period.

1.1.3 Consistency between Server and Cached Objects
This is a major issue in any web caching strategy. Once a document is cached there is no guarantee that the original document will remain unchanged. In most cases the document at the original location gets updated without the knowledge of the caches that have an older version of the document. In this situation, when the client requests for the document a stale document will be returned. This is a serious problem especially many websites today are moving towards delivery of real-time information instead of serving as static archive of information.

1.2 Solutions

We summarize some of the solutions here as follows:

1.2.1 Cache Size
One solution to overcome this limitation is to share the storage space of several servers to achieve a greater capacity while at the same time acting as one logical cache server. The Cache Array Routing Protocol (CARP) [1] and Web Cache Communication Protocol (WCCP) support such cooperation of several servers. These servers however need not to be located in the same location.

1.2.2 Consistency between Server and Cached Objects
The solutions available for the cache consistency fall into one of two categories, namely strong consistency or weak consistency. Weak consistency is achieved by using a Time To Live (TTL) algorithm [2]. When a cached document is requested the cache server will check if the TTL has lapsed before returning the document. If the TTL has not lapsed, the cached copy is considered valid and is delivered to the client.

Otherwise the copy is discarded and a new copy is fetched from the origin server. Strong consistency could be achieved by polling or by using an invalidation protocol [3]. Polling involves the cache checking the validity of the document from the origin server, each time it is requested. Invalidation protocol involves the original server keeping track of all the caches where the document is cached and then sending an invalidation command to the caches once the document is updated.

In this paper we propose a revolutionary distributed web caching system. The proposed theoretical model has the largest combined storage space and has a guaranteed data consistency.

2 Desirable Properties of Distributed Web Caching

2.1 Fast access. Access latency is an important measurement of the quality   of Web service. A desirable caching system should aim at reducing Web access latency. In particular, it should provide user a lower latency on average than those without employing a caching system.

2.2 Robustness. Robustness means availability, which is another important measurement of quality of Web service. Users desire to have web service available whenever they want.

2.3 Transparency. A Web caching system should be transparent for the user, the only results user should notice are faster response and higher availability.

2.4 Scalability. We have seen an explosive growth in network size and density in last decades and are facing a more rapid increasing growth in near future. The key to success in such an environment is the scalability. We would like a caching scheme to scale well along the increasing size and density of network.

2.5 Efficiency. We would like a caching system to impose a minimal additional burden on the network. This includes both control packets and extra data packets incurred by using a caching system.

2.6 Adaptivity. The adaptivity involves several aspects: cache management, cache routing, proxy placement, etc. This is essential to achieve optimal performance.

2.7 Stability. The schemes used in Web caching system shouldn't introduce instabilities into the network.

2.8 Load balancing. It's desirable that the caching scheme distributes the load evenly through the entire network.

2.9 Simplicity. We would like an ideal Web caching mechanism to be simple to deploy.

3 Problems in Distributed Web Caching

3.1 Extra Overhead. Extra Overload increases when all the proxy servers keep the records of all the other proxy servers which results congestion on all proxy servers. They all have to keep check on the validity of their data which results in extra overhead on proxy servers.

3.2 Size of Cache. If Cache Size is large then Meta data become unmanageable because in traditional architectures each proxy server keep records for data of all other proxy servers. In this way if Cache size becomes large then maintenance of Meta data is a problem.

3.3 Cache Coherence Problem. When client send requests for data to proxy server that data should be up-to-date. This results into Cache Coherence problem.

3.4 Scalability. Finally, By Clustering we can also solve the problem of scalability, add more number of clients, and data of these clients will be managed on the basis of geographical region based Cluster. A particular cluster will only have to manage the id's and update the meta data of all the proxy servers fall under the , particular geographical region cluster.

4 Proposed Solution for Distributed Web Caching

Extra overhead on proxy server, problem of unmanageable data, Cache coherence and Scalability. Extra Overhead increases when all the proxy servers keep the records of all the other proxy servers which results congestion on all proxy servers. They all have to keep check on the validity of their data which results in extra overhead on proxy servers. Clustering reduces this extra overhead. By making clusters on the basis of Geographical region we can solve this problem. From now one proxy will manage the Meta data regarding the proxy servers which fall under the same cluster region. If Cache Size is large then Meta data become unmanageable because in traditional architectures each proxy server keeps records for data of all other proxy servers. In this way if Cache size becomes large then maintenance of Meta data is a problem. When client send requests for data to proxy server that data should be up-to-date. This results into Cache Coherence problem. This can be solved by having a timer with origin server, after a particular time period if there is any fresh page then origin server will check for it and send the fresh pages to any of proxy server which in turn forward this information to all other proxies and one cluster region have to maintain the record for cache updation for that cluster only. This gives proper updation of data and also less workload. With all the data pages there will be a time stamp field, now if there is any fresh page then origin server will check for it and send the fresh pages to any of proxy server which in turn forward this information to all other proxies and one cluster region have to maintain the record for cache updation for that cluster only. This gives proper updation of data and also less workload. Finally, By Clustering we can also solve the problem of scalability by this, add more number of clients, and data of these clients will be managed on the basis of geographical region Cluster. A particular cluster will only have to manage the id's and update the meta data of all the proxy servers fall under the , particular geographical region cluster. and data of these clients will be managed on the basis of geographical region Cluster. A particular cluster will only have to manage the id's and update the meta data of all the proxy servers fall under the , particular geographical region cluster.

5 The Proposed Caching System

In this section, we first define the structure for which our proposed caching model is intended. This is followed by a detailed description of the caching model. We then discuss some interesting properties of the proposed system.

5.1 Structure of Network

At the highest level origin server are scattered around the world. These origin servers arc connected to proxy server via various form of communication medium. These proxy servers are in turn connected to client computer whose purpose are just to send the request and get response. Proxy servers are arranged at middle level which acts as both client and servers. For origin server they act as client and for client computers they act as servers. All the proxy servers are arranged in the geographical region based .After adding the concept of clusters now it is easy to maintain the data in the cache of proxy servers. To maintain the data consistency we arrange a timer with the origin server so that if there is any fresh page after that time interval then origin server keep check for that and forward fresh pages to the proxy servers on any port which in turn forward data to other proxy servers to maintain metadata. Each Proxy server is having metadata in its cache which keeps the record about data in other proxy servers. Each proxy server in one cluster is having metadata about proxy servers which fall in corresponding geographical based cluster.

5.2 Proposed Architecture

According to this architecture browsers are at the lower level, proxy servers at the middle level and origin servers at the highest level.

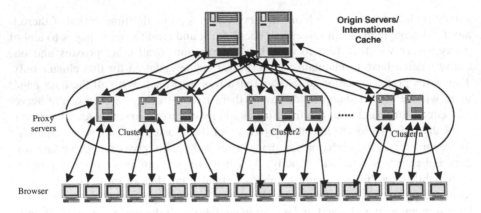

Working: In this arrangement whenever client request for a page that request goes to proxy server, Proxy server maintains metadata for each and every page, proxy server check for match in meta data for the requested page. If the match found is for current proxy then search for data and send it to client. Otherwise make connection with the other matched proxyserver. If there is no match found then request forward to the origin server.

5.3 Proposed Algorithm

5.3.1 Proxy Server
/* queuelength: It is associated with every proxy server, which tells how many client's requests can be made to a proxy server.*/
CIP: Client's Internet Address.
PS: Proxy Servers.
Noofservices: tells how many connections are active with proxy server. Reply: has either requested page or message "NO".
Rpage: Requested page or file.
Ps_ip []: is a stack of Internet Addresses of all the proxy servers in same Cluster.
OS []: is a stack of Internet Addresses of all the Origin Servers.

Cluster []: is a stack of Internet Addresses of all Clusters.
Step 1: noofservices=0
Step 2: If Request from OS [] for connection then
A. Establish connection with the origin server.
B. Connection Established.
  i.   A new thread is established.
  ii. Receive data from origin server.
  iii. Update its metadata and broadcast information to all clusters.
Step 3: Proxy Server will wait for connection with clients or from other proxy servers.
Step 4: If request is to update data by any other proxy server then update metadata.
Step 5: if noofservices<=queuelength then
Step 6: As a connection is established by creating a new thread to deal with it.
Step 7: Get client's locative on in IP address in CIP.

Step 8: Check if CIP is in Ps_ip [] then/*request is from proxy server*/.
Step 8.a Get request from CIP as Rpage.
Step 8.b Search for Rpage in its metadata.
Step 8.c Noofservices=noofservices-1
Step 8.d Return Rpage to CIP
Step 9: Else/*request is from client*/
Step 9.a Get request from CIP as Rpage.
Step 9.b Find a match for Rpage in metadata.
Step 9.c If matchfound then
a. If matchfound=currentproxy then
1. Search for Rpage in cache.
2. Noofservices=noofservices-1
3. Return Rpage to CIP.
b. Else
1. Establish connection of client   with matched proxy server.
2. Go to step 4.
Step9.d Else
a. Establish Connection with OS [].
b. Send request for Rpage and look for reply.
c. If reply=Rpage then
  i. Load Rpage into its Cache memory.
 ii. Update metadata and broadcast information for adding new data to all proxies.
iii. Noofservices=noofservices-1
iv. Return Rpage to CIP.
d. Else Message "NO" to proxy server.
Step 10: Else
Step10.a Establish connection with some other proxy server in Cluster.
Step10.b Go to step 4.

5.3.2 Origin Server

/* Whole data files resides at origin server's secondary memory at a fixed directory path of c:\pages*/
Step 1: Start timer / time_counter
Step 2: If(time_counter>=3min) then
Step2.a: Create metadata of updated pages.
Step2.b: Check and list the updated pages.
Step3: Try to establish connection with a proxy server.
Step 3.a: Connection established
i. Send metadata to proxy server.
Step4: Wait for the connection with proxy servers at a specified port.
Step 5: Connection is established
Step 5.a: A new thread is created to deal with proxy server's connection with origin server.
Step 5.b: As proxy server makes a request for a page then:
i. Fixed directory path is searched for requested page or file.
ii.If page exists then Desired file/page is returned to proxy server.
iii. Else "No" is returned.

5.3.3 Client Algorithm

/* Hierarchies are used so clients know IP addresses of their proxy servers, to which they will connect and send request.*/

Step 1: Establish connection of client with proxy server

Step 2: Client sends a request for a page to proxy server and starts a timer "delay".

Step 3: if delay<=3 minutes then

a) if desired page is returned then execute the page

b) else

  Write message "No such file exists! Please check the spellings and try   again!"

Step 4: else

c) Write "Page request is expired! Try again".

6 Conclusions

Web service becomes more and more popular, users are suffering network congestion and server overloading. Great efforts have been made to improve Web performance. Web caching is recognized to be one of the effective techniques to alleviate server bottleneck and reduce network traffic, thereby minimize the user access latency. In this work, I give an algorithm to reduce the Extra Overhead, solves the problem of Cache Coherence (Get if Modified), problem of Scalability along with solving all these problems it also improves the Hit Ratio and the Latency Time .By surveying previous works on Web caching, we notice that there are still some open problems in Web caching such as proxy placement, cache routing, dynamic data caching, fault tolerance, security, etc. The research frontier in Web performance improvement lies in developing efficient, scalable, robust, adaptive, and stable Web caching scheme that can be easily deployed in current and future network. Further we can improve performance by adding page replacement algorithm and till now we have used static hierarchies can improve by adding concept of dynamic hierarchies.

References

1. Valloppillil, V., Ross, K.W.: Cache Array Routing Protocol v1.0 (February 1998)
2. Gwertzman, J., Seltzer, M.: World Wide Web cache consistency. In: Proceedings of the 1996 Usenix Technical Conference, Boston, MA. Harvard College (1996)
3. Worrel, K.: Invalidation in large scale network object caches., Technical report, Master's Thesis, University of Colorado, Boulder (1994)

TRING: A New Framework for Efficient Group Key Distribution for Dynamic Groups

D.V. Naga Raju[1] and Dr.V. Valli Kumari[2]

[1] Research Scholar Acharya Nagarjuna University, Guntur, India
[2] College of Engineering Andhra University, Visakhapatnam, India
{nagudatla,vallikumari}@gmail.com

Abstract. Many emerging applications like audio/video conferencing, stock quote updates, interactive gaming etc., require secure group communication. In these group based applications, data is to be delivered from one or more legitimate sources to a group of legitimate receivers. The critical issue in any group communication protocols is that the group membership is highly dynamic with frequent member addition and member eviction. Security can be achieved only though the renewing of the existing key material with every possible event like member addition and member leave. As these events are performed more often, the renewing and distribution of the key material to the entire group should be done in an efficient and scalable manner. Any network application requires minimum computational and communication costs. Generally with cryptographic protocols the computation cost is influenced by the number of encryptions/decryptions. This paper proposes two protocols one using the broadcast ring and the other using the combination of the ring and tree based protocol to minimize the communication overhead as well as computation burden.

1 Introduction

Many group based applications like audio/video conferencing, stock quote updates, interactive gaming are gaining popularity with latest advancements in the Internet technologies especially with increase in the bandwidth. In this group oriented applications the participation number is very high and highly dynamic. In any group based applications the data need to be delivered to a group of legitimate users from one or more legitimate sources. The confidentiality can be maintained by sharing a common group key among the group members. The critical issue with any group communication protocols is the dynamic nature of the membership. As the member addition into the group and the member leave from the group are most frequently performed activity during the group communication, security can be maintained only through the refreshment of the existing key material. This process of refreshment of key material is known as rekeying. Since the rekeying is the frequently performed activity, key generation and distribution should be done in an efficient and scalable manner by best utilizing the network resources. Multicasting is the optimum technique for these applications. Group key management is highly difficult for large and dynamic multicast groups. Any group key management protocols need to address two important issues: Forward secrecy and backward secrecy. Forward secrecy ensures that the evicted

N. Meghanathan et al. (Eds.): CNSA 2010, CCIS 89, pp. 55–65, 2010.

member should not have access to any future communication. Backward secrecy ensures that the new member should not have access to the past communication. In order to maintain the forward and backward secrecy the group key need to be changed with every membership change. The other factors that also influence the performance of group based protocols are the minimum key maintenance by the member, less number of encryptions/decryptions, minimum communication cost etc.

2 Related Work

The existing Group key management protocols can classified into three categories: centralized, decentralized and contributory key management protocols. The centralized key management schemes [1], [2], [3], [4], [5], [6] assume a trusted server known as Key Distribution Server (KDC) which takes the responsibility of generation and distribution of the keys to group members. These protocols suffer from a single point of failure. In decentralized approach [7], [8], [9], [10], [11], a hierarchy of key managers takes the responsibility of the distribution of the group key to the group members in order to avoid the single point of failure. Contributory key agreement schemes [12], [13], [14], [15], [16] take the equal share of every member in the generation of the common group key.

The centralized key management scheme proposed by Wong et al. [3], is one of the efficient method where a logical key hierarchy is maintained. The members occupy the leaf nodes possesses all the keys along their key path. The key generation and distribution is carried out by the KDC which suffers from a single point of failure. Moreover LKH reduces the number of rekey messages during membership change using the hierarchical approach. The FDLKH [7] which belongs to the decentralized category inherits the key hierarchy of the LKH [3].Unlike LKH, FDLKH does not maintain any central server. Hence no single point of failure. The FDLKH also uses a binary key where the intermediate nodes are associated with symmetric keys. Unlike the members of LKH, the members of FDLKH have no individual keys. Hence the number of keys maintained at each member is one less than that of LKH. FDLKH gives the responsibility and distribution of the keys to captains using DH key exchange protocol. Rakesh Bobba, Himamshu Khurana [12] proposed DLPKH: Distributed Logical Public Key Hierarchy where they also followed the concept of Logical Key Hierarchy. In this scheme they used public key trees for the secure distribution of the updated keys which have the advantage of secure distribution of the keys without establishing any secure channel. In this scheme, each member who occupies at leaf node will know all the private and public keys of their ancestor nodes and also the public keys of the nodes that are siblings to the set of nodes on the path from the leaf to the root. The responsibility of generation and distribution of keys is given to the sponsors and cosponsors. The major weakness of this protocol is that the private keys of the nodes will be revealed which is totally against the concept of public key cryptography. The schemes used in this paper uses the logical key tree hierarchy like LKH[4], share of dynamically selected members for the generation and distribution of group key like FDLKH[7]and DLPKH[12]. The proposed schemes have certain advantages like no single point of failure unlike [3], no need of secure channel establishment unlike [3], [7]. Not revealing the private keys unlike [12]. Moreover the number of encryption/decryptions as well as communication cost is also less with the proposed schemes.

3 Notations and Terminology

Mi	Member occupies the position i (i=1, 2, 3…)
(l, m)	m^{th} node at level l in a tree
P_bK,	Public Key associated with a member
P_rK	Private Key associated with a member
P_bK^{I}	updated Public Key
P_rK^{I}	updated Private Keys
SK	Shared key
E (K, X)	Encryption of data X using a key K
GK	Group key
AS	Authenticated server
AS_n	Number of Authentication servers
DH	Diffie-Hellman key exchange protocol
n	Number of members in a group
p, g	ElGmal group parameters

4 Broadcast Ring Based Group Communication

This section describes the basic principle and assumptions of broadcast ring based group key management protocol. The proposed scheme assumes a unidirectional logical broadcast ring. There is an Authentication Server (AS) for the entire group. The Authentication server validates the authenticity of the user and some times is also participates in the generation and distribution of the group key. Each member occupies a position in the ring. Each member is associated with its private and public key, a group key and a shared key. Each member knows the public keys of its successors and shared keys of its predecessors. The group key is generated with the help of a dynamically selected member known as sponsor. The members change their private and public keys using the equations.

$$\text{New public key} = \text{old Public key} \times g^{newGK} \mod p \qquad (1)$$

$$\text{New private key} = \text{old Private Key} + \text{new GK} \mod p \qquad (2)$$

$$\text{New Shared key} = H (\text{old shared key} \| \text{new GK}) \qquad (3)$$

4.1 Join Protocol

When a member wants to join, it broadcasts a join request. The join request includes the public key of the joining member. After the validation of the new member is done by the Authentication server, the new member is allowed to join the group. All the existing members store the public key of the new member. The joining point is always the predecessor of the Authentication server. The predecessor of the Authentication server (before the member joins the group) is selected as the sponsor. For the group size of one, the new member and the Authentication server will exchange the new group key using the Diffie-Hellman key exchange algorithm. For group size greater than one, the Authentication server and the sponsor exchange the new group key using Diffie-Hellman key exchange algorithm. The sponsor broadcasts the new group key encrypted with the old group key. All the members except the new member get the new group key. The sponsor also sends to the joining member the new group key and all the updated shared keys it had, encrypted with the public key of the new member and also the complete ring structure. Now all the members get the new group key and update their key pair and the public keys of their successors and shared keys of their predecessor using the equations (1) , (2) and (3).

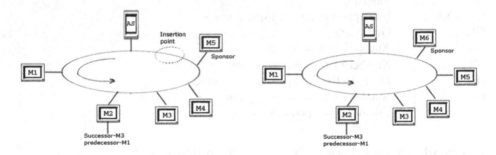

Fig. 1. Ring before join   **Fig. 2.** Ring after join

Suppose M6 wants to join the group, it broadcasts a join request. The Authentication Server validated the new member and if it satisfies then it can be allowed to be a member of the group. The sponsor in this case is M5. Now sponsor (M5) and the authentication server exchange the new group key using DH key exchange algorithm. The sponsor (M5) broadcasts the new group key encrypted with the old group key. The sponsor also sends to the joining member the new group key and all the updated shared keys it had, encrypted with the public key of the new member.

M5 $\rightarrow$ G   : E (Old GK, new GK);

M5 $\rightarrow$ M6: E (P$_b$K of M6, (SK^1 of M4, SK^1 of M3, SK^1 of M2, SK^1 of M1, new GK))

4.2 Leave Protocol

When an existing member wants to leave the group, it broadcasts a leave request. Unlike join protocol in leave, two members known as sponsor and co-sponsor are selected for the generation and distribution of the new group key. There are three cases of leave. Case-1: if the leaving member is neither the successor nor the predecessor of the Authentication server then the predecessor of the leaving member is selected as sponsor and the successor of the leaving member is selected as co-sponsor. The sponsor and the co-sponsor exchange the new group key using DH key exchange algorithm. The sponsor encrypts the new group key with its private key and broadcast. Now all the predecessors of the leaving member will get the new group key. Similarly the co-sponsor encrypts the new group key with its shared key. Now all the successors of the leaving member will get the new group key. All the members will update the keys the possesses using (1),(2) and (3).

Case-2: If the leaving member is the successor of the authentication server, then the Authentication server is selected as sponsor.

Case-3: If the leaving member is the predecessor of the authentication server, then the Authentication server is

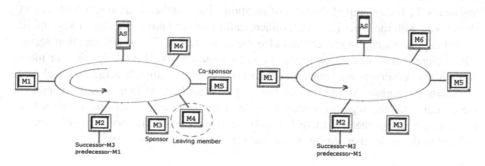

Fig. 3. Ring before leave   **Fig.4.** Ring after leave

Suppose M4 wants to leave, it broadcasts a leave request. The sponsor and co-sponsor are selected independently by the existing group members. In this case the sponsor is M3 and the co-sponsor is M5. The sponsor (M3) and the co-sponsor (M5) exchange the new group key using the DH key exchange algorithm. Sponsor (M3) encrypts the new group key with its private key and the co-sponsor (M5) encrypts the new group key with its shared key and broadcasts.

M4→ leave request

M3→G: E (P_rK of M3, New GK)

M5→G: E (SK of M5, New GK)

5 Group Communication Using the Combination of Ring and Tree

This section describes the basic principle and assumptions of the scheme that uses the combination of both ring and tree based protocols for efficient conference key distribution. The entire group is divided into several regions. Each region headed with An Authentication server. All the existing Authentication servers form a logical broadcast ring. A logical tree hierarchy is maintained with root as an Authentication server. The tree is assumed to be a binary tree. Members occupy the leaf nodes. Each member is associated with its public key, private key a group key. The keys of the intermediate nodes are assumed to be shared keys that it can share with the members. The root is associated with a public, private key and a shared key. Each member holds all the shared keys of its ancestor nodes including the public key and the shared key of the root. Each Authentication server maintains the count of the number of members it is currently associated. Generally with the tree based protocols, the keys maintained by the member increases with the increase in the depth of the tree. In this scheme we restrict the depth of the tree (a threshold value) i.e. each tree (region) has a certain capacity i.e. the number of members it can have. If the tree reaches the threshold value, another group (region) will be formed with another Authentication server as a root by all the existing authentication servers (roots). Each authentication server maintains the time stamp of the time of creation. Each Authentication server shares its shared key with the other i.e. each Authentication server knows the shared keys of all the other Authentication servers and also the time stamps. The Authentication server where there is a room for new members will announces its ID publicly. Two or more Authentication servers may announce their ID at the same time. It is the user's choice to choose the region. All the regions have equal priorities. Without loss of generality we assume that the region capacity is eight. Key-path can be defined as the set of intermediate nodes that are there between the member and the root. Co-path can be defined as the nodes that are siblings to the set of nodes on the key-path.

5.1 Join Protocol

When a member wants to join a particular region, it sends a join request to that authentication server. The join request includes the public key of the joining member and the region ID where it wants to join. After the validation of the member is over, then it is allowed to join the group. The insertion point and sponsor is always the right most shallowest leaf node. The share of a dynamically selected member known as sponsor is taken for the generation of the new group key. The criteria for selection of sponsor and member addition: i) if the insertion point is a leaf node then it is selected as a sponsor. Two new nodes are created and added to the insertion point. The sponsor currently associated with the leaf node is give to the left child and the right child became the new member and is given the public key of the new member. ii) Otherwise if the insertion point is a non leaf node with a child existing already this child is selected as sponsor. A new node is created and becomes the new member. iii) Otherwise the sponsor of the sibling of the new member is selected as the sponsor.

The sponsor and the root exchange the new group key using the Diffie-Hellman key exchange protocol. The sponsor encrypts the new group key with the old group key and broadcasts it. All the members of this region will get the group key. The sponsor also sends the new group key, updated public key of the root and the updated shared keys of the ancestor nodes of the new member encrypted with the public key of the new member. The authentication server where the join event is happened

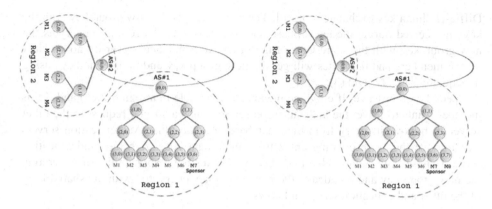

Fig. 5. Tring before join   **Fig. 6.** Tring after join

encrypts the new group key with the shared keys of the other Authentication servers it knows. Once the members getting the new group key, they will updated the keys using equations (1), (2) and (3).

Suppose a member M8 wants to join in a region #1, it broadcasts a join request. The join request contains the region ID as AS#1and its own public key. All the members of this region (#1) receive this join request and independently determine the insertion point and sponsor. Here the sponsor is M7. The sponsor (M7) and the root (AS) will exchange the new group key using DH key exchange algorithm. The sponsor (M7) encrypts the new group key using the old group key and broadcasts it. The sponsor also encrypts the new group key and updated shared keys of the ancestor nodes of the new member and updated public key of the root with the public key of the new member. All the members update the keys using equations (1), (2) and (3).

M8→join request

Sponsor (M7) →G: E (old GK, new GK)

Sponsor(M7)→M8: E(P_bK of M8,(SK of (2,3),SK of(1,1), P_bK of (0,0))

AS#1→AS#1: E (SK of AS#2, new GK)

5.2 Leave Protocol

When a member wants to leave from a region, it broadcasts a leave request. The leave request includes the ID of its region and also the shared keys of the ancestor nodes of the leaving member. Like join, in leave also the share of a dynamically selected member known as sponsor is taken in the generation of the new group key. The criteria for selection of the sponsor: i) if the leaving member has a sibling then it will be selected as the sponsor. ii) Otherwise the sponsor of the subtree rooted at the sibling node of leaving node's parent will be selected as the sponsor. All the co-path members of the leaving member will send their shared keys encrypted with the public key of the root. Sponsor and the root will exchange the new group key using

Diffie-Hellman key exchange protocol. The root encrypts the new group key with the keys it received during the leave phase and broadcasts it. The root also encrypts the new group key with the share keys of the other Authenticated server it knows. Now all the members and the nodes will get the new group key and update the keys using the equations (1), (2) and (3).

Special case of leave: If only one member is available in a region (tree) and if this member wants to leave, the authentication server sends a special request to the other server to remove its entry from their database. All the other Authentication servers will remove the corresponding entry from their data base. A senior authentication server (whose time stamp value is higher) will takes the responsibility of generating the new group key and broadcasts the new group key encrypted with the shared keys of the other authentication servers it knows.

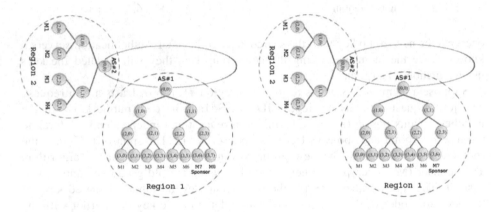

Fig. 7. Tring before leave   **Fig. 8.** Tring after leave

Suppose M8 wants to leave from the group, it broadcasts a leave request. The leave request includes the region id and the ancestor nodes of the leaving member. The co-path nodes leaving member ((2, 2), (1, 0)) send their shared keys to the root encrypted with the public key of the root. The sponsor (M7) will exchange the group key using DH key exchange protocol. The root encrypts the new group key with the keys it receives during the leave request and broadcast it.

M8→ leave request (#1, SK (2, 3), SK (1, 1))

(2, 2)→(0, 0): E (P_bK of (0, 0), SK (2, 2))

(1, 0)→(0, 0): E (P_bK of (0, 0), SK (1, 0))
(0, 0)→(1, 0): E (SK (1, 0), new GK)
(0, 0)→(2, 2): E (SK (2, 2), new GK)
(0, 0)→(1, 0): E (SK (1, 0), new GK)
(0, 0)→(1, 1): E (SK (1, 1), new GK)
(0, 0)→(2, 3): E (SK (2, 3), new GK)
AS#1→AS#2: E (SK of AS#2, new GK)

6 Analysis

6.1 Number of Keys at Each Member

S.No	Protocol	Keys
1	Proposed scheme-1	$n+3$
2	Proposed scheme-2	$l+5$
3	FDLKH	l
4	LKH	$l+1$

6.2 Cost of Join

Scheme	Entity	DH	Encs	Decrs
Proposed scheme-1	AS	1	-	-
	Sponsor	1	2	-
	New member	-	-	1
	Other members	-	-	1
Proposed scheme-2	*AS	1	$ASn-1$	-
	Other ASs	-	-	1
	Sponsor	1	2	-
	New member	-	-	1
	Other members	-	-	1
FDLKH (Dedicated)	New member	l	-	-
	Other Member	-	-	2
	per Captain	1	1	$(l-1)/2$
FDLKH (Distributed)	New member	1	-	$l-1$
	Other Member	-	-	2
	per Captain	$(2l-1)/l$	$(2l-2)/l$	$(l-1)(l-2)/2l$
LKH	Key server	-	$2l$	-
	New member	-	-	1
	Per member	-	-	2

*The AS who is responsible for the region where the join event is happened.

6.3 Cost of Leave

Scheme	Entity	DH	Encs	Decrs
Proposed scheme-1	AS	-	-	-
	Sponsor	1	1	-
	Co-sponsor	1	1	-
	leaving member	-	-	-
	Other members	-	-	1
Proposed scheme-2	*AS	1	$l-1$	$l-1$
	Sponsor	1	1	-
	leaving member	-	-	-
	Each Co-path node	-	1	1
	Other members	-	-	1

FDLKH (dedicated)	leaving member	-	-	-
	Other Member	-	-	2
	per Captain	1	1	$(l-2)/2$
	Buddy Captain	$l-1$	$l-2$	-
FDLKH (Distributed)	Leaving member	-	-	-
	Other Member	-	-	2
	per Captain	$(2l-2)/l$	$(2l-3)/l$	$(l-1)(l-2)/2l$
LKH	Key server	-	-	-
	New member	-	-	2
	Per member	-	$2l$	-

*The AS who is responsible for the region where the leave event is happened.

7 Conclusion

Maintaining security in a large dynamic group is highly difficult with frequent joins/leaves. The generation and distribution of the new key material to the entire group should be done in a scalable and efficient manner with effective utilization the network resources and with minimum burden. The two schemes proposed in this paper achieve confidentiality with minimum efforts. The advantages of the two schemes includes no single point of failure, no need of secure channel establishment, minimum computational burden and minimum communication overhead.

References

[1] Harney, H., Muckenhirn, C.: Group Key Management Protocol (GKMP) Architecture. RFC 2093 (July 1997)
[2] Harney, H., Muckenhirn, C.: Group Key Management Protocol (GKMP) Specification. RFC 2094 (July 1997)
[3] Wong, C.K., Gouda, M., Lam, S.S.: Secure Group Communication Using key Graphs. IEEE/ACM Transactions on Networking 8(1), 16–30 (2000)
[4] Blundo, C., De Santis, A., Herzberg, A., Kutten, S., Vaccaro, U., Yung, M.: Perfectly-secure key distribution for dynamic conferences. In: Brickell, E.F. (ed.) CRYPTO 1992. LNCS, vol. 740, pp. 471–486. Springer, Heidelberg (1993)
[5] McGrew, D.A., Sherman, A.T.: Key establishment in Large Dynamic Groups using One-Way Function Trees. IEEE Transactions on Software Engineering 29(5), 444–458 (2003)
[6] Waldvogel, M., Caronni, G., Sun, D., Weiler, N., Plattner, B.: The VersaKey Framework: Versatile Group Key Management. IEEE Journal on Selected Areas in Communications (Special Issues on Middleware) 17(8), 1614–1631 (1999)
[7] Inoue, D., Kuroda, M.: FDLKH: Fully Decentralized Key Management scheme on a Logical Key Hierarchy. In: Jakobsson, M., Yung, M., Zhou, J. (eds.) ACNS 2004. LNCS, vol. 3089, pp. 339–354. Springer, Heidelberg (2004)
[8] Ballardie, A.: Scalable Multicast Key Distribution. RFC 1949 (May 1996)
[9] Chaddoud, G., Chrisment, I., Shaff, A.: Dynamic Group Communication Security. In: 6th IEEE Symposium on Computers and Communication (2001)

[10] Oppliger, R., Albanese, A.: Distributed registration and key distribution (DiRK). In: Proceedings of the 12th International Conference on Information Security IFIP SEC 1996 (1996)

[11] Rafaeli, S., Hutchison, D.: Hydra: a decentralized group key management. In: 11th IEEE International WETICE: Enterprise Security Workshop (June 2002)

[12] Bobba, R., Khurana, H.: DLPKH: Distributed Logical Public Key Hierarchy. In: McDaniel, P., Gupta, S.K. (eds.) ICISS 2007. LNCS, vol. 4812, pp. 110–127. Springer, Heidelberg (2007)

[13] Ingemarson, I., Tang, D., Wong, C.: A Conference Key Distribution System. IEEE Transactions on Information Theory 28(5), 714–720 (1982)

[14] Steiner, M., Tsudik, G., Waidner, M.: Diffie-Hellman key distribution extended to group communication. In: 3rd ACM Conference on Computer and Communications Security, pp. 31–37 (March 1996)

[15] Lee, P.P.C., Lui, J.C.S., Yau, D.K.Y.: Distributed Collaborative Key Agreement Protocols for Dynamic Peer Groups. In: Proc. IEEE International Conference on Network Protocols, ICNP (November 2002)

[16] Perrig, A.: Efficient Collaborative Key Management Protocol for Secure Autonomous Group Communication. In: Proc. of International Workshop CrypTEC (1999)

Image Classification for More Reliable Steganalysis

R. Shreelekshmi[1], M. Wilscy[2], and C.E. Veni Madhavan[3]

[1] Department of Computer Science and Engineering, College of Engineering
Trivandrum, Kerala -695016
shreelekshmir@cet.ac.in
[2] Department of Computer Science, University of Kerala, Trivandrum
wilsyphilipose@hotmail.com
[3] Department of Computer Science and Automation, Indian Institute of Science,
Bangalore 560012
cevm@csa.iisc.ernet.in

Abstract. We propose a simple method for classifying images to increase the reliability of steganalysis techniques in digital images. RS Steganalysis Method(RSM), Sample Pair Method(SPM), and Least Square Method(LSM) are the most reliable steganalysis methods in the literature for LSB replacement steganography on digital images in spatial domain. These methods give highly accurate results on most of the images. However all these methods show very high embedding ratio when no data or very small amount of data is hidden in some images. We propose a simple method to identify images which give very accurate results and images which give highly inaccurate results. The novelty of our method is that it does not require any knowledge about the cover images. The image classification is done based on certain statistical properties of the image, which are invariant with embedding. Thus it helps the steganalyst in attaching a level of confidence to the estimation he makes.

1 Introduction

Steganography hides the secret message in cover objects to obtain stego objects. Digital images, videos, sound files and other computer files that contain perceptually irrelevant or redundant information are used as cover objects to hide secret messages. The goal of steganalysis is to detect/ estimate /retrieve potentially hidden information from observed data with little or no knowledge about the steganographic algorithm or its parameters. The purpose of steganography is to hide the presence of communication, as opposed to cryptography, which aims to make communication unintelligible to those who do not possess the right keys [4].

In this paper we focus on LSB replacement steganography on digital images in spatial domain. Many methods (see [1], [2], [3], [5], [6], [7] and [8]) have been proposed in the literature for steganalysis of digital images. These methods give very accurate results on most of the images.

Attempts were made in estimating the error in various steganalysis methods. Ker derived error distribution in Least Square steganalysis[9]. It shows that

N. Meghanathan et al. (Eds.): CNSA 2010, CCIS 89, pp. 66–74, 2010.
© Springer-Verlag Berlin Heidelberg 2010

LSM, one of the most reliable steganalysis methods, gives very accurate results on most of the images, but shows estimation errors on some images due to image specific properties.

With the development of very accurate steganalysis methods, methods have been proposed for increasing reliability of LSB steganography also. Fridrich et. al developed a general coding method called matrix embedding[10] that can be applied to most steganographic schemes for improving their steganographic security.

Luo et.al [11] developed a method for increasing security of LSB steganography based on chaos system and dynamic compensation. The dynamic compensation is done after hiding the data in the image. After doing dynamic compensation the most accurate methods like RS, SPM and LSM and their improved versions detect stego images with very high payload as cover images. However dynamic compensation causes the cover images to be detected as cover images only.

In this paper we present a simple image classification to identify a class of images that give accurate results and another class of images that give highly inaccurate steganalysis results. The method we propose is based on the statistical properties of the image. Certain statistical properties of the image are invariant with embedding. Since the classification proposed makes use of the properties of image which are invariant with embedding, it helps in identifying the stego images giving accurate results/highly inaccurate results without any knowledge about the cover images.

The rest of this paper is organized as follows: Section 2 explains the notations we use in this paper. Section 3 introduces the new method for image classification. Section 4 shows the experimental results we obtained. Section 5 is the conclusion.

2   Notations

P : Multiset of sample pairs (u, v) drawn from digital image
X_n : Sub multi set of P that consists of sample pairs drawn from cover signal and whose values differ by n and in which even value is larger
Y_n : Sub multi set of P that consists of sample pairs drawn from cover signal and whose values differ by n and in which odd value is larger
C_m : Sub multi set of P that consists of sample pairs drawn from cover signal and whose values differ by m in the first $(b-1)$ bits (i.e., by right shifting one bit and then measuring the difference of m)
D_0 : Sub multi set of P that consists of sample pairs drawn from cover signal and whose values differ by 0
p : Estimated length as percentage of number of pixels in the image

3   Classification of Images for More Reliable Steganalysis

RSM[1], SPM[2], and LSM[3] accurately estimate length of data hidden in images. According to the literature, SPM performs better than RSM and LSM outperforms SPM in general. These methods are based on probabilities of transitions between sample pairs due to LSB embedding operations.

LSM and SPM are based on the finite state machines shown in Fig. 1 and Fig. 2. The arrows are labelled with the probability of transition. The precision of SPM [3] depends on following hypotheses

$$E\{| X_{2m+1} |\} = E\{| Y_{2m+1} |\} \tag{1}$$

or a more relaxed condition

$$E\{| \bigcup_{m=i}^{j} X_{2m+1} |\} = E\{| \bigcup_{m=i}^{j} Y_{2m+1} |\}, 1 \leq i \leq j \leq 2^{b-1} - 1 \tag{2}$$

LSM [3] makes the hypothesis that there is a small parity difference occur in natural signals for each m. Estimation errors occur when the hypotheses do not hold.

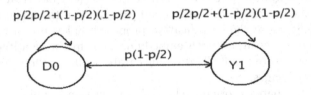

Fig. 1. Finite state machine associated with C_0

Apart from parity difference, there are other factors causing error. Both the methods partitions P into $C_m, 0 \leq m \leq 2^{b-1} - 1$. Each $C_m, 1 \leq m \leq 2^{b-1} - 1$ is further partitioned into sub multi sets X_{2m-1}, X_{2m}, Y_{2m} and Y_{2m+1} and C_0 is partitioned into D_0 and Y_1. When data is embedded into the image, sample pair in one sub multi set change to another sub multi set and thus the cardinalities of these sub multi sets change with embedding.

In fact cardinalities of sub multi sets in each $C_m, 0 \leq m \leq 2^{b-1} - 1$ increase /decrease monotonically with ratio of embedding and at 100% embedding these cardinalities become equal. Typical change in cardinalities of sub multi sets in a $C_m, 1 \leq m \leq 2^{b-1} - 1$ and C_0 are shown in Fig. 3.

In most of the images, $| X_{2m-1} | > | X_{2m} | \approx | Y_{2m} | > | Y_{2m+1} |$ and $| D_0 | > | Y_1 |$. Hence due to embedding $| X_{2m-1} |$ decreases and that of $| Y_{2m+1} |$ increases. $| X_{2m} |$ and $| Y_{2m} |$ increase or decrease depending on their initial values. At 100% embedding, all these cardinalities become equal. From the monotonic increase or decrease in cardinalities of sub multi sets the p value is calculated.

In cover images, $| X_{2m+1} | \approx | Y_{2m+1} |, 0 \leq n \leq 2^b - 1$ and with embedding the difference between $| X_{2m+1} |$ and $| Y_{2m+1} |$ increases and the difference is maximum at 100% embedding.

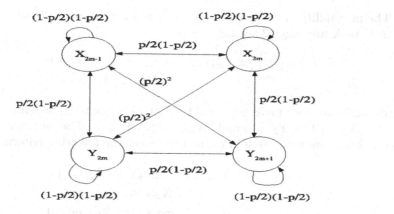

Fig. 2. Finite state machine associated with C_m, $m \geq 1$

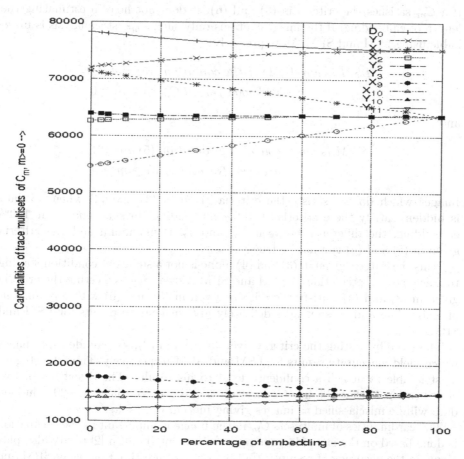

Fig. 3. Change in cardinalities of sub multi sets of C_m due to embedding in general

The probability of transition from trace multi set X to multi set Y and that from Y to X are same. Therefore when

$$| X_{2m-1} | \approx | Y_{2m+1} | \approx | X_{2m} | \approx | Y_{2m} |, m > 0 \qquad (3)$$
$$| D_0 | \approx | Y_1 |, m = 0 \qquad (4)$$

cardinalities of trace multi sets would not change due to embedding. In a cover image $| X_{2m-1} | \approx | Y_{2m-1} |$ and $| X_{2m+1} | \approx | Y_{2m+1} |$ Therefore a cover image meeting the condition given in (3) and (4) meet the following criteria.

$$| Y_{2m-1} | \approx | X_{2m-1} | \approx | Y_{2m+1} | \approx | X_{2m+1} | \approx$$
$$| X_{2m} | \approx | Y_{2m} |, m > 0 \qquad (5)$$
$$| D_0 | \approx | Y_1 | \approx | X_1 |, m = 0 \qquad (6)$$

If a C_m satisfies the criteria in (5) and (6), it does not help in estimating the length of embedding. If the image contains only such C_ms, steganalysis is unreliable using LSM and SPM. More precisely

LSM is unreliable if the conditions (5) and (6)
hold good for all C_m, $5 \geq m \geq 0$ $\qquad (7)$

and

SPM is unreliable if the condition (5) and (6)
are true for all C_m, $31 \geq m \geq 0$ $\qquad (8)$

Images which do not satisfy the criteria given in (3) and (4) when no data is hidden, satisfy these criteria at 100% embedding. In such images at 100% embedding, the difference between X_n and Y_n is maximum and the criteria given in (5) and (6) can not be true.

Thus the criteria given in (3) and (4) alone is not a sufficient condition leading to inaccuracy of prediction by LSM and SPM. Cover images meeting the criteria given in (3) and (4), satisfy the criteria given in (5) and (6) with any amount of embedding and these images definitely give inaccurate results for LSM and SPM.

Therefore by testing the criteria given in (7) and (8), we can identify images which yield inaccurate results for LSM and SPM respectively. Thus the steganalyst is able to attach a confidence level to his results. The drawback of this classification is that the images meeting the above criteria with 100% hidden data will be misclassified as images giving inaccurate results.

The cardinalities of multi sets C_m in the image is important as the estimation is done based on the law of large numbers. As pointed out in [2] parity also play a role in the accuracy of results. $| C_0 |$ is involved in estimation using SPM and LSM. When $| C_0 |$ is very large, the negative effect of parity is minimum. $| C_0 |$ does not change with embedding. So for an image if $| C_0 |$ is sufficiently large, we can conclude that the image does not show very high embedding ratio when no data is hidden or small amount of data is hidden. i.e, such an image gives reliable results. However image might give moderately inaccurate results due to the effect of parity.

The images which meet the criteria in (7) and (8) will show very high amount of hidden data when no data is hidden by LSM and SPM respectively. Hence an image which does not meet the criteria in (7) and (8) and where $| C_0 |$ is large, the estimated results are highly accurate. Image classification we suggest involves finding $| C_0 |$ and checking the criteria in (7) and (8). Using this classification we can detect images which give accurate results and images which give highly inaccurate results.

The novelty of the proposed classification is that it is done based on the statistics from the stego image. This classification helps in reducing the estimation error and thus increasing the reliability of the classification method. Since the classification is done using the statistics of the stego image, the steganalyst is able to add a confidence level also along with the results he gives.

The drawback of our method is that some of the images which are predicted to give good steganalysis results show small amount of initial bias. It is due to parity. Moreover some images for which $| C_0 |$ is small and parity difference is almost nil, also give highly accurate results. As parity is a variant with respect to embedding, from the stego image the effect caused by parity can not be predicted.

4   Experimental Results

4.1   Identification of Images Which Give Highly Inaccurate Results

We downloaded few hundred images which were originally stored as high-quality JPEG images. We identified one hundred 24 bit color images which meet the condition (7) and (8). We embedded messages of length 3%, 5%, 10%, 20%, .. 100% onto these images and estimated the message length. The estimated length for sample images are given in table 1.

In the case of type 1 images, SPM is not able to estimate length as the determinant turns out negative and LSM shows very high embedding (above 90% even when no pay load is hidden). Type 2 images give very high embedding for both methods. From the results it is clear that the images meeting criteria given in (7) and (8) show very high embedding even when no data is hidden. Hence by testing the above criteria which is an invariant with embedding we can predict whether the results given by these steganalysis methods are correct or not.

In short by testing the above criteria we can identify stego images which definitely give inaccurate results by these steganalysis methods. By filtering out stego images which show inaccurate results we increase the reliability of these steganalysis methods.

Table 1. Estimated length of hidden message when the cardinalities of sub multi sets of C_m are almost equal in cover image

Length of embedding (%)	Image Type I		Image Type II	
	SPM	LSM	SPM	LSM
0	nan	90.20	60.80	94.70
3	nan	90.90	62.70	95.20
5	nan	91.10	64.80	95.80
10	nan	91.70	68.20	96.90
20	nan	93.40	75.40	99.30
30	nan	95.80	80.20	101.4
40	nan	96.00	86.60	105.4
50	nan	97.50	90.80	110.1
60	nan	98.30	94.40	118.3
70	nan	99.10	95.80	98.6
80	nan	99.20	97.70	97.8
90	nan	99.20	100.5	99.1
100	nan	99.30	100.0	92.9

Table 2. Average estimated message length (in percent) for one hundred images with $|C_0| > 50\%$

Embedded message length (%)	SPM	LSM
0	0.38	0.17
3	3.41	2.91
5	5.21	4.91
10	10.60	10.21
20	21.20	20.35
30	31.22	30.45
40	40.65	40.24
50	50.42	49.98
60	60.35	60.14
70	70.20	70.17
80	78.17	79.35
90	89.57	89.97
100	97.02	98.85

4.2   Identification of Images Which Give Accurate Results

We downloaded a set of 24-bit color images from *www.nationalgeographic.com* (mostly Photo of the day images from National Geographic Channel), which were originally stored as high-quality JPEG images. For our test purposes, we resized them to $800X600$ pixels. Then we selected one hundred images from this set meeting the classification criteria $(C_m > 50\%)$ we proposed.

We created a series of stego images by embedding messages of length 0%, 3%, 5%, 10%, ...,100% into these images using random LSB replacement method. Then we estimated the hidden message length from these stego images using SPM and LSM, the two most accurate steganalysis methods in the literature. We got test results which are given in table 2.

Thus the classification proposed causes to identify images which give accurate results. These images do not show very high initial bias. It doesn't mean that all the images which do not meet the classification criteria always give high initial bias. The proposed classification is done based on the properties of the stego image. Hence steganalyst without having knowledge on the cover image can be sure that the results are accurate if the said criteria is met.

5   Conclusion

In this paper we discussed a method for classifying images for increasing the reliability of steganalysis methods on digital images in spatial domain employing LSB replacement steganography. The proposed classification is done based on certain properties of images which are invariant with embedding. Using the image classification proposed, the steganalyst can identify images that give accurate results and images which give highly inaccurate results. If the image is identified as giving accurate results by the proposed method, then the steganalyst can be sure that the estimated length is very accurate. If the image is identified as giving highly inaccurate results then steganalyst can be sure that the results shown are highly unreliable. Thus steganalyst can attach a confidence level to his results. This classification decreases the false alarm rate and increases the accuracy of prediction by identifying images which give accurate results. Thus the image classification we proposed increases the reliability of staganalysis of digital images in spatial domain employing LSB replacement steganography. Influence of other factors like parity on accuracy of steganalysis results of images in spatial domain are to be investigated further.

References

1. Goljan, M., Fridrich, J., Du, R.: Detecting lsb steganography in colour and grey-scale images. Magazine of IEEE Multimedia, Special Issue on Security (October-November 2001)
2. Wu, X., Dumitrescu, S., Wang, Z.: Detection of lsb steganography via sample pair analysis. IEEE Transactions on Signal Processing 51(7), 1995–2007 (2003)
3. Tang, Q., Lu, P., Luo, X., Shen, L.: An improved sample pairs method for detection of lsb embedding. In: Fridrich, J. (ed.) IH 2004. LNCS, vol. 3200, pp. 116–127. Springer, Heidelberg (2004)
4. Anderson, R.J., Petitcolas, F.A.P.: On the limits of steganography. IEEE Journal of Selected Areas in Communications (Special issue on copyright and privacy protection) 16 (1998)

5. Du, R., Fridrich, J., Meng, L.: Steganalysis of lsb encoding in colour images. In: Proceedings of IEEE International Conference on Multimedia and Expo. New York City, NY, July 30-August 2 (2000)
6. Tao, Z., Xijian, P.: Reliable detection of lsb steganography based on the difference image histogram. In: Proc. IEEE ICAAP, Part III, pp. 545–548 (2003)
7. Ker, A.D.: Improved detection of lsb steganography in greyscale images. In: Fridrich, J. (ed.) IH 2004. LNCS, vol. 3200, pp. 97–115. Springer, Heidelberg (2004)
8. Liu, B., Luo, X., Liu, F.: Improved rs method for detection of lsb steganography. In: Gervasi, O., Gavrilova, M.L., Kumar, V., Laganá, A., Lee, H.P., Mun, Y., Taniar, D., Tan, C.J.K. (eds.) ICCSA 2005. LNCS, vol. 3481, pp. 508–516. Springer, Heidelberg (2005)
9. Ker, A.: Derivation of error distribution in least squares steganalysis. IEEE Transactions on Information Security and Forensics 2, 140–148 (2007)
10. Fridrich, J., Soukal, D.: Matrix embedding for large payloads. IEEE Transactions on Information Security and Forensics 7, 12–17 (2008)
11. Yang, C., Luo, X., Hu, Z., Gao, S.: A secure lsb steganography system defeating sample pair analysis based on chaos system and dynamic compensation. In: ICACT 2006, pp. 1014–1019 (2006)

Security for High-Speed MANs/WANs

Professor (Dr) C.S. Lamba

HOD Department of Computer Science & Engineering
Rajasthan Institute of Engineering & Technology
Jaipur, Pawan Kumar Tanwar
kunjean_lamba@yahoo.com

Abstract. This research paper deals with a range of secure high-speed networking over a metropolitan or wide area. Since this is quite active research area, a full report is given of the interfaces that thrive in removing the bandwidth burden from long distance networks. Only those with the status or potential of a standard are taking into consideration. Next, the position of security is evaluated. It is recommended that the access Interface enjoy certain advantages over the upper layers. Hence, the results of this work are directly applicable to virtually any layered communication architecture. Amongst the security protocols that are available, the IEEE802.11 represents the only viable solution to have the CLS service properly secured. This protocol is designed for a different type of environment and the implications of this are known. In the real sense, IEEE802.11 proves to be a very valuable tool to built multi-level secure private and public networks using the most recent MAN/WAN technologies. Furthermore, it shows how to enhance the security issues related to Metropolitan and Wide Area Network considering the required security services and mechanism.

Keywords: MAN/WAN, Security threats, protocols, ATM.

1 Introduction

Security plays a very important role in expansion and convenient use of the broadband service and there is a growing interest in the development of broadband services and networks for commercial use in both local area and wide area networks. The early drive some years ago was improvement of Asynchronous Transfer Mode (ATM) for use on broadband networks, under the banner of broadband ISDN (B-ISDN). Recently there is a genuine realistic drive for broadband service to meet up the demand for increased bandwidth for remote site inter-connection, and high-speed data transfer. This implies that distributed systems are more prone to attacks. The need for sensible solutions for secure network systems management is becoming more and more important.

In developing these solutions, some vital issues need to be carefully addressed from a key depth. First it is important to recognize clearly the functionalities and interfaces of the trusted security management mechanism. Then it is necessary to consider whether some of these trusted management authorities could be grouped together to make things easier for the overall management depending on some factors

N. Meghanathan et al. (Eds.): CNSA 2010, CCIS 89, pp. 75–82, 2010.

such as the relationship between organization or unit concerned in the network environment and the types of services offered as well as performance conditions.

Wide Area Networks (WANs). The term Wide Area Network (WAN) typically refers to the network that covers a large geographical area and use communications circuits to connect the intermediate nodes. Transmission rates are typically 2 Mbps, 34 Mbps, 45 Mbps, 155 Mbps, 625 Mbps or more. Several WANs have been constructed, including public packet networks, large corporate networks, military networks, banking networks, stock brokerage networks, and airline reservation networks. Some WANs are very widespread across the globe, but majority do not provide true global coverage. Organizations supporting WANs by means of the Internet Protocol are well known as Network Service Providers (NSPs). These form the foundation of the Internet. By relating the NSP WANs together using links at Internet Packet Interchanges (sometimes called —peering points) a universal communication infrastructure is formed. NSPs do not usually handle individual customer accounts but instead of transacting with intermediate organizations that they can be charged for higher capacity communications. In general, they have an agreement to exchange definite volumes of data at a certain —quantity of service ‖ with other NSPs. So practically any NSP can get in touch with any other NSP, but may need the use of one more other networks to reach the required destination. NSPs differ in terms of the transit delay, transmission rate, and connectivity offered. Fig 2.1 Typical "mesh" connectivity of a Wide Area Network

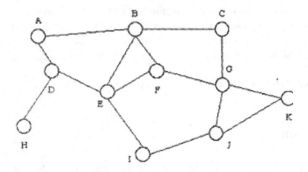

A typical network is shown in the figure above.

This connects a number of End Systems (ES) (e.g. A, C, H, K) and a number of Intermediate Systems (IS) (e.g. B, D, E, F, G, I, J) to form a network over which data may be communicated among the End Systems (ES). In view of the fact that the topologies of WANs are more complex than those of LANs, routing algorithms also receive more emphasis. Many WANs also employ sophisticated monitoring measures to account for which users use the network resources. This in some cases, used to generate billing information to charge individual users.

Metropolitan Area Networking. Metropolitan Area Networks (MANs) are public networks that are targeted to offer high-speed networking over metropolitan area distances. Desire to communicate over a wider geographical area has motivated the concept of Metropolitan Area Networks (MAN). A MAN is loosely defined, because to most people it is a way of enabling diverse computer facilities to communicate over high speed links within the citywide area. It provides a high speed data connections, across the city wide areas up to 50 km diameter between the following: local area networks that hold on to a published recognized standard; hundreds of PC's terminals, or host to host communication; work station to host communication. In existence for over a decade now, MANs have usually been designed for voice transmission based on time division multiplexing (TDM) technology. Then, voice traffic was significantly more important than data traffic. As a result, synchronous optical network/synchronous digital hierarchy (SONET/SDH) and Wavelength Division Multiplexing (WDM) became the main standard on these networks. This technology has been able to meet the initial requirements of MANs quite adequately and today, most of them are based on SONET/SDH technology. With the sudden increase in the demand for bandwidth for data transmission, it became relatively understandable that SONET/SDH networks needed to be reengineered to handle data traffic in a more efficient way. This lead to the emergence of next-generation SONET/SDH and also the increasing number of networks based on dense wavelength division multiplexing (DWDM) and Ethernet technologies.

Technologies in MAN SONET/SDH has been a basis of MAN over the last decade, serving as a primary transport layer for TDM-based circuit switched networks and most overlay data networks. Though it is measured to be very resilient technology but it's quite expensive to implement. Its inefficiencies in adapting data services and an inflexible multiplexing hierarchy remain a big concern. Another problem is its inability to configure and provision of end-to-end services, since it lacks a universal control mechanism to configure networks.

ATM was considered to be very accepted on the market because of it ability to encapsulate different protocols and traffic types into a common arrangement for transmission over SONET infrastructure. It is very strong in Metropolitan Area Networks since it can accommodate higher speed line interfaces and provides managed virtual circuit services while offering traffic management capabilities.

Dense Wavelength Division Multiplexing (DWDM) is another very important technology related to MAN. One of its main characteristics is that it can suit the traffic demands for high-capacity networks. DWDM systems tolerate carriers to develop current network capacity 80 times or more. They increase network capacity by splitting light into individual wavelengths, each containing an independent signal, and transmitting all wavelengths simultaneously through a single fiber. A key advantage of DWDM is that it's protocol and bit rate independent and this is why it's widely used with MANs. **FDDI** The fiber distributed data interface (FDDI) is a multiple access packet-switching local area network (LAN) that performs operation at 100 megabits (Mb) per second. The physical layer of FDDI - links several stations, which helps to spread information to any other station in the network.

1.1 Security Threats

Information is a major asset of organizations. Companies' uses the information gather as an advantage in a competitive market. The threat comes from others who would like to get information or reduce business opportunities by intrusive attitude towards the normal business processes. The main aim of security is to protect important or sensitive organizational information at the same time as making it readily available. Attackers trying to wreck a system or disrupt normal business operations by taking an advantage of vulnerabilities using different techniques, methods, and tactics. System administrators need to be sensitive about various aspects of security to improve the procedures and policies to protect assets and limit their vulnerabilities.

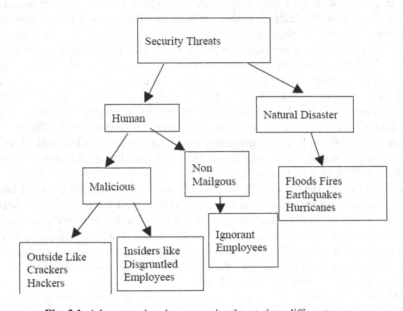

Fig. 3.1. A layout to break up security threats into different areas

Natural Disasters
Nobody can prevent the environment from taking its course. Earthquakes, hurricanes, floods, lightning, and fire can cause brutal damage to high speed networks. Information can be nowhere to be found; downtime or damage to hardware can affect other important services. Few safeguards can be carried out against natural disasters. The main approach is to have disaster recovery plans and unanticipated event plans in place. Other threats such as riots, wars, and terrorist attacks could be incorporated here.

Human Threats
Malicious threats consist of attacks within by restless or malicious employees and outside attacks that are not part of the establishment looking to harm and disrupt an organization networks. Mainly dangerous attackers are usually former the employees, for the fact that they know many of the codes and security measures that are set in place in an organization. Insiders are possibly having some intend or goals and objectives despite all the legal access to the network system, which gives them, more chances to break into the network. Employees are the mostly conversance with the organization's computers and applications, and are most likely to be acquainted with damages caused by any action on the network. Insiders can set viruses, Trojan horses, or worms, and they can look through the file system. They can have an effect on all

components of computer security. By browsing through a system, confidential information could be uncovered. Trojan horses are a threat to both the integrity and privacy of information in the system. They can affect ease of use by congesting the system's processing or storage capacity, or by making the system to break down. Malicious attackers usually will have a specific aim and objective for an attack on a system. These motives could be to interrupt services and the progress of business operations by using denial-of-service (DoS) attack tools. They might as well want to steal information or hardware such as laptop computers. Hackers can market information that can be valuable to competitors.

Non-malicious threats usually come from employees who are inexpert in computers and are ignorant of security threats and vulnerabilities. Users who open up Microsoft Word documents by means of Notepad to edit the documents, and then save them could cause damage to the information stored on the document. Users, data entry clerks, system operators, and programmers frequently make unintended errors that create to security problems, directly and indirectly. At times, such as a data entry error or a programming error that crashes a system is a threat. In other cases, errors create vulnerabilities. Errors can take place in all areas of the system life cycle.

1.2   Threat Identification

Implementing a security plan needs an evaluation of the risks of both Internal and external threats to the information and system. It does extremely little good to apply a high security environment to keep a company from the outside if the threat is within the company.

Internal Threats
This includes worker scam, abuse or alteration of data, and theft of property. These threats involve that both policies and systems be set in place to recognize and mitigate these possibilities. The key roles for computer security professionals are investigating and making recommendations to management on technical changes and policies.

The majority of the well-publicized internal threats involve financial abuses. A few of these abuses are total fraud or theft. These types of threats, mostly in a computer intensive environment can be very complex to notice and examine. From a computer security viewpoint, an internal threat can be as a result of negligence or failure in both financial, operational, and computer security controls.

External Threats
On the other hand, External threats are growing rapidly. Today, a lot of companies use online databases, take information, process payments, and track shipments, supervise inventory, and manage others vital information using complicated systems. These systems are linked with the private corporate records, trade secrets, strategic plans, and many other types of important information. It has occurs when the security breaches remained insecure for years with no knowledge by the company that a compromise ever occurred. One of the greatest things is when skilled criminals create and make use of this type of security breach. Early methods of cracking systems were primitive. Nowadays, software packages exist that locate targets automatically and then systematically attack the target to locate its vulnerabilities. This type of work is very interesting and involves a lot of skills that will be learning in this thesis.

1.3 Security Concerns and TCP/ IP

The Transfer Control Protocol/ Internet Protocol network protocol, used by most corporate networks, was planned to allow communications in a trustful setting. This protocol was mainly experimental and used by most schools and governmental agencies for research. While it is vigorous in its error handling, it is unsecured. Several network attacks occur through the TCP/ IP protocol. Unfortunately, TCP/ IP is more protected than many of the protocols still installed on networks today. Practically all-large networks, at the same time as the Internet are built on the TCP/ IP protocol, which has become an international standard for large and small networks. TCP/ IP were intended to connect different computer systems into a robust and consistent network/The protocol offers a richness of capabilities and maintains different protocols. Because it is user-friendly and well documented network, the emphasis in this section is on the types of connections and services.

TCP/ IP Attacks
Attacks on TCP/ IP usually take place between Host-to-Host or Internet layers. Any layer of the protocol is potentially susceptible though. TCP/ IP are weak to attacks from both outside and inside an organization. The chances for external attacks are to some extent limited by the devices in the network, including the router. The router blocks a lot of the protocols from exposure to the Internet. Some protocols, such as ARP, are not routable and are not usually at risk to outside attacks. Other protocols, such as SMTP and ICMP, pass through the router and include a normal part of Internet and TCP/ IP traffic. TCP, UDP, and IP are all weak to attack. The particular attacks that a TCP/ IP based network is vulnerable to when using, in various cases are:

Network Sniffers
A network sniffer is simply a device that captures and displays network traffic. Network cards usually only pass information up to the protocol load if the information is planned for that computer; any network traffic not proposed for that computer is disregarded. Promiscuous mode is where the NIC card is placed upon and it allows the NIC card to take into custody all information that it sees on the network. Most networks are bus oriented, during which all traffic is sent to all internal computer systems. Devices such as routers, bridges, and switches can be used to break up or section networks within a larger network. Every traffic in a specific part is visible to all stations in that section. By using a sniffer, an insider can capture all of the information transported by the network. Lots of advanced sniffers can reconstruct packets and create complete messages including user IDs and passwords. This susceptibility is mainly sensitive in environments where network connections are easily easy to get to by the outsiders.

Port Scans
A TCP/ IP network makes a lot of the ports accessible to outside users through the router. These ports will act in response in a predictable manner when queried. For example, TCP will attempt bringing together when a session initiation occurs. An attacker can query a network to verify on which services and ports are insecure. This process is called port scanning, and it can make known all about a network. Port scans

can be done both internally and externally. Many routers, unless configured properly, will let the entire protocols pass through them.

1.4 Physical Security

The computers and networks can be kept secure in different technical aspects of the systems and networks in which the physical environment and the business exist. This involves evaluating the physical security, social engineering issues, and environmental issues.

Physical Barriers
A main aspect of access control involves physical barriers. The aim of a physical barrier is to avoid access to computers and network systems. Mainly, effective physical barrier implementations need more than one physical barrier be crossed to get access. This type of approach is called a multiple barrier system.

1.5 Security Services and Mechanisms

Preferably, security enhancements should have a minimum impact on existing routing and switching infrastructure, segmentation and access control techniques, and the similar to organizational structures that support these systems. Four elements support this:

- Presence: The network relies on the ease of use of certain controls within discrete nodes on the network, which seem to be the identity, access control, data inspection, and communication security, as well as newer application-aware capabilities that handle peer-to-peer content. Web services, voice services, and
dynamic mobile content.
- Context: A user enters a network, instead of focusing only on permissions at the time. It's more effective to grant or cancel permissions based on behavior and associated context for the period of the user's connection with the network.
- Linkages: In order to deal with the latest forms of threats and misuse, networks have established linkages between devices through routing protocols. These linkages should extend all the way to the source and the destination of network traffic.
- Trust: In the past, trust has been tied mainly to the identity of a device or user.

1.6 Why a New Approach Is Needed

As we progress into an information-driven universal economy, today's networks must be able to act in response to attacks while maintaining availability and trustworthiness. Rather than giving way, networks must be able to take up attacks and remain prepared, much in the similar way the human immune system functions still in the presence of infections. Mainly, the abilities of the adaptive defenses, which-are built into the concept of a self defending network, include the following benefits:

- Remain active at all times
- Perform unobtrusively
- Minimize propagation of attacks
- Quickly respond to as-yet unknown attacks.

These capabilities can cause a reduction of the windows to be more vulnerable and minimize the, impact of attacks, and develop the overall infrastructure availability and reliability. They also assist in creating autonomous systems that can quickly react to an occurrence with little to no human intervention. Such a self-defending system should include the following elements explained below:

- Endpoint Protection: By detecting and preventing viruses and worms from getting a foothold at an endpoint, you can prevent them from propagating across a network.
- Admission Control: Allows you to know the level of network access to grant to an endpoint based on its security position, which is based on the security state of the operating system and associated applications
- Infection Containment: expand the security checks carried out at the time of admission for the period of the network connection.
- Intelligent Correlation and Incident Response: offer services such as real-time correlation of events, quick assessment of the security impact of an event, the ability to choose what action to take, and the ability to know the closest control point to implement a response.
- Application Security: To tackle new classes of threats, security software should offer granular traffic inspection services to critical network security enforcement points, thereby containing malicious traffic before it can be propagated across the network.

References

1. Ekstrom, D.: Securing a wireless local area network- using standard security
2. Goralski, W.: SONET/SDH. McGraw-Hill, Emeryville (2002)
3. Network, IEEE Communications Magazine (2002)
4. Nichols, K.R.: ICSA guide to cryptography (1999)
5. Ballart, R., Ching, Y.-C.: SONET: Now It's a Standard Optical
6. Shepard, S.: SONET/SDH Demystified. McGraw- Hill Companies, Blacklick (2001)
7. Varadharajan, V.: Security issues in emerging high speed networks, July 4 (1996)
8. Varadharajan, V.: Design and management of a secure networked administration system, June 7 (1996)

Behavioral Analysis of Transport Layer Based Hybrid Covert Channel

Koundinya Anjan and Jibi Abraham

Dept. of Computer Science and Engineering,
M.S.Ramaiah Institute of Technology,
Bangalore,India

Abstract. Covert Channels are malicious conversation in a legitimate secured network communication that violates the security policies laid down. Covert channels are hidden, unintended design in the legitimate communication whose motto is to leak information. Trapdoors are unintended design with a communication system that exists in network covert channels as a part of rudimentary protocols. Subliminal channel, a variant of covert channel works similarly as network covert channel except that trapdoor is set in cryptographic algorithm. A composition of covert channel with subliminal channel is the Hybrid Channel or Hybrid Covert Channel. Hybrid Covert Channels are a major threat for security which is clearly unacceptable in presence of secured network communication. The objective of the present paper is to make microscopic analysis of behavior of hybrid covert channel with a clearly understanding of theoretical literatures of composed covert channels. Paper proposes practical implementation of transport layer based hybrid covert channeling based on TCP and SSL.

Keywords: Network Security, Covert Channel, Subliminal Channel, Kleptography, Covert Communication.

1 Introduction

Computer Network is unpredictable due to information warfare and is prone to threats, attacks and vulnerabilities. Such activities on the network fail to deliver the most important attribute, the privacy. Most of the attacks and threats are based on channel called "Covert Channel". The word "Covert" means hidden data or information leaks.

Covert Channel [4] [7] [9] is a malicious conversation within a legitimate network communication. Covert Channels clearly violate the security policies laid down by the network environment allowing the information leak to the unauthorized or unknown receiver. Covert Channels often do not have concrete definition and are scenario oriented. This is because such channel can exist between processes in operating system or amongst distributed objects. Covert process entities should adhere to confinement problem [7] [13] to resolve them. Covert Channel in this paper refers to network covert channel between a pair of users.

N. Meghanathan et al. (Eds.): CNSA 2010, CCIS 89, pp. 83–92, 2010.
© Springer-Verlag Berlin Heidelberg 2010

One unique nature of Covert Channel is that they consume or sore the legitimate bandwidth. Figure 1 visualizes the covert activity in a network. A covert channel does not need to be end to end, that is middle man can also involve in such channeling. Figure 1 depicts the covert communication model employed in the covert channel with pre-shared information encoding and decoding scheme between the covert users.

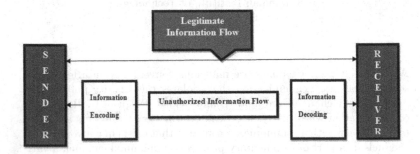

Fig. 1. Covert Channel Visualization

Covert Channel has broad classification although the overall motto is to promote the covertness in one or other form in the legitimate network. Subliminal channel is one of the forms of covert channel that focuses only on information leaks in cryptographic protocols. A channel composed of simple covert channel and the subliminal channel is the hybrid covert channel. Hybrid Covert Channel has no concrete composition of covert channel components. Detection or even identification of such channel is found to be unimaginable in many cases. This paper aims to visualize the theoretical boundaries of covert channels in legitimate network communication and also proposes the practical implementation of hybrid covert channels based on TCP and SSL.

Further section of this paper covers the importance of covertness and covert channel in brief. Section 2 describes feasible patterns of covert communication amongst covert users. Section 3 highlights the urgent need to focus on covertness used in layers of attack modeling. Section 4 focuses on variants of covert channels and hybrid covert channel. Section 5 describes about transport layer based hybrid covert channels.

2   Covert Communication

In Network communication, covert communication amongst a pair of users can take two forms; (a) covert data exchange and (b) covert indication. In covert data exchange, covert data is exchanged between the covert users by hiding covert data in rudimentary protocols. This form of covert communication can best be understood with pipeline problem, where there exists two pipes p_1 and p_2 of diameters d_1 and d_2 respectively, one inside the other such that $d_2 < d_1$. These pipes are setup between two geographical places for the transportation of crude oil. The inner pipe p_2 of diameter d_2 is the covert pipe not known in the design and used for smuggling oil.The outer pipe p_1 is the legitimate pipe.

Second form of covert communication is the covert indication. Covert users communicate in a language not known to others. In Figure 1, the covert sender and receiver share an information encoding scheme to leak information. This information encoding scheme is the language that covert users employ to communicate in a secured legitimate network environment. The best real time example of such communication is Examination Problem. Student X leaks the answers to Student Y for an objective type examination paper in an examination hall in presence of invigilating officer. For each choice in a question, student X make a gesture that triggers an event to student Y, For instance to communicate choice A to student Y, student X coughs. Same holds well in case network communication where covert user X triggers continuous clock events that communicate some form of action to be performed by covert user Y.

3   Importance of Covertness and Layers of Attack

Most of the attacks, threats and vulnerabilities depend on pre-established covert channel whose objective is to send hidden data or program, unseen to any security methods in a legitimate network communication in a hassle free manner. Attacks based on covert channel are studied in Kleptography [6] [9]. Practically, the hidden data can be anything: it can contain a piece of malicious code to gain access or control over the target system. Hidden data are also termed as "Trapdoors" or "Backdoors"[9]. Bandwidth of legitimate channel will be greater than or equal to covert channel as illustrated by classical pipeline problem in Section 2. Once the covert channel is established, attacker has many ways to deploy attacks; such attacks are specially labeled as Kleptographic attacks [6]. Figure 2 illustrates the layers of attacks based on covert channel to accomplish the attack objectives set by any attacker.

Kleptographic attacks depend on subliminal channel [6]. Covert channel and Subliminal channel have been used in different manner with slight distinction,

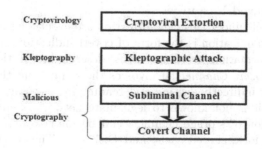

Fig. 2. Layers of Attack

to accomplish more or less the same objectives; further these distinctions can be understood better in section 5. Kleptographic attacks are a miniature form of catastrophic attacks called cryptoviral attacks. In fact, Kleptography is branch of Cryptovirology, which describes about best Kleptographic method for crypto viral breeding in the network. One of the devastating attacks of Cryptovirology is "Cryptoviral Extortion" where victim has to compromise on security and is forcefully compelled to give the ransom demanded by the attacker.

4   Covert Channel Variants

Covert Channel exists in various forms. It is purely scenario oriented and therefore it does not have concrete theoretical definition. Covert Channels exhibit some characteristics irrespective of their type: Capacity, Noise and Transmission mode [7]. Capacity of covert channel is the quantity of covert data that has to be transmitted. Noise is the amount of disturbance that can interfere with the covert data when transmitted in the network channel. Transmission mode is many times found to be synchronous but can also be asynchronous. The covert channels are broadly classified into:

a. **Based on Communication Parties**
    Any network covert channel has to be either noisy or noiseless type.
    - *Noisy Covert Channel* [4] is a communication channel which has presence of both legitimate and covert users. Attacks based on such channel are generally termed as "Information snatching and victimizing".

    - *Noiseless Covert Channel* [4] is the communication channel used solely by covert parties. This channel can be characterized by the traffic flow between the covert parties. Traffic generated by noiseless covert channel is more regular than traffic generated by legitimate network users. Traffic practically means the regularity in interarrival times. Detecting such activity requires to model entire process using queuing theory [8] concepts.

b. **Based on Shared Resources**
    Covert Channels under this categorization are event triggered. The pattern of covert communication is the form of covert indication, which is based on pre-shared information encoding scheme described in Section 1.
    - *Storage Covert Channel* [4] involves the sender and the receiver either directly or indirectly writing and reading in to storage location in such way that it is not known to legitimate network environment. Further classification of storage channels can be made by the type of storage used; File-lock, shared cache and Disk-arm. The covert sender in file-lock based storage covert channel constantly set and reset the lock on shared file. This produces an observable bit stream to its covert receiver

that deduces some covert information. The same working principle can be employed in other forms of storage covert channel with shared storage medium between the covert parties.

- *Timing Covert Channel* [4] [5] involves the sender signaling the information by modulating the resources in such a way that real response time is observed by the receiver. Receiver then derives an information from fluctuating response time. For instance sender pulsates a shared clock at 1 KHz constantly indicating some information to its covert receiver. Variable clock pulsation is the information encoding scheme previously shared by the covert parties. Clock triggers events in the channel to which the receiver has to respond.

c. Based on Trapdoor Setting

- *Simple Network Covert Channel* [4] (SNCC) exists by creating a trap door in rudimentary protocols used in TCP/IP protocol suite. This is accomplished by potentially using the unused fields in the protocol header or employing an encoding scheme by manipulating the fields in the protocol.
- *Subliminal Channel* [3] [9] exists within a cryptographic protocol like authentication system, signature that transmits additional information to a special receiver. It is concerned with leaking of information in most popularly employed cryptographic algorithms like DSA, RSA, DH and so on. Notion of subliminal channel can be best understood with classical Prisoner Problem [2] by G.Simmons. Subliminal Channel has further variants based on the backdoors creation; Newton Channel, Oracle Channel and Legendre Channel [9].

d. Hybrid Covert Channels

A new era of covert channel where there is co-existence of two or more different variants of covert channels and is termed as Hybrid Channel or Hybrid Covert Channel. For instance Simple Network Covert Channel and storage channel can exist together in network environment. Various possibilities of hybrid channeling can exist, for example noisy covert channel in transport layer with subliminal channel in network layer or application layer. Such combinations of covert channels are greatest threat to legitimate network environment. Hybrid Covert Channel behaves as a single channel which is very difficult to detect. Further elimination of such hybrid channel is a costly affair.

5   Transport Layer Based Hybrid Covert Channel

In this paper we propose a new Hybrid Covert Channel which is a composition of noisy covert channel in the transport layer and subliminal channel in the SSL/TLS. Figure 3 visualizes this composition. There can be 'n' different possible compositions of using covert channel variants in hybrid channeling. Efforts are made to understand end-to-end covert channeling only. Noisy covert channel is implemented as Simple Network Covert Channel (SNCC) with the trapdoor set in transport layer protocols. Practical network communication involves both the legitimate and the covert parties; hence it is a noisy covert channel.

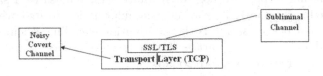

Fig. 3. Hybrid Covert Channel (Hybrid NCT/SCSL)

To uniquely identify this combination for later discussion, let us name this channel as "Hybrid-NCT/SCSL" (NCT- Noisy Covert Channel in transport layer, SCSL - Subliminal Channel in SSL). This composition is significant and one of the strongest form of hybrid channeling as the focus is on end-to-end transport layer based channeling. SSL is a basic security service that any network can provide and transport layer is crucial layer for communication over packet switched network[19]. Such composition of hybrid channeling can create a chaos in the legitimate network environment. Hybrid - NCT/SCSL can be implemented by creating a noisy covert channel (NCT) with a trap door set in Transmission Control Protocol (TCP) and then subliminal channel in Secure Socket Layer (SSL) protocol.

5.1 NCT - SNCC Implementation

TCP in the transport layer plays vital role in this channeling and format is as per RFC 793 described in [12]. Focus here is the covert data placement [1] [14] in most suitable TCP fields. Assume that the covert users have pre-shared information encoding/decoding scheme. It requires slight modification of TPDU(Transport Layer Protocol Data Unit) [12], during the processing at the transport layer which is described in 4. SSL encrypts the data from the application layer and appends its header. Modified TCP header with the SSL data (TPDU) is sent across the network. The initiator of covert channel has to share the information encoding schema with the other party by sending the schema as padded data in TCP header for the first time. At covert 2, TPDU at the transport layer is decoded by schema shared before. This extracts the covert data and rest is then sent to SSL and TCP. Feel of covert channel is not experienced at the legitimate protocol handlers. The following fields of TCP header can be used for covert data placement:

- **Padding 31bits/packet** - This is the most common form of placing the covert data since this field has no significance, but stuff dummy zero bits. This field requires the receiver to just extract the covert data in the padding fields before the TCP handler. Such field does not even demand the covert users to share common scheme for information encoding/decoding. Length of padding depends on presence or absence of options field in the TCP header, hence under an absence it is 31bit or else 8bit/packet.

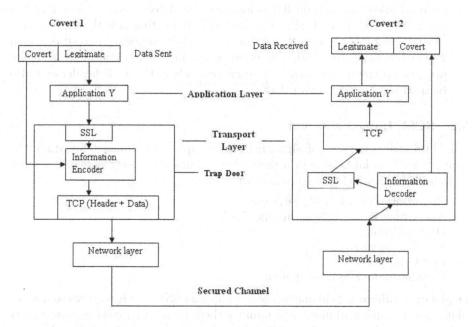

Fig. 4. Depicting the information encoding /decoding as trapdoors and also the modified packet processing in the transport layer in presence of covert users

- **Initial Sequence Number ISN 32bits/connection** - TCP employs "three way handshake" process for protocol negotiation. ISN serves as a perfect medium to ensure reliable delivery in case of packet loss due to various circumstances. In this method, the sender generates an ISN corresponding to actual covert data. Covert receiver extracts this field and does not give an ACK for it. Covert sender keeps on sending the same packet with different covert data embedded in ISN. This is the simplest form of using this field for placement of covert data.

- **TCP Acknowledge Sequence Number Field 32bits/connection - Bounce** - This method is based on spoofing of IP address where sending machine's packet is bounced off by a remote server. Consider a scenario with remote server A and communicating systems; System 1 and System 2. System 1 communicates with System 2 by bouncing on the server system A. ACK is of length 4 bytes in the TCP header. Assume that entire message is divided into 5 blocks . With pre-calculated acknowledgement numbers at System 1, these blocks are sent to Server A with system 2 as its source address. Bounce of ACK at remote server A will not generate new ACK numbers. Reassembling these on the other side, a channel can be retrieved. Most of the time, this method creates suspicious packets and leads to detection.

– **Manipulation of Flag bits and the usage of Reserved field- TCP** is intended for end-to-end reliable delivery therefore this connection oriented protocol makes use of 6 bit flag fields, also called "code bits". These flag bits are URG, ACK, PSH, RST, SYN, and FIN, indicating how the TCP packet (TPDU) has to be handled. 6 bit has 64 possible combinations out of which 29 combinations are valid. Therefore remaining combination can be made use to send the covert data. The reserved fields in the TCP header can also be used to place the covert data.

5.2   SCSL Implementation

SSL/TLS has wide range of algorithms in its cipher suite meant to satisfy the security services laid down in a secured communication over network. Cipher suite in SSL/TLS include algorithms for

– Confidentiality like RSA, DES etc.,
– Authentication and Signature like DSA
– Digital Certificate
– Key Exchange DH
– Key Generation
– Pseudo-random Number generation

Deploying a subliminal channel is not as simple as SNCC as it requires to manipulate the modular arithmetic and number theory concepts, used as base in any cryptographic algorithm. Most of the algorithms stated in SSL/TLS versions are black-box, deterministic and have polynomial run time. Black-box cryptosystem [9] are theoretically abstract and the underlying implementation cannot be scrutinized. Assuming that we are aware of the fundamentals of cryptography [10], the easiest way to illustrate the subliminal channel is through the Ong-Shamir digital signature scheme[3]. Digital signature scheme in general, comprises of key generation, signature generation and signature verification phases. Subliminal message or covert message $m^{''}$ can be included in any of the phases. Key generation phase generates private key x and public key y. Private key x is generated using a pseudo random number algorithm [11] and the generator algorithm is a deterministic finite automata with a predictable number of states transitions. Making use of this nature of pseudo randomness, covert user can manipulate random number to send covert message $m^{''}$. This pattern of covert communication is covert indication form established in the subliminal channel. Further this hampers the private key x and indirectly public key y, because key generation is based on randomness or random numbers. One more way of sending a subliminal message $m^{''}$ is to stuff it with the message m and send it in such a way that the signatures are not violated.

First let us go through the normal process of digital signature steps to understand the different phases clearly.

▶ **Key Generation**
  – Sender S_x chooses n such that it is computationally infeasible to factorize.
  – S_x then chooses random u, such that $(u, n) \equiv 1$ or $u \bmod n = 1$ and calculate $k = u^{-2} \bmod n$. u is kept as a secret.
  – u and k are the keys generated.

▶ **Signature Generation**
  – Given message m to be signed such that $(m, n) \equiv 1$. S_x chooses r such that $(r, n) \equiv 1$ r is kept secret.
  – S_x now calculates s_1 and s_2, $s_1 = \frac{1}{2}(\frac{m}{r}+r) \bmod n$, $s_2 = \frac{u}{2}(\frac{m}{r}-r) \bmod n$ and the signed message $m' = (m, s_1, s_2)$ is prepared.

▶ **Signature Verification**
  – Receiver R_x calculates after receiving (m,s1,s2)

$$a = (s_1^2 + k.s_2^2) \bmod n$$

  – If a= m then message is accepted as authentic.

Now let see how to deploy a subliminal channel in the signature phase. To transmit the covert message m'', sender S_x has to send signed message m' in the legitimate channel with covert message m'' in the subliminal channel such that any third party is able to verify the authenticity of the of signed message m' and not aware of about the presence of the subliminal channel.

Signature generation for m + m'' at Sender S_x

  – Given a message m, $(m, n) = 1$ and subliminal message $(m'', n) \equiv 1$
  – S_x calculates $s_1 = (\frac{m}{m''} + m'') \bmod n$, $s_2 = \frac{u}{2}(\frac{m}{m''} - m'') \bmod n$ and the signed message $m' = (m, s_1, s_2)$ to be transmitted.

Designated receiver is aware of how to get the subliminal message m'' by knowing u, as shown below.

$$m'' = \frac{m}{(s_1 + s_2.u^{-1})} \bmod n$$

Thus retrieving the hidden message m'' from the signature, a successful subliminal channel is established.

6   Conclusion and Future Work

Hybrid covert channels are clearly a threat to legitimate network since their exact composition is difficult to detect or even analyze. Our work put forward in this paper aims at finding out clearly the theoretical boundaries of Covert Channel with further exploration of hybrid form of Covert Channel in transport layer.

Future works will concentrate on a detailed analysis of all the possible combinations of hybrid channeling,the analysis with respect to rudimentary protocols like ICMP, OSPF, SIP, FTP, HTTP,security protocols like IPsec, HTTPs and so on. For each of the feasible combinations we would like to draw correct line of inference on detection and elimination mechanism to achieve the overall goal of covert free network.

References

1. Bharti, V.: Practical Development and Deployment of Covert Communication in IPv4. Journal on Theoretical and Applied Information Technology (April 2007)
2. Simmons, G.J.: The Prisoner's Problem and the Subliminal Channel. Springer, Heidelberg (1996)
3. Simmons, G.J.: The Subliminal Channel and Digital Signatures. Springer, Heidelberg (1998)
4. Cabuk, S., Brodley, C., Sheilds, C.: IP Covert Channel Detection. ACM Transaction on Information and System Security, Article 22, 12 (April 2009)
5. Cabuk, S., Brodley, C., Sheilds, C.: IP Covert Timing Channels: Design and Detection. In: CCS 2004 (October 2004)
6. Golebiewski, Z.: Stealing Secrets with SSL/TLS and SSH -Kleptographic Attack. Lecture Notes at Institute of Mathematics and Computer Science, pp. 3–11. Wroclaw University of Technology
7. Lampson, B.W.: A Note on the Confinement Problem. Communication of the ACM (1973)
8. Willig, A.: A Short Introduction to Queuing Theory. Lecture Notes at Technical University, Berlin (July 1999)
9. Young, A.: Malicious Cryptography, 1st edn., pp. 220–240. Wiley Publishing, Chichester (February 2004)
10. Stallings, W.: Cryptography and Network Security, 3rd edn. Pearson Publishing, London (2006)
11. Banks, J., et al.: Discrete Event System Simulation, 3rd edn. Prentice Hall, Englewood Cliffs (January 2001)
12. Tannebaum, A.: Computer Networks, 4th edn. Pearson Education, London (2008)
13. Gold, S.M., et al.: Program Confinement in KVM/370. In: Proceeding of The ACM Annual Conference, pp. 404–441 (1977)
14. Murdoch, S.: Embedding Covert Channel in to TCP/IP. In: Information Hiding Workshop (July 2005)

Efficient Encryption of Intra and Inter Frames in MPEG Video

V. Vijayalakshmi, L.M. Varalakshmi, and G.F. Sudha

Department of ECE, Pondicherry Engineering College, Puducherry. India
vijayalakshmi.visu@gmail.com, vvijiyalakshmi@gmail.com

Abstract. The growth in multimedia based Internet applications can be seen in the quantity of growth in video telephony, video on demand, media server etc. With the current cyber threats, sensitive video need to be protected before transmission. Streaming video applications requires high security as well as high computational performance. The need for video data protection is on rise hence encryption of video is imperative. In highly sensitive videos such as military applications, confidential video broadcasting where every part of the video is important it is required Intra and Inter frames need to be encrypted. A new video encryption scheme is proposed for sensitive applications. In this paper the objective is to analyze a secure and computational feasible video encryption algorithm for MPEG video, to improve the security of existing algorithm by combining encryption in Intra and Inter frames and to test the algorithm against the common attacks.

Keywords: Encryption, Shamir's secret sharing, MPEG, Intra and Inter frames.

1 Introduction

With the ever-increasing growth of multimedia applications, security is an important issue in communication and storage of encryption/decryption videos, and encryption is one the ways to ensure security. The need for efficient encryption algorithms for multimedia data will become increasingly important. Examples of such future applications include video e-mail and video-on-demand.

While encryption standard algorithms like AES (Advanced Encryption Standard) or DES (Data Encryption Standard) can be used to encrypt the entire video file, it has two main drawbacks. First, since multimedia data is usually large and requires real-time processing, DES and AES incur significant overhead. Recent video encryption algorithms have focused on protecting the more important parts of the video stream to reduce this overhead. Second, these techniques hide the synchronization information in the video stream, making it impossible to adaptively shape the stream to match available network resources and making it harder to recover from transmission errors in the network.

Owing to the large size and real-time applications of video, two types of encryption algorithms are generally in vogue. They are selective encryption and light-weight encryption which trades off security for computational time.

N. Meghanathan et al. (Eds.): CNSA 2010, CCIS 89, pp. 93–104, 2010.

Streaming video application requires high security as well as high computational performance. In video encryption, traditional selective algorithms have been used to partially encrypt the relatively important data in order to satisfy the streaming performance requirement. Most video selective encryption algorithms are inherited from still image encryption algorithms, the encryption on motion vector data is not considered. The assumption is that motion vector data are not as important as pixel image data. Unfortunately, in some cases, motion vector itself may be sufficient enough to leak out useful video information. Normally motion vector data consume over half of the whole video stream bandwidth, neglecting their security may be unwise.

1.1 MPEG Coding Methodology

A MPEG [1] video is composed of a sequence of Group of Pictures (GOPs). Each GOP consists of three types of frames namely I, P and B. I frames are called Intra-coded frames and are compressed without reference to any other frames. The P and B frames are forward predictive and bi-directional predictive coded frames, called as Inter frames respectively. These are subjected to compensation by subtracting a motion compensation prediction. Fig.1. shows the block diagram of the MPEG video coding scheme. The typical steps performed in video compression (e.g., MPEG and H.263) include motion estimation, DCT transform, quantization, and entropy encoding [2]

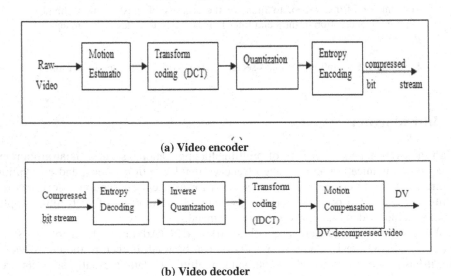

(a) Video encoder

(b) Video decoder

Fig. 1. MPEG Video encoder and decoder

1.2 Video Security Algorithms

Several encryption algorithm have been proposed to secure MPEG video.

E.Choo and group [3] proposed a light-weight encryption algorithm named Video Encryption Algorithm (VEA). It uses simple XOR of sign bits of the DCT coefficients of an I frame using a secret m-bit binary key. The Zigzag-Permutation algorithm, which permutes the AC coefficients, is one of the earliest algorithms designed for MPEG encryption. In this technique, the DCT coefficients are encoded in a different order than the standard MPEG video zigzag order .This algorithm is very fast but has been shown to have serious security problems.

Qiao and Klara [1] proved that Tang's encryption suffers from the known-plaintext and ciphertext-only attack. They also proposed a new encryption algorithm called Video Encryption Algorithm (VEA). In this algorithm, a chunk of an 'I' frame is divided into two halves. Both the halves are XORed and stored in one half. The other half is encrypted with a standard encryption algorithm-DES. This algorithm provides good security. It also employs fewer number of XOR operations than DES. However, it cannot be implemented in real-time for high resolution and high bit rate video sequences. Shi and Bhargava [4] proposed a light-weight encryption algorithm, in which a secret key randomly changes the sign bits of all the DCT coefficients of every I-frame in MPEG video. The authors further extended the algorithm by encrypting the sign bits of motion vectors of P and B frames. However, as with most of the light-weight algorithms known so far, the algorithm of [4] is also susceptible to known-plaintext and cipher text-only attacks [5].

The selective encryption algorithms typically use heavy-weight encryption algorithms (eg.DES, AES etc.,). Consequently, time taken for the encryption using them is high making them unsuitable for real-time applications. On the other hand, as mentioned earlier, most of the known light-weight algorithms are susceptible to known plaintext and cipher text-only attacks [5]. Therefore, there is a need for a new secure video encryption algorithm perhaps designed by combining these two classes, which retains their respective advantages, while minimizing the disadvantages.

Qiao and Nahrstedt [6] have proposed an MPEG video encryption algorithm based on the statistical analysis of the MPEG video stream. They observed that a video stream has a more uniform distribution of byte values. The analysis of the distribution of the byte value, the pair of two adjacent bytes, and the pair of two bytes with a fixed distance in between reveal that there is no repeated byte pattern within any 1/16 chunk of an I-frame. The algorithm first divides a chunk of the MPEG video stream into two byte lists: an odd list and an even list. Then it performs the XOR operation to encrypt the odd list, and uses another encryption function to encrypt the even list to get the cipher text. Since this chunk of data is a non-repeated pattern, it is considered to be perfectly secure.

Further algorithms, such as Motion Vector Encryption Algorithm (MVEA) [6] and Real Time Video Encryption Algorithm (RVEA) [7] are used to encrypt motion vectors efficiently.

The algorithm MVEA is an improvement to the algorithm VEA described above. It includes the following additions: the sign bits of differential values of motion vectors in P and B-frames can also be randomly changed. This type of improvement makes the video playback more random and more non-viewable. When the sign bits of differential values of motion vectors are changed, the directions of motion vectors change as well. The authors found that the encrypting of sign bits of motion vectors makes the encryption of sign bits of DCT coefficients in B- and P-frames unnecessary.

Finally, the algorithm RVEA is significantly secure approach than the previously described algorithms. This approach is considered to be robust under both cipher text-only attack and known-plaintext attack. The difference between RVEA and MVEA/VEA algorithms is that RVEA uses conventional symmetric key cryptography to encrypt the sign bits of DCT coefficients and the sign bits of motion vectors. The selective approach significantly speeds up the process of conventional encryption by only encrypting certain sign bits in the MPEG stream.

In the Algorithm RVEA, the sign bits of DCT coefficients and motion vectors are simply extracted from the MPEG video sequence, encrypted using a fast conventional cryptosystem such as AES, and then restored back to their original position in the encrypted form. The effect of this is similar to VEA/MVEA where the sign bits are either flipped or left unchanged.

2 Proposed Encryption Method

In highly sensitive videos such as military applications, confidential video broadcasting where every part of the video is important it is required Intra and Inter frames need to be encrypted. A new video encryption scheme is proposed for sensitive applications.

In this paper, a selective cum light-weight encryption algorithm is proposed for Intra frames which are fast enough for real-time applications, yet possessing practically acceptable levels of security without much overhead on the MPEG encoding and decoding process. A key ingredient of our solution is a suitably adapted and randomized version of Shamir's Secret Sharing scheme. Further more, the proposed algorithm, unlike most of the video encryption algorithms, has an inbuilt error-tolerance, which could be handy in many practical applications.

The proposed algorithm is a selective and light-weight encryption algorithm. It takes the DC component of each DCT block and depending on the number of ACs in that block distributes the DC among the ACs and itself, based on the method of secret sharing.

DCT is popularly used to compress images and videos. It decomposes an image signal into multiple frequency components. DCT transformation is considered to be the most efficient transformation for image and video coding, since it is found to be best in energy compaction among the existing transformation techniques. The transform coefficients can be classified into two groups namely, DC and AC coefficients. The DC coefficient is the mean value of the image block and carries most of the energy in the image block. The AC coefficients carry energy depending on the amount of detail in the image block. In practice, most of the energy is compacted in the DC coefficient and a few AC coefficients.

2.1 Secret Sharing

Secret sharing was invented by both Adi Shamir and George Blakley independently in 1979. Secret sharing is a way to distributing secret among a group of members such that each member owns a share of the secret. Only some specific combinations of shares can reconstruct the secret. Individual shares reveal nothing about the secret.

2.2 Shamir's Secret Sharing Scheme

In this section, the concept of Shamir's Secret Sharing (SSS)[8] is described briefly. A (k, n) threshold-based secret sharing describes how a secret is shared among n participants. It constructs a $k - 1$ degree polynomial $f(x)$ as

$$f(x) = (d_{k-1}x^{k-1} + \ldots + d_1x + d_0) \bmod p$$

Where the value d_0 is the secret, $d_1 \ldots d_{k-1}$ are random numbers and p is a prime number. The secret shares are the pair of values (x_i, y_i) where $y_i = f(x_i)$, $1 \leq i \leq n$. The polynomial function $f(x)$ is destroyed after each shareholder possesses a pair of values (x_i, y_i) so that no single shareholder knows the secret value d_0. In fact, no group of $k - 1$ or fewer secret shares can discover the secret d_0. On the other hand, when k or more secret shares are available, then we may form at least k linear equations $y_i = f(x_i)$ for the unknown d_i's. The unique solution to these equations shows that the secret value d_0 can be obtained from the Lagrange's interpolation. The SSS is regarded as a Perfect Secret Sharing (PSS) scheme since knowledge of any $(k - 1)$ values does not reveal any information about the secret. The trusted dealer performs the following tasks to share the secret among n users:

(i)   Choose a prime p larger than n and the secret S.
(ii) Construct $f(x)$ by selecting $(k-1)$ random coefficients $d_0, \ldots, d_{k-1}$.
(iii) Compute the shares S_i by evaluating $f(x)$ at n distinct points.
(iv) Securely distribute S_i to user P_i $(1 < i < n)$.

Encryption Algorithm: For Intra frames
     for Each and Every DCT block do
        Step 1: Initialize nac = number of non-zero ACs
        Step 2:
   if nac < 10 and nac > 5 then
       perform (4,5) secret sharing with
       DC, AC1, . . . , AC3 as input and
       store the result in DC, AC1, AC2, AC3, ACnac
   end if
   if nac < 20 then
       perform (8,9) secret sharing with
       DC, AC1, . . . , AC7 as input and
       store the result in DC, AC1, AC2, . . . , AC7, ACnac
   end if
   if nac > 20 then
       perform (12,13) secret sharing with
       DC, AC1, . . . , AC11 as input and
       store the result in DC, AC1, . . . , AC11, ACnac
   end if
   end for

In highly sensitive video where every part of the video is important it is also required that, the motion vector (P and B frames) is also encrypted along with the I frames. P and B frames can be encrypted as substitutes to I frames, without loss in security level. But this cannot be applied to highly sensitive videos where every part of the video is important. To further increase the security, encryption and decryption are done at I frame along with P and B frames.

In the proposed scheme the I frame are encrypted along with the motion vectors. First the Shamir's secret sharing scheme was implemented I frames, that is, the DC component of each DCT block is taken and depending on the number of AC coefficients in that block, the DC values is distributed among the AC coefficients. Next P and B frames are encrypted by generating random array and XORed with the motion vectors.

The encryption of motion vector consists of two stages. The first stage is to generate the key randomly for every frame in the GOP which is obtained from the Galois's field polynomial.

Key generation

A GF polynomial is created for generating the key randomly with the given initial values. For an example consider a GF polynomial $f(x)$ of order one as given below.

$$f(x) = a_1x + a_0 \; ; \; x: \quad \text{initial seed value (ranges from 0 to 255)}$$
$$a_1, a_0: \quad \text{coefficients of the polynomial (ranges from 0 to 255)}$$

The polynomial is created in such a way that seed of the first value which is obtained by solving the GF polynomial from the given initial value is fed as input to the GF polynomial for generating next key values. The second step of the encryption process is to XOR the motion vectors with the pseudorandom array along with seed. A pseudorandom bit generator (PRBG) is a deterministic algorithm which, given a truly random binary sequence of length k, outputs a binary sequence of length l, k which "appears" to be random. The input to the PRBG is called the seed, while the output of the PRBG is called a pseudorandom bit sequence.

2.3   Decryption of Intra and Inter Frames

The decryption process involves in two steps, first the I frames are decrypted using the SSS scheme the authorized user first has to generate a set of random numbers using the key as the input to PRNG and then precede with constructing k equations from n values then use Lagrange's interpolation to get back the DC and AC coefficients of each block to get the original I frames. The secret S can be recovered by constructing the polynomial given in eqn.

$$f(x) = \sum_{i=0}^{t-1} y_i \prod_{0 \le j \le t-1, j, i} (x - x_i) / (y - y_i)$$

From any t of the n shares, and computing $f(0)$. Even if receiver loses $n - k$ values (only one value in the current setting), he can retrieve all the DCT coefficients correctly.

An unauthorized user cannot get back the secret because of the property that any $k - 1$ shares doesn't reveal anything about the secret. The second step is to decrypt the motion vectors for this the user has to feed the correct seed to the pseudorandom array generator. Next the motion vectors are XORed with random array with correct seed for P and B frames to get the original P, B frames. The output of the decryption system gives the original video.

3 Security Analysis

To test robustness of the proposed scheme, security analysis was performed. Key space analysis and statistical analysis were carried out to demonstrate the effectiveness of the new scheme.

3.1 Key Space Analysis

An encryption algorithm is said to provide acceptable level of security if the cost of breaking the encryption requires more investment than buying the key. Also encryption algorithm is secure, if it can withstand cipher text-only and known- plaintext attacks. In the cipher text-only attack, the attacker has to find the original video from the encrypted video.

According to encryption algorithm, for a given block the computational cost of breaking the key would be 255^6 this makes it practically infeasible. Since two GF polynomial of order one is used for Intra and Inter frames key generation and since each polynomial requires 3 digits, each of the digits ranging from 0-255 the overall key space is increased to 255^6. Thus, the algorithm is robust to cipher text-only attack.

In the known-plaintext attack, unauthorized user has both original and the corresponding encrypted pixel values. The GF polynomial is created in such a way that seed of the first value which is obtained by solving the GF polynomial from the given initial value is fed as input to the GF polynomial again for generating next key values. Since a freshly generated seed (key) is used for encrypting each I, P, B frames of the video, it is obvious that the algorithm is secure against known-plaintext attack.

3.2 Statistical Analysis

In the statistical analysis, two tests are performed on the new scheme, histogram analysis and correlation coefficient analysis.

3.2.1 Histogram Analysis
To prevent the leakage of information to an opponent, it is also advantageous if the cipher image bears little or no statistical similarity to the plain image. The image-histogram of I, P, B frames illustrates how pixels in an image are distributed by graphing the number of pixels at each intensity level. It is observed that the histogram of the original frame after the encryption is significantly different from that of the original frame. The histogram results of the original and encrypted I, B, P frames are depicted in Fig.2

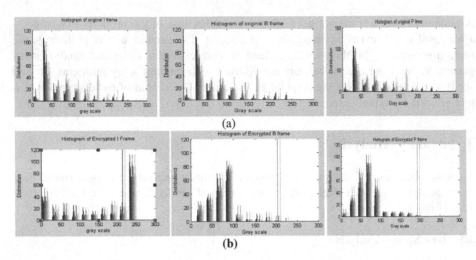

(a)

(b)

Fig. 2. Histogram of (a) original I, B, P frames and (b) encrypted I, B, P frames

3.2.2 Correlation Coefficient Analysis

In addition to the histogram analysis the correlation between two vertically adjacent pixels, two horizontally adjacent pixels and two diagonally adjacent pixels in original and encrypted frames are analysed respectively. The correlation coefficient analysis indicaties the relationship among the pixels in the encrypted frame. In the new scheme the correlation among adjacent pixels is lower than that of the original image.

Fig.3. shows the I, B, P frame correlation distribution of two horizontally adjacent pixels pixels in the original and encrypted frame respectively

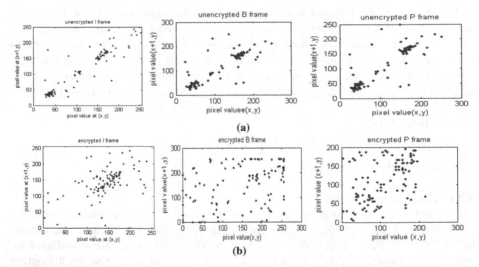

(a)

(b)

Fig. 3. Horizontal Correlation of (a) original I,B,P frame and (b) encrypted I,B,P frame

Fig.4. shows the I, B, P frame correlation distribution of two vetically adjacent pixels pixels in the original and encrypted frame respectively

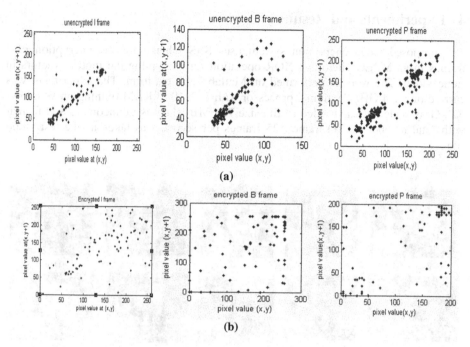

Fig. 4. Vertical Correlation of (a) original I,B,P frame and (b) encrypted I,B,P frame

Fig.5. shows the I, B, P frame correlation distribution of two vetically adjacent pixels pixels in the original and encrypted frame respectively.

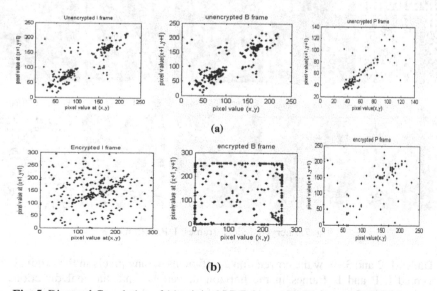

Fig. 5. Diagonal Correlation of (a) original I,B,P frame and (b) encrypted I,B,P frame

4   Experiments and Results

The proposed video encryption system uses SSS scheme for the encryption of I frames in an MPEG video and XOR operation for encrypting the motion vectors in same video. The work is performed on Matlab 7.4.0 platform. The experiment was carried on a 2.4 GHz Pentium 4 processor with 512MB of RAM running on Windows XP. Gray scale news.avi video of file size 7.26MB which is in uncompressed format with total number of 300 frames, 25 frames per second was taken as the test video file.

Fig. 6. Original video sequence

Fig. 7. Encrypted video frames: I, P, B frames

Tables 1, 2 and 3 show the correlation coefficients among pixels in the original and encrypted I, P and B frames in the horizontal, vertical and diagonal directions of adjacent pixels. From the table it is clear that the pixel values of the original and

Fig. 8. Decrypted video frames: I, P, B with correct key

Table 1. Correlation coefficients of original and encrypted I frame

Direction of Adjacent pixels	Original I frame	Encrypted I frame
Horizontal	0.9351	0.2103
Vertical	0.7950	0.1579
Diagonal	0.8995	0.1294

Table 2. Correlation coefficients of original and encrypted B frame

Direction of Adjacent pixels	Original B frame	Encrypted B frame
Horizontal	0.7995	0.2177
Vertical	0.9371	0.4995
Diagonal	0.9004	0.3749

Table 3. Correlation coefficients of original and encrypted P frame

Direction of Adjacent pixels	Original P frame	Encrypted P frame
Horizontal	0.9285	0.2328
Vertical	0.7905	0.1383
Diagonal	0.9004	0.4601

encrypted frames are completely decorrelated. For original frames the correlation coefficeint ranges from 0.7905 to 0.9371 where the range of the encrypted frame is between 0.1294 to 0.4995.

5 Conclusion

In this paper, a new video encryption scheme has been proposed in which the security of existing algorithm is improved by combining encryption in the DCT block and the Motion Vector Block. The I frames are encrypted based on the method of Secret Sharing is done in which the strength of the DC coefficient is distributed among the AC values of DCT based on Shamir's Secret Sharing Scheme. To further increase the security, encryption and decryption are done at I frame along with P and B frames. P and B frames are encrypted by means of XORing with randomly generated pseudo random sequence.

According to encryption algorithm, for a given block the computational cost of breaking the key would be 255^6 this makes it practically infeasible to break. Thus, the algorithm is robust to cipher text-only attack. Since a freshly generated seed (key) is used for encrypting each I, P, B frames of the video, it is obvious that the algorithm is secure against known-plaintext attack. The proposed video encryption algorithm was subjected to both security and statistical analysis. For original frames the correlation coefficeint ranges from 0.7905 to 0.9371 where the range of the encrypted frame is between 0.1294 to 0.4995.In the new scheme the correlation coefficient among adjacent pixels is lower than that of the original image.

In the new scheme encryption is done DCT block and motion vector block. With the advances in the transformations other transforms such as DWT, packet transforms can be used for encryption. The proposed video encryption algorithm can be extended to future research work by doing encryption in the audio.

References

[1] Tang, L.: Methods for Encrypting and Decrypting MPEG Video Data Efficiently. In: Proceedings of ACM Multimedia, Boston, USA, pp. 219–229 (November 1996)

[2] Agi, I., Gong, L.: An Empirical Study of Secure MPEG Video Transmissions. In: Proceedings of the Internet Society Symposium on Network and Distributed System Security, San Diego, CA, Febuary 22-23, pp. 137–144 (1996)

[3] Choo, E., Jehyun, L., Heejo, L., Giwon, N.: SRMT: A lightweight Encryption Scheme for Secure Real-Time Multimedia Transmission. In: Multimedia and Ubiquitous Engineering, Seoul, April 26-28, pp. 60–65 (2007)

[4] Liu, Z., Li, X., Dong, Z.: Enhancing Security of Frequency Domain Video Encryption. In: Proceedings of ACM Multimedia, New York, USA, pp. 304–307 (September 2004)

[5] Shi, C., Bhargava, B.: A Fast MPEG Video Encryption Algorithm. In: Proceedings of ACM Multimedia, Hingham, MA, USA, pp. 81–88 (September 1998)

[6] Liu, Z., Li, X.: Motion vector encryption in multimedia streaming. In: Proceedings of 10th International Conference of Multimedia Modeling Conference, Brisbane, Australia, pp. 64–71 (January 2004)

[7] Tosun, A.S., Feng, W.-C.: Lightweight Security Mechanisms for Wireless Video Transmission. In: International Conference on Information Technology: Coding and Computing, Las Vegas, NV, USA, April 2-4, pp. 157–161 (2001)

[8] Shamir, A.: How to share a secret. In: Proc. of Communications of the ACM, vol. II, pp. 612–613 (1979)

VLSI Design and Implementation of Combined Secure Hash Algorithm SHA-512

R. Kayalvizhi, R. Harihara Subramanian, R. Girish Santhosh,
J. Gurubaran, and V. Vaidehi

Department of Electronics, MIT Campus, Anna University, Chennai-44
kavikkayal@annauniv.edu, hhs_2222@yahoo.co.in,
girish_santhosh@yahoo.co.in, jguranb4@gmail.com,
vaidehi@annauniv.edu

Abstract. Secure Hashing Algorithm (SHA) is increasingly becoming popular for the online security applications, specifically, for mobile and embedded system platforms. Hash functions have many information security applications, notably in digital signatures, message authentication codes (MACs), and other forms of authentication. This necessitates a high performance hardware implementation of the SHA algorithms (SHA–512). In this paper we propose a new method for generating digital signature based on SHA-512 hash algorithm. This design uses two SHA-512 modules in parallel which operate simultaneously to provide highly secure, more efficient and high throughput mechanism to compute a 1024- bit Message Digest (MD) or Hash.

Keywords: Combined SHA-512, MAC, MD and VLSI.

1 Introduction

The need for protecting the integrity and confidentiality of information is increasing ever. With many applications getting computerized day by day the requirement for protecting information is mounting with the possibility of threats for security of data. Hash functions are common and critical cryptographic primitives. Their primary application is combined use with public-key cryptosystems in digital signature schemes The most widely known is the SHA-512 version, which produces a message digest of 512 bits [1]. Due to the use of the HMAC in the IPSec, e-payment and VPN applications, the throughput of the cryptographic system, especially the server, has to reach the highest degree of throughput. Especially in these applications as the transmission and reception rates are high, any latency or delay on calculating the digital signature of the data packet leads to degradation of the network's quality of service. Software implementations are presenting unacceptable performance for high speed applications [2]. So we implement and verify our design in VLSI using Verilog HDL.

2 SHA-512 Implementation

The SHA hash functions are a set of cryptographic hash functions designed by the National Security Agency (NSA) and published by the NIST as a U.S. Federal

N. Meghanathan et al. (Eds.): CNSA 2010, CCIS 89, pp. 105–113, 2010.

Information Processing Standard. The new family of hashing algorithms known as SHA-2, use larger digest messages, making them more resistant to possible attacks and allowing them to be used with larger blocks of data [4]. The SHA-512 algorithm can be described in two stages [1]:

- Preprocessing
- Hash Computation

2.1 Preprocessing

Preprocessing shall take place before hash computation begins. This preprocessing consists of three steps: padding the message, M, parsing the padded message into message blocks, and setting the initial hash value.

Padding the message
The message, M, shall be padded before hash computation begins. The purpose of this padding is to ensure that the padded message is a multiple of 1024 bits.

Parsing the Message
Before the message pads, it must be parsed into N m-bit blocks before the hash computation begins. The padded message is parsed into N 1024-bit blocks, M(1), M(2),..., M(N). The 1024 bits of the input block may be expressed as sixteen 64-bit words, the first 64 bits of message block i are denoted M0(i), the next 64 bits are M1(i) upto M15(i)

Setting Initial Hash Values
The system is initialized with certain values to start the recursive algorithm and compute the hash. These words were obtained by considering the first sixty-four bits of the fractional parts of the square roots of the first eight prime numbers.

2.2 Hash Computation

Message Scheduler
This unit generates 80 message-dependent words Wt. The first 16 words are the first 16 words of the input message block. The remaining words are computed using simple feedback function, based on rotations, shifts and XOR operations. Message Scheduler receives a 1024-bit message block in 64-bit chunks through X_{in}.

According to Fig.2 this module has a 16×64-bit shift register and one multiplexer. During the first 16 pulses of the system clock, whole message block enters into the shift register and then the multiplexer selects Win to provide feedback for the shift register. The each clock pulse the message scheduler generates W_{out} for the hash algorithm. For every round the module takes the (Round$_i$) W_{in} and X_{in} as an input to produce the W_{out} [4].

According to NIST Standard, SHA-512 uses the sequence of eighty constant 64-bit words, K0, K1..., K79. These words represent the first 64 bits of the fractional parts of the cube roots of the first eighty prime numbers. To store the constant values, an

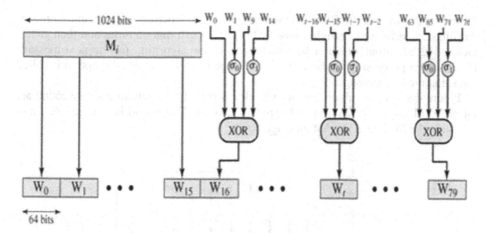

Fig. 1. Message Scheduler

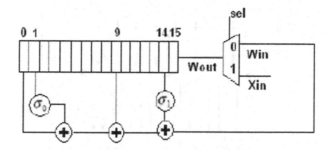

Fig. 2. Message Scheduler using Shift register Memory

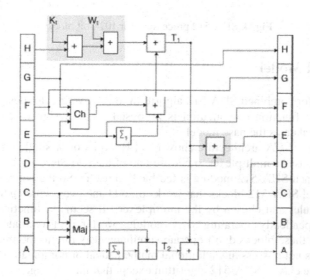

Fig. 3. SHA-512 Round Algorithm

80×64-bit Xilinx specific Block ROM was used. Fig. 3 depicts the execution of standard hash algorithm of a single round. This round performs 80 times and then generates a 512-bit output which is an initial value of the algorithm for the next message block. After processing all the 1024-bit message blocks, final 512-bit output is called the signature of a message.

Figure 4 shows the algorithm in expanded form. The inputs to a single round are 64 bit word, 64 bit constant ki and registers a,b,c,..h. This round is repeated 80 times to obtain the final hash for that message block.

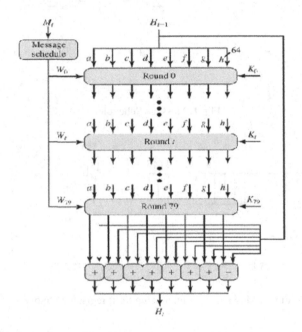

Fig. 4. SHA-512 processing for 1024-bit block

3 Proposed Model

A new design for combined SHA-512 algorithm to achieve greater design complexity and faster hash function computation is proposed. The design of combined SHA given in [4] is taken as the base model.

The combined SHA architecture shown in [4] works on a single 64 bit word per clock cycle. It uses a multiplexer to choose one of the two SHA -512 modules. Also the output of each SHA-512 module is fed back to itself. So the entire module looks like two parallel SHA-512 blocks that works on odd and even words generated by the message scheduler and chosen by the multiplexer. It seems to function as if it contains two independently operating SHA modules working on alternate words of the message. And these blocks don't operate simultaneously due to the multiplexing action. So it does not possess any additional mathematical or computational complexity compared to the classic SHA-512 algorithm except that the message digest obtained is 1024 bits.

In this proposed model as in fig 5, two SHA-512 blocks are designed to operate simultaneously on alternate 64-bit words. The outputs of the SHA-512 rounds are cross connected to the other module. This is done in order to ensure that the two blocks are dependent on each other which means the output of each block is also dependent on the other output of each block is dependent on the other. So the work factor for birthday attack is 2^512. Improving the data dependency increases mathematical complexity and thus makes the final digest more secure.

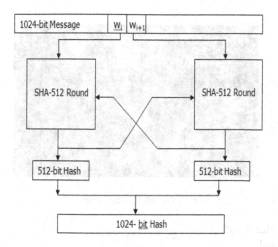

Fig. 5. Proposed design for Combined SHA-512

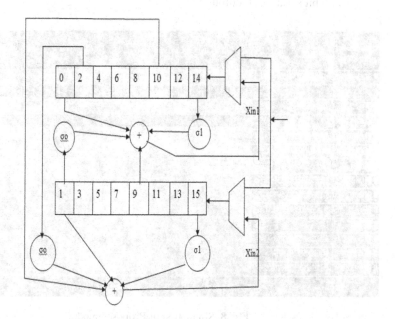

Fig. 6. Modified Message Scheduler

To generate two words in a single clock cycle, 128 bits of message is taken as input to the scheduler block. This model uses two 8*64 bit shift register instead of a single 16*64 bit shift register [4]. The 128 bit message input is then split up as two 64 bit chunks and is fed to the two register banks simultaneously. This is done for the first 8 clock cycles. After that the 64 bit words are generated according to message scheduler equation as shown in fig 6.

The overall system consists of the following I/O signals to implement in FPGA as shown in fig 7.

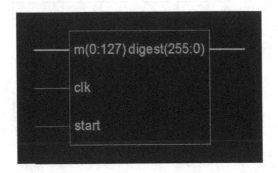

Fig. 7. Overall System design

128 bit serial input
Clock signal
Start signal
256 bit serial hash output

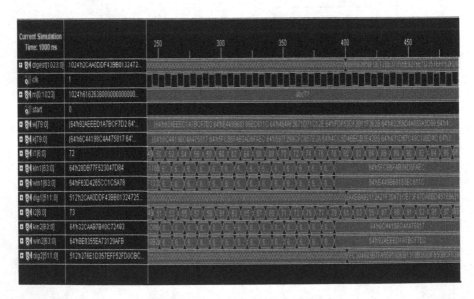

Fig. 8. Simulation of Proposed model

Fig 8 shows the simulation result of our design. The 1024-bit output is obtained in 40 clock cycles with clock period of 10 ns. But the earlier designs generated 512-bit hash in 80 clock cycles.

4 Performance Analysis

All modules were synthesized, placed and routed on Xilinx Virtex4 xc4vsx35ff668-12 target device. In the case of SHA-512 the utilization of slices was 1921 out of 15360 (12%) and number of consumed slice flip flops was 2240 out of 30720 (7%). The timing analysis shows 118.043 MHz as the maximum frequency of the design.

Maximum data throughput can be simply computed by the following equation:

$$\text{Throughput} = S \times F / R \tag{1}$$

where

S: message block size
F: Maximum clock frequency
R: Number of rounds

Maximum expected throughput is: 1.51Gbps (1024b × 118.043MHz / 80).

For the combined SHA-512 method[4], the utilization of slices is 3541 out of 15360 (23%) and number of slice flip flops is 4490 out of 30720 (14%) with the maximum clock frequency of 117.845 MHz and maximum throughput of 2.51Gbps.

For our proposed model, the design analysis shows that it requires 2930 (19%) slices and 2549 (12%) flip flops for implementation and timing analysis show that maximum operating frequency is 126.985 MHz. So the throughput of our design is 3.25 Gbps since it operates for 40 clock cycles.

5 Security Analysis

The security of hash functions is determined by the size of their outputs, referred to as hash values, n. The best known attack against these functions, the "birthday attack", can find a pair of messages having the same hash value with a work factor of approximately $2^{n/2}$.

So the complexity of birthday attack for this design is 2512 which is high compared to basic SHA-512 algorithm and the design in [4]. The combined SHA-512 model proposed [4] contains two independent SHA modules operating alternatively on a message. So the complexity is same as that of a SHA-512 module.

Since this design uses two cross connected SHA-512 modules operating simultaneously on two consecutive words of a message the hash function complexity is high.

The complexity of the hash function can be further increased by using the permutation unit [4]. If a 1024-bit secret key is used, permutation complexity becomes which yields the total complexity of $2^{10!} \times 2512$.

But in order to store the key it requires 1024*10 bit memory which is very huge for light weight applications. So depending upon the application and the level of security to realize the permutation unit may be used or ignored.

Table 1. Comparisons of SHA-512, Combined SHA [4] and Proposed Model

FEATURES	CLASSIC SHA-512	COMBINED SHA [4]	PROPOSED MODEL
Clock Cycles	80	80	40
Flip-flops %	7	14	12
Slices %	12	23	19
Frequency (MHz)	118.043	117.845	126.985
Throughput (Gbps)	1.51	2.51	3.25
Digest Length	512	512	1024
Time delay (ns)	677.719	814.629	314.931
Pre-image attack	2512	21024	21024
Birthday attack	2256	2256	2512

6 Conclusion

In this paper a novel technique to generate message digest based on SHA-512 algorithm proposed. The implementation and simulation results show the superiority of this method over the basic algorithm in considering the aspects of throughput and security features. A main feature of this design is that it incorporates parallelism without any compromise on data dependency.

The throughput performance of the design is approximately 1.3 times better than the design proposed in [4]. The net time delay to compute the message digest is reduced by 2.5 times due to improved performance and also reduced the number of clock cycles required to compute the message digest. Security analysis shows that the design is more secure due to increased computational complexity.

This work can be applied efficiently in the implementation of digital signature algorithms, keyed hash message authentication codes. This can also be used efficiently in applications which operate at high data rates.

References

1. Federal Information Processing Standards Publication 180-2, August 1 (2002)
2. Aisopos, F., et al.: A Novel High-Throughput Implementation of a Partially Unrolled SHA-512. In: IEEE Melecon 2006, Benalmádena (Málaga), Spain, May 16-19 (2006)
3. Chaves, R., et al.: Cost-Efficient SHA Hardware Accelerators. IEEE Transactions on VLSI Systems 16(8) (August 2008)
4. Emam, S.A., Emami, S.S.: Design and Implementation of a Fast, Combined SHA-512 on FPGA. International Journal of Computer Science and Network Security 7(5) (May 2007)
5. Mladenov, T., Nooshabadi, S.: Implementation of Reconfigurable SHA-2 Hardware Core. In: IEEE Asia Pacific Conference on Circuits and Systems (2008)

Performance Comparison of Multicast Routing Protocols under Variable Bit Rate Scenario for Mobile Adhoc Networks

N. Bhalaji[1], P. Gurunathan[2], and Dr.A. Shanmugam[3]

[1] Research Scholar, Anna University Coimbatore
[2] School of Engineering, Vels University, Chennai
[3] Principal, Bannari Amman Institute of Technology

Abstract. An ad hoc network is formed by wireless mobile nodes (hosts) that operate as terminals as well as routers in the network, without any centralized administration. Mobile ad hoc networks (MANETs) are characterized by lack of any fixed network infrastructure. In a MANET, there is no distinction between a host and a router, since all nodes can be sources as well as forwarders of traffic. Moreover, all MANET components can be mobile. MANETs differ from traditional, fixed-infrastructure mobile networks; MANETs require fundamental changes to conventional routing and packet forwarding protocols for both unicast and multicast communication. Wireless ad-hoc networks have gained a lot of importance in wireless communications. Wireless communication is established by nodes acting as routers and transferring packets from one to another in ad-hoc networks. Routing in these networks is highly complex due to moving nodes and hence many protocols have been developed. This Paper thesis concentrate mainly on routing protocols and their functionality in Ad-hoc networks with a Variable Bit Rate (VBR) discussion being made on four selected protocols MAODV, ADMRP, ODMRP and ABAM, ending with their comparison.

Keywords: Multicast routing protocols, ADMRP, ABAM, ODMRP, Manet, Glomosim.

1 Introduction

Multicasting is the transmission of datagram to a group of hosts identified by a single destination address and hence is intended for group-oriented computing [1]. In MANET, multicast can efficiently support a variety of applications that are characterized by close collaborative efforts. A multicast packet is typically delivered to all members of its destination group with the same reliability as regular unicast packets. Multicast can reduce the communication costs, the link bandwidth consumption, sender and router processing and delivery delay. In addition, it can provide a simple and robust communication mechanism when the receiver's individual addresses are unknown or changeable. Multicast routing protocols for ad hoc networks have been proposed [2] [3] [4] in order to save the network bandwidth and node resource because they are the protocols for powerful communication used in multi-hop applications, and are more efficient than the approach of sending the same information from

N. Meghanathan et al. (Eds.): CNSA 2010, CCIS 89, pp. 114–122, 2010.

the source to each of the receivers individually. The presence of wireless communication and mobility makes an ad hoc network unlike a traditional wired network and requires that the routing protocols used in an ad hoc network be based on new and different principles. Routing protocols for traditional wired networks are designed to support a tremendous numbers of nodes, but they assume that the relative position of the nodes will generally remain unchanged [8]. In a mobile ad hoc network, however, there may be fewer nodes among which to route, and the network topology changes can be drastic and frequent as the individual mobile nodes move.

2 Multicasting Protocols in MANET

MAODV. [1, 2] protocol is the multicast extension of AODV [8] which is used for unicast traffic. It creates a group tree, shared by all sources and receivers for a multicast group. The root of each group tree is a multicast source or receiver for that group that has been designated as a group leader which is the first member of a multicast group. This leader takes the responsibility of maintaining multicast group sequence number and propagating this number to the entire group through proactive GROUP HELLO message. Members use the GROUP HELLO message to update request table, and distance (hop) to group leader.

The MAODV discovers multicast routes on demand using a broadcast route-discovery mechanism which is based on a ROUTE REQUEST and ROUTE REPLY cycle. A mobile node originates a ROUTE REQUEST message when it wishes to join a multicast group, or when it requires a route to send data to a multicast group. A member of the multicast tree with a current route to the destination responds to the ROUTE REQUEST with a ROUTE REPLY message. Non-member nodes just simply rebroadcast the ROUTE REQUEST message. Each node on receiving the ROUTE REQUEST updates its route table and records the sequence number and next hop information for the source node. This information is unicast through ROUTE REPLY message back to the source. If the source node receives multiple ROUTE REPLY message from its neighbor for its route request, it then chooses only one ROUTE REPLY message having the freshest sequence number or the least hop count. Then the MULTICAST ACTIVATION (MACT) message is sent to set up multicast state between source node and the node sending the reply. If a source node does not receive a MACT message within a certain period it broadcasts another RREQ. After a certain number of retries (RREQ RETRIES), the source assumes that there are no other members of the tree that can be reached and declares itself as the group leader. MANET multicast protocols should work efficiently with the dynamic topology changes. A tree-based protocol, e.g., MAODV (Multicast Ad hoc On demand Distance Vector), AMRoute (Adhoc Multicast Routing) [7] and AMRIS (Ad hoc Multicast Routing protocol) [6], maintains and enhances a multicast tree structure specialized in MANET scenarios. On the other hand, a mesh-based protocol such as ODMRP (On Demand Multicast Routing Protocol), and CAMP (Core-Assisted Multicast Protocol) [8] uses a multicast mesh structure that allows redundant paths between a source and a member. With a mesh structure, members can receive multicast data packets from any of their forwarding neighbor nodes. Thus, a mesh topology improves the connectivity of a network and the availability of multicast routes in the presence of dynamic topology changes.

ODMRP. [1, 5], like MAODV and ADMR, is also on-demand multicast routing protocol. However, ODMRP is a mesh based rather than tree based protocol so it has multiple paths from the sender to the receivers, contrary to the MAODV or ADMR which is a tree based protocol and has only one path to the receivers. When a node has information to send but no route to the destination, a JOIN QUERY message is broadcasted. The next node that receives the JOIN QUERY updates its routing table with the appropriate node id from which the message was received for the reverse path back to the sender (backward learning). Then the node checks the value of the TTL (time to live) and if this value is greater than zero it rebroadcasts the JOIN QUERY. When a multicast group member node receives a Join Query, it broadcasts a JOIN REPLY message. A neighborhood node that receives a JOIN REPLY consults the join reply table to see if its node id is the same with any next hop node id. If it is the same then the node understands that it is on the path to the source and sets the FG_FLAG (Forwarding Group flag). ODMRP is a soft state protocol, so when a node wants to leave the multicast group it is over passing the group maintaining messages [1], [5], [7] and [8].

ADMR. [1], [3], builds source-specific multicast trees, using an on-demand mechanism that only creates a tree if there is at least one source and one receiver active for the group. To join a multicast group, an ADMR receiver floods a MULTICAST SO-LICITATION message throughout the network. When a source receives this message, it responds by sending a unicast KEEP-ALIVE message to that receiver, confirming that the receiver can join that source. The receiver responds to the KEEP-ALIVE by sending a RECEIVER JOIN message along the reverse path which sets up forwarding state along the shortest paths. In addition to the receiver's join mechanism, a source periodically sends a network-wide flood of a RECEIVER DISCOVERY message. Receivers that get this message respond to it with a RECEIVER JOIN if they are not already connected to the multicast tree. To detect broken links within the tree, the ADMR routing layer at a multicast source monitors the packet forwarding rate to determine when the tree has broken or the source has become silent. If a link has broken, a node can initiate a repair on its own (local repair), and if the source has stopped sending then any forwarding state is silently removed. Receivers likewise monitor the packet reception rate and can re-join the multicast tree if intermediate nodes have been unable to reconnect the tree. The receivers do a repair by broadcasting a new MULTICAST SOLICITATION message. Nodes on the multicast tree send a REPAIR NOTIFICATION message down its sub-tree to cancel the repair of downstream nodes. The most upstream node transmits a hop-limited flood of a RECONNECT message. Any forwarder receiving this message forwards the RECONNECT up the multicast tree to the source. The source in return responds to the RECONNECT by sending a RECONNECT REPLY as a unicast message that follows the path of the RECONNECT back to the repairing node. Unlike MAODV, ADMR does not employ any periodic control packet exchanges, such as neighbor sensing or periodic flooding, and does not rely on lower layers within the protocol stack to perform such functions [3]. Thus, it performs both its route discovery and route mechanism functions on demand.

ABAM. [6] is Associativity-Based Ad hoc Multicast and on-demand source-based routing protocol for mobile ad-hoc networks (MANETs). It establishes multicast sessions on demand and utilizes the association stability concept that is adopted in the ABR for mobile ad-hoc unicast routing. For each multicast session a multicast tree is established primarily based on association stability. ABAM consists of 3 phases: 1.Multicast Tree Establishment 2.Multicast Tree Reconfigurations 3.Multicast Tree Deletion.

3 Experimental Setup and Performance Metrics

We have used Glomosim simulator for simulation, most widely used network simulator and freely downloadable. We simulated network for simulation time of 1000 sec and area of 1000 m *1000 m. Further increase in these values increased the time taken for completing simulation, to a limit which is not feasible due to various constraints. We have used Throughput, Average Message Latency, Routing Overhead and Group Reliability as performance parameters while varying various network parameters such as Number of Nodes. To perform various operations during the simulation. The enable parameters use to configure the evaluation environment by checking its behavior. The following performance metrics that are needed to be taken into consideration in order to analyze and compare the performance of these protocols are

(a)Number of Nodes: Number of nodes may be varying parameter as it plays important role in performance. Various performance parameters versus No. of. Nodes. The total number of packets with different types: Sent, Received, Forwarded and Dropped, which were transmitted between mobile nodes in the period of simulation. This metric provides us with an overview of how the simulated ad-hoc network, with the defined parameters, reacts to topology changes while nodes are moving.

(b)Throughput: Throughput or Network throughput is the average rate of successful message delivery over a communication channel.

(c)Average Message Latency: Latency is measure from the time a request (e.g. a single packet) leaves the client to the time the response (e.g. An Acknowledgment) arrives back at the client from the serving entity. The unit of latency is time. Throughput on the other hand is the amount of data that is transferred over a period of time.

(d)Routing overhead: Routing overhead is the ratio between the numbers of control bytes transmitted to the number of data bytes received. This is the ratio of overhead bytes to delivered data bytes.

(e)Group reliability: The ratio of number of packets received by all multicast receivers to number of packets sent. Thus, for this metric, a packet is considered to be received only if it is received by every member of the multicast group.

4 Simulation Result

Throughput. The general trend we observe from Figure 1 is that, especially at high mobility, flooding performs better than ODMRP which in turn performs better than MAODV. Comparing flooding to ODMRP, we notice that at lower speeds the difference in packet delivery ratio is between 5% and 7%. However, at higher speeds the gap in packet delivery ratio starts widening. In the case of ODMRP, increased mobility requires that forwarding group members be updated more frequently. One way to address this problem is to update forwarding group members more often through more frequent Join-Queries. This of course would result in higher control overhead and possibly greater packet loss due to contention. Comparing ODMRP with MAODV, we observe that ODMRP exhibits better (by roughly 10%) packet delivery ratios. Since ODMRP maintains meshes, it has multiple redundant paths to receivers and is not affected by mobility as greatly as MAODV. Increased mobility causes frequent link changes and requires MAODV to reconfigure the multicast tree more frequently to prevent stale routing information. This in turn requires higher control traffic which can have a negative effect of increased packet loss due to contention and hidden terminals.

As a starting set of simulations we have varied the number of senders to evaluate the protocol scalability based on the number of multicast source nodes and the traffic load. We inferred from the Figure 3 that ADMR is over 37% more effective than ODMRP in throughput as the number of senders incremented from 0-15. While ABAM is over 30% more and 25% less in throughput compared to that of MAODV and ODMRP. We have also observed that both protocols have not performed well if the number of senders increased above 20.

Average Message Latency. In terms of latency, overall it is shown in Figure.4 that MAODV experiences the highest latency compare to both ADMR and ODMRP. It is due to the longer paths that data packets have to follow within the shared tree. ODMRP's latency is the lowest. It is due to the frequent state discovery floods, it uses the shortest forwarding path among the three protocols. Meanwhile, though ADMR's latency is higher than ODMRP, but it is shown that its latency remarkable nearly consistent across all scenarios. In this scenario, we study the behavior of MAODV, ODMRP and ADMR as node mobility is increased from 1 m/s to 20 m/s. The number of senders and receivers is fixed to 1 and 20 respectively. We observe that, with mesh topology ODMRP is generally having a slight effect to the mobility on achieving.

The ADMR's robust performance is based on its ability to switch to flooding mode in high mobility situation. On the other hand, tree structure in MAODV is very fragile to mobility drops significantly. In terms of latency (Fig 2), ADMR and ODMRP have nearly consistent latency for all mobility scenarios. Conversely, mobility leads to higher latency for MAODV. Since MAODV proactively maintains the single shared multicast tree, the topology is very fragile to mobility. Thus, in any breaks in link that may occurs it does not have alternative paths between source and destination and requires longer times to repair the topology which in turn affect the longer delay delivering data to the receivers.   Both ODMRP and MAODV protocols uses on-demand route discovery but with different routing mechanisms. In general, from Graph-4 ODMRP outperforms group reliability than the MAODV. But ODMRP hasn't had good Message Latency and Routing Overhead as the number of senders or the group size increases. Figure 4 shows the comparison of Average message latencies of all the four protocols, by this comparison we can see the decrement of the delay by 60% as that for ADMR and 20% as that for MAODV.

Routing Overhead. Figure 3 plots control overhead per data byte transferred as a function of mobility. Note that flooding's overhead does not change with mobility as only data header packets contribute to overhead. In ODMRP, the Join-Query interval was fixed at 3 seconds and hence control overhead remains fairly constant with node mobility. The slight increase in overhead at higher speeds (around 55 km/hr) is due to the fact that the number of data bytes delivered decreases with increased mobility. In the case of MAODV, increased mobility causes frequent link breakages and data packet drops; link outages also generate repair messages increasing control overhead. From Figure 5 it is clear that ABAM protocol speeds up its performance better than other three protocols. ADMR and ODMRP have its routing overhead with 42 to 45 while for MAODV it is nearing 40. Thus ABAM outperforms in this case.

Group Reliability. Figure 4 plots group reliability as a function of node speed. From the Figure it can be seen that flooding is most effective in delivering packets to all group members (as expected). Moreover, flooding is able to keep group reliability fairly constant even at higher speeds. Both ODMRP and MAODV exhibit poor performance even at low mobility (group reliability lower than 50% for speeds higher than 10 km/hr). However, as expected, ODMRP exhibits better group reliability than MAODV. Although ODMRP can maintain multiple routes to receivers, the mesh connectivity is largely dependent on the number of senders and receivers. In case of 5 senders, mesh connectivity is insufficient to ensure packet delivery to all group members (especially, with node mobility) resulting in low group reliability. Since MAODV delivers packet along a multicast tree, a single packet drop upstream can prevent a large number of downstream multicast receivers from receiving the packet. The absence of redundant routes affects performance greatly as node mobility results in frequent link breakages and packet drops. From Figure 6 the reliability of the group is higher for ABAM compared to other cases. In this scenario, we study the behavior of MAODV, ABAM, ODMRP and ADMR as node number is increased from 1 to 15. We observe that, with mesh topology ODMRP is generally having a slight effect to the mobility on achieving Group Reliability. The ADMR's robust performance is based on its ability to switch to flooding mode in high mobility situation.

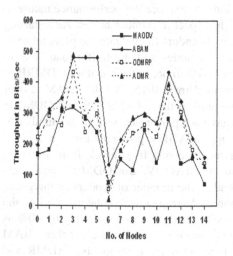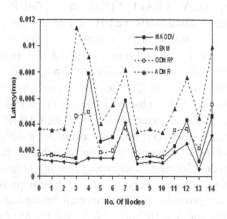

Fig. 1. Throughput vs.Nodes   **Fig. 2.** Message Latency vs. Nodes

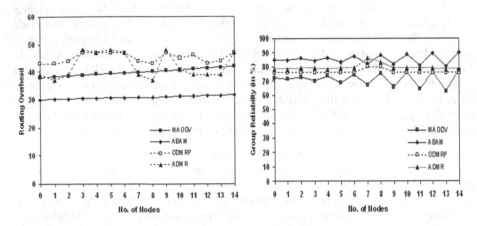

Fig. 3. Routing overhead vs. Nodes   **Fig. 4.** Group Reliability vs. Nodes

5 Conclusion and Future Work

In this paper, we reported on simulation-based experiments evaluating two different approaches to multicast communication in mobile ad hoc networks (MANETs), namely mesh- and tree-based multicast. One of the chief contributions of this work is our objective analysis of these two multicast routing protocol categories in order to characterize their behavior under a wide range of MANET scenarios, including different mobility and traffic load conditions as well as multicast group characteristics (e.g., size, number of sources, multiple multicast groups, etc.). The following metrics considered for routing/multicast protocol performance evaluation (a). Throughput (b). Average Message latency (c). Routing overhead (d). Group Reliability.

We have performed a number of experiments to explore the performance nature of MAODV, ABAM, ADMR and ODMRP with respect to number nodes. As a starting set of simulations we have varied the number of senders to evaluate the protocol scalability based on the number of multicast source nodes and the traffic load. We inferred from the Figure.3 that ADMR is over 37% more effective than ODMRP in throughput as the number of senders incremented from 0-15. While ABAM is over 30% more and 25% less in throughput compared to that of MAODV and ODMRP. We have also observed that both protocols have not performed well if the number of senders increased above 20. Both ODMRP and MAODV protocols uses on-demand route discovery but with different routing mechanisms. In general, from Figure 4 ODMRP outperforms group reliability than the MAODV. But ODMRP hasn't had good Message Latency and Routing Overhead as the number of senders or the group size increases. Figure 2 shows the comparison of Average message latencies of all the four protocols, by this comparison we can see the decrement of the delay by 60% as that for ADMR and 20% as that for MAODV. From Figure 3 it is clear that ABAM protocol speeds up its performance better than other three protocols. ADMR and

ODMRP have its routing overhead with 42 to 45 while for MAODV it is nearing 40. Thus ABAM outperforms in this case.

From Figure 4 the reliability of the group is higher for ABAM compared to other cases. In this scenario, we study the behavior of MAODV, ABAM, ODMRP and ADMR as node number is increased from 1 to 15. We observe that, with mesh topology ODMRP is generally having a slight effect to the mobility on achieving Group Reliability. The ADMR's robust performance is based on its ability to switch to flooding mode in high mobility situation. On the other hand, tree structure in MAODV is very fragile to mobility thus Group Reliability drops significantly. The sharp degradation of reliability is experienced by MAODV can also be explained as the cost of high control overhead generated by MAODV to adapt the increasing speed of the nodes. In terms of latency MAODV and ODMRP have nearly consistent latency for all scenarios. Thus, in any breaks in link that may occurs it does not have alternative paths between source and destination and requires longer times to repair the topology which in turn affect the longer delay delivering data to the receivers.

Our simulation results demonstrate that even though the performance of all multicast protocols degrade in terms of packet delivery and group reliability as node mobility and traffic load increases, mesh-based protocols (e.g., flooding and ODMRP) perform considerably better than tree-based protocols (e.g., MAODV). The general conclusion from the comparative analysis was that flooding, which is the simplest routing mechanism provides higher delivery guarantees than ODMRP and MAODV for most scenarios considered. ODMRP exhibits decent robustness on account of its mesh structure. MAODV did not perform as well as the other protocols in terms of packet delivery ratio and group reliability but has the lowest routing overhead among the protocols considered. One of the conclusions from our study is that given the diversity of MANETs, it is impossible for anyone routing protocol to be optimal under all scenarios and operating conditions. One possible solution would be to develop specialized multicast solutions for each type of network and the means for integrating those solutions. Our results show that ABAM, ADMR and ODMRP outperform MAODV across all scenarios which typically generate high delivery ratio with low average latency. Even in harsh environment, where the network topology changes very frequently, ABAM ADMR and ODMRP effectively delivers packets with a high Packet delivery ratio. While MAODV is scalable and effective in terms of packet delivery ratio as long as the number of senders is low. On the other hand, it does not scale well with number of multicast senders. Based on our analysis, the poor performance of MAODV is due to the shared multicast tree structure, hard state approach, requiring periodic control packet exchanges employed by the protocol. On the contrary, ABAM, ADMR is per-source tree and a soft state protocol, which attempts to reduce as much as possible any non-on-demand components. As a result, though being a tree based protocol, the performance of ABAM, ADMR is comparable to mesh-based protocol such as ODMRP which also utilize soft-state approach.

For future work, we intend to compare it with other multicast routing protocols, considering new performance metrics such as energy-based mobility and link stability metrics. We also intend to implement the protocol with different group mobility models that are suitable for multicast applications.

References

1. Kaur, J., Li, C.: Simulation and Analysis of Multicast protocols in Mobile Ad Hoc Networks using NS2. In: Faculty of Engineering and Applied Science, Memorial University of Newfoundland, St. John's, Newfoundland, A1B 3X5
2. Deering, S.: Host extensions for IP multicasting. RFC 1112 (August 1989), http://www.ietf.org/rfc/rfc1112.txt
3. Ballardie, T., Francis, P., Crowcroft, J.: Core Based Trees (CBT) – An architecture for scalable inter-domain multicast routing. In: Proceedings of ACM SIGCOMM 1993, San Francisco, CA, pp. 85–95 (October 1993)
4. Deering, S.E., Cheriton, D.R.: Multicast Routing in Datagram Internetworks and Extended LANs. ACM Transactions on Computer Systems 8(2), 85–110 (1990)
5. Deering, S., Estrin, D.L., Farinacci, D., Jacobson, V., Liu, C.-G., Wei, L.: The PIM Architecture for Wide-Area Multicast Routing. IEEE/ACM Transactions on Networking 4(2), 153–162 (1996); ACM SIGCOMM 1993, San Francisco, CA, pp. 85--95 (October 1993)
6. Moy, J.: Multicast Routing Extensions for OSPF. Communications of the ACM 37(8), 61–66, 114 (1994)
7. Royer, E.M., Perkins, C.E.: Multicast operation of the ad-hoc on-demand distance vector routing protocol. In: Proceedings of the 5th ACM/IEEE Annual Conf. on Mobile Computing, pp. 207–218 (1999)
8. Bagrodia, R., Gerla, M., Hsu, J., Su, W., Lee, S.-J.: A performance comparison study of ad hoc wireless multicast protocols. In: Proc. of the 19th ComSoc IEEE Conf., pp. 565–574 (2000)
9. Madruga, E.L., Garcia, J.J.: Scalable multicasting: the core assisted mesh protocol. Mobile Networks and Application Journal 6, 151–165 (2001)
10. Mohapatra, P., Li, J., Gui, C.: Multicasting in Ad Hoc Networks. Kluwer Press, Dordrecht (2004)
11. Lee, S.-J., Gerla, M., Chiang, C.-C.: On-demand multicast routing protocol. In: Proceedings of IEEE WCNC, pp. 1298–1302 (1999)
12. Kunz, T.: Multicasting: From fixed networks to ad-hoc networks. In: Handbook of Wireless Networks and Mobile Computing, pp. 495–507. John Wiley & Sons, Chichester (2002)
13. Jetcheva, J.G., Johnson, D.B.: Adaptive demand-driven multicast routing in multi-hop wireless ad-hoc networks. In: Proceedings of the 2nd ACM International Symposium (2001)
14. Toh, C.-K.: Associativity-Based Routing For Ad Hoc Mobile Networks. Wireless Personal Communications Journal: Special Issue on Mobile Networking and Computing System 4(2), 103–139 (1997)

A Trust Based Technique to Isolate Non-forwarding Nodes in DSR Basedmobile Adhoc Networks

N. Bhalaji[1] and Dr.A. Shanmugam[2]

[1] Research Scholar, Anna University Coimbatore
[2] Principal, Bannari Amman Institute of Technology
Bhalaji.80@gmail.com

Abstract. In this manuscript we deal with securing routing protocol of mobile adhoc network against Non forwarding nodes which originate selfish or passive attack .due to its unique feature of open nature, lack of infrastructure and central management, node mobility and change of dynamic topology, prevention methods from attacks on them are not enough. Further most of the mobile adhoc routing protocols assume that nodes are trust worthy and cooperative this renders them vulnerable to various types of attacks. In this scheme the nodes which originate the passive or selfish attacks are identified and isolated from the routing and data forwarding function. We considered DSR protocol in NS-2 for our simulation. The results obtained illustrates that the proposed scheme outscores the traditional DSR in all metrics.

Keywords: Adhoc networks, Secured routing, Nonforwarding nodes, malicious nodes, Passive attacks.

1 Introduction

Mobile ad hoc network (MANET) is relatively new communication paradigm. MANET does not require expensive base stations of wired infrastructure. Nodes within radio range of each other can communicate directly over wireless links, and those that are far apart use other nodes as relays. Each host in a MANET also acts as a router and routers are mostly multi hop [1]. MANET is self-organized in such a way that a collection of mobile nodes without a fixed infrastructure and central management is formed automatically. Each node is equipped with a wireless transmitter and receiver that communicate with other nodes in the vicinity of its radio communication range. If a node decides to send a packet to a node that is outside its radio range, it requires the help of other nodes in the network. Due to the fact that mobile nodes are dynamic and they constantly move in and out of their network vicinity, the topologies constantly change. Initially, MANET was designed for military applications, but, in recent years, has found new usage. For example, search and rescue mission, data collection, virtual classes and conferences where laptops, PDA or other mobile devices are in wireless communication. Since MANET is being used widespread, security has become a very important issue. The majority of routing protocols that have been proposed for MANET assumes that each node in the network is a peer and not a malicious node. Therefore, only a node that compromises with an attacking

N. Meghanathan et al. (Eds.): CNSA 2010, CCIS 89, pp. 123–131, 2010.

node can cause the network to fail. MANET relies on the cooperation of all the participating nodes. The more nodes cooperate the more powerful a MANET becomes. But supporting MANET requires detecting routes and forwarding packets [2] which may cost them to loose their energy [3]. Therefore there is a strong motivation for a node to deny packet forwarding to other, while at the same time using their services to deliver own data. Current schemes of detecting node misbehaviour in MANET are mostly centered on using incentives, reputation [4] or price-based mechanisms [5] to achieve the desired effect of nodes cooperation. In an adhoc network one of the major concerns is how to increase the routing security in presence of malicious nodes.

2 Security Attacks in MANET

The main assumption of the ad hoc routing protocols is that all participating nodes do so in good faith and without maliciously disrupting the operation of the protocol [6][7][8]. However, the existence of malicious entities cannot be disregarded in any system, especially in open ones like ad hoc networks. The RPSEC IETF working group has performed a threat analysis that is applicable to routing protocols employed in a wide range of application scenarios [9]. Cryptographic solutions can be employed to prevent the impact of attackers by mutual authentication of the participating nodes through digital signature schemes [10]. However, the underlying protocols should also be considered since an attacker could manipulate a lower level protocol to interrupt a security mechanism in a higher level. The nodes which do not send the received packets (used for storing battery life span to be used for their own communications) are called Selfish nodes [11] [12]. A Selfish node impacts the normal network operations by not participating in routing protocols or by not sending packets.

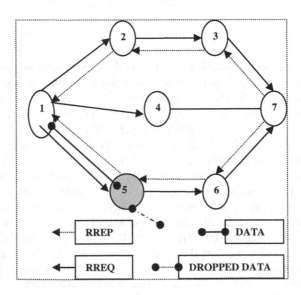

Fig. 1. Attack Scenario

The selfish node does not perform the packet forwarding function [3, 4]. When this behavior is selected, the packet forwarding function performed in the Nodes is disabled for all packets that have a source address or a destination address different from the current selfish node. However, a selfish node that operates following this model participates in the Route Discovery and Route Maintenance phases of the DSR Protocol. As an example consider the scenario in figure 1. Here node 1 is the source node and node 7 is the destination node. Nodes 2 to 6 acts as the intermediate nodes. Node 5 acts as a malicious node. When source wishes to transmit data packet, it first sends out RREQ packets to the neighbouring nodes. The malicious nodes being part of the network also receives the RREQ. The source node transmits data packets after receiving the RREP from the destination. As node 5 is also the part of routing path will receive the data packets and drops some of them while forwarding others. The consequence of the proposed model in terms of consumed energy is that the selfish node will save a significant portion of its battery life neglecting data packets, while still contributing to the network maintenance. This paper focuses on nodes which do not forward but drop packets and we believe that the selfishness problem is of great interest because nodes of a mobile ad hoc network are often battery-powered, thus, energy is a precious resource that they may not want to waste for the benefit of other nodes.

3 Related Works

The routing misbehavior is mitigated by including components like *watchdog* and *pathrater* in the scheme proposed by Marti, Guiti, Lai and Baker [13]. Every node has a Watchdog process that monitors the direct neighbors by promiscuously listening to their transmission. Main draw back of this idea is that it enables the misbehaving node to participate in the network cooperation without punishing.

The CONFIDANT protocol [14] [15] works as an extension to reactive source routing protocols like DSR [17]. The basic idea of the protocol is that nodes that does not forward packets as they are supposed to, will be identified and expelled by the other nodes. Thereby, a disadvantage is, if a node is found to be intolerable then all the routes which consists of this node will be deleted.

The Grudger Protocol As explained in [16] it is an application from a biological example proposed by Dawkins [17] which explains the survival chances of birds grooming parasites off each others head. Dawkins introduces three categories of the birds namely Suckers, Cheats, Grudger. In an ad hoc network, grudger nodes are introduced which employ a neighbourhood watch by keeping track of what is happening to other nodes in the neighbourhood, before they have a bad experience themselves. They also share information of experienced malicious behaviour with friends and learn from them.

A Security policy model namely, resurrecting duckling suggested by Stajano and Anderson [18] describes a secure transient association of a device with multiple serialized Owners.

4 Other Related Work

Threshold Cryptography and *diversity coding* schemes are introduced by Zhou and Haas [19] to build a highly secure network. Highly available key management service is established by distributing trust among a set of servers, employing share refreshing to achieve proactive security and adapting to changes in the network in a scalable way.

A self-organized public-key infrastructure is developed by Hubaux, Buttyan and Capkum [20]. The certificate directories are stored and distributed by users. The *shortcut hunter algorithm* is proposed to build local certificate repositories for the users. Between any pair of users, they can find certificate chains to each other using only their local certificate repositories. A *secure routing protocol* (SRP) is presented by Papadimitratos and Haas [21]. This route discovery protocol mitigates the detrimental effects of such malicious behaviour, so as to provide correct connectivity information. It guarantees that fabricated, compromised or replayed route replies would either be rejected or never reach back the querying node. *Ariadne* is another secure routing scheme proposed by Hu and Perrig [22]. This routing protocol is designed to protect against active attackers. The routing security is achieved through digital signatures, TESLA authentication or by MAC authentication. Malicious nodes are not addressed here. SEAD, *Secure Efficient Ad hoc Distance vector routing Protocol* is proposed by Hu, Johnson and Perrig [23] which uses one way hash chains for authentication. This protocol is based on DSDV-SQ protocol. The routing messages like sequence number and path length are authenticated on a hop to hop basis. Hence, malicious nodes cannot claim to have bogus links. In a mobile environment, there is a significant increase in overhead which may lead to congestion. The Authenticated Routing for Ad-hoc Networks (ARAN) [24] secure routing protocol relies on the use of digital certificates and can successfully operate in the managed-open scenario where no network infrastructure is predeployed, but a small amount of prior security coordination is expected.

5 The Proposed Scheme

In a mobile adhoc network the nodes constantly moving and leaving the network. This initiates association between nodes to be short lived one. As the time span of these associations is considerable, we are able to analyse about the nature of a node and its behaviour with respect to its neighbouring nodes.

5.1 Nature of Association between Neighbouring Nodes in an Ad Hoc Network

In our proposed scheme we classify the Association among the nodes and their neighbouring nodes in to three types as below. In an adhoc network the Association between any node **x** and node **y** will be determined as follows.

UNKNOWN: Node x have never sent/received any messages to/from node y, Trust levels between them are very low, Probability of malicious behaviour is very high, Newly arrived nodes are grouped in to this category,

KNOWN: Node x have sent/received some messages to/from node y, Trust levels between them are neither low nor too high, Probability of malicious behaviour is to be observed.

COMPANION: Node x have sent/received plenty of messages to/from node y, Trust levels between them are very high,

Probability of malicious behaviour is very less.

5.2 Association Estimator Technique

The Association status which we discussed in the previous section depends up on the trust value and threshold values. The trust values are calculated based on the following parameters of the nodes. We propose a very simple (1) for the calculation of trust value between any two node in the network.

$$T_V = \tanh(R1 + A) \tag{1}$$

Where

T_V = Trust value, **A** = Acknowledgement. (0 or 1) if the acknowledgment is received for data transmission from the destination then nodes in that path are assigned value 1 else value 0 is assigned.

The threshold trust level for an unknown node to become a known to its neighbour is represented by T_K and the threshold trust level for a known node to become a companion of its neighbour is denoted by T_C. The Associations are represented as

A (node x → node y) = C when $T \geq Tc$, A (node x → node y) = K when $T_K \leq T < T_C$

A (node x → node y) = UK when $0 < T \geq T_K$

Where

T = Threshhold,   K = known, UK= unknown, C = companion

Also, the Association between nodes is asymmetric, (i.e.,) A (node x → node y) is an Association evaluated by node x based on trust levels calculated for its neighbour node y. A (node y → node x) is the Association from the Association table of node y. This is evaluated based on the trust levels assigned for its neighbour. Asymmetric Associations suggest that the direction of data Flow may be more in one direction. In other words, node x may not have trust on node y the same way as node y has trust on node x or vice versa. The Threshold parameters are design parameters. Simulation is to be carried out with suitable values or all the parameters and the threshold trust levels so as to obtain optimum performance.

5.3 Routing Mechanism

When any node wishes to send messages to a distant node, its sends the ROUTE REQUEST to all the neighbouring nodes. The ROUTE REPLY obtained from its neighbour is sorted by trust ratings. The source selects the most trusted path. If its one hop neighbour node is a Companion, then that path is chosen for message transfer. If its one-hop neighbour node is a known, and if the one hop neighbour of the second best path is a companion choose C. Similarly an optimal path is chosen based on the degree of Association existing between the neighbour nodes.

Table 1. Path Chosen Based On Proposed Scheme

Next hop neighbour in the best path P1	Next hop neighbour in the next best path P2	Action Taken
C	C	C is chosen in P1 or P2 based on the length of path
C	K	C is chosen in P1
K	C	C in path P2
K	K	K is chosen in P1 or P2 based on the length of the path
C	UK	C is chosen in P1
UK	C	C in path P2

C = companion, K= known, UK = unknown.

6 Simulation Set Up

The simulation is implemented In Network Simulator 2 [25], a simulator for mobile adhoc networks. The routing protocol we use is DSR. We simulate the network with 1000m*1000m space and 50 mobile nodes. The simulation time is 900seconds. We implement the random waypoint movement model for the simulation with a maximum speed of 20m/s the pause time is 10seconds, which represents a network with moderately changing topology. The communication pattern we use was constant bit rate (CBR). In random way model a node starts at a random position, waits for the pause time, and then moves to another random position with a velocity chosen between 0 m/s to the maximum simulation speed. A packet size of 512 bytes and a transmission rate of 4 packets/s, congestion of the network are not likely to occur. We assumed 20 selfish nodes in each of the simulation, which is almost more than 40 percent of total number of nodes.

7 Results and Discussions

For the performance analysis of the Association based DSR protocol the throughput is compared with the standard DSR in presence of the malicious nodes. The other parameters [26] to be considered are packet delivery ratio and dropped data packets.

In our simulations we use several performance metrics to compare the proposed DSR protocol with the existing one. The metrics considered for the comparison were Packet Delivery Ratio, Throughput, Average Latency: Byte Overhead. Fig. 3 depicts the performance results for the DSR protocol in the presence of malicious nodes. The results indicate that the throughput of the protocol rapidly drops with the increase in the number of malicious nodes. The throughput drops in DSR rapidly when the number of malicious nodes increases. Fig. 4. Shows the percentage of packet delivery ratio under the threat of increasing malicious nodes. Here too the proposed protocol performs better than the conventional one. We conducted another simulation to determine the percentage of dropped data packets for proposed and standard protocol. When no malicious nodes are present the standard DSR has less dropped data packets but these changes when the number of malicious nodes increases. The results are shown in Fig. 5. The simulation results in Fig 6. & Fig.7 illustrates that the average latency and byte over head are slightly higher than the conventional one due to the trust based routing.

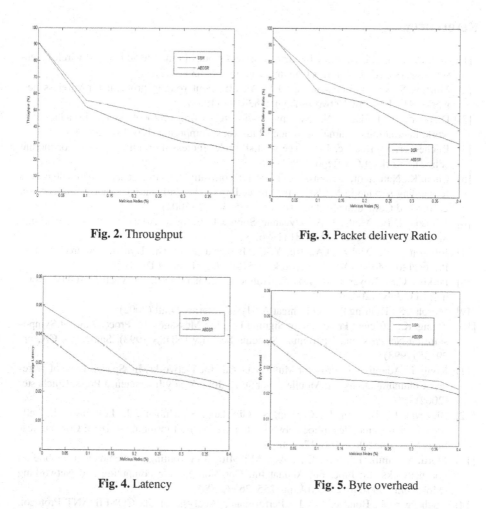

Fig. 2. Throughput   Fig. 3. Packet delivery Ratio

Fig. 4. Latency   Fig. 5. Byte overhead

8   Conclusion

Mobile adhoc networks are commonly targeted by participating malicious node to attack the network. Many experiments have shown that techniques like cryptography, hashing, authentication are not enough and implementation of those techniques imposes certain unessential requirements. In order to combat the nature of dynamic nature of Manet, in this article we have used association based approach by enforcing trust between the nodes. Each node in the network will monitor its surrounding neighbours and based on certain criteria decides the nature of association between them. This enhances the nodes to select the reliable routes instead of standard shortest route. Through relevant simulations we have proved that the throughput of the proposed DSR remains significantly higher than the existing protocol in the presence of malicious nodes.

References

[1] Sun, B., Young, L.O.: Intrusion detecti on techniques in mobile ad hoc and wireless sensor networks. IEEE Wireless Communications, 56–63 (2007)

[2] Murthy, S., Garcia-Luna-Aceves, J.J.: An effi cient routing protocol for wireless networks. ACM Mobile Networks Appl., 183–197 (1996)

[3] Djenouri, D., Badache, N.: New power- aware routing protocol for mobile adhoc network. International Journal of Adhoc Ubiquitous Computing, 126–136 (2006)

[4] Buchegger, S., Boudec, J.-Y.: The sel fish node: Increasing routing security for mobile adhoc networks. LCA-Report-2001-008

[5] Chen, K., Nahrstedt, K.: IPass: An incentive compatible auction scheme to enable packet forwarding service in MANET. In: Proceeding of the 24th International Conference on Distributed Computing System, Tokyo, pp. 534–542 (2004)

[6] Johnson, D.B., Maltz, D.A.: Dynamic Source Routing in Adhoc wireless networking. Mobile Computing 353, 153–181 (1996)

[7] Johnson, D.B., Maltz, D.A., Hu, Y.-C., Jetcheva, J.G.: The Dynamic Source Routing Protocol for Mobile Ad hoc Networks, DSR (2002) (Internet Draft)

[8] Perkins, C.E., Royer, E.M., Das, S.: Adhoc On-demand Distance Vector (AODV) Routing. RFC 3561 (2003)

[9] Murphy, S.: Routing Protocol Threat Analysis. Internet Draft (2002)

[10] Zhang, K.: Efficient Protocols for Signing Routing Messages. In: Proceedings of Symposium on Network and Distributed Systems Security (NDSS 1998), SanDiego, CA, pp. 29–35 (1998)

[11] Kong, J.: Adaptive Security for Multi-layer Ad Hoc Networks. In: Special Issue of Wireless Communications and Mobile Computing. John Wiley Interscience Press, Chichester (2002)

[12] Blazevic, L., Buttyan, L., Capkun, S., Giordano, S., Hubaux, J., LeBoudec, J.: Self-organization in mobile ad-hoc networks: the approach of terminodes. IEEE Communications Magazine 39(6), 166–174 (2001)

[13] Marti, S., Giuli, T.J., Lai, K., Baker, M.: Mitigating routing misbehavior in mobile ad hoc networks. In: Proc. 6th Annual Int. Conf. on Mobile computing and Networking (MobiCom 2000), Boston, MA, pp. 255–265 (2000)

[14] Buchegger, S., Boudec, J.-Y.: Performance Analysis of the CONFIDANT Protocol. Cooperation of Nodes - Fairness in Dynamic Ad-hoc Networks. Technical Report (IC/2002/01), EPFL I&C, Lausanne (2002)

[15] Buchegger, S., Boudec, J.Y.L.: Performance analysis of the CONFIDANT protocol. In: Proceedings of the 3rd ACM International Symposium on Mobile ad Hocnetworking & Computing, Lausanne, Switzerland, pp. 226–236 (2002)

[16] Buchegger, S., Boudec, J.-Y.L.: Nodes Bearing Grudges towards Routing Security, Fairness and robustness in Mobile ad hoc networks. In: Proceedings of the Tenth Euromicro Workshop on Parallel, Distributed and Network–Based Processing, pp. 403–410 (2002)

[17] Dawkins, R.: The selfish Gene, 1980th edn. Oxford University Press, Oxford

[18] Stajano, F., Anderson, R.: The Resurrecting Duckling: Security Issues for Ad hoc Wireless Networks. In: Proceedings of 7th International Workshop on Security Protocols, Cambridge, UK, pp. 172–194 (1999)

[19] Zhou, L., Haas, Z.: Securing ad hoc networks. IEEE Network Magazine, Special Issue on Networking Security 13(6), 24–30 (1999)

[20] Hubaux, J., Buttyan, L., Capkun, S.: The quest for security in Mobile Ad hoc Networks. In: Proceedings of the ACM Symposium on Mobile Ad hoc Networking and Computing, MobiHOC (2001)

[21] Papadimitratos, P., Haas, Z.J., Samar, P.: The secure routing protocol (SRP) for ad hoc networks. In: Proceedings of the 2nd ACM Workshop on Wireless Security, San Diego, CA, USA, pp. 41–50 (2003)

[22] Hu, Y.C., Perrig, A., Johnson, D.B.: Ariadne: a secure on-demand Routing protocol for ad hoc networks. In: Proceedings of 8th ACM International Conference on Mobile Computing and Networking (2002)

[23] Hu, Y.-C., Johnson, D.B., Perrig, A.: SEAD: Secure Efficient Distance Vector Routing for Mobile Wireless Ad hoc Networks. In: Proceedings of 4th IEEE Workshop on Mobile Computing Systems and Applications, Callicoon, NY, pp. 3–13 (2002)

[24] Dahill, Levine, Royer, Shields: A Secure routing protocol for adhoc networks. In: Proceedings of the International Conference on Network Protocols (ICNP), pp. 78–87 (2002)

[25] Fall, K., Varadhan, K.: The ns manual, http://www.isi.edu/nsnam/ns/doc/index.html

[26] Broch, J., Johnson, D., Maltz, D., Hu, Y., Jetcheva, J.: A Performance Comparison of Multihop Wireless Ad Hoc Networking Protocols. In: Proceedings of 4th ACM/IEEE International Conference on Mobile Computing and Networking (1998)

Ensured Quality of Admitted Voice Calls through Authorized VoIP Networks

T. Subashri, B. Gokul Vinoth Kumar, and V. Vaidehi

Department of Electronics, MIT Campus, Anna University, Chennai-44
tsubashri@annauniv.edu, bgokul1989@gmail.com,
vaidehi@annauniv.edu

Abstract. IP based voice transmission technology is a flexible, simpler and a cost effective implementation of voice transmission. It provides a real convergence of various networks. This voice transmission technology does not support a quality that is equivalent to digitized voice, which is available in the existing PSTN networks. In addition to this, data network vulnerabilities affect the VOIP service causing a drop in the utilisation of voice communication. In this paper, the quality of service for voice calls is ensured with the integration of CAC mechanism with the bandwidth link utilization which makes an estimation of the demanded bandwidth. In terms of security, prevention of ARP cache poisoning attack is done by use of the signed MAC address response in local area networks. It makes the network confident that the admitted user is the authorized user and also it verifies that only the authorized users' information is exchanged over the local area network. Also an approach that makes it difficult for the hacker to hack the data exchanged over the quality channel is proposed.

Keywords: Bandwidth link utilization, CACA, LU-CAC, MAC addresses Hash value.

1 Introduction

With the growing speed of large scale internet industry it is now possible to transmit all real time data over the internet protocol. The internet protocol plays a major role in the real time services offered in the internet world. One such technology is voice over internet protocol. Sending digitized voice over the internet protocol is an approach to make voice call. VOIP is an attractive technology and it is adopted in home and business environments, because of their cheaper call rates compared to the PSTN based fixed networks. And it provides greater flexibility in terms of added features in addition with the existing voice communication techniques. In case the IP based networks did not have CAC mechanisms the new flow would suffer packet loss and/ or significant delay. To prevent this insufficient QoS, guarantees for both new and existing calls by the decision making process of CAC mechanism is introduced in IP networks. In the PSTN network there is a call admission control mechanism. If the number of call attempts exceeds the capacity of links, the request for setting up new calls will be rejected while all the other calls in progress continue without any problem. The admission of a voice call is done by the CACA (Call Admission Control

N. Meghanathan et al. (Eds.): CNSA 2010, CCIS 89, pp. 132–142, 2010.
© Springer-Verlag Berlin Heidelberg 2010

Agent) [1]. But in the case of IP based VOIP networks, this CAC mechanism is not provided, and hence QoS will not be guaranteed. There is new traffic which keeps entering the network even beyond the networks capacity limit, consequently causing both the existing and the new flows to suffer packet loss and /or significant delay [2]. By the CAC mechanism integrated with the call manager, the rejection of voice calls and QoS is guaranteed. A very important aspect from the corporate point of view for the lack of success of VOIP technology is its security. VOIP technology is integrated with the workplace making the hacker's job easier if it is routed through unsecured data packets on a public network.

The transmissions of speech across data networks are mostly vulnerable to attacks. Thus the attacker poses a threat to the security services which is available in the VOIP network. Different attacks cause several changes towards the secured information. Depending on the kind of attack several changes have to be made to the security of a network. Some of the security attacks may prevent use of all the available user resources. Thus all the services and features available to the enhanced users are destroyed making the purpose of the VOIP communication a failure due to this security problem. Quality ensured user authentication is very important for VOIP conversation. Without this verification of authentication, all the calls may get dropped even if the user resource quality is enhanced. In this paper, an approach which ensures that the authorized user is able to get the enhanced QoS guaranteed channel for their communication   is provided by the integration of CAC mechanisms with user authentication procedure at the server [3].

2 Admission of Voice Calls Using Delay Analysis Method in Differentiated Services

Call manager provides the overall framework for communication within a corporate environment. Gatekeeper provides address translation and admission control services to the calls. Call manager and gatekeeper communicate with each other by using the H.323 signaling protocol shown in Figure 1. A location defines the topological area connected to other areas by links with a limited bandwidth that are registered to a call manager. A zone is a collection of H.323 endpoints that have been registered

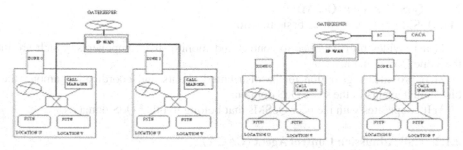

Fig. 1. Block Diagram of the VOIP system   **Fig. 2.** Block Diagram of QoS Provisioning VoIP system

with the gatekeeper. Call Manager as well as Gatekeeper performs admission control for calls between locations in a zone or calls between zones, aiming to provide a certain degree of QoS to voice over IP networks. To call within a zone, only the CallManager located in the enterprise environment is invoked to perform CAC. However, for a call traversing multiple zones, not only CallManagers but also the related Gatekeeper may be involved to perform CAC.

The QoS-provisioning system is integrated into the current VoIP systems to enable both SU-CAC and LU-CAC to be well utilized and supported. With this system, the overhead of resource reservation at the core routers will be pushed to the agents in the QoS-provisioning system, which overcomes the weakness of the current VoIP system in applying the LU-CAC performing resource allocation to better support the SU-CAC mechanism. This VOIP QoS-provisioning system consists of a Call Admission Control Agent (CACA) and the integration component (IC) as shown in Figure 2. The CACA has two modules. They are Utilization Computation Module and Admission Decision Module. The Integration Component (IC) integrates CACA with the existing VoIP systems. IC in the VOIP system provides call signaling process modules to monitor and intercept the call setup signaling from Gatekeeper or Call-Manager, and withdraws the useful message and passes it on to the CACA. Call admission decision is made by the CACA.

2.1 Components of the Qos-Provisioning System

Qos-Provisioning VoIP System consists of three different types of components:

1) QoS Manager (QoSM),
2) Call Admission Control Agent (CACA), and
3) Integration Component (IC).

The main functions of these components are as follows:

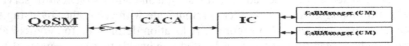

Fig. 3. Components of the QoS-provisioning system

2.1.1 QoS Manager (QoSM)
The QoSM implements three basic functions:

1) It provides user interface to control and monitor the components, which are in the same QoS domain.
2) It provides registration to the distributed agents and coordination among the distributed agents in the same QoS domain.
3) It cooperates with the peer QoSMs that belong to other QoS domains.

2.1.2 Call Admission Control Agent (CACA)
The CACA has two modules:

1) Utilization Computation Module, which performs deterministic or statistic delay analysis to obtain the maximum bandwidth utilization.

2) Admission Decision Making Module, which performs admission control with specific CAC mechanisms.

2.1.3 Integration Component (IC)

The IC integrates CACA into existing VoIP systems and provides call signaling processing modules to monitor and intercept call setup signaling from Gatekeeper or Call-Manager, withdraws the useful message and passes it to CACA, and executes call admission decision made by CACA.

2.2 Design of a Call Admission Control Agent (CACA)

The Call Admission Control Agent (CACA) is a key component in the QoS-provisioning system. It consists of two modules. The utilization computation module performs delay analysis and computes the maximum bandwidth utilization. It usually runs at the configuration time. The computed utilization will be allocated to LU-CAC mechanism. At the runtime, the admission decision making module will make an admission decision for each incoming call request, based on the allocated bandwidth utilization (by the utilization computation module) and the currently consumed bandwidth. The maximum link utilization is the maximum value of the link utilization under which the end to end delay can be guaranteed with LU-CAC.

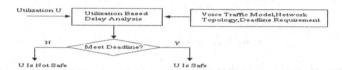

Fig. 4. Utilization verification procedure

The utilization computation module has a sub module called Link Utilization Computation. The main task of this sub module is to compute the maximum link utilization for LU-CAC by calling a procedure, named the utilization verification procedure. It is shown in Fig.3, Given the voice traffic model, the network topology, and the voice traffic deadline requirement, for any input of link utilization u, we can compute the worst-case delay (deterministic case) or delay distribution (statistical case) with our delay analysis methods. Then, we can verify whether the link is safe or not for making the end-to-end delay meet the deadline. Generally, there are two distinct types of delays suffered by a voice packet from source to destination: fixed and variable. Fixed delays include propagation delay, transmission delay, and so on. Variable delays arise from queuing delays in the output buffers. All fixed delays can be obtained by well-known experimental data or by using existing tools. However, it is difficult to obtain the variable delays. Therefore, all the calls currently established in the network must be known in order to compute queuing delays.

2.3 Utilization-Based Deterministic Delay Analysis

If the deadline requirement is deterministic the worst-case queuing delay dk, suffered by any voice packet the buffer of output link k is bounded by

$$d_k \leq (c_k\text{-}1/c_k\text{-}u_k)\, u_k\, [(\sigma/\rho) + y_k] \tag{1}$$

$$c_k = (\textstyle\sum_{j\epsilon lk} c_j)/ c_k \tag{2}$$

Where ck is the capacity of the link. σ is the burst size, ρ is the average rate at the entrance of the network, u_k is the utilization of the link. We also define $d_k{}^\wedge$ as the worst case delays bound suffered by any real time packet layer –k link servers and y_k as the worst case queuing delay bound suffered by any packet upstream from layer-k is given by,

$$y_k = \sum_{l=1}^{k\text{-}1} d_l{}^\wedge \tag{3}$$

$$d_k{}^\wedge = r((\sigma/\rho) + y_k) \tag{4}$$

By using the equation (3) and (4) we get,

$$d_k{}^\wedge\text{-}d{}^\wedge{}_{k\text{-}1} = rd{}^\wedge{}_{k\text{-}1} \tag{5}$$

$$d_k{}^\wedge = (r+1)d{}^\wedge{}_{k\text{-}1} = (r+1)^\wedge(k\text{-}1)d_l{}^\wedge \tag{6}$$

We know that $d_l{}^{\wedge} = r(\sigma/\rho)$, therefore, $d_k{}^{\wedge}$, the maximum of worst-case delays suffered by any voice packet at layer-k link servers, can be bounded as follows,

$$d_k{}^\wedge \leq r((r+1)^{k\text{-}1})*(\sigma/\rho) \tag{7}$$

y_k the maximum of worst-case delays suffered by any voice packets from layer-k link server can be bounded as,

$$y_k \leq \sum_{l=1}^{k\text{-}1} d_l{}^\wedge \leq \sum_{l=1}^{k\text{-}1} r(r+1)^\wedge(l\text{-}1)\,(\sigma/\rho) = ((r+1)^{k\text{-}1}\text{-}1) \tag{8}$$

Therefore the maximum end to end delay can be bounded as

$$d^{e2e} \leq y_{h^\wedge+1} \leq ((r+1)^\wedge h\text{-}1)(\sigma/\rho) \tag{9}$$

2.4 Utilization-Based Statistical Delay Analysis

If the deadline requirement is probabilistic, as in this case, d_k is a random variable and D_k is denoted as its deadline. The violation probability of delay for any voice packet with the highest priority suffered at the buffer of output link k is bounded by

$$P\{d_k > D_k\} \leq \begin{cases} 1/\sqrt{2\pi}[exp(-24*(1-u_k/u_k^2)*(D_k/(\sigma/\rho))], & u_k \geq D_k/(\sigma/\rho) \\ 1/\sqrt{2\pi}[exp(-6*(1-u_k)/u_k^3)*(u_k+\{D_k/(\sigma/\rho)\})^2], & u_k < D_k/(\sigma/\rho) \end{cases} \qquad (10)$$

The end to end deadline violation probability can be bounded as,

$$P\{d^{e2e} > \sum_{k \in R} D_k\} \leq 1 - \pi_{k \in R}(1 - P\{d_k > D_k\}) \qquad (11)$$

The utilization-based delay analysis techniques show that, under the given network topology and traffic model, the queuing delay or deadline violation probability at each output queue depends on link bandwidth utilization. By limiting the utilization of link bandwidth, the overall delay or deadline violation probability can be bounded. Given the deadline requirement, with the utilization-based delay analysis techniques, the maximum link utilization computation can obtain the maximum link utilization, which will be applied in the LU-CAC mechanism to perform admission control.

3 Proposed Method for Securing ARP Cache Poisoning Attack

Here, an approach for the secured ARP request and response between the client and the server is proposed. The block diagram of ARP cache prevention architecture is presented in figure 5. Domain Name system (DNS) provides the network IP address to the requested client. In addition to that, client A needs the MAC address of the client 2 in the network for making communications. ARP program in client 1 gives the MAC address of client 2 from its ARP cache table. If client 2's address is not found in the ARP cache table, it sends the request to the server and tries to find the MAC address of client 2. The ARP table contains the IP and MAC address of the clients. The table is available for the use of the two clients involved in the communication and remains invisible to the other clients. The other clients are not allowed to change the entries of the ARP cache table. In the server, broadcasting of ARP request results in forged ARP replies from the hackers and causing false communication between the client and the hacker. Instead of broadcasting the request to the entire network, the newly created relay agent is used for treating the secure ARP request and response. Server relay agent takes the responsibility of sending the request and replies to the client in a secured manner, thereby establishing a proper user communication between the sender and the receiver.

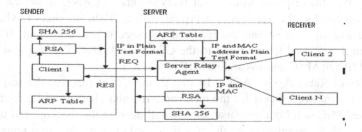

Fig. 5. Block diagram of ARP cache prevention architecture

After the client sends a request, the server relay agent sends a response which is hashed with SHA-256 algorithm and encrypted using the RSA algorithm. Therefore only the correct authorised clients who are all connected to the server relay agent are permitted to exchange these ARP requests and responses in a secured manner. Therefore only the authorised client can decrypt and use this secured response from the server relay agent. After a time period, if client 1 is no longer communicating with client 2, then the system will age out the entry in the ARP table. So it is difficult for eavesdrop to poison the ARP request and reply. Since the clients can only request server to get the destination's MAC address and the network broadcast overhead of ARP request is also reduced.

3.1 Secure ARP Request and Response between LAN

1) Client 1 → Server Relay Agent: ARP req + MIC 1: Message Integrity Code 1. In Step 1, A sends the request in encrypted form using RSA and the MIC1. The MIC1 is generated using a collision-free one-way hash function SHA256. Message digest using SHA 256 is calculated for the encrypted IP address.

2) Server Relay Agent1→ Broadcast the request to all the servers: ARP req + MIC 1. In step 2, once the server relay agent1 in LAN1 receives the request from the Client1, it calculates the message digest for the received encrypted IP address to create a similar MIC1 (say, MIC1*). If MIC1= MIC1*, then the request is accepted else it will be rejected. It will check the corresponding MAC address in its ARP table. The request will be the IP address of the Client1 which is in LAN2. Since the requested MAC address is in some other LAN the server relay agent cannot reply directly to Client1. Hence the request will be broadcasted to other server relay agent outside the network.

3) Server Relay Agent 2 → Server Relay Agent 1 A: ARP res + MIC 2. In step 3, the server relay agents in other LANs receive the request and check whether the corresponding MAC address for the request is there in its ARP table. If suppose server relay agent2 in LAN2 is having the MAC address for the requested IP address, it will reply to the server relay agent1 in LAN1. Server relay agent2 of LAN2 will get the public key of server relay agent1 of LAN1. Then it will encrypt the IP and MAC address and will calculate the message digest using SHA256 for the encrypted value. The response will be an encrypted value and MIC2 created using SHA256.

4) Server Relay Agent → A: ARP res + MIC 3. In step 4, the server relay agent1 in LAN1 receives the response from server relay agent2 in LAN2. It will calculate the message digest for the received encrypted value. Then it checks whether the calculated message digest and the received message digest are equal. If both are equal, then it will send the response to the Client1 in LAN1. The response includes encrypted IP and MAC address and its MIC say MIC3.

5) A→ Server Relay Agent: ACK. In step 5, the Client receives the response and calculates the message digest for the received MIC and checks for the equality with the received MIC's. If both are equal, then it will decrypt the message and update the ARP table with the received time, else it will discard the reply and start requesting the server for the MAC address. Finally, the host A sends an acknowledgment.

4 Experimental Results for Admission of Voice Calls Using Delay Analysis Method

By using NS2, Utilizations of the links are plotted and the maximum bandwidth is obtained. From maximum bandwidth utilization we can find whether the utilization is safe or not. Figure 6 represents the Xgraph for estimated utilization of the link bandwidth as a function of time. The estimated utilization represents the overall utility of link that can be used by the voice traffic. Figure 7 represents the Xgraph for actual utilization of the link bandwidth as a function of time. The actual utilization represents the final utility of link for incoming voice traffic through a CAC mechanism.

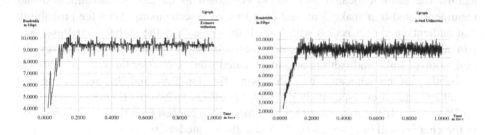

Fig. 6. Xgraph for Estimated Link Utilization   **Fig. 7.** Xgraph for Actual Link Utilization

4.1 Performance of Authenticated Voice User Admission Procedure in VOIP Network

A call admission control mechanism has 2 calls where service can be offered simultaneously. Due to limitations in space, only 4 calls are accepted for servicing. The arrival pattern is in possion distribution with 12 calls per calls day. The service time in both the calls is exponentially distributed with $\mu = 8$ calls per day. Then the average number of calls in the service station, the average number of calls waiting for service and the average time a call spends in the system can be calculated by using following method.

The performance of authenticated and unauthenticated user success to access the channel for voice calls are analyzed by using probability based method. For example Given $\lambda = 12/day$ S=2 and k=4 $\mu = 8/day$

$$P0 = [\sum_{N=0}^{S-1} [1/n \, (\lambda/\mu) \, n + 1/S! \, (\lambda/\mu) \, s \sum_{n=s}^{K} (\lambda/\mu S)^{\,n-S}]^{-1} = 0.1960 \qquad (12)$$

$$E\,(Nq) = P0 \, (\lambda/\mu) \, S * \rho/S! \, (1-\rho) \, 2 \, [1 - \rho^{K-S} - (K-S)(1-\rho)^{K-S}] = 0.4134 \text{ calls} \qquad (13)$$

Where $\rho = (\lambda/\mu S)$

E (N) average number of calls in the service station

$$E(N) = E(Nq) + S - \sum_{N=0}^{S-1}(S-n)\,P_n = 0.4134 + 2 - \sum_{N=0}^{1}(2-n)\,P_n = 1.73 \text{ calls} \qquad (14)$$

$$E(W) = 1/\lambda\, E(N) \qquad (15)$$

$$\text{Where } \lambda = \mu\,[S - \sum_{N=0}^{S-1}(S-n)\,P_n] = 0.1646 \text{ day} \qquad (16)$$

if the probability that authenticated user wins the channel access in CAC procedure against the unauthenticated user access is known to be 2/5. If authenticated and unauthenticated user make 3 request each to CAC mechanisms. Then the probability that authenticated user access with lose all the three calls the authenticated user will win all the 3 trials and authenticated user win at most one trail can convey the utilization of link bandwidth to an authenticated user. Consider the 1, 2 and 3 are the probability of authenticated user that wins the 1st, 2nd and 3rd request against unauthenticated user respectively P (1) = P (2) =P (3) = (2/5), P (1`) = P (2`) =P (3`) = 1-(2/5) = 3/5. If the probability for first method is chosen then the entire bandwidth of the channel will only be reserved for unauthenticated users.

4.2   Verification of Prevented ARP Cache Poisoning Attack Using Message Integrity and Message Authentication

Client to server communication was created and simulated by using java socket programming. By using the link, clients send their IP address and MAC address to the corresponding LAN server. In the servers' ARP caches table the present clients' entries are updated. Any client in the same LAN can find the MAC and IP addresses of the other clients that exist in the network which acts as the destination node. ARP request and response completes these processes. The Figure 8 shows that the updated entry for two clients in the ARP cache table which is in server. If the IP address of the destination node is known, then the client makes a request to the server for the MAC address. This action of getting MAC address with the ARP request is given in the

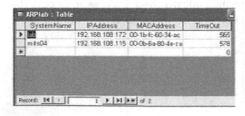

Fig. 8. Server ARP cache table updating 2 clients

Fig. 9. Finding MAC address of the for destination by using ARP Request

Figure 9. In the client, destination IP address is encrypted and its hashed code value is formed. Figure 10 shows the exchange of the encrypted IP and MAC addresses and the figure 11 shows the decryption of these addresses and thereby the correct IP and MAC addresses are obtained after the transmission. Thus the IP and MAC addresses are secured in the ARP request and response.

The transmitted and received hash values are equal and it's displayed. By applying the received hash value, the decryption process is continued. Figure 11 shows that the decryptions of the MAC address by the client. Verification of the generated key and received key in the secured ARP response. Decryption of the secured ARP response provides the destination MAC address to the server and the ARP cache table in the server is updated. By comparing hashed code of received and the generated values the authentication of the user is verified. Now the ARP response to the client provides only the authenticated destination's MAC address for communication.

Fig. 10. Encrypted IP address of the destination and its hashed value

Fig. 11. Decryption of the destination's IP Address and finding its match

5 Conclusion

By integrating the Call Admission Control Agent (CACA) into the current VoIP system, the overall system can achieve high resource utilization while invoking relatively low overhead. In this paper, one of the confidentiality threats viz. ARP cache poisoning attack is considered and solution to the VOIP network system is proposed. Also, only secured clients are connected to the server and the server is restricted to provide client's IP-MAC mapping and their connectivity only to the other intended client on the server's entry table. To provide message integrity for both client and the server, cryptographic hash function SHA256 is used. And for providing authentication for both the ends, RSA public key cryptosystem is used. RSA encrypts the network IP address and Client's MAC address so that only the intended participants are allowed to decrypt and verify authentication at both end. If the hacker is trying to eavesdrop between the client and server, he will not be able to generate the message digest value of the client. So the Client's MAC address cannot be viewed by the hacker and hence the communication is made secure.

References

1. Wang, S., Xuan, D., Bettati, R., Zhao, W.: Providing Absolute Differentiated Servicesfor Real-Time Applications in Static Priority Scheduling Networks. IEEE/ACM Trans. Networking 12(2), 326–339 (2004)
2. Wang, S., Xuan, D., Bettati, R., Zhao, W.: Differentiated Services with Statistical RealTime Guarantees in Static-Priority Scheduling Networks. In: Proc. IEEE Real-Time Systems Symp. (December 2001)
3. Chong, S., Li, S.: Characterization Based Connection Control for Guaranteed Servicesin High Speed Networks. In: Proc. IEEE Infocom (April 1995)
4. Agrawal, G., Chen, B., Zhao, W., Davari, S.: Guaranteeing Synchronous Message Deadlines with the Timed Token Protocol. In: Proc. IEEE Int'1 Conf. Distributed Computing Systems (June 1992)
5. Jamin, S., Shenker, S., Danzig, P.: Comparison of Measurement-Based Admission Controller-Load Service. In: Proc. IEEE Infocom (April 1997)
6. Abad, C.L.: An analysis on the schemes for detecting and preventing ARP cache poisoning attack. In: IEEE Processing ICDCSW 2007 (2007)

Wireless Mesh Networks: Routing Protocols and Challenges

Pavan Kumar Ponnapalli, Ramesh Babu Battula,
Pavan Kumar Tummala, and Prof. Srikanth Vemuru

Computer Science and Engineering, KLUniversity, Vaddeswaram, Guntur District,
Andhra Pradesh
pavancse@ymail.com, ramsbattula@gmail.com,
pavankumar_ist@klce.ac.in, srikanth_ist@klce.ac.in

Abstract. In this paper, a survey on routing protocols, challenges and applications in wireless mesh networks (WMNs) is conducted. Wireless Mesh network is a type of distributed, self-organizing, self-configuring and self-healing network. When access points in Wireless Local area Networks start to communicate and get networked in an ad hoc fashion to relay packets for their neighbors, a wireless mesh network comes into being. Wireless Mesh Networks are a promising way to provide internet access to fixed and mobile wireless devices. In mesh networks, traffic between mesh nodes and the Internet is routed over mesh gateways. In this paper, we discuss some of the routing protocols (i) OLSR, an Optimized Link State Routing Protocol and (ii) FSR, Fish-eye state routing protocol in detail and present various ad hoc routing protocols and their properties.

Keywords: Wireless Mesh Networks, Self-organizing, Self-configuring, Access point, mesh, ad hoc networks.

1 Introduction

Wireless Mesh Networks (WMNs) are dynamically self-organized and self-configured networks that employ multihop communications to transmit data traffic to and from Internet entry points. WMNs are comprised of three types of nodes: access points, mesh routers, and mesh clients. Access points are special routers with a high-bandwidth wired connection to the Internet and they serve as interfaces of WMNs. Mesh clients, which can be desktop computers, laptops, PDAs, cellular phones, are the ultimate users in WMNs. Most mesh clients run on batteries and only have limited radio transmission range. For mesh routers, they provide multihop connectivity between mesh clients and access points. Mesh routers have power supplies and minimal mobility. In addition to mesh networking among WMNs, the gateway/bridge functions in mesh routers enable the integration of WMNs with various other networks. The network of mesh routers and access points creates a wireless backhaul communication system, which provides each mesh client with a low-cost, high-bandwidth and seamless multi hop connection to Internet. Despite recent advances in the research and development in WMNs, many challenging problems still remain.

N. Meghanathan et al. (Eds.): CNSA 2010, CCIS 89, pp. 143–151, 2010.

It is believed that an optimum routing protocol for WMNs must capture the following features:

- Many existing routing protocols use minimum hop as the performance metric to select the routing path; but this has been demonstrated to be inefficient in WMNs.
- Setting up and maintaining a routing path in a WMN will take a long time due to the large size of a WMN network. Thus, it is critical to have a scalable routing protocol in WMNs.
- The routing protocol in WMNs must be robust to link failures or congestions.

To this end, several routing protocols have been proposed and they consider some of these features. In the following sections, we will present two of these routing protocols and routing metrics in detail.

2 Routing Layer Challenges

Despite the availability of many routing protocols for ad hoc networks, the design of routing protocols for WMNs is still an active research area. We believe that an optimal routing protocol for WMNs must capture the following features:

• **Multiple Performance Metrics**: Many existing routing protocols use minimum hop-count as a performance metric to select the routing path. This has been demonstrated to be ineffective in many situations.

• **Scalability:** Setting up or maintaining a routing path in a very large wireless network may take a long time. Thus, it is critical to have a scalable routing protocol in WMNs.

• **Robustness:** To avoid service disruption, WMNs must be robust to link failures or congestion. Routing protocols also need to perform load balancing.

• **Efficient Routing with Mesh Infrastructure**: Considering the minimal mobility and no constraints on power consumption in mesh routers, the routing protocol in mesh routers is expected to be much simpler than ad hoc network routing protocols. With the mesh infrastructure provided by mesh routers, the routing protocol for mesh clients can also be made simple. Existing routing protocols for ad hoc networks have already considered some of these features. However none of them has captured all of these features, as explained in the following routing protocols.

3 Routing Metrics

In this section, we present some routing metrics that are currently used in WMNs. We are considering the following metrics: Hop Count, Blocking Metric, Expected Transmission Count (ETX), Expected Transmission Time (ETT), Modified Expected Number of Transmissions (mETX).

3.1 Hop Count

Hop count is the most commonly used metric in wireless multi hop networks. The path selected is the one minimizing the number of links between a given source and destination node.

3.2 Blocking Metric

A simple improvement over hop count has been presented in [13] order to account for the interference along a certain path. In this work, the interference level referred to as Blocking Value is defined as the number of neighbors a node is interfering with. Each node is therefore weighted according to this Blocking Value. The Blocking Metric of a path is then defined as the sum of all the blocking values along the path. The paths with minimum cost will consequently be used to carry the traffic flows.

3.3 Expected Transmission Count (ETX)

Expected Transmission Count is defined as the number of transmissions required to successfully deliver a packet over a wireless link [1]. The ETX of a path is then defined as the sum of the ETX of each link along the path. Let pf and p, be the packet loss probability in the forward and reverse directions. The probability p of an unsuccessful transmission is:

$$p = 1 - p(1 - p_f)(1 - p_r)$$

Therefore, the expected number of transmissions to successfully deliver a packet in 1 hop can then be expressed as:

$$\text{ETX} = \sum_{k=1}^{\infty} Kp^k(1-p)^{k-1} = \frac{1}{1-p}$$

3.4 Expected Transmission Time (ETT)

ETT is an improvement over ETX as it includes the bandwidth in its computation [2]. Let S be the packet size and B the bandwidth of the link considered, then ETT is computed as follows:

$$ETT = ETX \frac{S}{B}$$

Similar to ETX, the expected transmission time of a path is computed as the sum of the links' ETT along the path [2]. This metric was designed to favor channel-diverse paths. For a path p, WCETT is defined as follows:

$$WCETT(p) = (1 - \beta) \sum_{link1\epsilon p} ETT\, t + \beta \max_{1 \le j \le k} Xj$$

Where, β is a tunable parameter less than 1 and X, represents the number of times channel j is used along path p.

4 Routing Protocols

Despite the availability of many routing protocols, the design of routing protocols for WMNs is still challenging. To this end, several routing protocols have been proposed and they consider some of these features. In this section, we will present three routing protocols and compare their performance in detail and we describe two of the routing protocols that can be implemented in wireless Mesh Networks namely OLSR, optimized Link state routing protocol and FSR, Fish-eye state routing protocol.

MANET and independent research groups have produced many different ad hoc routing protocols. Among them, the following proposed protocols will be analyzed in the next sections: Optimized Link State Routing Protocol (OLSR), Fisheye State Routing Protocol (FSR), Dynamic Destination-Sequenced Distance Vector (DSDV), Wireless Routing Protocol (WRP), Cluster head Gateway Switch Routing (CGSR), Zone-based Hierarchical Link State (ZHLS), Ad Hoc On Demand Distance Vector (AODV), Temporally-Ordered Routing Algorithm (TORA), Dynamic Source Routing (DSR).

4.1 Optimized Link State Routing (OLSR) Protocol

4.1.1 Description
OLSR [9] is an optimization of the classical link state algorithm tailored to the requirements of a mobile wireless LAN. The key concept used in the protocol is that of multipoint relays (MPRs). MPRs are selected nodes which forward broadcast messages during the flooding process. This technique substantially reduces the message overhead as compared to a classical flooding mechanism, where every node retransmits each message when it receives the first copy of the message. In OLSR, link state information is generated only by nodes elected as MPRs. Thus, a second optimization is achieved by minimizing the number of control messages flooded in the network. As a third optimization, an MPR node may chose to report only links between itself and its MPR selectors. Hence, as contrary to the classic link state algorithm, partial link state information is distributed in the network. This information is then used for route calculation. OLSR provides optimal routes (in terms of number of hops). The protocol is particularly suitable for large and dense networks as the technique of MPRs works well in this context.

The HELLO messages permit each node to learn the knowledge of its neighbors up to two hops. On the basis of this information, each node performs the selection of its multi point relays. These selected Multi point relays are indicated in the HELLO messages with the link status MPR. On reception of these HELLO messages each node can construct its MPR selector table with the nodes who have selected it as a Multipoint relay.

In the neighbor table, each node records the information about its one hop neighbors, the status of the link with these neighbors, and a list of two hop neighbors these one hop neighbors give access to.

4.2 Fish-Eye State Routing Protocol

4.2.1 Description
FSR [11] is an implicit hierarchical routing protocol. It uses the "fisheye" technique proposed by Kleinrock and Stevens, where the technique was used to reduce the size of information required to represent graphical data. The eye of a fish captures with high detail the pixels near the focal point. The detail decreases as the distance from the focal point increases. FSR is functionally similar to LS Routing but the difference is the way in which routing information is disseminated. In LS link state packets are generated and flooded into the network whenever a node detects a topology change. In FSR, link state packets are not flooded. In order to reduce the size of update

messages without seriously affecting routing accuracy, FSR uses the fisheye technique. The scope is defined as a set of nodes that can be reached within a given number of hops. In our case, three scopes are shown for 1, 2 and >2 hops respectively. Nodes are colorcoded as black, grey and white accordingly. The number of levels and the radius of each scope will depend on the size of the network.

4.3 Destination Sequenced Distance Vector (DSDV)

4.3.1 Description
DSDV [11] is a hop-by-hop distance vector routing protocol where each node has a routing table that stores next-hop and number of hops for all reachable destinations. Like distance-vector, DSDV requires that each node periodically broadcast routing updates. The advantage with DSDV over traditional distance vector protocols is that DSDV guarantees loop-free routes. To guarantee loop-free routes, DSDV uses a sequence number. A route is considered more favorable it has a greater sequence number. To reduce the amount of information in these packets, there are two types of update messages defined: full and incremental. The full broadcast carries all available routing information and the incremental broadcast only carries the information that has changed since the last broadcast.

4.4 The Wireless Routing Protocol (WRP)

4.4.1 Description
The Wireless Routing Protocol (WRP) [12] is a table-based distance-vector routing protocol. Each node in the network maintains a Distance table, a Routing table, a Link-Cost table and a Message Retransmission list. The Distance table of a node x contains the distance of each destination node y via each neighbor z of x. It also contains the downstream neighbor of z through which this path is realized. The Routing table of node x contains the distance of each destination node y from node x, the predecessor and the successor of node x on this path. It also contains a tag to identify if the entry is a simple path, a loop or invalid. Storing predecessor and successor in the table is beneficial in detecting loops and avoiding counting-to-infinity problems. Nodes exchange routing tables with their neighbors using update messages periodically as well as on link changes. On receiving an update message, the node modifies its distance table and looks for better paths using new information. Any new path so found is relayed back to the original nodes so that they can update their tables. The node also updates its routing table if the new path is better than the existing path. On receiving an ACK, the mode updates its MRL. A unique feature of this algorithm is that it checks the consistency of all its neighbors every time it detects a change in link of any of its neighbors.

4.5 Clusterhead Gateway Switching Routing Protocol (CGSR)

4.5.1 Description
Clusterhead Gateway Switch Routing (CGSR) [13] uses as basis the DSDV Routing algorithm described in the previous section. The protocol differs in the type of addressing and network organization scheme employed. Instead of a "flat" network,

CGSR is a clustered multihop mobile wireless network. It routes traffic from source to destination using a hierarchical cluster-head-to-gateway routing approach. Mobile nodes are aggregated into clusters and a cluster-head is elected. All nodes that are in the communication range of the cluster-head belong to its cluster. A gateway node is a node that is in the communication range of two or more cluster-heads.

4.6 Zone Based Hierarchical Link State Routing Protocol (ZHLS)

4.6.1 Description
In Zone-based Hierarchical Link State [14], the network is divided into non overlapping zones. ZHLS defines two levels of topologies: 1) node level and 2) zone level. A node level topology describes how nodes of a zone are connected to each other physically. A virtual link between two zones exists if at least one node of a zone is physically connected to some node of the other zone. Zone level topology tells how zones are connected together. Unlike other hierarchical protocols, there are no zone heads. The zone level topological information is distributed to all nodes. There are two types of Link State Packets (LSP) as well: node LSP and zone LSP. A node LSP of a node contains its neighbor node information and is propagated within the zone whereas a zone LSP contains the zone information and is propagated globally. Given the zone id and the node id of a destination, the packet is routed based on the zone id till it reaches the correct zone. Then in that zone, it is routed based on node id. A <zone id, node id> of the destination is sufficient for routing so it is adaptable to changing topologies.

4.7 Ad Hoc On Demand Distance Vector Routing (AODV)

4.7.1 Description
Ad hoc On-demand Distance Vector Routing (AODV) [15, 16] is an improvement on the DSDV algorithm. AODV minimizes the number of broadcasts by creating routes on-demand as opposed to DSDV that maintains the list of all the routes. To find a path to the destination, the source broadcasts a route request (RREQ) packet with sequence numbers to neighbor which in turn broadcast the packet to their neighbors until it reaches an intermediate node that has recent route information about the destination or until it reaches the destination. When a node forwards a route request packet to its neighbors, it also records in its tables the node from which the first copy of the request came to construct route reply packet and hence symmetric. If the source moves then it can reinitiate route discovery to the destination. If one of the intermediate nodes move then the moved nodes neighbor realizes the link failure and sends a link failure notification to its upstream neighbors and so on until it reaches the source upon which the source can reinitiate route discovery if needed.

4.8 Temporally-Ordered Routing Algorithm- TORA

4.8.1 Description
Temporally Ordered Routing Algorithm (TORA) is a distributed source-initiated on-demand routing protocol [17], designed to minimize reaction to topological changes. A key concept in this design is that control messages are typically localized to a very

small set of nodes. It guarantees that all routes are loop-free (although temporary loops may form), and typically provides multiple routes for any source/destination pair. TORA can be separated into three basic functions: 1) creating routes, 2) marinating routes, and 3) erasing routes. TORA associates a height with each node in the network. All messages in the network flow downstream, from a node with higher height to a node with lower height. Routes are discovered using Query (QRY) and Update (UPD) packets. This QRY packet will propagate through the network until it reaches a node that has a route or the destination itself. Such a node will then broadcast a UPD packet that contains the node height. Every node receiving this UPD packet will set its height to a larger height than specified in the UPD message. The node will then broadcast its own UPD packet which can result in multiple routes.

4.9 Dynamic Source Routing- DSR

4.9.1 Description

Dynamic Source Routing (DSR) [18] is a source-routed on-demand routing protocol means that each packet in its header carries the complete ordered list of nodes through which the packet must pass. DSR uses no periodic routing messages thereby reducing network overhead and avoiding large routing updates throughout the ad-hoc network. The two basic modes of operation in DSR are 1) route discovery and 2) route maintenance. When the source node wants to send a packet to a destination, it looks up its route cache to determine if it already contains a route to the destination. If it finds that an unexpired route to the destination exists, then it uses this route to send the packet. But if the node does not have such a route, then it initiates the route discovery process by broadcasting a route request packet. To limit the number of route requests propagated, a node processes the route request packet only if it has not already seen the packet and it's address is not present in the route record of the packet.

A route reply is generated by the node with information regarding the route to destination. Route record is formed when route request propagates in the network which is placed in the reply packet. On the other hand, if the node generating the route reply is an intermediate node then it appends its cached route for the destination to the route record of route request packet and puts that into the route reply packet. To send the route reply packet, reverse of route record can be used if symmetric links are supported. In case symmetric links are not supported, the node can initiate route discovery to source and piggyback the route reply on this new route request.

5 Application Scenarios

Wireless mesh networks can be established and applied in many areas such as university campuses, convention centers, airport, hotel, shopping malls and sport centers [3]. The typical application scenarios are as listed below.

5.1 Wireless Broadband Home Networking

Wireless broadband home networks implemented over wireless local area networks afford various facilities for us. Despite this, some drawbacks exist in this type of networking. Dead spot is a typical problem. If wireless mesh networking is employed for broadband home networks, these problems can be solved easily. In wireless mesh networks, mesh routers will take the place of those access points. It is efficient because wiring mesh routers to the access modem is not required. Also, we can improve the dead spot problem effectively just through establishing more mesh routers [4].

5.2 Enterprise Networking

Currently, offices in many companies are equipped with wireless enterprise networks. These wireless networks are realized based on wireless local area networks. If these networks need to be connected, the wired Ethernet connection is the only way, which is a high network cost for enterprises [7]. If those access points in wireless local area networks are substituted with mesh routers, the Ethernet wiring becomes unnecessary and all nodes in the networks can share access modems in the whole network through mesh routers.

5.3 Broadband Community Networking

Connecting to DSL or a cable through a wireless router is the most common home Internet access method in community. With the wireless mesh networking establishment, homes can faster share information and more conveniently communicate with each other in community. In addition, the high bandwidth gateway can be shared by multiple homes, which greatly reduces the cost. Roofnet is a typical example of broadband community networking.

6 Conclusion

In this paper, a comprehensive survey on the developments, routing protocols and applications of wireless mesh networks is conducted. Some open issues and challenges existing in design of routing layer in wireless mesh networks are also discussed. Wireless mesh network can be formed from wireless local area network and ad hoc network, thus, wireless mesh network combines the advantages of wireless local area network and ad hoc network. No wired infrastructure, easy installation, flexible operation and low cost prove wireless mesh network is superior to wireless local area network. Covering a larger area through connecting mesh routers and integrating with multiple different networks are the merits ad hoc network can not gain. Therefore, wireless mesh networking is a very promising technology for the next generation networking. In order that this technology can be earlier applied in more areas, more efforts need to be devoted.

References

[1] De Couto, D., Aguayo, D., Bicket, J., Morris, R.: A high-throughout path metric for multi-hop wireless routing. In: Proceedings of the 9th Annual International Conference on Mobile Computing and Networking, MobiCom (2003)

[2] Koskal, C.E., Balakrishnan, H.: Quality-aware routing metrics for time-varying wireless mesh networks. IEEE Journal on Selected Areas in Communications 24(11), 1984–1994 (2006)

[3] Draves, R., Padhye, J., Zill, B.: Comparisons of Routing Metrics for Static Multi-Hop Wireless Networks. In: ACM Annual Conf. Special Interest Group on Data Communication (SIGCOMM), pp. 133–144 (August 2004)

[4] Draves, R., Padhye, J., Zill, B.: Routing in Multi-Radio, Multi-Hop Wireless Mesh Networks. In: ACM Annual Int'l. Conf. Mobile Comp. and Net (MOBICOM), pp. 114–128 (2004)

[5] Belding-Royer, E.M.: Multi-level Hierarchies for Scalable ad hoc Routing. ACM/Kluwer Wireless Networks (WINET) 9(5), 461–478 (2003)

[6] Frey, H.: Scalable Geographic Routing Algorithms for Wireless Ad Hoc Networks. IEEE Network Mag., 18–22 (July/August 2004)

[7] Zhang, Y., Luo, J., Hu, H.: Wireless Mesh Networking - Architectures. In: Protocols and Standards. Auerbach Publications (2007)

[8] Pei, G., Gerla, M.: Tsu-Wei chen Fisheye State Routing: A routing scheme for Ad hoc wireless networks. IEEE Transactions (2003)

[9] Jacquet, P., Muhlethaler, P., Clausen, T., Laouiti, A., Qayyum, A., Viennot, L.: Optimized Link state routing for Ad Hoc Networks IETF Internet Draft 2004 (2004)

[10] Wei, H.-Y., Ganguly, S., Izmailov, R., Haas, Z.: Interference-aware IEEE 802.16 wimax mesh networks. In: Proceedings of the IEEE Vehicular Technology Conference, VTC (2004)

[11] Perlman, R.: Interconnections: Bridges, Routers, Switches, and Internetworking Protocols, 2nd edn. Addison Wesley Longman, Inc., Reading (2000)

[12] Murthy, S., Garcia-Luna-Aceves, J.J.: An Efficient Routing Protocol for Wireless Networks. In: ACM Mobile Networks and Applications, Routing in Mobile Communication Networks, pp. 183–197 (October 1996)

[13] Chiang, C.: Routing in Clustered Multihop, Mobile Wireless Networks with Fading Channel. In: Proceedings of IEEE SICON 1997, pp. 197–211 (April 1997)

[14] Joa-Ng, M., Lu, I.: A Peer-to-Peer zone-based two-level link state routing for mobile Ad Hoc Networks. IEEE Journal on Selected Areas in Communications, Special Issue on Ad-Hoc Networks, 1415–1425 (August 1999)

[15] Perkins, C., Royer, E.: Ad Hoc On Demand Distance Vector(AODV) Routing. IETF Internet draft (November 1998)

[16] Perkins, C.E., Royer, E.M.: Ad-hoc On-Demand Distance Vector Routing. In: Proceedings of 2nd IEEE Workshop of Mobile Computer Systems and Applications, pp. 90–100 (February 1999)

[17] Park, V., Corson, M.: A Highly Adaptive Distributed Routing Algorithm for Mobile Wireless Networks. In: Proceedings of INFOCOM 1997 (April 1997)

[18] Johnson, D., Maltz, D.: Dynamic Source Routing in Ad Hoc Networks. Mobile Computing, 152–81 (1996)

Comparative Analysis of Formal Model Checking Tools for Security Protocol Verification

Reema Patel[1], Bhavesh Borisaniya[1], Avi Patel[1], Dhiren Patel[2],
Muttukrishnan Rajarajan[3], and Andrea Zisman[3]

[1] Sardar Vallabhbhai National Institute of Technology Surat, India,
{reema.mtech,borisaniyabhavesh,avi2687}@gmail.com
[2] Indian Institute of Technology Gandhinagar, India
dhiren@iitgn.ac.in
[3] City University London, UK
R.Muttukrishnan@city.ac.uk, a.zisman@soi.city.ac.uk

Abstract. With the proliferation of *universal clients* over Internet, use
of security protocols is rapidly on rise to minimize associated risks. Security protocols are required to be verified thoroughly before being used
to secure applications. There are several approaches and tools exist to
verify security protocols. Out of these one of the more suitable is the
Formal approach. In this paper, we give an overview of different formal
methods and tools available for security protocol verification.

Keywords: Security Protocols, Formal Methods, State Exploration, Verification, Falsification.

1 Introduction

The usage of Internet has rapidly risen in our day-to-day life. Internet based
applications such as online banking, online reservation, e-governance and many
more use sensitive information and therefore need higher levels of security. To secure such applications, various security protocols have been developed. Security
protocols ensure secure communication over a hostile network by performing
security related functions using appropriate cryptographic primitives. Several
protocols have been shown to have flaws in computer security literature. Badly
designed security protocols make it easy for the intruder to observe, delay, redirect or replay the messages. In order to make these protocols secure they need
to be verified using a systematic approach.As manual analysis of such security
protocols is extremely difficult and time consuming, alternative methods and
automatic tools are required for the protocol verification.

1.1 Two Approaches for Protocol Verification

Security protocols achieve secure communication using cryptographic primitives
like *Key Distribution* or *Key Agreement, Authentication, Symmetric* or *Asymmetric Encryption, One Way Hash Function (OWHF)* or *Message Authentication Code* (MAC), etc. The main aim of the security protocol verification is to

N. Meghanathan et al. (Eds.): CNSA 2010, CCIS 89, pp. 152–163, 2010.

verify whether a security protocol satisfies the security requirements. Primarily, there are two approaches for security protocol verification [1]. They are computational approach and the formal method approach.

Computational Approach. Computational approach considers cryptographic primitives as a function on a string of bits. Security properties are defined in terms of probability of successful attacks.

The intruder is modeled as a *Turing machine* which has access to an oracle. However the oracle aims to find the decryption key. Protocol is considered good if oracle cannot find the decryption key or it will consume computational power to find the decryption key. Computational approach finds all probabilistic polynomial-time attacks but proofs are difficult to automate, which is quite hard to understand.

The Formal Method Approach. Contrast to a computational approach, Formal approach assumes perfect cryptography. It states that cipher-text can only be decrypted by applying the appropriate decryption key. Intruder is modeled as an agent that controls the network but cannot do a cryptanalysis [2].

There are a number of automatic security protocol verification tools based on formal approach. In formal approach, protocol description, security properties and intruder capabilities are defined formally. Formal method verification tool verifies the security protocol in the presence of the intruder, and if it is found to be faulty then it provides a counter example that represents how protocol violates the security requirement. Providing a counter example is an easy way to understand how attack can be performed on that protocol.

Rest of the paper is organized as follows: Section 2 discusses various approaches of formal verification of security protocols. Section 3 discusses different formal model checking tools. We give an example of protocol verification in section 4. In section 5 we give a comparative analysis of model checking tools. Finally section 6 gives the conclusion to this comparative study.

2   Formal Verification of Security Protocols

There are three approaches for formal verification of security protocols viz; *belief logic, theorem proving approach* and *state exploration* [2]. We hereby provide a brief overview of each approach.

2.1   Belief Logics

Belief logic was the first attempt to automate the verification of security protocols.

BAN Logic: BAN [3] logic, developed by Mike Burrows, Martin Abadi, and Roger Needham; is the most significant and prominent belief logic. It describes beliefs of communicating principles and evaluates those beliefs using inference rules. Inference rules derive a final goal statement from all previously evaluated statements which represent either protocol is correct or not.

Its main characteristic is its simplicity but minor disadvantage is their assumptions. They include: strength of cryptography algorithm, principals are trustworthy, and principals can recognize and ignore their own messages. BAN Logic can only be used to verify authentication properties.

GNY: **G**ong, **N**eedham and **Y**ahalom extended the BAN logic [4]. BAN logic does not consider the release of message contents and the interaction of the protocol runs at different time. Thus a successful but complicated approach was proposed called GNY [4]. The GNY approach puts more considerations on the difference between content and meaning of messages. GNY logic has been difficult to apply, due to its many inference rules. GNY Logic also used to verify only authentication protocols.

BGNY: BGNY logic, introduced by **B**rackin [5] is an extended version of GNY. This belief logic is used by software that automatically proves the authentication properties of cryptographic protocols. Similarly to GNY logic, BGNY addresses only authentication. However, BGNY extends the GNY logic by including the ability to specify protocol properties at intermediate stages and being able to specify protocols that use multiple encryption and hash operations, message authentication codes, hash codes as keys, and key-exchange algorithms [6].

2.2   Theorem Proving Based Approaches

The Theorem proving approach considers a formal version of mathematical reasoning about the system. Tools which used this approach are based on either *Higher Order Logic* (HOL) or *First Order Logic (FOL)*. Examples of theorem proving tools are HOL theorem prover, the ACL2 theorem prover, Isabelle theorem prover etc. Using a theorem prover, one formalizes the system (infinite number of principles running infinite number of sessions along with the intruder) as a set of possible communication traces. Theorem proving approach provides a formal proof [2]. This approach is not fully automatic and therefore time consuming approach. This approach provides poor support for flaw detection.

2.3   State Exploration

In this approach, a verification method searches all possible execution paths of the protocol and verifies each reachable state that satisfies some conditions. *Unbounded verification* considers unbounded number of principles and unbounded number of protocol sessions. So the state space generated from analyzing a protocol may be infinite. Here, intruder can also generate infinite number of messages. Such kind of a problem where the state space grows too large is known as state explosion. In *bounded verification*, principles and protocol sessions are fixed. Verification method finds out a particular state in which security property gets violated and a counter example is built by exploiting a trace from that incorrect state to an initial state. State exploration methods are found to be powerful and automatic. Starting with an overview of Dolev-Yao method, followed by model checking tools which are used state exploration method, we discuss most important state exploration tools.

Dolev and Yaos Method Dolev-Yao method [7] mainly focuses on a formal model of an intruder. In this model, the network is assumed to be under the full control of an intruder who can read all message traffic, modify and destroy any messages, create any messages, and perform any operation, such as encryption or decryption that is available to legitimate users of the system. Most of the model checking tools use Dolev-Yao intruder model with minor changes.

3 Model Checking Tools

Majority of security protocol verification tools are based on model checking approach rather than on theorem proving approach. Some of the tools which use model checking approach based on state-exploration method are discussed below.

FDR/Casper: FDR (Failures-Divergence Refinement) is used to verify CSP (Communicating Sequential Processes) Programs. Gavin Lowe, found a flaw in NSPK (Needham-Schroeder Public-Key) protocol [8], and approached the verification of security protocols using Hoares calculus of CSP. FDR takes two CSP processes as input. One is the implementation of protocol, where all agents and intruder are modeled as CSP process. The second is specification of protocol which represents "correctly achieves authentication" or "secrecy" and models them as CSP process. It then verifies, whether implementation refines the specification or not. If FDR finds out that the specification is not met then it results the trace of system that does not satisfy specification. This trace consider as an attack on that protocol.

The process of converting a protocol description into CSP program is very difficult and time-consuming. For that Lowe developed a Casper compiler [9] that compiles abstract security protocol description into CSP program.

OFMC: Basin introduced On-the-Fly Model-Checker (OFMC) in 2003 [10]. OFMC is based on two lazy techniques: the first is lazy demand-driven search and second is the lazy intruder, which reduces the computational effort. Protocol description is specified in HLPSL (High-Level Protocol Specification Language) that allows user to write the protocol in *Alice-Bob* style notation. HLPSL2IF automatically translates it to IF (Intermediate Format) which OFMC takes as input.

Lazy demand-driven search uses lazy data types to model infinite state-space of protocol. Lazy data types model the protocol and attacker as infinite tree on the fly, in a demand driven way. The nodes of the tree are traces and children represent the next step of protocol or an action of an attacker. Properties of nodes represent the security properties. Lazy intruder techniques model a lazy Dolev-Yao intruder whose actions are generated in a demand-driven way. Now OFMC is renamed as Open source Fixed-point Model-Checker.

CL-Atse: Chevalier et al. developed the Constraint-Logic based ATtack SEarcher [11]. It is OCaml-based (programming language) implementation of the deduction rules. These rules allow user to interpret and automatically execute the protocols in every possible way in the presence of Dolev-Yao intruder Capabilities.

Protocol description is specified as a set of rewriting rules in IF format. The main design goals of CL-Atse are modularity (easily extend the class of the protocols to be analysed) and performance (obtain the results using large number of protocol sessions). Any state-based properties (like secrecy, authentication etc) and algebraic properties of operators like XOR, exponentiation can be modelled and analysed.

SATMC: SAT-based Model Checker is an open and flexible platform for SAT-based bounded model checking [12]. Protocol descriptions are specified as rewrite formalism in IF format. SAT compiler generates the formula for each step of the protocol using encoding techniques. Each formula is then tested using SAT solver - whether formula is satisfiable or it leads to an attack. SATMC performs bounded analysis by considering finite sessions of the protocol with Dolev-Yao intruder capabilities.

TA4SP: Tree Automata based on Automatic Approximations for the Analysis of Security Protocols (TA4SP) was developed by Genet and Klay in 2000 [13], and is based on abstraction-based approximation method. Abstraction provides a way to prove correctness or security of a protocol by over-estimating the possibility of failure. This tool language represents an over-approximation or under-approximation of the intruder knowledge with an unbounded number of sessions.

The tool Is2TiF, composed in TA4SP automatically converts the input protocol specification file (HLPSL format) into Timbuk (a tree automata library). Tree automata library contains an approximation function, a term rewriting system representing the protocol, the intruder's abilities to analyze message and an initial configuration of the network. Timbuk taking the protocol specification file and then test, three kinds of conclusions can be deduced from the results: either a protocol is flawed (under-approximation), or a protocol is secured (over-approximation), or no conclusion can be raised.

AVISPA: AVISPA, a push-button tool for the Automated Validation of Internet Security-sensitive Protocols and Applications was developed by Basin *et al.*, in 2004 [14]. A number of protocol verification tools analyze small and medium-scale protocols such as Clark/Jacob library [15]. But AVISPA can analyze both small and medium-scale protocols as well as large scale Internet security protocols. Protocol description is specified in High Level Protocol Specification Language (HLPSL). Then HLPSL2IF converts it into rewrite IF format. Current

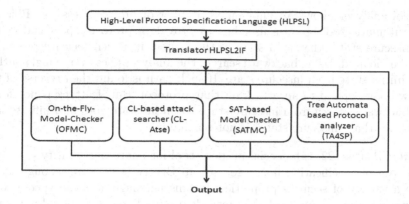

Fig. 1. The Architecture of the AVISPA tool

version of the AVISPA tool integrates four back-end tools which are: OFMC [10], CL-Atse [11], SATMC [12], and TA4Sp [13]. Now IF specifications are given as input to the all back-end tools. There is different output for each back-end tool. AVISPA tool provides a web-based graphical user interface that supports the editing of protocol specifications and allows the user to upload protocol specification. If an attack is found, the tool displays it using message-sequence chart which is very easy to understand. Figure 1 shows the architecture of AVISPA tool [14].

HERMES: Bozga *et al.* introduced HERMES in 2003 [16]. This tool is specialized to verify secrecy properties with unbounded number of sessions and principles. Hermes has no restriction on the size of messages.

Hermes provides a frond end (EVA). Hermes provides either an attack or proof tree for the protocol correction. Hermes uses three back-end tools to verify secrecy which are: Cryptographic Protocol Verification (CPV) [17], Hermes [16] and SECURIFY [18].

Interrogator: Interrogator, developed by Millen *et.al* in 1987 [19] is a Prolog program that searches for security vulnerabilities in network cryptographic key distribution protocols [20]. Here, a Protocol is modeled as communicating state machines in which intruder can destroy, intercept, and modify every message. Given a protocol description and a final state i.e. goal of the intruder in which message is supposed to be secret, the interrogator searches for every possible attack scenario with intruder abilities and verify the protocol against that final state.

NRL protocol analyzer: Catherine Meadows developed the NRL Protocol Analyzer [21] in US Naval Research Laboratory (NRL) in 1994. It is special-purpose tool that uses a theorem proving technique such as Inductive method for security protocol analysis. NRL uses the same model as interrogator. NRL protocol analyzer allows an unbounded number of protocol sessions. It is not fully automatic tool because user has to provide a protocol specification and also insecure state that is, a state of the system in which security properties has been violated. Using backward search, the analyzer tries every single path to reach initial state from insecure state. If such path is found then reverse of this path will correspond to an attack on that protocol. But if attack is not found then backward search from insecure state to initial state goes into infinite loop and proves that "insecure state" is not reachable.

Brutus: Brutus [22] is a special-purpose tool for analyzing security protocols. The Protocol specification language used in Brutus is powerful enough to describe a variety of security properties. In this language user can specify what information participants (including intruder) must know and should not know. Brutus can only check a finite number of states and a full proof of protocol correctness cannot be obtained. Advantage of Brutus is that the intruder model is inbuilt into the tool so user has to not explicitly specify intruder abilities.

Murφ: The Murφ [23] verification system is a finite-state machine verification tool. Mur is also a description language. Murφ uses either breadth-first or depth-first search for the finite state space generation. The protocol specification is modeled in Murφ. Security properties can be specified by invariants, which are those Boolean conditions that are true in all reachable state. If a state is reached in which some invariant is violated, Murφ prints an error trace - a sequence of states from the start state to the state exhibiting the problem.

Pro Verif: ProVerif, developed by Bruno Blanchet [24] represents protocol specification by Horn clauses. ProVerif accepts two kinds of input files: Horn clauses and a subset of the Pi-calculus. Protocol is analyzed with unbounded number of protocol sessions by using some approximations. Dolev-Yao intruder model is inbuilt into the tool so there is no need to explicitly model the attacker. Sometimes it can generate false attacks too [25].

Athena: Athena is an automatic model checking tool developed by Dawn Song and Perring in 2001 [26]. Thayer, Herog and Guttman proposed a Strand Space Model (SSM) for protocol representation [27]. Athena developed a new logic suitable for SSM for describing security protocols and their intended properties. Athena uses techniques from both model checking and theorem proving to extend SSM to represent protocol execution.

Athena allows arbitrary protocol configuration, e.g. unbounded number of principles and protocol sessions. To improve efficiency Athena uses pruning theorems for avoiding state-space explosion problem. One disadvantage of Athena is that the verification procedure is not guaranteed to terminate in unbounded verification. Termination can be forced by bounding the number of protocol sessions and the length of messages.

Scyther: Scyther and Scyther GUI were developed by Cas Cremers in 2007 [25]. Scyther is an automatic push-button tool for the verification and falsification of security protocols. Scyther provides a graphical user interface which incorporates the Scyther command-line tool and python scripting interfaces. Scyther tool takes protocol description and optional parameters as input, and outputs a summary report and display a graph for each attack. Figure 2 shows prototype of Scyther tool [25].

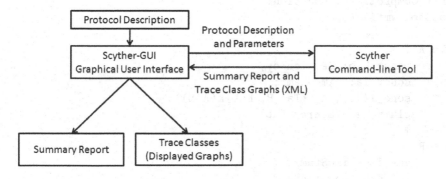

Fig. 2. The prototype of the Scyther tool

The description of a protocol is written in SPDL. Security properties are modeled as claim events. For the protocol verification, Scyther can be used in three ways. 1) Verification of claims: Scyther verifies or falsifies security properties. 2) Automatic claims: if user does not specify security properties as claim events then Scyther automatically generates claims and verifies them. 3) Characterization: Each protocol role can be "characterized". Scyther analyzes the protocol, and provides a finite representation of all traces that contain an execution of the protocol role.

Scyther generates attack graph for counter example. Scyther represents individual attack graph for each claim. It combines a number of novel features with the state-ofthe art performance viz; Scyther is guaranteed to terminate for an unbounded number of sessions, represents infinite sets of traces in terms of patterns, and facilitates multiprotocol analysis.

4   Protocol Verification Using Scyther

In this section we discuss how a protocol is verified using Scyther tool. Let us consider Wide-Mouthed-Frog (WMF) protocol. The WMF protocol is a server-based Symmetric key protocol which aims to provide shared key using trusted server and timestamp. The description of WMF protocol is as follows:

1. $A \rightarrow S : A, \{Ta, B, Kab\} Kas$
2. $S \rightarrow B : \{Ts, A, Kab\} Kbs$

In Scyther, a protocol is described in SPDL language in which each agent and the server is defined as a role. The WMF protocol specification in SPDL is given here.

#Protocol description in SPDL Language

```
usertype SessionKey,TimeStamp;
secret k: Function;
const Compromised: Function;
protocol wmf(A,B,S)
{
role A {
      const Kab: SessionKey;
      const Ta: TimeStamp;
      send_1(A,S, A, {Ta, B, Kab}k(A,S));
      claim_A1(A,Secret,Kab);
      }
role R {
      var Ts: TimeStamp;
      var Kab: SessionKey;
      read_2(S,B, {Ts, A, Kab}k(B,S));
      claim_B1(B,Secret,Kab);
      claim_B2(R,Nisynch);
      }
role S {
      var Kab: SessionKey;
      const Ts: TimeStamp;
      var Ta: TimeStamp;
      read_1(A,S, A,{Ta, B, Kab}k(A,S));
      send_2(S,B, {Ts, A, Kab}k(B,S));
      }
}
```

In first message, an agent A sends a message to S which contains his own identity i.e A, and Timestamp Ta, identity of B and session key Kab encrypted using symmetric key Kas. In SPDL, $send\_1(A,S,A,\{Ta,B,Kab\}k(a,s))$; is the message .This same message is taken as a read event in server role. In second message, server replays to B and sends Timestamp Ts, As identity, and a session key Kab encrypted using symmetric key Kbs. This message is written as a send event in server role and as a read event in agent B role.

Security properties are defined as claim events. In this protocol session key Kab should be kept secret, in order to define $claim\_A(A, secret, Kab)$. Scyther verifies WMF protocol and finds flaws in it and generates attack graph, which is shown in Figure 3.

Here Scyther finds out a replay attack which is already discovered by Lowe, as follows:

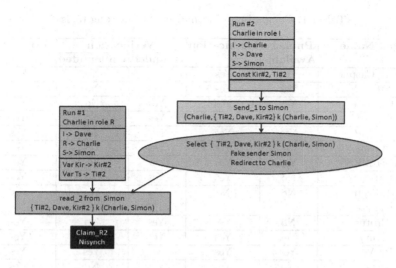

Fig. 3. Attack graph for WMF protocol

I.1 A → S: A, {Ta, B, Kab}Kas
I.2 S → B: {Ts, A, Kab} Kbs
II.2 I(S) → A: {Ta, B, Kab}Kas

In this attack, A thinks that B has established two sessions with him, when B thinks he has established only one session with A. $I.1$ and $I.2$ are actually correct messages of session I, however, there is also a possibility that intruder can reply the first message as if generated from the server.

5 Comparative Analysis of Formal Method Model Checking Tools

The comparison of formal model checking tools is given in Table 1 in relation to falsification, verification, and termination.

Tools perform falsification if it provides response when protocol is flawed. Verification of protocol can be taken as bounded if the tool verifies it with fixed number of principles and sessions or unbounded if number of principles and sessions are not fixed. While termination indicates that verification procedure will end successfully or not.

Athena is strong contender for protocol verification because it also provides bounded and unbounded verification but it's not publicly available.Publicly available tools such as FDR, OFMC, SATMC etc. also performs falsification,but their application is limted only to bounded verification. Hence, from comparison it's clear that AVISPA and Scyther are the most suitable tools for model checking.

Table 1. Comparison of formal model checking tools

Tool Name	Publicly Available	Falsification	Verification		Termination
			Bounded	Unbounded	
FDR/Casper	Yes	Yes	Yes	No	Yes
OFMC	Yes	Yes	Yes	No	Yes
CL-Atse	Yes	Yes	Yes	No	Yes
SATMC	Yes	Yes	Yes	No	Yes
TA4SP	Yes	Yes	No	Yes	Yes
Avispa	Yes	Yes	Yes	Yes	Yes
HERMES	Yes	Yes	No	Yes	Yes
Interrogator	No	Yes	Yes	No	Yes
NRL Protocol analyzer	No	No	No	Yes	Yes*
Brutus	No	Yes	Yes	No	Yes
Murφ	Yes	Yes	Yes	No	Yes
ProVerif	Yes	Yes	No	Yes	Yes
Athena(Bounded)	No	Yes	Yes	No	Yes
Athena(Unbounded)	No	Yes	No	Yes	No
Scyther	Yes	Yes	Yes	Yes	Yes

* It may not guarantee to terminate if the protocol is flawed.

6 Conclusion

Tools using formal approach are more appropriate for verifying security properties of a given protocol. Comparison shows that a fully automated Scyther and AVISPA formal verification tools are efficient to verify and falsify security protocols.

References

1. Abadi, M., Rogaway, P.: Reconciling two views of cryptography (the computational soundness of formal encryption). In: TCS 2000: Proceedings of the International Conference IFIP on Theoretical Computer Science, Exploring New Frontiers of Theoretical Informatics, pp. 3–22 (2000)
2. Juan Carlos, L.P., Monroy, R.: Formal support to security protocol development: A survey. Computacion y Sistemas 12(1), 89–108 (2008)
3. Burrows, M., Abadi, M., Needham, R.: A logic of authentication. ACM Trans. Comput. Syst. 8(1), 18–36 (1990)
4. Gong, L., Needham, R., Yahalom, R.: Reasoning about belief in cryptographic protocols. In: IEEE Symposium on Security and Privacy, p. 234 (1990)
5. Brackin, S.H.: A hol extension of gny for automatically analyzing cryptographic protocols. In: CSFW 1996: Proceedings of the 9th IEEE Workshop on Computer Security Foundations, p. 62 (1996)
6. Chen, Q., Zhang, C., Zhang, S.: Overview of security protocol analysis. In: Chen, Q., Zhang, C., Zhang, S. (eds.) Secure Transaction Protocol Analysis. LNCS, vol. 5111, pp. 17–72. Springer, Heidelberg (2008)

7. Dolev, D., Yao, A.C.: On the security of public key protocols. In: Annual IEEE Symposium on Foundations of Computer Science, pp. 350–357 (1981)
8. Lowe, G.: An attack on the needham-schroeder public-key authentication protocol. Inf. Process. Lett. 56(3), 131–133 (1995)
9. Lowe, G.: Casper: A compiler for the analysis of security protocols. Journal of Computer Security, 53–84 (1998)
10. Basin, D.A., Mödersheim, S., Viganò, L.: Ofmc: A symbolic model checker for security protocols. Int. J. Inf. Sec. 4(3), 181–208 (2005)
11. Basin, D.A.: Lazy infinite-state analysis of security protocols. In: Proceedings of the International Exhibition and Congress on Secure Networking - CQRE (Secure) 1999, pp. 30–42 (1999)
12. Armando, A., Compagna, L.: Satmc: A sat-based model checker for security protocols. In: Alferes, J.J., Leite, J. (eds.) JELIA 2004. LNCS (LNAI), vol. 3229, pp. 730–733. Springer, Heidelberg (2004)
13. Boichut, Y., Heam, P.C., Kouchnarenko, O., Oehl, F.: Improvements on the Genet and Klay Technique to Automatically Verify Security Protocols. In: Proc. Int. Workshop on Automated Verification of Infinite-State Systems (AVIS 2004), joint to ETAPS 2004, pp. 1–11 (2004)
14. Vigan, L.: Automated security protocol analysis with the avispa tool. Electronic Notes in Theoretical Computer Science 155, 61–86 (2006)
15. Clark, J.A., Jacob, J.L.: A survey of authentication protocol literature. Technical Report 1.0 (1997)
16. Bozga, L., Lakhnech, Y., Périn, M.: Hermes: An automatic tool for verification of secrecy in security protocols. In: Hunt Jr., W.A., Somenzi, F. (eds.) CAV 2003. LNCS, vol. 2725, pp. 219–222. Springer, Heidelberg (2003)
17. Goubault-Larrecq, J.: A method for automatic cryptographic protocol verification. In: IPDPS 2000: Proceedings of the 15 IPDPS 2000 Workshops on Parallel and Distributed Processing, pp. 977–984 (2000)
18. Cortier, V.: A guide for securify. Technical Report 13 (2003)
19. Millen, J.K., Clark, S.C., Freeman, S.B.: The interrogator: Protocol secuity analysis. IEEE Trans. Softw. Eng. 13(2), 274–288 (1987)
20. Tarigan, A., Rechnernetze, A., Systeme, V., Bielefeld, U.: Survey in formal analysis of security properties of cryptographic protocol (2002)
21. Meadows, C.: The nrl protocol analyzer: An overview. The Journal of Logic Programming 26(2), 113–131 (1996)
22. Clarke, E.M., Jha, S., Marrero, W.R.: Verifying security protocols with brutus. ACM Trans. Softw. Eng. Methodol. 9(4), 443–487 (2000)
23. Mitchell, J.C., Mitchell, M., Stern, U.: Automated analysis of cryptographic protocols using murφ. In: SP 1997: Proceedings of the 1997 IEEE Symposium on Security and Privacy, p. 141 (1997)
24. Blanchet, B.: An efficient cryptographic protocol verifier based on prolog rules. In: CSFW 2001: Proceedings of the 14th IEEE Workshop on Computer Security Foundations, p. 82 (2001)
25. Cremers, C.: Scyther - Semantics and Verification of Security Protocols. Ph.D. dissertation, Eindhoven University of Technology (2006)
26. Song, D., Berezin, S., Perrig, A.: Athena: a novel approach to efficient automatic security protocol analysis. Journal of Computer Security 9, 2001 (2001)
27. Thayer Fbrega, F.J., Herzog, J.C., Guttman, J.D.: Strand spaces: Why is a security protocol correct? In: Proceedings of the 1998 IEEE Symposium on Security and Privacy, pp. 160–171 (1998)

Secured Paradigm for Mobile Databases

D. Roselin Selvarani

Dept. of Computer Science, Holy Cross College, Trichirappalli – 2,
Tamil Nadu, India
jmjroselin@yahoo.co.in

Abstract. Mobile databases are gaining popularity as portable devices have become need based and common. One key aspect of these database systems is their ability to deal with disconnection. Many businesses today are no longer solely conducting business within the confines of their buildings. They have employees who travel, who work in different geographic areas, or occasionally work from home. Many organizations allow the mobile workers to carry their sensitive data outside the physical boundaries in order to increase the productivity and revenue. But when the device is not protected properly all the data stored in the device will be exposed to outsiders including competitors. So security for the database that resides in the mobile device is the major concern for such type of organizations. In order to secure the mobile database a secured architecture is proposed in this paper.

Keywords: Mobile Database, Disconnection, Data Security, Client-Server Security, Secured Architecture.

1 Introduction

Database security is an important issue in database management because of the sensitivity and importance of data and information of an organization. The goal of the database security is the protection of data against threats such as accidental or intentional loss [1]. The main requirements of database security are Confidentiality, Integrity, Authentication, Authorization and Non-repudiation [2]. Mobile environment has to face additional risks and challenges for securing its database along with the conventional problems. The new risks are caused by the mobility of users, the portability of hand held devices and wireless links [3].

In today's dynamic, fast-paced business environment, the truly agile business is the mobilized business [4]. Mobile applications and services in e-commerce or m-commerce have to be supported by databases. The mobile computing environment involves communication between the central database server and the mobile database application platforms such as laptops, PDAs, and mobile phones. A central database server consists of large databases and a mobile database application platform contains a mobile database and the applications using that database. Mobile users access the data residing in a central database through the database applications. The central database can be accessed by a variety of users such as local, remote and mobile [5].

N. Meghanathan et al. (Eds.): CNSA 2010, CCIS 89, pp. 164–171, 2010.

When the mobile user wants to get some data from the central database through an application, the mobile application first connects to the central database. Then, it retrieves the needed data and formats the data so that it can be displayed on the cell phone. The mobile application need not be connected to the central database, if the information is already stored in the mobile device. This is where the mobile databases come into the picture. Mobile database is a portable database and physically separate from a centralized database server but is capable of communicating with that server from remote sites allowing the sharing of corporate data [1, 6]. Mobile database applications are an effective way to streamline business processes and ensure that end users always have access to the critical corporate information they need, to do their jobs. Although large enterprises tend to be the ones that invest most heavily in mobility, smaller businesses can benefit from mobilizing their data [7].

2 Related Works

2.1 Encryption

Security approaches based on encryption play a vital role in securing mobile database. The need for encryption is strongly recommended to mitigate the risk of intentional or accidental disclosure of sensitive data in portable devices [8]. Cryptographic algorithms can be broadly categorized into three classes – Symmetric ciphers, Asymmetric ciphers and Hashing algorithms [9]. Among these three classifications, Asymmetric key cryptography and hashing algorithms are highly computationally intensive compared to Symmetric key cryptography. Therefore, for resource constraint mobile devices, Symmetric key algorithms are more suitable [8, 10, 11, 12]

2.2 Issues

In [13], the authors have categorized the issues and solutions for designing the mobile database as Responsiveness, Data consistency and Concurrency, Synchronization and Conflict resolution, Security, High Availability, Data size, Screen Size, Slow Transmission Speed, Slow Processing Speed and Cost. In [14], Darin Chan and John F. Roddick have addressed the important issues of Mobile databases as the relative unreliability of connections (and the variability of bandwidth when connected), the limitations on storage capacity and the security and privacy issues created when a computer is in a mobile environment.

After reviewing the issues of the mobile databases from many literatures, it is found that all the authors have invariably addressed the Security and Privacy as one of the important critical issue. Having studied many research articles none of the papers had focused on the security of the Mobile Database. So, we have proposed a secured paradigm for Mobile database.

2.3 Architecture

Architecture for a mobile database includes a small database fragment residing in the mobile device derived from the main database called central database. Two types of architectures are found in the literature: Client-Server architecture [13, 14, 15, 16, 17] and Server/Agent/Client architecture [14, 16, 18].

Client-server architecture consists of a server, fixed clients and mobile clients. A mobile client is in disconnected state when it enters the shadow area of wireless network. In order to save power and expensive wireless communication cost and provide faster response time, it may want to execute transactions in disconnected state intentionally. A mobile host has mobile database hoarded from the server to process transaction locally during disconnection. Whenever wireless connectivity improves or a wired link is available, the mobile client connects with the server and incorporates effects of the transaction committed during disconnection into the server database.

In Server/Agent/Client architecture, the role of the agent may vary between different implementations and may reside either in the server or in a mobile device. The architecture of mobile database based on agent has three layers: Mobile terminal layer, Mobile agent layer and Server layer. Each layer has some agents and each agent is responsible for a specific task.

In the second type of architecture, additional security measurements are needed to protect the agent itself. So only the Client-Server architecture is considered in the proposed paradigm. The study reveals that among the Client-Server architectures found in the literature, none of the architecture has focused on the security concept. In [13], the authors have described only the mobile database design methodology for designing appropriate databases for mobile business applications. In [14], the authors have addressed both the type of architectures. In Client-Server architecture, the main database is located with the server and the summery database resides within the client or mobile device. In [15], Publication/Subscription framework is used, which can also be considered as a Client - Server architecture. In this framework, the Publisher object acts as a Server whereas the Subscriber object acts as a Client. The authors have used this model for Object- Oriented data synchronization of mobile databases over mobile ad-hoc network.

In [16], the authors have discussed the characteristics of mobile and embedded databases and provided the methods to improve the data accessing, efficiency, stability, maintainability and uniformity of the database but not on the security. In [17], 3-tier replication architecture (Mobile client – Synchronization Server – Database Server) is used to solve the synchronization problem in embedded database based Mobile Geospatial Information Service.

3   Proposed Architecture

Our proposed model follows Client-Server architecture. In this model, the server side consists of a database server, an application server and a Mobile server. Database server has a central database, other databases required for the organization and a credential of the server. Application server contains applications pertaining to the various manipulation of the central database and takes care of providing the data in the format that is required for updating the central database. The Mobile server contains the master information from the organization and the data captured from the mobile. The main functionality of the mobile server is to synchronize the mobile database with the central database. The client side contains a web enabled mobile device with mobile

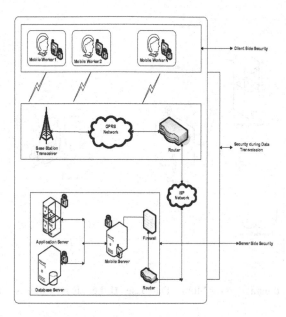

Fig. 1. Secured paradigm for Mobile Database (If Wireless Connection Exists)

database and needed application for remote transactions along with a mobile client. In the proposed model, the synchronization between the mobile database and the central database is done over the GPRS network using SSL protocol, if the wireless connectivity exists.

When a mobile worker (Mw) wants to hoard data into his mobile device from the central database, he has to authenticate himself as a correct user. In addition to the user authentication, device authentication is also mandatory in mobile database scenario. After the successful verification of the user and the device authentication, the required portion of the database is installed in the mobile device in an encrypted form. In order to initiate the transaction at the remote side, the Mw must be authenticated by the mobile device. This client side authentication prevents the unauthorized user to access the mobile device. During the transaction, the mobile database is updated first and then the updated values are seamlessly integrated with the central database through GPRS network in a secured way using SSL protocol, if the wireless connectivity exists (Fig. 1).

To establish a secured communication for the synchronization, the client as well as the server should authenticate each other. After the successful authentication at both sides, the data is encrypted using the secret key before being transmitted, which prevents the intruders from eavesdropping. At the server side, the encrypted data is decrypted using the same key.

If there is no wireless connectivity, then the Mw directly updates the mobile database with the server at the end of the day or at the end of the transaction through wired connection (Fig. 2). In this scenario the Mw should come to the office to update the data stored in his mobile device with the server. This is something similar to updating the data from one computer to another computer.

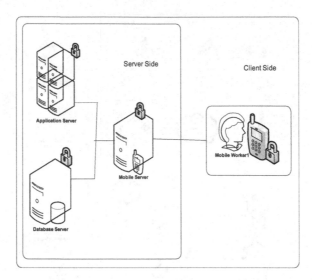

Fig. 2. Secured paradigm for Mobile Database (If there is no wireless Connection)

3.1 Server Side Security

The mobile worker (Mw) initiates his work by login to the server using username and password (Uname1 , Pw1). The Uname1 is generated based on the role of the Mw and given to him initially whereas the Pw1 is selected by the Mw. The server checks the parameters with the database which contains the identification of all the mobile workers. If valid, it prompts the user for device authentication. Mw enters IMEI of his mobile device. The server validates IMEI. If correct, both Mw and the device are authenticated successfully. Then the server generates a secret key (Sk) based on Pw1 and IMEI, which is used for cryptography. It stores Sk in the encoded form on the mobile device as well as in its database. It also installs it's security certificate on the mobile device which contains it's public key. Then the server installs the needed portion of the database on the mobile device after encrypting it.

3.2 Client Side Security

At the client side, the authentication is done in two levels. The Mw enters username and password (Uname2, Pw2) and which are verified by the device with the parameters stored in the memory in an encoded form. This is the first level authentication. In the second level authentication, the device challenges the Mw by displaying four digits number and prompts the Mw to enter his response. If the Mw enters the sum of the four digits as response, he is further authenticated to access the database from the device. In this authentication process, each user is assigned a different challenge function to compute. Because there are many possible challenge functions, an intruder who captures the username and password cannot necessarily infer the proper function. When the Mw initiates his transaction, first he must decrypt the encrypted database using the secret key, Sk. During the transaction, the mobile database is first updated and then the updated values are seamlessly integrated with the central database through GPRS network in a secured way using SSL protocol, if the connectivity exists.

3.3 Security during Data Transmission

To initiate the synchronization process, the content of the credential is decoded with Sk and the public key of the server (S_Pubk) is extracted. Then the parameters Uname1, Pw1 and IMEI of the mobile device are encrypted using 128 bit AES symmetric algorithm(AES) with SK first. The encrypted information is further encrypted with S_Pubk using AES. The doubly encrypted information is being sent to the server for authentication. At the other end, the server decrypts the information with its Private key (S_Prik) using AES and further decrypts the decrypted information with SK using AES to get back the original parameters. It checks these values in the database and if there is a match, it notifies the client with ok message otherwise an error message is being sent to the client. When it passes the reply, first the message is encrypted with AES using S_Prik . Then the encrypted message is further encrypted using AES based on Sk. At the client side, the message is decrypted with Sk first and then again decrypted with S_Pubk. In this authentication process, the end to end security is maintained.

3.4 Advantages of the Proposed Architecture

3.4.1 Confidentiality and Integrity
In the Client side, confidentiality of the database is achieved by encrypting the database based on symmetric key cryptography using the secret key, which is generated based on the password and IMEI.

In the server side, the confidentiality and integrity is assured by not permitting the unauthorized users to disclose and modify the database. The server checks the parameters namely username1 and password1 entered by the Mw at the time of accessing the server database. If there is no match, it will not permit the Mw to access the database.

Even if the device is lost, the data can not be revealed to the unauthorized users as it is encrypted. Moreover when the device is lost or stolen, Mw is expected to report to the organization immediately about the lost so that "remote wiping" will be carried out to clean all the data stored in that device.

3.4.2 Authentication
At the client side, two factors authentication is implemented. Mw is authenticated by entering Uname2 and Pw2. The mobile device checks these values with the parameters which are already stored in the memory in an encrypted form. If valid, the client will display a four digit number and prompts the Mw to enter the response. If the response is the sum of the individual digits of the given number he is further authenticated to access the data.

At the server side, Mw is authenticated based on the Uname1 and Pw1. The Uname1 is generated randomly based on the role. Role Based Access Control is implemented in the server. If the parameters are valid, the Mw is permitted to access the server otherwise access is denied.

Both in the client and server side, number of attempts a user can make to login is restricted, after which the application will be locked. This will prevent an unauthorized user trying to access the device or server by brute-force.

Client-Server authentication is also done at the time of synchronization. The client sends Uname1, Pw1 and IMEI in doubly encrypted form to the server. The server decrypts them and checks for the validity of the parameters. If valid, it permits the synchronization by sending ok message, which is also encrypted doubly at the server side. In this procedure, when the client is sending the message, the server alone can decrypt, since the decryption needs private key of the server and secret key of the client, which are unknown to others. Similarly the response from the server is decrypted only by the Mw as it needs the public key of the server and secret key of the mobile device.

3.4.3 Non-repudiation
In the server side, a log file is maintained for auditing purpose. Whenever Mw hoards the database into his device and synchronizes it to the server, a record is created and stored in the server. Therefore Mw can not deny that he has not hoarded/sent the database from/to the server.

3.4.4 Availability
In mobile database environment, as the database resides on the mobile device itself, at anytime it is possible for Mw to access the data, even during the disconnection state.

4 Conclusion

Securing the Mobile database environment is an important task for the organizations which permit the mobile workers to carry their data outside the physical boundary. A secured architecture for mobile database is proposed based on the encryption cryptographies. Keeping the limitations of the mobile platforms in mind, a secured paradigm is proposed using asymmetric cryptography for key exchange and symmetric cryptography for data encryption.

References

1. Singh, S.K.: Database Systems: Concepts, Design and Applications. Dorling Kindersley (India) Pvt. Ltd., New Delhi (2006)
2. Leung, A., Sheng, Y., Cruickshank, H.: The Security Challenges for Mobile Ubiquitous Services. Elsevier, Science Direct, Information Security Technical Report 12, pp. 162–171 (2007)
3. Lubinski, A.: Database Security meets Mobile Requirements. In: IEEE International Symposium on Database Technology and Software Engineering, pp. 445–450 (2000)
4. ftp://ftp.compaq.com/pub/solutions/
   WEF_MaximizingBusinessAgilityFlyer_4-01-03.pdf
5. Weider Yu, D., Amjad, T., Goel, H., Talawat, T.: An Approach of Mobile Database Design methodology for Mobile Software Solutions. In: The 3rd International Conference on Grid and Pervasive Computing - Workshops. IEEE, Los Alamitos (2008)
6. Connolly, T., Begg, C.: Database Systems: A Practical Approach to Design, Implementation and Management, 3rd edn. Dorling Kindersley (India) Pvt. Ltd., New Delhi (2002)
7. http://EzineArticles.com/?expert=Eric_Giguere

8. Diaa Salama Abdul, E., Kader, H.M.A., Hadhoud, M.M.: Performance Evaluation of Symmetric Encryption Algorithms. International Journal of Computer Science and Network Security 8(12) (2008)
9. Ravi, S., Raghunathan, A., Hattangady, S.: Security in Embedded Systems: Design Challenges. ACM Transactions on Embedded Computing Systems 3(3), 461–481 (2004)
10. Chandramouli, R., Bapatla, S., Subbalakshmi, K.P.: Battery Power-Aware Encryption. ACM Transactions on Information and System Security 9(2), 162–180 (2006)
11. Ruangchaijatupon, N., Krishnamurthy, P.: Encryption and Power Consumption in Wireless LANs. In: The Third IEEE Workshop on Wireless LANS (2001)
12. Han, J., Chang, H.-Y., Park, M.: EMCEM: An Efficient Multimedia Content Encryption scheme for mobile handheld devices. In: International Conference on Information Science and Security. IEEE, Los Alamitos (2008)
13. Weider Yu, D., Amjad, T., Goel, H., Talawat, T.: An Approach of Mobile Database Design methodology for Mobile Software Solutions. In: The 3rd International Conference on Grid and Pervasive Computing - Workshops. IEEE, Los Alamitos (2008)
14. Chan, D., John Roddick, F.: Summarisation for Mobile databases. Journal of Research and Practice in Information Technology 37(3), 267–284 (2005)
15. Li, Y., Zhang, X., Gao, Y.: Object-Oriented Data Synchronization for Mobile Database over Mobile Ad-hoc Networks. In: International Symposium on Information Science and Engineering. IEEE, Los Alamitos (2008)
16. Li, W., Yang, H., He, P.: The research and application of embedded mobile database. In: International Conference on Information Technology and Computer Science. IEEE Computer Society, Los Alamitos (2009)
17. Yun, Z., Mu, Z., Fuling, B.: A Tiered Replication Model in Embedded Database Based Mobile Geospatial Information Service. IEEE, Los Alamitos (2008)
18. Li, J., Wang, J.: A New Architecture Model of Mobile Database Based on Agent. In: First International Workshop on Database Technology and Applications. IEEE, Los Alamitos (2009)

Energy Analysis of RSA and ELGAMAL Algorithms for Wireless Sensor Networks

R. Kayalvizhi, M. Vijayalakshmi, and V. Vaidehi

Department of Electronics Engineering, Madras Institute of Technology Campus
Anna University, Chennai-44, India
kavikayal@annauniv.edu, om_vijisep03@yahoo.co.in,
vaidehi@annauniv.edu

Abstract. Sensor networks are primarily designed for real-time collection and analysis of low level data in hostile environments. Basically sensor networks are application dependent. Wireless sensor network (WSN) applications can be classified into two - event based and continuous monitoring. This paper focuses on continuous monitoring application. One of the major challenges of wireless sensor network is security. The security of WSNs poses challenges because of the criticality of the data sensed by a node and in turn the node meets severe constraints like minimal energy, computational and communicational capabilities. Taking all the above mentioned challenges energy efficiency or battery life time plays a major role in network lifetime. Providing security consumes some energy consumed by a node, so there is a need to reduce the energy thus the cost incurred by security algorithm.In this paper the performance of the RSA cryptography algorithm is compared with the ELGAMAL cryptography algorithm by evaluating their energy efficiency and network lifetime. A cluster based wireless network topology environment is constructed in NS2 and the performances of different cluster are compared. From the simulated output the RSA algorithm consumes less energy than ELGAMAL algorithm.

Keywords: RSA, WSN, Security, Public Key, ELGAMAL, Cryptography.

1 Introduction

Recent advancement in wireless communication and electronics has enabled the development of low cost wireless sensor networks. A sensor network is composed of a lots of sensor nodes that are densely deployed either inside the phenomenon or very close to it. These sensor nodes consist of sending, data processing, and communication components. They use their processing abilities to locally carry out simple computations and transmit only the required and partially processed data [1].

The position of sensor nodes need not be engineered or predetermined. This allows random deployment in inaccessible terrains or disaster relief operations. Therefore, the sensor networks are expected to lead to a wide range of applications. WSN is an emerging technology that has already proved its applicability in surveillance, precision agriculture, smart home, industry, habitat monitoring, disaster control etc.

N. Meghanathan et al. (Eds.): CNSA 2010, CCIS 89, pp. 172–180, 2010.

Depending on the environment where nodes are deployed, appropriate protection measures should be taken for data confidentiality, integrity and authentication between communicating entities, while taking into account the cost, storage, energy and communication efficiency requirements. To support such security services one needs key management techniques that are resilient to both external and internal attacks. The required trade - off, makes it an important challenge to design secure and efficient key establishment techniques for wireless sensor networks [2].

Security is important for performance and energy efficiency in many applications. Besides application within the war zone, security is also crucial for premise protection and surveillance as well as critical communities like airports, hospitals, etc. Due to the property of sensor devices, the sensor networks may easily be compromised by attackers who send forged or modified messages.

To prevent information and communication systems from illegal delivery and modification, message authentication and identification needs to be examined through certificated mechanisms. Therefore, the receiver has to authenticate messages transmitted from the sensor nodes over a wireless sensor network. This is done through cryptography. It is a challenge to find out suitable cryptography for wireless sensor networks due to limitations in power efficient, computationally efficient and good storage capabilities [2].

Many schemes based on public or symmetric key cryptography are investigated [3]. Most previous schemes proposed for the security of network have used symmetric cryptography and asymmetric cryptography.

This paper concerns, a RSA (Rivest, Shamir and Aleman) cryptography algorithm for secure wireless sensor network and comparing with traditional public key cryptography technique. RSA require simple arithmetic primitive and few operands. Also RSA is an asymmetric key with simple algorithm it consumes less energy.

The main goal of this paper is to provide the secure communication among sensor nodes and also in turn reduce the overall energy consumption of the wireless sensor networks [4]. This is mainly to provide confidentiality, integrity, authentication, and availability of information during communication between sensor nodes. Also increase the lifetime of the network is to be taken care by being energy efficient.

The manuscript is organized as follows. Section II lists some of the advantages of the asymmetric key security scheme when compared to symmetric security schemes, Section III describes about RSA and ELGAMAL algorithm for event detection application using wireless sensor network, section IV discusses about the result and implementation of the RSA algorithm and ELGAMAL algorithm based on the energy consumption, section V describes the comparison of RSA and ELGAMAL algorithm and finally the section VI concludes the paper.

2 Cryptography for WSN

It is a challenge to find out suitable cryptography for wireless sensor networks (WSN) due to limitations of power, computation capability and storage resources [4]. Many schemes based on public or symmetric key cryptography are investigated. In this paper consider RSA (Rivest Shamir Adelman) and ELGAMAL algorithm, which can be used for key distribution as well as encryption/decryption.

2.1 Need of Asymmetric Key Cryptosystem

A symmetric key approach uses a single key to secure communication between two users in the entire network. So, (n-1) keys are required for each user, if network size is n. However, in a typical sensor network with thousands of sensor nodes, the storage requirement for this approach is beyond the memory limitations of sensors. Example of symmetric key cryptography are DES (Data Encryption Standard), AES (Advanced Encryption Standard), RC4 (Rivest Cipher four) and Diffie Helman algorithm. Nowadays most of the wireless environment devices use RC4 cryptosystem. These algorithms require large computation, so they consume more energy. This is the main drawback of symmetric key cryptography.

When compared with the symmetric key cryptography, the public key cryptography eliminates the key distribution problem [5]. Here one of the two keys must be kept secret. It is impossible or at least impractical to decipher a message without knowing the private key. Knowledge of the algorithm plus one of the keys plus samples of ciphertext is insufficient to determine the other key. This is a one-way trap door function and its calculation of the function is easy. Whereas the inverse calculation of RSA is infeasible, so information is more secured. It provides Confidentiality, Date Authentication, Availability and Data Integrity etc. Keys and Key length can also be changed. Group key management is also easy [6]. Hence, public key cryptography is suitable for wireless sensor networks.

3   Crypt Algorithms for WSN

Many schemes based on public key cryptography are investigated. Those algorithms are RSA (Rivest Shamir Adelman), Elgamal and ECC (Elliptic curve cryptography) [7]. This paper consists of RSA (Rivest Shamir Adelman) algorithm, which can be used for key distribution and decrypting the message and it is also suitable for general kind of network and also taken the key generation and encryption scheme is based on the RSA (Rivest Shamir Adelman) algorithm and ELGAMAL algorithm. Public-key algorithms rely on one key for encryption and other is used for decryption.

3.1   RSA Algorithm

Security purposes, we use a RSA algorithm, hence a public key and private key is generated in every node. In this paper generate the public key and private keys of all the nodes are assigned in a key table and put in a node which is called as the base station.

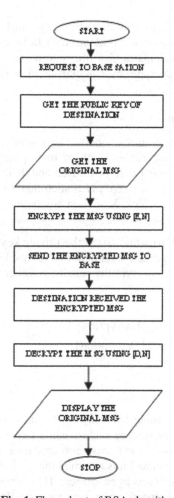

Fig. 1. Flow chart of RSA algorithm

The base station also contains the routing table, having the exact location of all the other nodes. Based on the routing table the base station assigns two other nodes, which are nearer to the base station as cluster heads. Lastly two other nodes are assigned as a source node and destination node randomly with respect to each and every application.

The security of RSA (Rivest Shamir Adleman) is inherent in the difficulty of factoring large numbers. The RSA encryption and decryption algorithms require a single modular exponentiation operation. The size of the modulus determines the security strength of the cipher [8]. The RSA ingredients are the following [9],

P,q, two prime numbers,   (private , chosen)

n =pq   (public, calculated)

e, with gcd (φ(n),e) =1; 1<e< φ(n)   (public, calculated)

d≡ e-1 mod φ(n)   (private, chosen)

The private key consists of {d, n} and the public key consists of {e, n}. Suppose that user Alice has published its public key and that user Bobs wishes to send the message M to Alice [9]. Then Bobs calculates C = Me mod n and transmits C. On receipt of this cipher text, user Alice decrypts by calculating M = Cd mod n [9]. The this is shown in Fig.1.

3.2 ELGAMAL Algorithm

This public key cryptosystem, require a modular exponentiation operation. The size of the modulus determines the security strength of the cipher. Key generation requires large strong random prime number p, to be chosen and their product computed. Select d to be a member of the group G= < Zp*, X > such that 1 • d • p-2. Select e1 to be a primitive root in the group G = < Zp*, X >.Then compute

$$e_2 = e_1^d \bmod p$$

The public key is the {e1, e2, p} while {d} is the private key. To encrypt a secret m, it is represented as a binary integer less than n and have to select the random integer r in the group G = < Zp*, X >. To decrypt the resulting cipher text c1, c2, it is raised to the power d modulo p.

$$c_1 = e_1^r \bmod p$$
$$c_2 = (m^* e_2^r) \bmod \qquad \{\text{Encryption}\}$$
$$m = [\, c_2\, (c_1^d)^{-1}] \bmod p \quad \{\text{Decryption}\}$$

4   Simulation Results

The wireless sensor network is simulated using NS2 which consists of ten sensors nodes. Consider the five nodes act as sensing nodes, while two nodes act as cluster heads. Among the different sensor nodes, there exists a source node, destination node / controller and a base station. In the Figure 2 it is assumed that node 1 acts as source node, node 8 acts as base station and node 9 acts as controller. The 10 nodes are randomly deployed in any hostile environment. For security purposes, we use a RSA algorithm, hence a public key and private key is generated in every node. These keys of all the nodes are assigned in a key table and made available in a node called as the base station.

The base station also contains the routing table, having the exact location of all the other nodes. Based on the routing table the base station assigns two nodes, which are nearer to the base station acts as cluster heads [10]. Finally the 2 nodes are assigned as a source node and destination node randomly with respect to each and every application [11].

The information has to be encrypted at source node and the cipher text sends to destination node via the cluster heads, and base station and the cipher text decrypted by a destination node.

The source node collects the public key of the destination node from the base station, to encrypt the information sensed by it. The encrypted information to the nearest cluster head in turn is send to the base station, and it sends it to the other nearest cluster directing it towards destination cluster head. The destination node decrypts the encrypted information by using its private key. The network architecture design is shown in the Fig. 2.

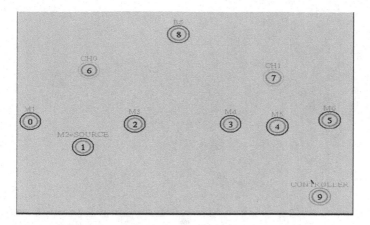

Fig. 2. Screenshot of network architecture design

Sensor networks often have one or more points of centralized control called base stations. A base station is typically a gateway to another network, a powerful data processing or storage centre, or an access point for human interface. They can be used as a nexus to disseminate, control information into the network or extract data from it [13]. Base Stations have also been referred to as sinks. The sensor nodes establish a routing forest, with a base station at the root of every tree [11]. Base stations are many orders of magnitude more powerful than sensor nodes.

Typically, base stations have enough battery power to surpass the lifetime of all sensor nodes, sufficient memory to store cryptographic keys, stronger processors, and means for communicating with outside networks. Active attacks present the opposite characteristics of passive attacks [8]. Whereas passive attacks are difficult to detect, measures are available to prevent their success. On the other hand, it is quite difficult to prevent active attacks absolutely, because to do so would require physical protection.

Encryption and decryption are done by using RSA and ELGAMAL algorithm. These algorithms are processed at each node, for developing the public key and private key [12]. These keys are used for encrypting the sensed information and decrypting the encrypted data at the destination node.

4.1 ELGAMAL Algorithm-Energy Diagram

The computational efficiency of ELGAMAL is determined by the efficiency of the modular exponentiation and the modular inversion operations. The bit operation of encryption or decryption in ELGAMAL cryptosystem is polynomial. It requires more energy for generation of keys, encryption and decryption of the information.

The following energy diagram Fig. 3 describes the energy consumption of using ELGAMAL algorithm in a wireless environment.

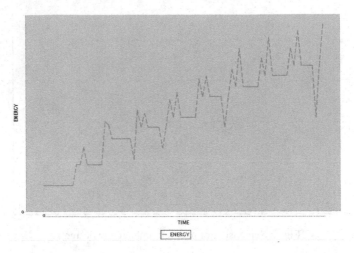

Fig. 3. Screenshot of energy diagram of ELGAMAL algorithm

4.2 RSA Algorithm-Energy Diagram

The computational efficiency of RSA is determined by the efficiency of the modular exponentiation and the modular inversion operations [9]. The bit operation of encryption or decryption in RSA cryptosystem is polynomial. It requires the less energy for generation of keys, encryption and decryption of the information.

The following energy diagram Fig.4 describes the energy consumption of using RSA algorithm in a wireless environment.

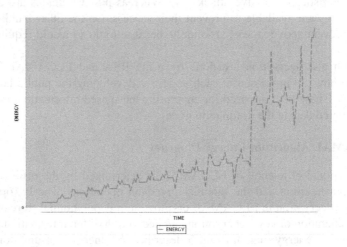

Fig. 4. Screenshot of energy diagram for RSA algorithm

5 Comparison of RSA and ELGAMAL

The wireless sensor node, which is a very small device, can only be equipped with a limited power source. Sensor node lifetime depends upon the power source and, therefore, shows a strong dependence on battery lifetime.

The main task for a sensor node in a sensor field is to detect events, perform data processing, and then transmit data. Power consumption can hence be divided into three domains: sensing, communication and data processing.

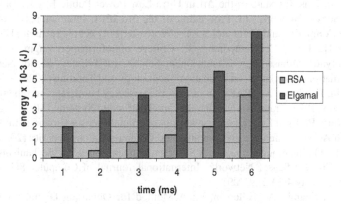

Fig. 5. Energy Loss Diagram

This paper estimates the energy consumption of RSA and ELGAMAL algorithm. From the simulated output, observed that RSA algorithm consumes 12.5x10-3J and ELGAMAL algorithm consumes 27x10-3J [12].

The energy utilization of RSA and ELGAMAL algorithm, is compared and shown in Fig.5, which shows that RSA algorithm is energy efficient than ELGAMAL [12]. The RSA has less computation power and hence increases the network lifetime.

6 Conclusion

Both algorithms perform the key distribution and encryption/decryption process. The RSA has one-way trap door function to generate different keys for encryption and decryption process. The RSA algorithm does not allow the inverse modular exponentiation. Hence, intruder cannot find the sensed information without knowing the private key even if he knows the public key. This is the main advantage of RSA algorithm and also there is no (n-1) key distribution problem found in symmetric key algorithms. The standard recommends the size of p and q is 154 decimal digits, which makes the size of n is 309 decimal digits. These are main advantages of RSA algorithm [12].

The RSA consumes less power and hence increases the network lifetime when compared with ELGAMAL. From the observations RSA algorithm provides better security for wireless sensor networks and it consumes 14.5% less energy than the ELGAMAL algorithm. Therefore, the RSA is adoptable for the wireless sensor networks.

References

1. Wander, A.S., Gurat, N.: Energy Analysis of Public-Key Cryptography for Wireless Sensor Networks. In: Proceeding of the 3rd IEEE International Conference on Pervasive Computing and Communications. University of California, Berkeley (2005)
2. Whitfield, D., Hellman, M.: New directions in cryptography. IEEE Transaction on Information Theory 22 (1976)
3. Delgosha, F.: Senier member of IEEE, A multivibrate key establishment scheme for wireless sensor networks. IEEE Transaction on Wireless Communication 18 (April 2009)
4. Gaubatz, G., Jens, E.: State of the Art in Ultra-Low Power Public Key Cryptography for Wireless Sensor Networks. In: Proceeding of the 3rd IEEE International Conference on Pervasive Computing and Communications. Worcester Polytechnic Institute, USA (2005)
5. Tong-sen, H., Deng, C., Xian-zhong, T.: College of information Engineering, An Enhanced Polynomial-based Key Establishment Scheme for Wireless Sensor Networks. In: 2008 International Workshop on Education Technology and Training (2008)
6. Ma, L., Liu, F., cheng, X.: iPAK: An in situ pair wise key bootstrapping scheme for wireless networks. IEEE Transaction on Parallel and Distributed Systems 18(8) (August 2007)
7. Liu, D., Ning, P.: Establishing pairwise keys in distributed sensor networks. In: Proceeding of the 10th ACM, Conference on Computer and Communications Security (2003)
8. Padmavathi, G., Shanmugapriya, D.: A Survey of Attacks, Security Mechanisms and Challenges in Wireless Sensor Networks. International Journal of Computer Science and Information Security 4(1&2) (2009)
9. Rivest, R.L., Shamir, A., Adleman, L.: A Method for Obtaining Digital Signatures and Public-Key Cryptosystems. Communications of the ACM 21 (February 1978)
10. Du, X., Xiao, Y.: A routing driven elliptic curve cryptography based key management scheme for heterogeneous sensor networks. IEEE Transaction on Wireless Communications 8(3) (March 2009)
11. Luo, X., Zheng, K.: Encryption algorithms comparisons for wireless networked sensors. In: 2004 IEEE International Conference on Systems, Man and Cybernetics, College of Computer Science. Zhejiang University, China (2004)
12. Zhang, Z., Cui, G.: A Cluster Based Secure Cryptography for Sensor Networks. In: 2008 International Conference on Computer Science and Software Engineering. Huazhong University of Science & Technology, China (2008)

Detection and Mitigation of Attacks by Colluding Misbehaving Nodes in MANET

Poonam, K. Garg, and M. Misra

Dept. of Electronics & Computer Engineering
IIT Roorkee, Roorkee, India
{pgeradec,kgargfec,manojfec}@iitr.ernet.in

Abstract. A Mobile Ad-hoc Network (MANET) is an infrastructure-less network, operated and managed by the nodes themselves. Inherently secure routing protocols are must for operational continuity of such networks which requires sustained and benevolent behavior by all participating nodes. A number of secure routing protocols based on trust have recently been proposed, which are able to detect routing misbehavior in the direct neighborhood of a node. However, collusion of misbehaving nodes has not been adequately addressed yet. In this paper, we present and evaluate a protocol, in which multipath routing combined with trust information of the nodes involved, are used to detect misbehaviors on data delivery formed by one or more misbehaving nodes in an ad hoc network. Data and control packets are transmitted through node-disjoint trustworthy paths. Our protocol is able to withstand against attacks carried out by multiple malicious nodes acting in collusion. We take advantage of the existence of multiple paths between nodes in an ad hoc network to increase the confidentiality and robustness of transmitted data. We have evaluated the misbehaving node detection rate and the performance of our method along a number of parameters through simulation. Results show that our method increases the throughput of the network while also discovering a secure route.

Keywords: Trust, misbehaving node, colluding misbehaving nodes, Multipath routing.

1 Introduction

A mobile ad-hoc network (MANET) is a collection of wireless mobile nodes organized to create a temporary connection between them. All nodes act both as hosts and routers, and thus cooperatively provide multi-hop strategy to communicate with other nodes outside their transmission range. Nodes in the network execute a pre-agreed routing protocol to route the packets. The accurate execution of these protocols requires sustained and benevolent behavior by all participating nodes.

The problem of all the current ad hoc routing protocols is that all the nodes are considered as trust worthy and assumed that they behave properly. Therefore, they are vulnerable to attacks launched by misbehaving nodes. According to [1] misbehaving nodes can be categorized as *selfish* or *malicious*. Misbehaving nodes participate in the route generation process to sabotage the network. Several secure routing protocols

N. Meghanathan et al. (Eds.): CNSA 2010, CCIS 89, pp. 181–190, 2010.

have been proposed recently to detect routing/forwarding misbehavior in a node's one-hop neighborhood. However, considering only the one-hop neighborhood disregards an important security problem: the collusion of misbehaving nodes. Colluding misbehaving nodes are able to cloak the actions of each other in order to prevent detection of misbehavior. This kind of misbehavior is more dangerous and difficult to detect and defend. To the best of our knowledge, there is no solution that handles all misbehaving nodes actions. In this paper, we propose an end-to-end method aimed at safeguarding data transmission from the node misbehavior in ad hoc networks using trust based multipath routing. Source node distributes the load in such a manner that the delay per packet or average end to end delay is lower. Reliability of data transfer is also increased without duplicating it, by selecting the trustworthy path excluding misbehaving nodes. The performance of our method is compared with a trust based DSR routing protocol and multipath protocol. We have evaluated our method at scenarios where misbehaving nodes are present, even in the form of collusion.

The rest of this paper is organized as follows. In Section 2 the related work is given, followed by a detailed description of our solution in Section 3. In Section 4 we analysis the security of our method showing how it withstands different attacks. In section 5 we evaluate the efficiency of our method through exhaustive simulation. The last section concludes the paper and gives suggestions for further work in this area.

2 Related Work

Wang et al. [4] have also proposed a Routing Algorithm based on Trust. They have assumed that the trust values of all nodes are stored at each node in advance. Trust for the route is calculated at the source node based on the weight and trust values are assigned to the nodes involved in the path at the source node. However, they have used a forward trust model to find the trust worthy path from source to destination. But, trust has asymmetric characteristic, so mutual trust information should be used.

SRP [9] manages to find multiple node-disjoint paths. It is very efficient and protects from several attacks of malicious nodes. However, the route request propagation is inherently weak to the racing phenomenon, which may prevent the discovery of existing node-disjoint paths. Thus, a malicious node may participate with fake identities to several paths, rendering the multipath routing insecure.

The secure multipath routing protocol Multipath [10] is based on the Ford- Fulkerson MaxFlow algorithm exhibits high security characteristics. It discovers all existing node disjoint paths bounded by a TTL field. However, the propagation of the route request query is not efficient in terms of computation and space costs. Furthermore, the use of digital signatures by the intermediate nodes of each route request message costs both in delay and processing power and may not be affordable for typically available equipment.

Djenouri et al. [11] propose an alternative approach for detecting forwarding misbehavior which suggests the usage of authenticated two-hop acknowledgments per message. However, this solution causes a high traffic overhead and fails to address collusion among misbehaving nodes.

SMR (Split Multi-path Routing) [12] SMR based on DSR [3] attempts to discover maximally node disjoint paths. The routes are discovered on demand in the same way as it is done with DSR. From the received RREQs, the destination then select two multiple node disjoint paths and sends a Route REPly (RREP) packet. However, no method to take care of colluding misbehaving nodes has been implemented.

In summary, these networks are considered as vulnerable if nodes are colluding in order to hide their misbehavior. All the existing methods have used cryptographic and authentication methods to mitigate the effect of attack of colluding misbehaving nodes. But key distribution is a non-trivial problem in MANETs. Nodes may join and exit a network at any point of time. Moreover, a key distribution server may not be able to communicate with all the nodes.

3   Trust Based Multipath DSR

A Trust based multi path DSR protocol [2] has been proposed which uses a multi-path forwarding approach to address the above vulnerability. Each node forwards the RREQ if it is received from different path. Through this method we detect and avoid misbehaving nodes due to vulnerability in DSR route discovery [3]. In our protocol each node broadcasts the packet embedding trust information about its immediate neighbor. At the source node, a secure route to the destination is calculated as the weighted average of the number of nodes in the route and their trust values.

However, to minimize overhead of the above protocol while ensuring good throughput, modification has been done to give an efficient Trust based Multi-path Dynamic Source Routing protocol (TMDSR) [13]. Unlike the previous protocol which is based on broadcast of RREQ and which ignore the path from the one hop neighbor of the destination, TMDSR consider such paths as RREQ packets are unicasted from one hop neighbor of destination. The source node selects the most trust worthy path from the multiple paths discovered. We have assumed that each node creates a Trust Table to store the trust value of its one-hop neighbors. The trust value of a node ranges from 0 to 1. The trust value of well behaved node is >= 0.5 and node having trust value less than 0.5 are characterized as malicious node. A Neighbor table is maintained at each node to store the one hop neighbor of destination.

3.1   Route Discovery at Source Node

The source node initiates a route discovery process by broadcasting a RREQ packet. The RREQ packet header is modified by adding a *p_trust* field. *p_trust* denotes the trust value of the path up to that node and is initialized as 0 at source node.

$$RREQ: \{IPd, IPs, Seq\,num\}\| \, p\_trust \qquad (1)$$

After broadcasting the RREQ packet, the source node sets a timer whose time period T is equal to the 1-way propagation delay and is calculated using formula given below:

$$T = 2*TR / S + C \qquad (2)$$

Where TR is maximum transmission range, S is Speed of the wireless signal, C is constant value, TR/2*S as used in our simulation. The value of timer indicates the time needed to receive a RREP packet from one hop neighbors. If the packet arrives before the timer expires, it is accepted if path length is equal to 1 else it is rejected and the neighbor table is also updated.

3.2 RREQ Processing at Intermediate Nodes

An intermediate node is not allowed to reply from its route cache. In our method, an intermediate node forwards the RREQ packet if it received from a different node and itself is not included in the source route of RREQ to avoid route loop. Each RREQ packet is modified to include the trust value of the node from which the packet is received. For example, if there are two nodes A and B in the network, when B broadcasts a RREQ packet and node A receives it, it updates the *p_trust* field as:

$$p\_trust = p\_trust + T_{AB} \tag{3}$$

where T_{AB} is the trust value that is assigned by node A to B.

3.3 RREP at Destination Node

The RREP packet header is modified by the inclusion of other two fields *p_trust* and *n_trust*. The updated RREP is:

$$RREP : \{IPs, IPd, Seq\ num\} \| \ p\_trust \ \| \ n\_trust \tag{4}$$

where *p_trust* is assigned from the RREQ packet and *n_trust* is initialized to 0. It has the same importance as *p_trust* in the RREQ packet and denotes the trust value of the path up to that node from the destination.

3.4 RREP Processing at Intermediate Nodes

When an intermediate node receives a RREP, it checks if it is the intended next recipient. If yes, it modifies *n_trust* in the same manner as *p_trust*. For example, when node X receives RREP from node Y, it updates *n_trust* as:

$$n\_trust = n\_trust + T_{XY} \tag{5}$$

3.5 Path Decision at Source Node

When the RREP packet reaches the source node, the most secure path is selected by it. It is calculates *path_trust* which is the trust value associated with the path. It is defined as weighted average of *p_trust* and *n_trust* received in the RREP packet and the number of nodes in the path as shown in equation 6, 7. The path selected is the one which has the maximum path trust.
Trust value of i_{th} path:

$$path\_trust_i = ((p\_trust + n\_trust)/2) * w_i \tag{6}$$

$$\text{where,} \ w_i = 1/n_i / \sum_{i=1}^{n} 1/n_i \tag{7}$$

$$\text{and,} \ path\_trust_{s-d} = \max(path\_trust_i) \tag{8}$$

n_i is the number of nodes in i_{th} path, n is the total number of paths from s to d, w_i is the weight assigned to the i_{th} path and *path_trust_i* is the trust value of the i_{th} path.

However, presence of colluding malicious nodes would mutually cooperate to give high trust values to each other, hence strengthening launch of black hole attacks. To eliminate the above problem, we propose E-TMDSR, which increases the reliability of data transmission and provides load balancing.

4 Extended - Trust Based Multi-path Dynamic Source Routing (E-TMDSR)

Multipath routing consists of finding multiple routes between a source and destination node. These multiple paths can be used to compensate for the dynamic and unpredictable nature of ad hoc networks. While designing a multipath routing protocol, following major fundamental issues have to be dealt with:

4.1 Discovery of Multiple Paths

To discover multiple node-disjoint paths from a source to a destination, we have modified the route discovery mechanisms of DSR protocol to discover a maximum number of node-disjointed and trust-worthy paths. We prohibit RREP from the intermediate nodes. An intermediate node forwards the RREQ if it is received from a different node and itself is not in the source route. The RREQ is forwarded in a unicast manner if the node is one hop neighbor of destination node else it is broadcasted.

4.2 Path Selection

Once all node-disjointed have been discovered, there arise other issues, like how to select a suitable path or a set of paths from all the discovered paths and what node should make this selection namely, the source or the destination. In our method that path is selected which induces minimum delay in the network and it does not include any misbehaving nodes. The selection process is carried at both source and destination.

Path selection at destination node. The destination node RREP for the first received RREQ satisfying equation 9. Thus the selected the path has minimum delay and having average node trust value as 0.5. So, this is fastest replied trust-worthy path also called as primary path. Afterwards, destination node sends the RREP for RREQ which are node disjoint from the primary path. n_i is the number of nodes in i_{th} path.

$$p\_trust / n_i >= 0.5 \tag{9}$$

Path selection at source node. When the selected RREP packet reaches the source node, the secure paths are selected. The source node computes the *path_trust* of each of RREP received it select the path which are node disjoint and having *path_trust* greater than threshold. Through exhaustive simulation we have set threshold as 0.6.

4.3 Traffic Allocation

When a path or a set of paths are selected, next we decide how to use these while sending data packets. Paths selected satisfy the reliability constraint of the network, they are selected based on the mutual trust information of the nodes involved. A source node transmits data along the primary trust-worthy path which has shortest delay. Next it distributes the load among the paths so that the delay per packet or average end to end delay is lower. *Path multiplexing* is used to distribute the load fairly and to avoid congestion at the node. Intuitively, path multiplexing distributes the forwarding overhead of communication between source and destination over the network, thus preventing concentration of the workload on a small number of nodes. This is done by multiplexing packets over a set of paths interchangeably, instead of on a single path. We use a simple multiplexing policy which switches path among the multiple paths explored by the multipath routing after p numbers of packets are sent. In our protocol we have a specific $p=5$ *value* that performs best for each routing performance metric.

4.4 Route Maintenance

If a node X realizes that an established link with a neighboring node Y is broken, then it sends a Route ERRor (RERR) packet in the upstream direction of the route. The RERR contains the route to the source, and the immediate upstream and downstream nodes of the broken link. Upon receiving this RERR packet, the source removes every entry in its route table that uses the broken link (regardless of the destination). Route rediscovery is delayed as the active session is delayed if there exist at least a valid route. When the source is informed of a route disconnection, it uses the remaining valid route to deliver data packets.

5 Security Analysis of E-TMDSR

We analyze the security of our method by evaluating its robustness in the presence of some of the attacks as described below.

5.1 Protection against Malicious Colluding Nodes

This is the basic security property that the protocol is designed for and is achieved through multipath routing. By using k node-disjoint paths of communication, an adversary should compromise at least k nodes or at least one node in each route, in order to control the communication. According to the operation mode, our method offers different levels of protection. In parallel mode, the protocol is resilient against $k - 1$ collaborating malicious nodes. In single operation mode the adversary can disrupt communication by compromising only the active path.

5.2 Black Hole and Gray Hole Attacks

This type of attack involves forging routing packets to cause all routes to go through a misbehaving node. The malicious node then drops all or some packets for the destination, thus carrying out the black hole or gray hole attack respectively. In our method, forged routing packets are detected due to mutual trust information in the route discovery packets provided by neighboring nodes. Therefore the path including such misbehaving nodes is excluded by the source node based on the *path_trust*.

5.3 Cache Poisoning

When a RREP packet from the destination node is tunneled back to the source node, through misbehaving nodes or colluding malicious nodes, a shorter path is recorded at intermediate nodes and source node, resulting in an attack called cache poisoning. But in our approach we prohibit the RREP from the intermediate node so that these nodes do not maintain a route cache. Ultimately space is saved at intermediate nodes and misbehaving nodes are not able to launch the cache poisoning attack.

6 Performance Analysis of E-TMDSR

We have used the QUALNET network simulator (version 4.5) developed by Scalable Network Technologies Inc. [14] to evaluate the effectiveness of the proposed method. Different scenarios are defined in a 1000 * 1000 m square area with 50 nodes. The source and destination nodes are randomly selected. The IEEE 802.11 Distributed Coordination Function (DCF) [15] is used as the medium access control protocol. A traffic generator was developed to simulate constant bit rate (CBR) sources. In every scenario, the nodes move in a random direction using the random waypoint model with a speed randomly chosen within the range of 0–20 m/s. The transmission range of each node is 100 m. We assume that there are 0-40% malicious nodes in the network.

6.1 Metrics

To evaluate the performance of the proposed scheme, we use the following metrics:

Route Selection Time: It is defined as the total time required for selecting a path set for routing.

Routing Packet Overhead: It is defined as the ratio between the total number of control packets generated to the total number of data packets received during the simulation time.

Average Latency: It is defined as the mean time in seconds, taken by the data packets to reach their respective destinations.

Throughput: It is the ratio of the number of data packets received by the destination node to the number of packets sent by the source node.

6.2 Discussion of Results

The results obtained from exhaustive simulation are shown as graphs in fig.1 to fig.4. These correspond to standard DSR, SMR, TMDSR and E-TMDSR.

The *route selection time* for all algorithms is presented in Fig. 1. Since DSR selects the first path it receives as the path set, the route selection time of DSR is minimum. The disjoint multi-path routing algorithm SMR [12] has to wait for at least two disjoint paths till it can select a path set. TMDSR takes the longest time in route selection as it selects the path from all the available paths. E-TMDSR has longer time than DSR, since it requires trusted path which may take a longer time to come. But in cases where all the nodes of the path received first are trusted, the route selection time of the E-TMDSR can be equal to that of a DSR. Hence, we observe that there is a compromise between security and route selection time, which is generally the case with most security algorithms. We have achieved a balance between these two concepts in order to provide maximum security level without causing a substantial delay, by choosing the first trust worthy path.

The higher packet delivery rate of the trusted protocols also lowers the *routing overhead* which is computed per received data packet. The overhead is increased in SMR and DSR with increase in misbehaving nodes as no procedure has been adopted to mitigate the effect of these nodes. In E-TMDSR, the data packets which finally do reach their intended destinations in the presence of malicious nodes have traversed the path that contains no black hole. Therefore when number of malicious nodes increases to 40% in the network, the packet delivery rate is substantially high compared to DSR and SMR as path is free from misbehaving nodes as in fig. 2. TMDSR has more overhead as a single route is used for each session, so it decreases the packet delivery rate.

However, as the trusted protocols endeavor to find the most trusted paths in the network, the selected paths may sometimes deviate considerably from the optimal paths. This increases the length of the paths, thereby increasing the latency of the network. But the *average latency* of the network is lower for the multipath protocols compared to DSR, where routing decisions are only made once. E-TMDSR has the lowest average latency as in fig. 3 because it uses multi path simultaneously and if one of route is disconnected the data is transmitted to next available route. Hence no route acquisition latency is required. As number of misbehaving nodes increases in the network it simultaneously increases the rate of route recovery due to the attack launched by misbehaving nodes. But average latency in DSR and SMR increases significantly with respect to increase in misbehaving nodes in the network. In E-TMDSR, all the paths are node disjoint so the impact of node misbehavior or link failure is limited only to specified path.

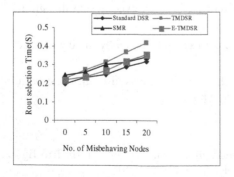

Fig. 1. Route Selection Time

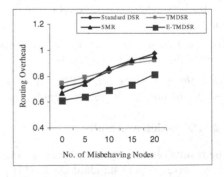

Fig. 2. Routing Overhead

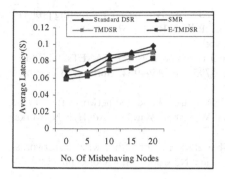

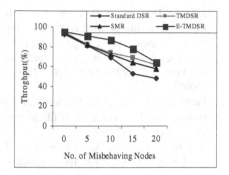

Fig. 3. Average Latency   **Fig. 4.** Throughput

When the network is free from malicious nodes the throughput of TMDSR and DSR is the same but SMR and E-TMDSR have high throughput due to multipath feature. Throughput for DSR and SMR steeply degrades with the increase in number of misbehaving nodes in the network as shown in Fig. 4. Throughput of TMDSR also decreases with the increase of malicious nodes but it is very less compared to DSR and SMR. ETMDSR makes effective use of its inherent multipath feature and selects the trustworthy path excluding misbehaving nodes, hence it is able to forward a large number of packets at all traffic loads with minimal loss as seen in fig. 4.

7   Conclusions and Future Work

In this paper, we have proposed E-TMDSR protocol for detecting and mitigating attacks by colluding misbehaving nodes in MANETs. It is an on-demand protocol that builds node disjoint and trusted paths to mitigate attack by colluding misbehaving nodes. It also avoids certain links from being congested. Providing multiple paths is useful in ad hoc networks because when one route is disconnected, the source can simply use other available routes without performing the route recovery.

Simulation results obtained from E-TMDSR are compared against the results obtained using traditional algorithms such as normal DSR, trust based DSR and multipath routing using disjoint paths. Our proposed technique proved to be much more secure. In the future, we plan to investigate and design a more efficient algorithm for increasing throughput with increase of misbehaving nodes in the network.

References

1. Kargl, F., Schlott, S., Klenk, A., Geiss, A., Weber, M.: Securing Ad hoc Routing Protocols. In: EUROMICRO 2004 (2004)
2. Poonam, G.K., Misra, M.: Trust based multi path DSR protocol. In: Proceedings of IEEE Fifth International Conference on Availability, Reliability and Security, Poland, pp. 204–209 (February 2010)

3. Johnson, D.B., Maltz, D.A., Hu, Y.C., Jetcheva, J.G.: The dynamic source routing protocol for mobile ad hoc networks (DSR). In: Internet draft IETF RFC 3561 (2003), http://www.ietf.org/rfc/rfc3561.txt

4. Wang, C., Yang, X., Gao, Y.: A Routing Protocol Based on Trust for MANETs. In: Zhuge, H., Fox, G.C. (eds.) GCC 2005. LNCS, vol. 3795, pp. 959–964. Springer, Heidelberg (2005)

5. Pirzada, A.A., Datta, A., McDonald, C.: Propagating trust in ad-hoc networks for reliable routing. In: Proceeding of IEEE International Workshop Wireless Ad Hoc Networks, Finland, pp. 58–62 (2004)

6. Pirzada, A.A., Datta, A., McDonald, C.: Trust-based routing for ad-hoc wireless networks. In: Proceeding of IEEE International Conference Networks, Singapore, pp. 326–330 (2004)

7. Papadimitratos, P., Haas, Z.: Secure routing for mobile ad hoc networks. In: Proceedings of the SCS Communication Networks and Distributed Systems Modeling and Simulation Conference (CNDS), TX, San Antonio (January 2002)

8. Burmester, M., Van Le, T.: Secure multipath communication in mobile ad hoc networks. In: Proceedings of the International Conference on Information Technology: Coding and Computing (ITCC 2004). IEEE, Las Vegas (April 2004)

9. Djenouri, D., Badache, N.: Cross-Layer Approach to Detect Data Packet Droppers in Mobile Ad-Hoc Networks. In: de Meer, H., Sterbenz, J.P.G. (eds.) IWSOS 2006. LNCS, vol. 4124, pp. 163–176. Springer, Heidelberg (2006)

10. Lee, S., Gerla, M.: Split multipath routing with maximally disjoint paths in ad hoc networks. In: Proceedings of the IEEE ICC, pp. 3201–3205 (2001)

11. Poonam, G.K., Misra, M.: Trust Enhanced Secure Multi-Path Routing Protocol for Detecting and Mitigating Misbehaving Nodes. In: Proceedings of ACM International Conference and Workshop on Emerging Trends in Technology, pp. 109–114 (2010)

12. QUALNET simulator, http://www.scalable-networks.com

13. IEEE Computer Society LAN MAN Standards Committee, Wireless LAN Medium Access Protocol (MAC) and Physical Layer (PHY) Specification, IEEE Std 802.11-1997. The Institute of Electrical and Electronics Engineers, New York, NY (1997)

A Flow Based Slow and Fast Scan Detection System

N. Muraleedharan and Arun Parmar

Centre for Development of Advanced Computing (C-DAC)
Electronics City, Bangalore, India
{murali,parmar}@ncb.ernet.in

Abstract. Attackers perform port scan to find reachability, liveness and services in a system or network. Current day scanning tools provide different scanning options and capable of evading various security tools like firewall, IDS and IPS. So in order to detect and prevent attacks in early stages, an accurate detection of scanning activity in real time is very much essential. In this paper we present a flow based protocol behavior analysis system to detect TCP based slow and fast scan. This system provides scalable, accurate and generic solution to TCP based scanning by means of automatic behavior analysis of the network traffic. Detection capability of proposed system is compared with SNORT and results proves the high detection rate of the system over SNORT.

Keywords: Scan detection, Flow, IPFIX, Anomaly, Entropy.

1 Introduction

Current day security attacks like malware, worm and botnet happens through multiple stages. In the initial stage, an attacker tries to understand the livens, reachability, services in the system and vulnerabilities in it. Once attacker identifies these details, he can accurately plan the attack and get maximum benefit out of it with less probability of attack detection. So from security perspective, it is very important to detect the scanning attempt of a system or network accurately with the identity of attacker and victim.

Since scanning is the first stage of an attack, if we can detect it properly in real time, multi stage attack prevention can be done through the scan detection. But, nowadays the sophistication of scanning tools are increasing and by using a single tool itself, an attacker can conduct different types of scanning on a network or system. Moreover, some of the scanning tools provide features for evading firewall rules or sneaking past intrusion detection or prevention systems [1].

In this paper we present a flow based port scan detection technique which provides a generic solution for different types of TCP scan and detects both slow and fast scan. Reasons for selecting TCP based scanning for our considerations are, firstly, TCP works in connection oriented mode, and therefore provides high accuracy in scan results and due to this advantage attackers prefer TCP based scanning over UDP. Secondly all scanning tools provide TCP scanning

N. Meghanathan et al. (Eds.): CNSA 2010, CCIS 89, pp. 191–200, 2010.

as a defacto scan. Thirdly, compared to UDP based scanning, number of options available with TCP scanners are more which can help to provide more information about the victim.

We are approaching port scan detection problem through transport layer protocol behavior analysis. Scanning tools make use of the RFC definition of protocol for identifying the status of the port. So a generic approach to detect scan using different protocols (TCP and UDP) may generate false alarms. This system collects flow data as input for the analysis and defines flow records using IPFIX protocol [2]. The advantage of IPFIX over other flow definitions is that, the user defined parameters can be incorporated in IPFIX flow definition.

The remainder of this paper is organized as follows. The related works are introduced in section 2. Section 3 explains the architecture and detection techniques of our system. In section 4, the experiment set-up details are described and results are explained in section 5. Result analysis are done in section 6. Section 7 concludes this paper.

2   Related Work

Researchers have proposed different techniques for detecting scan activities in a network or a system. Allman et al [3] examine scanning phenomenon in time dimension and describes a method for scan detection by means of connection and host classification. Their approach is based on the notion that connection attempts that do not result in established connection may be a possible scan. Our detection technique is also working with this concept, but parameters for detection mechanism are very much different. Moreover for scan detection, we do not do any classification based on connection or host. Jung et al [4] developed a technique known as Threshold Random Walk (TRW) based on sequential hypothesis for testing fast scan. This technique is limited to the detection of fast scan alone but our method addresses both fast and slow scan detection. A stealthy port scan detection mechanism is explained in [5] by storing the anomalous packets. This system works on packets and anomalous packets are stored for a long period for identifying slow scan, which may create processing overhead in current day high speed networks.

Recently, instead of packet based analysis, flow based security analysis and attack detection are getting attention from researchers. Quyen at al [6] explains a port scan technique by considering small volume flows. Myung-Sup Kim et al [7] also uses small sized flows for scan detection. But simply relay on small volume flows for scan detection can miss some scanning attacks if the attacker changes the size of the packets. Also some of the scanning tools provide option to change the size of scan packets. In [8] a flow based aggregation algorithm is using for identifying the distribution in the cluster. The algorithm relies on information-theoretic techniques and identifies the clusters of attack flows in real time and aggregates those large number of short attack flows into a few meta flows. Another work based on flow monitoring is explained in [9] which works on monitoring the four predefined metrics that capture the flow statistic of the network. This method is capable to detect UDP flood, ICMP flood and scanning, by using Holt-Winters Forecasting technique. This technique make projection about future performance based on historical and current data of the network. The prediction which come out by this technique may arise false alarms because network behavior is not static. Myung et al [10] suggests that by aggregating packets of the identical flow, one can identify the abnormal traffic pattern that appear during attack. They formalize detection function for attack detection, which are composed of several traffic parameters and constant values. Our system computes threshold by providing weight after considering the deviation in the values of parameters because of which results will be more accurate. Entropy estimation is a general technique but recently, the use of entropy has received a lot of attention and is suggested for fine-grained detection of abnormal behavior [11,12,13]. Our work is also uses entropy based detection techniques for slow scan. For detecting network scan researchers use probabilistic approaches [14]. However, Attackers can reduce the likelihood of detection by spreading the scan for long period.

3   Proposed System

3.1   Architecture

As a generic anomaly detection system, this system is also works in a profile and detection mode. In profile time, the system identifies the normalcy of the traffic and derives a base line (threshold) for normalcy. In detection time, system calculates threshold using real time data and compare the calculated threshold with profile time threshold. Figure 1 illustrates the scan detection system architecture. Detailed description of each component is explained below.

Input : Network traffic flow plays an important role in network monitoring and security, both for anomaly detection and corresponding defense. Flow can be defined as uni-directional sequence of packets from source to destination for a particular time duration with same protocol and port number[15]. Compared to packet based analysis, flow data have the advantage of less volume. So from performance perspective, flow data can provide faster responses and real time analysis is also possible through flow data.We uses flow data as the input of this system and to export the flow data from flow probe to collector IPFIX protocol is used. Since this system addresses only TCP based scan detection, from the received flow data, using protocol field, it filters out TCP flows. Due to the uni-directional property of flow, for every TCP connection two flows available, one from sender to receiver and another from receiver to sender.

Fig. 1. Architecture Diagram

Profiler : Traffic profiler collects the flow data and identify the normal traffic patterns of the traffic. In the initial stage, system will be in profile mode, and after the profile interval (γ) the system moves into detection mode. The profile period duration should be long enough to capture the entire network traffic behavior in a network. Profile interval is sub divided into profile periods (δ). In each profile period, the system calculates the threshold values and at the end of profile interval, average of profile period threshold are calculated and fix the final threshold. The profiler component have two subsections in it, Short Term Profiler (STP) and Long Term Profiler (LTP).

Short Term Profiler (STP). Fast scan attacks last for a short period of time and it makes deviation in the normal traffic pattern. STP profiles these traffic behavior to detect fast scan activities in a network or host. STP works with flow duration, number of packets in a flow, average packet size, number of flows and count of single packet flows to fix baseline (T2) for fast scan. Short term profiler uses a time based profile technique to fix the threshold values for fast scan.

Long Term Profiler (LTP). Since the slow scan attacks last for long duration, to detect it accurately a long term traffic profiling is required. To identify the slow scan activities, LTP uses a count based profile technique. Independent of time, LTP waits for 'n' flows and if it receives 'n' flows then checks for slow scan activities in those data set.The reason to selects count based profile for long term profiler is that, firstly, network traffic is dynamic in nature. So if we set a fixed time interval for long term profiler, with in that time period, traffic behavior can be different. Secondly, since we uses an entropy based method for detecting slow scan activities, if the number of record is fixed in the data set maximum entropy value also be same for all data set. Thirdly, long term profiler stores data for a long period to find the behavior changes. So if it is a time based profile, due to the dynamic nature of network traffic, number of data records are different. Hence, required storage space is also variable. LTP takes source IP, destination IP, source port, destination port and packet size as parameters and applies an entropy based method for setting the baseline (T1) for slow scan. In our system, during detection time, STP check for fast scan and if it is not finds any scan activities then only LTP considers those data set for updation.

Anomaly Detector: Once the profile interval is over, system moves into the detection mode. In detection mode, for every δ time, using current traffic, system calculates the threshold values and compares it with profile time threshold. If the threshold value changes with profile threshold, anomaly detector analyzes the data and identifies the scanning activities. As mentioned in the profiler, anomaly detector is categorized in to two types. Short Term Anomaly Detector (STAD) and Long Term Anomaly Detector (LTAD). STAD process the data and after every δ time it will check for fast scan activities. LTAD detects slow scan activities by means of higher δ value and related parameters.

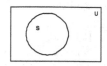

Fig. 2. Single Packet Flow Vs Scan Flow

3.2 Detection Methods

TCP protocol uses three-way handshake procedure to establish a connection [16]. Since data transfer can be possible only through the established connection, for any successful TCP communication need to have more than three packets. But in the scanning time, an attacker's intention is only to verify status of the port, most of the connection will terminate before the completion of three way handshake process [17]. Moreover, if three-way handshake does not happen, connection details cannot be identified by log analysis.

Due to the unidirectional property of the flow, every connection will create two flows and each flow will contains at least one packet in the connection establishment process itself. After the connection establishment, data transfer and/or connection release has to be done. So the total number of packets in a proper TCP flow will be more than one. But in scanning time, since proper handshake process is not done, each flow will have single packets only ie, for every scanning attempt it will create two flows with single packets. Single packet TCP flow can be generated due to different other reasons like inactive time of the flow and TCP keepalive feature [18]. Figure 2 represents these options. U is the universal set of single packet flows and S is the scan flows and $S \leq U$. In scanning time number of S will be high and $S \approx U$.

Fast Scan Detection: In our previous work, [19], we consider single packet flow as the main parameter for scan detection, because at the time of scanning single packet flow rate will be high. Since scan tools knock more ports on a system or more number of machines in a network, the number of flow increases in scan time. Other than these two parameters, we consider average packet size, average number of packets in a flow and average flow duration for scan detection. Due to the dynamic nature of network traffic, the number of flows can vary from time to time. So if we are considering the number of flow as a parameter for setting a common threshold for different time periods, it can lead to false positives. To avoid the possibilities of these false alarms we are considering a threshold setting method which is independent on the number of flows. In our approach we are considering the percentage of single packet flows in total flows.

The behavioral changes of different parameters on scan time and the impact on those in the detection is depicted in Table1. For setting the threshold, we calculates the corresponding deviations in the parameters values. To reduce the possibility of occurrence of false alarm, we are providing different weight to parameters. During scan time, the percentage of single packet flow is very high compared to normal traffic, we have assigned 60 percentage weight to that parameter. Weight distribution between other parameters are, 15 for average packet

Table 1. Fast scan detection parameters

Parameter	Behavior		Mean	Std	Weight	Total
	Normal	Scan time				
Percentage of Single packet flow	low	high	$\mu1$	$\sigma1$	w1=.60	T1
Average packet size	high	low	$\mu2$	$\sigma2$	w2=.15	T2
Average no of packets in a flow	high	low	$\mu3$	$\sigma3$	w3=.15	T3
Average flow Duration	high	low	$\mu4$	$\sigma4$	w4=.10	T4

size, 15 for average number of packets in a flow and 10 for flow duration. Based on profile period data, the system learns the network behavior and keeps track of the required parameters for setting the threshold. The formula for setting threshold for fast scan detection is given as

$$
\begin{aligned}
AVG &= \sum_{i=1}^{4} \mu i \\
STD &= \sum_{i=1}^{4} \sigma i \\
Ci &= \frac{\mu i + \sigma i}{AVG + STD} \\
Ti &= Ci \times Wi \\
Threshold &= T2 + T3 + T4 - T1
\end{aligned}
\tag{1}
$$

In detection time, the system calculates thresholds using current time flow data set. Equation 2 describes the steps to calculate the threshold values at detection time.

$$
\begin{aligned}
AVG &= \sum_{i=1}^{4} \mu i \\
Ci &= \frac{\mu i}{AVG} \\
Ti &= Ci \times Wi \\
Threshold &= T2 + T3 + T4 - T1
\end{aligned}
\tag{2}
$$

In scan traffic, the calculated threshold value will be less than the profile threshold because of the increase of single packet flow ratio (T1) will reduce the thresholds value. In normal traffic the detection time threshold will be greater than the profile threshold.

Slow Scan Detection. Long Term Profiler (LTP) identifies and stores all single packet flows for a profile period. Since the profile period value of LTP is more, it has a long term details of single packet flows. Since scan flow also have single packet in it, through single packet flow profiling, we can collect the scan traffic and number of single packet flows are comparatively very less in entire traffic flow. Hence it requires less storage space and less processing power. Another feature of this system is that once the fast scan detector detects scanning using Short Term Profiler (STP), flow records in that profile period will not be updated by Long Term Profiler. This can be done because the duration of the profile period of STP is less than that of LTP.

We are using entropy based detection techniques for identifying slow scan activities. In information theory, entropy is a measure of the uncertainty associated with a random variable and entropy of a random variable X is defined as $H(X) = -\sum_{i=1}^{N} p(x_i) \log_2(p(x_i))$ where $p(x_i)$ is the probability that X takes the value i. For standardizing the value of entropy between 0 and 1, we have taken normalized entropy using $\frac{H}{\log(N_0)}$ where N_0 is the number of distinct x_i values present in the data set. To detect slow scan activities, we extract source address, destination address, source port, destination port and flow size from the single packet flow data set. After that we calculate the entropy values of those parameters.

4 Experiments

4.1 Test Set-Up

For this experiment, we collected data from a live network which have around 250 machines with different operating systems and application. This network is connected through a 2 Mbps link and Internet is accessed through a proxy machine. We have collected flow data from a gateway machine which is connected to the mirrored port of the switch. So all incoming, outgoing and internal traffic can be accessed by the probe for flow creation. Once the probe creates flow, it export flow record's into a collector machine. Collector machine keep track of flow data and analyze it for scanning activity. Proposed system and Snort [20] intrusion detection system are deployed in the port mirrored switch through a hub. So both the systems can access the same traffic which include incoming, outgoing and internal traffic. The 'sfportscan' preprocessor of snort is enabled and configured to detect the scan activities.

We have identified two machine inside our network, one to initiate scan and other as victim of the scan. Time synchronization of the attacker machine and flow analyzer is done through the 'ntp' service. Using 'nmap' tool, we have done different TCP based scanning from attacker machine to victim machine. Once the flow analyzer detects the scanning, it generates an alert and after verification of the scanning activity, we calculates the detection delay. Similarly, we verified the scan detection capability of Snort using the generated alerts.

5 Result

To test detection capabilities of the system, we have configured profile interval of STP as one day and profile period as 10 seconds. Flow probe exports flow records for every 10 seconds and flow analyzer checks for scan activity. Table 2 shows the summary of fast scan results. Using nmap tool, 13 different types of scan activities have done in a victim machine from the attacker machine and detection delay is calculated as the difference between detection time and start time of the scan. We configured the profile interval for slow scan profiler (LTP) for one day. Instead of setting profile period based on time, we have taken 20000 single packet flow records for a single profile period. In profile time, LTP collects a group of 20000 records and calculate the entropy values for source IP, Destination IP, source port, destination port and packet size. Using slow scan option (-T sneak) in 'nmap' we conducts a slow scan and collects those scan data details form LTP. nmap sneak scan has taken 27529.794 seconds (7.64 Hours) to complete the scan in a single host. We have calculated the entropy values of the parameters from 20000 records of those scan data.

Table 2. Fast scan detection Result

No	Scan Type	Scan Duration(sec)	Detection Delay(sec)	
			Proposed System	Snort
1	SYN	3.908	44	1
2	Connect	3.670	48	1
3	ACK	1.919	48	Not Detected
4	NULL	2.038	46	Not Detected
5	FIN	2.167	40	Not Detected
6	XMAS	1.979	50	Not Detected
7	OS finger printing	5.849	48	1
8	Maimon	2.138	50	Not Detected
9	Window	1.966	45	Not Detected
10	Fast Scan	2.343	45	1
11	Datalength	6.000	44	Not Detected
12	Version Detection	109.642	49	1
13	Polite scan	670.304	50	Not Detected

6   Result Analysis

6.1   Fast Scan Detection

From table 2, it is clear that the system capable to detects conventional TCP based scan like SYN, Connect and ACK scan. Another feature of this system is that, it detects stealthy scans like NULL, FIN and XMAS accurately even though those scans are capable to sneak through certain non-stateful firewalls and packet filtering routers. Since we are not depend on the packet size for scan detection, our system can detects scan using nonstandard size TCP packets , those are capable to evade security systems like firewall and IDS, like '–data_length' option in nmap scan. 'nmap' tools provides a fine-grained timing control for scanning under the '-T' option. Polite scan is one scan available in that category which waits for 0.4 seconds between scan probes moreover, it is slower than default nmap scan. The results reveals that the proposed system has the capability to detect different types of scan over snort. Out of conducted 13 different scan, snort detects only 5 of them (detection rate 38.46). Compared to Snort, the proposed system have an advantage on stealth scan like XMAS, NULL, FIN. Scan using ACK flags in TCP header can be generally detected using state-full mechanism but proposed system is able to detect ACK scan.

6.2   Slow Scan Detection

Table 3 summarizes the impact of scan in entropy values to different parameters. Column 2 indicates the average standard entropy values of different parameters in normal traffic and column 3 shows the standard deviation. Fourth column shows the entropy values at scan time and last column indicates the difference in entropy values in normal and scan time. In scan time, by default, nmap uses

Table 3. Slow scan detection Result

Parameter	Normal Traffic entropy		Scan Traffic	Difference
	Average	Std		
Source IP	0.27480	0.01370	0.27012	-0.00468
Source Port	0.81019	0.00761	0.73403	-0.07616
Destination IP	0.39932	0.02310	0.23494	-0.16438
Destination Port	0.32155	0.03148	0.41293	0.09138
Packet Size	0.12361	0.01043	0.05446	-0.06914

same source port to send different packets. Since most of the flows have same source port, the entropy value of those parameter is less than that of normal traffic. During vertical scan, all the scan traffic goes in to same destination. So the entropy value of destination IP at vertical scan time should be less than normal traffic entropy value. Since we have done a vertical scan, scan traffic entropy value of destination IP is less.

In vertical scan, attacker probes different ports of same machine and it creates different flows with different destination port. So the entropy value of destination port is high in scan time. In normal data set, the entropy values of packet size is almost similar and it is more than 0.1. But in scan time, it is reduced in to 0.05446. Scan tools uses same sized packets for probing different port, hence it reduces the entropy value of packet size during scan time. Since we have done the scan from same machine, minor change in source IP is visible in the scan data. If it is a distributed scan, the source IP entropy also indicates the difference. Similarly, in horizontal scan, if attacker targets a specific service on the network, destination port entropy value will be less and destination IP entropy value will be more. From this result, we can conclude that, even in slow scan there are changes in the entropy values of destination port, packet size, destination IP and source port. By means of a proper profiling and threshold setting, we can identify the slow scan activities.

7 Conclusion

In this paper, we have presented a system for detecting TCP based scan activities using IPFIX flow. This system provides a generic, scalable and accurate method to detect TCP based fast and slow scan.Since the scanning behavior are different for slow and fast scan, we have selected different methods and parameter for detecting slow and fast scan. Using the properties of flow definition, we have developed a method for identifying fast scan, and uses entropy based approach to detect slow scan activity.

The experimental results shows that the system effectively detects different types of fast scan. Regarding slow scan, the system takes minimal storage and resources for detection and detects scan even the scan activity last for very long period.

References

1. Firewall/IDS Evasion and Spoofing, Nmap Reference Guide,
   http://nmap.org/book/man-bypass-firewalls-ids.html
2. RFC 5101, Specification of the IP Flow Information Export (IPFIX) Protocol for the Exchange of IP Traffic Flow Information
3. Allman, M., Paxson, V., Terrel, J.: A Brief History of Scanning. In: IMC 2007 Proceedings of the 7th ACM SIGCOMM Conference on Internet Measurement. ACM, New York (2007)
4. Jung, J., Paxson, V., Berger, A.W., Balakrishnan, H.: Fast Port scan detection using sequential hypothesis testing. In: Proceedings of the IEEE Symposium on Seurity Privacy (May 2004)
5. Staniford, S., Hoagland, J.A., McAlerney, J.M.: Practical automated detection of stealthy portscans. Journel of Computer Security 10 (2002)
6. Quyen, L.T., Zhanikeev, M., Tanaka, Y.: Anomaly identification based on flow analysis. In: 2006 IEEE Region 10 Conference on TENCON 2006 (November 2006)
7. Kim, M.-S., Kong, H.-J., Hong, S.-C., Chung, S.-H., Hong, J.W.: A flow-based method for abnormal network traffic detection. In: Network Operations and Management Symposium, NOMS 2004 (2004)
8. Hu, Y., Chiu, D.-M., Lui, J.C.S.: Entropy Based Adaptive Flow Aggregation. In: IEEE/ACM (December 2007)
9. Nguyen, H.A., Van Nguyen, T., Kim, D.I., Choi, D.: Network traffic anomalies detection and identification with flow monitoring. In: WCON 2008 (May 2008)
10. Kim, M.-S., Kang, H.-J., Hong, S.-C., Chung, S.-H., Hong, J.W.: A Flow-based Method for Abnormal Network Traffic Detection. In: IEEE/IFIP Network Operations and Management Symposium (2004)
11. Gu, Y., McCallum, A., Towsley, D.: Detecting anomalies in network traffic using maximum entropy estimation. In: Proc. IM 2005 (2005)
12. Nychis, G., Sekar, V., Andersen, D.G., Kim, H., Zhang, H.: An empirical evaluation of entropy-based traffic anomaly detection. In: 8th ACM SIGCOMM Conference on Internet (2008)
13. Wagner, A., Plattner, B.: Entropy based worm and anomaly detection in fast IP networks. In: 14th IEEE International Workshops on Enabling Technologies 2005 (2005)
14. Leckie, C., Kotiagiri, R.: A probabilistic approach to detecting network scans. In: 2002 IEEE/IFIP Network Operations and Management Symposium (2002)
15. Introduction to cisco IOS netflow - a technical overview,
    http://www.cisco.com/en/US/prod/collateral/iosswrel/ps6537/ps6555/ps6601/prod_white_paper0900aecd80406232.html
16. RFC793 - Transmission Control Protocol (September 1981)
17. de Vivo, M., Carrasco, E., Isern, G., de Vivo, G.O.: A review of port scanning techniques. ACM SIGCOMM Computer Communication Review (April 1999)
18. RFC1122 - Requirements for Internet Hosts – Communication Layers (October 1989)
19. Muraleedharan, N.: Analysis of TCP Flow data for Traffic Anomaly and Scan Detection. In: 16th IEEE International Conference on Networks (2008)
20. Snort Manual, http://www.snort.org
21. nmap Reference guide, http://nmap.org/book/man.html

A New Remote Mutual Authentication Scheme for WI-FI Enabledhand-Held Devices

Amutha Prabakar Muniyandi[1,*], Rajaram Ramasmy[1,**], and Indurani[2,***]

[1] Thiagarajar College of Engineering, Madurai, Tamil Nadu, India
[2] Alagapa University, Karaikudi, Tamil Nadu, India
ap_sse@tce.edu, rrajaram@tce.edu

Abstract. User authentication is a continual problem, particularly with mobile and handheld devices such as Personal Digital Assistants (PDAs), Smartcard, Laptops. User authentication is a difficult for every system providing safe access to precious, private information, or personalized services. User authentication is the primary line of defence for a handheld device that comes into the hands of an unauthorized individual. Password or Personal Identification Number (PIN) based authentication is the leading mechanism for verifying the identity of actual device users. Remote mutual authentication is the best solution for remote accessing in Wi-Fi environment. In this paper we propose a new remote mutual authentication scheme in wireless environment without maintaining the password table. This is based on ElGamal's. It provides high security and mutual authentication at a reasonable computational cost. Furthermore it restricts most of the current attacking mechanisms. It is simple and can be adopted in any kind of lightweight devices.

Keywords: Authentication, ElGamal, Wi-Fi devices, smartcard, mobile devices.

---

* He received the B. E. degree in Computer Science and Engineering, in 2003; the M. E. in Computer Science and Engineering, in 2005. He had worked as a lecturer in the department of Computer Science and Engineering, R. V. S. College of Engineering and Technology, India from 2004-2007. Now he is doing his Research in the area of cryptography and security under anna university - coimbatore. He worked as a Research Associate in Smart and Secure Environment Lab under IIT, Madras. Now he is working as a lecturer in department of Information Technology, Thiagarajar College of Engineering, Madurai. His current research interests include Cryptography and Security.

** He is working as Dean of CSE/IT in Thiagarajar College of Engineering, has BE degree in Electrical and Electronics Engineering from Madras University in 1966. He secured the M Tech degree in Electrical Power Systems Engineering in 1971 from IIT Kharagpur, and the Ph.D. degree on Energy Optimization from Madurai Kamaraj University in 1979. He and his research scholars have published/presented more that 45 research papers in Journals and Conferences.

*** She is working as a research associate in SSE project Alagapa university campus. She is doing her PhD in network security.

N. Meghanathan et al. (Eds.): CNSA 2010, CCIS 89, pp. 201–213, 2010.
© Springer-Verlag Berlin Heidelberg 2010

1 Introduction

The fundamentals of data networking and telecommunication are being changed and integrated networks are becoming a reality owing to the wireless communication revolution. Personal communications networks, wireless LAN's, mobile radio networks and cellular systems, harbour the promise of fully distributed mobile computing and communications, anytime, anywhere by freeing the user from the cord.

In wireless networking, we have several security issues. The communication channel employed in wireless environment is air which provides plenty of possibilities for information snoop from nodes by un-authorized user that are pretending as the valid one, thus being the reason for the several security issues. Hence, to have reliable proper security over the wireless environment it is necessary to provide certain security measures, e.g., authenticity

Authentication is a process whereby a verifier is assured of the identity of a prover involved in a protocol, and that the prover has actually participated. All security access methods are based on three fundamental pieces of information: who you are, what you have, and what you know. For proving who they are, users can provide their name, email address, or a user ID. For proving what they have, users can produce service cards (i.e., ATM cards), physical keys, digital certificates, smart cards, or one-time login cards such as the Secure ID card. For proving what they know, users can provide a password or pass phrase, or a personal identification number (PIN). This information is essentially a secret that is shared between the user and the system.

Password authentication is the foremost mechanism for verifying the identity of computer users. In the existing traditional setup the ID and PW are maintained by the remote system in a verification table. If a user wants to log in a remote server, he has to submit his ID and PW to the server. The remote server receives the login message and checks the eligibility of the user by referencing the password or verification table. If the submitted ID and PW match the corresponding pair stored in the server's verification table, the user will be granted access to the server.

A remote password authentication scheme is used to authenticate the legitimacy of the remote user over an insecure channel. In such a scheme, the password is often regarded as a secret shared between the authentication server (AS) and the user, and serves to authenticate the identity of the individual login. Through knowledge of the password, the remote user can create a valid login message to the authentication server. AS checks the validity of the login message and provides the access right.

1.1 Problems in the Traditional Method

Two problems are found in this existing traditional mechanism.

    1. The administrator of the server will come to know the password, because the server maintains the password table.

    2. An intruder can impersonate a legal user by stealing the user's ID and PW from the password table.

To add to the woes, the current Internet is vulnerable to various attacks such as denial of service attack, forgery attack, forward secrecy attack, server spoofing attack, parallel session attack, guessing attack, replay attack, and stolen verifier attack. In this paper we propose a new remote mutual authentication scheme without password table, which circumvents most of these attacks. In the proposed method the remote system does not maintain the password able, but instead maintains the one-time registration date and time of the users. In this paper, we propose an improved remote user authentication scheme based on ElGamal. We have incorporated mutual authentication, which enhances the security mechanism further. Our proposed scheme resists most of the attacking mechanisms.

2 Related Work

In 1981 Lamport proposed a remote password authentication scheme using a password table to achieve user authentication. The Lamport scheme is not secure, due to some vulnerability. Since smartcards is the device which requires more security, we had chosen the algorithms existing in the smartcard as the base and proposed our algorithms.

A remote user authentication scheme using smart cards was proposed by Hwang–Li [7]. Hwang–Li's scheme is based on the ElGamal's [2] public key scheme. This scheme can withstand the replaying attack by including time stamp in the login message. Moreover, the remote system does not need to store a password table for verifying the legitimacy of the login users. The system only needs to maintain a secret key, which is used to compute user passwords, based on user submitted identities in the authentication phase. As the security of the scheme relies on the difficulty of computing discrete logarithms over finite fields, it is difficult for the users to compute the secret key of the system from known information. This scheme is breakable only by one of its legitimate users. A legitimate user can impersonate other legal users by constructing valid pairs of user identities without knowing the secure key of the system. Later, Shen [15] analyzed impersonation attack of Chan [8] on

Hwang Li's [7] scheme, and suggested methods to repulse it.

Awasthi–Lal [14] presented a remote user authentication scheme using smartcards with forward security. Forward security ensures that the previously generated passwords in the system are secure even if the system's secret key is compromised. Yoon et al. [23] citing Awasthi Lal [14] proposed a hash based authentication scheme based on the work of Chien et al.[13]. In the authentication phase, the system cannot validate the login request message to compute the password of the user.

Yoon et al. [23] presents an enhancement to resolve the problems in the abovementioned scheme based on hash function. This scheme enables users to change their passwords freely and securely without the help of a remote server. It also provides secure mutual authentication In 2004 Kumar [21] proposed a scheme, which is secure against forgery. To obtain this security, this scheme suggests some modification in login and authentication phases. This scheme is the modified form of the Hwang et al. [15] scheme and uses one more function CK to generate the check digit of Kumar [21] for each registered identity. In this scheme, only the AS can generate a valid identity and the corresponding check digit. Ku et al. [19] proposed an improvement to prevent the reflection attack mentioned by Mitchell [3] and an insider attack discussed by Ku et al. [16]. In addition, they showed that Chien [13] scheme is vulnerable and can be compromised. Furthermore, Ku et al. [19] proposed an improvement to Chien [13].

3 Authentication

Security of user authentication associated issues comes into view over the use of mobile and handheld devices; handheld devices progressively build up sensitive information and over time gain access to wireless services and organizational intranets. The wired and the wireless network community are affected by one of the major security issues, Authentication. Therefore, it is necessary to attain authenticity which is an essential prerequisite achieved by employing cryptographic systems in most applications where security matters. Authentication is utilized as an initial process to authorize a mobile terminal for communication through secret credentials so as to provide security services in wireless networks.

Authentication can be defined as the act of establishing or confirming something (or someone) as authentic, that is that claims made by or about the thing are true.

A claimed identity is verified in this process i.e., someone (user, machine, etc.) is verified whether they are really the one who he/she/it claims to be.

3.1 Authentication Factors

Strong user authentication is the term used occasionally to describe any authentication process that increases the probability of the correct verification of the identity of base station. Long complicated passwords or combination of two or more authentication factors are used to accomplish it.

In general, three authentication factors are distinguished as

1 Knowledge factor – the user has to present the information known by him/her, i.e., some secret information such as, a password, PIN.
2 Possession factor –the user has to present something possessed by him/her, i.e., some physical object for instance- tokens or keys.
3 Being factor – In contrast to the former two factors, the user has to present something that is a part of him/her, for example- physical parameters. i.e., some biometric data e.g., fingerprint, iris pattern

The classification of the numerous authentication mechanisms and protocols that exist into two large groups, or patterns: Direct Authentication and Indirect Authentication are useful.

In direct authentication, pre-shared symmetric or asymmetric keys are utilized by the two parties for verifying each other and the flow of data between them. Whereas, a trusted third party, i.e. a Certification Authority, is made responsible for certifying one party to another party in the indirect authentication . As the node and the Main server, both are not familiar to each other, we are proposing Indirect Authentication in our protocol. Succinctly, indirect authentication is suitable for this kind of situation.

3.2 Indirect Authentication

In both wired and wireless network, indirect authentication is the most widely used protocols. Indirect authentication means that entities use intermediary entities to authenticate each other. A trust third party is involved in the indirect authentication protocol. Certification of the two communication parties is the responsibility of this third party such as certification Authority. In indirect authentication, authentication server is commonly used to perform the authentication.

There are two authentication procedures in indirect authentication. When the user logs into his wireless device (such as mobile phones) it is the first phase. The authentication of the wireless device itself by the services is included in the second phase. As user interaction is not necessary, this method of authentication to the services is more flexible.

4 Proposed Authentication Scheme

In this paper, we propose a new remote mutual authentication scheme for handheld. Our proposed scheme is composed by an initial phase, a registration phase, a login phase and an authentication phase. Whenever a new user registers through the registration phase, the server issues the username and password, which holds the related information, and sends it through the secure channel. To access the remote server, user provides his username and password. The server authenticates the user in the authentication phase.

4.1 Initial Phase

The Authentication Server (AS) generates the following parameters

p : a large prime number

$f(.)$: A one–way function

X_s : the secret key of the system, maintained by the server

T_R : Registration Timestamp of every user, maintained by the server in an encrypted form, using the server's secret key.

4.2 Registration Phase

A user U_i who wants to register to access the server services, submits its ID_i to the AS. AS computes PW_i as

$$PW_i = (ID_i \oplus T_R)^{X_s} \bmod p$$

Here T_R is the one–time registration time and date of the user U_i as got from the system clock and maintained by the server. Registration centre issues a password PW_i.

4.3 Login Phase

User U_i enters the ID_i and PW_i. The client will perform the following operation.

Step 1.   Generate a random number r.

Step 2.   Compute $C_1 = PW_i^r \bmod p$.

Step 3.   Compute $t = f(T \oplus PW_i) \bmod (p-1)$ where T is the current date and time of client.

Step 4.   Compute $M = PW_i^t \bmod p$.

Step 5.   Compute $C_2 = M \times (C_1^t) \bmod p$.

Step 6.   Sends a login request $C = (ID_i, C_1, C_2, T)$ to the remote

system

(Authentication Server AS).

4.4 Authentication Phase

Assume AS receives the message C at time T_c, where T_c is the current date and time
of the AS. Then AS takes the following actions,

Step 1.   Check the format of ID_i. If the identity format is correct, then
AS will accept the login request. Otherwise, the request will
be rejected.

Step 2.   Check the validity of the time interval between T and T_c.

Step 3.   Check   whether   the   following   equation,
$C_2 (C_1)^{t-1} = (PW_i)^{f(T \oplus PW_i)} \bmod p$ is satisfied. It is
difficult for user U_i to compute the secret key X_s and find
the registration time T_R of the system from the equation,

$$PW_i = (ID_i \oplus T_R)^{X_s} \bmod p.$$

Step 4.   Now mutual authentication message is composed as follows

$$t = f(T_s \oplus PW_i)$$
$$S = f(PW_i \oplus T_s \oplus r)$$
$$C_3 = t \oplus r$$
$$C_4 = t \oplus S$$

Here r is the
random number.

Step 5.   User U_i receives the mutual authentication message
(C_3, C_4, T_s) and checks the validity of the message.

$$t^* = f(T_s \oplus PW_i)$$
$$r = t \oplus C_3^*$$
$$S^* = t \oplus C_4^*$$
$$S^{**} = f(PW_i \oplus T_s \oplus r)$$

If S^* and S^{**} is equal then accepts, otherwise rejects and generates a
new login request.

5   Security Analysis of Our Scheme

In this section we discuss the enhanced security features of the proposed scheme. Our proposed scheme withstands most of the attacking methods.

5.1   Denial of Service Attack

In our proposed scheme, the login request is generated based on a password and the current time. The login request generation does not depend on any previous information: every time it is a new one with current time. The attacker cannot create or update the false information to login.

5.2   Forgery Attack

The attacker cannot create a valid password without knowing the registration time T_R and the secret key of server X_s. So the attacker cannot create a valid login request and act as a legal user.

5.3   Password Guessing Attack

In our scheme, the password is computed as follows $PW_i = (ID_i \oplus T_R)^{X_s} \bmod p$ suppose an adversary intercepts the login request $C = (ID_i, C_1, C_2, T)$ of a user U_i. It is not possible to recover the original password from the login request message. The T_R value is unique and X_s is the secret key of the remote system.

5.4   Parallel Session Attack

Suppose an adversary intercepts the login message $C = (ID_i, C_1, C_2, T)$, the adversary cannot create a valid new login message. Here C_1 and C_2 values are fresh for every time. The adversary cannot find the value of r and $t = (T \oplus PW_i)$.

5.5   Mutual Authentication

The user U_i wants to log on to the remote system AS and sends a login request to AS. Suppose an adversary intercepts the login request and attempts to impersonate as remote system AS. The adversary cannot calculate the valid S^* without knowing the value PW_i, and cannot get the PW_i value from the login message. The adversary again fails to impersonate the remote system AS.

6   Security Analysis

Table 1 shows the security requirements of the related schemes. Hwang's, Awasthi–Lal scheme are based on the public key ElGamal scheme.

Table 1. Security Comparison

Schemes	S1	S2	S3	S4	S5	S6	S7	S8
Hwang–Li [7]	Y	N	N	N	Y	Y	Y	Y
Awasthi [14]	Y	Y	Y	N	Y	Y	Y	Y
Our Scheme	Y	Y	Y	Y	Y	Y	Y	Y

In this table we consider all the attacks identified and defined by Tsai–Lee–Hwang [22]. They are the ones described below. In the table, Y stands for achieved and N for non–achieved.

S1 – Denial of Service Attacks: An attacker can update false verification information of a legal user for the next login phase. Afterwards, the legal user will not be able to login successfully anymore

S2 – Forgery Attacks (Impersonation Attacks): An attacker attempts to modify intercepted communications to masquerade the legal user and log in the system

S3 – Forward Secrecy: It ensures that the previously generated passwords in the system are secure even if the system's secret key has been revealed in public by accident or has been stolen

S4 – Mutual Authentication: The user and the server can authenticate each other. Not only can the server verify the legal users, but the users can also verify the legal server. Mutual authentication can help withstand the server spoofing attack where an attacker pretends to be the server to manipulate sensitive data of the legal users

S5 – Parallel Session Attack: Without knowing a user's password, an attacker can masquerade as the legal user by creating a valid login message out of some eavesdropped communication between the user and the server

S6 – Password Guessing Attack (Offline dictionary attack): Most passwords have such low entropy that the system is vulnerable to password guessing attacks, where an attacker intercepts authentication messages, stores them locally and then attempts to use a guessed password to verify the correctness of his/her guess using these authentication messages

S7 – Replay Attacks: Having intercepted previous communications, an attacker can impersonate the legal user to log in the system. The attacker can replay the intercepted messages.

S8 – Stolen–Verifier Attacks: An attacker who steals the password–verifier (e.g., hashed passwords) from the server can use the stolen–verifier to impersonate a legal user to log in the system

7 Implementation Results and Discussions

Table 2. Cost comparison between Our Scheme and Related Schemes

Scheme	Registration Phase	Login Phase	Authentication Phase
Our Scheme	1 *Dis–Log*	1 *Hash* + 2 *Dis-log*	2 *Hash* + 3 *Dis-log*
Hwang–Li's [7]	1 *Dis–Log*	1 *Hash* + 2 *Dis-log*	1 *Hash* + 2 *Dis-log*
Awasthi [14]	1 *Dis–Log*	1 *Hash* + 2 *Dis-log*	1 *Hash* + 2 *Dis-log*

Dis–log–discrete logarithm and *Hash*–hash function.

In this section, we present a comparison between our scheme and two other schemes. All the 3 schemes are based on ElGamal's, but only proposed scheme facilitates mutual authentication. Obviously due to inclusion of mutual authentication, our scheme entails a higher computational cost. The table 2 illustrates the complexity of proposed scheme with related schemes.

7.1 Experimental Setup

The setup for the experiment is as shown in figure 9. The server used was an IBM compatible PC with Intel P4 processor. The server had Windows XP professional installed on it. The server is connected to the access point with 100 Mbps Ethernet link. The access point used for the experiments is wireless module. The wireless devices considered in the experiment are laptop, Pocket PC and Handheld PC. The Transmission of data is from the wireless devices to the server through the wireless link using TCP/IP protocol.

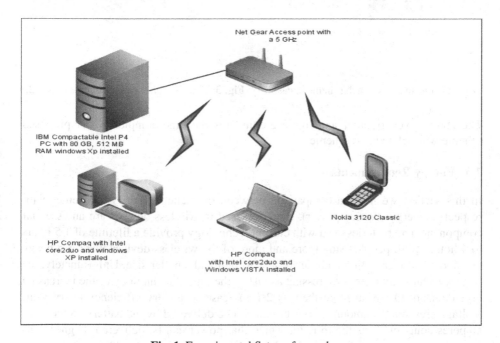

Fig. 1. Experimental Setup of our scheme

7.2 Time Complexity

In this section we make a comparison between our scheme and two schemes with respect to time taken. In this the time taken to execute each scheme is calculated (for login phase only since it only mainly takes place in user side) in Pentium 4 processor (2.97 GHz clock speed) and a NOKIA 3120 Classic mobile phone. We had taken two cases for each scheme, and time taken is calculated and compared.

Case1: Prime Number: 999983, X_s=123456, r=999999, ID_i=111111.

Case2: Prime Number: 9999991, X_s=1234567, r=9999999, ID_i=1111111.

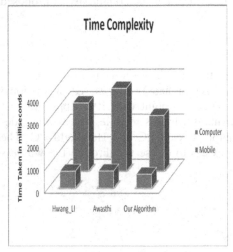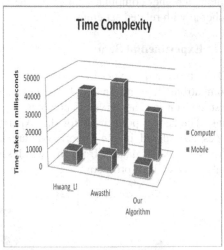

Fig. 2. Time taken for each scheme in case1   **Fig. 3.** Time Taken for each scheme in case2.

The above given figure 1 and figure 2 compares the time complexity our proposed scheme with related two schemes.

7.3 Energy Requirements

In this section we make a comparison between our scheme and two schemes with respect to energy (battery power). Batteries used in wireless devices are an essential component. The batteries used with current technology provide a lifetime of 1.5 hours to 4 hours. With people using more and more of the wireless devices there is a heavy demand for longer lasting batteries of less weight and smaller size. Unfortunately, the battery technology is not progressing as fast as the digital technology or the increasing user demand. On an average there is 2% increase in battery efficiency every year. Voltage presents the amount of power that can be delivered by the battery and a milliamperes hour (mAh) is the time for which that power can be delivered. Higher voltage is preferred since if battery has lower output voltage then additional circuit is required to convert the voltage to higher values.

In our setup, we use NOKIA 3120 Classic, mobile phone, with battery specification Standard Battery, Li- Ion 1000 mAh, BL-4U 3.7 V.

To demonstrate how the calculations were done consider Table 3 as an example of the observations for a scheme.

Table 3. Sample table of observations

Observation	Number of iteration	Percentage Battery Left
1	10	98
2	20	97
3	30	95
4	40	94
5	50	92

Next we calculate the difference in iterations between different observations as follows.

Table 4. Sample table of observations and Battery consumption per iteration

Observation	Difference in iteration	Change in % battery left	Battery Consumed Per Iteration
1,2	10	1	0.1
2,3	10	2	0.2
3,4	10	1	0.1
4,5	10	2	0.2

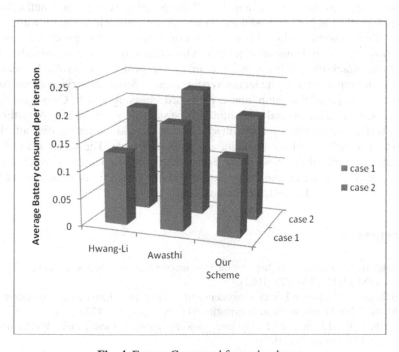

Fig. 4. Energy Consumed for each scheme

The average battery consumed per iteration can thus be calculated as follows
Average battery Consumed per iteration = (0.1 + 0.2 + 0.1 + 0.2)/4 = 0.15

Thus the statistics for reliability was gathered by taking every battery life change divided by runs to get battery life per run over the period of the experiment.

We had taken the same two cases for each scheme, and battery consumed is calculated and compared.

Case1: Prime Number: 999983, X_s=123456, r=999999, ID_i=111111.

Case2: Prime Number: 9999991, X_s=1234567, r=9999999, ID_i=1111111.

8 Conclusion

This paper presents an enhanced remote user authentication scheme. Since the secret key of the AS is a long-term key therefore it requires further security. In the situation, when the secret key of the AS is revealed or compromised by an accident or stolen etc, then it is not better to replace/alter the whole system at the AS. It is also not efficient to replace/alter the secret key of the AS with the previously registered identities and their corresponding passwords. However, the secret key of the AS requires further security in term of forward secrecy: the revelation or publication of the secret key of the AS does not result in compromise of the security of the previously registered identities and their corresponding passwords. The proposed scheme also provides forward secrecy to the AS. Hwang Li [7] proposed a remote user authentication scheme. Awasthi Lal [14] proposed a remote user authentication scheme with forward security. Both schemes suffer different types of attacks. In this paper we propose a new remote mutual authentication scheme. Our proposed scheme withstands most of the current attacking mechanisms. The proposed protocol is provably secure to withstand the replay attack, the stolen verifier attack, denial of service attack, impersonation attack, parallel session attack, password guessing attack. Consequently, the proposed scheme adds mutual authentication, session key generation. Awasthi Lal's scheme suffers from stolen verifier attack. In our method, stolen verifier attack will not work. The server will not maintain any password table. The server maintains the registration time of all the users in the encrypted format by using its secret key. It is difficult for the attacker to find the password without knowing the registration time of the user and the secret key of the remote system.

References

[1] Lamport, L.: Password authentication with insecure communication. Communication of the ACM 24(11), 770–772 (1981)

[2] ElGamal, T.: A public key cryptosystem and a signature scheme based on discrete logarithms. IEEE Transactions on Information Theory 31(4), 469–472 (1985)

[3] Mitchell, C.: Limitation of challenge–response entity authentication. Electronics Letters 25(17), 1195–1196 (1989)

[4] Chang, C.C., Wu, T.C.: Remote password authentication with smart cards. IEE Proceedings 138(3), 165–168 (1993)

[5] Chang, C.C., Hwang, S.J.: Using smart cards to authenticate remote passwords. Computers and Mathematics with Applications 26(7), 19–27 (1993)

[6] Wu, T.C.: Remote login authentication scheme based on a geometric approach. Computer Communication 18(12), 959–963 (1995)

[7] Hwang, M.S., Li, L.H.: A new remote user authentication scheme using smart cards. IEEE Transactions on Consumer Electronics 46(1), 28–30 (2000)

[8] Chan, C.K., Cheng, L.M.: Cryptanalysis of a remote user authentication scheme using smart cards. IEEE Transactions on Consumer Electronics 46, 992–993 (2000)

[9] Li, L.H., Lin, L.C., Hwang, M.S.: A remote password authentication scheme for multi-server architecture using neural networks. IEEE Transactions Neural Networks 12(6), 1498–1504 (2001)

[10] Tang, Y.L., Hwang, M.S., Lee, C.C.: A simple remote user authentication scheme. Mathematical and Computer Modelling 36, 103–107 (2002)

[11] Lee, C.C., Hwang, M.S., Yang, W.P.: A flexible remote user authentication scheme using smart cards. ACM Operating Systems Review 36(3), 46–52 (2002)

[12] Lee, C.C., Li, L.H., Hwang, M.S.: A remote user authentication scheme using hash functions. ACM Operating Systems Review 36(4), 23–29 (2002)

[13] Chien, H.Y., Jan, J.K., Tseng, Y.M.: An efficient and practical solution to remote authentication: smart card. Computers & Security 21(4), 372–375 (2002)

[14] Awasthi, A.K., Lal, S.: A Remote User Authentication Scheme using Smart Cards with Forward Security. IEEE Transactions on Consumer Electronics 49(4), 1246–1248 (2003)

[15] Shen, J.J., Lin, C.W., Hwang, M.S.: A modified Remote User Authentication Scheme using Smart Card. IEEE Transactions on Consumer Electronics 49(2), 414–416 (2003)

[16] Ku, W.C., Chen, C.M., Lee, H.L.: Cryptanalysis of a variant of Peyravian–Zunic's password authentication scheme. IEICE Transaction on Communication E86-B(5), 1682–1684 (2003)

[17] Lee, S.-W., Kim, H.-S., Yoo, K.-Y.: Comment on a Remote User Authentication Scheme using Smart Cards with Forward Secrecy. IEEE Transactions on Consumer Electronics 50(2) (May 2004)

[18] Kumar, M.: Some Remarks on a Remote User Authentication Scheme Using Smart Cards with Forward Secrecy. IEEE Transactions on Consumer Electronics 50(2) (May 2004)

[19] Ku, W.C., Chen, S.M.: Weakness and improvement of an efficient password based user authentication scheme using smart cards. IEEE Transactions on Consumer Electronics 50(1), 204–207 (2004)

[20] Awasthi, A.K., Lal, S.: An enhanced remote user authentication scheme using smart cards. IEEE Transactions on Consumer Electronics 50(2), 583–586 (2004)

[21] Kumar, M.: New remote user authentication scheme using smart cards. IEEE Transactions on Consumer Electronics 50(2), 597–600 (2004)

[22] Tsai, C.S., Lee, C.C., Hwang, M.-S.: Password Authentication Schemes: Current Status and Key Issues. International Journal of Network Security 3(2), 101–115 (2006)

[23] Tian, X., Zhu, R.W., Wong, D.S.: Improved Efficient Remote User Authentication Schemes. International Journal of Network Security 4(2), 149–154 (2007)

[24] Yongliang, L., Gao, W., Yao, H., Yu, X.: Elliptic Curve Cryptography Based Wireless Authentication Protocol. International Journal of Network Security 5(3), 327–337 (2007)

Concurrent Usage Control Implementation Verification Using the SPIN Model Checker

P.V. Rajkumar[1], S.K. Ghosh[1], and P. Dasgupta[2]

[1] School of Information Technology,
Indian Institute of Technology Kharagpur, 721 302, India
vrj@sit.iitkgp.ernet.in, skg@iitkgp.ac.in
[2] Department of Computer Science and Engineering,
Indian Institute of Technology Kharagpur, 721 302, India
pallab@cse.iitkgp.ac.in

Abstract. The $UCON_A$ usage control authorization model supports concurrency and the model left issue of synchronizing usage control processes to the implementation. Manual verification of application specific concurrent usage control implementation is a hard problem. In this paper, we show the usage of a formal verification tool, the SPIN model checker, for verifying the correctness of the concurrent usage control implementation. We also provide an illustrative case study.

Keywords: Usage control, Concurrency, Software Implementation and Model Checking.

1 Introduction

Recent times, multi-core processors are commonly deployed from desktop computers to high-end server machines. Software industries also began to write concurrent software applications to exploit the computation power provided by multi-cores. Most of the applications, like web services which are concurrent in nature, provides services to multiple users with varying access permissions. In this context, security of an application is a problem of confining the information/service access within the vicinity of users' permissions. Usage control is one of the component to achieve such a confinement.

Usage control in concurrent software applications, besides maintaining usage confinement, must be flexible enough to allow concurrent execution of user tasks to avoid performance degradation. The functions within the usage control also needs to support the concurrent execution of user tasks. The $UCON_A$ [1] usage control authorization is a comprehensive usage control model which is made to fit for concurrent applications. This model is build over the set of usage control actions, and usage rights are defined using these actions. Usage decisions are based on the objects' attribute values. These attributes are variables of particular data type and can be dynamically modified by the update actions within the usage control; it also allows continuous usage control enforcement.

N. Meghanathan et al. (Eds.): CNSA 2010, CCIS 89, pp. 214–223, 2010.

Expressivity [1], formal specification [2] and safety analysis [3] constitutes three important aspects of the usage control model. Safety analysis procedure can ensure the model level correctness, however security of the usage control in the software application depends on both the safety of the model as well as the correctness of its implementation. Usage control system implementation in a typical software application consists of

- Functions to check and enforce the usage constraints,
- Update actions to modify the attribute values,
- Mechanism to synchronize various concurrent usage control actions.

Above mentioned elements are specific to the application and its usage control policy. Note that even if the model is theoretically safe, the errors in any of these elements leads to security violation. Formal method based techniques plays a vital role in security verification [4]. Model checking is one of the well known formal method and it is successfully been applied for ensuring the correctness of many safety critical systems. This paper, we use the SPIN model checker to verify the concurrent usage control implementation in software applications.

Remaining part of the paper has been organized as follows. Section 2 presents the related work. Section 3 presents the overview of software model checking. Section 4 presents the concurrent usage control implementation verification using SPIN model checker. Section 5 presents an illustrative case study. Section 6 presents the conclusion.

2   Related Work

The logical specification [2] of usage control model and its safety analysis [3] has been explored. Safety analysis procedure can ensure the model level correctness, however the correctness of usage control in software application depends on both the safety of the model as well as correctness of its implementation. In this section, we briefly present an outline of methods proposed to verify the correctness of access control implementation.

Naldurg et al. [5] presents a tool to find the information-flow vulnerabilities by using the access control meta-data i.e. access control entries in the access control list implementation. This tool takes an instance of access control configuration and derives the relational expression through which the information-flow vulnerabilities could be identified. Guelev et al. [6] presents model checking approach for verifying the consistency of access control policy specification and Zhang et al. [7] presents a method to synthesize XACML tags from the verified policy. Martin et al. [8] presents a method to test XACML policies using fault models. Pretschner et al. [9] presents the Z-specification of mechanisms for usage control models. Janicke et al. [10] presents the concurrent enforcement method for the usage control policies. This paper focuses on leveraging the developments in software model checking for verifying the correctness of concurrent usage control implementation.

3 Overview of Software Model Checking

Software model checking is a formal verification method to ensure the correctness of software programs with respect to specified properties. Software model checking tools takes a program and the correctness properties as input and exhaustively explores the program's state space for finding property violations. Software programs may have infinite state space. The tools like BLAST [11]and Magic [12] work directly on the C language source code and they do well for finding bugs in the program. These tools statically constructs an *over-approximate* finite state model using the predicates over the state variables in the program and verifies the properties over the model. If there occurs any violation due to the approximation they refine the model and repeat the verification over the refined model. They continue the refinement and verification cycle until they find either a violation in the actual code or no violation in the model.

The SPIN [13] and NuSMV [14] are the two well-known finite state model checkers which works on the specification of the system implementation. They have their own language for system implementation specification and they use temporal logic for specification of correctness properties. Here, the system specification is a finite state transition model and the verification algorithm exhaustively searches for all possible behaviors in the finite state space for finding a property violation. If any property violation is found, they terminate with a *counter example* which illustrates the system behavior that leads to the violation. If there is no violation, they terminate with a guarantee that the implementation is a *model* of the property. In this work, we use the SPIN model checker for verification of usage control implementation.

3.1 The SPIN Model Checker

The SPIN model checker's specification language PROMELA supports concurrency and its syntactic constructs are similar to C programming language. It would be much easier for the software programmers to write the implementation specification in PROMELA compared to the NuSMV's specification language. Correctness properties can be expressed using the assertions denoting the invariants or using the Linear Temporal Logic (LTL) formulae. The SPIN converts the PROMELA specifications into a finite state automaton and the LTL formula into a Buchi automaton. The verifier constructs the synchronous product of the two automata and searches for the property violation in the product automaton. The SPIN also supports inline assertions and deadlock detection in the implementation.

4 Concurrent Usage Control Authorization Implementation Verification

The $UCON_A$ usage control authorization is a group of core models defined in $UCON_{ABC}$ [1] usage control model and it supports concurrency. The $UCON_A$ defines usage rights based on the valuation of the authorization predicates. State of usage control authorization is defined by the value of objects' attributes [2]. Usage control defines three types of actions to change the attribute values namely, *pre-update*, *on-update* and *post-update*, and these actions are performed by the system *before* the access ,*during* the access process and *after* the access respectively. The updates actions change the state of usage control system.

The formal model of $UCON_A$ [2] is defined as quatriple: $M = (S, P_A, A_A)$, where S is a set of sequence of states, P_A is a finite set of authorization predicates and A_A is a finite set of update actions. Usage control decisions are based on the predicates (P_A) defined over the subject and object attributes. The decision can be made before the usage–*preAuthorization* or during the usage–*ongoingAuthorization* of the right. Authorization specification may have update actions before the usage–*preUpdate* or during the usage–*onUpdate* or after the usage–*postUpdate* of access right. Usage control decision along with different update actions forms eight sub-models. Detailed specifications of the sub-models in the $UCON_A$ are given in [2].

The $UCON_A$ allows concurrent usage processes, the model assumes that the processes are properly synchronized such that they maintain the ACID property. However, the software application which implements the model should implement an application specific synchronization mechanism. This paper primarily focuses on verifying the correctness of such application specific synchronization implementations.

Each concurrent user task may change the usage control state of the application. State based dynamic usage control policy enforcement methods performs the constraint check at every change in state; hence, it may result in loss of concurrency. Safety analysis ensures that a given initial configuration is free from unauthorized usage of rights in all feature states. Hence, the implementation of the *safe* usage control model can allow concurrent state changes. This will enable the applications to efficiently utilize the computational power of the multi-core systems.

4.1   Verification Using the SPIN

The subjects, objects and the usage rights in the application along with the implementation details of primitive usage control functions can be specified in the SPIN's system specification language PROMELA. It supports

– Composite data type specification using *typedef,*
– Specification of concurrent processes using the *proctype,*
– Communication between the various active processes through *shared variables* as well as the message channel *chan.*

Apart from them, it supports *symbolic constant* specifications and *inline* functions. Concurrency in PROMELA is supported through interleaved execution, and it also provides *atomic* operator to avoid the undesirable interleaving.

Usage control system of the application can be specified as a set of active processes. Communication between the usage control system and other functional modules can be specified using message channels. Usage control policies of the application can be specified using Linear Temporal Logic(LTL) formulae over the state variables. The SPIN model checker verifies correctness of usage control implementation with respect to the specified LTL formulae. After verification, we can use the PROMELA compiler [15] to translate the PROMELA specification into C language functions. The remaining functional features of the application can be embedded into the C language source code. We shall illustrate this approach using a case study.

5   Case Study

Usage control requirements [16] [17] of a typical web based conference management application can be cited to illustrate our approach. For example, consider the following usage control requirements

- Authors can submit papers but they should be excluded from reviewing their own papers.
- After submission, the program committee members can choose papers to review.
- Reviewers are allowed to write and submit reports without exceeding 250 words. After submission, no modification should be allowed.
- Reviewers can read others' reports after submitting their own report. After reading a report, they should not be allowed to submit reports about the same paper.
- After reading reviewer's report, the chair is allowed to make the acceptance decision.
- After acceptance decision is made, authors can view the acceptance status of their papers and copy their review reports.

In this example, the conference web server may allow reviewers to concurrently write their review reports. If dynamic state based usage control policy is enforced at the web server then there will be a severe delay in response time, because, it requires a coarse grained task synchronization. Such a problem may create more serious issues in many other real time applications like online banking, where large number of users avail the service at the same time. In this section, we illustrate the static usage control policy enforcement which allows concurrent task execution.

5.1   Safe Usage Control Authorization Model Design

Initial configuration of usage control begins with a few permissions, when the users execute permissions, the configuration changes over time. Safe usage control model design is the problem of choosing an initial configuration such that no sequence of user actions can lead to an *unsafe* configuration where a user obtains an unauthorized permission.

Usage control model for the above mentioned application has the following basic elements

- **Subjects:** Authors, Program Committee (PC) Members and the Chair.
- **Objects:** Papers and Review Reports.
- **Rights:** submit, read, write, take-reviewership, make-decision and copy.

The subjects and objects have a set of finite valued attributes. Authorization predicates and update functions are defined using these attribute values. Usage of rights, excepting the copy right, makes changes in usage control state. For example, usage of *take-reviewership* right enables the user to write and submit review reports, at the same time it restricts the user to *read* others' review reports. These changes are captured in the pre-update functions of the model. The following specification shows the concurrent *"write"* and *"submit"* permissions in the usage control model.

$$
\begin{aligned}
permitaccess(s,o,write) \rightarrow\ &\blacklozenge(tryaccess(s,o,write) \wedge IsReportType_a(o) \wedge \\
&IsReviewer_a(s,o) \wedge \neg IsReportSubmitted_a(o) \wedge \\
&IsReportWithInLimit_a(o)) \\
permitaccess(s,o,write) \rightarrow\ &\Diamond(onUpdate(o.WordCount) \wedge \Diamond endaccess(s,o,write)) \\
onUpdate(o.WordCount)\ :\ &o.WordCount \leftarrow TokenCount(o.Report," ")
\end{aligned}
$$

$$
\begin{aligned}
permitaccess(s,o,submit) \rightarrow\ &\blacklozenge(tryaccess(s,o,submit) \wedge IsReportType_a(o) \wedge \\
&IsReviewer_a(s,o) \wedge \neg IsReportSubmitted_a(o) \\
&\wedge IsReportWithInLimit(o)) \wedge \\
&\blacklozenge preUpdate(o.ReportSubmitted) \wedge \\
&\blacklozenge preUpdate(s.ReportSubmitted)
\end{aligned}
$$

$$
\begin{aligned}
IsReportType_u(o)\ :\ &o.Typc = Report \\
IsReviewer_a(s,o)\ :\ &s.ID = o.Reviewer \\
IsReportSubmitted_a(o)\ :\ &o.Submitted = True \\
IsReportWithInLimit_a(o)\ :\ &o.WordCount \leqslant 250 \\
preUpdate(o.ReportSubmitted)\ :\ &o.ReportSubmitted \leftarrow True \\
preUpdate(s.ReportSubmitted)\ :\ &s.ReportSubmitted \leftarrow True
\end{aligned}
$$

The complete usage control authorization for conference management application can be found in our earlier work on application specific usage control implementation verification using a semi-formal method [17].

5.2 Usage Control Implementation Verification

The key elements of the PROMELA specification in the usage control implementation of conference management application are given as follows

- The subjects and objects along with their attributes are implemented as composite state variables.

```
typedef Object
{
    ObjectType Type;
    ObjectID ID;
    SubjectID ReviewersList[MAX];
    ObjectID ReportID[MAX];
    bool ReportSubmitted;
    int WordCount;
    bool DecisionMade;
    char Report[MAX_BUF_SIZE];
};

typedef Subject
{
    ObjectType Type;
    ObjectID ID;
    SubjectID ReviewersList[MAX];
    ObjectID ReportID[MAX];
    bool ReportSubmitted;
    int WordCount;
    bool DecisionMade;
    char Report[MAX_BUF_SIZE];
};
```

— Usage *rights* are coded as symbolic constants as follows

```
mtype={submit, read, write,...};
```

— *Set of primitive usage control functions*, which directly operates over the object attributes, like *predicates* and the *update* are specified using the inline functions

```
inline IsReportType(O)
{
    assert(O.Type==ReportType);
}

inline preUpdateReportSubmission(O.ReportSubmitted)
{
    O.ReportSubmitted=true;
}
```

— *Set of usage control functions* which implements the core usage control system are specified as active processes. It uses the structure variables, symbolic constants and the primitive usage control functions.
— *Set of usage control sensitive functions* are used to model the functional part of the application. The functional processes specifies the way in which the usage control system is used within the application.
— *Communication* between the usage control system and the usage control sensitive functions are implemented using the message channel *chan*.

The usage control processes in the application are specified as active processes in PROMELA and they can make use of all the above mentioned features. For example, a function in the usage control implementation of conference management application is specified as follows

```
active[PMAX] proctype UsageControlTakeReviewership()
{
    Subject s;
    Object o;
    bool preCond;
    do
    ::UserUCtrl?tryaccess(s,o,TakeReviewerShip)->
            if ::IsPaperType(s,o) && NotAuthor(s,o) && IsPCMember(s,o) && NotReviewer(s,o)

                        preUpdateReviewersList(s,o);
                        preUpdateReviewPaperIDList(s,o);
                        preUpdateReviewReportID(s,o);
                        preUpdateReportsRead(s,o);
                        UCtrlUser!permitaccess(s,o,TakeReviewerShip);

            ::else ->

                        UCtrlUser!denyaccess(s,o,TakeReviewerShip);

            fi;
    od;
}
```

The *active* construct in the above specification creates instances of concurrent process. The *UCtrlUser* is a message channel, "*?*" is the receive operation and "*!*" is the send operation. The inline functions like *IsPaperType and NotAuthor* are authorization predicates and the inline functions like *preUpdateReviewersList* are the preUpdate actions in the usage control implementation.

All possible valuation of the attribute variables constitutes the usage control protection state-space and the active processes make transitions within the state space. Usage control policy defines the *acceptable* protection states and transitions within states. Note that every usage control sensitive user action is abstracted and modeled as active processes which communicates with the primitive usage control functions. The model checking tool, the SPIN, verifies the implementation for correctness with respect to the policies specified as a LTL formula. For example, the usage control policy *"Authors can submit the papers and they should be excluded from reviewing their own paper"* can be specified in LTL as follows

$$\Box(ObjectList[i].Author! = NULL \rightarrow$$
$$\Box(ObjectList[i].Author! = ObjectList[i].ReviewersList[j]))$$

The first condition *"ObjectList[i].Author!=NULL"* will be true once an author submits a paper. After the submission he should not be allowed to review that paper, this notion is captured in the second part of the formula *"ObjectList[i].Author!=ObjectList[i].ReviewersList[j]"*. Verification of this property involves 3867989 state visits with each state-vector of size 836 bytes and the verification process takes 143 seconds. In case of property violations, the model checker produces counter examples.

Success of verification in the SPIN model checker needs a right kind of implementation abstraction. Verification time and accuracy mainly depends on the chosen abstraction. Abstraction eliminates property irrelevant code details; it varies from one application to another as well as one property to another. Note that the complete specification of usage control implementation in the SPIN may not scale well due to *state space explosion*. For the conference management application, we manually choose those parts of implementation that are specific to every property and verified the implementation correctness.

The process models in PROMELA are very much similar to the functions in C language. The PROMELA compiler [15] can be used to convert the process models into subroutines in C. Primary usage control processes in the PROMELA specification may become usage control decision function in resulting C source code. Rest of the task is to embed the functional part of the application within the C source code of usage control system.

6   Conclusion

This paper presented an approach to verify application specific concurrent usage control implementation using the SPIN model checker. The SPIN model checker's counter examples are useful in correcting the concurrency errors. Such an approach can be used to verify usage control implementations in small scale software applications. It may also be useful for software developers to test and debug the concurrency errors in usage control implementations during the development phase.

References

1. Park, J., Sandhu, R.: The $UCON_{ABC}$ usage control model. ACM Transactions on Information and System Security 7(1), 128–174 (2004)
2. Zhang, X., Parisi-Presicce, F., Sandhu, R., Park, J.: Formal model and policy specification of usage control. ACM Transactions on Information and System Security 8(4), 351–387 (2005)
3. Zhang, X., Sandhu, R.: Safety analysis of usage control authorization models. In: Proceedings of the 2006 ACM Symposium on Information, Computer and Communications Security, Taipei, Taiwan, pp. 243–254 (2006)
4. Wing, J.M.: A symbiotic relationship between formal methods and security. In: Proceedings of the Computer Security, Dependability and Assurance: From Needs to Solutions, York, UK, pp. 26–38 (1998)
5. Naldurg, P., Schwoon, S., Rajamani, S., Lambert, J.: NETRA: Seeing through access control. In: The 4th ACM Workshop on Formal Methods in Security Engineering, Fairfax, Virginia, pp. 55–66 (2006)
6. Guelev, D.P., Ryan, M., Schobbens, P.: Model checking access control policies. In: Proceedings of the Seventh Information Security Conference, Palo Alto, USA, pp. 219–230 (2004)
7. Zhang, N., Guelev, D.P., Ryan, M.: Synthesising verified access control systems through model checking. Journal of Computer Security 16(1), 1–6 (2007)
8. Martin, E., Xie, T.: A fault model and mutation testing of access control policies. In: Proceedings of the 16th ACM International Conference on World Wide Web, New York, USA, pp. 667–676 (2007)
9. Pretschner, A., Hilty, M., Basin, D., Schaefer, C., Walter, T.: Mechanisms for usage control. In: ACM Symposium on Information, Computer and Communications Security, Tokyo, Japan, pp. 240–244 (2008)

10. Janicke, H., Cau, A., Siewe, F., Zedan, H.: Concurrent enforcement of usage control policies. In: Proceedings of the IEEE Workshop on Policies for Distributed Systems and Networks, Palisades, NY, USA, pp. 111–118 (June 2008)
11. Henzinger, T.A., Jhala, R., Majumdar, R., Sutre, G.: Software verification with blast. In: Ball, T., Rajamani, S.K. (eds.) SPIN 2003. LNCS, vol. 2648, pp. 235–239. Springer, Heidelberg (2003)
12. Chaki, S., Clarke, E., Groce, A., Jha, S., Veith, H.: Modular verification of software components in c. IEEE Transactions on Software Engineering 30(6), 388–402 (2004)
13. Holzmann, G.J.: The model checker spin. IEEE Trans. on Software Engineering 23, 279–295 (1997)
14. Cimatti, A., Clarke, E., Giunchiglia, F., Roveri, M.: Nusmv: A new symbolic model verifier. In: Proceedings of the 11th International Conference on Computer Aided Verification,Trento, Italy, pp. 495–499 (1996)
15. Lffer, S., Serhrouchni, A.: Creating implementations from promela models. In: Proceedings of Second SPIN Workshop, New Jersey, USA (1996)
16. Rajkumar, P.V., Ghosh, S.K., Dasgupta, P.: An end to end correctness verification approach for application specific usage control. In: Proceedings of the Fourth IEEE International Conference on Industrial and Information Systems, pp. 122–136 (December 2009)
17. Rajkumar, P.V., Ghosh, S.K., Dasgupta, P.: Application specific usage control implementation verification. International Journal of Network Security and Its Applications 1(3), 116–128 (2009)

Pipelining Architecture of AES Encryption and Key Generation with Search Based Memory

T. Subashri, R. Arunachalam, B. Gokul Vinoth Kumar, and V. Vaidehi

Department of Electronics, MIT Campus, Anna University, Chennai-44
tsubashri@annauniv.edu, bgokul1989@gmail.com,
r_arun21@yahoo.co.in, vaidehi@annauniv.edu

Abstract. A high speed security algorithm is always important for wired/wireless environment. The symmetric block cipher plays a major role in the bulk data encryption. One of the best existing symmetric security algorithms to provide data security is AES. AES has the advantage of being implemented in both hardware and software. We implement the AES in hardware because the hardware implementation has the advantage of increased throughput and offers better security. In order to reduce the constraint on the hardware resources while implementing the look-up table based s-box we propose a search based s-box architecture. Also the pipelined architecture of the AES algorithm is used in order to increase the throughput of the algorithm. The key schedule algorithm of the AES encryption is also pipelined.

Keywords: AES pipelining, Key pipelining, Search Based Memory, VLSI.

1 Introduction

In general network security has three major security goals: confidentiality, availability and message integration between senders to destination. Many of the algorithms are available in each of these three goals of security. And they are faced to different kind of the attacks also. In this respect one of the frequently used security algorithms in block cipher is the AES algorithm. This is considered in our work. Basically high speed security decisions are important to support multimedia data transmission. Due to the large data transmission of voice data in VOIP it has to check the speed of the algorithm in terms of less computation time.

In general cost of an algorithm covers the computational efficiency and storage requirement for different implementations such as hardware, software or smart cards. And the algorithm should have implementation flexibility and simplicity. This gives development of the algorithm. We try to incorporate these characteristics in the AES algorithm. In this paper, section 2 describes the introduction to the AES algorithm; section 3 describes the pipelining of the AES algorithm, section 4 describes the search based memory, section 5 describes the pipelining of the key scheduling algorithm, section 6 shows the comparison of the different synthesized hardware utilization and finally section 7 presents the conclusion.

N. Meghanathan et al. (Eds.): CNSA 2010, CCIS 89, pp. 224–231, 2010.

2 AES (Advanced Encryption Standard)

The standard comprises three block ciphers, AES-128, AES-192 and AES-256, adopted from a larger collection originally published as Rijndael. Each AES cipher has a 128-bit input block size, with key sizes of 128, 192 and 256 bits, respectively. The AES ciphers have been analyzed extensively and are now used worldwide [1], [2], [5], [6]. The AES algorithm organizes the data block in a four-row and row-major ordered matrix. In both encryption and decryption, the AES algorithm uses a round function.

The step involved are given below

1.   Key Expansion using Rijndael's key schedule
2.   Initial Round
  o AddRoundKey
3.   Round
  o Sub Bytes—a non-linear substitution step where each byte is replaced with another according to a lookup table.
  o Shift Rows—a transposition step where each row of the state is shifted cyclically a certain number of steps.
  o Mix Columns—a mixing operation which operates on the columns of the state, combining the four bytes in each column
  o AddRoundKey—each byte of the state is combined with the round key; each round key is derived from the cipher key using a key schedule.
4.   Final Round (no Mix Columns)
  o Sub Bytes
  o Shift Rows
  o AddRoundKey

This is the iterative looping architecture of the AES. VERILOG code is written for the AES encryption algorithm for finding cipher for any given plaintext input. The next section describes the pipelining of the AES algorithm.

3 Pipelining of AES Encryption

As it can be seen from the figure 1 the pipelined architecture is just a modification of the iterative looping architecture except that in between two rounds a register is included. These registers help us in achieving the pipelining of the AES.

Basically pipelining means to process the data that is given as input in a continuous manner without having to wait for the current process to get over. This pipelining concept is seen in many processors. In the architecture in the figure 1 the registers are used to store the current output of the round that is being executed. Now instead of passing the output of each round to the next round directly we use a register which would act as a bypass or an internal register. Since the current rounds' value is stored in the register the next input to the current round can be given as soon as the current output is obtained. And the input to the next round is given from the register thus avoiding a direct contact between the two rounds. This is not possible in the iterative looping architecture because the next input can be given only after the whole round based processing is over since the same hardware is used over and again in the process of obtaining the cipher text. Thus, the pipelined architecture increases the speed of execution of the obtaining of cipher text but at the cost of increased hardware cost. In the substitute bytes we use a look up table based S-box. This contributes for some of the hardware in the form of block RAMs. With the help of a search based look up table (LUT) we can reduce the hardware cost to a considerable extent. This is described in the next section.

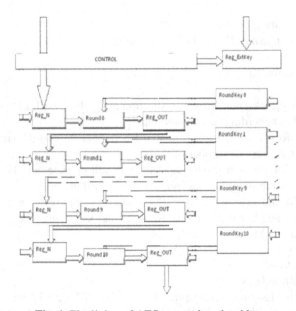

Fig. 1. Pipelining of AES encryption algorithm

From the results, it is very clear that as the number of inputs is greater than 4 there will be progressive decrease in the time at which the output is obtained when compared to the AES iterative looping structure. Thus by using the AES pipelined architecture we have seen an increase in the throughput whose proportions increase as the size of data increases. Invariably, the size of inputs is going to be high in real time application as large volumes of data are fragmented in to 128 bits each and fed as input. But the hardware utilization is higher than that of the iterative looping architecture. But this is a trade off that needs to be done in order to achieve higher speeds in encryption.

4   Search Based Memory

It's a kind of storage technique which includes comparison logic with each bit of storage. A data value is broadcast to all words of storage and compared with the values there. Words which match are flagged in some way. Subsequent operations can then work on flagged words, e.g. read them out one at a time or write to certain bit positions in all of them. It is similar to a special type of computer memory used in certain very high speed searching applications.

Unlike standard computer memory (RAM) in which the user supplies a memory address and the RAM returns the data word stored at that address, this is designed such that the user supplies a data word and the algorithm searches its entire memory to see if that data word is stored anywhere in it. If the data word is found, the algorithm returns a list of one or more storage addresses where the word was found (and in some architecture, it also returns the data word or other associated pieces of data). This search based memory concept can be used in the S-box which results in the reduction of the number of block RAMs used thereby reducing the hardware utilization and making the pipelining more efficient.

5 Pipelining of Key Schedule Algorithm

Apart from Encryption and Decryption Module, another main component is Key Expansion Schedule. The security factor of the AES Encryption / Decryption Standard mainly depends on this part. For better security, in AES Algorithm first round user key is XORed with the original Plain / Cipher Text. And next round onwards Expanded Key from Expanded Key Schedule is XORed with data. The expansion algorithm of the AES is fixed [5]. To speed up the process of Key Generation, it is preferable opt for pipeline architecture

5.1 Pipelined Architecture for Key Expansion Module

The figure 2 presents the hardware architecture for Key Expansion Module which is one of the main components of the Grand Key. Key Expander comprises of EX-OR, Pipelined Data Registers. Since there are 44 words used in the key expansion process 44 data registers will be used, four in each stage of the pipeline.

From the figure 2 we can clearly see that registers are included between each round and thereby we are creating a sort of buffer between each round enabling us to provide the input without having to wait for the whole process to get over. So since the inputs are given at a faster rate and outputs are also obtained at a faster rate. So if without pipelining the second output is obtained at the end of 22 cycles with the help of pipelining the output is obtained at the end of 12 cycles thereby speeding up the process of obtaining the output.

6 Comparison of Hardware Utilization

- As can be seen from the table 1 below, the hardware utilization of the pipelined architecture far exceeds that of the iterative architecture. But when a search

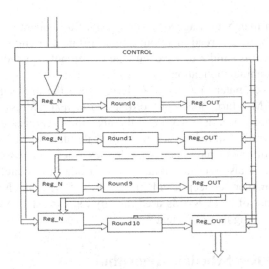

Fig. 2. Architecture of the pipelined key schedule algorithm

based s-box is used in AES pipelined architecture some of the important device consumption are reduced or completely eliminated.

- Number of block RAMs which are important resources in any chips are completely reduced to NIL when a search based s-box is used in AES pipelined algorithm whereas there is 2% consumption of block RAMs in iterative architecture without search based s-box and 19% in AES pipelined architecture on a virtex 5 board.
- Also the Number of fully used Bit Slices is substantially reduced in *AES* pipelined architecture with a search based memory which is even lower than in the iterative architecture.
- The input/output device utilization is understandably constant in all the three architectures.
- All other devices such as slice registers, flip-flops and LUTs are understandably lower in case of iterative architecture.
- Thus with the help of search based s-box in AES pipelined algorithm some of the key resource utilization is reduced which is agog trade-off between iterative architecture and pipelined architecture and at the same time ensuring the tremendous throughput as in pipelined feature.

The table 2 shows the comparison of the synthesized hardware utilization of the key expansion algorithm, with and without pipelining. It is clear from the table that the hardware utilized by the pipelined architecture is higher than utilized by the ordinary key expansion algorithm. But the up side is that there is a definite increase in the speed at which the output that's obtained. So there is a little trade-off that has to be made in the hardware utilization in order to get faster output.

Table 1. Comparison of synthesized hardware utilization of different architectures of the AES algorithm

TITLE	AES ITERATIVE LOOPING ARCHITEC-TURE	AES PIPELINED ARCHITEC-TURE	AES PIPELINING WITH SEARCH BASED S-BOX
Slice Logic Utilization			
Number of Slice Registers	402 out of 138240 0%	2700 out of 138240 1%	3898 out of 138240 2%
Number of Slice LUTs	565 out of 138240 0%	2948 out of 138240 2%	13020 out of 138240 9%
Number used as Logic	565 out of 138240 0%	1796 out of 138240 1%	11868 out of 138240 8%
Number used as Memory	-	1152 out of 36480 3%	1152 out of 36480 3%
Number used as SRL	-	1152	1152
Slice Logic Distribution			
Number of Bit Slices used	694	3076	14125
Number with an unused Flip Flop	292 out of 694 42%	376 out of 3076 12%	10227 out of 14125 72%
Number with unused LUTs	129 out of 694 18%	128 out of 3076 4%	1105 out of 14125 7%
Number of fully used Bit Slices	273 out of 694 3	2572 out of 3076 83%	2793 out of 14125 19%
IO Utilization			
Number of IOs	388	387	387
Number of bonded IOBs	388 out of 680 57%	386 out of 680 56%	386 out of 680 56%
Specific Feature Utilization			
Number of Block RAM/FIFO	5 out of 212 2%	41 out of 212 19%	NIL
Number of BUFG/ BUFGCTRLs	1 out of 32 3%	1 out of 32 3%	1 out of 32 3%

Table 2. Comparison of synthesized hardware utilization of key expansion with and without pipelining

TITLE	KEY EXPANSION WITHOUT PIPELINING	WITH PIPELINING
Number used as Logic:	311 out of 19200 1%	4480 out of 19200 23%
Number of Slice LUTs:	311 out of 19200 1%	4608 out of 19200 24%
Number of Bit Slices used:	311	5760
Number with an unused Flip Flop	311 out of 311 100%	3200 out of 5760 55%
Number with an unused LUT:	0 out of 311 0%	1152 out of 5760 20%
Number of fully used Bit Slices:	0 out of 311 0%	1408 out of 5760 24%
Number of IOs:	258	258

7 Conclusion

The speed of encryption is of prime importance in applications where data is to be transmitted at high speeds. Thus, with use of fully pipelined architecture the throughput and hence the speed of encryption is increased tremendously. But there is an increase in area because of pipelining. In an attempt to reduce this area search based s-box was implemented and this was successful in reducing the number of block RAMs. The hardware implementation provides faster speed and better security when compared to software models. Thus the proposed method could be successfully implemented in currently developing technologies like VoIP systems where encryption of both voice and data takes place and where the speed of encryption is very critical. Also a pipelined architecture of the key pipelining was proposed which can be utilized in the environment where the key needs to be changed at a faster rate.

References

1. Elbirt, J., Yip, W., Chetwynd, B., Paar, C.: An FPGA Implementation and Performance evaluation of the AES Block Cipher Candidate Algorithm Finalist. In: The third AES Conference (AES3), New York (April 2000), http://csrc.nist.gov
2. Elbirt, A.J., Yip, W., Chetwynd, B., Paar, C.: An FPGA Implementation and Performance evaluation of the AES Block Cipher Candidate Algorithm Finalist. IEEE Transactions on Very Large Scale Integration (VLSI) Systems 9(4) (August 2001)
3. Zhang, X., Parhi, K.K.: Implementation Approaches for the Advanced Encryption Standard Algorithm. IEEE Circuits and Systems Magazine 2(4), 24–46 (fourth quarter 2002)

4. Gaj, K., Chodowiec, P.: Hardware performance of the AES finalists survey and analysis of results, http://citeseer.ist.psu.edu/460345.html
5. National Institute of Standards and Technology, Specification for the Advanced Encryption Standard (AES). FIPS PUB 197 (2001), http://csrc.nist.gov
6. Stallings, W.: Cryptography and Network Security- Principles and Practice, 3rd edn. Pearson Education, London
7. Rabaey, J.M.: Digital Integrated Circuits. Prentice-Hall, Englewood Cliffs (1996)

A SAT Based Verification Framework for Wireless LAN Security Policy Management Supported by STRBAC Model

P. Bera[1], Soumya Maity[1], S.K. Ghosh[1], and Pallab Dasgupta[2]

[1] School of Information Technology
[2] Department of Computer science and Engineering
Indian Institute of Technology, Kharagpur-721302, India
bera.padmalochan@gmail.com, soumyam@iitkgp.ac.in, skg@iitkgp.ac.in,
pallab@cse.iitkgp.ernet.in

Abstract. The widespread proliferation of wireless networks (WLAN) demands formal evaluation and analysis of security policy management in enterprise networks. The enforcement of organizational security policies in wireless local area networks (WLANs) requires protection over the network resources from unauthorized access. Hence it is required to ensure correct distribution of access control rules to the network access points conforming to the security policy. In WLAN security policy management, the role-based access control (RBAC) mechanisms can be deployed to strengthen the security perimeter over the network resources. Further, there is a need to model the time and location dependent access constraints. In this paper, we propose WLAN security management system supported by a spatio-temporal RBAC (STRBAC) model and a SAT based verification framework. The system stems from logical partitioning of the WLAN topology into various security policy zones. It includes a *Global Policy Server* (GPS) that formalizes the organizational access policies and determines the high level policy configurations; a *Central Authentication & Role Server* (CARS) which authenticates the users and the access points (AP) in various zones and also assigns appropriate roles to the users. Each policy zone consists of an *Wireless Policy Zone Controller* (WPZCon) that co-ordinates with a dedicated *Local Role Server* (LRS) to extract the low level access configurations corresponding to the zone access router. We also propose a formal spatio-temporal RBAC (STRBAC) model to represent the global security policies formally and a SAT based verification framework to verify the access configurations.

Keywords: WLAN Security, Security Policy, STRBAC model, Formal verification.

1 Introduction

The security management in wireless networks (WLAN) is becoming increasingly difficult due to its widespread deployment and dynamic topology characteristics. Mobile users remotely access the internal network from various network zones; may

N. Meghanathan et al. (Eds.): CNSA 2010, CCIS 89, pp. 232–241, 2010.
© Springer-Verlag Berlin Heidelberg 2010

violate the organizational security policies. Typically, security policy provides a set of rules to access network objects by various users in the network. It requires a strong security policy management system with appropriate access control models.

The policy based security management is useful for enforcing the security policies in organizational LAN. The key idea of policy based security management lies in partitioning the network topology into different logical policy zones and enforcing the security policies in the policy zones through a set of functional elements. It requires distribution of the system functionalities into various architectural elements. However, the deployment of policy based security management in wireless network (WLAN) require appropriate access control models (such as role-based access control (RBAC), spatio-temporal RBAC) for representing and enforcing the security policies. This is due to the dynamic topology characteristics of wireless networks (wireless nodes may not bind to a specific IP address). The background and standards for policy based security management can be found in *RFC 3198* [5]. In wireless LAN security management, the STRBAC model can be used where the users associated to a role can access network objects, iff they satisfy certain location and time constraints. For example, in an academic network, Students are not allowed to access internet from their residential halls during class time (say, 08:00-18:00 in weekdays). However, they are always allowed to access internet from the academic departments. In this paper, we propose a WLAN security policy management system supported by a spatio-temporal RBAC model and a SAT based verification framework.

The rest of the paper is organized as follows. The related work in the areas of Wireless LAN policy based security management and spatio-temporal RBAC models has been described in section 2. In section 3, we describe the architecture and operational flow of the proposed WLAN policy management system. Section 4 describes the proposed spatio-temporal RBAC model to support our policy management system. Section 5 describes the SAT based verification procedure for analyzing the access configurations with respect to the global policy.

2   Related Work

Several research has been performed in the area of network policy based security management. Westrinen et al. [5] standardizes the terminologies and functional elements for policy based management. The IETF Policy working group developed a framework for network policy based admission control [4]. It consists of a central policy server that interprets the policies, makes policy decisions and communicates them to various policy enforcement points. The research outcome of IST-POSITIF project [1] is policy-based security framework in local area networks. J Burns et al. propose a framework [3] for automatic management of network security policies based on central policy engine. But, the framework considers very simple set of policy constraints. A recent work [2] has been proposed by Lapiotis et al. on policy based security management in wireless LAN. However, they do not describe the type of security policies enforced and also do not describe the formal validation of the policies.

Several works [7] [8] has been done to improve RBAC functionalities incorporating time and location information. Ray and Toahchoodee [8] propose a Spatio-Temporal Role-Based Access Control Model incorporating both time and location information. We introduce the notion of wireless policy zone to represent location in our model. The role permissions to access network objects are modeled through policy rules containing location and temporal constraints.

The application of spatio-temporal RBAC model in wireless network security is in its infancy. Laborde et al. [10] presents a colored Petri Net based tool which allows to describe graphically given network topology, the security mechanism and the goals required. In this work, the authors model the security policies through generalized RBAC without considering time and location dependent service access. Tomur et al. [9] uses spatio-temporal RBAC in wireless network. They present a layered security architecture to control access in wireless networks based STRBAC model. However, this work does not describe the modeling of STRBAC policies using existing ACL standards. In our proposed WLAN policy management system, the global access policies are represented through a formal STRBAC model and enforced through distributed policy zone controllers. This makes the task of policy enforcement and validation easier and efficient.

3   WLAN Security Policy Management System

The proposed WLAN policy management system shown in Fig.1 stems from the notion of Wireless policy zones. A policy zone comprises of one or more wireless Access Points (AP), a dedicated *Wireless Policy Zone Controller* (WPZCon) and a *Local Role Server* (LRS) separated from other zones by a zone router. The authentication of the users and the access points are managed by a special authentication server (AS) called *Central Authentication & Role Server* (CARS) which can be a RADIUS or an AAA server [14]. It also assigns appropriate roles to the authenticated users based on user credentials and policy zone (location) information. Each time a new node enters in the range of an AP, AS authenticates it and communicates the information to LRS while associating the node in the corresponding zone. When a node leaves the range of an AP, using the baecon packet AP can sense it and requests the AS to remove the information regarding the node from the zone. The LRS is responsible for maintaining the AP and user-role information in a policy zone. The *Global Policy Server* (GPS) formalizes the global security policy (GP) through a spatio-temporal RBAC model. The detail of the STRBAC model is described in section 4. It also determines and validates high level policy configurations for various policy zones. Each WPZCon coordinate with the local role server to derive low level access configuration for the policy zone and validates it with corresponding high level configuration. Finally, the implementation access rules corresponding to the low level access configurations are distributed to various zone access points. The operational flow of the system is shown in Fig.2. In our framework, the distributed policy zone architecture makes the task of policy enforcement and validation easier and efficient. We also propose a formal spatio-temporal RBAC model for representing the security policies described in the next section.

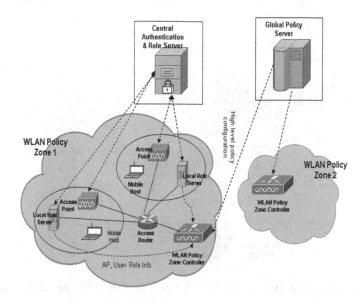

Fig. 1. Wireless LAN Security Policy Management System

4   Proposed Spatio-temporal RBAC Model for WLAN Policy Management

Typically, the spatio-temporal RBAC model incorporates the location and time information to the basic RBAC entities through various relations. The basic RBAC entities are users, roles, objects, permissions and operations. The modeling of location and time information to support the proposed WLAN policy management system has been described further below.

Modeling Location: In our model, the network location is represented in terms of policy zones. The policy zones physically represent different sections in an organizational WLAN. For example, in a typical *academic* network, the policy zones can be *Academic sections*, *Hostels* or *Administration*. A policy zone is formally defined as follows:

Definition 1: [Policy Zone] *A Policy Zone* $PZon_i$ *is defined as a set of IP addresses*, $\{IP_i, IP_j, ..., IP_n\}$. *The IP addresses can be contiguous or discrete.*

Example of a contiguous IP address block is [10.14.0.0 − 10.14.255.255]. Example of a discrete IP address block is [10.14.0.0 − 10.14.255.255, 10.16.0.0 − 10.16.255.255].

Modeling Time: The time must be modeled with appropriate granularity to provide temporal object access. The granularity of time may depend on the organizational access control requirements. To represent time in our model, we use the notion of time instant and time interval.

A time instant is a discrete point on the time line. A time interval is a set of time instances. The interval can be continuous and non-continuous. Example of

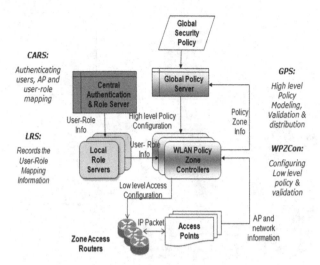

Fig. 2. Operational Flow of the WLAN Security Policy Management System

a continuous interval is 09:00-15:00 on 24th July. Example of a non-continuous time interval is 09:00-19:00 on Monday to Friday in the month of July. A time instant t_i in the interval T is indicated as $t_i \in T$.

4.1   Modeling Basic RBAC Entities in the Proposed System

The basic RBAC entities are Users, Roles, Objects, Permissions and Operations. In our model, Permissions and Operations associated to various roles are modeled as Policy Rules.

Users: The users are mobile hosts, communicate to wireless access points (AP) in a policy zone. The CARS authenticates the users and the AP(s) based on user credentials (mainly, MAC address), locations (policy zones) and AP credentials (device ID and network-ID). The location of an user is the policy zone from which it communicates. The policy zone of an user u during time interval T can be identified by the function $UserPZone(u, T)$. Multiple users can be associated to a single policy zone at any given point of time.

Network Objects: In the proposed model, the network objects are logical. A network object is identified by a network service and a service policy zone.

Definition 2: [Network Object] *A network object $Obj_i < Serv_j, Z_k >$ represents a network service $Serv_j$ associated to a service policy zone Z_k.*

Network services refer to any network applications conforming to TCP/IP protocol. For example, some of the known network services are *ssh, telnet, http* etc. The service policy zone is the destination location associated to the service. For example, *ssh* service access to a policy zone Z_d can be represented by a network object $Obj_i < ssh, Z_d >$.

Roles: Roles represent group of users. For example, typical roles for an academic institution may be *faculty, student, administrator, guest* etc. In our model, the assignment of roles to the users is location and time dependent. Thus, valid users must satisfy the spatial and temporal constraints before role assignment. $RoleAssignZone(r_i)$ represents the policy zone(s) where the role r_i can be assigned. $RoleAssignTime(r_j)$ represents the time interval when the role r_j can be assigned.

The predicate $UserRoleAssign(u_i, r_j, T, Z_k)$ states that the user u_i is assigned to role r_j during the time interval T and policy zone Z_k. This predicate must satisfy the property: $UserRoleAssign(u_i, r_j, T, Z_k) \Rightarrow (UserPZone(u_i, T) = Z_k) \wedge (Z_k \subseteq RoleAssignZone(r_j)) \wedge (T \subseteq RoleAssignTime(r_j))$.

4.2 Modeling of Global Policy

The global policy of an organization can be modeled through a set of policy rules that *"permit"/"deny"* user accesses to various network objects from different policy zones during specified time intervals. A policy rule represents the network object accessibility permissions (*"permit"* or *"deny"*) of a role from a policy zone to the network objects during certain time interval.

Definition 3: [Policy Rule] *A Policy Rule $PR_i < r_j, Z_l, Obj_k, T, p >$ defines that the role r_j is assigned the* permission p *("permit"/"deny") to access the object obj_k from the policy zone $PZon_l$ during the time interval T.*

Each policy rule must satisfy the following predicates: (1) $T \subseteq RoleAssignTime(r_j)$, i.e., time interval T must be contained in $RoleAssignTime(r_j)$; (2) $Z_l \subseteq RoleAssignZone(r_j)$, i.e., source zone Z_l contained in $RoleAssignZone(r_j)$. The global policy is represented as ordered set of policy rules $\{PR_1, ..., PR_N\}$.

High Level Policy Configuration: To enforce the security policy in the wireless LAN, the rules in the global policy model GP must be properly distributed to various policy zone controllers (WPZCon). Thus, GP is represented as a distribution of zonal rule sets $< GP_{Z_1}, GP_{Z_2}, ..., GP_{Z_N} >$, where GP_{Z_i} represents the zonal rule set for policy zone, Z_i. To ensure correct distribution, following property must be satisfied, *Property2:* $(GP_{Z_1} \wedge GP_{Z_2} \wedge ... \wedge GP_{Z_N}) \Rightarrow GP$. A policy rule PR_i is included in the zonal rule set GP_{Z_k} corresponding to zone Z_k, iff the zone of PR_i is contained by Z_k. This is formalized as follows: $\forall PR_i \in GP, \exists Z_k \subseteq Any, (Z_k \subseteq PR_i[Z] \Rightarrow (PR_i[Z] \Uparrow GP_{Z_k}))$. Here, $(PR_i \Uparrow GP_{Z_k})$ indicates the inclusion of PR_i in GP_{Z_k}. Thus, $\forall k, GP_{Z_k} \subseteq GP$. In our model, $< GP_{Z_1}, GP_{Z_2}, ..., GP_{Z_N} >$ represents the high level policy configuration corresponding to the global policy GP.

Low Level Access Configuration: The global policy server (GPS) distributes the high level policy rule sets to various policy zone controllers (WPZCons). Each WPZCon translates the zonal rule set to low level configuration based on the local policy zone information coordinating with the local role server (LRS) and access points (AP). The low level access configuration LP_{Z_k} represents a collection of implementation rules $\{IR_1, IR_2, ..., IR_N\}$ corresponding to the zonal rule set GP_{Z_k} of policy zone Z_k.

Definition 4: [Implementation Rule] *An Implementation rule $IR_x < u_i, r_j, Serv_k, Z_s, Z_d, T, p, net_l >$ defines that an user u_i associated to the role r_j is assigned the permission p to access the network service $Serv_k$ from the source zone Z_s to destination zone Z_d during time interval T; where, net_l represents the access router or the network interface to which the rule is physically mapped.*

For each implementation rule, IR_i, the service $Serv_k$ and destination policy zone Z_d can be determined from the associated network object ($PR_i[Obj]$) corresponding to the policy rule PR_i. More importantly, the following property ensures the correct user-role mapping,
Property1: $UserRoleAssign(u_i, r_j, T, Z_k) \Rightarrow (UserPZone(u_i, T) = Z_k) \wedge$
$(Z_k \subseteq RoleAssignZon(r_j)) \wedge (T \subseteq RoleAssignTime(r_j))$.

The validation of the low level access configuration is ensured by the property,
Property3: $\forall (LP_{Z_i}, GP_{Z_i}), LP_{Z_i} \Rightarrow GP_{Z_i}$. It states that each low level access configuration, LP_{Z_i} must conform to the corresponding high level policy rule set GP_{Z_i}. In our earlier work [15], the detailed formalization and analysis of the proposed STRBAC model has been described. Next section describes the verification of the security properties of the proposed STRBAC model.

5   SAT Based Security Property Verification

In SAT based approach, the verification problem is reduced into boolean formula and its satisfiability is checked. In the present work, the STRBAC model, Global policy (GP), high level policy configurations ($< GP_{Z_1}, GP_{Z_2}, ..., GP_{Z_N} >$) and low level access configurations ($< LP_{Z_1}, ..., LP_{Z_N} >$) are reduced into set of boolean clauses. Then, security properties, i.e., *Property1, Property2* and *Property3* [described in section 4] are reduced into boolean clauses which are fed as SAT query to the SAT solver [12]. The SAT solver checks the satisfiability of the properties to asses the access configuration with respect to the global policy.

5.1   Boolean Modeling STRBAC Entities and Policy Configurations

The proposed STRBAC model includes the following entities: *users, roles, time, source* and *destination policy zones* and *network services*. Here, a *network service* and a *destination policy zone* compositely define a *network object*.

Each *user or host* is identified by a MAC address which is a 48 bit number. So, *users* are modeled as 48 boolean variables, namely, $(u_0, u_1, ..., u_{47})$. Similarly, *roles* are modeled as 4 boolean variables, namely, $(r_0, r_1, ..., r_3)$ where we consider 16 different roles. The *source* and *destination* zones are represented as IP address blocks and are modeled with 32 boolean variables each, namely, $(s_0, s_1, ..., s_{31})$ and $(d_0, d_1, ..., d_{31})$ respectively. A range of IP addresses can be translated using disjunction ($\vee$) operator. Similarly, protocol type and service port numbers are mapped into 5 and 16 boolean variables, namely, $(p_0, p_1, ..., p_4)$ and $(i_0, i_1, ..., i_{15})$ respectively. A *network service* is modeled as conjunction ($\wedge$) of protocol and service port number. A *network object* is modeled as conjunction ($\land$) of a service and destination zone. *Time* constraints are modeled as disjunction of its valid periods. Each valid time period may contain *day of week, hours* and *minutes* etc. access permissions ("permit" or "deny") are modeled using a variable A. The components of a valid time period are mapped into a set of boolean variables, namely, (dt_0, dt_1, dt_2), $(th_0, th_1, ..., th_4)$ and $(tm_0, tm_1, ..., tm_5)$ respectively. The *UserPZone, RoleAssignTime, RoleAssignZone* and *UserRoleAssign* functions are modeled through four boolean functions, namely $FUZone(u_i, T_i, Z_i)$, $FRATime(r_i, T_i, Z_i)$, $FRAZone(r_i, Z_i, T_i)$ and (u_i, r_i, T_i, Z_i) respectively.

In both the policy and access configuration models, rule components are same except the network *access router* information in the low level access configuration. As access router IP address corresponding to a policy zone contained in the zone IP address block, it is modeled through same set of boolean variables as source policy zone, namely, $(s_0, s_1, ..., s_{31})$.

Reduction of Global Policy and High level Policy Configurations: Global policy is represented as collection of policy rules with following components: *roles, source-policy zone, network object* and *permissions*. The global policy (GP) is reduced into two boolean functions, "permit"(PT^{gp}) and "deny" (PF^{gp}) where each function incorporates corresponding "permit" and "deny" rules through disjunction($\lor$) operator. The formulation is described as follows:
$PR_i \Leftrightarrow (FR_i \land SIP_i \land Obj_i \land T_i \land A_i)$; where, $Obj_i \Leftrightarrow (P_i \land I_i \land DIP_i)$
$PT^{gp} \Leftrightarrow (\bigvee PR_j)$, $\forall PR_j(action) =$ "permit"
$PF^{gp} \Leftrightarrow (\bigvee PR_k)$, $\forall PR_k(action) =$ "deny".
Similarly, the high level policy configuration is represented as collection of zone-wise policy rule sets and hence reduced to two boolean functions for each zone Z_x, namely, PT^{Z_x} and PF^{Z_x} respectively. This is formalized as follows:
$PT^{Z_x} \Leftrightarrow (\bigvee PR_j)$, $\forall PR_j(action) =$ "permit" $\land PR_j(SIP_j) = Z_x$
$PF^{Z_x} \Leftrightarrow (\bigvee PR_k)$, $\forall PR_k(action) =$ "deny" $\land PR_k(SIP_j) = Z_x$.

Reduction of Low level Access Configurations: Low level access configuration is represented as zone-wise distribution of low level access rules (IR). Each low level access rule contains the following components; *user, role, network service, source policy zone, destination policy zone, time constraints, permission* and *access router* (or wireless policy zone interface) IP address. In our model, the access router IP is considered as the first IP address in the corresponding wireless zone IP block. The low level access configuration for each policy zone Z_x is reduced into two boolean functions LAT^{Z_x} and LAF^{Z_x}. The low level access rules and access configurations are formalized as follows:
$IR_i \Leftrightarrow (u_i \land r_i \land SIP_i \land DIP_i \land T_i \land A_i \land ARIP_i)$, where, $ARIP_i \oplus SIP_i = 000..01$.
$LAT^{Z_x} \Leftrightarrow (\bigvee IR_j)$, $\forall IR_j(action) =$ "permit".
$LAF^{Z_x} \Leftrightarrow (\bigvee IR_j)$, $\forall IR_j(action) =$ "deny" $\land IR_j(SIP_j) = Z_x$.

5.2   SAT Solver and SAT Query Formulation

The security property verification problem has been reduced to SAT query and verified through *zChaff* SAT solver [12]. It takes SAT query in conjunctive normal form (CNF) and checks its satisfiability. We use *DIMACS* [13] format for storing

CNF formulae in ASCII files. SAT query for the present problem is conjunction of *Property1*, *Property2* and *Propwerty3* (refer section 4). This is represented as the boolean expression: $F = Pr1 \wedge Pr2 \wedge Pr3$, where,

$Pr1 \Leftrightarrow [UserRoleAssign(u_i, r_j, T, Z_k) \Rightarrow (UserPZone(u_i, T) = Z_k) \wedge (Z_k \subseteq RoleAssignZon(r_j)) \wedge (T \subseteq RoleAssignTime(r_j)];$

$Pr2 \Leftrightarrow [GP_{Hall} \wedge GP_{Academic} \wedge GP_{Admin} \Rightarrow GP]$ and

$Pr3 \Leftrightarrow [(LP_{Hall} \Rightarrow GP_{Hall}) \wedge (LP_{Academic} \wedge \Rightarrow GP_{Academic}) \wedge (LP_{Admin} \Rightarrow GP_{Admin})]$. /*Here, the properties are shown considering a typical *academic* network with three network zones, namely, *Hall*, *Academic* and *Admin**/.

In our framework, the formula F is translated into CNF using standard algorithm for 3-CNF satisfiability [11]. The algorithm forms truth tables for every sub-expression containing disjunctions of conjunctions and converts it into CNF applying De-Morgan's rules where each clause contains at most 3 literals. For example, equivalent CNF for the the the formula $Pr2 \Leftrightarrow [GP_{Hall} \wedge GP_{Academic} \wedge GP_{Admin} \Rightarrow GP]$ can be represented as $(\neg Pr2 \vee \neg GP_{Hall} \vee \neg GP_{Academic} \vee \neg GP_{Admin}) \wedge (Pr2 \vee GP_{Hall}) \wedge (Pr2 \vee GP_{Academic}) \wedge (Pr2 \vee GP_{Admin}) \wedge (Pr3 \vee \neg GP)$. The formula F (in DIMACS CNF format) is provided as input to *zChaff*. It checks the SAT/UNSAT of the formula. The SAT result implies that the low level access configuration conforms to global policy whereas UNSAT result indicates that the low level access configuration is incorrect. In that case the unsatisfiable instance indicates the violating rule.

6   Conclusion

In this paper we present a security policy management system for wireless network (WLAN) supported by a formal spatio-temporal RBAC model. In the proposed system, the global security policy is enforced through distributed policy zone controllers (WPZCons) which are populated by extracting the high level policy configurations from the global policy server (GPS). This makes policy enforcement and validation simple and efficient. We present a spatio-temporal RBAC model to support the policy management system which ensures time and location dependent authorized access to the network objects and hence provides strong security perimeter over an organizational WLAN. We also present a SAT based verification framework for checking correct enforcement of the access policies in the wireless access routers.

References

1. Basile, C., Lioy, A., Prez, G.M., Clemente, F.J.G., Skarmeta, A.F.G.: POSITIF: a policy-based security management system. In: 8th IEEE International Workshop on Policies for Distributed Systems and Networks (POLICY 2007), Bologna, Italy, p. 280 (June 2007)
2. Lapiotis, G., Kim, B., Das, S., Anjum, F.: A Policy-based Approach to Wireless LAN Security Management. In: International Workshop on Security and Privacy for Emerging Areas in Communication Networks, Athens, Greece, pp. 181–189 (September 2005)

3. Burns, J., Cheng, A., Gurung, P., Rajagopalan, S., Rao, P., Rosenbluth, D., Martin, D.: Automatic Mnagement of Network Security Policy. In: Proceedings of the 2nd DARPA Information Survivability Conference and Exposition (DISCEX II), Anaheim, California, pp. 12–26 (June 2001)
4. Yavatkar, R., Pendarakis, D., Guerin, R.: RFC 2753: A Framework for Policy-based Admission Control. Internet Society, 1–20 (January 2000)
5. Westrinen, A., Schnizlein, J., Strassner, J., Scherling, M., Quinn, B., Herzog, S., Carlson, M., Perry, J., Wldbusser, S.: RFC 3198: Terminology for Policy-Based Management. Internet Society, 1–21 (November 2001)
6. Ferraiolo, D.F., Sandhu, R., Gavrila, S., Kuhn, D.R., Chandramouli, R.: Proposed NIST standard for Role-Based Access Control. ACM Trnsactions on Information and Systems Security 4(3) (August 2001)
7. Joshi, J.B.D., Bertino, E., Latif, U., Ghafoor, A.: A Generalized Temporal Role-Based Access Control Model. IEEE Transactions on Knowledge and Data Engineering 17(1), 4–23 (2005)
8. Ray, I., Toahchoodee, M.: A Spatio-Temporal Role-Based Access Control Model. In: Barker, S., Ahn, G.-J. (eds.) Data and Applications Security 2007. LNCS, vol. 4602, pp. 211–226. Springer, Heidelberg (2007)
9. Tomur, E., Erten, Y.M.: Application of Temporal and Spatial role based access control in 802.11 wireless networks. The Journal of Computers & Security 25(6), 452–458 (2006)
10. Laborde, R., Nasser, B., Grasset, F., Barrere, F., Benzekri, A.: A Formal Approach for the Evaluation of Network Security Mechanisms Based on RBAC policies. Electronic Notes in Theoritical Computer Science 121, 117–142 (2005)
11. Hofmeister, T., Schoning, U., Schuler, R., Watanabe, O.: A Probabilistic 3-SAT Algorithm further improved. In: Alt, H., Ferreira, A. (eds.) STACS 2002. LNCS, vol. 2285, pp. 192–202. Springer, Heidelberg (2002)
12. Mahajan, Y., Fu, Z., Malik, S.: Zchaff 2004: An efficient SAT solver. In: Hoos, H.H., Mitchell, D.G. (eds.) SAT 2004. LNCS, vol. 3542, pp. 360–375. Springer, Heidelberg (2005)
13. Dubois, O., Andre, P., Boufkhad, Y., Carlier, J.: SAT versus UNSAT, Second DIMACS challenge. In: Johnson, D.S., Trick, M.A. (eds.) (1993)
14. Bhagyavati, Summers, W.C., Dejoie, A.: Wireless security techniques: an overview. In: Proceedings of 1st International Conference on Information Security Curriculum Development (InfoSecCD 2004), Georgia, pp. 82–87. ACM Press, New York (2004)
15. Bera, P., Dasgupta, P., Ghosh, S.K.: A Spatio-temporal Role-based Access Control Model for Wireless LAN Security Policy Management. In: Proceedings of 4th ih International Conference on Information Systems, Technology and Management (ICISTM 2010), Thiland, pp. 76–88. Springer, Heidelberg (2010)

Detection and Classification of DDoS Attacks Using Fuzzy Inference System

T. Subbulakshmi[1], Dr. S. Mercy Shalinie[2], C. Suneel Reddy[3], and A. Ramamoorthi[4]

[1] Senior Grade Lecturer, Department of Computer Science and Engineering,
Thiagarajar College of Engineering, Madurai
subbulakshmitce@yahoo.com
[2] HODCSE, Department of Computer Science and Engineering,
Thiagarajar College of Engineering, Madurai
shalinie_m@yahoo.com
[3] II MECSE, Department of Computer Science and Engineering,
Thiagarajar College of Engineering, Madurai
suneelreddyc@gmail.com
[4] I MECSE, Department of Computer Science and Engineering,
Thiagarajar College of Engineering, Madurai
armoorthi@gmail.com

Abstract. A DDoS attack saturates a network by overwhelming the network resources with an immense volume of traffic that prevent the normal users from accessing the network resources. When Intrusion Detection Systems are used, a huge number of alerts will be generated and these alerts consist of both False Positives and True Positives. Due to huge volume of attack traffic, there is a possibility of occurring more False Positives than True Positives which is difficult for the network analyst to classify the original attack and take remedial action. This paper focuses on development of alert classification system to classify False Positives and True Positives related to DDoS attacks. It consists of five phases : Attack Generation, Alert Collection, Alert Fusion, Alert Generalization and Alert classification. In Attack Generation, DDoS attacks are generated in experimental testbed. In Alert Collection, snort IDS will be used to generate alerts for the generated traffic in testbed and alerts are collected. In Alert Fusion, the repeated alerts will be fused together to form meta alerts. In Alerts Generalization, the alerts indicating traffic towards the servers will be taken for further analysis. In Alert Classification, using fuzzy inference system the alerts will be classified as True Positives and False Positives. This reduces the difficulty of the network analyst by eliminating the false positives. This system is tested using an experimental testbed.

Keywords: Alert Classification, Alert Generalization, Alert Fusion, DDoS, False positives, Intrusion Detection, Fuzzy Inference System.

1 Introduction

One of the major problems faced by IDS is huge number of false positive alerts, i.e. alerts that are mistakenly classified normal traffic as security violations. A perfect

N. Meghanathan et al. (Eds.): CNSA 2010, CCIS 89, pp. 242–252, 2010.
© Springer-Verlag Berlin Heidelberg 2010

IDS does not generate false or irrelevant alarms. In practice, signature based IDS found to produce more false alarms than expected. This is because of the overly general signatures and lack of built in verification tool to validate the success of the attack. The huge amount of false positives in the alert log makes the process of taking remedial action for the true positives, i.e. successful attacks, delayed and labor intensive.

Same intrusion event can trigger hundreds of similar alerts. For example, a single network scan may cause to generate several alerts which differ by a small amount of time. These alerts can be fused together before passing to human analyst. Also, different types of alert will be having same underlying event as the root cause. Each attributes of all alerts can be generalized to find out the correlated alerts. This will help in the process of root cause analysis and hence eliminate more number of false positives. Alert generalization also helps to speed up alert verification some times. For example, suppose a large number of IIS exploit attack comes to port 80 of a particular machine which is running an Apache web server and Linux, obviously all of these can be marked as irrelevant since they are not successful.

In intrusion detection, machine learning has so far been primarily used to build systems that classify network connections or system call sequences into one of several predefined classes. This task proved to be very difficult because it aimed at building IDSs only from training examples. Lee [6] developed a methodology to construct additional features using data mining. He also showed the importance of domain-specific knowledge in constructing such IDSs. The key advantage of this work is that it employs the real-time data and classify alerts generated by IDSs, whereas other conventional methods use the existing data to build IDS. So the possibility of new attacks and their recognition can be easily accomplished by this research work.

2 Review of Literature

Alert aggregation and verification are often part of Alert correlation [3], but it has a different goal, to reconstruct incidents from alerts and to find attack scenarios.. Kruegel, Robertson and Vigna [3] proposed a method for alert verification using both active and passive verification methods. In their implementation they use active alert verification extensively while only passive alert verification is used in this work. Pietrazek and Tanner [1] propose a two stage alert classification mechanism for reducing false positives. Alert correlation [7] tries to solve a different, though related goal of alert processing, namely reconstructing attacks and incidents from alerts. Attacks most often occur in distinctive groups, which are called incidents or multi staged attacks [8]. In the general case, it is not possible to reconstruct incidents from alerts.

Hemler et al. [4] applied RIPPER [10] on system calls to generate small and concise set of rules to classify intrusions for host based IDS. He has investigated incremental learning algorithms and their application to intrusion detection. They underline the significance the symbolic representation language and human understanding of background knowledge and learned concepts and criticize a neural network approach. Human understanding is important because should the system act in a way that is harmful to humans, then the concepts responsible for this behaviour can be inspected and modified.

An approach for evolving fuzzy classifiers using genetic algorithms has been proposed[11]. Genetic algorithm with special operations (Gene Addition and Gene deletion) is used to create fuzzy rules for normal and abnormal classes. kddcup '99 data set with 42 attributes and 4,94,021 records is used for experiments. Several statistical methods have been applied to reduce the dimensionality of the problem. Our work differs from this work by solving the issues related to Real time attack and alert generation schemes.

A method is proposed[12] using 'anfis' as a classifier to detect intrusions. The system evaluates the performance of anfis in the forms of binary and multiclass classifier. The kddcup '99 dataset with 42 attributes and 48840 training and 4884 testing records have been used for detection task. Since in this research there are more records and more types of attack classes the system developed can be readily used online.

A real valued negative selection algorithm is proposed [13] and improved using deterministic crowding to generate fuzzy detector rules in the non-self space that can determine if new sample is normal or abnormal. Genetic Algorithm is used with deterministic crowding as the niching technique since it was better than sequential crowding. In evolving fuzzy detector rules first the condition part of the rules is represented using chromosome and fitness of the rules is calculated and the hamming distance is used to perform the deterministic crowding. The experiments were calculated with three different datasets Machey-Glass, Darpa 99, kddcup '99 and two algorithms Efficient Rule detectors and Parallel Hill Climbing of fuzzy rule detectors is found to be better than the other algorithms.

3   System Architecture

In this paper a five phase alert classification system is described. Fig. 1 gives an overview about this architecture.

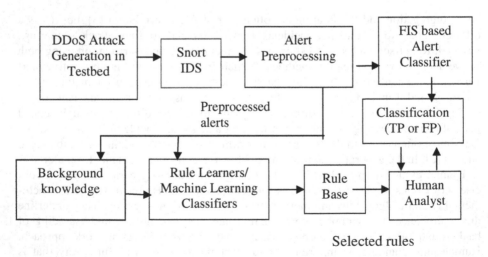

Fig. 1. DDoS Attack Detection /Classification System Architecture

3.1 Anomaly Detection Dataset

The DDoS attacks are generated in an experimental testbed using 'packit' network packet injection tool. In testbed, first the number of test nodes will be selected based on the attack scenario. In the case of Denial of Service(DoS) attack only one Source node and one Sink node will be selected and in the case of Distributed Denial of Service(DDoS) attacks two or more Source nodes and one Sink node will be selected. The user has to upload the Source and Sink programs to the Server and specify the corresponding Source and Sink nodes in which the programs has to be executed. The user should also specify the time interval in which the programs should be executed. In the specified time interval the programs will be transferred from Server to corresponding Source and Sink nodes and executed. The Source program uses IP spoofing with IP address of the available testbed nodes and generates ICMP, TCP and SYN requests towards the sink node. During the execution of programs the specified Source programs will generate traffic towards Sink nodes. The sink program uses traffic recording program. During the time interval the traffic along the Sink nodes will be recorded using the tshark traffic/protocol analyzer and dumped into a file. The dumped traffic contains both the generated traffic and the normal network traffic. When the time interval expires the dumped file will be transferred to Server.

3.2 Alert Generation

The dumped file is taken from the Server and given as input to the open source light-weight intrusion detection system 'Snort'. The default snort rule base contains rules for detecting all types of attacks like DDoS, Remote to Local, User to Root and Probing. By default all the rules will be enabled for detecting all the types of attacks. The snort rules have been modified to detect the DDoS attacks. The rules for detecting DDoS attacks, ICMP and TCP rules have been changed for the environment in which the test is conducted. When the dump file is given as input to the snort, it will generate the alerts. The alerts will be recorded in Comma Separated Value(CSV)files for further processing.

The alerts generated from snort consists of six tuples

```
("msg", "proto",  "srcip", "srcport", "dstip", "dstport")
```

3.3 Alert Preprocessing

Alerts generated by one or more IDS can be set to log into a centralized database. If different types of IDS are used, (Application, Network and Host based) the attack messages also will be in different formats. So preprocessing step has to be done, before passing into the clustering component. While preprocessing the alert best effort values will be supplied for the missing attributes. Also the timestamp is converted into seconds for the purpose of comparison.

Since different IDS may use different naming conventions for the same event, there is a need to standardize the messages. For example, the messages 'scanning', 'nmap scan', 'port scan' all belongs to the category 'port scan'. The standard names are chosen either from CVE or Bugtraq and in some cases names from one of the IDS is taken as standard. In addition, a unique id is also added to every alert for the purpose of tracking the alerts.

3.3.1 Alert Fusion

First, alerts with same attributes are fused together for the purpose of alert reduction. This is possible since multiple IDS may be there in the network which produces redundant alerts and same event may cause to trigger hundreds of similar alerts. Alert fusion also makes the process of generalization fast. Alerts with same attributes are fused together to form meta-alerts and the number of alerts is added at the end as seventh tuple 'count'.

The format of alerts is

```
("msg", "proto",  "srcip", "srcport", "dstip", "dstport",
"count")
```

3.3.2 Alert Generalization

For the purpose of generalization of alerts, hierarchical background knowledge has to be incorporated for each attribute. A sample hierarchy is shown in Fig.2. Human understandable descriptions of alert clusters are preferred since human intervention may be required for advanced analysis. Generalization is carried out as a step by step process. On every iteration, one of the selected attribute is generalized to the next higher level of hierarchy and those alerts which have become similar by this generalization are grouped together. This process is repeated until one of the generalized alerts reach a threshold count. The selection of this threshold is left as a design choice. Since it is assumed that the attacks are originated from the outside source unique internal destination ips are extracted from the previous step.

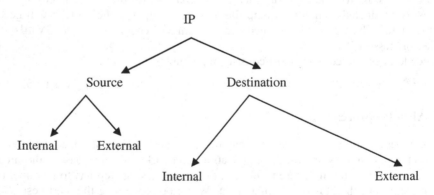

Fig. 2. Sample Hierarchy

3.3.3 Alert Verification

Alert verification is done based on the static asset information collected about the machines inside the network. The process of collecting services and vulnerability information is done with Nessus [9] client. The false positives and irrelevant alerts are marked separately for further analysis. Alert verification is of two types, active and passive. In active verification, whenever an alert is received an information gathering process is initiated to verify the correctness of alert. This method requires more resources and it may slow down the whole alert management process. As an alternative, passive alert verification system is employed this depends on a priori gathered information about the host and network. A drawback of passive alert verification is that the information may be redundant. But still, for real-time environments, the performance of passive verification suits well. The human analyst can optionally examine the output of this step for advanced root cause analysis and for updating firewall and IDS rules for avoiding irrelevant and false positive alerts. The labeled alerts are passed to the next phase.

3.4 Alert Classification Using Fuzzy Inference System

Unfortunately, alerts generated by IDS have to be reviewed by a mentor since no rule can assure hundred percent true positive or true negative rates. In this phase, the labeled alerts from first phase are used for training the automatic classifier which uses RIPPER algorithm for learning the classification rules. The main aim of this phase is to build an automatic alert classifier that reduces the workload of the human analyst.

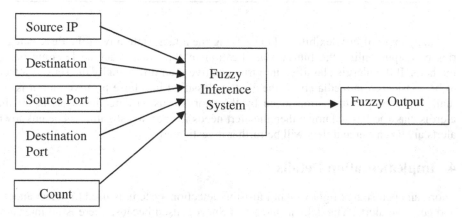

Fig. 3. Fuzzy Alert Classification System

The analyst examines the rules formed by the classifier and modifies if required. The qualified rules are updated to an Alert filter which classifies the alerts as true and false positives. Some algorithms can give confidence level of classification. In this case, the one with high level of confidence can be safely removed as false positives. The alerts which have been classified as false positive by the human analyst can be considered for training purpose. In addition to training examples, background knowledge is used to learn improved classification rules. These rules are then used by the classifier to classify alerts. The analyst can inspect the rules to make sure they are correct. Fuzzy logic is used to identify the alerts as either true positive or false positive. Fuzzy Inference system with five input variables and one output variables is used. The input and output variables and their membership functions are given in Table 1.

Table 1. Fuzzy Input/Output Membership Functions

Sl. No	Input /Output	Name of the Input or Output	Membership functions
1	Input	Source IP	Int_server, int_client, ext_host
2	Input	Destination IP	Int_server, int_client, ext_host
3	Input	Source port	legal, illegal, unknown
4	Input	Destination port	legal, illegal, unknown
5	Input	Count	Low, medium, high
6	Output	Classification	TP, FP, Unknown

Fuzzy logic offers flexibility of classifying the attacks into any of the three categories of output unlike the binary classification of the other machine learning based methods. If the alert is classified into true positive then it is actually the serious attack to be considered immediately. If the alert is classified into false positive then it is actually the wrong information given by the snort intrusion detection system. If the alert is classified as unknown then the alert needs further investigation. The unknown alerts are taken out and they will be further investigated.

4 Implementation Details

Snort, an open source light weight intrusion detection system, is used to detect attacks and generate alerts. The default rule set of Snort is used because there is no intension to evaluate the performance of Snort as IDS. Separate IDS is placed for wireless and wired networks inside the campus. The alerts generated are logged into a file. Each alert is represented as a seven filed record containing the following attributes: time-stamp, signature ID, Source and destination IP addresses, message name and protocol.

The alerts generated for a period of 24 hours have been collected for the purpose of analysis. Alerts from multiple IDS are combined and considered for preprocessing. The preprocessed alerts are then normalized with standard naming conventions as discussed earlier. After normalizing similar alerts are fused together for eliminating redundancy. The alerts are then generalized for root cause analysis and alert verification. The background knowledge for generalization is represented as a tree structure. The whole system was developed in java.

For the fuzzy logic based alert classification system the alerts are classified into attacks based on the rules. The rules are written to classify the alerts into the three output categories. Some example rules are

- If source IP is ext_host and destination IP is int_server and source port is unknown and destination port is illegal and count is high then output is TP

- If source IP is ext_host and destination IP is int_client and source port is unknown and destination port is illegal and count is high then output is TP

- If source IP is ext_host and destination IP is ext_host and source port is unknown and destination port is legal and count is high then output is unknown

- If source IP is int_host and destination IP is int_server and source port is unknown and destination port is illegal and count is low then output is FP

Some more information is added as background knowledge for the purpose of learning. Attribute valued representation of background knowledge [1], which is most suitable for machine learning algorithms, is used in this experiment. Eight more attributes to the alerts generated by snort has been added. The background knowledge sets used are IP address classification and operating system for source and destination IP addresses, Aggregate 1 containing number of alerts in the time window of one minute with same source or destination IP address and total number of alerts in the same time window, Aggregate 2 contains fields same as Aggregate 1 but within the time window of 5 minutes. WEKA implementation of RIPPER algorithm is used in the experiments.

5 Results and Discussion

The result of Alert Correlation Steps is shown in Table2. It is shown that about 81% of the false positives were successfully identified by the system. This may not be the case always. The alerts collected were mostly repeated and redundant.

Table 2. Results of Alert Classification

Name of Alert Correlation Steps	Reduction in number of alerts
Alert Detection	63592
Alert Preprocessing – Fusion	3207
Alert Preprocessing – Generalization	2515
Alert Classification – threshold based method	679
Alert Classification – Fuzzy method	400

Table 3. Results of Ripper algorithm using Background Knowledge

Background Knowledge	Precision	Recall	F-measure
Full	0.972	0.954	0.962
Partial	0.954	0.996	0.975

The labeled alerts after verification have been sent to the experiments in WEKA with two sets of background knowledge. The results, as shown in Table 3, indicates that RIPPER performs well with full background knowledge set.

Table 4. Results obtained Machine learning classifiers

ALGORITHM	Precision	Recall	F-Measure	ROC
RandomForest	0.958	0.965	0.961	0.625
DecisionStump	0.954	0.996	0.975	0.473
RIPPER	0.954	0.996	0.975	0.580
NNge	0.959	0.954	0.956	0.554
oneR	0.954	0.993	0.973	0.496
PART	0.955	0.985	0.970	0.668
FIS based AC	0.999	0.963	0.971	0.552

The result of 10-fold cross validation is given in Table 4. Cross validation results indicates the suitability of classifier for future instances. In algorithms like RIPPER, the classifier with no background knowledge performs worse than the classifier with simple classifications of IP addresses and operating systems running on the machines in terms of false positives. Using the background knowledge consisting of the classifications above and aggregates significantly reduces the false positive rate and increases the true positive rate. Full background knowledge performs much better to the reduced one. So all attributes of background knowledge were used in this research.

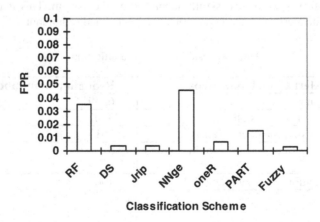

Fig. 4. Graph showing False Positive Rates (FPR) for different classification schemes

A good measure for fitness of algorithms is to take the ones with area under ROC (Receiver Operating Characteristics) curve greater than 0.5. Table 4 provides a comparison of all the six algorithms used on the basis of ROC curve area. PART and

Random Forest algorithm performs well in this manner, but compared to FIS Based AC the false negative ratio is higher for these algorithms (Figure 4). FIS based AC has only minimum false negative rate which is tolerable. Also, it supports incremental learning for batch classification of alerts and provides classification confidence for each rule produced. Fuzzy Inference Systems based Alert Classification gives better classification results. This can be very much useful in a system which processes alerts autonomously. The outputs with high classification confidence can be passed without verification by the analyst. Putting it all together, FIS based Alert Classification comes out to be the most suitable algorithm for false positive reduction.

5.1 Key Findings of the Research

- Fuzzy Inference System based Alert Classification produces three classes of outputs true positive, false positive and unknown alerts which is different from the other machine learning methods which produces binary classification. Even though the machine learning methods produce multi class classification the classes of output will be the types of attacks or normal class.

- Fuzzy Inference system produces output based on the nature of attacks and the output value of the alerts [0,1] specifies the severity of the attack.

  - o If value is nearer to '1', then the attack should be considered as highly severe and it will be classified as True Positive

  - o If value is '0.5' then the attack should be considered as moderately severe and it will be classified as unknown

  - o If value is nearer to '0' then the attack should be considered as less severe and it will be classified as false positive

- The False Positive Rate (FPR) of the FIS based Alert Classification is found to be lower than the other machine learning algorithms Random Forest, Decision Stump, JRipper, NeuralNetworks Generalization, OneR, PART. The FIS based Alert Classification produces less false positives and it is more effective since it produces the classes of alerts along with their severity ratings. The alerts which have high severity can be attended immediately and low severity alerts will be removed from the system which helps in building an effective classifier.

6 Conclusion

The Alert Classification System is implemented using Fuzzy Inference System based Alert Classification and machine learning techniques. Alert preprocessing helped in eliminating about 63% of the false positives. After the process of passive verification 18% of the alerts were marked as irrelevant. So a total of 81% reduction is achieved through Fuzzy Inference System based Alert Classification which is actually really impressive. The result may slightly vary from organization to organization since in our network most of the attack types and alerts were repeated. Most of the attacks were originated from inside the network, which also helped in generalization. The classification accuracy can be further improved by classifying using Machine learning algorithms with feature selection and on line classification.

Acknowledgement

This work was supported by grants from National Technical Research Organization of Government of India, as a part of "Smart and Secure Environment". The authors sincerely thank the Management and Principal of Thiagarajar College of Engineering, Madurai, India for their support and encouragement.

References

1. Pietraszek, T., Tanner, A.: Data mining and machine learning-Towards reducing false positives in intrusion detection. Information Security Technical Report 10, 169–183 (2005)
2. Pietraszek, T.: Using adaptive alert classification to reduce false positives in intrusion detection. In: Jonsson, E., Valdes, A., Almgren, M. (eds.) RAID 2004. LNCS, vol. 3224, pp. 102–124. Springer, Heidelberg (2004)
3. Kruegel, C., Robertson, W., Vigna, G.: Using alert verification to identify successful intrusion attaempts. K.G. Saur Verlag, Munchen (2004)
4. Helmer, G., Wong, J.S.K., Honavar, V., Miller, L.: Automated discovery of concise predictive rules for intrusion detection. The Journal of Systems and Software 60(2), 165–175 (2002)
5. Debar, H., Wespi, A.: Aggregation and correlation of intrusion detection alerts. In: Lee, W., Mé, L., Wespi, A. (eds.) RAID 2001. LNCS, vol. 2212, pp. 85–103. Springer, Heidelberg (2001)
6. Lee, W.: A Data Mining Framework for Constructing Features and Models for Intrusion Detection Systems, PhD thesis, Columbia University (1999)
7. Cohen, W.W.: Fast effective rule induction. In: Prieditis, A., Russell, S. (eds.) Proceedings of the 12th International Conference on Machine Learning, Tahoe City, CA, pp. 115–123. Morgan Kaufmann Publishers, San Francisco (1995)
8. Howard, J.D., Longstaff, T.A.: A common language for computer security incidents, Technical report, CERT (1998)
9. Cohen, W.W.: Fast effective rule induction. In: Prieditis, A., Russell, S. (eds.) Proceedings of the 12th International Conference on Machine Learning, Tahoe City, CA, pp. 115–123. Morgan Kaufmann Publishers, San Francisco (1995)
10. Helmer, G., Wong, J.S.K., Honavar, V., Miller, L.: Automated discovery of concise predictive rules for intrusion detection. The Journal of Systems and Software 60(2), 165–175 (2002)
11. Gomez, J., Dasgupta, D.: Evolving Fuzzy Classifiers for Intrusion Detection. In: Proceedings of the 2002 IEEE Workshop on Information Assurance (2002)
12. Toosi, A.N., Kahani, M., Monsefi, R.: Network Intrusion Detection Based on Neuro-Fuzzy Classification. In: Proceedings of IEEE International Conference on Computing and Informatics. IEEE, Los Alamitos (2006)

Detection and Recognition of File Masquerading for E-mail and Data Security

R. Dhanalakshmi[1] and Dr. C. Chellappan[2]

[1] Research Scholar, Department of computer science and Engg.,
Anna University , Chennai
[2] Professor , Department of computer science and Engg., Anna University , Chennai
dhanalakshmisai@gmail.com, drcc@annauniv.edu

Abstract. Due to the tremendous improvement of internet technology and increasing importance of privacy, security, and wise use of computational resources, the corresponding technologies are increasingly being faced with the problem of file type detection. Digital forensics deals with an investigation of digital evidence to enable investigators to detect the facts for the offences. In digital forensics, there are numerous file formats in use and criminals have started using either non-standard file formats or change extensions of files while storing or transmitting them over a network. This makes recovering data out of these files difficult. This also poses a very severe problem for the unauthorized users to send malicious data across the network and it is essential to tackle this e-crime which may harm the entire organization and network . File type detection has the most usage and importance in the proper functionality of operating systems, firewalls, intrusion detection systems, anti viruses, filters, steganalysis and computer forensics. Certain organizations may ban specific file formats via their intranet or E-mail services and the technique to change file extension in sending across has to be severely monitored. Identifying the type of file format of a digital object will be a crucial function on ingest to a digital repository thereby attaining improved security and fraud prevention .This paper focuses on identifying the true file type , detect the presence of embedded data types to improve analysis efficiency in Digital forensic .

Keywords: Digital forensics, File structure, Signature, Fileprints, Validation.

1 Introduction

Computer forensics is defined as the application of computer investigation and analysis techniques to determine potential evidence. Large companies and organizations have at their disposal dozens of knowledge repositories located in different parts of the world, accessible through intranets. Simply changing the file extension on a Windows-based computer will often allow a user to make an image file masquerade as another type of file. A particular file format is often indicated as part of a file's name by a file name extension (suffix). Conventionally, the extension is separated by a period from the name and contains three or four letters that identify the format. A malicious user may attempt to change the extension of the file (For example star.exe

N. Meghanathan et al. (Eds.): CNSA 2010, CCIS 89, pp. 253–262, 2010.

may be changed or renamed as star.zip) ,save as a different file format(star.doc is saved as star.html) or the file extension may be deleted . All of the above scenarios may be used to transmit the malicious data or banned file formats in a network which may corrupt the same. Forensic investigators have a number of tools at their disposal that can overcome this simple ruse. Such tools often look for "magic numbers" that can identify whether or not a given file matches the type indicated by its extension. However there are some file types for which there are no magic numbers or there may be instances where the sequence of bytes represents a partial file that no longer includes the magic number.

An efficient, automated algorithm to perform this kind of file type recognition would be of tremendous benefit to organizations needing to perform forensic analyses of computer hard drives. It could also be used by virus protection software, intrusion detection systems, firewalls, and security downgrading packages to identify the true nature of programs passing through the protected systems. This paper proposes an content based algorithm for generating "fingerprints" of file types based on a set of known input files, then using the fingerprints to recognize the true type of unknown files based on their content, rather than metadata associated with them. Recognition is performed by various options such byte frequency analysis, byte frequency cross-correlation analysis, file header/trailer analysis and statistical methods using Linear discriminant model.

2 Problem Definition

In digital forensic, there are numerous file formats in use and criminals have started using either non-standard file formats or changing extensions of files while storing or transmitting them over a network. This makes recovering data out of these files difficult. It is required to produce a tool that can identify the format of any file including compound file .Identifying correct file formats despite modification by malicious users, when transmitted over a network . Certain organizations ban specific file formats(For example unable to transmit .exe file attachments in Gmail but the file type may be changed and transmitted via the same) A file identification tool will prevent users from sending disguised documents.

2.1 Design Goals

The design goals to be attained are
  ➢ To attain higher accuracy to identify file types.
  ➢ To automatically generate file type fingerprints and they should be minimized
  ➢ To attain speed thereby making the comparisons as fast as possible irrespective of the fingerprint file size.
  ➢ To provide a tradeoff between speed and accuracy

2.2 File Type Detection Methods

True identification of a file format is a tedious task. File type detection methods can be categorized into three kinds: extension-based, magic bytes-based, and content-based methods, each of them has its own strengths and weaknesses, and none of them are comprehensive or foolproof enough to satisfy all the requirements .The fastest and easiest method of file type detection is the extension-based method. The Microsoft's operating systems use such approach almost exclusively. All the file types, at least in the Windows based systems, are generally accompanied by an extension. This approach can be applied to both binary and text files. While it does not need to open the files, it is by far the fastest way to classify the files. However, it has a great vulnerability while it can be easily spoofed by a simple file renaming.

The second method of file type detection that is devoted to the binary files is based on the magic bytes. The magic bytes are some predefined signatures in the header or trailer of binary files. Magic bytes may include some extra information regarding the tool .The magic bytes method is taken by many UNIX based operating systems. However, it has some drawbacks: the magic bytes are not used in all file types. They only work on the binary files and are not an enforced or regulated aspect of the file types. They vary in length for different file types and do not always give a very specific answer. There are several thousand file types for which magic bytes are defined and there are multiple lists of magic bytes that are not completely consistent. Some programs or program developers may never put any magic bytes at the beginning of their file types. This approach can be also spoofed. Altering the magic bytes of a file may not disturb its functionality but can defeat the true file type detection.

The third method of file type detection is to consider the file contents and using the statistical modeling techniques. It is a new research area and is the only way to determine the spoofed file types. It is based on the byte values inside of different computer files. Each computer byte consists of eight bits so it can accept 256 different values varying between 0 and 255. The BFD of a file can be simply found by reading the contents of that file and counting the number of times that each byte value occurs. It is believed that different files of the same type have the same characteristics, which can be extracted to be used in the file type detection. In this approach, several sample files of the same type is given and a fileprint, something similar to a fingerprint, is produced from the sample files. Whenever an unknown file is examined, its fileprint will be produced with the same process and it will be compared with the collection of previously produced fileprints. To produce a fileprint some features of the file type should be selected and extracted. The original principle is to use the BFD of file contents and manipulate with its statistical features. Such statistical measurements together form a model of the chosen file type, sometimes called a centroid. It is also possible to produce several centroids from a file type (multi-centroids). The centroids are then compared to an unknown sample file or data fragment, and the distance between the sample and the centroids is then calculated. If such distance is lower than a predefined threshold, the examined file is categorized as being of the same file type that the centroid represents.

3 Literature Survey

The most common and the simplest way to identify file type is to look at the file's extension [22], but this can be easily spoofed by users with malicious intent. Novice users could also unintentionally change the file extension while renaming the file name. Malwares could also easily hide themselves by having file extensions that virus scanners skip. Another method to identify file type is to look at magic numbers in the file [23]. For example, GIF files begin with ASCII representation of either GIF87a or GIF89a depending on the standard. ZIP files always have the magic number "PK" at the beginning of the file. However, only binary files have magic numbers so it is not applicable to text files. As with the file extension, it can also be easily spoofed. Various techniques proposed fall under the broad categories of

- Byte Frequency Distribution Techniques
- Metrics Based Techniques

3.1 Byte Frequency Distribution Techniques

McDaniel and Heydari [9] introduce three algorithms to identify file types by analyzing file content. In byte frequency analysis algorithm (BFA), they calculate byte-frequency distribution of different files and generate "fingerprint" of each file type by averaging byte-frequency distribution of their respective files. They also calculate correlation strength as another characterizing factor. They take the difference of the same byte in different files. If the difference gets smaller, the correlation strength increases towards 1 or vice versa. In byte-frequency cross correlation algorithm, they find the correlation between all byte pairs. They calculate the average frequency between all byte pairs and correlation strength similar to the BFA algorithm. In file header/trailer algorithm, the file headers and trailers are byte patterns that appear in a fixed location at the beginning and end of a file. They maintain an array of 256 for each location and the array entry corresponding to the value of the byte is filled with correlation strength of 1. They construct the fingerprint by averaging the correlation strength of each file. In these algorithms, they compare the file with all the generated fingerprints to identify its file type. Wei-Hen Li et al.[19] identify file types using n-gram analysis. They calculate 1-gram frequency distribution of files and build 3 different models of each file type: single centroid (one model of each file type), multi-centroid (multiple models of each file type), and exemplar files (set of files of each file type) as centroid. They refer them as "fileprint". In single and multi-centroid models, they calculate mean and standard deviation of 1-gram frequency distribution of files, and use Mahalanobis distance to compare these models with 1-gram distribution of given file to find the closest model. In exemplar file model, they compare 1-gram distribution of exemplar file with that of given file (there is no variance computed), and Manhattan distance is used instead of Mahalanobis distance. Their solution cannot identify files having similar byte-frequency distributions such as MS Office file formats (such as Word and Excel) but treat them as one group or one abstract file type.

Karresand and Shahmehri [3] [4]proposed the _Oscar_ method for identifying the types of file fragments. They build the single centroid file prints but use quadratic distance metric and 1-norm as distance metric to compare the centroid with the byte frequency-distribution of file. Although Oscar identifies any file type, they optimized their algorithm for JPG file using specific byte pairs in the file, and reported 99.2%

detection rate with no false positives. They also use rate of change of bytes, i.e. the difference of two consecutive byte values where they consider the ordering information of bytes.

3.2 Metric Based Techniques

Veenman [17] extracts three features from file content. These features are 1) byte frequency distribution, 2) entropy derived from byte-frequency distribution of files, and 3) the algorithmic or Kolmogorov complexity that exploits the substring order . The Fisher linear discriminant is applied to these features to identify the file type.

Calhoun and Coles [18] extended Veenman's work by building classification models (based on the ASCII frequency, entropy, and other statistics) and apply linear discriminant to identify file types. They also argued that files of same type probably have longer substrings in common than that of different types. Our recursive scheme also uses the byte-frequency distribution as a feature and linear discriminant analysis for classification. However, the main difference of ours from Veenman's scheme[17] is the way we build the classification model for each file type. Veenman computes one discriminant function for each file type using all its sample files. However, our scheme combines the similar byte frequency files in groups irrespective of their file types using clustering, and computes the linear discriminant function for each file type in each group. Hence multiple functions could be computed for each file type.

4 Proposed Technique

In this approach, several sample files of the same type is given and a fileprint, similar to a fingerprint, is produced from the sample files. Whenever an unknown file is examined, its fileprint will be produced with the same process and it will be compared with the collection of previously produced fileprints. To produce a fileprint some features of the file type should be selected and extracted. There are some methods that can be used for the feature extraction. The original principle is to use the BFD of file contents and manipulate with its statistical features. Such statistical measurements together form a model of the chosen file type, sometimes called a centroid. It is also possible to produce several centroids from a file type (multi-centroids). The centroids are then compared to an unknown sample file or data fragment, and the distance between the sample and the centroids is then calculated. If such distance is lower than a predefined threshold, the examined file is categorized as being of the same file type that the centroid represents. The proposed methodology combines the features of Header /trailer Algorithm and in the worst case if it fails , looks into Fisher Linear Discriminant model as illustrated in Fig 1

It consists of following modules:

- FHT Analysis – File Identification module
- MDA – File Identification module
- Compound File Detection module

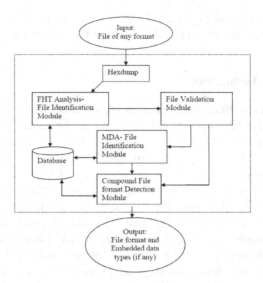

Fig. 1. Architecture

4.1 File Header/Trailer Analysis

If the patterns are not easily identifiable , the file headers and file trailers can be analyzed and used to strengthen the recognition of many file types. The file headers and trailers are patterns of bytes that appear in a fixed location at the beginning and end of a file. If H is the number of file header bytes to analyze, and T is the number of trailer bytes to analyze, then two two dimensional arrays are built, one of dimensions H X 256 and the other of dimensions T x 256. For each byte position in the file header (trailer), all 256 byte values can be independently scored based upon the frequency with which the byte value occurs at the corresponding byte position.

It takes the input file or a fragment as input and analyses its contents to determine the file format.A fileprint is constructed using the header and trailer of various file formats. Given an input file, it is compared with existing fileprints and a score generated for the input file with each file format. The format which gives the maximum score is the resultant format.

To generate Fingerprint Score

$$NFPA=(OFPA*PNF)+NA/(PNF+1)$$

> NFPA-New Fingerprint Array entry.   OFPA-Old Fingerprint Array entry.
> PNF-previous number of files.   NA-New Array Entry

To identify file type

> Generate the score using the following equation.

$$S=I_1F_1+I_2F_2+... I_nF_n / (F_1+F_2+...+ F_n)$$

I-> correlation strength for the byte value extracted from the input file for each byte position.

F ->correlation strength of the byte value in the fingerprint array with the highest correlation strength for the corresponding byte position.

Compare the unknown file with fingerprint and cross-correlation values and pick out the best match. It takes the input file or a fragment as input and analyses its contents to determine the file format.

4.2 Multiple Discriminant Analysis/Compound File Type Detection

Matrices are constructed with ascii, low, entropy and correlation values computed for each file format. Discriminant analysis is performed and the results tabulated. Given an input file, the specified statistical measures are computed and a score is generated. This score on comparison with existing file formats gives the format the file belongs to.

- *Training Session*

   Matrices are constructed for all combinations of pairs of file formats, with the rows representing the file format and the columns representing the statistics taken for each format. File statistics such as correlation are used to detect formats given just a fragment of the file.

- *Input session*

   Statistics are similarly computed for the input file and the resultant file format arrived at.

- Statistical Measures Used:

   Average

   The average is taken by averaging the byte values for each window i and averaging the set of window averages. N denotes the number of bytes in the window. The graph of averages will show how the range of values in each window changes across the file

$$AM = \frac{1}{n} \sum_{i=1}^{n} a_i$$

   Standard deviation

   The standard deviation of the byte values of a window from the average for the window. This essentially identifies how chaotic elements values within a window are and how tightly knit the elements are to the median; i.e. are there many outliers in the window or are the values mostly consistent?

$$\sigma = \sqrt{\frac{1}{N} \sum_{i=1}^{N} (x_i - \mu)^2},$$

5 Tested Environment

The proposed algorithm has been tested with the following algorithms and environments given in the Table 7.1.

Table 7.1. Tested Conditions and results

S. NO	INPUT	ALGORITHMS		
		FHT	MDA	CFD
1	Any file with misleading extension	Identifies correct file format	Identifies correct file format	No embedded data type
2	Any file converted to a different format	Identifies correct file format	Identifies correct file format	No embedded data type
3	Any file with corrupted header	Fails (Gives incorrect file format)	Identifies correct file format	No embedded data type
4	Compound file (File with embedded data types)	Identifies correct file format	Identifies correct file format	Identifies the format of embedded file

FHT – File Header / Trailer Algorithm
MDA – Multi Discriminant Analysis Algorithm
CFD – Compound File Detection Algorithm

6 Conclusion

The tool aims at identifying the file types in various scenarios such as using Header / Trailer methods and in case if the header is corrupted it focuses on the respective content structure which is completely header-independent and uses the whole contents of files. It does not depend on the positions of data fragments of the files and can detect the file type even if the file header is changed or corrupted. The proposed method can be optimized by taking several approaches. Design goals were identified for the file type recognition algorithm. Three of the goals were accuracy, speed, and flexibility. These three factors proved to be closely related. In addition, speed is directly proportional to the number of fingerprints that have been created (although it is independent of the size of files that were originally added into the fingerprint.) Flexibility was provided by allowing for three options that could be used independently or in combinations. The options provided different methods of file comparison with different accuracies and speed of execution.

7 Future Work

Many file types have recurrent patterns throughout the body that could be used for identification as well. A novel approach to identify those patterns is much essential As an improvement to the proposed work , this file analysis method based on the contents may be utilized for identifying malcode bearing documents , to detect the viruses in a file, to detect the encrypted and stegoed files if it carries any malicious content .

Acknowledgment

This work is supported by the NTRO, Government of India. NTRO provides the fund for collaborative project "Smart and Secure Environment" and this paper is modeled for this project. Authors would like to thanks the project coordinators and the NTRO members.

References

1. Hall, G.A., Davis, W.P.: Sliding Window Measurement for File Type Identification. In: Proceedings of IEEE Workshop on Information Assurance Workshop (June 2006)
2. Haggerty, J., Taylor, M.: FORSIGS; Forensic Signature Analysis of the Hard Drive for Multimedia File Fingerprints. In: IFIP TC11 International Information Security Conference, Sandton, South Africa (2006)
3. Karresand, M., Shahmehri, N.: Oscar: File Type Identification of Binary Data in Disk Clusters and RAM Pages. In: Proceedings of IFIP International Information Security Conference: Security and Privacy in Dynamic Environments (SEC 2006), Karlstad, Sweden, pp. 413–424. Springer, Heidelberg (May 2006)
4. Martin, K., Nahid, S.: File type identification of data fragments by their binary structure. In: Proceedings of the IEEE Workshop on Information Assurance (2006)
5. Ahmed, I., Lhee, K.-s., Shin, H., Hong, M.: On Improving the Accuracy and Performance of Content-based File Type Identification. In: Boyd, C., González Nieto, J. (eds.) ACISP 2009. LNCS, vol. 5594, pp. 44–59. Springer, Heidelberg (2009)
6. Ahmed, I., Lhee, K.-s., Shin, H., Hong, M.: Fast File-type Identification. In: Proceedings of the 25th ACM Symposium on Applied Computing (ACM SAC 2010). ACM, Sierre (March 2010)
7. Martin, K., Nahid, S.: Oscar - file type identification of binary data in disk clusters and RAM pages. In: IFIP Security and Privacy in Dynamic Environments, pp. 413–424 (2006)
8. Martin, K., Nahid, S.: File type identification of data fragments by their binary structure. In: Proceedings of the IEEE Workshop on Information Assurance, pp. 140–147 (2006)
9. McDaniel, M., Heydari, M.H.: Content Based File Type Detection algorithms. In: IEEE Proceedings of the 36th Hawaii International Conference on System Sciences (2003)
10. Amirani, M.C., Toorani, M., Shirazi, A.A.B.: A New Approach to Content-based File type Detection. In: Proceedings of the 13th IEEE Symposium on Computers and Communications (ISCC 2008), pp. 1103–1108. IEEE ComSoc, Marrakech (July 2008)

11. Erbacher, R.F., Mulholland, J.: Identification and Localization of Data Types within Large-Scale File Systems. In: Proceedings of the 2nd International Workshop on Systematic Approaches to Digital Forensic Engineering, Seattle, WA (April 2007)
12. Roussev, V., Garfinkel, S.: File Classification Fragment-The Case for Specialized Approaches. In: Systematic Approaches to Digital Forensics Engineering (IEEE/SADFE 2009), Oakland, California (2009)
13. Lechich, R.: File Format Identification and Validation Tools. In: Integrated Library & Technology Systems. Yale University Library, New Haven
14. Harris, R.M.: Using Artificial Neural Networks for Forensic File Type Identification. Master's Thesis, Purdue University (May 2007)
15. Ware, R.: File Extension Renaming and Signaturing. Digital Forensics (September 19, 2006)
16. Moody, S.J., Erbacher, R.F.: SÁDI – Statistical Analysis for Data type Identification. In: 3rd International Workshop on Systematic Approaches to Digital Forensic Engineering (2008)
17. Veenman, C.J.: Statistical disk cluster classification for file carving. In: IEEE Third International Symposium on Information Assurance and Security, pp. 393–398 (2007)
18. Calhoun, W.C., Coles, D.: Predicting the types of file fragments. In: Digital Forensic Research Workshop. Elsevier, Amsterdam (2008)
19. Li, W.-J., Wang, K., Stolfo, S.J., Herzog, B.: Fileprints: Identifying File Types by n-gram Analysis. In: Proceedings of the 2005 IEEE Workshop on Information Assurance (2005)
20. Lin, X., Xiong, Y.: Detection and analysis of table of contents based on content association. International Journal of Document Analysis (2006)
21. Mohay, G., Anderson, A., Collie, B., De Vel, O., Mc Kemmish, R.: Computer and Intrusion Forensics. Artech House, Inc. (2003)
22. File extensions, http://www.file-extension.com/
23. Magic numbers,
    http://qdn.qnx.com/support/docs/qnx4/utils/m/magic.html
24. File Format Registry,
    http://hul.harvard.edu/~stephen/Format_Registry.doc

Privacy Preserving Mining of Distributed Data Using Steganography

D. Aruna Kumari[1,*], Dr.K. Raja Sekhar Rao[2,**], and M. Suman[3,***]

Department of Electronics and Computer Engineering
K.L.E.F University Vaddeswaram,
Guntur(dist) 522502, A.P, INDIA
enteraruna@yahoo.com, rasekhar.kurra@klce.ac.in,
suman.maloji@gmail.com

Abstract. Privacy preserving mining of distributed data has numerous applications. Several constraints can imposed by the applications, it includes how the data is distributed; when the data is distributed privacy should be preserved...etc. Data mining has operated on a data warehousing model of gathering all data into a central site, then running an algorithm against that data. Privacy considerations may prevent this approach. This paper presents steganography techniques and shows how they can be used to solve several privacy-preserving data mining problems. Steganography is a technique to hide secret information in some other data (we call it a vessel) without leaving any apparent evidence of data alteration.

Keywords: Distributed data mining, privacy, steganography.

1 Introduction

Data mining technology has emerged as a means for identifying patterns and trends from large quantities of data. Data mining and data warehousing go hand-in-hand: most tools operate on a principal of gathering all data into a central site, then running an algorithm against that data (Figure 1).

There are a number of applications that are infeasible under such a methodology, leading to a need for distributed data mining. Distributed data mining extracts important knowledge from large volumes of data sets. These collections (data sets) are distributed over several sites, i.e data are partitioned either horizontally or vertically. The problem is not simply that the data is distributed, but that it must be distributed. There are several situations where this arises:

1. Connectivity. Transmitting large quantities of data to a central site may be infeasible.
2. Heterogeneity of sources. Is it easier to combine results than combine sources?
3. Privacy of sources. Organizations may be willing to share data mining results, but not data.

---

* Asst. Professor.
** Professor.
*** Assoc. Professor.

N. Meghanathan et al. (Eds.): CNSA 2010, CCIS 89, pp. 263–269, 2010.
© Springer-Verlag Berlin Heidelberg 2010

This research will concentrate on issue 3 and issue1 : obtaining data mining results that are valid across a distributed data set, with limited willingness to share data between sites. When the data is to be transmitted between the sites, data should not be accessed by the unauthorized persons; so to ensure this security this paper is proposing a new method of privacy preserving using steganography

There are many variants of this problem, depending on how the data is distributed, what type of data mining we wish to do, and what restrictions are placed on sharing of information. Some problems are quite tractable, others are more difficult.

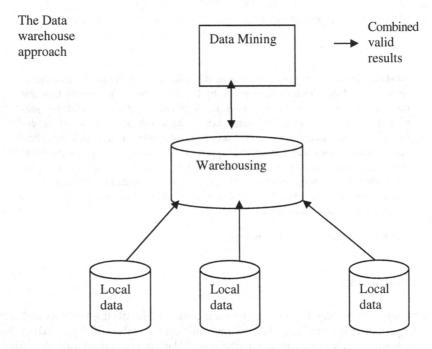

Fig. 1. Data warehouse approach to distributed data mining

There are algorithms to efficiently find all association rules with a minimum level of support. We can easily extend this to the distributed case using the following lemma: If a rule has support > k% globally, it must have support > k% on at least one of the individual sites.1 A distributed algorithm for this would work as follows: Request that each site send all rules with support at least k. For each rule returned, request that all sites send the count of items they have that support the rule, and the total count of all items at the site. From this, we can compute the global support of each rule, and (from the lemma) be certain that all rules with support at least k have been found. An example of how this works is shown in Figure 2.

This is straightforward, but as we vary the problem the challenge becomes more difficult. What if we want to protect not only the individual items at each site, but also how much each site supports a given rule? The above method reveals this information. Another variant where this approach fails is when the data is partitioned vertically: a single item may have part of it's information at one site, and part at another. We are building a research program that will address a broad spectrum of data mining and privacy issues.

In this paper we propose a new approach for preserving privacy at individual sites by stegonograpphy techniques.

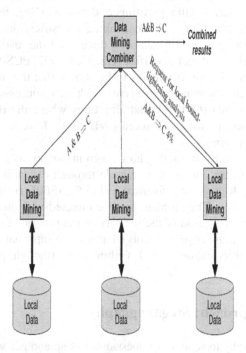

Fig. 2. Example of Computing Association rules from individual sites

2 Related Works

Why is there research to be done here? What happens if we run existing data mining tools at each site independently, then combine the results? This will not generally give globally valid results.

Situations that cause a disparity between local and global results include:

1. Values for a single entity may be split across sources. Data mining at individual sites will be unable to detect cross-site correlations.

2. The same item may be duplicated at different sites, and will be over weighted in the results.

3. Data at a single site is likely to be from a homogeneous population. Important geographic or demographic distinctions between that population and others cannot be seen on a single site.

Data mining algorithms that partition the data into subsets have been developed [SON95]. In particular, work in parallel data mining that may be relevant [Zak99, KC00]. Although the goal of parallelizing data mining algorithms is performance, the communication cost between nodes is an issue. Parallel data mining algorithms may serve as a starting point for portions of this research.

Algorithms have been proposed for distributed data mining. Cheung et al. proposed a method for horizontally partitioned data[CNFF96], this is basically the approach outlined in the Figure 2. Distributed classification has also been addressed. A meta-learning approach has been developed that uses classifiers trained at individual to develop a global classifier [Cha96, Cha97, PCS00]. This could protect the individual entities, but it remains to be shown that the individual classifiers do not release private information. Recent work has addressed classification in vertically partitioned data [CSK01], and situations where the distribution is itself interesting with respect to what is learned [WBH01]. However, none of this work addresses privacy concerns.

There has been research considering how much information can be inferred, calculated or revealed from the data made available through data mining algorithms, and how to minimize the leakage of information [LP00, AS00]. However, this has been restricted to classification. The problem has been treated with an \all or nothing" approach. We desire quantification of the security of the process. Corporations may not require absolute zero knowledge protocols (that leak no information at all) as long as they can keep the information shared within strict (though possibly adjustable) bounds.

3 Proposed Approach: Steganography

People use cryptography to send secret messages to one another without a third party overseeing the message. Steganography is a type of cryptography in which the secret message is hidden in a digital picture.

Steganography is the art and science of hiding communication; a steganographic system thus embeds hidden content in unremarkable cover media so as not to arouse an eavesdropper's suspicion. In the past, people used hidden tattoos or invisible ink to convey steganographic content. Today, computer and network technologies provide easy-to-use communication channels for steganography.

Approach:

Before each site sends the count of items and its support, we add some random noise to the information and then we send this information by embedding in to an image (encoding) . That image will be sent over the network to the destination party. Let us see the traditional approach of sending messages.

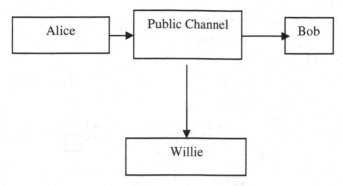

Fig. 3. Traditional Approach

In the traditional approach fig 3, there is a possibility for the attacker to learn the message.

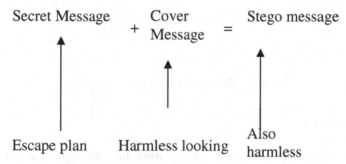

Here we obscure the data, so called cover message. Fig 4 and Fig 5 show how the messages can be sent using steganography.

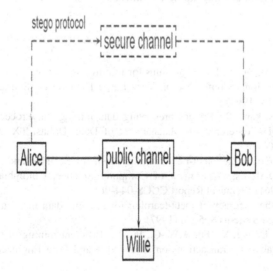

Fig. 4. Security provided by Stego protocol

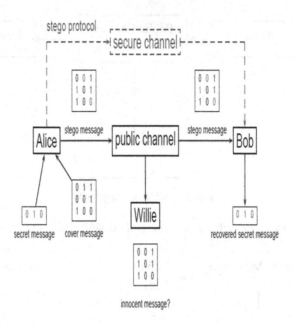

Fig. 5. Sending message using steganograpghy

4 Conclusions

Distributed data mining is a natural choice when the data mining environment has distributed data, computing resources, and users. This paper focused on privacy preserving of distributed data mining using steganograpghy. Its is new approach, it show better performance than cryptographic techniques.

References

[1] Agrawal, R., Srikant, R.: Fast algorithms for mining association rules. In: Proceedings of the 20th International Conference on Very Large Data Bases, Santiago, Chile, VLDB, September 12-15 (1994)

[2] Agrawal, R., Srikant, R.: Privacy-preserving data mining. In: Proceedings of the 1997 ACM SIGMOD Conference on Management of Data, Dallas, TX, May 14-19. ACM, New York (2000)

[3] Chan, P.: An Extensible Meta-Learning Approach for Scalable and Accurate Inductive Learning. PhD thesis, Department of Computer Science, Columbia University, New York, NY (1996) (Technical Report CUCS-044-96)

[4] Chan, P.: On the accuracy of meta-learning for scalable data mining. Journal of Intelligent Information Systems 8, 5–28 (1997)

[5] Cheung, D.W.-L., Ng, V., Fu, A.W.-C., Fu, Y.: Efficient mining of association rules in distributed databases. Transactions on Knowledge and Data Engineering 8(6), 911–922 (1996)

[6] Chen, R., Sivakumar, K., Kargupta, H.: Distributed web mining using bayesian networks from multiple data streams. In: The 2001 IEEE International Conference on Data Mining, November 29-December 2. IEEE, Los Alamitos (2001)

[7] Goldreich, O., Micali, S., Wigderson, A.: How to play any mental game - a completeness theorem for protocols with honest majority. In: 19th ACM Symposium on the Theory of Computing, pp. 218–229 (1987)

[8] Kargupta, H., Chan, P. (eds.): Advances in Distributed and Parallel Knowledge Discovery. AAAI/MIT Press (2000)

[9] Lindell, Y., Pinkas, B.: Privacy preserving data mining. In: Bellare, M. (ed.) CRYPTO 2000. LNCS, vol. 1880, pp. 36–54. Springer, Heidelberg (2000)

[10] Prodromidis, A., Chan, P., Stolfo, S.: Meta-learning in distributed data mining systems: Issues and approaches, ch. 3. AAAI/MIT Press (2000)

[11] Savasere, A., Omiecinski, E., Navathe, S.B.: An e±cient algorithm for mining association rules in large databases. In: Proceedings of 21th International Conference on Very Large Data Bases, VLDB, September 11-15, pp. 432–444 (1995)

[12] Wirth, R., Borth, M., Hipp, J.: When distribution is part of the semantics: A new problem class for distributed knowledge discovery. In: Ubiquitous Data Mining for Mobile and Distributed Environments workshop associated with the Joint 12th European Conference on Machine Learning (ECML 2001) and 5th European Conference on Principles and Practice of Knowledge Discovery in Databases (PKDD 2001), Freiburg, Germany, September 3-7 (2001)

[13] Yao, A.C.: How to generate and exchange secrets. In: Proceedings of the 27th IEEE Symposium on Foundations of Computer Science, pp. 162–167. IEEE, Los Alamitos (1986)

[14] Zaki, M.J.: Parallel and distributed association mining: A survey. IEEE Concurrency, special issue on Parallel Mechanisms for Data Mining 7(4), 14–25 (1999)

Proxy Re-signature Scheme That Translates One Type of Signature Scheme to Another Type of Signature Scheme

N.R. Sunitha[1] and B. Bharat Amberker[2]

[1] Dept. of Computer Science & Engg., Siddaganga Institute of Technology, Tumkur, Karnataka, India
[2] Dept. of Computer Science & Engg., National Institute of Technology, Warangal, Andhra Pradesh, India

Abstract. In 1998, Blaze, Bleumer, and Strauss (BBS) proposed proxy re-signatures, in which a semi-trusted proxy acts as a translator between Alice and Bob to translate a signature from Alice into a signature from Bob on the same message. The proxy, however, does not learn any signing key and cannot sign arbitrary messages on behalf of either Alice or Bob. In the 12th ACM Conference on Computer and Communications Security (CCS 2005), Ateniese and Hohenberger formalised the definition of security for a proxy re-signature and presented two secure proxy re-signature schemes based on bilinear maps. They left open the problem of determining whether or not a proxy re-signature scheme can be built that translates one type of signature scheme to another i.e. a scheme that translates Alice's Schnorr signatures into Bob's RSA based ones.

In this paper we address this open problem. We construct proxy signature scheme that translates Alice's Schnorr/ElGamal signature to Bob's RSA signature. We construct this by generating suitable proxy re-sign keys by establishing communication among delegatee, proxy signer and the delegator. At no point of conversion the security of Schnorr, ElGamal and RSA signature schemes are compromised. The Signatures generated by regular signature generation algorithm and the proposed re-signature algorithm are indistinguishable.

Keywords: Signature translation, Proxy re-signature, Proxy Signature, Proxy revocation, Proxy key.

1 Introduction

In Eurocrypt 98, Blaze, Bleumer, and Strauss (BBS)[5] proposed proxy re-signatures, in which a semi-trusted proxy acts as a translator between Alice and Bob. To translate, the proxy converts a signature from Alice into a signature from Bob on the same message. The proxy, however, does not learn any signing key and cannot sign arbitrary messages on behalf of either Alice or Bob. Since the BBS proposal, the proxy re-signature primitive has been largely ignored, until Ateniese and Hohenberger [1] showed that it is a very useful tool

N. Meghanathan et al. (Eds.): CNSA 2010, CCIS 89, pp. 270–279, 2010.

for sharing web certificates, forming weak group signatures, and authenticating a network path.

The proxy signatures introduced by Mambo, Usuda and Okamoto [10,11] must not be confused with proxy re-signatures. A proxy signature [10,11,8,7] allows one user Alice, called the original signer, to delegate her signing capability to another user Bob, called the proxy signer. After that, the proxy signer Bob can sign messages on behalf of the original signer Alice. Upon receiving a proxy signature on some message, a verifier can validate its correctness by the given verification procedure. By this the verifier is convinced of the original signer's agreement on the signed message. In proxy re-signature, a proxy translates a perfectly-valid and publicly-verifiable signature, $\sigma_A(m)$, from Alice on a certain message, m , into a signature, $\sigma_B(m)$, from Bob on the same message m. Notice that, in proxy re-signature, the two signatures, one from Alice and the other from Bob as generated by the proxy, can coexist and both can be publicly verified as being two signatures from two distinct people on the same message. Moreover, the proxy can convert a single signature into multiple signatures of several and distinct signers, and vice-versa.

Ateniese and Hohenberger [1] re-opened the discussion of proxy re-signature by providing four separate results: (1) motivation for the need of improved schemes, by pointing out that the original BBS scheme [5], while satisfying their security notion, is unsuitable for most practical applications, including the ones proposed in the original paper, (2) formal definitions and a security model, (3) provably secure proxy re-signature constructions from bilinear maps, and (4) new applications. Nevertheless, they left open the following problem: Determining whether or not proxy re-signature scheme can be built that translate from one type of signature scheme to another i.e. like a scheme that translates Alice's Schnorr signatures into Bob's RSA based ones.

To address the open problem of Ateniese and Hohenberger, we present construction of schemes which converts Alice's Schnorr/ElGamal signature to Bob's RSA signature. We construct this by generating suitable proxy re-sign keys which are computed by establishing communication among delegatee, proxy signer and the delegator. At no point of conversion the security of Schnorr, ElGamal and RSA signature schemes are compromised. Signatures of Schnorr and ElGamal get converted to RSA signatures by providing only the signature and re-sign keys as input to Re-sign algorithm.

The organisation of our paper is as follows: In Section 2, we define the proxy re-signature. In Section 3, we explain two conversion schemes i.e Schnorr to RSA Conversion Scheme and ElGamal to RSA Conversion Scheme along with proxy revocation and properties of the scheme. In Section 4, we discuss the security of our scheme. In section 5, we discuss the application of conversion of signatures. Lastly in Section 6, we conclude.

2   Definition of Proxy Re-signature Scheme

We follow the definitions given in [1]. A proxy re-signature scheme is a tuple of polynomial time algorithms (KeyGen, ReKey, Sign, ReSign, Verify), where,

(KeyGen, Sign, Verify) form the standard key generation, signing, and verification algorithms.

On input $(pk_A, sk_A^*, pk_B, sk_B)$, where (pk_A, sk_A^*) is the public key - secret key pair of A and (pk_B, sk_B) is the public key - secret key pair of B, the re-signing key generation algorithm, ReKey, outputs a key $rk_{A \to B}$ for the proxy. By providing this key as input to ReSign algorithm, the proxy converts a signature from Alice into a signature of Bob on the same message. The proxy, however, does not learn any signing key and cannot sign arbitrary messages on behalf of either Alice or Bob. (Note: $rk_{A \to B}$ allows to transform A's signatures into B's signatures, thus B is the delegator and A is the delegatee). The input marked with a * is optional as in case of public proxy re-signature scheme.

On input $rk_{A \to B}$, a public key pk_A, a signature $\sigma_A(m)$, and a message m, the re-signature function, ReSign, outputs $\sigma_B(m)$ if Verify$(pk_A, m, \sigma_A(m)) = 1$ and an error message otherwise.

The correctness of the scheme has two requirements. For any message m in the message space and any key pairs $(pk, sk), (pk', sk') \leftarrow KeyGen(1^k)$, let $\sigma = Sign(sk, m)$ and $rk \leftarrow ReKey(pk, sk, pk', sk')$. Then the following two conditions must hold:

$$Verify(pk, m, \sigma) = 1$$

$$Verify(pk', m, ReSign(rk, \sigma)) = 1.$$

That is, all signatures formed by either the signing or re-signing algorithms will pass verification.

3   Proxy Re-signature Scheme to Translate One Type of Signature Scheme to Another Type

In this section we develop proxy signature scheme for translating the following signatures:

1. Schnorr Signature to RSA Signature
2. ElGamal Signature to RSA Signature

In these schemes, signatures generated by signature generation algorithm and the re-signature algorithms are indistinguishable. Further, Proxy signer revocation is also possible.

3.1   Schnorr Signature Scheme to RSA Signature Scheme

Following protocols are used to translate Alice's Schnorr Signature to Bob's RSA Signature:

1. Key generation for Schnorr Signatures
2. Key generation for RSA Signatures
3. Re-Signature key generation
4. Schnorr Signature generation

5. Schnorr Signature verification
6. Re-Sign Algorithm
7. RSA Signature verification.

In the following subsections we discuss the above protocols.

1. **Key Generation for Schnorr Signature Scheme:**
   (a) Alice chooses a random large prime p such that $p - 1 = kq$ for some integer k and large prime q.
   (b) She chooses randomly a secret key x in the range $0 \le x \le q - 1$ and generator $\alpha \in Z_p^*$ of order q.
   (c) She computes $\beta = \alpha^{-x} \bmod q$. Alice's Public key is (p, q, α, β) and Secret key is x.

2. **Key Generation for RSA Signature Scheme:**
   (a) Bob generates two large distinct random primes p_1 and q_1, each roughly of the same size.
   (b) He computes $n = p_1.q_1$ and $\phi(n) = (p - 1)(q - 1)$.
   (c) He selects a random integer e, $1 < e < \phi(n)$, such that $gcd(e, \phi(n)) = 1$.
   (d) He computes the unique integer d, $1 < d < \phi(n)$, such that $ed \equiv 1 (\bmod \phi(n))$.
   (e) Bob's Public key is (n, e) and Private key is d.

3. **Re-Signature Key Generation (Re-Key):** Four re-signature keys $rk1_{A \to B}$, $rk2_{A \to B}$, $rk3_{A \to B}$ and $rk4_{A \to B}$ are required for this conversion.
   (a) *The re-signature key $rk1_{A \to B}$ is generated as follows:*
      i. Bob randomly chooses $k \in Z$ and sends $k.\phi(n)$ to Alice.
      ii. Alice computes $x \equiv x_1 \bmod (k.\phi(n))$ and sends it to proxy. Note that if $x \equiv x_2 \bmod \phi(n)$ then $x_1 \equiv x_2 \bmod \phi(n)$.
      iii. Proxy sets re-sign key as $rk1_{A \to B} = x_1 \bmod (k.\phi(n))$.
   (b) *The re-signature key $rk2_{A \to B}$ is generated as follows:*
      i. Bob randomly chooses $l \in Z$ and sends $l.\phi(n)$ to Alice and to Proxy.
      ii. Proxy randomly chooses $r \in Z_{l.\phi(n)}$ and sends it to Alice.
      iii. Alice computes $r + x \bmod (l.\phi(n))$ and sends it to Bob.
      iv. Bob computes $r + x + d \bmod (l.\phi(n))$ and sends it to proxy.
      v. Proxy sets the re-sign key as $rk2_{A \to B} = x + d \bmod (l.\phi(n))$.
   (c) *The re-signature key $rk3_{A \to B}$ is generated as follows:*
      i. Proxy sends a random $r \in Z_q$ to Alice.
      ii. Alice sends $r + x \bmod (q - 1)$ to Bob,
      iii. Bob sends $r + x + d \bmod (q - 1)$ to the proxy.
      iv. Proxy recovers $d + x \bmod (q - 1)$ and sets the re-sign key $rk3_{A \to B} = d + x \bmod (q - 1)$.
   (d) *The re-signature key $rk4_{A \to B}$ is generated as follows:*
      i. Bob sends $\alpha^d \bmod q$ to Proxy.
      ii. Proxy sets the re-sign key $rk4_{A \to B} = \alpha^d \bmod q$.

4. **Schnorr Signature generation:**
   (a) Alice selects a random integer k, such that $0 \le k \le q - 1$.
   (b) She computes $r = \alpha^k \bmod q$, $v = H(m||r) \bmod q$ and $s = (k + x.v) \bmod q$, where H is a collision-resistant hash function.
   (c) The signature of Alice on the message m is (v, s), which is sent to Proxy.

5. **Schnorr Signature verification:** On receiving Alice's signature on m, proxy does the following to verify the signature:
   (a) He computes $v' = H(m||r_v)$ where, $r_v = \alpha^s.\beta^{-v} \bmod q$.
   (b) He accepts the signature if and only if $v' = v$.
6. **Re-signature (Re-Sign)** On input re-signature keys $rk1_{A\rightarrow B}$, $rk2_{A\rightarrow B}$, $rk3_{A\rightarrow B}$ and Alice's Schnorr signature (v, s) on m, Re-Sign converts Alice's Schnorr signature to Bob's RSA signature in two steps.
   – **Step 1:** Compute $\sigma_1 = \alpha^{s-rk3_{A\rightarrow B}.v}.(rk4_{A\rightarrow B})^v$ and check that $\sigma_1 = 1$. The following calculations show that this is indeed true.

$$\sigma_1 = \alpha^{s-rk3_{A\rightarrow B}.v}.(rk4_{A\rightarrow B})^v.(\alpha^s.\beta^{-v})^{-1} \bmod q$$
$$= \alpha^{(k+x.v)-(d+x).v}.(\alpha^d)^v.(\alpha^s.\alpha^{-vx})^{-1} \bmod q$$
$$= \alpha^{k+x.v-dv-xv}.\alpha^{dv}.(\alpha^k)^{-1}$$
$$= \alpha^k.(\alpha^k)^{-1} \bmod q$$
$$= 1 \bmod q$$

Note that this step ensures that Alice uses the same key used during re-signature key generation to sign the message m.
   – **Step 2:** If $\sigma_1 = 1 \bmod q$, then compute

$$\sigma_2 = \mathcal{R}(m)^{rk2_{A\rightarrow B}}.\mathcal{R}(m)^{-rk1_{A\rightarrow B}} \bmod n,$$

where $\mathcal{R}$ is the public redundancy function [12].
Note that $\sigma_2 = \mathcal{R}(m)^d \bmod n$ is Bob's RSA signature. This is shown as follows:

$$\sigma_2 = \mathcal{R}(m)^{rk2_{A\rightarrow B}}.\mathcal{R}(m)^{-rk1_{A\rightarrow B}} \bmod n$$
$$= \mathcal{R}(m)^{d+x}.\mathcal{R}(m)^{-x_1} \bmod n$$
$$(\text{since } x \equiv x_1 \bmod \phi(n))$$
$$= \mathcal{R}(m)^d \bmod n.$$

Thus, Re-Sign has translated Alice's Schnorr signature to Bob's RSA signature.
7. **RSA Signature verification:** Any verifier can verify the RSA signature generated by Re-sign as follows:
   (a) Compute $\mathcal{R}(m) = C^e \bmod n$.
   (b) Verify $m = \mathcal{R}^{-1}(\mathcal{R}(m)) \bmod n$.

3.2   ElGamal Signature to RSA Signature Scheme

Following protocols are used to translate Alice's ElGamal Signature to Bob's RSA Signature:

1. Key generation for ElGamal Signatures
2. Key generation for RSA Signatures
3. Re-Signature key generation

4. ElGamal Signature generation
5. ElGamal Signature verification
6. Re-Sign Algorithm
7. RSA Signature verification.

In the following subsections we discuss the above protocols.

1. **Key generation for ElGamal Signatures:**
   (a) Alice generates a large random prime p and a generator α of the multi-plicative group Z_p^*.
   (b) She select a random integer s, $1 \leq s \leq p - 2$. s is the secret key.
   (c) She computes the public key $\beta = \alpha^s \bmod p$.
2. **Key generation for RSA Signatures:**
   (a) Bob generates two large distinct random primes p_1 and q_1, each roughly the same size.
   (b) He computes $n = p_1.q_1$ and $\phi(n) = (p-1)(q-1)$.
   (c) He select a random integer e, $1 < e < \phi(n)$, such that $gcd(e, \phi(n)) = 1$.
   (d) He computes the unique integer d, $1 < d < \phi(n)$, such that $ed \equiv 1 (\bmod \phi(n))$.
   (e) Bob's Public key is (n, e) and Private key is d.
3. **Re-Signature Key Generation (Re-Key):** Four re-signature keys $rk1_{A \rightarrow B}$, $rk2_{A \rightarrow B}$, $rk3_{A \rightarrow B}$ and $rk4_{A \rightarrow B}$ are required for this conversion.
   (a) *The re-signature key $rk1_{A \rightarrow B}$, is generated as follows:*
      i. Bob randomly chooses $k \in Z$ and sends $k.\phi(n)$ to Alice.
      ii. Alice computes $s \equiv s_1 \bmod (k.\phi(n))$. Note that if $s \equiv s_2 \bmod \phi(n)$ then $s_1 \equiv s_2 \bmod \phi(n)$
      iii. Proxy sets resign key as $rk1_{A \rightarrow B} = s_1 \bmod (k.\phi(n))$.
   (b) *The re-signature key $rk2_{A \rightarrow B}$ is generated as follows:*
      i. Bob randomly chooses $l \in Z$ and sends $l.\phi(n)$ to Alice and to Proxy.
      ii. Proxy randomly chooses $r \in Z_{l.\phi(n)}$ and sends it to Alice.
      iii. Alice computes $r + s \bmod (l.\phi(n))$ and sends it to Bob.
      iv. Bob computes $r + s + d \bmod (l.\phi(n))$ and sends it to proxy.
      v. Proxy sets the re-sign key as $rk2_{A \rightarrow B} = s + d \bmod (l.\phi(n))$.
   (c) *The re-signature key $rk3_{A \rightarrow B}$ is generated as follows:*
      i. Proxy sends a random $r \in Z_p$ to Alice.
      ii. Alice sends $r + s \bmod (p - 1)$ to Bob.
      iii. Bob sends $r + s + d \bmod (p - 1)$ to the proxy.
      iv. Proxy recovers $s + d \bmod (p-1)$ and sets $rk3_{A \rightarrow B} = s + d \bmod (p-1)$.
   (d) *The re-signature key $rk4_{A \rightarrow B}$ is generated as follows:*
      i. Bob sends $\alpha^d \bmod p$ to Proxy.
      ii. Proxy sets the re-sign key $rk4_{A \rightarrow B} = \alpha^d \bmod p$.
4. **ElGamal Signature generation:**
   (a) Alice selects a random secret integer k, $1 \leq k \leq p-2$ with $gcd(k, p-1) = 1$.
   (b) She computes $y_1 = \alpha^k \bmod p$.
   (c) She computes $y_2 = (H(m) - s.y_1)k^{-1} \bmod (p-1)$, where H is a collision-resistant hash function.
   (d) The signature (y_1, y_2) on message m is sent to the Proxy.

5. **ElGamal Signature verification:** The proxy verifies the received ElGamal signature as follows:
   (a) He accepts the signature if $\alpha^{H(m)} = \beta^{y_1} y_1^{y_2} \bmod p$.
6. **Re-signature (ReSign):** On input of re-signature keys $rk1_{A \to B}$, $rk2_{A \to B}$ and $rk3_{A \to B}$ and Alice's ElGamal signature (y_1, y_2) on m, Re-Sign algorithm converts Alice's ElGamal signature to Bob's RSA signature in two steps:
   - **Step 1:** Compute $\sigma_1 = y_1^{y_2} . \alpha^{-H(m)} . \alpha^{(d+s).y_1} . \alpha^{-d.y_1} \bmod p$ and check that $\sigma_1 = 1$. The following calculations show that this is indeed true.

$$\sigma_1 = y_1^{y_2} . \alpha^{-H(m)} . \alpha^{(d+s).y_1} . \alpha^{-d.y_1} \bmod p$$
$$= \alpha^{k.k^{-1}.(H(m)-s.y_1)} . \alpha^{-H(m)} . \alpha^{(d+s)y_1} .$$
$$\alpha^{-d.y_1} \bmod p$$
$$= \alpha^{H(m)} . \alpha^{-s.y_1} . \alpha^{-H(m)} . \alpha^{d.y_1} . \alpha^{s.y_1} .$$
$$\alpha^{-d.y_1} \bmod p$$
$$= 1 \bmod p.$$

Note that this step ensures that Alice uses the same key used during re-signature key generation to sign the message m.
   - **Step 2** If $\sigma_1 = 1 \bmod p$, then compute

$$\sigma_2 = \mathcal{R}(m)^{rk2_{A \to B}} . \mathcal{R}(m)^{-rk1_{A \to B}} \bmod n,$$

where $\mathcal{R}$ is the public redundancy function [12].
Note that $\sigma_2 = \mathcal{R}(m)^d \bmod n$ as shown below.

$$\sigma_2 = \mathcal{R}(m)^{rk2_{A \to B}} . \mathcal{R}(m)^{-rk1_{A \to B}} \bmod n$$
$$= \mathcal{R}(m)^{d+s} . \mathcal{R}(m)^{-s_1} \bmod n$$
$$= \mathcal{R}(m)^d . \mathcal{R}(m)^s . \mathcal{R}(m)^{-s} \bmod n$$
$$(\textbf{since } s \equiv s_1 \bmod \phi(n))$$
$$= \mathcal{R}(m)^d \bmod n$$

Thus, Re-Sign has translated Alice's ElGamal signature into Bob's RSA signature.
7. **RSA Signature verification:** Any verifier can verify the RSA signature generated by Re-sign as follows:
   (a) Compute $\mathcal{R}(m) = C^e \bmod n$.
   (b) Verify $m = \mathcal{R}^{-1}(\mathcal{R}(m)) \bmod n$.

3.3 Proxy Signer Revocation

In all the constructions discussed above, we can revoke the proxy signer from performing conversion of signatures from one type of signature scheme to another type by including the expiry date as part of the signature. If the current date is greater than the expiry date, the verifier stops the verification process. If a proxy signer is to be revoked before the expiry date, a proxy revocation list can be maintained in which the public key of proxy signers to be revoked are entered. The entry is retained only till the expiry date and later removed. This helps to maintain a small list of revoked proxy signers. The verifier performs the verification of the signature received from the proxy signer only if his public key is not available in the proxy revocation list and the current date is less than or equal to the expiry date.

3.4   Properties of the New Proxy Re-signature Schemes

1. Unidirectional: The re-signature keys allows the proxy to turn Alice's signatures into Bob's, but not Bob's into Alice's. This property allows for applications where the trust relationship between two parties is not necessarily mutual. Schemes that do not have this property are called bidirectional.
2. A message can be re-signed a polynomial number of times. That is, signatures generated by either the Sign or ReSign algorithms can be taken as input to ReSign.
3. Private Proxy: In a private proxy scheme, the re-signature keys are kept secret by an honest proxy. Thus, a single proxy may control which signatures get translated.
4. Transparent: The proxy is transparent in the scheme, meaning that a user may not even know that a proxy exists. More formally, we mean that the signatures generated by Bob on a message m using the Sign algorithm are computationally indistinguishable from the signatures on m generated by the proxy as the output of ReSign. Notice that this implies that the input and the corresponding output of the ReSign algorithm cannot be linked to each other.
5. Key Optimal: Alice is only required to protect and store a small constant amount of secret data (i.e., secret keys) regardless of how many signature delegations she gives or accepts. Here, we want to minimize the safe storage cost for each user.
6. Interactive: The proxy creates the re-signature keys by interacting with Bob (the delegator) and Alice (the delegatee).
7. Non-transitive: According to the property of transitivity, from $rk_{A\rightarrow B}$ and $rk_{B\rightarrow C}$, the proxy must be able to produce $rk_{A\rightarrow C}$. The new schemes are non-transitive as we are considering conversion of schemes between different public key crypto-systems and still there are no schemes to convert between RSA and ElGamal/Schnorr.
8. Temporary: Whenever a party delegates some of her rights to another party, there is always the chance that she will either need or want to revoke those rights later on. We have discussed this under proxy signer revocation.

4   Security of Our Schemes

Our security model protects users from two types of attacks: those launched from parties outside the system (External Security) and those launched from parties inside the system such as the proxy, another delegation partner or collusion between them (Internal Security).

External Security: Our security model protects a user from adversaries outside the system. This is equivalent to adaptive chosen-message attack where an adversary cannot create a new signature even for a previously signed message. For a non-zero $n \in poly(k)$ and algorithm A,

$$Pr[(pk_i, sk_i) \leftarrow KeyGen(1^k)_{i \in}, (t, m, \sigma) \leftarrow A^{O_{sign}(\cdot,\cdot), O_{resign}(\cdot,\cdot,\cdot,\cdot)} :$$
$$Verify(pk_t, m, \sigma) = 1] < 1/poly(k)$$

where the oracle O_{sign} takes as input an index j and a message $m \in M$, and produces the output of $Sign(sk_j, m)$; the oracle O_{resign} takes as input two distinct indices i, j, message m, and signature σ and produces the output of $Resign$. Here the proxy ie required to keep the re-signature keys private.

Internal Security: If the delegator and delegatee are both honest, then:

1. the proxy cannot produce signatures for the delegator unless the message was first signed by the delegatee and
2. the proxy cannot create any signature for the delegatee.

5   Conversion of One Type of Signature to Another Type: Applications

1. If we have schemes which convert different types of signatures to one type of signature, for example all types of signatures are converted to RSA signatures, then signatures can be easily aggregated and a single verification done to verify all the signatures which are originally of different type signatures.
2. By providing a variety of conversion schemes, a user can sign using any signature scheme and the required party can convert it into the signature type that it requires.
3. Using signature conversion schemes, documents can be easily transferred across organisations following different signature schemes.
4. Suppose Alice's ElGamal Signature is converted to Bob's RSA signature, Bob's signature is publicly available and there are chances of Bob's secret key being exposed than Alice's secret key. Thus the original signer Alice's secret key is more secure than Bob's secret key.

6   Conclusion

We have proposed a solution for the open challenge in the area of proxy re-signatures to determine whether or not a proxy re-signature scheme can be built that translates one type of signature scheme to another type i.e. a scheme that translates Alice's Schnorr signatures into Bob's RSA based ones. We have come up with schemes which convert Schnorr signatures to RSA and ElGamal signatures to RSA signatures. The signatures generated by regular signature generation algorithm and the proposed re-signature algorithm are indistinguishable.

All organisations do not follow a common signature scheme. With many more signature conversion schemes (all possible conversions for existing signature schemes) similar to that of ours are constructed, a user need not sign using the signature scheme followed by the organisation. He can always sign using one signature scheme of his choice, and the organisations can convert to the signature scheme that they use.

References

1. Ateniese, G., Hohenberger, S.: Proxy re-signatures: new definitions, algorithms, and applications. In: ACM CCS 2005, pp. 310–319. ACM Press, New York (2005)
2. Bellare, M., Rogaway, P.: Random oracles are practical: A paradigm for designing efficient protocols. In: ACM CCS 1993, pp. 62–73. ACM Press, New York (1993)
3. Libert, B., Vergnaud, D.: Multi-Use Unidirectional Proxy Re-Signatures, arXiv:0802.1113v1 [cs.CR], February 8 (2008)
4. Boneh, D., Lynn, B., Shacham, H.: Short signatures from the Weil pairing. In: Boyd, C. (ed.) ASIACRYPT 2001. LNCS, vol. 2248, pp. 514–532. Springer, Heidelberg (2001)
5. Blaze, M., Bleumer, G., Strauss, M.J.: Divertible protocols and atomic proxy cryptography. In: Nyberg, K. (ed.) EUROCRYPT 1998. LNCS, vol. 1403, pp. 127–144. Springer, Heidelberg (1998); SCN 2002, LNCS, vol. 2576, pp. 241–256. Springer, Heidelberg (2002)
6. Boldyreva, A., Palacio, A., Warinschi, B.: Secure proxy signature schemes for delegation of signing rights, http://eprint.iacr.org/2003/096
7. Kim, S., Park, S., Won, D.: Proxy signatures, revisited. In: Han, Y., Quing, S. (eds.) ICICS 1997. LNCS, vol. 1334, pp. 223–232. Springer, Heidelberg (1997)
8. Lee, B., Kim, H., Kim, K.: Strong proxy signature and its applications. In: Proceedings of the 2001 Symposium on Cryptography and Information Security (SCIS 2001), Oiso, Japan, January 23-26, vol. 2(2), pp. 603–608 (2001); pp. 127–144 (1998)
9. Lee, B., Kim, H., Kim, K.: Secure mobile agent using strong non-designated proxy signature. In: Varadharajan, V., Mu, Y. (eds.) ACISP 2001. LNCS, vol. 2119, pp. 474–486. Springer, Heidelberg (2001)
10. Mambo, M., Usuda, K., Okamoto, E.: Proxy signature: Delegation of the power to sign messages. IEICE Trans. Fundamentals E79-A(9), 1338–1353 (1996)
11. Mambo, M., Usuda, K., Okamoto, E.: Proxy signatures for delegating signing operation. In: Proc. of 3rd ACM Conference on Computer and Communications Security (CCS 1996), pp. 48–57. ACM Press, New York (1996)
12. Menezes, A., Van Orschot, P., Vanstone, S.: Handbook of Applied Cryptography. CRC Press, Boca Raton (1996)

Efficient Region-Based Key Agreement for Peer -to - Peer Information Sharing in Mobile Ad Hoc Networks

K. Kumar[1], J. Nafeesa Begum[2], and Dr. V. Sumathy[3]

[1] Research Scholar &Lecturer in CSE Government College of Engg, Bargur- 635104,
Tamil Nadu, India
[2] Sr. Lecturer in CSE, Government College of Engg, Bargur- 635104, Tamil Nadu, India
[3] Asst .Professor in ECE ,Government College of Technology,Coimbatore,
Tamil Nadu, India
{pkk_kumar,nafeesa_jeddy}@yahoo.com, sumi_gct2001@yahoo.co.in

Abstract. Peer-to-peer systems have gained a lot of attention as information sharing systems for the wide-spread exchange of resources and voluminous information that is easily accessible among thousands or even millions of users. However, current peer-to-peer information sharing systems work mostly on wired networks. With the growing number of communication-equipped mobile devices that can self-organize into infrastructure-less communication platform, namely mobile ad hoc networks (MANETs), peer-to-peer information sharing over MANETs becomes a promising research area. In this paper, we propose a Region-Based structure that enables efficient and secure peer-to-peer information sharing over MANETs. The implementation shows that the proposed scheme is Secure, scalable, efficient, and adaptive to node mobility and provides Reliable information sharing.

Keywords: Region –Based Key Agreement, Ad-Hoc networks, Peer –to-Peer Information Sharing, Elliptic Curve Cryptography.

1   Introduction

A peer –to – peer (P2P) system is a self organizing system of equal, autonomous entities which aims for the shared usage of distributed resources in networked environment avoiding central services. The P2P networks are a powerful architecture for sharing of resources and voluminous information among thousands of users. An important issue in P2P system is searching for resources (e.g., data, files, and services) available at one or more of the numerous host nodes. The distributed nature of p2p systems can be an advantage over client-server architectures. First, they tend to be more fault-tolerant as there is no single point –of – failure. Second, processing, network traffic and data storage can be balanced over all peers, which enables the network to scale well with the number of peers.

Group Key Agreement (GKA) protocols [1,3], which enable the participants to agree on a common secret value, based on each participant's public contribution, seem to provide a good solution. They don't require the presence of a central authority. Also, when the group composition changes, Group Controller can employ supplementary key agreement protocols to get a new group key.

N. Meghanathan et al. (Eds.): CNSA 2010, CCIS 89, pp. 280–295, 2010.
© Springer-Verlag Berlin Heidelberg 2010

Elliptic Curve Cryptography (ECC)[2,4,5] is a public key cryptosystem based on elliptic curves. The attraction of ECC is that it appears to offer equal security for a far smaller key size, thereby reducing processing overhead.

In this paper, we propose a reliable and secure Region-Based Key Agreement Protocol for peer-to-peer information sharing. Here, we break a group into region-based subgroups with leaders in subgroups communicating with each other to agree on a group key in response to membership change. In addition to showing that the forward and backward secrecy requirements are satisfied, we identify optimal settings of our protocol to minimize the overall communication and computation costs due to group key management.

The contribution of this work includes:

1. In this paper, we propose a new efficient method for solving the group key management problem for effective P2P information sharing over mobile ad-hoc network. This protocol provides efficient, scalable, reliable and secure P2P information sharing over ad-hoc network..

2. We introduce the idea of subgroup and subgroup key and we uniquely link all the subgroups into a tree structure to form an outer group and outer group key. This design eliminates the centralized key server. Instead, all hosts work in a peer-to-peer fashion to agree on a group key. Here we propose a new protocol ECRBGKA (Elliptic Curve Region-Based Key Agreement) for ad hoc networks. It is a combination of GECDH & TGECDH protocol so as to keep the group key secure among the group members in P2P group communication with a shorter key length and same security level as that of other cryptosystems.

3. We design and implement ECRBGKA protocol in peer-to-peer information sharing using Java and the extensive experiments show that the secure P2P information sharing in ad-hoc networks is achievable in addition to the performance issues like memory cost, communication cost and computation cost.

The rest of the paper is as follows, Section 2 presents the Proposed Schemes. Section 3 describes the Experimental Results and Discussion. Section 4 describes the performance analysis. and finally Section 5 concludes the paper.

2 Proposed Scheme

2.1 System Model

In this section we first provide an overview of our secure information sharing system, including the security model.

2.1.1 Overview of Region-Based Group Key Agreement Protocol

The goal of this paper is to propose a communication and computation efficient group key establishment protocol in ad-hoc network. The idea is to divide the multicast group into several subgroups, let each subgroup has its subgroup key shared by all members of the subgroup. Each Subgroup has subgroup controller node and a Gateway node, in which Subgroup controller node is the controller of subgroup and a Gateway node is controller of subgroups controller.

The layout of the network is as shown in below Figure.1.

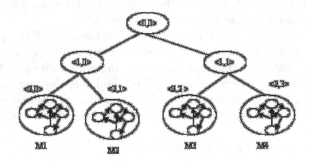

Fig. 1. Region based `Group Key Agreement

One of the members in the subgroup is subgroup controller. The last member join-ing the group acts as a subgroup controller. Each outer group is headed by the outer group controller. In each group, the member with high processing power, memory, and Battery power acts as a gateway member. Outer Group messages are broadcast through the outer group and secured by the outer group key while subgroup messages are broadcast within the subgroup and secured by subgroup key.

Let N be the total number of group members, and M be the number of the subgroups in each subgroup, then there will be N/M subgroups, assuming that each subgroup has the same number of members.

Assume that there are a total of N members in Secure Group Communication. Af-ter sub grouping process (Algorithm 1), there are S subgroups M_1, M_2... M_s with n_1, n_2 ...n_s members.

Algorithm. 1. Region-Based Key Agreement protocol

1.   The Subgroup Formation
        The number of members in each subgroup is
           N / S   < 100.
Where, N – is the group size. and   S – is the number of subgroups.
 Assuming that each subgroup has the same number of members.
2.   The Contributory Key Agreement protocol is implemented among the group
   members. It consists of three stages.
        a. To find the Subgroup Controller for each subgroups.
        b. GECDH protocol is used to generate one common key for each subgroup
           headed by the subgroup controller(i.e SubgroupKey),which performs
           encryption and decryption of sub group level messages broadcast to all
           subgroup members..
        c. Each subgroup gateway member contributes partial keys to generate a one
           common backbone key (i.e Outer group Key (KG)) ,which is used to
           encrypt and decrypt the messages broadcast among subgroup controllers,
           headed by the Outer Group Controller using TGECDH protocol.
    3.   Each Group Controller (sub /Outer) distributes the computed public key to all
        its members. Each member performs rekeying to get the respected group key.

A Regional key KR is used for communication between a subgroup controller and the members in the same region. The Regional key KR is rekeyed whenever there is a membership change event occurs due to member join / leave or member failure. The Outer Group key KG is rekeyed whenever there is a join / leave of subgroup controllers or member failure to preserve secrecy.

The members within a subgroup use Group Elliptic Curve Diffie-Hellman Contributory Key Agreement (GECDH). Each member within a subgroup contributes his share in arriving at the subgroup key. Whenever membership changes occur, the subgroup controller or previous member initiates the rekeying operation.

The gateway member initiates communication with the neighboring member belonging to another subgroup and mutually agree on a key using Tree-Based Group Elliptic Curve Diffie-Hellman contributory Key Agreement(TGECDH) protocol for inter subgroup communication between the two subgroups. Any member belonging to one subgroup can communicate with any other member in another subgroup through this member as the intermediary. In this way adjacent subgroups agree on outer group key. Whenever membership changes occur, the outer group controller or previous group controller initiates the rekeying operation.

Here, we prefer the subgroup key to be different from the key for backbone. This difference adds more freedom of managing the dynamic group membership. In addition, using this approach can potentially save the communication and computational cost.

An information sharing application should allow end users to:

> Search for information.
> Make their information available.
> Download information.

In order to secure this type of information sharing application we need to provide confidentiality and integrity of all communication and to enforce access control of resources i.e. communication channels and shared information.

Figure.1 shows the interactions between peers. A peer, P_1, searches for information by sending a *query* message to the subgroup. The subgroup controller sends the query message to outer group. Peers subgroup doesn't have content that matches the query, so they do not respond. Peer P_2 has content that matches the query, so it sends a *query response* message. P_1, can then request to download content from P_2 by sending a *transfer request* message. P_2 answers this request with the content

2.2 Network Dynamics

The network is dynamic in nature. Many members may join or leave the group. In such case, a group key management system should ensure that backward and forward secrecy is preserved.

2.2.1 Member Join

When a new member joins, it initiates communication with the subgroup controller. After initialization, the subgroup controller changes its contribution and sends public key to this new member. The new member receives the public key and acts as a group controller by initiating the rekeying operations for generating a new key for the subgroup. The rekeying operation is as follows.

New node $\xrightarrow{\text{Join request}}$ Subgroup Controller

Subgroup Controller $\xrightarrow{\text{change its contribution and send public key to}}$ New Node

New Node $\xrightarrow{\text{Acts as}}$ New Subgroup Controller

New Subgroup Controller $\xrightarrow{\substack{\text{puts its contribution to all the public key value \&} \\ \text{Multicast this public key value to}}}$ the entire member in the subgroup

Each Member $\xrightarrow{\text{put is contribution to the public value \& Compute}}$ New Subgroup Key

2.2.2 Member Leave

1. When a Subgroup member Leaves

When a member leaves the Subgroup Key of the subgroup to which it belongs must be changed to preserve the forward secrecy. The leaving member informs the subgroup controller. The subgroup controller changes its private key value, computes the public value and broadcasts the public value to all the remaining members. Each member performs rekeying by putting its contribution to public value and computes the new Subgroup Key. The rekeying operation is as follows.

Leaving Node $\xrightarrow{\text{Leaving Message}}$ Subgroup Controller

Subgroup Controller $\xrightarrow{\substack{\text{changes its private key value, compute the public key value and} \\ \text{Multicast the public key value to}}}$ All the remaining Member

Each Member $\xrightarrow{\text{Performs Rekeying and Compute}}$ New Subgroup Key

2. When a Subgroup Controller Leaves

When the Subgroup Controller leaves, the Subgroup key used for communication among the subgroup controller needs to be changed. This Subgroup Controller informs the previous Subgroup Controller about its desire to leave the subgroup which initiates the rekeying procedure. The previous subgroup controller now acts as a Subgroup controller. This Subgroup controller changes its private contribution value and computes all the public key values and broadcasts to all the remaining members of the group. All subgroup members perform the rekeying operation and compute the new subgroup key. The rekeying operation is as follows.

Leaving Subgroup Controller $\xrightarrow{\text{Leaving Message}}$ Old Subgroup Controller

Old Subgroup Controller $\xrightarrow{\substack{\text{change its private value, compute the all} \\ \text{public key value and Multicast}}}$ Remaining Member in the group

Subgroup Member $\xrightarrow{\text{Perform Rekeying and Compute}}$ New Subgroup Key

3. When an Outer Group Controller Leaves

When a Outer group Controller leaves, the Outer group key used for communication among the Outer group need to be changed. This Outer group Controller informs the previous Outer group Controller about its desire to leave the Outer group which initiates the rekeying procedure. The previous Outer Group controller now becomes the New Outer group controller. This Outer group controller changes its private contribution value and computes the public key value and broadcasts it to the entire remaining member in the group. All Outer group members perform the rekeying operation and compute the new Outer group key. The rekeying operation is as follows.

$$\text{Leaving Outer group Controller} \xrightarrow{\text{Leaving Message}} \text{Old Outer group Controller}$$

$$\text{Old Outer group Controller} \xrightarrow{\substack{\text{change its private value,compute the all} \\ \text{public key value and Multicast}}} \text{Remaing Member in the Outer group}$$

$$\text{Outer group Member} \xrightarrow{\text{Perform Rekeying and Compute}} \text{New Outer group Key}$$

4. When a Gateway member leaves

When a gateway member leaves the subgroup, it delegates the role of the gateway to the adjacent member having high processing power, memory, and Battery power and acts as a new gateway member. Whenever the gateway member leaves, all the two keys should be changed. These are

    i.   Outer group key among the subgroup.
    ii. Subgroup key within the subgroup.

In this case, the subgroup controller and outer group controller perform the rekeying operation. The Controller leaves the member and a new gateway member is selected in the subgroup, performs rekeying in the subgroup. After that, it joins in the outer group. The procedure is same as joining the member in the outer group.

2.3   Communication Protocol

The members within the subgroup have communication using subgroup key. The communication among the subgroup members takes place through the gateway member.

2.3.1   Communication within the Subgroup

The sender member encrypts the message with the subgroup key (KR) and multicasts it to all member in the subgroup. The subgroup members receive the encrypted message, perform the decryption using the subgroup key (KR) and gets the original message. The communication operation is as follows.

$$\text{Source Member} \xrightarrow{E_{KR}[\text{Message}] \ \& \ \text{Multicast}} \text{Destination Member}$$

$$\text{Destination Member} \xrightarrow{D_{KR}[E_{KR}[\text{Message}]]} \text{Original Message}$$

2.3.2   Communication among the Subgroup

The sender member encrypts the message with the subgroup key (KR) and multicasts it to all members in the subgroup. One of the members in the subgroup acts as a gate way member. This gateway member decrypts the message with subgroup key and encrypts with the outer group key (KG) and multicast to the entire gateway member among the subgroup. The destination gateway member first decrypts the message with outer group key. Then encrypts with subgroup key and multicasts it to all members in the subgroup. Each member in the subgroup receives the encrypted message and performs decryption using subgroup key and gets the original message. In this way the region-based group key agreement protocol performs the communication. The communication operation is as follows.

$$\text{Source Member } \xrightarrow{E_{KR}[\text{Message}] \& \text{Multicast}} \text{Gateway Member}$$

$$\text{Gateway Member } \xrightarrow{D_{KR}[E_{KR}[\text{Message}]]} \text{Original Message}$$

$$\text{Gateway Member } \xrightarrow{E_{KG}[\text{Message}] \& \text{Multicast}} \text{Gateway Member [Among Subgroup]}$$

$$\text{Gateway Member } \xrightarrow{D_{KG}[E_{KG}[\text{Message}]]} \text{Original Message}$$

$$\text{Gateway Member } \xrightarrow{E_{KR}[\text{Message}] \& \text{Multicast}} \text{Destination Member}$$

$$\text{Destination Member } \xrightarrow{D_{KR}[E_{KR}[\text{Message}]]} \text{Original Message}$$

2.4 Applying Elliptic Curve Based Diffie-Hellman Key Exchange

2.4.1 Member Join

User A and user B are going to exchange their keys(figure.2): Take p=211, Ep=(0,-4), which is equivalent to the curve $y^2 = x^3 - 4$ and G = (2,2). A's private key is nA = 47568, so A's public key PA =47568(2,2)=(206,121), B's private key is nB = 13525,so B's public key PB =13525(2,2)=(29,139). The group key is computed (Fig.[ ].) as User A sends its public key (206,121) to user B, then user B computes their Subgroup key as nB (A's Public key) = 13525(206,121) = (**155,115**). User B sends its public key (29,139) to User A, then User A compute their Subgroup key as nA(B's Public key)= 47568(29,139) = (**120,180**).

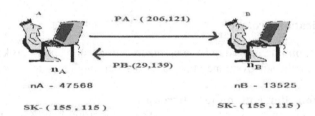

Fig. 2. User-A & User –B Join the Group

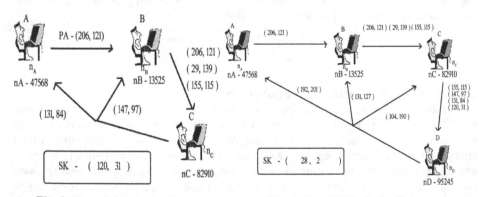

Fig. 3. User- C Join in the Group   **Fig. 4.** User-D Join in the Group

When User C is going to join in the group, C's private key becomes nC= 82910. Now, User C becomes a Subgroup Controller. Then, the key updating process will begin as follows: The previous Subgroup Controller User B sends the intermediate key as (B's Public key $ A's Public Key $ Group key of A&B)= ((29,139) $ (206,121) $ (155,115)) User C separates the intermediate key as B's Public key, A's Public Key and Group key of A&B=(29,139) , (206,121) and (155,115).Then, User C generates the new Subgroup key as nC (Subgroup key of A&B)= 82910(155,115) = (**120,31**). Then, User C broadcasts the intermediate key to User A and User B. That intermediate key is ((Public key of B & C) $ (Public key of A & C)) = ((131,84) $(147, 97)). Now, User B extracts the value of public key of A & C from the value sent by User C. Then User B compute the new Subgroup key as follows: nB (Public key of A&C)= 13525(147,97)= (**120,31**). Similarly, User A extracts the value of public key of B & C from intermediate key, sent by User C. Then User A compute the new Subgroup key as follows: nA (public key of B&C) = 47568(131,84) = (**120,31**). Therefore, New Subgroup Key of A, B and C = (**120, 31**) as shown in the figure.3.The same procedure is followed when User D joins as shown in the Fig.4.

2.4.2 Member Leave

When a user leaves (Fig.5.) from the Subgroup, then the Subgroup controller changes its private key. After that, it broadcasts its new public key value to all users in the Subgroup. Then, new Subgroup key will be generated. Let us consider, User B is going to leave, then the Subgroup Controller D changes its private key nD' =43297 ,so public key of User A & User C =(198,139)$(136,11). Then the new Subgroup Key generated is = 43297(198,139) = (**207,115**). Then, User A & User C computes the new Subgroup Key by using new public key. Therefore, the new Subgroup Key is (**207,115**)

2.4.3 Group Controller Leave

When a Subgroup controller leaves (Fig.6.) from the group, then the previous Subgroup controller changes its private key. After that, it broadcasts its new public key value to all users in the group. Then, new Subgroup key will be generated. Let us consider, Subgroup Controller User D going to leave, then the previous Subgroup controller User C act as Subgroup Controller and changes its private key nC' = 52898 , and computes the public key of B&C $ A&C = (16,111)$(181,2). Then the new Subgroup Key generated is = 52898(21,103) = (**198,139**). Then, User A & User B compute the new Subgroup Key by using new public key. Therefore, the new Subgroup Key is (**198,139**).

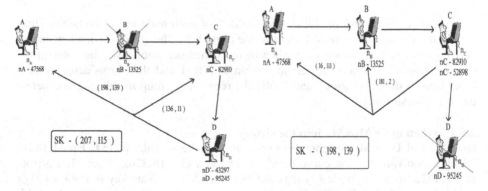

Fig. 5. User –B leave from the Group   **Fig. 6.** Group Controller Leave
                                                    from the group

2.5 Tree-Based Group Elliptic Curve Diffie-Hellman Protocol

The proposed protocol (Fig.7.), Tree-based group Elliptic Curve Diffie-Hellman (TGECDH), is a variant of TGDH based on ECDLP. In TGECDH, a binary tree is used to organize group members. The nodes are denoted as $< l, v >$, where $0 <= v <= 2^l - 1$ since each level l hosts at most 2^l nodes. Each node $< l, v >$ is associated with the key $K<l,v>$ and the blinded key $BK<l,v> = F(K<l,v>)$ where the function $F()$ is scalar multiplication of elliptic curve points in prime field. Assuming a leaf node $< l, v >$ hosts the member Mi, the node $< l, v >$ has Mi's session random key $K<l,v>$. Furthermore, the member Mi at node $< l. v >$ knows every key in the key-path from $< l, v >$ to $< 0, 0 >$. Every key $K<l,v>$ is computed recursively as follows:

$$
\begin{aligned}
K_{<l,v>} &= K_{<l+1,2v>} BK_{<l+1,2v+1>} \bmod p \\
&= K_{<l+1,2v+1>} BK_{<l+1,2v>} \bmod p \\
&= K_{<l+1,2v>} K_{<l+1,2v+1>} G \bmod p \\
&= F(K_{<l+1,2v>} K_{<l+1,2v+1>})
\end{aligned}
\tag{1}
$$

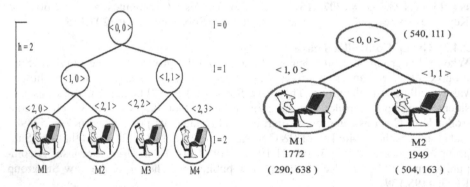

Fig. 7. Key Tree.   **Fig. 8.** User M_1 & M_2 Join the Group

It is not necessary for the blind key $BK<l,v>$ of each node to be reversible. Thus, simply use the x-coordinate of $K<l,v>$ as the blind key. The group session key can be derived from $K<0,0>$. Each time when there is member join/leave, the outer group controller node calculates the group session key first and then broadcasts the new blind keys to the entire group and finally the remaining group members can generate the group session key.

2.5.1 When node M_1&M_2 Join the Group
User M_1 and User M_2 are going to exchange their keys: Take **p=751, Ep=(1,188)** , which is equivalent to the curve $y^2=x^3 +x+188$ and **G = (0,376)**. User M_1's private key is **1772**, so M_1's public key is **(290,638)**. User M_2's private key is **1949**, so M_2's public key is (504,163) . The Outer Group key is computed (Figure.8) as User M_1 sends its public key **(290,638)** to user M_2, the User M_2 computes their group key as

PV(0,0) = X_{co} (PV(1,0) *PB(1,1)) and PB(0,0) = PV(0,0)*G =(**540,111**). Similarly, User M_2 sends its public key (**504,163**) to user M_1, and then the user M_1 computes their group key as (**540,111**). Here, Outer Group controller is User M_2.

2.5.2 When 3rd node Join

When User M_3 joins the group, the old Outer group controller M_2 changes its private key value from **1949** to **2835** and passes the public key value and tree to User M_3. Now, M_3 becomes new Outer group controller. Then, M_3 generates the public key (**623, 52**) from its private key as **14755** and computes the Outer group key as (**664,736**) shown in Figure.9. M_3 sends Tree and public key to all users. Now, user M_1 and M_2 compute their group key. The same procedure is followed by joining the User M_4 as shown in Fig.10.

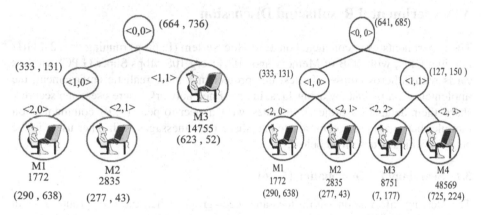

Fig. 9. User M_3 Join the Group   **Fig. 10.** User M_4 Join the group

2.5.3 Leave Protocol

There are two types of leave, 1.Gateway Member Leave and 2.Outer Group Controller Leave

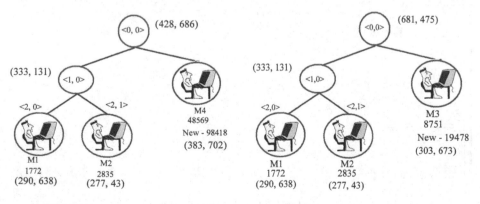

Fig. 11. User M_3 Leave from   **Fig. 12.** Outer Group Controller
the Group   Leave from the Group

1. Gateway Member Leave

When user M_3 leaves (Figure.11) the Outer group, then the Group controller changes its private key **48569** to **98418** and outer group key is recalculated as **(428,686)**. After that, it broadcasts its Tree and public key value to all users in the Outer group. Then, the new Outer group key will be generated by the remaining users.

2. When an Outer Group Controller Leaves

When an Outer Group Controller Leaves (Figure.12) from the group, then its sibling act as a New Outer Group Controller and changes its private key value 8751 to 19478 and recalculates the group key as **(681,475)**. After that, it broadcast its Tree and public key value to all users in the Outer group. Then, the new Outer group key will be generated by the remaining users.

3   Experimental Results and Discussion

The experiments were conducted on a Ad-Hoc System (Laptop) running on a 2.4 GHz Pentium CPU, with 2GB of Memory and 802.11 b/g 108 Mbps Super G PCI wireless cards with Atheros chipset. To test this project in a more realistic environment, the implementation is done by using Java, in an ad hoc network where users can securely share their data. This project integrates with a peer-to-peer (P2P) communication module that is able to communicate and share their messages with other users in the network which is described below.

3.1   Searching for Information [4,5,6]

Transferring information within the same peer group: when the peer group G is in need of searching for any messages within its members(Pi) , it needs to send a query message to all the members of G(i.e Pi) . Each peer, P_j in G, that receives the query message, checks whether any items match the query and responds directly to P_i with a

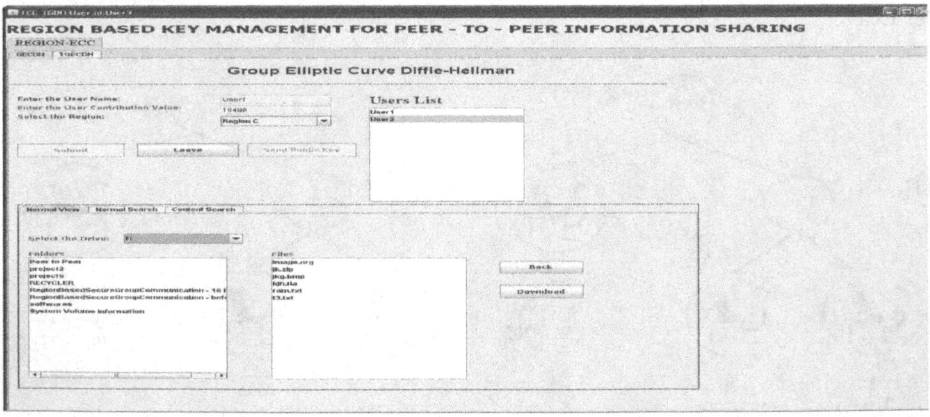

Fig. 13. Local Regional view

query response message that contains the metadata associated with the items that matched the query.

Transferring information between peers:. A peer P_i may request a transfer of information from a peer P_j, by sending a *transfer request message* to P_j. Pj, upon receiving this message checks whether it has the information item associated with the request. If P_j has the item then P_j transfers the requested information to Pi.

3.1.1 Local Region View

After the establishment of ECRBGKA protocol, the requested peer system files are displayed as shown in the figure.13.

3.2 Normal Search

As soon as the filename is entered and search button gets clicked, the path of the searched file will be enlisted and the desired file can be obtained in a fraction of time. Normal file search is performed as shown in the figure.14

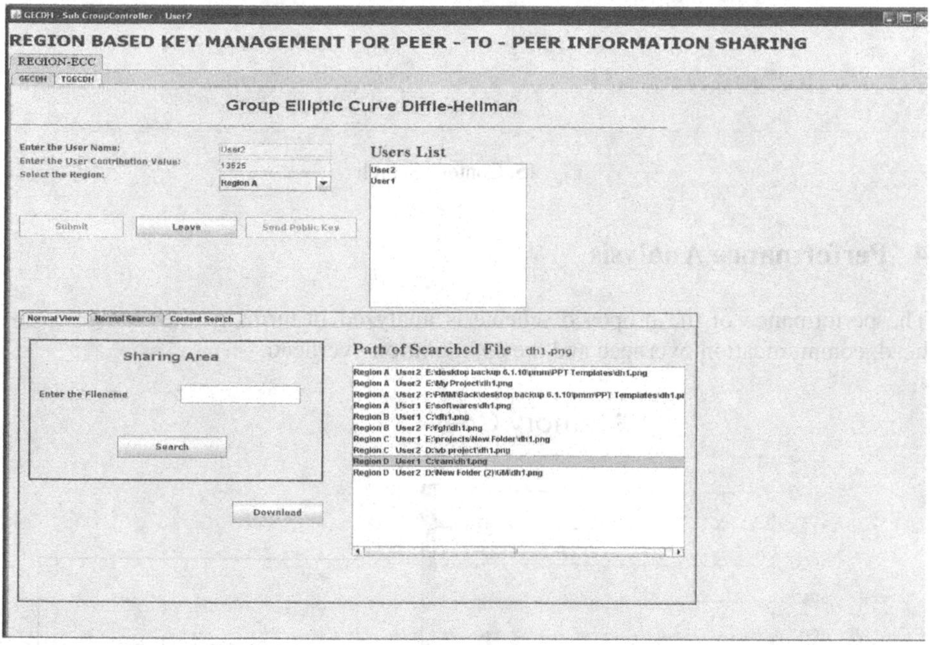

Fig. 14. Normal Search

3.3 Content Search

In this kind of search, the content of the specified file which we are looking for can be acquired instantly after clicking over the search button. Content search is performed as shown in the figure 15.

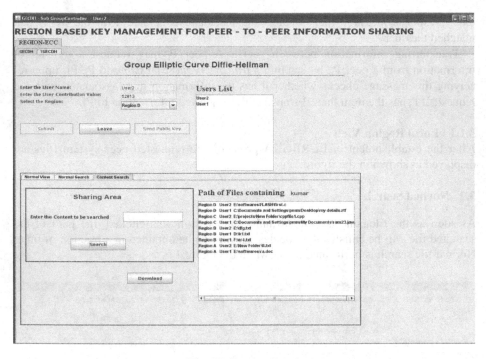

Fig. 15. Content Search

4 Performance Analysis

The performance of the proposed scheme is analyzed in terms of the storage overhead, communication overhead and the computation overhead.

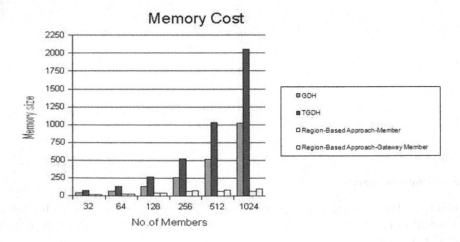

Fig. 16. Memory Cost

4.1 Storage Overhead

Storage overhead can be considered as the memory capacity required for maintaining the keys, which is directly proportional to the number of members if the key size are same. In this section, the storage cost is formulated, both at gateway member and at each member. Thus our approach consumes very less memory when compared to TGDH and GDH. TGDH and GDH occupy large memory when members go on increasing. But our Region-based Approach takes very less memory even when the members get increased. Consider (Figure- 16) there are 1024 members in a group our Region-based approach consumes 10% of memory when compared to GDH and 5% when compared to TGDH. The ratio of memory occupied is very less in our approach.

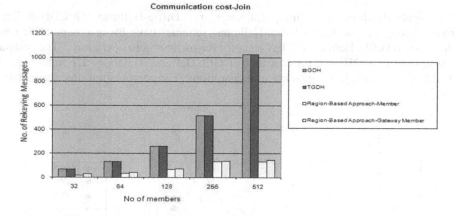

Fig. 17. Communication Cost - Join

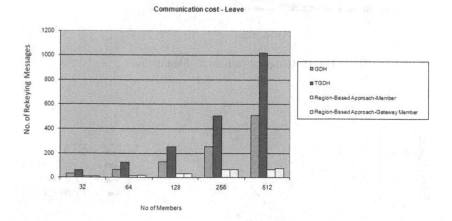

Fig. 18. Communication Cost - Leave

4.2 Communication Overhead

GDH is the most expensive protocol. TGDH consumes more bandwidth. The Communication and computation of TGDH depends on trees height, balance of key tree, location of joining tree, and leaving nodes. Hence GDH has more communication efficiency than TGDH protocol. But our approach depends on the number of members in the subgroup, number of Group Controllers, and height of tree. So the amount spent on communication is very much less when compared to GDH and TGDH.

Consider (Figure.17&18) there are 512 members in a group our approach consumes only 10% of Bandwidth when compared to GDH and TGDH. So our approach consumes low Bandwidth.

4.3 Computation Overhead

The figure.19 shows that Group Elliptic Curve Diffie-Hellman (GECDH)& Tree based Group Elliptic Curve Diffie-Hellman schemes have lower computation time than Group Diffie-Hellman (GDH) schemes for member join operations. The computation time of GDH is **2.2 times** that of GECDH and TGDH is **1.7** times that of TGECDH on average for member join operations. The computation time for member

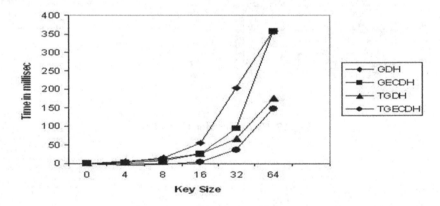

Fig. 19. Computation time for Member Join

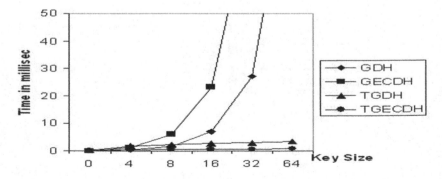

Fig. 20. Computation time for Member Leave

leave operations of TGECDH schemes are far better than group Diffie-Hellman schemes for member leave operations as shown in the figure.20. Performance wise our approach is took than GDH&TGDH methods, even for the very large groups.

The performance of GECDH&TGECDH over wireless ad hoc Networks can be summarized as follows:

1. It uses smaller keys.
2. It uses less computation time than the DLP-based scheme for the same security level.
3. Smaller packets are used to handle high bit error rate Wireless links.

5 Conclusion and Future Work

In this paper, we propose and evaluate a new ECDLP-based Diffie-Hellman protocols for secure Peer –to- peer Information sharing in mobile ad hoc networks. The experiment results show that ECRBGKA scheme is the best protocol in terms of overall performance for secure Peer –to- peer Information sharing in mobile ad hoc networks. Secure group information retrieval is most efficient if the group members have a common, shared key for securing the communication. Region-Based Group Key Agreement in Peer-to-peer Information sharing provides efficient, distributed, mechanisms for re-keying in case of dynamic groups, which generates a new key every time a membership change occurs to preserve forward secrecy. We have presented a Region-Based GKA of security mechanisms that can be used to provide ECC based security for peer-to- peer information sharing. Our solutions are based on established and proven security techniques and we utilize existing technologies. We make use of these mechanisms to provide efficient, scalable and secure delivery of queries and responses. Our future work will unsolve formalizing these protocols.

References

[1] Amir, Y., Kim, Y., Nita-Rotaru, C., Schultz, J., Stanton, J., Tsudik, G.: Exploring Robustness in Group Key Agreement. In: Proc. 21st IEEE Int'l Conf. Distributed Computing Systems, pp. 399–408 (2001)

[2] Rabah, K.: Theory and Implementation of Elliptic Curve Cryptography. Journal of Applied Sciences 5(4), 604–633 (2005)

[3] Steiner, M., Tsudik, G., Waidner, M.: Key Agreement in Dynamic Peer Groups. IEEE Trans. Parallel and Distributed Systems 11(8) (August 2000)

[4] Jin, H., Ning, X., Chen, H.: Efficient Search for Peer-to-Peer Information Retrieval Using Semantic Small World. In: Proc. 15th Int'l Conf. World Wide Web (WWW 2006), pp. 1003–1004 (May 2006)

[5] Yun Zhou, W.: Bruce Croft Brian Neil Levine. In: Content-Based Search in Peer-to-Peer Networks. Dept. of Computer Science, University of Massachusetts, Amherst, MA 01003 (2004)

[6] Berket, K., Essiari, A., Muratas, A.: PKI-Based Security for Peer-to-Peer Information Sharing. In: Fourth International Conference on Peer-to-Peer Computing, August 25-27 (2004)

A Power Adjustment Approach for Multi-channel Multi-AP Deployment Using Cognitive Radio Concept

Prabhat Kumar Tiwary, Niwas Maskey, and Suman Khakurel

Department of Electronics and Communication
NIT Surat, India
{prabhat393,niwasmaskey,167suman}@gmail.com

Abstract. The explosive growth in wireless network over the last few years resembles the rapid growth of the internet within the last decade. The increasing popularity of IEEE 802.11 demands enhancement in network performance. WLAN uses frequency spectrum for providing wireless access to nomadic nodes which is in fact a very scarce resource. One common issue in deployment of a multi-channel multi-AP (access point) wireless network is interference. Interference can be minimized by adjusting the transmission power. This paper focuses on transmission power adjustment of APs by using the concept of cognitive radio. The approach requires RSSI (Received Signal Strength Indication) information to be sent by all the mobile WSs (workstations) in the coverage area to the associated AP at regular intervals to keep the AP updated about their distance. Depending on the current position of WS, AP's power transmission level is adjusted (increased, decreased, remains same, transmission stopped). During adjustment of power level of the AP, cognitive radio concept is used to avoid the power level to reach beyond a maximum level so as to minimize the problem of interference. Each AP in the network considers itself to be secondary users as in a cognitive network and keeps it power level within a limit such that other APs (taken as primary users) do not face interference.

Keywords: IEEE 802.11, Cognitive radio, Access point, Power adjustment.

1 Introduction

Wireless access to data and resources is much desirable which has boosted the rapid growth in wireless network (IEEE 802.11). With increasing popularity of wireless LANs, solutions are required to increase the performance of network and minimize any insecurity, if present.

WLAN uses frequency spectrum for providing wireless access to nomadic nodes which is in fact a very scarce resource. Wireless network is created by placing a set of APs in a geographical area and connecting it to a distribution system, most commonly, Ethernet. But placing the APs blindly might cause interference.

Interference is the main reason why the capability of a network cannot be fully utilized. Two types of interferences can be distinguished: adjacent channel interference which is produced by transmissions from adjacent or partly overlapped channels; and co-channel interference which is caused by the same frequency channels.

N. Meghanathan et al. (Eds.): CNSA 2010, CCIS 89, pp. 296–301, 2010.

Interference is minimized using three basic methods [1]:

- AP placement
- adjusting the transmission power, and
- optimizing the AP frequency channel .

This work will be focusing on adjusting the transmission power of the APs by taking into consideration the co-channel non-adjacent APs.

According to IEEE 802.11 standard [2], the node will be associated to the AP that has the highest received signal strength indicator (RSSI) at the receiver. Association of more nodes to the AP will result in overloading at the particular AP. Beside this problem, for AP that uses the same channel or different overlapping channels, interference may occur among them. Pre-allocating the channels to each AP and adjusting the transmission power are the possible solutions to the stated problem.

This paper proposes a new model for wireless LAN (IEEE 802.11) network to improve the overall network system performance by adjusting the transmission power based on the estimation of the distance between the AP and the associated WS.

2 Related Work

A lot of work has been done to adjust the transmission power of the transmitter in a wireless network.

Previous researchers have done some work on adjusting the transmission power of the AP in a WLAN using cognitive radio network [3]-[7]. The main challenge of cognitive communication is to balance between the conflicting goals of maximizing the performance of secondary user, which is the cognitive radio (unlicensed) and minimizing the interference to the primary user (licensed).

Rafiza Ruslan and Tat-Chee Wan in their work [8] produced an initial algorithm for adjusting transmission power in an ESS of an infrastructure network adapting cognitive radio technique. However, they assumed the work stations to be fixed and immobile inside the ESS.

This paper focuses on transmission power adjustment for mobile workstations inside the ESS using the concept of cognitive network. The mobility of the workstations has been taken care of.

3 The Proposed Approach

In this section, we propose an algorithm which performs power level adjustment using the concept of CR technique in wireless LAN. The algorithm takes into consideration the distance between a WS and the associated AP in a multi-AP deployment.

In the scenario as shown in Fig. 1, the channels are pre-allocated to the APs in a way that it will not interfere with the adjacent AP. But there are possibilities that interference will occur from the non-adjacent co-channel APs.

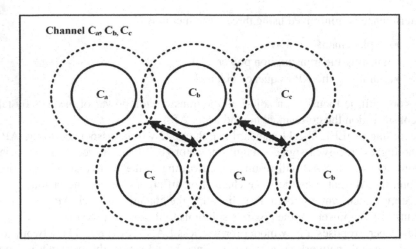

Fig. 1. The topology of non-adjacent co-channel APs

Let us simplify the topology as in Fig. 2. The network model consists of three APs and several WSs, where some of the WSs are associated to their respective APs. Each AP will have its own transmission range R_T with a radius of r_t and interference range R_I with a radius of r_i. The channel of the middle AP (AP$_2$) is different from the other two APs.

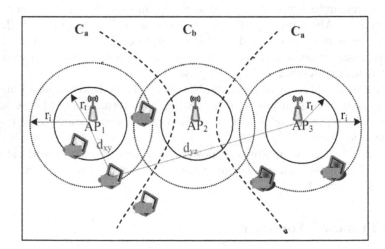

Fig. 2. The simulation scenario

It has been assumed that all transmissions are omnidirectional. The center of transmission range R_T and interference range R_I lies at the AP position.Therefore, by adjusting the transmission power, both ranges can be controlled. R_T is defined as the maximum range for a transmitter to transmit a signal that receiver can decode. Whereas, R_I is the interference range for the AP that may interfere with other co-channel APs or overlapping channel APs.

We assume all APs belong to the same wireless LAN network and thus are connected to the same Ethernet backbone. A constant bandwidth is provided by a channel at each AP regardless of the number of users and the reception sensitivity are the same for all nodes. This paper only considers AP to AP interference where power adjustment only can be done at the AP and not at the WS where the WSs have a fixed power level.

The idea behind the algorithm is to have an acceptable power level transmitted to the active WSs based on their estimated distance from the associated AP. The adjustment of the power levels are done until the maximum power is reached, or when the transmission begins to interfere with another non-adjacent co-channel AP.

The algorithm requires RSSI information to be sent by mobile WS to the AP at some convenient time interval according the expected mobility of WS in the service set. The AP gets updated about the distance of the WS with the help of the RSSI information received. Based on the current distance of WS from the AP, the algorithm will make some decision on the transmission power level required. This process would be repeated for every WS in the service set.

For a particular instant, we defined d_{xy} as the estimated distance between the WS and the associated AP (i.e, AP_1) . Whereas, d_{yz} is the estimated distance between the WS and the other non-adjacent co-channel AP (i.e, AP_3). d_{xy} falls within the R_I of AP_1 while d_{yz} is much greater than r_i of AP_3. The algorithm will check whether the WS is in the overlapping area or not. Transmission power will be incremented in order to obtain a successful transmission. The transmission powers received by the WS in the overlapping area will be checked. If, it is found that transmission power, $P_{tx}(AP_2)$ is greater than $P_{tx}(AP_1)$, the WS (located in the overlapping area) will be handed over to the adjacent AP (i.e, AP_2) otherwise it retains its association with AP_1.

The algorithm will be repeatedly adjusting the transmission power level rendering an appropriate power level for all the individual WSs to improve the overall network system performance. The transmission power level will be reduced, increased or kept the same every time a RSSI information is sent. The process of handover to another AP will also happen for the WS located in overlapping area if appropriate power is received from the new AP. Finally, if the WS is located beyond the R_I of an AP, no transmission will be executed since WS is out of coverage area.

By controlling the transmission power, the transmission and interference range can be adjusted. The proposed algorithm adapts cognitive radio for setting the value of maximum power an AP can transmit. Hence, that can be seen as the intelligence in maximizing the utilization of communication channels using reasonable power level. Each AP will be the secondary AP by assuming other APs as the primary APs.
For instance;

- AP_1 will assume AP_2 and AP_3 as the primary users;
- AP_2 will assume AP_1 and AP_3 as the primary users;
- AP_3 will assume AP_1 and AP_2 as the primary users;

Therefore, from each AP's perspective, the AP itself is the secondary user and other APs are the primary users. On the contrary, in a physical cognitive radio network, the secondary user (unlicensed users) may have access to the spectrum under the condition of no interference to the primary users (licensed users) [6], [7]. Thus, power adjustment decision is made based on the WS position, considering the co-channel inference as the limiting constraint. The relevant positions of WS which are taken under consideration in the proposed approach are:

- within the transmission range of an AP;
- in between transmission and interference range of an AP;
- in the overlapping area, OR
- beyond the interference range of an AP.

4 Algorithm for Power Adjustment

Step 1: RSSI information sent to AP
Step 2: /* decision making about power transmission and hand over*/
    if $d_{xy} \leq r_t(AP_1C_a)$ **then**
        /*node within R_T of AP_1 which is using channel C_a*/
        No change in AP_1's transmission power
    end if
    While $d_{xy} \leq r_i(AP_1C_a)$ AND $d_{yz} \geq r_i(AP_3C_a)$
    /* loop to attain an appropriate power level*/
        if $P_{tx}(AP_1C_a) \neq P_{max}(AP_1C_a)$ **then**
          /*if power not max*/
            if $r_t(AP_1C_a) \leq d_{xy} \leq r_i(AP_1C_a)$ then
            increase AP_1's power by one step
          end if

        else if $P_{tx}(AP_2C_b) > P_{tx}(AP_1C_a)$ **then**
          handover to AP_2
          /*switch to different channel AP_2*/
        end if
    end while
    if $d_{xy} \geq r_i(AP_1C_a)$ **then**
    /*outside the transmission range */
       no transmission
    end if
Step 3: Wait for new RSSI information
Step 4: Jump to Step 1 to work upon new RSSI information sent by the mobile WS.

5 Conclusion

The algorithm proposed in the paper provides a solution for power level adjustment for a multi-channel multi-AP configuration containing mobile work stations. The concept of cognitive radio has been used in order to limit the maximum power level that an AP can transmit. Thus, an attempt has been made to minimize interference in the network and enhance the performance of the network.

References

1. Vanhatupa, T., Hannikainen, M., Hamalainen, T.D.: Evaluation of planning. In: Proceedings of the 3rd International Conference on Quality Throughput Estimation Models and Algorithms for WLAN Frequency of Service in Heterogeneous Wired/Wireless Networks Waterloo, Ontario. ACM, Canada (2006)
2. IEEE802.11, Part 11: Wireless LAN Medium Access Control (MAC) and Physical Layer (PHY) Specifications, 2007th edn.
3. Shi, Y.: Algorithm and Optimization for Wireless Network. PhD Degree (2007)
4. Hoven, N., Sahai, A.: Power scaling for cognitive radio. In: 2005 International Conference on Wireless Networks, Communications and Mobile Computing, vol. 1, pp. 250–255 (2005)
5. Srinivasa, S., Jafar, S.A.: Soft Sensing and Optimal Power Control for Cognitive Radio. In: Global Telecommunications Conference, GLOBECOM 2007, pp. 1380–1384. IEEE, Los Alamitos (2007)
6. Qi, L., Zheng, Z., Cheng, Y., Yabin, Y.: The Coverage Analysis of Cognitive Radio Network. In: 4th International Conference on Wireless Communications, Networking and Mobile Computing, WiCOM 2008, pp. 1–4 (2008)
7. Wei, R., Qing, Z., Swami, A.: Power control in spectrum overlay networks: How to cross a multi-lane highway. In: IEEE International Conference on Acoustics, Speech and Signal Processing, ICASSP 2008, pp. 2773–2776 (2008)
8. Ruslan, R., Wan, T.-C.: Cognitive Radio-based Power Adjustment for Wi-Fi. IEEE, Los Alamitos
9. Forouzan, B.A.: Data Communication and Networking
10. Gast, M.S.: 802.11 Wireless Networks, The Definitive Guide.

Conscience-Based Routing in P2P Networks: Preventing Copyright Violations and Social Malaise

Ankur Gupta

Professor, Computer Science and Engineering
Model Institute of Engineering and Technology, Jammu, India
ankurgupta@mietjammu.in
http://www.mietjammu.in

Abstract. P2P networks are harbingers of copyright violations costing the music, movie and the software industries millions of dollars in lost revenue, through illegal sharing of content. Moreover, the anonymous social networking sites act as playgrounds for criminals and sexual predators, leading to a fast growing social malaise. Since, P2P networks are anonymous in nature, highly scalable and censorship-resistant by design, controlling shared content is non-trivial to say the least. Hence, there is an urgent need by the research community to counter these threats. We present the novel concept of **Conscience-Based Routing (CBR)** in which **Conscientious Peers (CPs)** actively block queries pertaining to illegal music/movies or those pertaining to topics such as national security or pornography. Moreover, CPs pass poisoned content to peers requesting illegal content so that their overall experience is severely diminished, discouraging them from seeking illegal content. Such an approach is suitable for a pure decentralized P2P network where individual peers perform overlay query routing. We establish the effectiveness of our approach through simulation and also discuss strategies to encourage "conscientious" behavior by peers in a real-world scenario.

Keywords: copyright violations in P2P networks, social networking, conscience-based routing, adaptive content poisoning, P2P query blocking.

1 Introduction

Peer-to-Peer (P2P) networks [1] and the computation that they facilitate have received tremendous attention from the research community because of the huge untapped potential of the P2P concept – extending the boundaries of scale and decentralization beyond the limits imposed by traditional distributed systems, besides enabling end users to interact, collaborate, share and utilize resources offered by one another in an autonomous manner. Moreover, P2P architectures are characterized by their ability to adapt to failures and a dynamically changing topology with a transient population of nodes/devices, thus exhibiting a high degree of self-organization and fault tolerance. P2P networks therefore have many desirable properties for designing massively distributed applications.

However, with the desirable properties P2P systems also have some characteristics which pose great challenges in designing robust, reliable and secure applications

N. Meghanathan et al. (Eds.): CNSA 2010, CCIS 89, pp. 302–313, 2010.
© Springer-Verlag Berlin Heidelberg 2010

around them. *Anonymity* of peers poses issues of trust and security, whereas frequent *node transience* does not allow any useful work to be performed apart from best-effort information sharing. Sharing of compute resources leads to vulnerability to a variety of *security attacks*, whereas overlay routing performed by peers raises issues of *data privacy*. *Lack of centralized control* and *censorship-resistance* leads to copyright violations and infringement of intellectual property rights. Thus, P2P systems have not been adopted by organizations even though their desirable properties can be leveraged to meet many organizational requirements effectively. Some organizations and network service providers have resorted to blocking P2P traffic entirely to prevent any potential impact on their operations.

P2P networks also have a far-reaching social impact [2]. Due to the anonymity offered by P2P networks, the social networking sites are fast becoming the playground of sexual predators, criminals and anti-social elements. The use of P2P-based social networking sites for selling and seeking drugs is well-known [3]. Recently some criminals used the social networking sites to lure, kidnap and murder Adnan Patrawala in Mumbai, India [4], exposing the dark side of the spurt in social networking. With 80% of the users of popular social networking sites estimated to be young teens and children, who tend to use the anonymity offered by P2P networks to lead a parallel digital existence, the possibility of their exploitation is real.

Hence, there is a real need to address this shortcoming of P2P networks to prevent copyright violations and social malaise from spreading further. This research paper proposes "Conscience-Based Routing" for pure P2P networks, where each peer is responsible for performing overlay routing. Conscience is a relative term and hence we define a "conscientious" peer as one which willingly blocks queries for music/movies, pornography, topics related to National security and the like. It scans the query and matches the query sub-string against its conscience-filters. It the match is successful the query is not propagated further. Rather poisoned content is passed back to the requesting peer. Thus, if sufficient number of CPs are present in the overlay network the disincentive for pirates seeking illegal content in terms of failed queries, longer response times, incorrect poisoned content etc. shall become significant enough, so that seeking illegal content is no longer worthwhile. Simulation helps establish the feasibility and effectiveness of this approach.

2   Related Work and Our Approach

This section discusses past attempts by researchers to counter the copyright violation problem in P2P networks. Some of the approaches discussed may not have been directly applied to solve the problem, but could be utilized to address some aspects of the problem.

2.1   Related Work

2.1.1   Authentication and Identity Management
The basis for peers to indulge in illegal content sharing is the cover of anonymity that P2P networks offer to participating peers. Thus, an easy way of controlling this menace would be to require peers to register with their real identities, obtain digital credentials and require strong authentication each time a registered peer joins the P2P network. However, since a multitude of P2P networks/applications are available

which place no such restrictions on peers are commonly available, there is no motivation for peers to join networks which require authentication.

Authentication [5] is needed to establish the unique identity [6] of the peer and to ensure that malicious peers cannot masquerade as genuine peers. Since, anonymity is a salient feature of P2P networks many authentication-based schemes establish virtual identities of peers and not their real identities. Moreover, malicious peers can indulge in spoofing, causing them to have multiple identities, thereby making it difficult to ensure the security of the P2P network. The use of Digital Signatures [7] has been proposed to establish irrefutable identities in the P2P domain. However, certificate issuing servers, introduce centrality in the otherwise distributed P2P network and constitute a single-point-of-failure for potential denial-of-service attacks, besides constituting a performance bottleneck. Also, implementing an authentication scheme in a purely decentralized P2P network is a big challenge.

2.1.2 Admission Control
Another related technique to prevent copyright violations is to have admission control in peer groups [8]. Admission control can work on various parameters, for instance only peers having the required credentials (digitally obtained on registration with a centralized authority) or trusted peers (from past interactions) can join a peer group. Then peers indulging in illegal sharing can be identified, isolated and their group membership revoked permanently.

2.1.3 Proactive Content Poisoning
To discourage pirates from downloading content Lou and Hwang [9] propose a proactive content poisoning approach. They propose the use of content distribution agents which respond to download requests for copyrighted material by sending poisoned chunks of requested data. The system ensures that pirates (identified by the use of digital signatures and their Peer Authentication Protocol (PAP)) are unable to download the required content even in repeated attempts. Although the scheme works as intended, It introduces centralized elements like the transaction server which keeps track of peer transactions, the key generator and distribution agents, through which all shared content must be downloaded. The use of distribution agents which are trusted peers operated by content owners to distribute content almost reduce this scheme to a client-server architecture and hence such a scheme is not suitable for a pure decentralized P2P network, where individual peers make routing decisions and share content.

2.1.4 Digital Rights Management (DRM)
DRM systems are designed to protect the Intellectual Property Rights pertaining to digital content. They encompass the legal, business and technical aspects involved in protecting digital content. Digital watermarking [10] is a machine readable pattern that is embedded in documents. Holt et al. [11] acquired a patent for a method for embedding an identification code in audio content as well. Technically, DRM systems make use of digital watermarking (embedding digital code into the content so that the origin of the content can be tracked and traced) and encryption (to make content unreadable) for content protection and relay on centralized elements like a license server and a content server to manage content downloads by clients. Such centralized elements are not intuitively suited to large-scale decentralized P2P networks, representing single point-of-failures and performance bottlenecks.

2.2   Our Unique Contributions

a.   Addressing Copyright Violations in Pure P2P Networks
Existing schemes do not address copyright violations in pure P2P networks, where content owners cannot rely on central distribution servers to distribute content in a controlled manner. Schemes such as [9] allow the content to be located and then rely on centralized distribution agents to send poisoned content. Our scheme relies on blocking queries for objectionable/illegal content at individual peer level which perform application layer routing in the P2P network.

b.   Two-Pronged Approach – Query Blocking and Content Poisoning
Not only does the proposed scheme block queries for illegal content it also indulges in content poisoning by sending poisoned chunks of data to the requesting peer. This causes a delay in the download times for the peer and serves as a disincentive for seeking illegal content.

c.   Conscience Filters at Each Peer for Query Blocking
Each peer has pre-defined conscience-based content filters, which match the query-substring against these filters, looking for illegal music, movies, pornographic material or words pertaining to national security. For music and videos, queries for purchase are however forwarded.

d.   Adaptive Content Poisoning by Considering Popular File Requests
The scheme does not work with pre-defined filters alone. It regularly builds up a database of most queries files offering the same files in its content advertisements. This would increase the lkelihood of queries being directed to it by other peers so that it can then send back the poisoned content. Thus, the scheme is adaptive in nature.

3   System Model

We consider a decentralized P2P network with each peer capable of performing overlay routing by caching content advertisements from other peers. We define two kinds of peers in the P2P network:

- **Malicious Peers (MPs)** – which advertise and actively seek illegal content or indulge in anti-social activities.
- **Conscientious Peers (CPs)** – which neither advertise nor seek illegal content. They instead block advertisements and queries for illegal/objectionable content from being propagated further, sending back poisoned content instead.

Figure 1 depicts the system model for the proposed scheme.

We consider a JXTA [12] (Juxtapose) based P2P network implementing a publish-subscribe model for content sharing. Peers advertise the content that they are willing to share through JXTA resource advertisements, which are basically XML files containing metadata about the content to be shared such as the file names, content categories etc. Alternately, peers can locate content by explicitly querying for it. This is done via the JXTA query-response interface which is implemented by each peer. Figures 2(a) and 2(b) provide examples of resource advertisements and the query-response messages. The query message has the following main elements:

- **HandlerName** – the name of the query handler specified by individual peers. Used by JXTA Resolver Service to match queries to their handlers.
- **QueryID** – again specified by individual peers. Used for query-response matching by the peer.

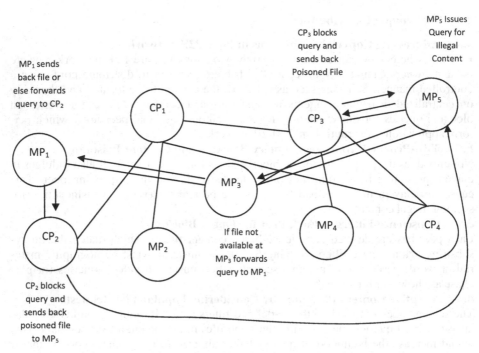

Fig. 1. A decentralized P2P network comprising CPs (Consientious Peers) and MPs (Malicious Peers)

- **HopCount** – the hop count for the query.
- **SrcPeerID** – the JXTA Peer ID of the peer issuing the query.
- **Query** – the actual query.

The "Query" element includes the following sub-elements:

- **pipeID** – the JXTA PipeID for the input pipe of the peer issuing the query. The responding peer uses the PipeID to send back a response/content
- **queryType** – hardcoded to "CS" (Content Search)
- **fileName** – name of the file to be searched or the substring to be searched in the file name.
- **category** – the broad category of content to which the file belongs – music, video, documents etc.

The peer issuing the query is responsible for matching the response with the issued query using the QueryID element, which is not modified by the responding peer. To simplify the response, the responding peer only sends back its PipeID in the response. The response indicates that the requested file or similar files from the same category are available. The peer then sends a download request to the specified pipeID to download the files. The actual query handling is performed by the individual peer, which implements the JXTA *QueryHandler* interface. It essentially involves implementing the following two methods:

- processQuery – handle queries forwarded by the JXTA *Resolver* service
- processResponse – handle the response to the issued query.

4 Protecting P2P Networks

4.1 Conscience Filters

Each CP implements a series of conscience filters which are a collection of known keywords for detecting queries pertaining to pornographic material, illegal music/movies, anti-social activities (rave parties, drug deals, prostitution etc.), national security (arms and ammunition, terrorist strikes, terrorist groups etc.).

```xml
<?xml version="1.0" encoding="UTF-8"?>
<!DOCTYPE jxta:ResolverQuery>
<jxta:ResolverQuery xmlns:jxta="http://jxta.org">
    <HandlerName>
        MyQueryHandler
    </HandlerName>
    <QueryID>
        1
    </QueryID>
    <HopCount>
        1
    </HopCount>
    <SrcPeerID>
        urn:jxta:uuid-
59616261646162614A78746150325033C97C25C756BB4D0195
    </SrcPeerID>
    <Query>
        <?xml version="1.0"?>
        <!DOCTYPE Peer:PeerQuery>
        <Peer:PeerQuery>
                <pipeId>
                urn:jxta:uuid-
59616261646162614E5047205032503393B5C2F6CA7A41FDB0
                </pipeId>
                <queryType>
                    CS
                </queryType>
                <fileName>
                    abc
                </fileName>
                <category />
                    document
                </category>
        </Peer:PeerQuery>
    </Query>
</jxta:ResolverQuery>
```

Fig. 2(a). XML representation of the "Content Search" query

```
<?xml version="1.0" encoding="UTF-8"?>
<!DOCTYPE jxta:ResolverResponse>
<jxta:ResolverResponse xmlns:jxta="http://jxta.org">
    <HandlerName>
        MyQueryHandler
    </HandlerName>
    <QueryID>
        1
    </QueryID>
    <Response>
        urn:jxta:uuid-
59616261646162614E50472050503250337672776D0D6945BDB2
    </Response>
</jxta:ResolverResponse>
```

Fig. 2(b). XML representation of the response query

These keywords can be updated and distributed to all CPs from time to time. For instance, one CP learns some new keywords which are being used by malicious peers to share illegal content. It can then update its keyword list and send the updates to other CP's. Fig. 3 illustrates a filter for detecting anti-social activities.

```
<?xml version="1.0" encoding="UTF-8"?>
<!DOCTYPE ConscienceFilter>
<Anti-Social>
    <FilterID>
        1
    </FilterID>
    <UpdatedBy>
        urn:jxta:uuid-
59616261646162614E50472050503250337672776D0D6945BDB2
    </UpdatedBy>
    <Keywords>
        Drugs, Dope, Ganja, Hashish, Heroin, Pot, Brown Sugar, Grass, Rave Parties,
Party Drugs, LSD, Liquid Gold, Cocaine, Rave Party, Rape Drug.
    </Keywords>
</Anti-Social>
```

Fig. 3. An example Anti-Social Filter to detect requests for narcostics

4.2 Content Poisoning

To discourage MPs from seeking and sharing illegal content, simply blocking their advertisements and queries may not be enough, since the sheer scale of P2P networks would allow them to exploit other peers for this purpose. Hence, an adaptive content-poisoning approach similar to the one employed in [9] is proposed. Our content poisoning scheme is completely distributed compared to the centralized approach wherein a few servers are responsible for content-poisoning. In this approach, any request for illegal material shall be responded to by the CP with a positive reply indicating the availability of the requested content. Then a large file containing junk is transferred to the requesting peer. This ensures that sufficient time is wasted in the content download process and reduces the user experience of the MP.

4.3 Audit Trails

Another aspect of the proposed solution is the use of encrypted audit trails at each peer. The audit trails record the activities of each peer, specifically the number of queries processed, the responses sent and the number of poisoned files shared. The audit trails would provide undeniable proof of a peer's conscience. In our scheme these audit trails shall be utilized to earn credit with the music/movie companies or national agencies for blocking/denying requests for illegal material. These credits can then be exchanged for instance to download legal music files from the authorized online music stores operated by the company. The audit trails are encrypted by the middleware so that the individual peer cannot read or modify it. The key for decrypting the audit trail is available only with the agencies sponsoring the conscientious behavior.

4.4 Circumventing Trust-Based Systems

In P2P networks which rely on trust ratings, the proposed scheme faces a few challenges. Everytime a CP transfers illegal content to an MP, the MP can potentially downgrade its trust/reputation rating which can prevent future queries from being routed to the CP. To overcome this challenge the group of CP's conspire to increase each other's trust ratings from time to time so that the queries still get routed to them. This would circumvent any trust-management schemes if implemented in the P2P network.

5 Result Analysis

The proposed scheme has been implemented and tested on the JXTA-based content sharing network comprising 50 peers. Peers share content by implementing a query-response interface (described in section 3) and exchanging their respective pipe IDs (JXTA communication end-points). To simulate the scheme, we randomly selected a few peers as CPs and the rest as MPs. The objective of the experiment was to determine the overall impact of the number of CPs (as a percentage of the total peer population) on the content sharing experience of MPs in terms of their query success,

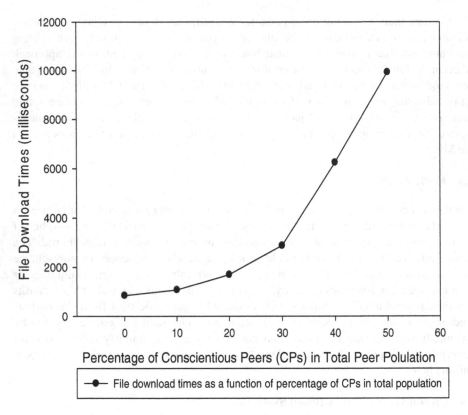

Fig. 4. Illegal file download times as a function of percentage of CPs in the total population of peers.

poisoned content received, time taken to download illegal files etc. Fig. 4 depicts the average time taken for MPs to download illegal content as a function on increasing percentage of CPs.

The average file size was kept at 1 MB It can be seen that as the percentage of CPs increases the time taken to download illegal content increases significantly. When the population of CPs crosses 30% of the total population, the file download times increase exponentially. From an average file download time of 847 msec when there are no CPs in the peer population, it increases to 2877 msec in the presence of 30% CPs and finally peaking at 9923 msec in the presence of 50% CPs. Fig. 5 shows the percentage of illegal queries receiving poisoned content as the number of CPs as a percentage of the total peer population increases. With 10% CPs, 13% of illegal queries receive poisoned content. This figure increases to 46% in the presence of 30% CPs, while 95% of illegal queries fail when 50% of the peer population consists of CPs. As can be seen from the preliminary results, a 30% population of CPs degrades the experience of MPs significantly. Future work shall involve devising new strategies to degrade the content sharing experience.

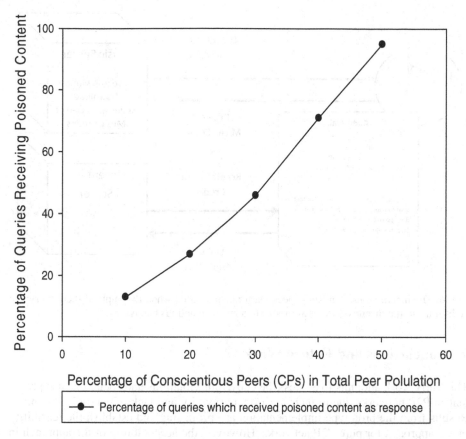

Fig. 5. Percentage of queries receiving poisoned content as a function of percentage of CPs in the total population of peers

6   Creating Real-World Conscience

Incentives have been widely employed in P2P networks to encourage "Good" behavior by participating peers, whether it is notional (Mojonation [13]) or linked to privileges (BitTorrent [14]) . Hence, CBR can be feasible only if there are sufficient incentives for individual peers to develop a conscience and block illegal content for being shared. An incentive scheme can be envisaged as a credit-based scheme implemented by the music/movie industry. Peers could upload their audit trails to the dedicated credit server sponsored by the music industry. Based on the analysis of the uploaded audit trails, credits could be awarded to individual peers on the basis of denied requests, advertisements blocked, poisoned files shared etc. These credits could be utilized by the peers to download legal music/videos/movies from the online stores operated by the media companies. Figure 6 provides an overview of this incentive mechanism.

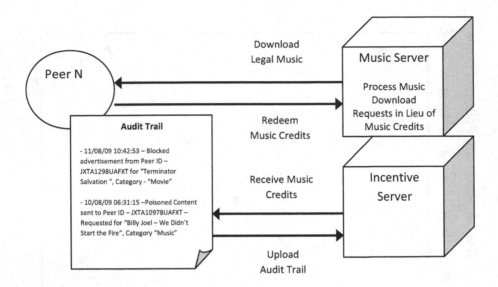

Fig. 6. The incentive mechanism - peers earn music credits when they upload their encrypted audit trails to the incentive server as proof of their conscientious behavior

7 Conclusions and Future Work

This early work attempts to address the copyright violations and social malaise prevalent in P2P networks due to their intrinsic anonymity and lack of centralized control. Results from the prototype implementation are promising and establish the feasibility of the approach for pure P2P networks. However, the acceptability of the approach in a real-world scenario requires to be carefully evaluated. For instance, what would it take for existing P2P networks to adopt this approach? Perhaps, legislation in national interest. The various stakeholders involved – national agencies, music/movie companies, open-source developer community, technology companies etc. would need to come together to work out the exact mechanisms for the implementation of such a scheme. Till then our work can serve as food-for-thought for more research to be taken up in this direction.

References

1. Oram, A. (ed.): P2P: Harnessing the Power of Disruptive Technologies. O'Reilly, Sebastopol (2001)
2. Glorioso, A., Pagallo, U., Ruffo, G.: The Social Impact of P2P Systems. In: Shen, X., Yu, H., Buford, J., Akon, M. (eds.) Handbook of Peer-to-Peer Networking. Springer, Heidelberg (2009)
3. Teens Find Drugs on Social Networking Sites, ABC News Press Coverage, http://abcnews.go.com/US/story?id=7540003&page=1

4. Adnan Patrawala Murder Case, News Story,
   http://www.ndtv.com/convergence/ndtv/
   processarchive.aspx?id=NEWEN20070023393
5. Gupta, R., Manion, T.R., Rao, R.T., Singhal, S.K.: Peer-to-Peer Authentication and Authorization, United States Patent: 7350074, March 25 (2008) (issued)
6. Lesueur, F., Me, L., Tong, V.V.T.: A Sybilproof Distributed Identity Management for P2P Networks. In: IEEE Symposium on Computers and Communications, pp. 246–253 (July 2008)
7. Modern Cryptography: Theory & Practice, Wenbo Mao, Prentice Hall Professional Technical Reference, New Jersey, p. 308 (2004), ISBN 0-13-066943-1
8. Kim, Y., Mazzocchi, D., Tsudik, G.: Admission Control in Peer Groups. In: Second IEEE International Symposium on Network Computing and Applications, p. 131 (April 2003)
9. Lou, X., Hwang, K.: Collusive Piracy Prevention in P2P Content Delivery Networks. IEEE Transactions on Computers 58(7), 970–983 (2009)
10. Szepanski, W.: A signal theoretic method for creating forgery-proof documents for automatic verification. In: Proceedings of the Carnahan Conference on Crime Countermeasures, Lexington, KY, USA, pp. 101–109 (1979)
11. Holt, L., Maufe, B.G., Wiener, A.: Encoded Marking of a Recording Signal, UK patent GB2196167 (1988)
12. JXTA HomePage, http://www.sun.com/jxta
13. The MojoNation Web Site, http://www.mojonation.net
14. BitTorrent Website, http://www.bittorrent.com/

Analysis of 802.11 Based Cognitive Networks and Cognitive Based 802.11 Networks

Niwas Maskey and Gitanjali Sachdeva

Sardar Vallabhbhai National Institute of Technology,
Surat, Gujarat, India
{niwasmaskey,gitanjali1602}@gmail.com

Abstract. Cognitive radio has emerged as a new design paradigm for next generation wireless networks that aims to increase utilization of scarce radio spectrum. Intelligent algorithms are used to learn the surrounding environment, and the knowledge thus obtained is utilized by trans-receiver to achieve the best performance. For IEEE 802.11 wireless LANs with multiple access points, it is critical to allocate limited number of radio channels dynamically and efficiently. In this paper, we are trying to implement the idea of using cognitive techniques to optimize access point configuration for IEEE 802.11 WLAN. Similarly, we can have 802.11 based cognitive networks in which CR (cognitive radio) can employ DCF (Distributed co-ordination function) protocol for contention based channel access. We have tried to interrelate between Cognitive and IEEE 802.11 WLAN networks and improve network's capability by taking useful part of other network.

Keywords: CR (Cognitive Radio, IEEE 802.11, DCF (Distributed Coordination Function), RSSI (Received Signal Strength Indicator), AP (Access Point), WS (Work Stations).

1 Introduction

Wi-fi (IEEE 802.11) is a renowned technology deployed in most of the places such as campuses, offices and some public areas. The rapid increasing of the wireless communications requires some solutions to enhance the network performance and avoid any bottleneck that occurred during data communication. Interference is the main reason why the capability of network cannot be fully utilized. Two types of interference can be distinguished: adjacent channel interference where it is produced by its transmissions on adjacent or partly overlapped channels; and co-channel interference which is caused by the same frequency channel. This work will be focusing on adjusting the transmission power of the APs by taking into consideration the co-channel non-adjacent AP. Transmission power affects directly the transmission range of an AP and cannot be simply adjusted.

According to IEEE 802.11 standard [1], the node will be associated to the AP that has the highest Received Signal Strength Indicator (RSSI) at the receiver. Consequently, more nodes will be connected to the highest RSSI that resulted in overloading at the particular AP. Beside this problem, for AP that uses the same channel or

N. Meghanathan et al. (Eds.): CNSA 2010, CCIS 89, pp. 314–322, 2010.

different overlapping channels, interference may occur among them. Pre-allocating the channels to each AP and adjusting the transmission power are the possible solution to the stated problem. In this paper we have analyzed a new model for Wi-Fi (IEEE 802.11) network to improve the overall network system performance by adjusting the transmission power based on the estimation of the distance between the AP and the associated WS using heuristic approach. Some heuristic approach using cognitive radio techniques may be feasible in order to better utilize the AP transmission power among the WSs in an ESS (Extended Service Set).

On the other hand, this paper considers a cognitive scenario in which multiple CR users attempt to access a channel licensed to a primary network. During spectrum sensing, it is assumed that all CR users must stay quiet, i.e., not transmitting data, to avoid self-interference. Upon detecting the primary network being idle, a CR user employs a modified 802.11 protocol ([1]) for contention-based channel access to avoid interference. In practice, spectrum sensing is imperfect and introduces false alarms and mis-detections. A false alarm occurs when a CR user mistakes an idle primary network as active and forgoes the opportunity to access the available channel. A mis-detection occurs when a CR user mistakes an active primary network as idle and can potentially cause harmful interference. To protect the primary network, it is required that the combined probability of mis-detection of all CR users must be below a specified threshold. Given this, varying the sensing time changes the probability of false alarm, i.e., the longer the sensing time, the lower the probability of false alarm. We provide an effective protocol design that adapts the standard 802.11 Distributed Coordination Function (DCF) to the frame-based CR operation. Specifically, we show how the 802.11 exponential backoff process should be carried out at the frame boundary.

The rest of this paper is organized as follows. In Section II, IEEE 802.11 architecture, cognitive radio in an infrastructure network and description of the proposed solution based on the heuristic approach of CR are given. And in Section III we have proposed the new cognitive design based on 802.11 DCF operations and its throughput analysis. Finally, we have concluded the paper in Section IV.

2   Heuristic Cognitive Approach for IEEE 802.11 WLAN

2.1   IEEE 802.11 Architecture

It is well known that the IEEE 802.11 MAC can be modeled based on the CSMA protocol for radio wireless. A CSMA/CA (carrier sense with collision avoidance) is used as a medium access control scheme. The access mechanism is based on the 'listen before talk' approach, i.e. each station that is willing to use the shared resource listens to the channel for the ongoing communication before attempting its own access. If the channel is sensed busy, the station refrains from transmitting.

Beside the above mentioned mechanism, the specification also contains a four-way frame exchange protocol called RTS/CTS mechanism. A station will send a control frame called Request-to-Send (RTS) and receive a Clear-to-Send (CTS) frame as a response to the station. Then the actual data frame is sent to the corresponding station and will receive an acknowledgement if the transmission is successful.

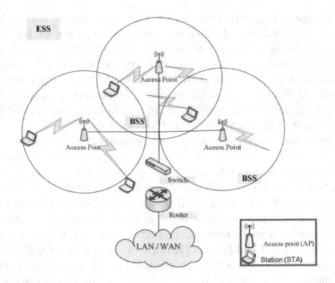

Fig. 1. IEEE 802.11 Architecture

In wireless network, each AP is associated with a transmission range, R_T and interference range, R_I. R_T and R_I directly depend on the node's transmission power [2]. Fig. 2 shows the specified R_T with a radius of r_t and R_I with a radius of r_i. R_T represents the range within which all transmissions are successful if there is no interference from other nodes.

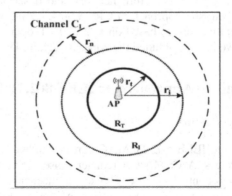

Fig. 2. Transmission Range and Interference Region

2.2 Cognitive Radio

Cognitive radio refers to wireless architecture where the communication system does not operate in a fixed assigned band but rather searches and finds an appropriate band to operate [3]. It can adjust its configuration based on the radio environment, so that other WSs can efficiently share the limited spectrum resources. Basically, cognitive radio network consists of a set of nodes; secondary transmitter, secondary receiver, primary transreceiver and primary receiver. The primary users are the user with license; whereas the secondary users are the unlicensed users. In order to find spectrum holes, the CR will dynamically adapt its transmission while minimizing the interference that may occur to the primary users. In a cognitive radio network, the secondary user (unlicensed user) will find an opportunity in sharing the spectrum without causing any interference to the primary user. CR will be employed according to a cognition cycle that was originally described by [4] as the fundamental activities in order to interact to the environment.

Cognitive radio merges artificial intelligence (AI) and wireless communication [5]. The research adapts the idea of using CR techniques that can intelligently decide on the transmission power level based on its environment. However, it only applies CR techniques heuristically in the AP without physically implementing the cognitive radio network.

2.3 Proposed Heuristic Model

This section describes the algorithm which performs power level adjustment using CR techniques in Wi-Fi. The algorithm takes into consideration the distance between a WS and the associated AP in a multi-AP deployment. However, the algorithm would be generic enough to be adapted in a single-AP deployment. The channels are pre-allocated to the APs in a way that it will not interfere with the adjacent AP. But there are possibilities that interference will occur from the non-adjacent co-channel APs.

A simplified topology is shown in Fig.3 as the proposed network model that consists of three APs and several WSs, where some of the WSs are associated to their respective APs. As mentioned earlier, in this initial work phase the WSs are static. Each AP will have its own transmission range, R_T with a radius of r_t and interference range, R_I with a radius of r_i. The channel of the middle AP (AP2) is different from the other two APs.

There are some assumptions made in the proposed model as pointed out below:

- Transmissions are to be omni-directional
- Transmission range, R_T and interference range, R_I for each transmitter (AP) is centered at the AP position. Therefore, by adjusting the transmission power, both ranges can be controlled.
- We assume that all APs belong to the same wireless LAN and thus are connected to the same Ethernet backbone.
- A constant bandwidth is provided by a channel at an AP regardless of the number of users and receive sensitivity are the same for all nodes.
- Our assumption considers AP to AP interference where power adjustment can be done at the AP and not at the WS.

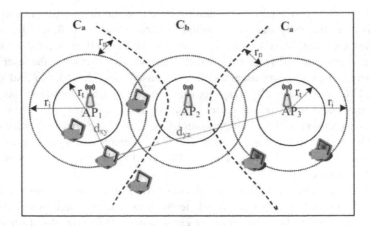

Fig. 3. The Algorithm Scenario

The WS which is within the R_T of the access point is guaranteed of any transmission without the node moving to other location. The main idea behind algorithm is to have acceptable power level transmitted to the active WSs from the AP. The power level transmitted is based on the estimated distance of the WS from the AP until the maximum power is reached or until the transmission begins to interfere with another non-adjacent co-channel AP.

So, in this heuristic approach, the algorithm will estimate the distance between the AP and WSs and accordingly distance will determine the power level of each AP. The distance is proportional to the RSSI for WSs. So, RSSI information as obtained by the WSs will be sent to the APs in one the frame of the RTS packet. Thus, on the basis of the estimated distance as calculated through the RSSI information, the algorithm makes some decision on the transmission power level. Henceforth, the algorithm will also consider other WS in the same range by repeating the process.

Consider the estimated distance between WS and associated AP is d_{xy} whereas d_{yz} is the estimated distance between WS and the other non adjacent co-channel AP. d_{xy} is within the R_I of the AP1, whereas d_{yz} is greater than r_i+r_n of AP3. Transmission power will be incremented until the successful transmission is obtained. Algorithm also checks whether WS is at the overlapping area or not. If the transmission power, $P_{tx(AP2)} > P_{tx(AP1)}$, then WS located at the overlapping area will be handover to the adjacent AP2.

Hence, based on the IEEE 802.11, WS will associate with the highest RSSI. Uniform traffic load is assumed among all APs. The algorithm will be repeatedly adjusting the transmission power level until it gets as appropriate power level for all the individual WSs to improve the overall network system performance.

The proposed algorithm adapts cognitive radio that can be seen as the intelligence in maximizing the utilization of communication channels using reasonable power level. Each AP will be the secondary AP by assuming other APs as the primary APs. Therefore, this AP should avoid interference to the primary APs. Other APs also assume the same thing where they consider themselves as secondary APs.

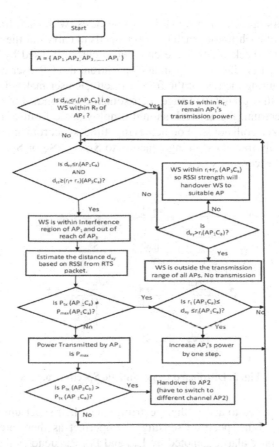

Fig. 4. Flowchart for the proposed Algorithm

This work applies the CR techniques on WI-FI where unlicensed band is used. Therefore, only secondary AP is being implemented. Thus, only one pair of secondary transmitters and receivers while all others are the primary transmitters and receivers. Therefore, from each AP's perspective, the AP itself is the secondary user and other APs are the primary users.

Finally, a centralized decision-making on power adjustment algorithm will be implemented to be added to the architecture of wireless LAN infrastructure network which considers multi-AP deployment where the co-channel inference is the main constraint.

3   802.11 Based Cognitive Radio Network

3.1   Operation Principles of the System

802.11 based cognitive radio network system is depicted in the Fig. 5. there are S_1, S_2,..... S_N, who want to transmit data to the destination D by making opportunistic use of the channel. The operation principles of the system are discussed below.

The N CR users operate on a frame by frame basis, with each frame of length T_f. At the beginning of each frame, each CR user needs to carry out the spectrum sensing for a duration T to check whether the channel is currently used by the primary network. If the channel is idle i.e. no primary operation, the CR user can attempt to access the channel during the rest of the frame. Each CR user makes independent channel decisions, i.e. they do not exchange their sensing outcomes. For achieving the full control of the spectrum, the network should employ some form of random access to avoid/reduce packet collisions. For achieving time synchronization in the system, either D periodically transmits timing beacons to S_1, $S_2...S_N$. or $S_1,S_2,.....S_N$ exchange their own timing beacons[1].

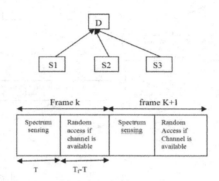

Fig. 5. Distributed Opportunistic Spectrum access

CR users are allowed to access the spectrum when their spectrum sensing indicates no primary action. But, spectrum sensing is imperfect as there are probabilities of misdetection and false alarm, denoted by P_{md} and P_{fa}. P_{md} denotes the probability that CR falsely detects the spectrum idle for the active primary network while P_{fa} is the probability that CR users mistake the idle primary network as active. The primary operation is affected when CR users have misdetections in spectrum sensing and proceed to transmit on the channel. To control this, it is required that the probability that at least one of the N CR users mis-detecting the primary network must not be more than P_{md}[6-8]. Apart from constraining the maximum mis-detection probability, primary operation is also protected by requiring CR users to carry out spectrum sensing frequently enough. Hence, T_f has been chosen to satisfy this requirement.

3.2 Overview of IEEE 802.11 DCF

Basic function of DCF 802.11 is based on CSMA/CA and can be briefly described as follows.

Carrier sense Multiple access: Before transmitting the data payload, each 802.11 station needs to sense the channel and have to wait until the channel is idle for the minimum specified period, i.e., DIFS(Distributed Inter-frame Space).

Random backoff: After waiting for DIFS time interval, each station selects random integer backoff time for preventing the collisions. The backoff counter is uniformly selected in the range of [0, w-1] where w is the contention window. The backoff counter is decremented in each backoff slot in which channel is sensed idle, and activated when a DIFS idle period is again observed. When backoff counter reaches zero, the station proceeds to transmit its data packet.

Adjusting contention windows: To avoid congestion, the contention window size of each window is adjusted according to the transmission outcomes. Initially, each station set w to the minimum $CW_{min,.}$ After each collision, w is doubled until it reached the maximum value CW_{max}. After a successful transmission, w is reset to CW_{min}.

There are two kinds of sensing operations, i.e., spectrum sensing to detect primary operation and carrier sensing carried out as part of the CSMA/CA protocol. The former is to be performed at very low detection SNR, thereby requires significant time and can introduce significant amount of mis-detections and false alarms. On the other hand, the later form of sensing, i.e., to detect an 802.11 peer transmission, is usually carried out at a much higher signal strength and therefore often assumed to be perfect (negligible false alarms and mis-detections) ([9]).

3.3 Proposed 802.11 Based Cognitive Design Spectrum Sensing

As discussed above, CR users need to follow a frame based operation to support the periodic spectrum sensing. After carrying out sensing for a duration τ, all users who detect an idle channel employ CSMA/CA during the rest of the frame. For 802.11 DCF protocol to be applicable in this frame based operation, following modification are to be done for the frame boundary effects.

- *Fixed sized packets*: It is required that CR users transmit fixed size packets, as opposed to the variable size packet transmission in 802.11.The advantages of the fixed sized packets are

- To enhance fairness when transmission time is limited to each frame.
- To avoid cases when users transmit long packets that goes beyond the frame boundary.

Let T_p denote the time to transmit the packet payload, T_s denote the duration of a successful transmission and T_c denote the duration of a collision.

- *Time-availability check*: After observing an idle period of DIFS, each CR user will only proceed with the backoff counting-down process if the time available until the end of the frame is not less than Ts.

- *Backoff counter control*: When the backoff counter of a CR user reaches zero, if the time available until the end of the frame is not less than Ts, the CR user proceeds to transmit a data packet, otherwise, the user resets its backoff counter to the value prior to the reactivation of the backoff counting-down process.

It is worth elaborating the above backoff counter control process. It can happen that, at the end of a frame, several CR users have their backoff counters reach zero but the time left is not enough for any of them to make a successful packet transmission. Then, the question is what the CR users should do? One naive option is to allow users with backoff counter reaching zero to start transmission at the beginning of the next frame. However, this would most likely result in collision if the packet size is large. Another option is to require these users to restart their backoff process, i.e., by picking a new random backoff time. However, this would be unfair for these users. An approach of asking all CR users to reset their backoff counters to the values prior to the reactivation of the counting-down process when there is not enough time to transmit a packet avoids both problems we just mentioned.

4 Conclusion

In the above discussion, we have analyzed and discussed an efficient algorithm which considers the overall power distribution between an AP and another co-channel non adjacent AP using CR techniques as well as control the switching to other APs to optimize the overall network performance. We also studied a distributed opportunistic spectrum access system where popular IEEE 802.11 DCF function was modified and frame based operation was introduced to support sensing/protecting of primary devices in the cognitive network.

Through comparative study of using CR Technique with Wireless 802.11 in this paper, we have analyzed that the concept of cognitive network and IEEE 802.11 network co-relates with each other. Each network complements each other for optimizing the network performances. Though there are various challenges like how to balance between the conflicting goals of maximizing the performance of secondary user, and minimizing the interference to the primary user in cognitive communication, yet a step by step approach in merging the two can lead to a much better performance. This will be the subject of our further research.

References

1. IEEE 802.11 WG, IEEE 802.11-2007, Wireless LAN MAC and PHY Specifications, Revised of IEEE 802.11-1999. IEEE LAN/MAN Standards Committee (June 2007)
2. Shi, Y.: Algorithm and Optimization for Wireless Network. PhD Degree (2007)
3. Sahai, A., Hoven, N., Tandra, R.: Some Fundamental Limits on Cognitive Radio. In: Forty-second Allerton Conference on Communication, Control and Computing, Monticello, IL (2004)
4. Mitiola, J.: Cognitive Radio: an integrated agent architecture for software defined radio. Royal Institute of Technology, KTH (2000)
5. Fette, B.: Cognitive Radio Technology, 1st edn. Newnes, Elsevier (2006)
6. Gardner, W.A.: Exploitation of spectral redundancy in cyclostationary signals. IEEE Signal Processing Magazine 8(2), 1436 (1991)
7. Sahai, A., Cabric, D.: Spectrum sensing: fundamental limits and practical challenges. In: Proc. IEEE International Symposium on New Frontiers in Dynamic Spectrum Access Networks (DySPAN), Baltimore, MD (November 2005)
8. Zeng, Y.H., Liang, Y.C.: Eigen value based sensing algorithms for cognitive radio. IEEE Trans. on Communications (2008) (to appear)
9. Bianchi, G.: Performance analysis of the IEEE 802.11 distributed coordination function. IEEE Journal on Selected Areas in Communications 18(3), 535–547 (2000)

Privacy Layer for Business Intelligence

Vishal Gupta and Ashutosh Saxena

SETLabs, Infosys Technologies Limited,
Lingampally, Hyderabad, Andhra Pradesh, India
{vishal_gupta10,ashutosh_saxena01}@infosys.com

Abstract. Business Intelligence brings information in an intelligent way that enable a requester of data to analyze, justify their views and make timely decisions. In all these processes a good amount of data may be exposed based on user profile and in varying degree of extent. Also, the recent trends in Information Management such as cloud computing and pervasive BI, has set forth many questions in the arena of legal compliance and information security. Especially when, millions of customer records of an organization are outsourced for testing, warehousing and data mining. In this paper, we present an approach that will require a new layer to be incorporated for business intelligence architecture and shall be used to preserve the privacy of sensitive information without changing the consolidated, processed and strategically aggregated data; keeping intact the analysis and mining needs of stakeholders within and outside the organization.

Keywords: Business Intelligence; Data Warehousing; Online Analytical Processing (OLAP); Data Mining; Privacy.

1 Introduction

From regular information reporting requirements at executive levels, the trend in Information management has seen a renewed focus on the way operational reports are generated and information is made more pervasive within organizations using advance analytics driven insight for driving operational execution [4]. Data mining techniques are widely used in advance analytics search through data looking for patterns, or correlations between identified variables. These techniques are used to analyze sales data, and also for applications in the area of fraud detection and customer churn analysis. The patterns and correlations thrown up by mining data having no logical foundation will have no business use. User expertise and experience is mandatory for mining data and presenting patterns which are meaningful for analysis. As most of the organizations may not posses these skills internally, the task may mostly be outsourced.

A recent literature published [7], has cited a survey result stating that more than fifty percent of the companies who share the sensitive data for project purposes do not preserve the privacy of data before sharing. Such data may be shared for regular project activities or to generate information using tools by professionals in various levels of organization hierarchy.

N. Meghanathan et al. (Eds.): CNSA 2010, CCIS 89, pp. 323–330, 2010.

The requirements of information at various levels in an organization are depicted in Fig 1. This information may be presented in the form of automated mails; reports or in dashboards and scorecards. A cube, generated using analytical tools, may be presented for what-if kind of analysis or information in a specified format can be presented to user. These are mostly controlled by information management governance body within an organization.

For example, the CXO is presented with an organization level summarization of data, and may drill down the report to the root of a particular measure. The operational level executive's report or automated mail may be restricted to only his role or area of work. He may not have the privilege of analyzing anything beyond the scope of data defined for him. For both to be able to make a common statement based on the data provided, the data consistency is necessary for such type of information generation, processing and distribution.

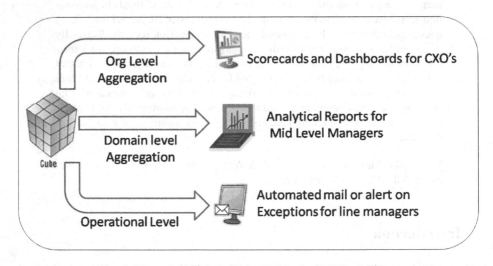

Fig. 1. Hierarchy Needs for Information via OLAP or Mining.

While the data is being shared at various levels of hierarchy, the exposure of sensitive data needs to be addressed. To contain the privacy of customer and business information, in this paper we present a solution where a privacy layer is embedded as part of the organization's information architecture.

The organization of the paper is as follows: Section 2 provides the approaches followed to preserve privacy of data; Section 3 provides the approach we propose in which the privacy layer and its constituents are detailed followed by conclusions.

2 Preserving Privacy

The data is being stored and repurposed for further use to achieve strategic benefits such as an output of analytics. The data may also be shared with software service providers, third party collaborations and others like public cloud for enhancing the customer experience or for more strategic cost and technology benefits. It is required that the various levels of application development; data storage and transfer are protected in a way that ensures the strategic need do not compromise the legal requirements of sensitive information and protects data against theft or misuse.

There are various techniques that are in use to preserve data privacy. Some of them are Substitution, Transposition, Encryption, Data Masking etc. and are very well suited for test data generation, especially for data that needs to be shared for development and maintenance. These techniques have their pros and cons and may not be suitable to retain the original format of the data especially for reports that require drill down analysis to granular levels [1] [8].

For data mining purpose, Vassilios *et al* [12] have provided a classification and an extended description of the various techniques and methodologies; like those developed in the area of privacy preserving data mining. No solution individually can support all the needs of the privacy and data mining together. Large organization may store the data in distributed databases and thus the privacy of data in such an environment would demand a different approach, relational decomposition, as prescribed by Marcin and Jakub [3]. Another approach suggested by Peter *et al* [6] talks about alert generation on sensitive data and leaves the decision on the users to manage the risks. For organization that have chosen to outsource data mining tasks, Ling et al [10] have proposed a bloom filter based solution to protect their business Intelligence and customer privacy. Meena *et al* [11] have suggested a weighted k-NN classification approach for mining data in cloud. For KPO, a synthetic data generation approach was suggested by Vishal *et al* [9], this synthesized data is not the same as original.

With analytical applications being developed having pervasiveness being kept in focus, the need for data access for a major percentage of the organization hierarchy becomes challenging. For preserving privacy, data cannot be replicated and stored for access based on role and privileges, and public domain access is still not a viable option for organizations. Hence, we need a solution with minimal use of hardware; data replication and maintenance requirements without compromising on the data needs of end users. The same solution can be used to outsource services on data without compromising on privacy.

3 Our Approach

As seen in various available techniques, the approach to preserving privacy mostly requires changing the real data and additional maintenance requirements for each new set of data that is generated or warehoused in the system. Most of the algorithms designed for preserving privacy may not be suitable for data requirements pertaining to data mining or analytical processing needs. Here we recommend having a privacy layer built in to the architecture of Business Intelligence. The approach we suggest here does not demand re-engineering of the traditional process to cleanse, consolidate in a warehouse.

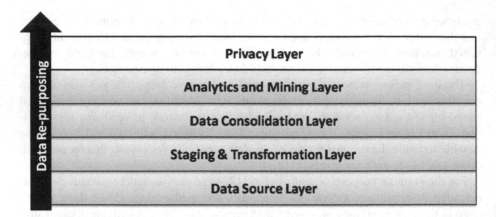

Fig. 2. Layered Architecture with Privacy Layer on the top

The Data Source layer is the existing sources within the organization identified for data consolidation and warehouse. Cleansing and Transformation are carried out on the source data and is made ready for consolidation in the staged area. Typically a data warehouse or a data mart, depending on the business goal to be achieved, is designed to house the consolidated data. Analytical processing is done on the consolidated data and is made ready with aggregations and calculated measures for reporting. For mining related activities the data at the raw level may be directly exposed to the experts.

The Privacy Layer will provide a secured way of processing data requests and also check for the level of details the user has access to and present him the data in a format based on definitions provided for his role by the governance team. Details about the other four layers can be found in [5] [6]. It will be prudent on our part to concentrate on the ingredients of the privacy layer which are detailed in the section below.

3.1 The Privacy Layer

The sensitive data access would be governed by the hierarchy in the organization and the role currently being played by the user requesting the data. Thus the role and data access privileges will be the key requirement for the functionality of Privacy Layer. Data and Object level security can be granted at database security level and can govern the depth of data a user has access. This access does not prohibit the exposure of business and customer sensitive information that can be queried from the consolidated data either at aggregated warehouse level or via cube analysis.

3.2 Components of Privacy Layer

The two key components of the privacy layer, Data Range Customizer and Rule Engine are shown in the Fig 3. These two components are discussed below.

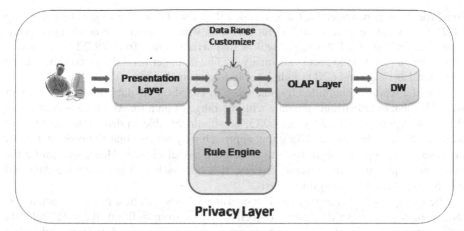

Fig. 3. A Rule Engine and Customizer for data ranges would be the key components of the Privacy Layer

The Rule Engine will maintain the following:

- A User Portfolio – access, role privileges

- Computational Algorithms – For each user, depending upon the role and privileges, it will calculate and present the desensitized data

- Rule Manager Interface – this will be required for the designated administrator for maintaining the engine and implement governance policies

The desensitizing technique using the customizer will generate class ranges and count the occurrences of instances in this range. The range for a dimension or fact measure for a particular user will be static and will alter if his role or privilege for this user is changed. Let us explain this further with some examples.

Table 1. For an actual age of customer = 21 the following ranges will be presented to the user

Role	Privilege level	Data	Range
Outsourced Vendor	Low	Age Group	21-30
Sales Rep 1	Medium	Age Group	21-25
Sales Rep 2	Medium	Age Group	18-22
Sales Manger	Medium-High	Age Group	20-22
CXO	High	Age Group	21

Table1 does not present the real view of data ranges, and is just a hypothetical one used for elaborating the data sensitizing technique of privacy layer.

The data range provided for outsourced vendor for analysis will provide a higher value of measures for this range as compared to Sales Rep 1 and 2. The two sales representatives, till the time they are playing this role, will have the range classes fixed for them as provided in Table 1. Sales Rep 1 will continue to get the age group 21-25 till the rule engine is altered for this user with a higher role or changed privilege. The data sets for Sales Rep 2 will be displaying ranges from 18-22 for all measures he has a privilege to access and analyze. The manager level data would be having a shorter data range and CXO might be able fetch actual values.

Now if a report is submitted by Sales Rep 1, based on his data range, the manager would be able to redistribute the data with the range of data for which he is entitled to. When his report is viewed by the CXO, he should be able to drill down to the real data available in the source. Using this approach may require that the presentation of the data in the reports might have to undergo a visual change. However, unlike the other techniques used to preserve privacy, this approach will not alter the data and will be useful for a meaningful analysis.

The management sponsorship and a governance body will be a must for such a system to be able to meet its desired objective. Apart from defining the role and data range sets for each level of user and measure or dimension, the data level and object level security would also be equally important to prevent unauthorized access.

The data ranges can be presented for both the measures in the fact tables and the dimensions for analysis. For instance:

- Sales Amount: USD 10,000 to USD 50,000
- Income Group: USD 1,000,000 to USD 10,000,000
- No of Visits: 1 to 10 by a class of customers
- Item Sold: 100-500 for a given class of products

The correctness of the ranges might not pass the Chi Square test, but the intent here is not to provide perfect ranges for the data, rather to preserve the privacy and not allow the unauthorized user to guess the real data and compromise on the privacy of individual customers and business information.

4   Conclusion

In this paper we have presented an approach to overcome the common drawbacks available in most of the techniques used for privacy preserving sensitive information. That is, by presenting data in ranges for analysis based on the role and privileges defined by the governance body within an organization.

This approach will be useful to preserve the original data as the data is not altered by using this technique, and there will be no additional data store required for duplicating the data for a separate set of users. The only additional storage requirements will be for the rules engine and additional code to be developed for the customizer. Further, there will not be any additional effort required to maintain data integrity as the original set of data is not changed and hence all types of users outsourced; pervasive or management will be able to get the data from the same data store, though controlled by a set of rules.

The algorithms once designed and implemented will not have to be remodeled with every fresh data load, and will have a minimal impact on any strategic change implemented at the data warehouse level. This is because, for every user, who has been granted access will be able to delve into the data sets till his profile exists in the privacy layer. Any additional data load even of large volumes; will not require specific modifications to the rule engine or customizer. When the user refreshes his query he can see the revised data set post the data load.

The data provided in the format suggested will have a low impact if the data is proliferated outside the legal bounds of the organization, say using P2P software. In a scenario for software as a service model, where there is a single consultant or expert serving the needs of a group or department within a organization, he will never be able to access the granular data, and would be able to provide his services with minimal or no deviation from the truth.

The only additional software and hardware required would be for the algorithms to group the data in ranges and an engine to check on the request and response. Further direction of this model is on the lines of SOA where the privacy layer can be fused as a service over the existing portfolio of information management.

This approach need not be restricted to a data warehouse model and can be utilized for entire organization wide data access from repositories meant for analysis. Therefore, this solution can become an integral part of an organizations data security and privacy model, and may find place in many verticals.

Acknowledgements

Authors would also like to acknowledge the suggestions provided by Dr. Radha Krishna Pisipati of Infosys technologies Ltd. India.

References

1. Edgar, D.: Data Sanitization Techniques, Net 2000 Ltd. Net 2000 Ltd. (2003-2004) (as on May/10/2010)
2. Fule, P., Roddick, J.F.: Detecting Privacy and Ethical Sensitivity in Data Mining Results. In: Estivill-Castro, V. (ed.) Proc. Twenty-Seventh Australasian Computer Science Conference (ACSC 2004), Dunedin, New Zealand. CRPIT, vol. 26, pp. 159–166. ACS (2004)
3. Gorawski, M., Bularz, J.: Protecting Private Information by Data Separation in Distributed Spatial Data Warehouse. In: Proceedings of the Second International Conference on Availability, Reliability and Security, ARES, April 10-13, pp. 837–844. IEEE Computer Society, Washington (2007)
4. HP, Top 10 trends in Business Intelligence for 2010, Business White Paper, Rev. 1 (February 2010), http://h20195.www2.hp.com/v2/GetPDF.aspx/4AA0-6420ENW.pdf (as on May/10/2010)
5. Inmon, W.H.: Building the Data Warehouse, 4th edn. John Wiley and Sons, Chichester (2005)
6. Kimball, R., Reeves, L., Ross, M., Thornthwaite, W.: The Data Warehouse Lifecycle Toolkit: Expert Methods for Designing, Developing, and Deploying Data Warehouses. John Wiley and Sons, Chichester (August 1998)

7. Korolov, M.: 'Vast Gaps' in Data Protection, Information Management Online (March 10, 2010),
   http://www.information-management.com/news/
   data_protection_security-10017342-1.html (as on May/10/2010)
8. Net 2000 Ltd., Data Scrambling Issues, Net 2000 Ltd. (2005),
   http://www.datamasker.com/
   datascramblingissues.pdf (as on May/10/2010)
9. Pannala, V., Bhattacharya, S., Saxena, A.: Synthetic Data for Privacy Preserving Data Mining. In: Proceedings of the 2007 International Conference on Data Mining, DMIN 2007, Las Vegas, Nevada, USA, June 25-28 (2007)
10. Qiu, L., Li, Y., Wu, X.: An Approach to Outsourcing Data Mining Tasks while Protecting Business Intelligence and Customer Privacy. In: Proceedings of the Sixth IEEE International Conference on Data Mining - Workshops, ICDMW, December 18-22, pp. 551–558. IEEE Computer Society, Washington (2006)
11. Singh, M.D., Krishna, P.R., Saxena, A.: A cryptography based privacy preserving solution to mine cloud data. In: Proceedings of the Third Annual ACM Bangalore Conference, COMPUTE 2010, Bangalore, India, January 22-23, pp. 1–4. ACM, New York (2010)
12. Verykios, V.S., Bertino, E., Fovino, I.N., Provenza, L.P., Saygin, Y., Theodoridis, Y.: State-of-the-art in Privacy Preserving Data Mining. SIGMOD Record 33(1) (March 2004)

Analysis and Comparative Study of Different Backoff Algorithms with Probability Based Backoff Algorithm

Narendran Rajagopalan and C. Mala

Department of Computer Science and Engineering,
National Institute of Technology, Tiruchirappalli,
Tamil Nadu, India-620015
narenraj1@gmail.com, mala@nitt.edu
http://www.nitt.edu

Abstract. Data Link Layer is the most important Layer in any type of Local Area Network. The main functions of the Data Link Layer is access control and flow control. The efficient implementation of access control protocol, decides the optimal usage of network resources. The backoff algorithm is a very important aspect in access control protocol implementation. Backoff algorithm is used to reduce the probability of frequent collisions when stations try to access the medium simultaneously. The basic Binary Exponential Backoff algorithm, Modified Binary Exponential Backoff algorithm and their drawbacks are analyzed and a new variation called Probability Based Backoff algorithm is proposed, which takes network traffic also into consideration.

Keywords: IEEE 802.11, CSMA/CA, DCF, PCF, Media Access Control, Backoff algorithm, Contention Window.

1 Introduction

Communication networks have gone through rapid evolution since its inception within a short span of time. Network systems are classified into *Local Area Networks* (LANs), *Wide Area Networks* (WANs) and *Metropolitan Area Networks* (MANs) based upon its area of coverage. LAN is an important classification which is widely used to connect standalone systems in offices or in institutions. The *Institution of Electrical and Electronics Engineers* (IEEE) is a technical professional society which standardizes specifications. IEEE came up with different standards for different LAN technologies such as IEEE 802.3 for wired ethernet LANs, IEEE 802.5 for wired token ring LANs, IEEE 802.11[1][2] for wireless LANs. Mobility has become one of the necessary requirements for users. IEEE 802.11b also known as Wireless Fidelity (WiFi) is becoming one of the widely used standards. Media access control is an important function in any Local Area Networks.

The main focus in this article is Access Control. Simultaneous access of the shared medium by many stations would lead to collision and retransmissions of

N. Meghanathan et al. (Eds.): CNSA 2010, CCIS 89, pp. 331–339, 2010.

data frames, resulting in degradation of the network bandwidth. Access control is a protocol by which decision is made as to who will access the medium at a given point of time. Flow control is another important function handled by the data link layer. The sender and the receiver come to an understanding on when and how much of data can be sent, so that it is convenient for both the sender and the receiver to optimize the bandwidth utilization. This function is called flow control. In this article, some of the protocols basically used for access control are analyzed.

As the nature of the media differs considerably, the wired media is scalable with the usage of higher bandwidth cables and also not subjected to interference and disturbance. The signal strength is uniform throughout the medium making it possible to sense for collision whenever two or more stations access it simultaneously. The protocol used for media access control in IEEE 802.3 is *Carrier Sense Multiple Access with Collision Detection* (CSMA/CD)[1]. But in the case of a wireless medium the frequency range is fixed and also highly vulnerable to interference and disturbance, making the same access control specifications unsuitable for both the media. In wireless LANs the signal strength decreases proportional to the square of the distance it travels, making it practically infeasible to sense a collision as the returned signal would be very mild which may go undetected.

IEEE 802.11 Media Access Control supports asynchronous and time bounded delivery of data frames. The standard supports mandatory *Distributed Coordination Function* (DCF)[3][4] and optional *Point Coordination Function* (PCF)[3][4].

In the case of PCF, one node is elected as the monitor such as an access point, which keeps polling the other nodes on whether they are interested to access the medium. It allocates the medium to one of the nodes based upon priority criteria. PCF is necessary for real time services. But ad-hoc networks cannot guarantee real time services as it is formed dynamically on the move by some stations and do not contain an access point.

In DCF two techniques are used in data transmission.

One technique is the basic two way handshaking mechanism in which the sender sends the data frame and the receiver sends a *Positive Acknowledgement* (PACK) after receiving the data frame. If the sender does not receive the PACK until timeout occurs, the frame is retransmitted. This handshaking mechanism is simple and easy, but results in wastage of bandwidth and very low throughput due to hidden terminal and exposed terminal problems[1].

If A,B and C are three stations, station A is transmitting packet to station B which is not visible to station C. Now if station C also tries to send a packet to station B, it would lead to a collision or interference at B. This problem is called *hidden terminal problem*.

Station C understands that stations A and B are in conversation by sensing the medium and refrains from sending any data to station D, eventhough station D is not in the interference range of both stations A and B. This is called as *exposed terminal problem*.

The other technique is a four way handshaking in which *Request To Send* (RTS) and *Clear To Send* (CTS) mechanisms are used to reserve the medium. This mechanism tries to overcome the hidden terminal and exposed terminal problems.

If stations A and B are in conversation, station A sends RTS to station B. Every station receiving the RTS irrespective of whether it is the intended recipient or not, must set their *Network Allocation Vector* (NAV)[9], which indicates the earliest time duration to be elapsed to access the medium. Station B responds with CTS, station C understands that stations A and B are in conversation and refrains from sending data to stations A or B. If station C needs to communicate with station D which is out of interference range of both the stations A and B, then station C sends RTS to station D which responds with the CTS hence enabling the communication between them without disturbing stations A and B.

This four way handshaking with RTS/CTS is used to implement *Carrier Sense Multiple Access with Collision Avoidance* (CSMA/CA)[4]. Even though the probability of collision of data frames is eliminated drastically due to the usage of CSMA/CA, there is a probability of collision of control frames, because two stations can try to access the medium by sending the RTS simultaneously, resulting in a collision. To overcome this issue the *Binary Exponential Backoff* (BEB) algorithm is used. It specifies the time span after which the system can attempt to access the medium again thus reducing the probability of collision.

2   Overview of Existing Backoff Algorithms

According to the BEB algorithm[5][6][7][8], if a station A tries to transmit data to station B and there is a collision, then station A would randomly choose a value with uniform probability from its contention window $[0 - CW]$ where CW is set to CW_{min} initially and then keeps doubling after every successive collisions until it reaches CW_{max}. It remains at CW_{max} until the transmission is successful or the number of retries exceed the specified limit which is 7 for RTS, wherein it is assumed that the station is unreachable. Whenever there is a successful transmission or the number of retries exceed the limit CW is reset to CW_{min}. This basic BEB algorithm assumes that the probability function of successful transmission of a data frame is independent of whether the previous frame was successfully transmitted or not.

In practicality, the probability function of successful or unsuccessful transmission of a data frame is dependent upon how many retries were attempted before the previous data frame was successfully transmitted. Hence Modified Binary Exponential Backoff (MBEB) algorithm was proposed in [6] to the BEB algorithm in which the contention window of previous transmitted data frame is retained for the current frame. If the transmission is successful, then the contention window is reduced by half i.e., $CW = CW/2$, which would be used as CW value for next frame transmission. If the transmission is unsuccessful, then the contention window is doubled $CW = CW \cdot 2$ until it reaches CW_{max} which is retained as it is, for further retries until successful. One more modification is, when the number of retries exceed the limit, the CW is not reset to CW_{min}, but retained as it is, for the next data frame transmission. Every time when the contention window is updated, it is verified whether the value falls below CW_{min}, if it falls below CW_{min}, then it is set to $CW_{min} + 1$. Similarly the new CW value is verified whether it exceeds CW_{max} and if it does, then the calculated new value is ignored and CW is set to $CW_{max} - 1$.

3   Proposed Probability Based Backoff Algorithm

A thorough study of BEB algorithm and the MBEB algorithm leaves with a question as to why the Contention Window should be increased or decreased by a factor of 2? A factor more than 2 will surely make Contention Window reach CW_{max} faster and also make the system to wait unnecessarily for a longer time duration before trying again to access the medium, thus hampering resource utilization. If the factor is less than 1 then it would result in very less backoff interval, hence resulting in frequent collision and waste of network resources. But surely the contention window can be increased or decreased by a factor between 1 and 2. Let α be the factor such that 2^α, is used to modify the contention window size. In the case of binary exponential backoff algorithm this value α, is set statically to 1, whenever there is a collision to set the contention window.

In the MBEB algorithm, the value of α is statically set to 1 whenever there is a collision, and to -1 whenever there is a successful transmission and also care is taken such that CW value does not exceed CW_{max} and also doesnot fall below CW_{min}. The contention window size is retained as it is, after the previous frame transmission.

In the proposed Probability Based Backoff (PBB) algorithm, the value of α is dynamically altered between the values 1 and -1 studying the network collision rate. Let S and C be two variables which keep count of number of successful transmissions, and collisions leading to backoff, respectively. The probability P indicates the collision rate of the network which will in turn affect the probability of successful transmission of the next data frame. This probability is given by $P = C/(S + C)$. This probability P must be used to decide the value of α. The value of α is determined by the equation,

$$\alpha = -1 + (P \cdot 2) \tag{1}$$

following a collision, and by equation,

$$\alpha = -1 + ((1 - P) \cdot 2) \tag{2}$$

following a successful transmission.

After calculating the value of α, the contention window is set by the following equation,

$$CW_{new} = CW_{Prev} \cdot 2^\alpha \tag{3}$$

The Probability Based Backoff Algorithm is as follows.

Step 1. The initial value of Contention Window CW is set to CW_{min}. The variables S and C which represent number of successful transmissions and number of collisions respectively are initialized to 0.

Step 2. After each attempt to transmit a data frame, S or C is incremented accordingly and the value of probability P is calculated using $P = C/(C+S)$.

Step 3. The value of α is calculated using the formula $\alpha = -1 + (P \cdot 2)$ following a collision and by formula $\alpha = -1 + ((1-P) \cdot 2)$ following a successful transmission.

Step 4. The value of CW is calculated by the formula,

$$CW_{new} = MAX[CW_{min} + 1, CW_{Prev} \cdot 2^{\alpha}] \qquad (4)$$

in the case of successful transmission and

$$CW_{new} = MIN[CW_{max} - 1, CW_{Prev} \cdot 2^{\alpha}] \qquad (5)$$

for unsuccessful transmission.

Step 5. Whenever the number of retransmissions exceed the number of retries, Contention window value is not reset but carried forward to the next frame transmission.

4 Comparative Analysis of BEB Algorithm, MBEB Algorithm and Proposed PBB Algorithm

Consider a scenario in which three data frame transmission attempts have been made, each of which may result in success or failure; success is represented by S and failure or collision is represented by C. Now when there is an attempt to transmit the fourth frame, the value of the contention window is calculated using the BEB algorithm, MBEB algorithm and the proposed PBB algorithm.

A comparative study is discussed in [5],[6],[7] on BEB algorithm and MBEB algorithm. [9] and [10] discuss its effect on throughput. From the basic BEB algorithm, it is known that the calculation of the contention window of a data frame does not depend on previous transmissions but only on the successive unsuccessful attempts. Let us assume that CW_{min} is the inital value of contention window (CW). Consider the first row of Table 1, the C states that the first transmission resulted in collision, hence CW was set to $CW_{min} \cdot 2$ for transmission 2. But again transmission 2 results in a collision thus making the value of CW set to $CW_{Prev} \cdot 2$ which is equal to $CW_{min} \cdot 2^2$. Similarly the CW for transmission 4 is set to $CW_{Prev} \cdot 2$ as transmission 3 also ended in collision. The CW value for transmission 4 is effectively equivalent to $CW_{min} \cdot 2^3$. In the second row it is observed that the first transmission and second transmission resulted in collision denoted by C, but the third transmission was successful in transmitting the frame. By the BEB algorithm, the initial value in CW at transmission 1 is

CW_{min}, at transmission 2 the value of CW becomes $CW_{min} \cdot 2$. At transmission 3 the value of CW becomes $CW_{min} \cdot 2^2$ as transmission 2 also was a failure. But transmission 3 was successful in transmitting the data frame, hence the CW value for the next transmission is reset to CW_{min} which is reflected in the table. Similarly examining the third row and fourth row, it can be observed that irrespective of the history of the transmission, if the previous transmission is successful CW value is reset to CW_{min}, as shown in rows 3 and 4.

Table 1. BEB Algorithm Results

Sl.No	Trans1	Trans2	Trans3	CW for Trans4
1	C	C	C	$CW_{Prev} \cdot 2$
2	C	C	S	CW_{min}
3	C	S	S	CW_{min}
4	S	S	S	CW_{min}

Table 1 gives the values of the CW after 3 transmissions in case of the basic BEB algorithm.

MBEB algorithm is applied to the same scenario and the CW value after each transmission is determined. Let CW be initialized to CW_{min} at transmission 1. As transmission 1 resulted in collision, the value of CW is $CW_{min} \cdot 2$ at transmission 2. As transmission 2 also a collision the value of CW is set to $CW_{min} \cdot 2^2$. Similarly the CW value is set to $CW_{min} \cdot 2^3$ which is numerically equivalent and represented as $CW_{Prev} \cdot 2$ in Table 2. The scenario in the second row differentiates MBEB algorithm from the BEB algorithm. As transmission 1 results in collision, CW value is set to $CW_{min} \cdot 2$. As transmission 2 also results in collision $CW = CW_{min} \cdot 2^2$ which is taken as the CW value for transmission 3. When transmission 3 is successful, the CW is not reset to CW_{min}, but it is set to $CW_{Prev}/2$ which is numerically equivalent to $CW_{min} \cdot 2$. The initial value of CW is assumed to be CW_{min} at row 3. As the first transmission is a failure, CW is set to $CW_{min} \cdot 2$. As the second transmission is a success, the CW is modified to $CW_{Prev}/2$ which is numerically equivalent to CW_{min}. Again the third transmission is a success which again reduces $CW = \text{MAX}[(CW_{Prev}/2$, $CW_{min} + 1$], hence making CW equal to $CW_{min} + 1$. Again as transmission 3 is also successful, CW is set to $\text{MAX}[CW_{Prev}/2$, $CW_{min} + 1$] again making it equal to $CW_{min} + 1$. Similarly applying the MBEB algorithm, the CW value at transmission 3 in rows 3 and 4 would be computed to $CW_{min} + 1$ which is represented as $CW_{Prev}/2$ in the Table 2.

Table 2 gives the values of CW in case of the MBEB algorithm.

The PBB algorithm is applied to the given scenario and the corresponding CW values are tabulated in Table 3. The initial value of CW is set to CW_{min}. Considering the first row of Table 3, after the first unsuccessful transmission which resulted in collision, the CW value is set to $CW_{min} \cdot 2$ because probability of congestion based on the previous transmission is 1. Hence $\alpha = -1 + (P \cdot 2$) which is computed to $\alpha = 1$. Thus CW gets computed to $CW = CW_{Prev} \cdot$

Table 2. MBEB Algorithm Results

Sl.No	Trans1	Trans2	Trans3	CW for Trans4
1	C	C	C	$CW_{Prev} \cdot 2$
2	C	C	S	$CW_{Prev}/2$
3	C	S	S	$CW_{Prev}/2$
4	S	S	S	$CW_{Prev}/2$

2^α, which reduces to $CW_{min} \cdot 2$. As transmission 2 has also ended in collision, the probability is again 1, hence making $CW = CW_{Prev} \cdot 2^\alpha = CW_{min} \cdot 2^2$. Similarly for the fourth transmission CW is set to $\mathrm{MIN}[CW_{min} \cdot 2^3 , CW_{Max} - 1]$ which is represented as $CW_{Prev} \cdot 2$ in Table 3. In the second row after the first and second transmission which is similar to the first row, CW is set to $CW = CW_{min} \cdot 2^2$. The transmission 3 is successful, hence the probability P becomes 2/3. $\alpha = -1 + (2 \cdot (1\text{-}P)) = -1/3$. Therefore $CW = CW_{Prev} \cdot 2^\alpha = (CW_{min} \cdot 2^2) \cdot 2^{-1/3} = CW_{min} \cdot 2^{5/3}$, which is represented as $CW_{Prev}/ \sqrt[3]{2}$ in Table 3 and numerically computes to the same value. In the third row, after the first unsuccessful transmission, the contention window CW is set to $CW_{min} \cdot 2$. But after the second transmission, which is a successful transmission, the probability P becomes 1/2. Hence $\alpha = -1 + (2 \cdot (1\text{-}P)) = 0$. As $\alpha = 0$, $CW = CW_{Prev} \cdot 2^\alpha = CW_{Prev} = CW_{min} \cdot 2$. As transmission 3 is also successful, P becomes 1/3 and $\alpha = -1 + (2 \cdot (1\text{-}P)) = 1/3$. The CW takes the value $CW_{Prev} \cdot 2^\alpha = CW_{min} \cdot 2 \cdot 2^{1/3} = CW_{min} \cdot 2^{4/3}$, which is represented as $CW_{Prev} \cdot \sqrt[3]{2}$ in Table 3 as it numerically computes to the same value. As all the transmissions are successful transmissions in row 4, the probability of a collision, P computes to 0, hence $\alpha = -1 + (2 \cdot P) = -1$. The value of $CW = CW_{Prev} \cdot 2^\alpha = CW_{Prev} \cdot 2^{-1} = CW_{min} \cdot 1/2$. But CW value is not allowed to go below CW_{min}. Hence $CW = \mathrm{MAX}[CW_{min} + 1 , CW_{Prev}/2]$ which would compute to $CW_{min} + 1$. The CW value remains at $CW_{min} + 1$, the minimum possible value as all are successful transmissions. This is represented by $CW_{Prev}/2$ in the Table 3.

Table 3 shows the values of CW when PBB algorithm is applied to the given scenario.

From the graph in figure 1, it can be observed that the BEB algorithm resets the CW value to CW_{min} after every successful transmission, hence the variance

Table 3. PBB Algorithm Results

Sl.No	Trans1	Trans2	Trans3	CW for Trans4
1	C	C	C	$CW_{Prev} \cdot 2$
2	C	C	S	$CW_{Prev}/ \sqrt[3]{2}$
3	C	S	S	$CW_{Prev} \cdot \sqrt[3]{2}$
4	S	S	S	$CW_{Prev}/2$

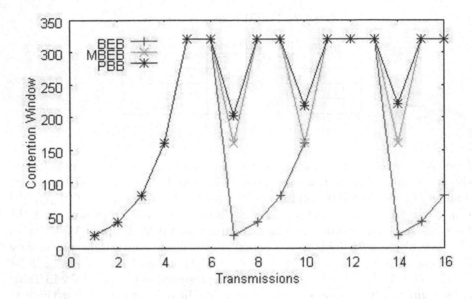

Fig. 1. Comparison of Different Backoff Algorithms

is too high. Though the variance is reduced in MBEB algorithm, probability based backoff algorithm represented by PBB reduces the variance even further.

5 Conclusion

This paper analyzes the performances of BEB algorithm, MBEB algorithm and compares it with the proposed PBB algorithm. It can be observed from the results tabulated in the tables that the value of CW grows exponentially in both the cases of BEB and MBEB algorithms without taking the network collision rate into consideration. The proposed PBB algorithm dynamically varies the value of α taking into consideration, the collision rate and the success rate of transmissions, thus making it more adaptable to the network.

References

1. Jochen, H.S.: Mobile Communications, 2nd edn. Pearson Education, London (2008), ISBN 81-297-0350-5
2. Wu, H., Peng, Y., Long, K., Cheng, S.: A Simple model of IEEE 802.11 Wireless LAN. In: ICII 2001, Beijing (2001)
3. HaiTao, W.U., Lin, Y., Cheng, S., Peng, Y., Long, K.: IEEE 802.11 Distributed Coordination Function, Enhancement and Analysis. Journal of Computer Science and Technology 18(5), 608 (2003)
4. Ziouva, E.: Theodore Antonakopoulos.: The IEEE 802.11 Distributed Coordination Function in Small-Scale Ad-Hoc Wireless LANs. International Journal of Wireless Information Networks 10(1) (January 2003)

5. Nasir, Q., Albalt, M.: Improved Backoff algorithm for IEEE 802.11 Networks. In: Proceedings of the 2009 IEEE International Conference on Networking, Sensing and Control, Okayama (2009)
6. Shin, H.-J., Shin, D.-R., Youn, H.-Y.: An Efficient Backoff Scheme for IEEE 802.11 DCF. In: Niemegeers, I.G.M.M., de Groot, S.H. (eds.) PWC 2004. LNCS, vol. 3260, pp. 180–193. Springer, Heidelberg (2004)
7. Chatzimisios, P.: A simple and effective backoff scheme for the IEEE 802.11 MAC protocol. In: Proceedings on CITSA (2005)
8. Moura, J.A., Marinheiro, R.N.: MAC approaches for QoS Enhancement in Wireless LANs. In: Proceedings on JETC (2005)
9. Bianchi, G.: Performance Analysis of the IEEE 802.11 Distributed Coordination Function. IEEE Journal on Selected Area in Communication 18(3), 514–519 (2000)
10. Bianchi, G.: IEEE 802.11-Saturation Throughput Analysis. IEEE Communications Letters 2(12), 318–320 (1998)

Proof Of Erasability for Ensuring Comprehensive Data Deletion in Cloud Computing

Mithun Paul and Ashutosh Saxena

Security and Privacy Group, SETLabs,
Infosys Technologies Ltd, Hyderabad
(Mithun_Paul,Ashutosh_Saxena01)@infosys.com

Abstract. In a typical cloud environment the client will be storing his data with a provider and paying as per the usage time. At the end of the contract the client, as the data owner, may like to see that the data should be properly shredded in the provider storage. In this paper we provide a scheme for Proof of Erasability (POE) for a client that a target data is completely destructed or is irreversibly rendered useless. The destruction of the data is achieved by a comprehensive destruction algorithm which systematically modifies the most significant bit(s) of every data chunk thereby making the data irrecoverably destructed and refuting any concerns on privacy and security.

Keywords: Erasability, MSB, Privacy.

1 Introduction

Clouds are a large pool of easily usable and accessible virtualized resources (such as hardware, development platforms and/or services). These resources can be dynamically re- configured to adjust to a variable load (scale), allowing also for an optimum resource utilization. This pool of resources is typically exploited by a pay-per-use model in which guarantees are offered by the Infrastructure Provider by means of customized SLAs [1].Cloud is fast being adapted as the de-facto standard by many industries and academic organizations.

The core idea in a cloud environment is that a user stores his personal files in a cloud, and can retrieve them irrespective of time and geographical barriers. In a cloud environment, the user's data will be stored in a third party infrastructure where he has virtually no access to the data once its stored and where the only safety is the SLA provided by the cloud storage facility provider.

Storage as a Service(SaaS) is being considered a boon for small or mid-sized businesses which generally lack the capability for a huge initial investment required for an elaborate infrastructure set up. Also when it comes to disaster recovery from geographically specific mishaps, and also for long-term storage of records for business continuity and availability, SaaS is being considered as a very credible option [2]. An obvious concern of data privacy forebodes such a setup though. To ensure data privacy for the client who is storing his data in the cloud, it is almost mandatory that the data be stored in an encrypted form.

N. Meghanathan et al. (Eds.): CNSA 2010, CCIS 89, pp. 340–348, 2010.
© Springer-Verlag Berlin Heidelberg 2010

Let's consider the following example: A User/Corporate 'A' wants to store sensitive data in the cloud with a storage provider/vendor 'B' for a particular period of time. Now at the end of a particular time period, 'A' wants to withdraw the data and dissociate with 'B'. The provider must ideally, as per the SLA, return the data to 'A' or delete it as A's requirement be. Now the difficulty here is, if the provider says that he has deleted the data from his infrastructure, what proof does 'A' have that the data has completely left the provider's network?

'A' will have to ensure a comprehensive destruction of that data from the storage, especially sensitive data that may be under regulatory compliance requirements. Even though a primary privacy protection is ensured by the encryption of the data before it is stored and even after assurances from the provider that the data has been completely erased/rendered useless from their disks, there is no methodology currently to verify it. It will create unfathomed issues if your data storage provider's data management infrastructure isn't compatible with your destruction requirements (e.g., the provider is able to delete the latest version, but is unable to delete data from archived storage) and some form of data remanence succumbs at last to data leakages. One example of such attack can be the recovery of supposedly erased data from magnetic media or random-access memory.

This paper involves development of a prototype model for data shredding in distributed environment. The focus is on a probing engine/destructor which will probe the environment and based on the rules on the data store, will shred them partially or fully. This prototype can further be extended as a service on Cloud. This destructor will systematically modify/update the Most Significant Bit of every data chunk, thus ensuring that the data is so corrupted/ impaired that no part of the data will make any sense to whomever gets hold of it later.

As per the SLA provided by 'B' this updation (which in this case is the comprehensive destruction of data through MSB modification) will be reflected in the rest of the copies of the database within the given exposure window. At the end of this exposure window, 'B' can retrieve certain bits of the values from one of these secondary databases, and compare them with the equivalent hashed value which was generated during the destructor run. A match of these two would mean that all the data stored with the provider has thus been rendered useless. This can be called a Proof of Erasability, viz a tangible proof given by the 'B' to 'A' that the data that is with 'B' is no more useful to anyone and hence proven destructed.

2 Related Work

Two methods of comprehensive data shredding methods have been consulted for this work, viz Kishi's comprehensive methodology by which data can be shredded within a storage subsystem and the Gutmann algorithm which provides a similar methodology for secure deletion of data [3] ,[4]. The work done on 'Proof of Retrievability', from which the name 'Proof of Erasability' is inspired, incidentally, by Jules and Kaliski [5] Shacham and Waters [6] has been also referred for arriving at this concept.

3 Our Scheme

We are proposing a methodology which would probe the storage infrastructure for sensitive data tags/flags and will do a periodic erasure. Our main interest in Proof of Erasability Scheme is related to the destructor based approach mentioned in the introduction. Before giving details, we outline the general protocol structure.

3.1 Setup Phase

Suppose a user U, has a huge chunk of sensitive data with him. U doesn't have the necessary storage facilities. As a solution to this U approaches one of the vendors, V, in the cloud who provides U the required storage space for a pre determined amount of time at cheap rates. Examples of such vendors include Amazon's EC2 [7], or any of the other popular vendors who offer Storage as a Service [8], [9].

3.2 SLA Details

The user U or his company would sign a service level agreement (SLA) with the Vendor V whereby the SaaS provider agrees to rent storage space on a cost-per-gigabyte-stored and cost-per-data-transfer basis and the company's data would be automatically transferred at the specified time over the storage provider's proprietary wide area network (WAN) or the Internet [10]. Under the same preamble, the user will be periodically accessing/updating the data through the multitude of application interfaces that he uses. E.g.: web services.

Though it is out of the scope of this discussion, it is understood that the SLA must be scrutinized for regulatory checks like back up services, encryption and compression algorithms involved etc [2].At this stage we are more concerned about the number of simultaneous storages that will be used for storing our data as per the SLA . The user must ensure that in the SLA the provider gives the details of the servers and, the respective geographic locations, on which their data will be simultaneously distributed. Generally in a cloud certain number of copies of the same data is created , regularly updated and stored at various geographical locations to ensure that a mishap in one of the geographical location doesn't affect the continuous data access process any of the client' applications might be doing.

Also a check must be done on the exposure window time mentioned in the SLA

3.3 Exposure Window

An exposure window is the time that is needed for a complete updation cycle across various copies of the data. The scenario is that the user application which is accessing the data through an interface, say a webservice, needs to update one row in one table in the database. So the application sends an update sql command to one of the databases to which it is connected. Suppose the cloud vendor is simultaneously storing your data in 4 different servers, viz D1,D2, D3 and D4. And assume that at the give time the data being shown to the user application is being retrieved from D1. Now the

Exposure Window (Δt) is the time, as per the SLA, that is required for this data to be updated in all the other 3 databases, viz D2,D3,D4 across the world i.e the time during which the data is exposed/not updated.

3.4 End of SLA Period

Suppose that at the end of a particular time period the user U is done with the necessity of storing the data in the cloud. Or maybe the user has found a better vendor who is providing the storage facility in a much cheaper rate. At this stage the user wants to pull out or ensure that the data is no longer with the vendor. Or even if the data remains at the already existing cloud storage vendor, even if it is in the encrypted state, it is rendered useless so that no privacy leakage occurs even if the data goes into wrong hands.

3.5 Destructor

So at this stage the User U, needs to make use of a DESTROYER application. Since the database schema was created by the user, he will know each and every tuple and changing what data will render the data useless.

What this application does is that given a data set, it will take the Most Significant Bit of all the bytes, and replace it with the opposite Boolean value. i.e a zero will be replaced with one and one will be replaced with zero. This essentially will render the byte useless. Fig1 and Fig 2 show how the Most Significant Bits have been manipulated before and after the destruction algorithm works on it.

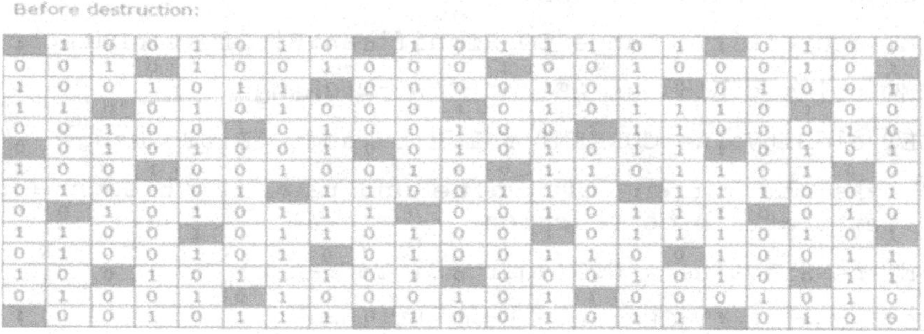

Before destruction:

Fig. 1. How the bits look before destruction

During this destructor process some specific details will be stored in a static storage media at the client end during every destruction operation. This includes the earlier and new values of the bit being modified, the relative address of the bit and the time during which the modification is happening. This destroyer application is invoked on the database to which the user application is currently connected to, viz D1 until each and every tuple in the data is systematically and comprehensively rendered useless.

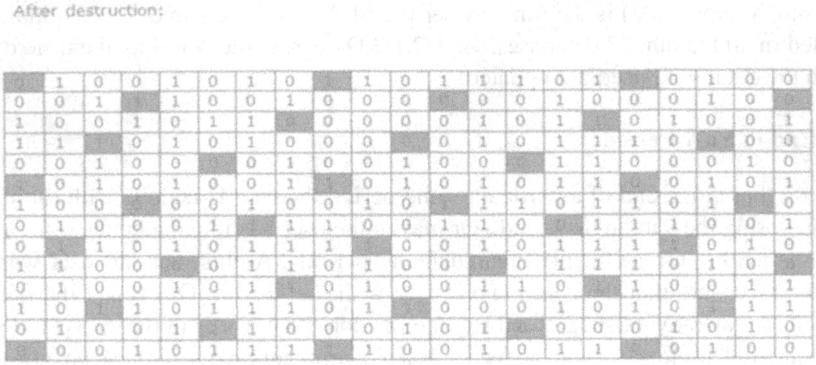

After destruction:

Fig. 2. How the bits look after destruction

The destructor algorithm can be elucidated by a pseudo code similar to the one mentioned below:

Destructor:

```
INITIATE nextChunkStart to StartOfDataChunk

WHILE nextChunkStart IS NOT EQUALTO Null

//Function for finding the Most/Least significant bit
of the given data chunk, a modification of which would
render the data useless.

SET addrOfBitToChange TO SignificantBitOfGivenDataChunk

SET relativeAddress AS addrOfBitToChange

SET oldBitValue CURRENT VALUE OF addrOfBitToCHange

//Take the current bit value and pass it through a NOT
Gate to attain destruction

SET newBitValue = NOT(addrOfBitToCHange)

SET addrOfBitToCHange = newBitValue


//While modifying a bit value, store the bit values,
previous and new, the current time and also the
relative address at which the change was made, in a
stable storage like database, so that this can be used
for data verification process - see below.

StoreOldandNewValues (oldValue, newValue,
relativeAddress)

//Assuming the data is not being stored contiguously
and hence there is a necessity for an algorithm which
```

```
would respawn the pointer to the address where the next
sequential data resides.

SET nextChunkStart TO NextDataChunk

END WHILE
```

3.6 Verifier

Once the destruction cycle is completed it is necessary that the user does a verification, to ensure that the bits have been modified/data has been destructed in the other copies of the database, viz the database servers provided by the cloud data storage provider, where all the data is copied, on which any data updation made on the first database, D1, will be updated after the exposure time mentioned in the database. For this purpose the verifier application will next connect to the other databases, D2,D3 etc. Here it will pick the bits of data from the same address location as that was modified in D1. A comparison of this bit value in the secondary databases with the equivalent bit value in D1, on which the destructor application had worked is done next.

The verifier algorithm can be elucidated by a pseudo code similar to the one mentioned below:

Verifier:

```
//Assuming all the modified bits and its corresponding
address values were stored as key-value pairs during
the destructor program run.EG:[OFFBC,0]

INITIALIZE flagCompleteMatch to TRUE

INTIALIZE countKeyValuePairs to Zero

INITIALIZE keyValuePairArray from Destructor Program
Run

// DeltaT, is the exposure time mentioned in SLA which
is the time taken by the provider to update other
copies of the update that is made in one database.


INTIALIZE DeltaT from SLA Value;

FOR EACH VALUE IN THE KeyValuePairs

//this is the address of the modified bit stored during
the destructor process.

SET BitAddress=CurrentkeyValuePair.Address;

SET timeOfFirstDestruction= keyValuePairArray.Time;

// For getting right results do the
verification/comparison only after the exposure time
elapses

WHILE (SUM (timeOfFirstDestruction + DeltaT ) GREATER
THAN currentTime)
```

```
                    SET bitValueFromDestructor =
keyValuePairArray.bitValue;

                    INPUT DatabaseName, Address

                    SET bitValueFromDBToCompare =
FindBitValue For a given Database and Address

      //We are comparing the value in the
auxiliary/copies of the database

IF bitValueFromDestructor NOT EQUAL TO
bitValueFromDBToCompare)

SET flagCompleteMatch EQUAL TO False

Exit

                    END IF

END WHILE

END FOR LOOP

If flagCompleteMatch IS EQUAL TO true

            PRINT "success-'Proof Of Erasability'
achieved"

END IF
```

4 Proof of Destruction/Proof of Erasability

Now the user needs to ensure that a similar data updation, which inherently destructs the data, has happened to the rest of the other database copies, viz D2,D3 and D4. As mentioned earlier, as per the SLA any updation done to D1 is reflected in D2, D3 and D4 with a time difference of (Δt).

For this verification the user asks the cloud storage provider to get relative bit location of certain bits in the D2,D3 and D4. These will be the relative MSBs noted by the destroyer application while rendering the database D1 useless. Once the bits are retrieved the provider is asked to to run those bits through the hash algorithm we provide, with the aforementioned key and the output is requested from the vendor.

This output is compared with the value recovered from the process one on database D1. If both these values match, we can ensure that the data with the provider is now rendered useless.

5 Analysis of Our Scheme

As mentioned, the scenario is that the cloud provider is providing a storage space, along with certain permissions for the applications from the client end to access and modify the data. It is on extension of the same postulation that a destructor algorithm is being proposed. As we are accessing the data through legitimate and well defined means, albeit for destructive purposes, the proposition can be considered meticulous and proper.

Considering security aspects, there are two possible vulnerabilities that can be raised. First, it can be argued that the provider can anytime make an extra copy of the data without informing the client. A legally binding Service Level Agreement will be the best solution for this. Within this SLA the provider will be mentioning the various archival methodologies he will be using to store client's data and also the copies and locations of the data which he will be creating to prevent local mishaps. A breach of such legal agreements will possibly be contested on the courts and any provider would want to avoid such a scenario and the loss of credibility that might arise along with.

Second argument can be that if the data provider gets to know that the data is being modified is with an intention of scrambling/destroying it, he might contemplate a need to secretly prevent/make a copy of the data. But since the data shredder calls are interlaced/masqueraded as the regular update calls that the application is permitted to make towards it's a data, there is absolutely no possibility that the storage provider can figure out whether the call/operation being performed on the database is a regular update operation or a destructor operation. Thus we won't be deviating anything from the agreed and SLA established fetch cycle because any destructor call will in effect works on the same application mode. Thus there is no possibility that anyone other than the owner of the data, in this case the client, knows that data is being destructed and not being updated. Thus, given the facts and methods mentioned in this document, it can be postulated as a fool proof scheme.

Performance wise, it must be mentioned that there is a scope of improvement with the given pseudo code. Optimizations can be incorporated with regard to the destructor and verifier processes.

6 Conclusion

We have presented here a scheme for Proof of Erasability (POE) in a distributed environment. The focus of our work is on a probing engine/destructor which will probe the environment and based on the rules on the data store, will shred them partially or fully. This prototype can further extended as a service on Cloud. This destructor will systematically modify/update the most significant bit of every data chunk, thus ensuring that the data is so corrupted/ impaired that no part of the data will make any sense to whomever gets hold of it later. On analyzing the scheme we found that our proposition can be considered meticulous and proper as we are accessing the data through legitimate and well defined means, albeit for destructive purposes. Our scheme enjoys full faith of the client as it provides him with the shredding capabilities without making a specific or a different call for the purpose. With the given pseudo code there is a scope of improvement and further optimizations can be incorporated with regard to the destructor and verifier processes. However, there is no possibility that anyone other than the owner of the data, in this case the client, knows that data is being destructed and not being updated. Implementation of our scheme is underway and we expect a good performance of the protocol.

References

1. Vaquero, L.M., Rodero-Merino, L., Caceres, J., Lindner, M.: A break in the clouds: towards a cloud definition. In: ACM SIGCOMM Computer Communication Review (December 2008)
2. What is Storage as a Service (SaaS)? - Definition from Whatis.com (February 2010), http://searchstorage.techtarget.com/sDefinition/ 0,,sid5_gci1264119,00.html
3. Kishi, G.: Method and system for shredding data within a data storage subsystem. Pat No: US 7308543B2 (March 2005)
4. Gutmann, P.: Secure Deletion of Data from Magnetic and Solid-State Memory (July 1996)
5. Juels, A., Kaliski, B.: Proofs of retrievability for large files. In: CCS 2007: Proceedings of the 14th ACM Conference on Computer and Communications Security, New York, pp. 584–597 (2007)
6. Shacham, H., Waters, B.: Compact proofs of retrievability. Cryptology ePrint Archive, Report 2008/073 (2008)
7. Amazon Elastic Compute Cloud (EC2) (February 2010), http://www.amazon.com/ec2/
8. 3X Systems private cloud (March 2010), http://www.3x.com/
9. The 100 Coolest Cloud Computing Vendors (February 2010), http://www.crn.com/storage/222600510
10. Service level agreement (February 2010), http://en.wikipedia.org/wiki/Service_level_agreement

A Roadmap for the Comparison of Identity Management Solutions Based on State-of-the-Art IdM Taxonomies

Srinivasan Madhan Kumar [1] and Dr. Paul Rodrigues[2]

[1] Education & Research,
Infosys Technologies, Mysore, India
madhan_srinivasan@infosys.com
[2] Department of IT,
Hindustan University, Chennai, India
deanit@hindustanuniv.ac.in

Abstract. In recent days, digital identity in a corporate environment needs to be treated with high priority. Irrespective of different applications we use in organization, resources need to be managed and allotted to the appropriate identity/user (i.e. Provisioning Management) with proper access rights (Access Management). Identity management or IdM refers to how humans are identified, authorized and managed across computer networks. It deals with issues such as creating identities to the users, different ways to protect those identities & related information and the technologies supporting that protection. This paper analyzes the latest IdM product vendors in today's market. Also this paper aims to provide a survey/roadmap to compare the identity management solutions based on various important identity factors. In this paper, we are analysing different IdM systems based on two state-of-the-art identity management taxonomies, such as features & capabilities and strategy & vision.

Keywords: Identity management, access management, digital identity, IdM taxonomies, identity management survey.

1 Introduction

In recent days, digital identity in a corporate environment needs to be treated with high priority. Irrespective of different applications/platforms we use in organization, resources need to be managed and allotted to the appropriate identity/user (i.e. Provisioning Management) with proper access rights (Access/Policy Management). This process is called Identity Management. To achieve Identity Management efficiently the digital identity need to be defined properly.

Identity management refers to the process of managing the identities of users in providing privileges and access rights within a company or an organization by employing emerging technologies. There is a need for automated application, which defines what data and applications each user can access, to reduce the time in general. Identity management aims at increased security and productivity reducing the costs associated with management of user identities, attributes and their credential. Identity management uses a middleware tool that identifies the users and manages the

N. Meghanathan et al. (Eds.): CNSA 2010, CCIS 89, pp. 349–358, 2010.

privileges and access rights to resources. It minimizes the multiple user identities across various networks to a single identity that is accepted globally. Secure identity management touches many diverse capabilities like self-service, single sign-on, content aggregation etc.

This paper aims at providing a survey report based on few important criteria, which are must for any enterprise. Also this paper attempts to bring out answers for some of the following client questions: Why should we shift to IDM? Which IDM suits my organization better? Should we change all our existing functionality/ infrastructure, if we want to proceed with IDM? etc.

2   Related to This Work

In existence we can see large number of IdM products from various vendors with different functional features. In practice, Identity Management is not just about a single application. The application areas of IdM are really huge and it holds lot more opportunities for large amount of sectors, which differs from academic research to commercial business related-applications.

In the work of Ruth Halperin & James Backhouse [2] the importance of identity in the information society is explained. Also it shows the different opportunities and areas for research on identity and its management. This work critically analyses the application areas of technology-based identity system like government, healthcare, commerce, and finance, etc. This survey adds some weightage to these factors, specifically.

3   Identity Management – A Survey

When we think of assessing the IdM market, initially we faced two primary issues. The first issue was that on whom we are going to evaluate? And the second was, on what? By now the IdM market is very vast with many vendors. And almost all of them are really doing the great job (at least on any one of the major functionality). By considering the mentioned fact we decided to depend on IdM related research organizations, in selecting vendors and evaluation factors.

3.1   Selection of Vendors for the Survey

In this paper we are considering five different identity management vendors for assessment (from ~15 top IdM vendors). These vendors are finalized based on the research results of two identity management research groups. They are Burton Group [5], [22] (www.burtongroup.com) and Forrester Research, Inc [9] (www.forrester.com). Forrester is being treated as one of the top research organization for independent technology and market research worldwide. And Burton Group is the leading research organization for IAM architecture and infrastructure related research. By considering various research reports by Forrester and Burton Group we are finalizing IBM, Novell, Sun, Oracle, and CA for this survey.

3.2 Selection of Evaluation Criteria

In the work of Andras Cser [9] from Forrester Research, Inc, the latest identity evaluation criteria were discussed and IdM solutions were evaluated on those taxonomies during 2008. This survey also deals with pricing scenarios and revenue of the product factors. We found that, those taxonomies, except pricing and revenue best suit for our survey.

The latest 2009 survey report of Lori Rowland and Gerry Gebel [5] from Burton Group, explores the major evaluation criteria. As equal to Forrester Research, we give top priority to Burton Group too in deciding our evaluation criteria.

3.3 State-of-the-Art IdM Taxonomies

As cited above, based on Forrester Research and Burton Group research results, we refined two state-of-the-art identity management taxonomies along with eight sub-factors. They are,

- Features & Capabilities
    - o Initial setup and system integration
    - o Data management
    - o Delegated administration and self-service
    - o Access management
    - o Policy and role management
    - o Customer references
- Strategy & Vision
    - o Identity management vision
    - o Breadth of identity management solutions

4 Review of Different IdMs

The reviews of selected IdMs are discussed here. After this section the results are compared and analyzed in the next section.

4.1 IBM Tivoli Identity Manager

IBM Tivoli Identity Manager (TIM) 5.0 version is being used for this survey. TIM uses custom agents that are installed on every managed resource, such as AD domain controllers, database servers, etc. IBM states [19] that many of its agents don't need to be installed on managed resources, but can manage multiple resources remotely from a single server.

Before TIM starts its activity, it must integrate some of the existing applications like client's directory, HR applications, etc. For this task, IBM uses TDI (Tivoli Directory Integrator), a Java application that functions as a junction of identity data, both for initial integration and as a permanent connector when needed. TDI can be installed on Windows & Linux platform. It helps the organization by offering a clear view of any managed resource. TDI assures the user with all integration tasks by providing easy methods to reformat dissimilar data, such as consistently formatting phone numbers, Social Security numbers, and birth dates, etc.

TIM's simulation feature is an advantage, which allows user to try policies like create approval steps, assign tasks, etc, before enabling them.

Paul Venezia [10] states that, the overall navigation of the UI wasn't so clear. He further states that when user tries to construct some action, they need to plug JavaScript code into (the small text field available) in the UI. This provides some power, but it's also significantly more complex and substantially less elegant than expected. Paul Venezia research describes that, the reporting engine of TIM is vast and complex. It's possible to generate reports containing nearly any data present in the system, but again, it's a little challenging to assemble the data in a logical form. Crystal Reports integration is also present in TIM.

4.2 Novell Identity Manager

Here we have used Novell's Identity Manager 3.6.1 version for this survey. Novell's identity management solution relies heavily on the company's directory server, eDirectory, which gives backbone support for all identity management activities. Novell's suite provides all identity management features including password management, role-based provisioning, cross-application user management, user deprovisioning, and corporate white pages functionality.

Identity Manager handles all IdM tasks with administrator-defined identity policies, by making communication between Identity Vault and the other applications on the network. All this depends on Identity Manager Drivers, which are the agents needed to manage all applications. Here communication between Vault, Drivers, and Identity Manager is totally based on XML.

Novell has an excellent UI, Designer. Designer proves the Novell solution as a masterpiece among others. But it's important to note that this is an optional add-on. Based on the Eclipse framework, Designer allows administrators to lay out almost the entire identity implementation visually and then drill down for configuration. Designer allows much of the configuration to be done in a simulated sandbox mode. The Designer is for policy management, workflow design and simulation, and documentation.

The only area where Novell uses outside tools is when wew need to merge two different AD's. First it uses Microsoft AD tools to migrate and then uses Identity Manager to manage all the data through its Identity vault. From administration to reporting, Novell Identity Manager proves to be one of the easiest to-use solutions in the collection. The addition of Designer adds even more automatic functionality on top of this suite.

Novell's policy management and delegated administration are split into two applications — which can be an inconvenience in large deployments [10]. Novell fares well in several of the functional areas of assessment; although it establishes leadership [9] in the data management, auditing and reporting, and architecture criteria sets, it trails in delegated administration and self-service, as well as in policy and role management. The disadvantage is that the product is dependent on eDirectory, which is one of the factors contributing to a skills gap that organizations often face and a need to bridge when selecting Novell for IAM.

4.3 Sun Java System Identity Manager

In Sun Java System Identity Manager 8.0 we can find a level of reliability and maturity that's rare in other IDM products. Sun's entire identity management suite consists of Access Manager, Directory Server Enterprise Edition, Federation Manager, Identity Auditor, Identity Manager, and Identity Manager Service Provider Edition.

Comparing with other IDM products Sun's is completely agentless. Its technology is fully responsible for monitoring and interacting with existing directory servers and applications without the need to deploy agents. For certain technologies, such as AD or Novell's directory, Sun deploys a black-box style software gateway for data translation, but this is not an agent, nor does it require changes to target systems in order to function. In practice [10], this looks very efficient. Sun uses Web-based, wizard-driven configuration tool to configure all resources, rules, users, and everything else.

When there is need to migrate one AD into another, Sun Identity Manager manages it without any use of Microsoft AD tools.

Sun's provisioning capabilities are extremely flexible. All events in the product can trigger workflows, which helps Sun Identity Manager meet very demanding customer requirements with minimal customization. Forrester Research survey [9] points that, Sun's Access Manager Solution is not up to the mark in the areas of centralized configuration management, policy definition, and adaptive authentication. Generally, the breadth of Sun's IAM portfolio is short of competitors Oracle and IBM (lacking E-SSO, identity audit, privileged user management, and entitlement management), and Sun has not yet fully implemented its open source strategy across the board of IAM products. Sun needs to focus on enhancing ERP connector capabilities and integrating audit log management systems more tightly with its products. Although the talent pool on the market for Sun's IAM skills is fairly rich, Sun has lost its exclusivity or elite status with SI partners, especially to Oracle.

4.4 Oracle Identity Management

Considering Oracle Corporation, we take its version of 11g for our analysis. In addition to Oracle Identity Manager (OIM) and Oracle Access Manager (OAM), its recent acquisition and integration of role management (Bridgestream/Oracle Role Manager [ORM]) and risk based authentication (Bharosa/Oracle Adaptive Access Manager [OAAM]) products will help Oracle position its IAM product set as the identity services foundation for all Oracle eBusiness products. In general Oracle's identity management platform has excellent enterprise role management capabilities [6], [16].

Functionality-rich connectors and a special staging area for intermediary data transformations allow for flexible data transformations. Oracle has retired all user management and workflow functionality features in OAM, and it plans to unify all such functionality, along with reporting and auditing, as a set of common services. The product directly supports rollback functions through Oracle's Total Recall feature, in addition to having workflow-enabled connections to endpoints. There is a wide array of options for detecting and dealing with orphaned accounts. Oracle's provisioning policy definition supports wildcards and nested roles. OAM natively supports chainable and pluggable authentication schemes, flexible policy design, and native multifactor authentication using OAAM. Oracle licenses Passlogix's E-SSO solution in an OEM agreement and integrates it with OIM for Windows-based password self-service.

ORM's advanced temporal role versioning and native support for multidimensional organizations and OAAM's easy-to-use multifactor and adaptive, risk-based authentication and fraud detection boost Oracle in front of the competition on functionality. Meanwhile, Oracle's focus on extending IAM from a security and systems management discipline to one of application architecture and development fuels its strategic leadership.

4.5 CA Identity Manager

CA has its recent Identity Manager r12 version for this analysis. CA has a leading Web SSO product with SiteMinder, but its Identity Manager still carries the burden of the legacy CA Admin provisioning engine, while only supporting CA Directory for the global user store [9].

CA's adaptable SiteMinder shares policies with Identity Manager's Delegated Administration Functionality, SOA Security Manager (the service-oriented architecture access management system), and SiteMinder Federation. Identity Manager's administrative model currently provides preventive — but not detective or corrective — SoD management (Segregation of Duties), a missing feature that will be present in CA's forthcoming Security Compliance Manager.

Based on the survey of Andras Cser [9] and his team, CA needs to eliminate the dependency on the inheritance CA Admin and CA Directory. Currently CA offers the Enterprise Entitlement Manager as an optional add-on to its IAM suite. But most of the customer survey states that, CA's Enterprise Entitlement Manager needs to be integrated into IAM suite to remain competitive in the market. CA's SiteMinder is still a tough competitor for any Web SSO implementation. But, it is having a drawback in its ability to chain independent pluggable authentication modules — a foundation feature for adaptive authentication. Customer references expressed concerns around 1) the scalability of CA Identity Manager's policies for large deployments and 2) CA's continuing ability to support its IAM products, as they witnessed a decline in technical support engineers expertise level.

5 Comparison Results

This section contains the comparison of our survey with results and graphical representation of the same. Those values and measurements we used are based on our research and references we came across. These are not final/official values any IdM product.

Table 1. Features & Capabilities

Features & Capabilities	IBM	Novell	Sun	Oracle	CA
Initial setup and system integration	6.8	6.6	6.8	7.2	4.8
Data management	6.2	8.9	8.8	8.8	5.7
Delegated administration and self-service	6.1	6.2	8	8.5	8.2
Access management	5.8	5.3	3.4	7.2	7.6
Policy and role management	5.8	5.4	7.5	6.2	4.2
Customer references	5.6	7.8	8.2	6.9	6.2

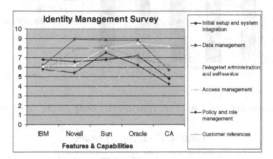

Fig. 1. Comparison of IdM's on Features & Capabilities factors

Table 2. Strategy & Vision

Strategy & Vision	IBM	Novell	Sun	Oracle	CA
Identity management vision	6.00	5.20	6.00	10.00	6.00
Breadth of identity management solutions	7.00	5.4	5.6	6.6	5.4

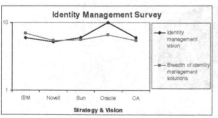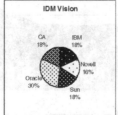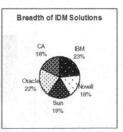

Fig. 2. (a) Comparison of IdM's on Strategy & Vision factors; (b) With respect to IdM vision; (c) Breathe of IdM solutions

Table 3. Comparison Results of Two Taxonomies

	Features & Capabilities	Strategy & Vision
IBM	6.05	6.5
Novell	6.70	5.30
Sun	7.12	5.2
Oracle	7.47	8.3
CA	6.12	5.7

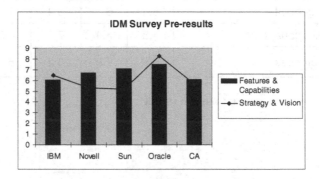

Fig. 3. Individual level-wise analysis on two state-of-the art taxonomies

Table 4. Final survey results

	Final Result
IBM	6.28
Novell	6.00
Sun	6.16
Oracle	7.89
CA	5.91

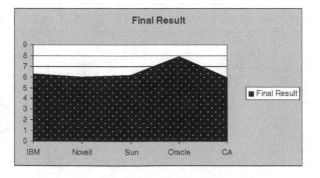

Fig. 4. Final survey results of all IdM's

6 Future Work

This survey analyzed and produced clear cut results of different IdM products. This research is done based on two taxonomies under which we have considered eight factors. The result of this survey is based only on these eight factors. Our future work will be concerned about improving the effectiveness of this research by including some more factors that are industry relevant as well as customer-need oriented. Also our future work will incorporate some more IdM products, if applicable and possible, those are revolting the market.

7 Conclusion

Identity management has successfully influenced many IT and business industries because of its composite nature in both features and benefits. Even after years of healthy adoption rates, the IdM market is actually just beginning its path toward broad adoption and deep penetration. IdM researches points that the utilization of identity and access management products in smaller enterprises (1,000 to 5,000 employees) is still an underserved market. A research report [21] projects that the IAM market will grow from nearly $2.6 billion in 2006 to more than $12.3 billion in 2014. With the base of the above remarks, this survey is an attempt to bring out the different views and aspects of selected IdM products. But, we are not concluding the best and worst out of these. Here we have given a roadmap for each product based on our own identity management taxonomies. Now, this roadmap can be used as a base for both vendors and organizations to proceed further with identity management based on their requirements.

References

1. Windley, P.J.: Digital Identity. O'Reilly Media, Inc., Sebastopol
2. Halperin, R., Backhouse, J.: A roadmap for research on identity in the information society. Identity in the Information Society Journal 1(1), paper no. 1, Identity Journal Limited, Springer (2008)
3. Irwin, C.S., Taylor, D.C.: Identity, Credential, and Access Management at NASA, from Zachman to Attributes. ACM, New York (2009)
4. Tynan, D.: Federation takes identity to the next level
5. Rowland, L., Gebel, G.: Provisioning Market 2009: Divide and Conquer. Burton Group Market Insight Report (2009)
6. Chanliau, M.: Oracle Identity Management 11g. An Oracle White Paper (February 2010), http://www.oracle.com/technology/products/id_mgmt/pdf/idm_tech_wp_11g_r1.pdf
7. Lai, E.: Novell to extend identity management to cloud, virtualized apps (December 2009)
8. Nawrocki, G.: Open Source Identity Management and the Grid
9. Cser, A.: Identity and Access Management. Forrester Research Report (2008)
10. Venezia, P.: The identity management challenge
11. Amiri, E.: CA Identity Manager: Capabilities and Architecture (2009)

12. Lavagnino, C.: Delivering Identity and Access Management as an Automated Service, CA (2009)
13. Fontana, J.: Novell, Sun, Oracle crank out identity management wares
14. Novell Inc., Novell Identity Manager 3 Demo,
    `http://www.novell.com/products/identitymanager/`
    `idm3_demo_viewlet_viewlet_swf.html`
15. Novell Inc., Novell Identity Manager Compare,
    `http://www.novell.com/products/identitymanager/compare.html`
16. Oracle Corporation, Oracle Identity Management 11g Datasheet,
    `http://www.oracle.com/technology/products/id_mgmt/pdf/`
    `idm_ds_11g_r1.pdf`
17. Volk, D.: Oracle Identity Manager 11g. Identity Management Experts Series, Identigral, Inc. (2009),
    `http://identigral.com/blog/2009/10/14/`
    `oracle-identity-manager-11g`
18. Sun Microsystems Inc., Sun Identity Manager 8.0 Workflows, Forms, and Views (2008)
19. IBM Corporation, IBM Tivoli Identity Manager Documentation,
    `http://publib.boulder.ibm.com/infocenter/tivihelp/v2r1/`
    `index.jsp?topic=/com.ibm.itim.doc/welcome.htm`
20. McAllister, N.: End-to-end identity management suites still coming together
21. Forrester Research Report, Identity Management Market Forecast: 2007 to 2014 (2008)
22. Burton Group Blogs, Identity and Privacy,
    `http://identityblog.burtongroup.com/bgidps/`
    `identity_management/`
23. Volk, D.: The rise of Suncle (volume 1). Identity Management Series, Identigral, Inc. (2009),
    `http://www.identigral.com/blog/2009/04/20/`
    `the-rise-of-suncle-volume-1`
24. Volk, D.: The rise of Suncle: Access Management. Identity Management Series, Identigral, Inc. (2009),
    `http://www.identigral.com/blog/2009/04/20/`
    `the-rise-of-suncle-access-management`
25. Volk, D.: The rise of Suncle: Directory Services. Identity Management Series, Identigral, Inc. (2009),
    `http://www.identigral.com/blog/2009/04/20/`
    `the-rise-of-suncle-directory-services`

BubbleTrust: A Reliable Trust Management for Large P2P Networks

Miroslav Novotny and Filip Zavoral*

Faculty of Mathematics and Physics,
Charles University in Prague
{novotny,zavoral}@ksi.mff.cuni.cz

Abstract. The open and anonymous nature of peer-to-peer (P2P) networks creates almost ideal environment for malicious activities. The trust management (TM) allows to establish trust relationships between peers in such hostile environment and makes using the P2P network more secure. In this paper we present a novel trust management system called BubbleTrust which use some new approaches. The system creates a bubble around the unknown peers which includes all peers which trust them. Each peer is evaluated separately as a participant in network services and as a participant in the TM. The peer credibility is derived only from verified information about transactions between peers. Our aim was to create a system which is applicable in large P2P networks and provides the reliable results.

Keywords: P2P Network, Security, Trust Management, DHT.

1 Introduction

A malicious peer behaviour is one of the most challenging research areas in the P2P networks. It is not rare when a part of peers try to exploit network for their own benefit or spoil using network services for other peers. The reliable P2P application must implement some methods which help to detect such peers and avoid collaboration with them. These methods are called trust managements (TM) and try to predict future peer behaviour on the basis of observation and evaluation peers past behaviour. The design of such system is difficult due to decentralized architecture and general distrust between unknown entities. Many trust managements with various ideas and targeted issues have been published in recent years [1], [2], [3], [4]. Although there are many proposed systems which try to implement TM in a P2P environment, the researches still propose new ones. The biggest threat is the peer or group of peers which have knowledge about the design of TM and know how to trick it. The defence against such behaviour presents the challenge for future research.

Trust management can be used in any community of entities which do not know each other previously and need to cooperate. For instance, in eCommerce

---

* This work was supported in part by grants GACR 202/10/0761, GACR 201/09/H05, and SVV-2010-261312.

N. Meghanathan et al. (Eds.): CNSA 2010, CCIS 89, pp. 359–373, 2010.

applications such as eBay, Amazon, and Yahoo the entities represent people which trade with a totally unknown partner. In social networks the trust can help to improve collaboration and mutual benefit for network members. TM has been used for identifying high-quality contribution in Wikipedia [5]. The file-sharing P2P applications exploit TM for filter out inauthentic content (pollution) [6] or penalize members who do not offer any resources (free-rides) [7]. The grid computing can use TM for identifying unreliable or irresponsible members [8].

In this paper we present a novel trust management system called BubbleTrust which use some new approaches. Each peer is evaluated separately as a participant in network services and as a participant in the TM. So, the system can distinguish the peers which provide honest service but do not participate correctly in providing references to other peers. The peer credibility is derived only from verified information about transactions between peers. The malicious peer cannot create fake transactions, hide information about their malicious transactions or alter information about other peers transactions.

The rest of the paper is organized as follows. The section 2 describes a basic concept of the proposed system. The details are explained in section 3 and section 4 suggests some optimizations. We evaluate performance and efficiency of the system in section 5. Section 6 concludes the paper and discusses future work.

2   Basic Concept

In this paper, we assume that the P2P network can be decomposed into a set of two-party transactions. In each transaction one party is designated as a consumer and the other as a provider. The provider is a peer which owns some resources and offers them to the public. The consumer is a peer which uses these resources. Each peer in the network can act as both a provider and a consumer.

After each transaction, the consumer can express its satisfaction with the quality of the acquired resource and transaction parameters. On the basis of all transactions with other peer the consumer can create an opinion about peer's reliability as a provider, this opinion is called provider rating.

The consumer offers this opinion to other peers in the network. In other words, the consumer evaluates every provider, which it cooperates with, and makes this evaluation accessible to the public. From the TM point of view the better notion for consumer is an evaluator. In the following text we use notion evaluator interchangeably with the notion consumer if we want to stress its evaluation function. Other peers download the provider rating from the evaluator and use it for its own calculation of the provider rating. From the other peers point of view the foreign provider rating is not as trustworthy as locally created ratings. We use notion recommendation for the provider rating acquired from other peers.

In the proposed system every peer has two ratings. First, it is the provider rating, which we defined above. The higher provider rating means that the peer is more likely to be a reliable resource provider. Second, the evaluator rating is connected with the evaluation function of the peers. The opinions from the peers with higher evaluator ratings are more trustworthy than opinions from the peers with lower evaluator ratings.

The provider rating can originate from direct transactions with evaluated peers or be calculated from the recommendations acquired from other peers. This rating corresponds to the notion of the trust commonly used in the contemporary TMs. The evaluator rating can be only calculated from the recommendations acquired from other peers which made opinions towards the same peer.

Every peer creates both ratings locally towards each peer which has required resources. The primary purpose of these ratings is to help peers to make a decision whether a given peer is reliable for cooperation. If the peer acts as a consumer, it is looking for a provider with a higher provider rating to ensure that the transaction will be successful. If the peer acts as a provider, it prefers the consumer with a higher evaluator rating to ensure that the transaction will be correctly evaluated and this evaluation will be trustworthy for other peers in the network.

The calculations of both ratings influence each other. The calculation of the provider rating requires the evaluator ratings of all peers which evaluated the given peer. Analogously, the calculation of the evaluator rating requires the provider ratings of all peers which were evaluated by the given peer. These two observations give us a brief outline of the calculation algorithm which will be explained below. The system creates a bubble around the unknown peers which contains the peers having references to them.

Most of the previously published trust managements used only one rating and this rating supplies the function of the both ratings in our system. The authors assumed that a quality provider should be a quality evaluator too and vice-versa. But this is not generally true. Especially peers which are members of malicious collectives can break this assumption in an effort to advantage some other members of the collective. The separation of ratings facilitates detection of such behaviour.

3   Calculation

Before each transaction the consumer needs the provider ratings of the all possible providers, on the basis of these ratings the consumer chooses the most reliable partner for cooperation. There are two possibilities how the consumer can get provider ratings. First, both peers have already cooperated in the past and the consumer has the rating created by itself. Second, the consumer has never cooperated with the remote peer and has to ask other peers for recommendations. These recommendations are used to compute the required rating.

Similar situation occurs on the provider's side. It need the evaluator rating of the consumer which ask for its service. The evaluator ratings are always calculated from the recommendations originated from the given evaluator. In this section we explain the calculation of both ratings. We start with the provider ratings, the calculation of the evaluator ratings is analogous. At first, we give several definitions:

Definition: Provider rating (V_P) is a real value in a range [-1,1] which expresses an opinion about the provider reliability. The positive value expresses the satisfaction and negative value dissatisfaction.

Definition: Evaluator ratings (V_E) is a real value in the range [0,1] which express an opinion about the quality of ratings offered by the evaluator. The higher value means more trustworthy rating.

We choose different ranges to stress the different interpretation of both values. The provider rating expresses two states: satisfaction and dissatisfaction whereas the evaluator rating expresses the quality of the opinion. The recommendation from an evaluator towards a provider is stored as a relation.

Definition: The relation is a 5-tuple r $= < E, P, v, w, t >$ where E is a transaction evaluator, P is a transaction provider, v is a provider rating, w is a transactions weight and t is a time of the last modification. We use a notation $r.E$, $r.P$, $r.v$, $r.w$ and $r.t$ for elements in the relation r.

Definition: The transactions weight expresses the consumer's opinion about the importance of the transactions between the consumer and the provider. This opinion is a real value in a range [0,1].

The relation can originate or be altered only after the transaction between involved peers takes place. The storing and seeking relations in the network is described in the 3.2. Meanwhile, we assume that all relations created in the network are available for every peer.

The transactions weight gives to the evaluator the opportunity to express the importance of the transactions, for instance on the basis of the size or character of the data. The importance of the whole relation is calculated from the transaction weight and the time of the last modification.

Definition: Weight function (W) determines the weight of the each relation and is defined by the formula:

$$W(r) = \alpha * f(r.t) + \beta * r.w \tag{1}$$

Where $\alpha + \beta = 1$ $\alpha, \beta \in [0, 1]$ are weight constants and $f(x) : N \rightarrow [0, 1]$ is a time function. The weight constants determine the ratio between time and weight component of the transaction and the time function maps the age of transaction into a range [0,1]. The design of time function and weight constants will be discussed later.

The next question is how the evaluator rating influence the opinion originated from the evaluator. We define the two dimensional function, called provider function, which expresses this dependency.

Definition: The provider function accepts two arguments, the provider rating originated from one evaluator and the evaluator rating of this evaluator. The result is altered provider rating which takes into account the evaluator trustworthiness. The function has a form: $pv(x_1, x_2) : [-1, 1] \times [0, 1] \rightarrow [-1, 1]$

Where x_1 is a provider rating originated from the remote evaluator and x_2 is an evaluator rating of the remote evaluator.

This function can have several interpretations, we analyse function requirements and provide possible interpretation in section 3.3.

Now we are able to give a formula to compute the provider rating. The basic idea is simple: The peer is a good provider if a majority of good evaluators agrees on it. The formula (2) takes into account the altered provider ratings and weights of all relations where the given peer acts as a provider.

Let R is a set of relation such $r \in R$ and $r.P = A$, the provider rating of peer A, $V_P(A)$, is calculated according the formula:

$$V_P(A) = \frac{\sum_{r \in R} pv(r.v, V_E(r.E)) * W(r)}{\sum_{r \in R} W(r)} \qquad (2)$$

The formula for computation of the evaluator rating is very similar. At first, we need the evaluator function.

Definition: The evaluator function accepts two argument, the provider rating originated from a given evaluator and the reference provider rating. The reference provider rating reflects the majority opinion of other peers or local provider ratings if it is available. The result is an evaluator rating of the given evaluator which takes into account the difference between both ratings. The function has a form: $ev(x_1, x_2) : [-1, 1] \times [-1, 1] \to [0, 1]$

Where x_1 is a provider rating originated from the remote evaluator and x_2 is a reference provider rating.

Similarly to provider function, this function can have several interpretations. We analyse function requirements and provide possible interpretation in section 3.3.

The idea behind the evaluator rating: the peer is a good evaluator if a majority of its ratings correctly evaluates the providers. The formula (3) takes into account the calculated evaluator ratings and weights of all relations where the given peer acts as an evaluator.

Let R is a set of relation such $r \in R$ and $r.E = A$, the evaluator rating of peer A, $V_E(A)$, is calculated according the formula:

$$V_E(A) = \frac{\sum_{r \in R} ev(r.v, V_P(r.E)) * W(r)}{\sum_{r \in R} W(r)} \qquad (3)$$

The aim of the trust management is to calculate the provider rating and the evaluator rating for the given peers. In the proposed system those values are computed locally on each peer. The calculated values are used only for decision on the local peer and are not exported to other peers. It means that each peer has a unique view on the network and the trust values towards one peer can be different on the different peers, the similar approach is used for example in Fuzzy [9] or Core [10]. The opposite approach represents the systems like EigenTrust [11] where the trust values are global: All peers share the same opinion towards others.

3.1 Basic Algorithm

In this section we describe the algorithms which implement the formulae (2) and (3). We demonstrate the algorithm which computes the provider rating, the calculation of the evaluator ratings is analogous. Both computations influence each other, we need to calculate evaluator ratings of all evaluators for a given peer if we want to calculate the provider rating for the given peer.

The basic algorithm works recursively, in each level computes either provider ratings or evaluator ratings of all peers in the input set. The first level computes provider ratings, the second level computes evaluator ratings, the third provider ratings and so on. The sequence of computation is illustrated in the figure 1.

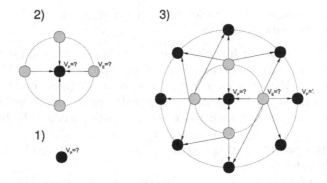

Fig. 1. The sequence of computation of the provider ratings. The dots are peers and the arrows represent relations. The direction is always from the evaluator to the provider. The dotted circles represent levels.

In each level the algorithm performs the following steps:

1. Find evaluators (or providers) for all peers in the input set.
2. Recursively computes the evaluator (or provider) ratings for new peers.
3. Computes provider (or evaluator) ratings according the formulae (2) or (3).

If the algorithm computes the provider rating (in step 3), it needs to find and compute the evaluator ratings of all evaluators (in step 1 and 2). The information about one peer is held in a data structure with following items:

```
node {
            VP = unknown|processing| [-1,1]
            VE = unknown|processing| [0,1]
            dividendP = 0;
            dividendE = 0;
            dividerP = 0;
            dividerE = 0;
}
```

The items V_P and V_E correspond to the provider rating and the evaluator rating. They can take the value unknown, processing or a number in the proper range. The newly discovered nodes have this value set to unknown, the value processing means that the calculation is in progress, and if the value is a number, this number matches the ratings. The data structure for the node itself has V_P and V_E set to 1, because every peer always trusts itself. The variable *dividend* and *divider* are auxiliary variables.

The following algorithm uses the function *get_relation(role,P)* to get all relations where a peer from the set P is in a given role. The role is either a provider or an evaluator. The function *evaluators(S)* returns all evaluators from the relations belonging to the set S and the function *evaluator_optimizations(S)* implements some optimizations which will be described further in the text. Meanwhile, let this function be empty. The basic algorithm for calculation of provider rating:

```
Input: Input - Set of nodes.
Output: Set items VP for all nodes from the input set.

function basic_provider_ratings(Input)
 1:  foreach p from Input {
 2:     if p.VP == unknown then {
 3:        p.VP = processing;
 4:        P = P + {p};
 5:     }
 6:  }
 7:  if empty(P) then return;
 8:  S = get_relations(provider,P);
 9:  evaluator_optimizations(S);
10:  E = evaluators(S);
11:  E = E \ P;
12:  basic_evaluator_ratings(E);
13:  foreach s from S {
14:     if s.evaluator.VE == processing then continue;
15:     s.provider.dividendP += pv(s.val,s.eval.VE) * W(s);
16:     s.provider.dividerP += W(s);
17:  }
18:  foreach p from P {
19:     if (p.dividerP != 0) then {
20:        p.VP = p.dividendP/p.dividerP;
21:     } else {
22:        p.VP = default_VP;
23:     }
24:  }
```

This algorithm sets the provider ratings for all peers in the input set at once. Every peer is able to calculate ratings for a larger number of peers in one algorithm run. This is a typical situation when the peer has several possible providers and needs to know the ratings of all. The function *basic_evaluator_ratings* is analogous, swap the words evaluator and provider and use the evaluator function instead of the provider function (line 15).

The algorithm visits each peer twice at the most, when calculates a provider rating and when calculates an evaluator rating. At the beginning all peers have the both ratings set to unknown. The function *basic_provider_ratings* accepts only peers with unknown provider ratings (line 2) and as the first step their ratings are set to *processing* (line 3). This ensures that any recursive call of this function does not deal with these peers again. At the end of the function all peers, which had unknown provider ratings, are set to numeric value (line 20 or 22). The algorithm also ignores the relations between peers in the input set (line 11) because these relations do not provide new information. The rules above ensure that the basic algorithm finishes after visiting all nodes in the network or if there are no relations from the visited nodes to the rest of the network.

In the practical application we cannot let the algorithm explore the whole network due to limited network performance and time requirements. Further in the text we introduce several methods how to reduce a number of visited nodes without significant degradation of the results.

3.2 Data Management

The algorithm described in the previous section needs function *get_relations* which discovers all relations for a given set of peers. It is not suitable to ask peers this information directly because the malicious peers can suppress some relations to improve their reputation. Instead we use a distributed hash table (DHT), like Chord [12], to store and seek relations.

We assume that every peer that takes part in the system has a unique identifier which is the hash value of the peers public key and this identifier serves as a key into the DHT. The relations are stored in the DHT by both the evaluator and the provider identifier. Hence the relations are searchable by both participants. The following protocol describe the creation and placing the relation between the peer A and the peer B into the DHT:

```
1.  A  ->  B:  Req(A,B,T)
2.  B  ->  A:  Ack(A,B,T,(A,B,T)PB)
3.  A <-> B:  Transaction
4.  A  -> DHT: Relation(A,B,R,W,T,(A,B,T)PB)PA
```

In the first step the peer A sends a request to the peer B, the request contains the identifiers of the both peers and the actual time stamp T. The peer B replies with an acknowledgement containing the digital signature of the items in the request. The peer B can refuse the request if the time stamp is significantly different from its local time or lower than in the previous transaction with the same peer. After the acknowledgement the transaction can be started. The peer A acts as an evaluator in this transaction and creates a relation record. This record contains identifiers of the both peers, transaction rating, weight and time stamp and the digital signature of the request received in step 2. The relation record is digitally signed by the peer A and stored into the DHT.

The first condition ensures that neither A nor B can create the relation itself, hence every relation is based on a legitimate transaction. The second condition provides data integrity, the transaction rating, weight and time are unmodified values created by the peer A. And the third condition ensures the search completeness. Any peer cannot suppress any relation involved in it.

The protocol above is vulnerable to sybil attack [13]. Every peer can generate many pairs of public/private keys and present multiple identities. So the protocol must implement the protection mechanism against such behaviour, for instance crypto puzzle. The function *get_relations* sends a DHT query for each peer from the input set. Those queries can be realized by one multi-query which lookups all keys concurrently.

3.3 Provider and Evaluator Function

The next task is to design the evaluator and the provider functions. Those functions have a crucial impact on the algorithm result. The provider function determines how the evaluator rating influences its recommendations. Analogously, the evaluator function determines how accuracy of the recommendation influences the evaluator rating of its originator. In this section we discuss the requirements on both functions and propose their formulations. We start with the provider function which has a form: $pv(x_1, x_2) : [-1, 1] \times [0, 1] \rightarrow [-1, 1]$

The first argument is a provider rating originated from an evaluator (recommendation) and the second one is the evaluator rating of this evaluator. The function result is the altered provider rating according evaluator trustfulness. This implies four natural conditions:

1. If $x_2 = 1$ then pv $= x_1$ (Let the recommendation unchanged.)
2. If $x_2 = 0$ then pv $= 0$. (Ignore the recommendation.)
3. The pv is an increasing function in x_2 for $x_1 > 0$.
4. The pv is a decreasing function in x_2 for $x_1 < 0$.

We introduce the fifth condition which allows us to parametrize the function by the parameter T_P. This parameter determines the degree of toleration and is in the range (0,1].

5. If $x_2 = 0.5$ then pv $= x_1 * T_P$.

In other words, if the evaluator trustfulness decreases to the mid-value, the recommendation is decreased by the parameter T_P. This parameter is called provider toleration. The simplest function which meets all five conditions:

$$pv(x_1, x_2) = x_2^{log_{0.5}(T_P)} * x_1 \qquad (4)$$

Figure 2A demonstrates the meaning of the parameter T_P. The bigger T_P implies that the pv decrease slowly, hence the system is more tolerant to the peers with lower evaluator ratings. In this figure, the function value in the point $x_2 = 0.5$ is equal to the value of T_P. And figure 2B illustrates the provider function for different x_1 value. The figure shows only positive values, the graph of negative values is symmetrical on axis x_2.

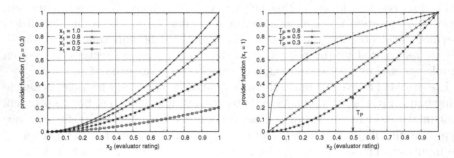

Fig. 2. Provider function with fixed x_1 and variable T_P and provider function with fixes T_P and variable x_1

The evaluator function is a little bit more complicated. It has a form:

$ev(x_1, x_2) : [-1, 1] \times [-1, 1] \to [0, 1]$

The first argument is a provider rating originated from a given evaluator and second argument is the reference provider rating. On the basis of those values the function determines the evaluator rating of the given evaluator. This implies three natural conditions:

1. If $x_1 = x_2$ then ev $= 1$ (Accurate recommendation)
2. If difference between x_1 and x_2 increases then ev decreases.
3. The decreasing rate depends on the absolute value of x_2. The smaller $|x_2|$ implies lower decrease rate.

We also introduce the next condition which allows us to parametrize the function by the parameter T_E. Similarly to the evaluator function this parameter can be interpreted as a degree of toleration.

5. If $x_2 = 1$ and $x_1 = x_2 * (1 - T_E)$ than ev $= 0.5$

In other words, if the known peer is complete trustful or complete distrustful and the recommendation differs by the parameter $(1 - T_E)$ than the given evaluator has an evaluator rating 0.5 (the mid-value). This condition is analogous to condition 5 for the evaluator function. The following function meets all conditions:

$$ev(x_1, x_2) = 0.5^{\left(\frac{x_1 - x_2}{(1 - T_E) * |x_1| - 1}\right)^2} \tag{5}$$

The figure 3 shows the evaluator function for fixed T_E and variable x_2. The maximum is in the points where $x_1 = x_2$ (accurate recommendation). The parameter T_E determines how quickly the function decreases from its maximum.

The last function is the time function which maps the age of transaction into a range [0,1]. There is only one simple condition: the older relation weights less than newer relation. The simplest implementation is the linear function with $f(0) = 1$ and $f(max\_time) = 0$. After max_time the relation is declared as obsolete and deleted. But in our system we use the exponential function which

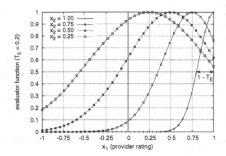

Fig. 3. Evaluator function with fixed T_E and variable x_2

better reflects dependency between time and the relation weight. We use the following exponential function with the parameter k in the range (0,1]:

$$f(t) = e^{-(\Delta t * k)^2} \tag{6}$$

4   Optimized Algorithms

The basic algorithm introduced in section 3.1 tries to reach all peers in the network. The load related with the basic algorithm can be unacceptable for real usage. In the following text we introduce several improvements which reduce the algorithm complexity without significant degradation of its efficiency.

4.1   Algorithm with Cutting Off

The first improvement is based on the idea that in the formula (2) or (3) it is not necessary to involve the relations which have small weight in comparison to other. Those relations have only limited influence on the result and can be neglected. The optimized algorithm ignores the peers whose relations have a low contribution to the calculated trust value and there is no point in dealing with them. We also implement the maximal number of nodes added in each level. The algorithm ensures that less important peers are removed first. The following function realizes the described restrictions and can implement the function *evaluator_optimizations(S)* in the basic algorithm:

```
function restrict_evaluator_nodes(S) {
  W = 0;
  foreach s from S {
    e = s.get_evaluator();
    e.weight += W(s);
    W += W(s);
    E.add(e);
  }
  foreach e from E { e.weight = e.weight/W; }
```

```
E = sort_weight(E);
removedWeights = 0;
foreach e from E {
  removedWeights += e.weight;
  if ((removedWeights <= limit) || (S.size() > maxNodes)) then
    E.remove(e);
}
foreach s from S {
  if (!E.contains(s.get_evaluator())) then S.remove(s);
}
return S;
}
```

The algorithm calculates cumulated weight for each evaluator, because this evaluator can have relations towards more peers in the input set. The algorithm removes the evaluators which cumulative weights towards all peers in the input set are smallest.

4.2 Limiting Depth

The basic algorithm finishes after visiting all nodes in the network or if there are no more relations from visited nodes to the rest of the network. The restrictions on number of nodes in each level results into increasing the depth of recursion, so it is necessary to limit the depth as well. The peers in the last level have assigned the default trust values. We choose the default provider rating equal to 0 and default evaluator rating to 0.5, both represents a mid-value. In simulations presented further in the text we recommend appropriate number of levels.

4.3 Using Values from Previous Runs

One algorithm run computes trust values for a large number of peers. It is efficient to use these values in the next runs. There are two issues related to this. First, not all trust values are equally reliable. For instance, the trust value which was calculated in level 6 is less reliable than the value from level 2. On level 6 there are less remaining levels to maximal depth and calculation is more limited. Second, the trust values obsolete in time because new transactions take place and relations are changed.

We introduce several simple rules for manipulating with the trust cache which take into account both issues:

1. The level where the trust value was calculated is stored into the cache along with the trust value.
2. The cache record is used in calculation only if the level of the record is less or equal to the current level in the calculation algorithms.
3. Each level has its time to live (TTL). After this time the level of the record is increased. If the record is on the maximal level, the record is deleted.

These rules ensure that the calculation is not less accurate than without using the cache. In fact, using cached values from the lower level than the current level increases accuracy, because the values on the lower levels are more precise.

5 Evaluation and Data Analysis

To evaluate performance of our method we implemented the simulation model. We generate a network with a given number of nodes and relations between them. The relations are generated according both zip's law and random distribution, each relation has a different size and time.

We focused on performance issues which can be measured by the average number of visited nodes for each query. The basic algorithm reaches as many peers as possible, if there are some relations from the visited peers to the rest of the network, the basic algorithm follows them. Hence the number of visited nodes depends on the density of relations in the network. The practical simulations showed that the average number of visited nodes for the basic algorithm and zipf's distribution is $1.4 *$ total number of the peers in the network. Remind that each peer can be visited twice.

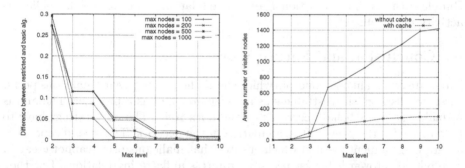

Fig. 4. a) The dependency between restriction parameters and calculation results. The network with 2000 nodes and 40000 relations with zipf's law distribution. b) Efficiency of using cache in the network with 1000 nodes and 20000 relations per day.

The optimized algorithm with cutting off and limiting depth reduces the maximal number of visited peers during one calculation to ($max\_nodes*max\_levels$). The parameter max_level limit the depth of the recursion and max_nodes limit the number of peers in each level. Obviously, the peers which are farther from the original peer have smaller influence on the calculated rating. Our goal is to set these parameters as low as possible with minimal impact to the result. The figure 4.a displays how the parameters max_nodes and max_levels change the function result. The graph shows the difference between outputs of the basic algorithm and restricted algorithm with the given parameters. As a result of this simulation, we recommend using the parameters $max\_nodes = 200$ and

$max\_levels = 5$ where the difference is less than 0.05. But the algorithm can still visit 1000 nodes, so the next optimization is necessary.

The cached version has a great potential to reduce the number of visited peers. We performed the simulation of the network with 1000 peers and 20000 relations per day with a zipf's distribution. The efficiency of this optimization depends on the peer activity. We suppose that the tested peers ask to the some others peer ratings every 10 minutes. The figure 4.b shows the simulation after two days. This simulation does not implement any other optimization. On recommended level 5 the number of visited peers falls to the one quarter. The rules for using cached values ensures that this optimization does not significantly change the result values.

Of course, further simulations are necessary to prove the algorithm efficiency against previously proposed mechanisms. In our future work we focus on this issue and provide detailed comparison against other mechanisms and malicious behaviour. We intend to use Matrix Model [14], among other things, to compare the results of different TM.

So far, we justify the efficiency of the proposed algorithm in brief discussion. The division of trustfulness into provider and evaluator rating allows better detection of malicious behaviour. Especially members of malicious collectives can have a low evaluator rating despite of their correct work as a provider. The BubbleTrust also has protection against fake relations which makes the malicious activity more difficult.

6   Conclusion and Future Work

There are two main new concepts which should help to fight with malicious peers. First, we distinguish trustfulness as an evaluator and as a provider. The aim is to make the peers behave correctly in the both roles. The both ratings have to be positive for the peers full participation in the network. The second concept is a data management method which ensures that malicious peers cannot create a fake relations towards honest peers or suppress unflattering relations. But they still can create fake relations towards allied malicious peers. In our future work we investigate the methods how to detect such relations.

Our method is based on a trust graph, similar to NICE [15]. In contrast, we do not try to find a trust path between a consumer and a provider, but we try to involve as many relations as possible into the decision process, we create a trust bubble. The method takes into account opinions of a great number of peers which have the strongest relations towards the queried peer. This method would not be possible without using a cache which significantly reduce the complexity of the algorithms.

In our future work we want to focus on the next reduction of the complexity of the algorithms. At the moment, every peer makes a decision on the basis of guaranteed information about transactions and performs all calculation. The most trustful peers can share information stored in the cache or participate on the neighbour calculation. And, as we mention before, we are preparing detailed evaluation of BubbleTrust with other TM.

References

1. Marti, S., Garcia-Molina, H.: Taxonomy of trust: Categorizing P2P reputation systems, Management in Peer-to-Peer Systems. Computer Networks 50, 472–484 (2006)
2. Fedotova, N., Bertucci, M., Veltri, L.: Reputation Management Techniques in DHT-Based Peer-to-Peer Networks. In: International Conference on Internet and Web Applications and Services, p. 4 (2007)
3. Suryanarayana, G., Taylor, R.N.: A Survey of TM and Resource Discovery Technologies in Peer-to-Peer Applications, Tech. Rep. UCI-ISR-04-6 (2004)
4. Novotny, M., Zavoral, F.: Reputation Based Methods for Building Secure P2P Networks. In: Proceedings of ICADIWT 2008, Copyright, pp. 403–408. IEEE Computer Society, VSB- Technical University of Ostrava (2008), ISBN 978-1-4244-2624-9
5. Adler, B.T., de Alfaro, L.: A content-driven reputation system for the wikipedia. In: Proceedings of the 16th International Conference on World Wide Web, New York, NY, USA, pp. 261–270 (2007)
6. Liang, J., Kumar, R.: Pollution in p2p file sharing systems. In: IEEE INFOCOM, pp. 1174–1185 (2005)
7. Feldman, M., Papadimitriou, C., Chuang, J.: Free-Riding and Whitewashing in Peer-to-Peer Systems. In: PINS 2004: Proceedings of the ACM SIGCOMM Workshop on Practice and Theory of Incentives in Networked Systems, pp. 228–236 (2004)
8. Alunkal, B.K., Veljkovic, I., von Laszewski, G., Amin, K.: Reputation-Based Grid Resource Selection. In: Workshop on Adaptive Grid Middleware, p. 28 (2003)
9. Aringhieri, R., Damiani, E., De Capitani Di Vimercati, S., Paraboschi, S., Samarati, P.: Fuzzy techniques for trust and reputation management in anonymous peer-to-peer systems., doi:10.1002/asi.20392
10. Michiardi, P., Molva, R.: Core: a collaborative reputation mechanism to enforce node cooperation in mobile ad hoc networks. In: Proceedings of the IFIP TC6/TC11 Sixth Joint Working Conference on Communications and Multimedia Security, pp. 107–121 (2002)
11. Kamvar, S.D., Schlosser, M.T., Garcia-Molina, H.: The EigenTrust Algorithm for Reputation Management in P2P Networks. In: Proceedings of the Twelfth International World Wide Web Conference. ACM, New York (2003)
12. Rowstron, A., Druschel, P.: Pastry: Scalable, distributed object location and routing for large-scale peer-to-peer systems. In: Guerraoui, R. (ed.) Middleware 2001. LNCS, vol. 2218, p. 329. Springer, Heidelberg (2001)
13. Douceur, J.R.: The Sybil Attack. In: IPTPS 2001: Revised Papers from the First International Workshop on Peer-to-Peer Systems, pp. 251–260 (2002)
14. Novotny, M., Zavoral, F.: Matrix Model of Trust Management in P2P Networks. In: 3rd International Conference on Research Challenges in Information Science, Fez, Morocco, pp. 519–528. IEEE Computer Society Press, Los Alamitos (2009)
15. Sherwood, R., Lee, S., Bhattacharjee, B.: Cooperative peer groups in NICE. In: Computer Networks: The International Journal of Computer and Telecommunications Networking. Elsevier, North-Holland, Inc. (2006)

Dynamic Policy Adaptation for Collaborative Groups

Madhumita Chatterjee* and G. Sivakumar**

Indian Institute of Technology
Department of Computer Science and Engineering
Mumbai, India 400 076
madhumita@cse.iitb.ac.in, siva@cse.iitb.ac.in

Abstract. Dynamic collaborative peer groups generally have constantly changing application requirements and varied security requirements, and require a secure and reliable group communication. Self-organizing groups like f/oss motivate the need for dynamic multi-level access control. Currently there are some integrated solutions for secure group communication, but very few allow dynamic multi-level access control based on trust. We propose a framework for collaborative groups which integrates authentication, admission control, policy based access control, adaptive trust and key management. Our model permits peers to regulate their own behavior by deploying access control policies dynamically based on the behavior and trust level of peers in the group and the current group composition. Peers can collaboratively modify policies governing their level. Our trust metric is a tunable metric based on context specific attributes. Functionality of members in a group is also dynamic and the group can dynamically prioritise requests for join. We tested the behavior of groups under different application scenario by implementing our framework in overlay simulator peersim integrated with Prolog. Our experiments show that dynamic polices based on the adaptive trust and changing group composition lead to better group efficiency as compared to static access control policies.

1 Introduction

Web based collaborative groups are becoming increasingly popular as peers with common interests form a network among themselves and automatically tend to create interest groups among each other, called communities. Such communities or groups need a communication model in which in which all the peers must collaborate in order to provide the basic services such as content or messages and normally assumes that all peers have equivalent capabilities. However the dynamic nature of peers and the changing topology of the network motivates the need to provide an environment for different functional roles of peers under the same overlay network. One motivating example is the Free and Open Source Software self-organizing P2P group F/OSS [24], which represents an approach

---

* Asst Professor in Ramrao Adik Institute of Technology.
** Professor in Indian Institute of Technology.

N. Meghanathan et al. (Eds.): CNSA 2010, CCIS 89, pp. 374–394, 2010.
© Springer-Verlag Berlin Heidelberg 2010

for communities of like-minded participants to create, distribute, acquire and use software and software-based services that are intended to be shared freely, rather than offered as closed commercial products. Participants within these communities often have different roles like core developer, module owner, code contributor, code repository administrator, reviewer or end-user. They contribute software content like programs, artifacts, and code reviews to Web sites within each community, and communicate information about their content updates via online discussion forums, threaded email messages, and newsgroup postings. F/OSS systems co-evolve with their development communities [21].

Consider an example of a developer's community for some critical security related open-source software. Depending on the sensitivity level of the code being developed, there could be hierarchial levels for the members of this forum. New members and existing members could be periodically rated or evaluated by existing members based upon the quality of their contribution. A member receiving a high rating value could be elevated to a higher level in the forum. A code developer could be updated to a reviewer if he has submitted a certain percentage of good code. The efficiency of the group may depend on the number of peers currently contributing to the development of code and reviewing of the code.

One possible approach to handle the dynamic and unreliable behavior of peers in such dynamic groups is to provide self organizing peer services or roles. These roles would differ in the context of a peer group. Peers could be allowed to dynamically make decisions based on specific conditions and assume additional functionality to ensure that the group reaches a certain satisfaction level. These type of decentralized and dynamic peer groups require a secure group admission policy and an adaptive access control mechanism where peers can collaboratively frame and revise access control decisions, based on behaviorial attributes, current group composition as well as trust evolved in the group. The changes must however be within the groups' constitution charter, so that loosening of access control is not permitted to such an extent that the group performance degrades. Further malicious peers should not be allowed to change the group's policies.

We propose a decentralized and integrated framework for authentication, admission control and access control in peer groups. The access control mechanism is dynamic, and allows peers to collaboratively modify policies and add new polices within the framework of the original group charter. Our framework allows us to test the evolution of peer groups based on different policies. Our trust metric is a tunable metric based on context specific attributes. There is a growth curve associated with every peer in the group which is affected by the environment and also depends on a peer's maximum intrinsic capability.

2   System Model

In our model peers with a common interest and unique ID join together to form a group. The peers in a group are governed under a set of rules that describe minimal conditions to be part of the group and they can be categorized as resource nodes and user nodes. Resource nodes provide services utilizing their resources such as shared files, memory and processors for users. The roles of resources and users are dynamic as a node can either be a resource or a node or both simultaneously. The following assumptions have been made in our model.

- Peers have an initial self proclaimed rating which is the initial trust value
- Peers are assigned different roles based on their functionality.
- Peers in a group can belong to different levels based on capability. A role of a peer is independent of the level which the peer is in.
- Peers are individually capable of performing tasks of authentication, voting, access control, key management etc.
- Peers can compute their own public-private key pair and provide self signed certificates, binding their identity with their public key.

2.1   Peer Behavior and Roles

A peer can either be a service provider or a rater. Quality of a peer as a service provider is independent of the quality of the peer as a rater. The additional functions that a peer is capable of performing in a group are storing and verifying certificates, authentication, voting, updating of levels, key management etc. The extent to which a peer performs these tasks is decided by the role the peer wants to play in the group. In our model [8], a peer can take on 3 different roles.

- *Member peer (MP)* A peer in this role is a minimal functionality peer who participates in the normal group activities but does not contribute to the admission of new peers, nor updating of levels of existing peers. Thus this peer is only a service provider.
- *Admission Peers (AP)* These are the peers which are allowed to register new group members.
- *Control peer (CP)* The control peers are the super nodes of the framework. Every group must have at least one control peer. These peers are responsible for broadcasting essential messages like
  1. Joining of a new peer
  2. Policy change(if it happens)
  3. Updated ratings of peers.
  Thus a peer in this role would have all the functional components and would participate in periodically updating levels of existing peers and also permitting change of role. These peers are also responsible for monitoring group activity and keeping a track of group performance index GPI. If GPI falls below a certain threshold then a CP can call for a consensus of AP's or MP's to decide on a policy change. Framing of new policies like adding a new level to the group can also be done by a CP.

Each peer (MP, AP or CP) has its own self proclaimed rating SPR and collects trust ratings from other peers in the group with whom it has Direct Interactions. The ratings are signed with the private key of the recommending peer. Final trust value of a peer is computed by a CP when a peer requests for updating of level.

2.2 Change of Roles

At any time a member peer may want to take up the role of an Admission Peer or control peer. Since the model focusses on the self-organizing and collaborative nature of peers, in order to achieve group efficiency, any peer which is part of the group may apply for a role change or level change. As peers belonging to CP or AP perform more operations, nodes with sufficient bandwidth or computing power may apply. Similarly if a CP decides to change its role to MP for some reason, such a peer would lose group membership unless it can transfer control to some other peer. If a peer is a single CP then it cannot be allowed to change its role. Thus change of role is also part of the global group policy.

3 Detailed Working of the Framework

The group has an initial admission control policy [1, 2] based on a dynamic threshold i.e t-out-of-n where t(no of peers collaborating) grows or shrinks in tandem with n(current group size). The admission policy can be changed collaboratively by peers and this change is enforced using voting. Peers wishing to join the group declare an initial self-proclaimed rating and request for some task allocation. Based on the join access policy he may be allowed to join at a lower level and would be allotted some role based on his self-proclaimed intrinsic capability. There can be different levels within a group and peers at each level can have different functionalities. Peers in one level can dynamically elevate their levels in a group. Peers can collaboratively modify policies at their level based on current group composition and trust level of existing peers. Thus low level join requests can be postponed in a group which has a certain threshold of peers already at the same level, by changing the join policy dynamically.

Once in the group peers are periodically rated by others based on our trust algorithm which combines Direct and Indirect trust along with context specific attributes, peer credibility and incentives for rating. Each peer may store his updated ratings in his local rating history table. Expert peers would store the ratings of all peers in their level, and would also update the ratings of peers in their level. Rating certificates are signed by recommending peers and hence cannot be modified. A peer may have some maximum potential or skill set and could rise only upto that potential. Each peer maintains information related to its own private-public key pair, signatures from other peers and the list of peers trusted by him.

Group access is done in stages. Group Discovery and Advertisement, Admission and Authentication, Access Control and Key management.

3.1 Group Discovery and Advertisement

A peer willing to serve as Control peer can create a new group and define an Initial Group Charter. The peer can then advertise and publish his group along with his charter which contains documents that specify the parameters of the group, such as group type, admission policies, group name, group members etc. Subsequent peers can then find this group and join it. The group advertisement should be periodically broadcast by the peers of the group.

3.2 Admission Request

This is the process by which a peer applies to be accepted into a group. During this the peer may receive credentials(keys,passwords,tokens)that it may use later to prove group membership. A new peer wishing to join a group first searches for an advertisement of a group that matches his requirements. He then submits a signed request to any peer which includes his credentials that he obtains from a CA say X.509 certificates or self-generated certificates, along with a request for the role that he wishes to join in. Given that each peer has his own certificate which could be self signed or signed by a CA, a peer credential is created by hashing the concatenation of unique user ID UUID and public key fields and then signing this hash with the private key of the user and using this digital signature as the identity of the peer. This identity is used as the peer's credential in the messages.

$$P_{new} \longrightarrow P_i : \{JoinREQ\}_{SK_{new}}, Cert_{new}$$

where

$$Cert_{new} = UUID_{new}, PK_{new}, RC_{new}, \{H[UUID\|PK_{new}]\}_{SK_{new}}$$

For a new peer his RC_{new} field will contain a single entry which is his self proclaimed rating SPR. The **Notations** used here are:

- P_{new} : New Peer
- P_i : Existing Peer
- SK_i : Private key of i
- PK_i : Public key of i
- $Cert_i$: Certificate of i which contains the ID, Public key, Level/rating, Validity period.
- $\{msg\}_{SK}$: Signed message

A rating certificate is used as a means of recommendation. This certificate contains the original trust value of the peer along with the signed recommended rating value given by each peer. The rating certificate also contains an expiry date to prevent the recommended peer from recycling good rating certificates beyond the specified period. The fields in the rating certificate are Recommending peer's identity, Recommended peer's identity, Original trust value, Issuing date and time, Expiry date and time, Contribution score and Signature of recommending peer.

3.3 Authentication

If the peer receiving this signed request is a member peer, he forwards it to an Admission peer who obtains the identity of the requesting peer from the

Certificate. If it is a signed certificate then the verification is easy. If however the Public Key pair is pseudo generated then the receiving peer will compute the hash of UUID and PK_i and tally this with received message. If the two hashes match then the user is authenticated and is granted access permissions based on the access control policy. If the user's credentials contain a rating field with a single entry he is treated as a fresh user.

We assume that each joining peer stores a local copy of the policy database. When a CP or an AP receives a join-request from a new peer it checks the policy file for the join policy. If all parameters match then the later gives a signed membership token $\{GC_{new}\}$ to the new peer.

$$P_i \longrightarrow P_{new} : \{GC_{new}\}_{G_{key}}$$

Since this is signed with the current group key which is unknown to the peer the later cannot modify it.

3.4   Key Management

After the peer receives the signed Group Membership certificate it is the task of the CP to perform the group rekeying at the necessary level. The new peer is allowed to join and his public key and unique user ID(i.e hash of his user ID and public key) is broadcast to the group. CP invokes the rekeying algorithm(TGDH) [19] and the new group key computed is sent to this peer encrypted with his public key, and to all other peers encrypted with the old group key. Every member keeps a list of keys and the associated set of members that share that key. The list is updated whenever a new key is generated.

The entry of the new peer is broadcast to all peers of the group. The membership token GC_{new} contains details of the access rights granted to the joining peer.

3.5   PDTBAC- Policy Driven Trust Based Access Control for P2P Applications

Authorization in a distributed environment should be determined as a result of evaluating the request of an authenticated user against various policies like privacy policy, trust policy, authorization policy and so on. In the context of dynamic self-organizing collaborative groups we define policy as a set of rules/ requirements associated with a group/peer/service/resource or domain. Trust is not a fixed value and can change dynamically depending on the behavior of the peer and the context in the environment. Our hybrid access control model is based on an integration of role based, policy based and trust based access control [3, 4].

Our model focusses on the genetic evolvement of groups based on group composition. We deploy access control policies flexibly and dynamically based on the behavior and trust level of peers in the group and the current group composition. Peers can collaboratively modify policies governing their level. The group policy can also dynamically prioritize requests for join. Join priorities depend on current group composition. Thus low level requests for join are postponed in a group which already has a large number of members performing the lower roles. Peers in one level are also allowed to be dynamically updated to a higher level. Update policy also depends on current group composition and behavior. A peer can also be collaboratively ejected from a higher level to a lower level or even out of the group if his behavior in the group degrades. It is also possible for peers in the highest level to introduce a new level in the group if the situation so demands. We define two levels of policies viz: Global Policies and Domain Specific Meta Policies.

Global policy

The Global policy forms part of the global group charter and contains rules specifying the number of levels in the group, bare minimum conditions to be allocated a particular role, rules for enabling a member to join or update his level in the group, rules for a member to change his role and so on. It also includes rules for group creation, admission of new peers, updating and leave of peers, discarding of malicious peers as well as rules for deciding the no of control peers needed to collaborate to frame new rules, or change existing rules. Some sample rules are:

- A peer can join as a member peer at level 1 of the group if his SPR is greater than some threshold and there is at least one control peer at that level.
- To join as admission peer or control peer at level 2 or 3, peer must have an accumulated trust rating greater than some threshold.
- To update level a peer must have an accumulated trust value $> x$ and should be an authenticated member at the lower level.
- A new level could be introduced if at least y no. of peers are present in the current highest level and all 100 % of them collaborate.
- For a new policy to be framed at least 75% of existing peers with trust value $>$ some threshold x must collaborate. This ensures that malicious peers cannot frame new policies.

Domain specific policy

This set of policies inherits the properties of the global policy and contains application specific policies. Say for example if we had a group for some multi-project software ecosystem and publish/subscribe etc, where peers could join as developers, reviewers, or moderators depending on their capability level. Further depending upon additional functionality each peer wishes to perform in the group a peer has different roles. A peer is allowed to elevate his level in the group based on some policy. Domain specific policies decide the optimum number of actors required at each level. Maybe some policy could prune down no of peers in a particular level/role to optimise group performance. Another domain specific policy could be the framing of adaptive trust policies, i.e the group works with trust framework TF_1 until it reaches a particular state and then adapts TF_2 and so on.

To address privacy issues the domain plays an important role. Domain or context specific policies refer to the set of rules/regulations/requirements of a domain to which an entity must conform to in order to be in that domain. To implement privacy based access, a variable can be attached to the information to indicate the privacy level of information. So if full privacy is chosen then the information will be sent with encryption and signature. Domain specific policies are part of a dynamic policy database and could be modified by peers, depending on peer behavior, group composition and evolving trust of peers in the group. Thus we have a policy based framework which interacts with the evolving trust parameters of peers in the group. Figure 1 depicts the interaction between global policies, application specific meta policies and the trust engine for peers having multiple roles in multiple levels.

Group Decisions for survival and evolution. Group decides on the type of group composition needed for efficiency i.e the % of MP,CP or AP. Based on this decision the join/leave policy of the group changes dynamically. So say if the current join policy permits peers with SPR 40,60 and 80 to join as MP, AP and CP respectively and if after a certain duration, the number of member peers exceeds 50% of the group size, making it difficult for the existing CPs to handle the group, thereby reducing GPI, then the group policy for join could change, postponing further low level join requests.

Peer Quality. A peer when he joins the group has an initial self proclaimed rating SPR, which is his initial trust value. As the peer performs in the group, this trust value changes based on the quality of service he provides and feedback

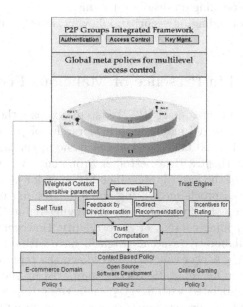

Fig. 1. Policy based framework

given by other peers. A peer can have some maximum intrinsic potential MIP beyond which his trust value cannot rise.

Multiple policy optimization focuses on optimizing the behavior of a peer so that it reaches its MIP. Groups in which every good peer reaches its MIP fast eventually survive.

As a rater, peer quality can be Good, Bad or Honest. A Good(Bad) peer sends absolutely correct(wrong) ratings each time based on truth. This is actually very difficult without a global view of the system, but we model it for studying extreme case of peer quality.

As a service provider Peers can be Good, Average, or O.K. We model good peers as expert peers who always provide excellent service. In the case of Average peers and OK peers the service quality gradually deteriorates.

Task Allocation Policies. The group has different tasks or modules at different difficulty levels. These tasks could be totally independent, sequential or concurrent or there could be some dependency among concurrent tasks. Say a peer could be allocated job C provided he has earlier met some pre-requisites. Task scheduling is done amongst peers based on peer capability, difficulty level of tasks and completion requirements. Consider a scenario where there are m peers with available resources needed by x peers for job completion. Each time k resources are generated by the system and each resource node can process only one job per time. If k $\geq$ m then different job allocation policies could be

- Allocate jobs to resources depending on their trust values/roles without considering the complexity of jobs.
- Allocate jobs depending on the complexity level.
- Allocate jobs depending on deadline to finish.
- Allocate jobs depending on security policy, i.e whether it needs encryption or not.

4   Trust Model in Presence of Malicious Peers

Anonymous nature of peer-to-peer (P2P) systems exposes them to malicious activity. We propose a layered model with a hierarchy of privileges, so peers are encouraged to exhibit good behavior and reach the upper layers of the community, which provides them with a better environment. A new peer joining our group starts at one of the lower layers since his behavior is not yet determined. He has an intrinsic self-proclaimed rating and a maximum capacity based on his potentials. Moving up the layers requires improving reputation score, which is done mainly by providing content of good quality. However this is application specific. Peers in collaborative systems might behave with different trust degrees in different situations. A peer can be moved down the reputation layers, resulting from a decrease in his reputation score computed by the group. Thus there is a growth curve associated with every peer in the group which is affected by the environment and also depends on a peer's maximum intrinsic capability.

4.1   Context Sensitive Layered Reputation Model

We assume some basic principles in our Trust Model.

- A peer's trustworthiness value depends on good behavior and enhances slowly, but drops rapidly in case he exhibits bad behavior.
- If the trust value of a peer falls below a certain threshold value then he is either removed from the group or his level is demoted.
- Calculation of trust value includes a peer's direct experiences as well as recommendations from other peers

The Basic trust metrics in our model are:

1. **Feedback Rating.** Reputation based systems rely upon feedback to evaluate a peer's trustworthiness. For e.g in ebay, buyers and sellers rate each other after every transaction. We include some attributes in this feedback and associate weights with these attributes. So for e.g in a F/OSS application, the attributes associated are various aspects of the S/W quality such as Lines of Code LOC, No of Bugs, Price, Delivery Time, etc. Let $a_i = a_1, a_2, a_3, \ldots\ldots a_n$ be the set of attributes. Let $f_E(x, y)$ denote an evaluation given by peer x for peer y at a transaction.
   Then
   $$f_E(x, y) = (f_{a1}(x, y), f_{a2}(x, y), f_{a3}(x, y), \ldots f_n(x, y))$$

   where $f_{ai}(x, y)\epsilon[0, 1]$ is the feedback score given by peer x about peer y for attribute ai. Relative importance assigned to each attribute can be modeled as weight w_{ai} such that $\sum w_{ai} = 1$. Peer y evaluates peer x against attributes ai and the rating thus computed is multiplied by w_{ai} which is the weight associated with attribute ai.

2. **Reputation.** This is a metric measuring overall quality of previous transactions between peer x and y. Here it is a value between 1 and 10 and is calculated from feedback ratings recorded by the peer. Assume that peer x stores upto n feedback ratings of previous transactions with peer y. Then reputation of peer y is calculated by peer x as

   $$R(x, y) = \frac{\sum_{i=1}^{n} \alpha^i . f_{Ei}(x, y)}{\sum_{i=1}^{n} \alpha^i} \tag{1}$$

   where $f_{Ei}(x, y)$ denotes the ith feedback given by peer y to x and $\alpha\epsilon[0, 1]$ is a decay factor which indicates how important the most recent interaction is to the user. Each user may set a different value of α for itself. The decay factor is important because trustworthiness is not always the same and may change with time.

3. **Indirect Reputation.** If a peer does not have sufficient number of transactions with a resource it can ask the opinion of other nodes to gain an overall evaluation T_{ID}. Assume that each user x receives job ratings for peer y from n references $k = (1, 2, \ldots n)$ and all nodes use the same decay factor α.

Then user x can compute the reputation $f_E(k_i, y)$ of each indirect peer k_i to resource y.

$$T_{ID}(x, y) = \frac{\sum_{i=1}^{n} I(x, y).R(k, y).T(k)}{\sum_{i=1}^{n} I(x, y)} \qquad (2)$$

4. **Context Factor.** To add incentives for rating we add the factor

$$\frac{F_x}{Ix, y}$$

where F_x is the total number of feedback ratings given by peer x.

5. **Credibility of evaluating peer.** The evaluator's credibility is important for a peer to decide whether to accept the reputation value or not. If an evaluator has low credibility, his evaluation will be ignored. Thus the effect of malicious peers can be avoided to some extent.

4.2   Design of Trust Model

We calculate a peer's trustworthiness from the direct and indirect reputations and determine the global reputation.

Direct Trust. This is derived from a peer's all Direct transaction experience, their credibility and the number of times the peer has been interacted with them.

$$T(D) = \frac{\sum I(x, y).R(x, y).T(y)}{\sum I(x, y).T(y)} \qquad (3)$$

where R(x,y) is the reputation which can be calculated using equation 1, I(x,y) is the number of times peer x interacted with peer y, T(y) denotes the trust value of peer y.

Global Trust value. Let T be the global trust value of a peer x. Then T is an aggregation of the direct experiences of every peer about peer x as well as the recommendations received about peer x, and the context factor.

$$T = \alpha * T_D(x, y) + \beta * T_{ID}(x, y) + \gamma * Context factor$$

where α is the weight associated with direct experience, β with indirect reputation and γ is a fine tuning constant to control the amount of reputation gained by rating others.

5   Modeling Dynamic Policies Using Prolog

In policy driven TBAC, the policy description language besides being expressive and easy to use must be flexible enough to allow extension of a policy by adding or modifying its constraints easily, without affecting existing policies. We use a logic programming system to realize our access control policies. We capture the policies using Prolog [20] rules. A prolog rule is an expression of the form

`Ro(uo):-R1(u1).......Rn(un)`

where Ri are predicates and ui are (possibly empty) tuples of variables and constants. The head of the rule is $Ro(uo)$ and the sequence of formulae on the R.H.S is the body of the rule.

A policy is a set of Prolog rules. We chose Prolog as our policy description language because it is declarative, supports back tracking and is a unification based language which allows writing policy templates. It is possible to reason from a set of Prolog rules, and Dynamic rules can be modeled using the assert and retract clauses. The Prolog inference engine provides a mechanism to derive consistent access control decisions at runtime.

New facts from independent policy sources can be added to the policy base before decisions are made, ensuring dynamic decisions at runtime. A policy interacts with its dynamic environment by consulting facts in the environment and constraining certain actions in the environment. In order to ensure that totally new policies outside the original group charter cannot be framed dynamically, we maintain a hash value of the original group charter with every peer. Thus a peer can at any time verify whether the policies being applied are as per the constitution framework.

5.1   Modeling Rules for Join

An example of rules for peer with unique identity to join as a admission peer in a group at level1 of a group is

$verify(Request,Rl,Level,Rate,SPR,Expert,Tot):-$
$join(Request),admission(Rl),Level=:=1,\ SPR>40.$

Verify function takes seven parameters as type of request, Role, Level, Overall Rating, Self proclaimed rating (SPR), percentage of expert peers and *Tot* as the total number of peers in the system. If the RHS is true for all given cases then function will return true.

A more stringent join policy which ensures that the percentage of expert peers is greater than 20, for a total group size upto 200 is

$verify(Request,Rl,Level,Rate,SPR,Expert,Tot):-$
$join(Request),\ admission(Rl),Level=:=2,\ SPR>50,\ Expert>20,\ Tot<200.$

5.2   Modeling Rules for Level Update

Similarly rule for update request is:

$verify(Request,Rl,Level,Rate,SPR,Expert,Tot):-$
$update(Request),maximal(Rl),Level=:=2,\ Rate\geq6,\ Expert<20.$

Here a peer is allowed to update his level1 to level2 if he is a maximal peer(or control peer) and his trust value is greater than or equal to 6 with a restriction that percentage of expert peers should not be more than 20 %.

5.3   Modeling Dynamic Rules

Here is an example rule which exhibits dynamism. It modifies the previous rule based on some parameter while simulation is running.

update_engine(Levels, MPs, APs, CPs, Total):- Total > 100,
retract(verify(Request,Rl,Level,Rate,SPR,Expert,Tot):-
join(Request), admission(Rl), Level=:= 1, SPR > 40,
assert(verify(Request,Rl,Level,Rate,SPR,Expert,Tot:-
join(Request), admission(Rl), Level=:= 1, SPR>40, Expert>20, Tot<200 .

The update_engine function can be used to update the new rule by retracting the old rule and then asserting a new rule. update_engine takes 5 inputs as Levels(no of levels), MPs(% of member peers), APs(% of admission peers), CPs(% of control peers) and Total(total number of peers). Above rule states that if total number peers in the system exceeds a threshold of 100 then update the old rule which permitted peer join without any restriction on percentage of expert peers and total number of peers allowed to join.

5.4   Overall Working of Framework with Prolog

Figure 2 shows the interaction between the events and policies in our framework. External events like join, leave, and internal events like level update, or application specific events like submitting a review, or submitting code, in case of F/OSS might trigger some other events, like change in policy. Change in policy in turn affects the way in which events like join, leave, update occur. All events are simulated in peersim simulator [12]. Simulator triggers the policy file which is prolog rules. Database contains all the information about all the peers. Prolog rules use the database and according to the changes in database, prolog rules or policy might change or be modified.

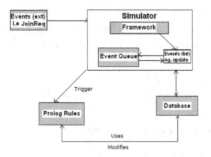

Fig. 2. Overall Framework

6   Application Framework

We simulated a typical F/OSS application with core developers, reviewers, documenter, moderators etc. For simplicity we mapped core developers of code to

Level1, reviewers to Level 2 and moderators to Level 3. Peers join the group either as Developers, Reviewers or Moderators and assume roles of Member peers, Admission Peers or Control peers depending on their functional capability. A peer in Developer Level for e.g can be updated to reviewer based on his performance and reputation earned in the group. At level 1 member peers develop code, while control peers do additional administrative tasks. The group permits peers to collaboratively work on different projects, and efficiency of the group is based on completion time, quality and price of the different projects.

6.1 Peer Behavior

For simplicity we assume that the Member peers behave as OK peers, Admission peers behave as average peers and Control peers behave as expert peers while providing services as well as while rating other peers. Further we assume that OK peers develop code with a certain higher percentage of bugs, at a slower rate as compared to Average and Expert peers. Similarly while rating, the Expert peers give more accurate ratings as compared to OK and Average peers.

The mapping between roles, levels and the entities of F/OSS model is shown in the figure 3.

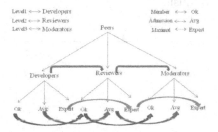

Fig. 3. Mapping of Roles and Levels

7   Implementation Details

We modeled the P2P groups using a java based overlay simulator namely Peer-Sim [12] which is a Peer-to-Peer simulator. We chose Interprolog as our bridge between Java and Prolog as it directly loads the prolog file from java. The global and domain specific policies were implemented using SWI-Prolog which we integrated with Peersim at runtime wherein java and prolog talk to each other by means of sockets.

The simulator starts with some initial peers in the group, and then events such as join, leave, update are triggered. The events have been triggered in the event mode of peersim. At the start of the simulation we define a project which requires some certain number of modules each having its own start time, difficulty level assigned and the expected time to finish that module. A module consists of parameters like Starting time, Current time, Time of completion,

Bugs, and Difficulty Level. According to the availability of peers and modules, peers are assigned modules. A module can have more than one peer working on it at a time. As soon as a module is finished, those peers will be allocated some other modules to work on. A priority queue is maintained based on the current time of start of a module so as to maintain the concurrency between the modules. Time is calculated on the basis of Poisson distribution where the lambda is the average time needed by a peer. Simulation runs until all modules of the project are completed. During the simulation, new peers can continuously join the group at any level depending on join policy and existing peers can also apply for update of levels. Dynamic leave of peers is also simulated. As a new peer joins he is allotted to a new module or a currently running module based on the allocation policy.

7.1   Simulations and Graphs

Some of the simulations that have been done are as follows:

Simulation1: Here we started with 40 peers in the system and allowed a maximum of 200 peers. Peers declare an initial SPR and are allocated jobs which are project development modules based on simple FCFS job allocation policy. Events such as join and leave occur dynamically as per the policies. Simulation ends when 1000 modules finish.

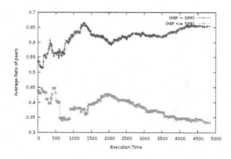

Fig. 4. Average Rating for oversmart vs honest peers

Analysis. The graph in Fig 4. is a plot of the average trust rating of oversmart versus honest peers. It is observed that for peers who declare an SPR which is much higher than their actual rating, the group eventually finds it out and the average trust value of the peer decreases. Thus for peers who over estimate their potential, the group eventually decreases their average trust value. Under estimation of initial trust value gives better performance than over estimation. The average trust value computed is used in the global policy to eject peers who give a very low performance or provide false ratings.

Simulation2: In this simulation we start with 40 peers in the system and allow a maximum of 300 peers. A total of 1000 modules are allowed to enter the system using a Poisson distribution.

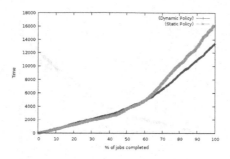

Fig. 5. Job Success with static and dynamic policy

We compare the performance of static versus dynamic policy. In the static join policy we restrict the total no of expert peers to 20 % of the group size. Thus when a peer wishes to join in the role of expert peer, he is permitted to do so only if current group composition has less than 20 % expert peers. In dynamic join policy we do not keep any restrictions till the group size reaches 100. Once the group size reaches 100, the join policy changes dynamically to restrict the expert peers to 20 % of group size and again for group size between 200 to 300 the policy changes to permit 30 % expert peers. This is done to study the effect of varying expert peers on group size.

Analysis. The graph in Fig 5. shows that initially till 50-60% of the job completion the two plots are very similar but after that as expert peers increases the time of completion decreases. Thus dynamic policy gives better results as compared to static.

Simulation3: Here we started with 100 peers in the system and allowed a maximum of 150 peers. The project contains 1000 modules. We defined jobs of different complexities as inputs, namely easy, medium and complex. Jobs enter the system in the ratio (60,20,20) meaning that 600 jobs are of easy complexity, 200 are medium and rest 200 are complex. We assume that most of the peers are truthful and have provided their accurate SPR.

The Job allocation to peers is varied as shown in table 1. In policy Alloc1, Easy jobs are allocated to peers having SPR between 0 to 40, Medium jobs between 40 to 70 and Difficult jobs between 70 and 100.

Table 1. Variation of job allocation

	Easy	Medium	Difficult
Alloc1	0 - 40	40 - 70	70 - 100
Alloc2	0 - 60	60 - 80	80 - 100
Alloc3	0 - 80	80 - 90	90 - 100

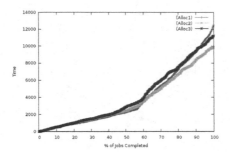

Fig. 6. Job Success with varying Job Allocation

Analysis. The graph in Fig 6. shows that the policy Alloc2 gave the best results as sufficient number of peers were available for easy jobs. Policy Alloc1 gave the worst result because of the less availability of peers for easy jobs. Initially till 50-60% of job completion Alloc1 gave better results because of proper distribution of peers for each job.

Simulation4: Initially we started with 100 peers in the system and then we permitted a maximum of 200 peer joins for this project.

The group choses a join policy which ensures that there are 30% ok peers, 40% average peers and 30% expert peers. The Job composition is varied as shown in table 2.

Table 2. Variation in job composition

	Easy	Medium	Difficult
Compos1	20	20	60
Compos2	40	20	40
Compos3	60	20	20

Analysis. Here we have taken composition of peer roles as (30, 40, 30), so there are equal number of OK and Expert peers in the system. The job compositions are varied in each policy. Thus in Compos 1, jobs arrive in the order of 20% easy jobs, 20 % medium jobs and 60 % difficult jobs. The job allocation policy is such that the difficult jobs are allocated to expert peers and easy jobs are allocated to OK peers. The graph in Fig 7. shows that in Compos2, the project completed very fast. This is because of the proper distribution of jobs and peers. Compos1 gives better results than Compos3 because of the large number of expert peers which decreases the overhead per expert peer. Thus job completion rate improves in a group which has a more stringent role and job allocation policy based on initial SPR of peer.

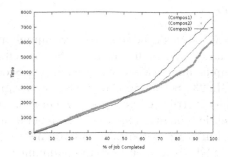

Fig. 7. Job Success with varying Job Compositions

Simulation 5 and 6: In simulation 5 we plotted graphs for static versus dynamic job allocation policies by fixing SPR at 40 and 60 respectively whereas in simulation 6 we kept both join policies as well as job policies dynamic. Graphs in Fig 8. and Fig 9. show that in both cases dynamic policy gives better result than static.

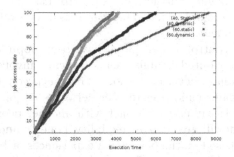

Fig. 8. Job Success with varying Job Compositions and SPR

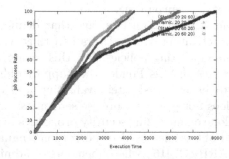

Fig. 9. Job Success with varying Job Compositions and varying join

8   Related Work

Security in collaborative groups is addressed by group membership, authentication, access control, and group key management. Several efforts have been made towards securing group communication systems, for e.g Secure Spread [22], and Secure group layer SGL [23]. Secure Spread [22] is a secure group communication system that uses a fully distributed group key generation protocol, but it does not provide any authentication or group access control mechanisms and focusses primarily on LAN and interconnected LAN environments.

Secure group layer SGL, is a secure group communication system aimed at WAN environments. It bundles a reliable group communication system, a group authorization and access control mechanism and a group key agreement protocol to provide a comprehensive and practical secure group communication platform. However the access control mechanism is not dynamic or scalable.

Some frameworks are focussed on peer to peer applications. Kim et al [1] [2] proposed an admission control framework which revolves around two basic elements, viz: a group charter which has well defined admission policies and a group authority which is an entity that can certify group admission. However their scheme lacks the attributes of peers and cannot simplify authorization in collaborative environments. Further access control has not been considered, all members have equal access rights, and neither does it integrate admission control with group key agreement.

Role based access control models [3] [4] have been popular in group communication systems. Distributed establishments typically involve peers that do not know each other and have never met before. This has precipitated work on trust and reputation mechanisms in peer-to-peer networks [5] [6]. Trust is a measure of how much a peer is willing to transact with another peer. It can be defined as a peer's belief in attributes such as reliability, honesty and competence of the trusted peer, either based on the peer's own experiences or based on recommendations by other peers. Reputation [7,9,10,11] is one specific way of establishing trust. It defines an expectation about a peer's behavior, based on recommendations received from other peer's or information about the peer's past behavior within a specific context at a given time.

Cassandra [13] is an authorization language that defines the actions of activating a role and deactivating a role. Users can thus write state-dependent and implicitly state manipulating policies, but this rather ad-hoc approach is inflexible. Some languages such as Ponder [14] support obligation policies. An obligation is a task to be executed after evaluating and enforcing an access request. However it does not provide a precise semantics for the state changes. Some work has been done on analyzing security properties in dynamic role-based systems, in the context of the role-based authorization language RT [15] and Administrative RBAC (ARBAC) [16], where members of administrative roles can modify the role membership and privilege assignments. In [18], policies written in Datalog can refer to facts in the authorization state, as in our model. Hezberg et al. propose in [17], a prolog-based trust management language, but do not focus on dynamically changing policies with the state of the environment.

9   Conclusion

We have modeled a dynamic policy driven trust based access control framework for collaborative groups. The model permits peers to regulate their own behavior and collaboratively frame, and modify policies at various levels. Our framework allows us to test the evolution of peer groups based on different policies. Join priorities can also be decided by the group policy and depend upon current group composition. We have proposed a tunable trust model which is based on context sensitive attributes. Thus malicious peers are not permitted to change the group's policies. We have run a few sets of experiments by modeling self-organizing group F/OSS. Experiments show that the dynamic polices permit the group to have a better job success rate than static policies. The group is able to compute the average trust value of a peer and peers providing false ratings or very bad service can be ejected. Collaborative applications like F/oss, multi-player online gaming and others can use this framework to test the evolution of peer groups and decide which policies to use to achieve a better job success rate.

References

1. Kim, Y., Mazzocchi, D., Tsudik, G.: Admission control in peer groups. In: Proceedings of the Second IEEE International Symposium on Network Computing and Applications, April 16-18, p. 131 (2003)
2. Saxena, N., Tsudik, G.: Admission Control in Peer-to- Peer: Design and Performance Evaluation. In: Proceedings of ACM Workshop on Security of Ad Hoc and Sensor Networks, SASN (2003)
3. Rotaru, C.N., Li, N.: A Framework for Role Based Access control in Group Communication Systems. In: IEEE Proceedings of the 17th International Conference on Parallel and Distributed Computing Systems, PDCS (2004)
4. Zhang, Y., Li, X., Huai, J., Liu, Y.: Access control in Peer to Peer collaborative Systems. In: ICDCSW 2005, IEEE-2005 (2005)
5. Tran, H., Hitchens, M., Varadharajan, V., Watters, P.: A trust based access control framework for P2P file sharing systems. In: Proceedings of the 38th Hawaii International Conference on Systems Sciences (2005)
6. Repantis, T., Kalogeraki, V.: Decentralized Trust Management for AdHoc Peer-toPeer Networks. In: MPAC, November 27-December 1. ACM, New York (2006)
7. Kamvar, S.D., Schlosser, M.T., Garcia-Molina, H.: Eigenrep: Reputation management in p2p networks. In: Proc. of 12th International WWW Conference, pp. 640–651 (2003)
8. Chatterjee, M., Sivakumar, G., Bernard, M.: Dynamic Policy Based Model for Trust Based Access Control in P2P Applications. In: IEEE International Conference on Communications 2009, ICC 2009, Dresden, Germany, June 14-18, pp. 1–5 (2009)
9. Xiong, L., Liu, L.: A Reputation-Based Trust Model for Peer-to-Peer eCommerce Communities. In: Proceedings of the Fourth ACM Conference on Electronic Commerce, San Diego, CA, USA, June 09-12, pp. 228–229 (2003)
10. Xiong, L., Liu, L.: PeerTrust: Supporting Reputation-Based Trust for Peer-to-Peer Electronic Communities. IEEE Transactions on Knowledge And Data Engineering 16(7) (July 2004)

11. Lai, K., Feldman, M., et al.: Incentives for Cooperation in Peer-to-Peer Networks. In: Proceedings of the Workshop on Economics of Peer-to-Peer Systems, Berkeley, CA, June 5-6 (2003)
12. PeerSim Simulator Documentation, http://peersim.sourceforge.net/
13. Becker, M.Y., Sewell, P.: Cassandra: Flexible trust management, applied to electronic health records. In: 17th IEEE Computer Security Foundations Workshop (CSFW), pp. 139–154 (2004)
14. Damianou, N., Dulay, N., Lupu, E., Sloman, M.: The Ponder policy specification language. In: International Workshop on Policies for Distributed Systems and Networks, pp. 18–38 (2001)
15. Li, N., Mitchell, J.C., Winsborough, W.H.: Beyond proof-of-compliance: security analysis in trust management. Journal of the ACM 52(3), 474–514 (2005)
16. Sasturkar, A., Yang, P., Stoller, S.D., Ramakrishnan, C.R.: Policy analysis for administrative role based access control. In: Workshop on Computer Security Foundations, pp. 124–138 (2006)
17. Hezberg, A., Mass, Y., Michaeli, J., Ravid, Y., Naor, D.: Access Control Meets Public Key Infrastructure. In: Proc. 2000 IEEE Symposium on Security and Privacy, Oakland, CA, pp. 2–14 (2000)
18. Dougherty, D., Fisler, K., Krishnamurti, S.: Specifying and reasoning about Dynamic Access control Policies. In: Third International Joint Conference on Automated Reasoning, IJCAR 2006, pp. 632–646 (2006)
19. Kim, Y., Perrig, A., Tsudik, G.: Tree-Based Group Key Agreement. ACM Transactions on Information and System Security 7(1), 60–96 (2004)
20. Prolog, http://en.wikipedia.org/wiki/Prolog
21. F/OSS Documentation, http://foss.in
22. Amir, Y., Nita-Rotaru, C., Stanton, J., Tsudik, G.: Secure Spread: An Integrated Architecture for Secure Group Communication. IEEE Transactions on Dependable and Secure Computing 2(3) (July-September 2005)
23. Agarwal, D.A., Chevassut, O., Thompson, M.R., Tsudik, G.: An Integrated Solution for Secure Group Communication in Wide-Area Networks. In: Proceedings of the 6th IEEE Symposium on Computers and Communications, Hammamet, Tunisia, July 3-5, pp. 22–28 (2001)
24. Scacchi, W.: Free/Open Source Software Development Practices in the Computer Game Community, Institute for Software Research. University of California, Technical Report (April 2003)

A Deviation Based Outlier Intrusion Detection System

Vikas Pareek, Aditi Mishra, Arpana Sharma, Rashmi Chauhan, and Shruti Bansal

Apaji Institute Of Mathematics and Applied Computer Technology
Banasthali Vidyapith, India-304022
er_pareekvikas@yahoo.co.in, aditimishra29@gmail.com,
shrutib23@gmail.com, chauhan.rashmiarya@gmail.com

Abstract. With the significant increase in use of networks, network security has become more important and challenging. An intrusion detection system plays a major role in providing security. This paper proposes a model in which Artificial Neural Network and Data Mining approaches are used together. In this model "Self Organizing Map" approach is used for behavior learning and "Outlier Mining" approach is used for detecting an intruder. The scope of the proposed model is for internet. This model improves the capability of detecting intruders: both masqueraders and misfeasors.

Keywords: Intrusion Detection, Artificial Neural Network, Data mining, Internet, Network Security.

1 Introduction

The use and importance of computers along with internet is increasing rapidly in everyone's life. The users can take benefits from the huge amount of information resource retrieval and fast communication in a very convenient manner. With the growth of the Internet and its potential there has been subsequent change in business model of organizations across the world. More and more people are getting connected to the Internet to take advantage of the new business model popularly known as e-Business.

There can be two aspects of business on the Internet. On one aspect, the Internet brings in tremendous potential to business in terms of reaching the users. At the same time it also brings in lot of risk to the business. A significant security problem for networked systems is hostile, or at least unwanted, trespass by users or software. One of the two most publicized threats to security is the intruder (the other is viruses), generally referred to as a hacker or cracker.

1.1 Intruder

Intruder is the person who tries to gain unauthorized access to the network or a host based system. Anderson identified three classes of intruders [1]:

1.1.1 Masqueraders
Masqueraders use authentication of other users to obtain corresponding privileges.

N. Meghanathan et al. (Eds.): CNSA 2010, CCIS 89, pp. 395–401, 2010.

1.1.2 Misfeasors

Misfeasors are legitimate users who have privileged access to the system and abuse it to violate security policies.

1.1.3 Clandestine

Clandestine users access the system with supervisory privileges and operate at a level below a normal audit mechanism, making it very difficult to detect them[1].

1.2 Intrusion

Intrusion is caused by attackers accessing the systems from the Internet, authorized users of the systems who attempt to gain additional privileges for which they are not authorized, and authorized users who misuse the privileges given to them.

1.3 Intrusion Detection

Intrusion detection is the process of monitoring the events occurring in a computer system or network and analyzing them for signs of intrusions, defined as attempts to compromise the confidentiality, integrity, availability, or to bypass the security mechanisms of a computer or network [2].

Thus it is necessary to maintain the security of the data to achieve the three pillars of information security (prevention, detection and response). Intrusion can be detected using the signature and behavior based knowledge of intruder (can be either masquerader or misfeasor) and intended user for a network based intrusion detection system. Artificial learning techniques as well as Data Mining techniques can be used combine to detect the intrusion.

2 IDS Classification

Intrusion Detection System (IDS) is categorized either as network-based or host based. In the former, header fields of the various network protocols are use to detect intrusions. In the later approach (host-based IDS), the focus shifts to the operating system level.

There are two types of approach to detect the intrusion. The first technique is misuse (signature) detection: this technique is similar to pattern matching. Initially the system has been designed on the basis of known attack patterns and the test data is checked for the occurrence of these patterns.

These systems have a high degree of accuracy, very effective at detecting attacks without generating an overwhelming number of false alarms. But they are unable to detect new attacks, Can only detect those attacks they know about—therefore they must be constantly updated with signatures of new attacks.

To overcome the drawback of misuse detection it is required to have the knowledge base system in which regular updates need to be made in order to add new intrusion scenarios. The second technique is *anomaly detection:* this technique works by analyzing the deviation from normal activities and usually at the user level or system level. They function on the assumption that attacks are different from "normal" (legitimate) activity and can therefore be detected by systems that identify these differences. They can detect unusual behavior and thus have the ability to detect symptoms of attacks without specific knowledge of details and can produce information that in turn be used to define signatures for misuse detectors but usually produce a large number of false alarms due to the unpredictable behaviors of users and networks [2].

3 Contemporary Research

Most of the models for IDS have been designed on the basis of k-means or k-monoids clustering technique of data mining but it suffers from various shortcomings like, this algorithm is very sensitive to outliers, and generally terminates at a local optimum. Secondly, it is necessary for K-means algorithm to determine the number K of clusters in advance. Therefore, the quality of the result is not satisfactory. The dependency on clusters effects critically on the clustering results. The models are not continuously learning the behavior thereby leading to the possibility that a new intrusion will not be detected and a false alarm may be generated [3].

The IDS model that we propose has the ability of continuous updation in behavior learning, which guarantees the system administrator that false alarms generated will be low. New intrusion will be detected because continuous updation in behavior learning is being made. We are considering some specific audit data for the confirmation of audit patterns, so it requires only a specific portion of audit records to be reviewed.

For learning the behavior of the system Artificial Neural Network approach "Self Organizing Approach (SOM)" has been used.SOM is a type of neural network that is trained using unsupervised learning. SOM use neighborhood functions which makes it different from other artificial neural networks.

4 Proposed Approach

4.1 Approach

We propose a model for Intrusion Detection, with the help of deviation based outlier and self organizing map approach, using signature and behavior based knowledge of intruder (masquerader & misfeasor) and intended user for a network based intrusion detection system. The Scope of this model is for Internet. When the intrusion detection system is learning the behavior, at the same time the network may experience an attack. In this interval of learning the system is open for attacks. Our system provides security with the help of network packet monitoring, audit logs and signature matching. This will also reduce false alarm rate.

4.2 Model

Deviation Based Outlier Intrusion Detection System is given in fig: 1

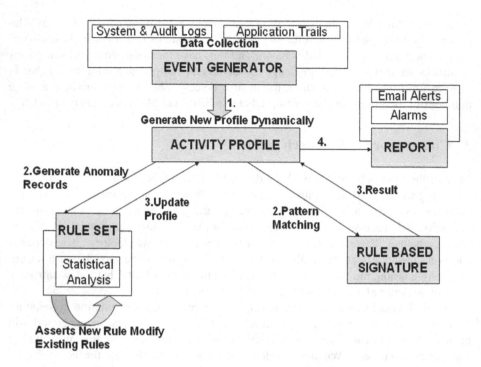

Fig. 1. Deviation Based Outlier Intrusion Detection System

4.2.1 Working of Model

Whenever the user logs into the system, some activities will be performed and there corresponding events will get traced in audit log files. Data will be collected for the event generated from audit log files. As soon as the data is collected the next step is generation of the activity profile of the current user on the basis of certain parameters, which has been selected from audit log files.

Initially some rules are defined on the basis of known attacks, which has been stored in the system repository. Once activity profile has been generated, two threads will be executed simultaneously. On one side, with the help of the existing rule pattern matching will be done which defines whether the behavior is of intruder or of legitimate user. The result will be reported back to activity profile and report will be generated in the form of alarms.

Now it may be possible that the behavior of legitimate user may change or there may be the possibility of new attacks, so it is necessary to update the existing rule set. Thus it requires continuous updation in the existing rule set. Therefore on the other side the second thread will executed which will update the existing rules in the rule based signature.

4.2.2 Description of Model

Event Generator: It is a data collector and the events may include audit records, system logs and application trails.

Activity Profile: It contains the variables that are used to calculate the behavior of the system based on some predefined statistical measure. The variables are associated with certain pattern specifications, which come into, play when filtering the event records.

Rule Based Signature: Involves an attempt to define a set of rules that can be used to decide that a given behaviour is that of an intruder. Rules are developed to detect deviation from previous usage patterns that searches for suspicious behaviour.

Rule Set: The rule set represents inferencing mechanisms, such as a rule-based system. It uses event records, anomaly records, and other data to Control the activity of the other components of the IDS and to update their state.

Report: Intrusions detection must be brought to attention. Reporting means Printed reports, email alerts, audible alerts, graphical displays etc [4].

4.2.3 Flow Diagram of Deviation Based Outlier Intrusion Detection System
Flow diagram of Deviation Based Outlier Intrusion Detection System is shown in figure 2. The system monitors the user's activity and collects audit logs corresponding to each event. When the logs are generated, system can have signature of current user who has just logged into it. This signature is then fed into two units.

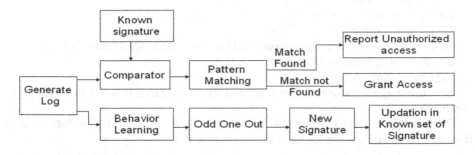

Fig. 2. Flow Diagram of Deviation Based intrusion Detection System

In one of the two units, the current signature and stored known signature (of attacker) will be compared. Here pattern matching will take place. If the patterns are matched that means signature of current user has matched with intruder's signature and report will be generated for unauthorized access.

In the other unit, the system will make use of signatures to learn the behavior of user's current activity. This behavior learning is necessary to have an updated system in order to have false alarm rate. For learning the behavior of the system Artificial Neural Network approach "Self Organizing Approach (SOM)" has been used.

They provide a way of representing multidimensional data in much lower dimensional spaces - usually one or two dimensions. This process, of reducing the dimensionality of vectors, is essentially a data compression technique known as *vector quantization*. SOM operates in two modes: training and mapping. We are using SOM during the behavior learning because it is unsupervised learning. In this we have taken certain parameters from the audit logs, and some weightage has been assigned to each parameter selected. Weightage is applied because on the basis of one or two parameters we cannot decide whether a person is an intruder or a legitimate user. Different parameters are holding different weightage, that is, a value is assigned to each parameter. This map is feed forward map which helps us to know about the future learning because under this each time the dataset will be updated.

In SOM we will be using U matrix. The U matrix value of a particular parameter is the average distance between the parameter and its neighborhood parameters. Euclidian distance is being used to calculate the value of U matrix. Whenever a new data set is being inputted in the network, that is whenever behavior learning is in process, and then the Euclidian distance to all the weight factors is computed. The parameter with weight factor most similar to the input is called Best Matching Unit (BMU). The magnitude of change that is the magnitude of learning new behavior decreases with time. This is so because more and more new cases have been already set as input as a case of learning. Hence change of magnitude decreases with time and with distance from BMU. The formula for updation of data set is given as follows:

$$Wv(t+1) = Wv(t) + \Theta(v, t) \, \alpha(t) \, (D(t) - W \, v(t)) \tag{1}$$

where:

$\alpha(t)$ is monotonically decreasing learning coefficient
A function is said to be monotonically decreasing whenever $x \leq y$ then $f(x) \geq f(y)$.
t is current iteration
α is limit on time iteration
Wv is current weight vector
$\Theta(t)$ is restraint due to distance from BMU usually called neighborhood function
$\alpha(t)$ is learning restraint due to time
D(t) is the input vector
$\Theta(v, t)$ is neighborhood function. It depends on the distance between the BMU and parameter p.

The U matrix is formed with the help of Euclidian distance. Euclidian distance between point's p and q is the length of the line segment pq

$$d(p,q) = \sqrt{(p_1 - q_1)^2 + (p_2 - q_2)^2 + \ldots\ldots\ldots\ldots + (p_n - q_n)^2} \tag{2}$$

Here each parameter has been assigned a weight factor. The size of the neighborhood function decreases with time. This process is repeated for each input vector, for a certain number of cycles in order to decrease the false alarm rate. [8, 9]

Algorithm:
1. Select the parameters.
2. Randomize the parameters with weight factors.
3. Learn the behavior. It can be new from the existing behavior.
4. Calculate the Euclidian distance for each parameter.
5. Track the parameter with the smallest distance. This gives the BMU of the parameter.
6. Update the parameter learning:
7. $Wv(t+1) = Wv(t) + \Theta(v,t) \, \alpha(t) \, (D(t) - W \, v(t))$
8. Increment t and repeat from step 2 while $t < \alpha$

We have make use of Outlier Mining, according to which we have been given a set of 'n' data points or objects and 'k' the expected number of outliers, find the top 'k' objects that are considerably dissimilar , exceptional or inconsistent with respect to the remaining data.

Here, we are using "Deviation Based Approach" for outlier mining. "Deviation Based Approach" identifies outliers by examining the main characteristics of objects in the group. Objects that deviate from this description are considered as outliers. We will sequentially compare the values in a given set. A set S of 'n' objects, a subsequence $\{S_1, S_2 \dots S_m\}$ of these objects is made with $2 \leq m \leq n$ such that S_{j-1} is subset of S_j.

In a given set of values it will return notification if the objects are similar to one another. Set a threshold value, if the difference is above the threshold value then alarm will be generated [4].

5 Conclusion and Future Works

Deviation Based Outlier Intrusion Detection System overcome the drawbacks of Rule based & statistical anomaly based approaches. We have put forward a new approach that contains advantages of Rule based & statistical anomaly based approaches by using self organizing maps and deviation based outlier approach.

The use of two methods for the intrusion detection system can raise the amount of resources of the system, able of finding attacks which may occur for an long period of time, a number of user sessions, or by many attackers working in concert.

Security of network and data is always very important for protecting data and to maintain its privacy. In future we plan to simulate and test this model with real network and information systems. This may confirm the claim made here.

References

[1] Pieprzyk, J., Hardjono, T., Seberry, J.: Fundamentals of Computer Security. Springer International Edition (2003)
[2] Bace, R., Mell, P.: NIST Special Publication on Intrusion Detection Systems (2000)
[3] Cannady, J., Harrell, J.: A Comparative Analysis of Current Intrusion Detection Technologies, Georgia Tech Research Institute,
    http://www.neurosecurity.com/articles/IDS/TISC96.pdf
[4] Hen, J., Kamber, M.: Data Mining- Concepts and Techniques. Morgan Kaufmann, San Francisco (2000)
[5] Seleznyov, A., Puuronen, S.: Anomaly Intrusion Detection Systems- Handling Temporal Relations between Events. University of Jyväskylä, Finland,
    http://www.raid-symposium.org/raid99/PAPERS/Seleznyov.pdf
[6] Jones, A.K., Sielken, R.S.: Computer system intrusion detection: A survey. Technical report, University of Virginia, Computer Science Department (1999)
[7] Stallings, W.: Cryptography and Network Security, 3rd edn. Prentice Hall, Englewood Cliffs (2003)
[8] Anderson, J.P.: Computer Security- Threat Monitoring and Surveillance. Technical Report, J.P. Anderson Company, Fort Washington, Pennsylvania (1980)
[9] Deepa, S.N., Sivanandam, S.N.: Principles of Soft Computing. Wiley, Chichester (2007)

Privacy Preserving Ciphertext Policy Attribute Based Encryption

A. Balu[*] and K. Kuppusamy[**]

Department of Computer Science & Engg.,
Alagappa University, Karaikudi, Tamil Nadu, India
balusuriya@yahoo.co.in, kkdiksamy@yahoo.com

Abstract. Ciphertext policy attribute based encryption (CP-ABE) allows to encrypt data under an access policy. The access policy can be formed with the logical combination of attributes.. Such ciphertexts can be decrypted by anyone with a set of attributes that satisfy the access policy. In CP-ABE, access policy is sent along with the ciphertext. We propose a method in which the access policy need not be sent along with the ciphertext, by which we are able to preserve the privacy of the encryptor. The proposed construction is provably secure under Decision Bilinear Diffe-Hellman assumption.

Keywords: Attribute based encryption, Access policy.

1 Introudction

Recently, much attention has been attracted by a new public key primitive called Attribute-based encryption (ABE). ABE has significant advantage over the traditional PKC primitives as it achieves flexible one-to-many encryption instead of one-to-one. ABE is envisioned as an important tool for addressing the problem of secure and fine-grained data sharing and access control.In an ABE system, a user is identified by a set of attributes. In their seminal paper Sahai and Waters [6] use biometric measurements as attributes in the following way. A secret key based on a set of attributes ω, can decrypt a ciphertext encrypted with a public key based on a set of attributes ω' , only if the sets ω and ω' overlap sufficiently as determined by a threshold value t. A party could encrypt a document to all users who have certain set of attributes drawn from a pre-defined attribute universe. For example, one can encrypt a recruitment related document to all recruitment committee members in the computer science department. In this case the document would be encrypted to the attribute subset { "Faculty", "CS Dept.", "Recruitment Committee"}, and only users with all of these three attributes in the university can hold the corresponding private keys and thus decrypt the document, while others cannot.

There are two variants of ABE: Key-Policy based ABE (KP-ABE)[5] and Ciphertext Policy based ABE(CP-ABE) [1,2,3,4]. In KP-ABE, the ciphertext is associated with a set of attributes and the secret key is associated with the access policy. The

---

[*] Research Associate.
[**] Associate Professor.

N. Meghanathan et al. (Eds.): CNSA 2010, CCIS 89, pp. 402–409, 2010.
© Springer-Verlag Berlin Heidelberg 2010

encryptor defines the set of descriptive attributes necessary to decrypt the ciphertext. The trusted authority who generates user's secret key defines the combination of attributes for which the secret key can be used. In CP-ABE, the idea is reversed: now the ciphertext is associated with the access policy and the encrypting party determines the policy under which the data can be decrypted, while the secret key is associated with a set of attributes.

1.1 Our Contribution

We present a scheme for constructing a Privacy preserving Ciphertext Policy Attribute based Encryption and provide security under the Decisional Diffie-Hellman assumption. In our scheme access policy can be expressed using AND, OR boolean operators, so that it is possible to express the access policy effectively. Each attribute w_i in the access policy can take multiple values. The access policy can be represented by an n-ary tree, the leaf nodes represents the attributes present in the access policy, interior nodes represents the AND, OR operators. Each attribute in the leaf node can take multiple values. The value assigned for the leaf node by the secret sharing method will be distributed to these multiple values. In our scheme, it is not necessary to put all the attributes in the access policy.

1.2 Related Work

Since the introduction of ABE in implementing fine-grained access control systems, a lot of works have been proposed to design flexible ABE schemes. There are two methods to realize the fine-grained access control based on ABE: KP-ABE and CP-ABE. They were both mentioned in [4] by Goyal et al. In KP-ABE, each attribute private key is associated with an access structure that specifies which type of ciphertexts the key is able to decrypt, and ciphertext is labeled with sets of attributes. In a CP-ABE system, a user's key is associated with a set of attributes and an ecrypted ciphertext will specify an access policy over attributes. The first KP-ABE construction [4] realized the monotonic access structures for key policies. Bethencourt et al. [2] proposed the first CP-ABE construction. The construction [2] is only proved secure under the generic group model. To overcome this weakness, Cheung and Newport [3] presented another construction that is proved to be secure under the standard model. To achieve receiver-anonymity , Boneh and Waters [10] proposed a predicate encryption scheme based on the primitive called Hidden Vector Encryption.

The first Anonymous Ciphertext policy Attribute-Based Encryption (ABE) construction was introduced by Nishide et al. [7]. They gave two CP-ABE schemes with partially hidden ciphertext policies in the sense that possible values of each attribute in the system should be known to an encryptor in advance and the encryptor can hide what subset of possible values for each attribute in the ciphertext policy can be used for successful decryption. The policy can be expressed as AND gates on multivalued attributes with wild cards. They describe their constructions in the multi-valued attribute setting where an attribute can take multiple values. The legitimate decryptor cannot obtain the information about the ciphertext policy.The Second construction was proposed by Keita Emura et al. [8] focusing Key anonymity with respect to the authority. In this model, even if an adversary has the master key, the adversary cannot guess what identity is associated with the ciphertext. The access structure used in their scheme is restricted to an AND gate only. Third construction was proposed by Jin li et al.[9] gave accountable, anonymous Ciphertext policy attribute based encryption. This is achieved by binding users identity in the attribute private key. They gave two constructions, one with short public parameters and the other with short ciphertext. They use two different generators to prevent the public verifiability of the ciphertext validity, which achieves hidden policy. In this method also the access structure can be specified as AND gate of multi valued attributes.

2 Preliminaries

2.1 Bilinear Maps

Let G and G_1 be two multiplicative cyclic groups of prime order p. Let g be a generator of G and e be a bilinear map, e : G x G $\rightarrow$ G_1. The bilinear map e has the following properties:

1. Bilinearity : for all $u, v \in$ G and $a, b \in Z_p$, we have
$$e(u^a, v^b) = e(u,v)^{ab}$$
2. Non-degeneracy : $e(g,g) \neq 1$.

We say that G is a bilinear group if the group operation in G and bilinear map e : G x G $\rightarrow$ G_1 are both efficiently computable. Notice that the map e is symmetric since $e(g^a, g^b) = e(g,g)^{ab} = e(g^b, g^a)$.

Decisional Bilinear Diffie-Hellman Assumption

A challenger chooses a group G of prime order p according to the security parameter. Let $a,b,c \in Z_p$ be chosen at random and g be a generator G. The adversary when given (g, g^a, g^b, g^c) must distinguish a valid tuple $e(g,g)^{abc} \in G_1$ from a random element R in G_1.

An algorithm $\mathscr{A}$ that outputs {0,1} has advantage ϵ in solving decisional BDH if G_0 if
$$\left| \Pr[\mathscr{A}(g, g^a, g^b, g^c, D=e(g,g)^{abc}) = 0] - \Pr[\mathscr{A}(g, g^a, g^b, g^c, D=R) = 0] \right| \geq \epsilon$$

Definition 1. The DBDH assumption holds if no polytime algorithm has a non-negligible advantage in solving the decisional BDH problem.

2.2 Access Structure

To achieve anonymity, it is desirable that the adversary A does not know which ciphertexts are related to which attributes. However, a ciphertext has to be decrypted by any decryptor without knowing an access structure. Therefore, in the above situation, a decryptor also cannot determine which secret keys are used for decryption. To solve this problem, we use access structure constructed by AND, OR gates on multi-valued attributes.

Definition 2. Let $U = \{ a_1, a_2, .., a_n \}$ be a set of attributes. For $a_i \; \varepsilon \; U$, $S_i = \{ v_{i,1}, v_{i,2}, ..., v_{i,n_i} \}$ is a set of possible values, where n_i is the number of possible values for a_i. Let $L = [L_1, L_2, .., L_n]$ $L_i \; \varepsilon \; S_i$ be an attribute list for a user, and $W = [W_1, W_2, .., W_n]$ $W_i \; \varepsilon \; S_i$ be an access structure. The notation $L \models W$ express that an attribute list L satisfies an access structure W, namely $L_i = W_i$ (i=1,2..,n). The notation $L \not\models W$ implies L not satisfying the access structure W.

2.3 Ciphertext Policy Attribute Based Encryption

A cipher text policy attribute based encryption scheme consists of four fundamental algorithms: Setup, Key Generation, Encryption and Decryption.

Setup: The setup algorithm takes no input other than the implicit security parameter. It outputs the public parameters PK and a master key MK.

Key Generation (MK,S): The key generation algorithm takes as input the master key MK and a set of attributes S that describe the key. It outputs a private key SK.

Encrypt (PK,A, M): The encryption algorithm takes as input the public parameters PK, a message M, and an access structure A over the universe of attributes. The algorithm will encrypt M and produce a ciphertext CT such that only a user that possesses a set of attributes that satisfies the access structure will be able to decrypt the message. Assume that the ciphertext implicitly contains A.

Decrypt(PK,CT,SK): The decryption algorithm takes as input the public parameters PK, a ciphertext CT, which contains an access policy A, and a private key SK, which is a private key for a set S of attributes. If the set S of attributes satisfies the access structure A then the algorithm will decrypt the ciphertext and return a message M.

2.4 Security Model for CP-ABE

Init. The adversary sends the two different challenge access structures W_0^* and W_1^* to the challenger.

Setup. The challenger runs the Setup algorithm and gives the public parameters, PK to the adversary.

Phase 1. The adversary sends an attribute list L to the challenger for a Key Gen query, where $(L \not\models W_0^*$ and $L \not\models W_1^*$) or $(L \models W_0^*$ and $L \models W_1^*$) The challenger answers with a secret key for these attributes.

Challenge. The adversary submits two equal length messages M_0 and M_1.

Note that if the adversary has obtained SK_L where $(L \models W_0^*$ and $L \models W_1^*$) then $M_0 = M_1$. The challenger chooses b randomly from $\{0,1\}$ and runs Encrypt(PK, M_b, W_b^*). The challenger gives the ciphertext CT* to the adversary.

Phase 2. Same as Phase 1.

Guess. The adversary outputs a guess b' of b.

The advantage of an adversary A in this game is defined as $\Pr[b'=b] - \frac{1}{2}$.

Definition 3. A ciphertext-policy attribute based encryption scheme is secure if all polynomial time adversaries have at most a negligible advantage in the above game.

3 Construction

Proposed solution consists of 4 phases, Setup Phase, Key Generation Phase, Encryption Phase and Decryption Phase.

Set Up:
The setup algorithm chooses a group G of prime order p and a generator g .

Step 1:   A trusted authority generates a tuple $G=[p,G,G_1,g \ \varepsilon \ G,e] \leftarrow Gen(1^k)$.

Step 2:   For each attribute a_i where $1 \le i \le n$, the authority   generates random value $\{a_{i,t} \ \varepsilon \ Z_p^*\} \ 1 \le t \le n_i$ and computes $\{T_{i,t} = g^{a_{i,t}}\} \ 1 \le t \le n_i$

Step 3: Compute $Y = e(g,g)^\alpha$ where $\alpha \ \varepsilon \ Zp^*$

Step 4: The public key PK consists of $[Y,p,G,G_1,e,\{\{T_{i,t}\} \ 1 \le t \le n_i\} 1 \le i \le n]$

The master key Mk is $[\alpha, \{\{a_{i,t} \ \varepsilon \ Z_p^*\} \ 1 \le t \le n_i\} \ 1 \le i \le n]$

Key Generation (MK,L): The Key Generation algorithm takes master key MK and the   attribute   list   of   the   user   as   input   and   do   the   following   Let $L=[L_1,L_2,...,L_n]=\{v_{1,t1},v_{2,t2},...,v_{n,tn}\}$ be the attribute list for the user who obtain the corresponding secret key.

Step1:   The trusted authority picks up random values $\lambda_i \ \varepsilon \ Z_p^*$ for $1 \le i \le n$ & $r \ \varepsilon$ Z_p^* and computes $D_0 = g^{\alpha - r}$.

Step2: For $1 \le i \le n$ the authority also computes $D_{i,1}$, $D_{i,2} = [g^{r+\lambda i \ a_{i,t}}, g^{\lambda i}]$ where L_i = $v_{i,ti}$. The secret key is $[D_0 \ D_{i,1} , D_{i,2}]$.

Encrypt(PK,M,W): An encryptor encrypts a message $M \in G_1$ under a cipher text policy $W=[w_1,w_2,..,w_n]$ and proceed as follows.

Step1 : Select $s \ \varepsilon \ Z_p^*$ and compute $C_0=g^s$ and $C^\sim = M. Y^s = M.e(g,g)^{\alpha s}$

Step2: Set the root node of W to be s, mark all child nodes as un-assigned , and mark the root node assigned.

Recursively, for each un-assigned non leaf node , do the following

a)   If the symbol is $\wedge$ and its child nodes are unassigned , we assign a random value s_i, $1 \le s_i \le p-1$ and to the last child node assign the value

$$s_t = s - \sum_{i=1}^{t-1} s_i \bmod p .$$ Mark this node assigned.

b)   If the symbol is $\vee$, set the values of each node to be s. Mark this node assigned.

c) Each leaf attribute a_i can take any possible multi values, the value of the share s_i is distributed to those values and compute $[C_{i,t,1}, C_{i,t,2}] = [\, g^{s_i}, \quad T_{i,t}^{\,s_i}\,]$. The cipher text CT is

$[C^{\tilde{}}, C_0, \{\{\ C_{i,t,1}, C_{i,t,2}\ \} \ 1 \le t \le n_i \} \ 1 \le i \le n\ \}]$.

Decryption(CT,SK$_L$):
The recipient tries to decrypt CT, without knowing the access policy W by using his SK_L associated with the attribute list L as follows

$$M = \frac{C^{\tilde{}} \prod_{i=1}^{n} e(C_{i,t,2}, D_{i,2})}{e(C_0, D_0) \prod_{i=1}^{n} e(C_{i,t,1}, D_{i,1})}$$

4 Security Analysis

Theorem. The anonymous CP-ABE construction is secure under the DBDH assumption.

Proof
We assume that the adversary $\mathcal{A}$ has non-negligible advantage ϵ to break the privacy of our scheme.

Then we can construct an algorithm $\mathcal{B}$ that breaks that DBDH assumption with the probability ϵ

Let (g, g^a, g^b, g^c, Z) be a DBDH instance.

Init. The adversary $\mathcal{A}$ gives $\mathcal{B}$ the challenge access structure W_0^* and W_1^*. $\mathcal{B}$ chooses b randomly from the set $\{\ 0,1\}$.

Setup. To provide a public key PK to $\mathcal{A}$, $\mathcal{B}$ sets $Y = e(g,g)^{ab}$, implies $\alpha = ab$.
Choose $a'_{i,j} \in_R Z_p^*$ ($i\epsilon [1,n], j\epsilon [1,n_i]$) and computes $T_{i,j} = g^{a'_{i,j}}$

The simulator, $\mathcal{B}$ sends the public parameters $(e,g, Y, \{\{\ T_{i,j}\ \} \ 1 \le j \le n_i \} \ 1 \le i \le n$ to $\mathcal{A}$.

Phase 1. A submits an attribute list $L = [L_1, L_2, ..., L_n]$ in a secret key query. We consider only the case where $(L \nVdash W_0^*$ and $L \nVdash W_1^*$).

For KeyGen query L, $\mathcal{B}$ choose $\beta_i \epsilon\ Z_p^*$ and set $r = -\beta_i a'_{i,j} - \alpha'$ and computes the secret keys as follows

$$D_0 = g^{\alpha+\beta_i a'_{i,j}+\alpha'}$$

$$= g^{(\alpha+\alpha')+\beta_i a'_{i,j}}$$

$$= g^{\gamma+\beta_i a'_{i,j}} \quad \text{where } \gamma = \alpha + \alpha'$$

$$D_{k,1} = g^{r+\lambda_i a_{i,t}}$$

$$= g^{-\beta_i a'_{i,j}-\alpha'+\lambda_i a_{i,t}}$$

$$= g^{-\alpha'}$$

$$D_{k,2} = g^{\lambda_i} = g^{\beta_i}$$

Challenge. A submits two messages $M_0, M_1 \in G_1$ if $M_0 = M_1$, B simply aborts and takes a random guess . The simulator flips a fair binary coin b, and returns the encryption of m_b. The encryption of m_b can be done as follows:

$$C_0 = g^c \quad , C^\sim = M_b \, e(g,g)^{ac} = M_b \, Z.$$

B generates, for w_b, the ciphertext components $\{\{ \ C_{i,t,1} \ , C_{i,t,2} \ \} \ 1 \le t \le n_i \ \} \ 1 \le i \le n$ as follows

Set the root node of W to be c, mark all child nodes as un-assigned and mark the root node assigned.

Recursively, for each un-assigned non leaf node , do the following

a) If the symbol is $\wedge$ and its child nodes are unassigned, we assign a random value hi $1 \le h_i \le p\text{-}1$ and to the last child node assign the value

$$h_t = \frac{c}{\sum_{i=1}^{t-1} h_i}. \text{ Mark this node assigned.}$$

b) If the symbol is $\vee$, set the values of each node to be c. Mark this node assigned.

Each leaf attribute w_i can take any possible multi values, the value of the share s_i is distributed to those values and compute

$$[C_{i,t,1} \ , C_{i,t,2} \ ] = [\ g^{h_i}, \quad T_{i,j}^{h_i} \ ].$$

Phase 2. Same as Phase 1.

Guess. From the above considerations, the adversary can decide that $Z = e(g,g)^{abc}$, when b = b' and can decide that $Z \in_R G_1$ otherwise. Therefore A breaks the DBDH problem with the probability $\in$.

5   Conclusion

We proposed an Attribute based encryption which preserves the privacy of the access policy, specified by the encryptor. This scheme is very expressive and provably secure under the decisional Bilinear Diffie-Hellman assumption.

Acknowledgment

This work was supported by National Technical Research Organization (NTRO), New Delhi, India.

References

1. Waters, B.: Ciphertext policy attribute based encryption: An expressive, efficient, and provably secure realization. In: Cryptology ePrint report 2008/290 (2008)
2. Bethencourt, J., Sahai, A., Waters, B.: Ciphertext policy attribute based encryption. In: IEEE Symposium on Security and Privacy, pp. 321–334 (2007)
3. Cheung, L., Newport, C.: Provably secure Ciphertext police ABE. In: CCS 2007: Proceedings of the 14th ACM Conference on Computer and Communications Security, pp. 456–465. ACM Press, New York (2007)
4. Goyal, V., Jain, A., Pandey, O., Sahai, A.: Bounded Ciphertext policy attribute based encryption. In: Aceto, L., Damgård, I., Goldberg, L.A., Halldórsson, M.M., Ingólfsdóttir, A., Walukiewicz, I. (eds.) ICALP 2008, Part II. LNCS, vol. 5126, pp. 579–591. Springer, Heidelberg (2008)
5. Goyal, V., Pandey, O., Sahai, A., Waters, B.: Attribute –based encryption for fine grained access control of encrypted data. In: ACM Conference on Computer and Communication Security, pp. 89–98 (2006)
6. Sahai, A., Waters, B.: Fuzzy Identity-based encryption. In: Cramer, R. (ed.) EUROCRYPT 2005. LNCS, vol. 3494, pp. 457–473. Springer, Heidelberg (2005)
7. Nishide, T., Yoneyama, K., Ohta, K.: ABE with partially hidden encryptor-specified access structure. In: Bellovin, S.M., Gennaro, R., Keromytis, A.D., Yung, M. (eds.) ACNS 2008. LNCS, vol. 5037, pp. 111–129. Springer, Heidelberg (2008)
8. Emura, K., Miyaji, A., Omote, K.: A ciphertext policy Attribute –Based Encryption scheme with strong Recipient Anonymity. In: The 4th International Workshop on Security (IWSEC), pp. 49–63 (2009)
9. Li, J., Ren, K., Zhu, B., Wan, Z.: Privacy aware Attribute based Encryption with user Accountability, http://eprint.iacr.org/2009/284
10. Boneh, D., Waters, B.: Conjunctive, Subset, and Range Queries on Encrypted Data. In: Vadhan, S.P. (ed.) TCC 2007. LNCS, vol. 4392, pp. 535–554. Springer, Heidelberg (2007)

Reliable Timeout Based Commit Protocol

Bharati Harsoor[1] and Dr. S. Ramachandram[2]

[1] Research Scholar, Dept of CSE, University College of Engg,
Osmania University, Hyderabad
[2] Professor, Dept of CSE, University College of Engg,
Osmania University, Hyderabad
bharati_a@rediffmail.com, schandram@gmail.com

Abstract. The issues related to mobile network like disconnection, node failures, message loss etc. needs to have reliable and efficient method of execution for transactions along with recovery of database into consistent state. The most widely used technique for database recovery is Log based recovery. During failure / crash to recover data values prior to modification and the new value after modification can be accessed with the transaction log. Checkpoints are used to reduce the number of log records that the system must scan when recovering from a crash.

In this paper we present an atomic commit protocol called Reliable Timeout Based Commit Protocol that uses notion of 2PC & TCOT for mobile environments. This model uses two alternative possible execution strategies for mobile transactions i.e. execution at MH & Execution at FH with using timeout based mechanism. The performance of our system is compared with the 2PC and TCOT in terms of message complexity, force writes etc. The proposal is also been made to have reliable execution of mobile transactions by maintaining logged information using flash memory at MH & BS by means of recovery algorithm, through which we can have durability in transactions.

Keywords: Mobile Transactions, Flash memory, Transaction Log, Transaction Recovery.

1 Introduction

The transaction is set of operations which transfers a database from a consistent state to another. The mobile transaction is the set of operations, with which we involve minimum of one mobile host. The user issues transactions from his/her mobile unit (MU), the transaction may not be completely executed at the MU so it is fragmented and distributed among database servers for execution. The final results come back to the same MU. This creates distributed mode of execution. The transactions executed in distributed networks often require an atomic execution. Guaranteeing atomicity in mobile networks involves a lot more challenges than in fixed-wired networks.

These challenges [3] mostly concern network failures, e.g. network partitioning and node disconnection, each of which involves the risk of infinite blocking and can lead to a high number of aborts. With this mode of execution it is difficult to enforce

N. Meghanathan et al. (Eds.): CNSA 2010, CCIS 89, pp. 410–419, 2010.

ACID properties in mobile transactions [5] Thus, new models are being created to deal with mobile transactions which implements an efficient transaction processing and ensures Atomicity & Durability properties by using updating techniques as log for backup in case of crash recovery with mobile and disconnected operations. The failures may also occur due to numerous reasons such as addressing error, wrong input RAM Failure, etc. This is accomplished with the help of mobile transaction recovery algorithm [7] and message logging i.e., they restore the database to a consistent state from where the transaction processing resumes. It uses the flash memory as log to retrieve the data in a fast & efficient manner.

2 Proposed Solution: Reliable Timeout Based Commit Protocol

Our work mainly aims at developing the reliable and efficient execution of transactions over mobiles using timeout mechanism (It is an extension to our work [8]) and tried to find the solution to overcome the issues of atomicity & durability. The crash recovery algorithm uses flash memory as logged area at each MH & FH to recover from failures over mobile database system.

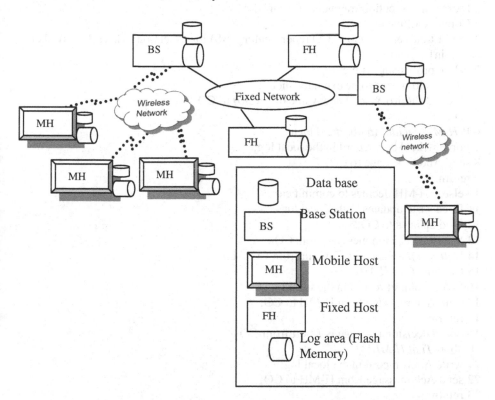

Fig. 1. Mobile Database Environment using Flash Memory as Logged area

This execution model has the Mobile Host (MH) and the Base Station (BS) communicating with each other through messages. The Mobile Transactions (MT) are initiated by the MH & are executed either at MH or at BS (BS is considered as coordinator-CO), Hence it uses distributed mode of execution between a MH & the data base servers (Part-FH) on the wired network. While executing such transactions, the bandwidth of the wireless channel is rather limited. Thus, logging of frequently accessed data in a mobile computer can be an effective approach to reduce contention on the narrow bandwidth wireless channel However; the recovery model is used to recover the mobile database back into consistent state in case of crash.

Fig 1 shows the architecture used with our proposed model, where each MH & BS have their own database along with logged area to maintain backup in case of recovery.

2.1. Transaction Execution at MH

Algorithm 1: MH's Algorithm

1 Initialize Ti at H-MH;
2 Extract its execution fragment ei0 from Ti;
3 Compute Et(ei0)
4 send Et(ei0) & Ti – ei0 to CO (coordinator - BS) for execution; where Ti = {ei0,ei1, ei2...ein}
5 While processing with ei0
    If Et (ei0) needs to be extended then
    Extend Et(ei0) & send new value of Et(ei0) to CO
    end
6 If H-MH decides to abort ei0 then
7 Force write Abort record in the local log;
8 send Abort message to CO;
9 return;
10 else // H-MH decides to commit $ei0$
11 force write updates to the local log;
12 send updates to CO;
13 Wait for decision message from CO
14 If decision message is Commit from CO then
15 Commit Ti at H-MH;
16 Write Commit record in the local log;
17 send Ack message from H-MH to CO;
18 return;
19 else // decision message is Abort from CO
20 abort Ti at H-MH;
21 write Abort record in the local log;
22 send Ack message from H-MH to CO;
23 return;
24 end
25 end

Algorithm 2: Coordinator's Algorithm

1 Wait for Et (ei0), *Ti- ei0* from H-MH, where Ti = {ei0, ei1, ei2…ein}
2 extract execution fragments of the Participants-FHs and sends them to their corresponding cohorts (CP)
3 Let $Cp = \{Cp1, \ldots, Cpm\}$ set of all the Cohort processes (CP) / fragments of Ti-ei;
4 Calculate Tm = max(Et(Cp1) , Et(Cp2) , Et(Cp3),…………. , Et (Cpm)
5 While waiting for Tm to expire do
6 if new / extended value of Et (Cpi) is received by the CO then recompute Tm, wait for Tm to expire.
7 collect all the votes from all cohort processes & H-MH;
8 if *all votes were yes then*
9 send Commit message to all members of the cohort processes & H-MH;
10 return;
11 else // at least one of the votes is No
12 if Abort *message received or within the Tm expiry if CO doesn't receive any message from any one of the Cohort processes or H-MH, then*
13 send Abort message to all members of the cohort processes and H-MH;
14 return;
15 end
16 rcturn;
17 write all received updates to local log;
18 end
19 end

Algorithm 3: Execution of fragments at Cohorts (Cp's)

1 Wait for corresponding execution fragments
2 Compute Et (Cpi) where i=1, 2,….., n cohort processes of their respective fragments & send it to CO
// continue with the steps from 5 to 25 of algorithm 1 of section 2.1 Substituting Et (ei0) with Et (Cpi)

In the above algorithms, i.e. execution at H-MH, the transaction is initiated by the MH & the part of the transaction ei0 is executed at MH & the other part of transaction i.e. Ti-ei0 is at CO. While executing ei0 at MH it calculates the Et & along with the Et of ei0 it sends Ti - ei0 to the CO for the execution of remaining fragments. On receiving (Ti-ei0) the CO splits into set of fragments & distributes among various cohorts (Part-FH) at the wired network. At the cohorts side, once after receiving the fragments they calculate the Et's as per their requirements and sends them to CO. Once after receiving all Et's, the CO calculates maximum Time (Tm= Max (Et0, Et1,…..,Etn) required to execute the transaction at H-MH & Part-MH A small value of Et may generate a large number of extension requests.

The MH begins processing of ei0 & after successful completion, sends updates of data items to the local log. During processing, if any of the nodes needs to extend the Et, they extend & sends the same copy to CO then CO calculates Tm based on extended Et's; if CO does not receive Commit message or if it receives an Abort message before the expiry of Tm then the CO decides abort Ti, else it decides to commit

& send the same updates to all, based on which the H-MH & Part-MH updates their database.

2.2 Transaction Execution at Coordinator i.e. at BS

Algorithm 1: MH's Algorithm

1 Initialize *Ti at H-MH*;
2 send *Ti (whole transaction)* to CO (coordinator);
3 After processing at CO,
4 if *updates are received for commit from CO,*
5 *Write* all received updates at H-MH to the local log
6 else (abort)
7 Abort the transaction.
8 end

Algorithm 2: Coordinator's Algorithm

1 after receiving Ti from H-MH
2 While *processing Ti* at CO do
3 Extract execution fragments Ti (ei0, ei1, ei2, ei3...,ein) for the Participants-FHs and sends them to their corresponding cohorts
4 Let $Cp = \{Cp1, \ldots, Cpm\}$ set of all the Cohort processes (*CP*) / fragments of Ti;
5 Calculate Tm = max(Et(Cp1) , Et(Cp2) , Et(Cp3), ..., Et(Cpm)
6 While waiting for Tm to expire do
7 If new / extended value of Et(Cpi) is received by the CO then recompute Tm , wait for Tm to expire.
8 While CO collects the votes from all cohort processes;
9 if *all votes were yes then*
10 send Commit message to all members of the cohort processes & H-MH;
11 return;
12 else // at least one of the votes is No
13 if Abort *message received or within the Tm expiry if CO doesn't receive any message from any one of the Cohort processes,* then // at least one of the vote is No
14 CO decides to Abort
15 send Abort message to all members of the cohort processes & to H-MH;
16 return;
17. Write all received updates to local log;
18 end
19 end.

Algorithm 3: Execution of fragments at Cohorts (Cp's or DBS):

1 Wait for the corresponding execution fragments
2 Compute Et(Cpi) where i=1, 2... n cohort processes of their respective fragments & send it to CO
// continue with the steps from 5 to 19 of algorithm 1 of section 2.1.

With another execution model, while executing transaction at CO i.e. at BS (above Algorithms 1-3 of Section 2.2), the whole transaction Ti is executed at CO by originating at MH. The CO in turn sends fragmented transactions Ti (ei0, ei1, ei2,......, ein) to all the participating FH's (Cohorts) at the wired network. The part-FH calculates the Et (Execution Time – Et0,Et1,Et2.....,Etn) of their respective fragments & sends them to the CO, then the CO calculates Maximum Time Tm= Max (Et0, Et1,.....,Etn) Each FH begins processing of ei & after successful completion, sends updates to the local log. During processing, if it needs to extend Et, Part-FH extends & sends the same copy to CO within the Et; if CO does not receive Commit message or if it receives an abort before Tm expires, then CO decides to abort Ti else decides to commit & send the same to all, based on which the H-MH & Part-MH update their database.

2.3 Recovery Model

The recovery of mobile transaction (MT) which is executed at MH can be performed without any complications by maintaining logs locally at MH. Rolling back in case of communicated actions, the BS has to explicitly identify the actions need to be rolled back. The rollback algorithm for mobile transaction environment is described below in Algorithm 1. This algorithm uses the concept of immediate update recovery technique. The transaction manager creates Transaction table (Commit table) & Active table according to the log creation. In case of recovery to rollback the database, the recovery manager creates Rollback LSN along with Transaction Id & tries to find its equivalent LSN in the log area from the point of checkpoint and assigns it to the Undonxtlsn. The Recovery manager reads the records based on the type of log record (Logrec.Tyoe) of undonxtlsn, accordingly the active table transactions are undone & commit table transactions are redone.

Algorithm 1: Rollback Algorithm

1. Rollback (RollbackLSN.TrID)
/* RollbackLSN is generated by the Respective log of MH which met with crash */
2. Undonxt = tr_table[trid].undonextlsn
3. Logrec: = LogRead (UndoNxt)
4. SELECT (logrec.Type)
5. WHEN (commit) assign all the data item to its AFIM for undo operations/ make changes to data item according to the commit table
6. WHEN (update) assign all the data item to its BFIM for redo operations /make changes to data item according to the active table.
7. Otherwise
8. UndoNxt: = LogRec.PrevLSN;
9. End SELECT /* Log Rec Type */
10. End Rollback

The recovery model uses the logged data which is maintained using flash memory at H-MH & Part-FH and to make them available at any time during the transaction failure. Log records on the flash memory are organized depending on the checkpoints to provide fast references in the reconstruction of failed transactions.

3 Performance Analysis of Reliable Timeout Based Commit Protocol

Execution Timeout (Et) as in TCOT [4] defines an upper bound timeout value within which a node of a commit set completes the execution of its *ei*. The value of *Et* may be node specific. It may depend on the size of *ei* and the characteristics of the process-ing unit. We identify *H-MH's* timeout by *Et*(H-*MH*) and Part-FH timeout by *Et*(Part-FH). The relationship between these two timeouts is $Et(MH) = Et(\text{part-FH}) + \text{¢}$. The ¢ accounts for the characteristics such as poor resources, disconnected state, availability of wireless channel, etc., compared to part-FH.

Furthermore, the value of a timeout for an *ei* depends on its *MH*, thus, $Et(MHi)$ may not be equal to $Et(MHj)$, $(i \mathrel{!=} j)$. It is possible that a *MH* may take less time than its *Et* to execute its *ei*. We also do not rule out the possibility that in some cases *Et* (Part-FH) may be larger than *Et* (*H-MH*). *Et* typically should be just long enough to allow a fragment to successfully finish its entire execution in a normal environment (i.e., no failure of any kind, no message delay, etc.)

Shipping timeout (St) [4] defines the upper bound of the data shipping time from *H-MH* to Part-FH. Thus, at the end of *Et* the CO expects the updates to be shipped to the Part-FH and logged there within *St*. In TCOT the *St is computed* as *Time to compose updates (Ut)* + *Time for the updates to reach CO (Sh)*. The total time required in TCOT will be Et + St, with our protocol because of maintaining logs locally we could be able to reduce its time by only Et. In the above algorithms (both the cases), we are not calculating St (ei0, ei1,......,ein) as in TCOT [4], Because the shipment time in TCOT is used to shift the updates (done during transaction processing) to the CO from H-MH & Part-MH. But in our case, we use local logs at H-MH & Part-MH to maintain the updates so no need of shipment time during processing. With our algo-rithm the blocking time can be reduced because the CO waits only up to the Et expires for any of either part-MH or H-MH. In this section, we make comparison on the analysis performance of message complexity & force writes and also the throughput of Reliable Timeout Based Commit Protocol with TCOT and conventional 2PC. The average Commit Time (CT) and the throughput of TCOT with Reliable Timeout Based Commit Protocol,

Compute CT for TCOT as: CT = St + Time to compute St + Commit messages

CT starts when the first commit message or the update shipment (at the end of execu-tion) is dispatched to the CO and it ends when CO declares Ti's commit.

CT for Reliable Timeout Based Commit Protocol = 0 + 0 + Commit messages

CT starts only when CO declares Ti's commit, hence the time-consuming activity in TCOT is the computation of Et and St, which is not present in our protocol (no need of calculating St + time to compute St). As the name suggests with our protocol, the timeout mechanism uses the Execution time (Et) of MH / FH + CT for the execution of transactions, within which the transaction is to be committed / aborted. This mechanism facilitates to increase the average commit time, through put & blocking time is reduced.

We have implemented our protocol in such a way that its working is also comparable to 2PC as this is the most widely accepted commit protocol in use today. In actuality, we use Reliable Timeout Based Commit Protocol with one less message during commit than traditional 2PC

Table 1. Performance Table

Protocol	Message rounds	Message complexity	Force writes	Message delay
2pc	02	4n	2n+1	02
TCOT	01	2n	n+1	01
Timeout based protocol – Execution at MH (In case of commit)	1.5	3n	n+1	1.5
(In case of aborts)	01	2n	n+1	01
Execution at FH (In case of Commit)	1.5	3n	n+1	1.5
(In case of aborts)	01	2n	n+1	01

The above Table 1 gives a comparison between our execution model and 2PC in terms of message rounds, no. of force writes and message complexity. In this table, n denotes the number of participants and the time delay to deliver a message. The latency of an atomic commitment protocol is the time spent between the submissions of the commit demand by the application until the reception of the decision by the participants. This factor is important since it determines the time after which a participant can relax the resources held by a transaction. We can show that, the total number of messages, force writes of Timeout based protocol will be almost similar to what is used in TCOT. Therefore, from the message viewpoint, the performance of TCOT is similar.

With the proposed model the mobile units holding logs locally overcome the issues like Disconnection, where the MH & FH can process individually & can locally log the information, after getting connected both can transfer the information to each other accordingly. The other advantages over TCOT are less reliable, i.e. if BS fails, the execution of entire process will stop; instead with Timeout based commit protocol, the MH can continue processing with locally logged Information. Logging Bottleneck Problem, the logging traffic at BS will be manageable (is not possible in TCOT) as MH maintains logs locally & each MH need not wait for logged information available at BS during recovery.

3.1 Results

We have modeled mobile transactions execution through explicit recovery model and messages in the form of simulation. The algorithms & flow diagrams for execution of transaction processing at MH & FH, crash recovery for partial and total rollback in a mobile transaction environment have been designed and the implementation of the same is done using the Java Runtime version 1.4.2_or newer with Microsoft Windows XP Professional SP2 / Symbian OS 60.

4 Conclusion and Future Work

This paper illustrates design & implementation of an efficient & reliable approach for transactions executing in mobile environment with recovery model to handle failures in case of crashes. It makes use of flash memory as logging area for more reliable & faster access storage. The check points are used to reduce the number of log records accessed during recovery. Primarily our protocol uses timeout mechanism with which we can encompass atomicity & durability properties. We extended the scope of the usage of the timeout, to identify the successful end of an activity within the defined time period. Thus, in our approach, timeout not only enforces the termination condition but the entire execution duration as well. We compared its performance with a well-known 2PC & TCOT commit protocol and observed that, the Reliable Timeout Based Commit Protocol offered better performance in terms of commit time, throughput, and significantly reduced the messaging cost . The logging is done at MH & also at BS, due to which it overcomes the issues like disconnection, handoff & blocking problem, hence it lead to be more reliable in case of failures.

The next step is making comparison with the existing methods based on their performance and to extend it to the following execution models

. Distributed Execution among several MHs
Distributed Execution among MHs and FHs

And Produce efficient Mobile Transaction model that maintains ACID properties.

References

[1] Bobineau, C., Pucheral, P., Abdallah, M.: A Unilateral Commit Protocol for Mobile and Disconnected Computing. In: PDCS, USA (2000)
[2] Ding, Z., Meng, X., Wang, S.: O2PC-MT: A Novel Optimistic Two-Phase Commit Protocol. In: Mayr, H.C., Lazanský, J., Quirchmayr, G., Vogel, P. (eds.) DEXA 2001. LNCS, vol. 2113, p. 846. Springer, Heidelberg (2001)
[3] Bobineau, C., Labbé, C., Roncancio, C., Alvarado, P.S.: Comparing transaction commit protocols for mobile environments. In: Proceedings of the 15th International Workshop on Database and Expert Systems Applications (DEXA 2004). IEEE, Los Alamitos (2004)
[4] Kumar, V., Prabhu, N., Dunham, M.H., Seydim, A.Y.: TCOT- A Timeout-Based Mobile Transaction Commitment Protocol. IEEE Transactions on Computers 51(10) (2002)

[5] Serrano, P., Roncancico, C., Adiba, M.: A Survey of mobile transactions. Distributed and Parallel Databases 16, 193–230 (2004)

[6] Bose, J.-H., Bottcher, S., Gruenwald, L.: An integrated commit protocol for mobile network databases. In: The Proceedings of 9th International Database Engineering & Application Symposium (IDEAS 2005). IEEE, Los Alamitos (2005)

[7] Goreyand, M.M., Ghosh, R.K.: Recovery of Mobile Transactions. In: Proceedings of the 11th International Workshop on Database and Expert Systems Applications (DEXA 2000). IEEE, Los Alamitos (2000), 0-7695-0680-1/00 ©

[8] Harsoor, B., Ramachandram, S.: Reliable Execution of Mobile Transactions. In: The Proceedings of 2nd International Conference on Wireless Information Networks & Business Information Systems (WINBIS- 10)

Proposed Security Model and Threat Taxonomy for the Internet of Things (IoT)

Sachin Babar*, Parikshit Mahalle, Antonietta Stango, Neeli Prasad,
and Ramjee Prasad

Center for TeleInFrastruktur, Aalborg University, Aalborg, Denmark
{sdb,pnm,as,np,prasad}@es.aau.dk
http://www.gisfi.org/

Abstract. IoT is an intelligent collaboration of tiny sensors and devices giving new challenges to security and privacy in end to end communication of things. Protection of data and privacy of things is one of the key challenges in the IoT. Lack of security measures will result in decreased adoption among users and therefore is one of the driving factors in the success of the IoT. This paper gives an overview, analysis and taxonomy of security and privacy challenges in IoT. Finally, Security Model for IoT has been proposed.

Keywords: Security, Privacy, Internet of Things, trust, authentication, authorization.

1 Introduction

The Internet has undergone severe changes since its first launch in the late 1960s as an outcome of the ARPANET with number of users about 20% of the world population. "7 trillion wireless devices serving 7 billion people in 2017". This vision reflects the increasing trend of introducing micro devices and tools in future i.e. IoT. In such ambient environment not only user become ubiquitous but also devices and their context become transparent and ubiquitous. With the miniaturization of devices, increase of computational power, and reduction of energy consumption, this trend will continue towards IoT[1]. One of the most challenging topics in such an interconnected world of miniaturized systems and sensors are security and privacy aspects. Having every 'thing' connected to the global future IoT communicating with each other, new security and privacy problems arise, e. g., confidentiality, authenticity, and integrity of data sensed and exchanged by 'things'.

This paper is structured as follows : Section 2 talks about the IoT objectives with detailed description of each. Section 3 focuses on the security requirements in terms of privacy, trust and authentication for IoT. Section 4 describes the possible threats to IoT. Section 5 analyzes related work for IoT security. Section 6 proposes a security model for IoT. Section 7 concludes the paper.

---

* Corresponding author.

N. Meghanathan et al. (Eds.): CNSA 2010, CCIS 89, pp. 420–429, 2010.

2 IoT Objectives

The IoT scenarios, like individual wireless device interfacing with internet, constellation of wireless devices, pervasive system and sensor network, are associated with new network service requirements that motivate rethinking of several Internet architecture issues. Several mobile/wireless features may require mechanisms that cannot be implemented through the conventional IP framework for the Internet, or if they can, may suffer from performance degradation due to the additional overhead associated with network protocols that were originally designed for static infrastructure computing. We discuss a set of objectives related to the networking requirements of the representative IoT scenarios identified earlier. Fig. 1 shows the IoT Objectives followed by their description.

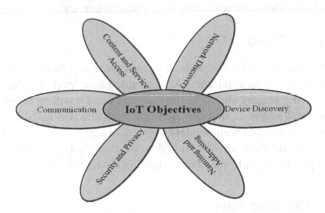

Fig. 1. IoT Objectives

2.1 Naming and Addressing

Today's Internet addressing scheme is rather rigid; it is well suited to a static, hierarchical topology structure. It provides a very efficient way to label (and find) each device interface in this hierarchy. To support mobility and routing the next generation Internet must provide ways to name and route to a much richer set of network elements than just attachment points. A clean architectural separation between name and routable address is a critical requirement [2].

2.2 Device Discovery and Network Discovery

The current Internet is text-dominated with relatively efficient search engines for discovering textual resources with manual configuration. An Internet dominated by unstructured information supplied from large numbers of sensor devices must support efficient mechanisms for discovering available sensor resources. The new architecture must support methods for the registering of a new sensor system in the broader network [3].

2.3 Content and Service Access

A new architecture should provide data cleansing mechanisms that prevent corrupted data from propagating through the sensor network. In particular, services that maintain device calibration and monitor/detect adversarial manipulation of sensor devices should be integrated into sensor networks. This could be realized through obtaining context information, metadata, and statistical techniques to locally detect faulty inputs.

2.4 Communication

Wireless devices should be able to operate independently of the broader Internet. In particular, there may be times during which the connection of a wireless device or network to the Internet is not available. During these times, wireless devices should be able to operate stably in modes disconnected from the rest of the infrastructure, as well as be able to opportunistically establish "local" ad-hoc networks using their own native protocols. In particular, this means that issues such as authorization and updating the device state should be seamless, with minimal latency.

2.5 Security and Privacy

Wireless networks can be expected to be the platform of choice for launching a variety of attacks targeting the new Internet. At the most basic level, wireless devices will likely have evolving naming and addressing schemes and it will be necessary to ensure that the names and addresses that are used are verifiable and authenticated. One parameter uniquely associated with wireless networks is the notion of location. Location information provided by the network should be trustworthy [4]. Additionally the architecture should provision hooks for future extensions to accommodate legal regulations.

3 Security Requirements

3.1 Key Properties of IoT

There are a number of key properties of IoT that create several issues for security and raises additional requirements for security. These key properties are listed below:

Mobility. IoT devices are mobile and often generally connect to the Internet via a large set of providers.
Wireless. These devices typically connect to the rest of the Internet via a wide range of wireless links, including Bluetooth, 802.11, WiMAX, Zigbee and GSM/UMTS. With wireless communications, any nearby observer can intercept unique low-level identifiers that are sent in the clear, e.g., Bluetooth and 802.11 device addresses.
Embedded Use. Major IoT devices have a single use (e.g., blood pressure or heart monitors and household appliances). As a result, the detection of communication patterns unique to a specialized device allows users to be profiled[5].
Diversity. These devices span a range of computational abilities from full-fledged PCs to low-end RFID tags. Privacy designs must accommodate even the simplest of devices.
Scale. These devices are convenient, growing in number daily, and increasingly embed network connectivity into everyday settings. This makes it difficult for users to monitor privacy concerns.

3.2 Challenges

Following are the challenges which need to be tackled in the world of pervasive devices.

- Management, scalability and heterogeneity of devices
- Networked knowledge and context
- Privacy, security and trust will have to be adapted to both devices and information

This will involve the development of highly efficient cryptographic algorithms and protocols that provide basic security properties such as confidentiality, integrity, and authenticity, as well as secure implementations for the various kinds of mostly resource constrained devices.

3.3 High Level Security Requirements

In business process, security requirements are described as follows :

Resilience to attacks. The system has to avoid single points of failure and should adjust itself to node failures.

Data authentication. As a principle, retrieved address and object information must be authenticated.

Access control. Information providers must be able to implement access control on the data provided.

Client privacy. Measures need to be taken that only the information provider is able to infer from observing the use of the lookup system related to a specific customer; at least, inference should be very hard to conduct.

Fig. 2 summarizes the high level security requirements for IoT.

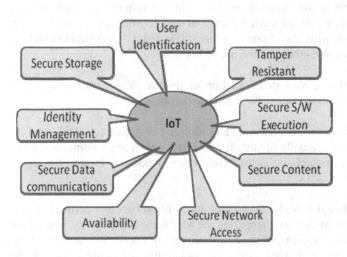

Fig. 2. High level Security Requirements for IoT

User identification. It refers to the process of validating users before allowing them to use the system.

Secure storage. This involves confidentiality and integrity of sensitive information stored in the system.

Identity Management. It is broad administrative area that deals with identifying individuals / things in a system and controlling their access to resources within that system by associating user rights and restrictions with the established identity.

Secure data communication. It includes authenticating communicating peers, ensuring confidentiality and integrity of communicated data, preventing repudiation of a communication transaction, and protecting the identity of communicating entities.

Availability. Availability refers to ensuring that unauthorized persons or systems cannot deny access or use to authorize users.

Secure network access. This provides a network connection or service access only if the device is authorized.

Secure content. Content security or Digital Rights Management (DRM) protects the rights of the digital content used in the system.

Secure execution environment. It refers to a secure, managed-code, runtime environment designed to protect against deviant applications.

Tamper resistance. It refers to the desire to maintain these security requirements even when the device falls into the hands of malicious parties, and can be physically or logically probed.

4   Security and Threat Taxonomy for IoT

IoT is coupled with new security threats and alters overall information security risk profile. Although the implementation of technological solutions may respond to IoT threats and vulnerabilities, IoT security is primarily a management issue. Effective management of the threats associated with IoT requires a sound and thorough assessment of risk given the environment and development of a plan to mitigate identified threats. Following Fig. 3 presents threat taxonomy to understand and assess the various threats associated with the use of IoT [6].

Identification covers determination of unique device/user/session with authentication, authorization , accounting and provisioning.

Communication threats covers a Denial-of-Service attack (DoS) and it occurs when an attacker continually bombards a targeted AP (Access Point) or network with bogus requests, premature successful connection messages, failure messages, and/or other commands.

Physical threat includes micro probing and reverse engineering causing serious security problem by directly tampering the hardware components. Some types of Physical attack requires expensive material because of which they are relatively hard to perform. Some examples are: De-packaging of chip, Layout reconstruction, Micro-probing.

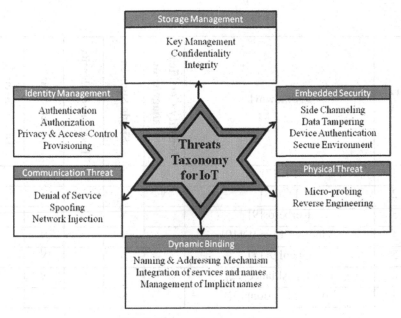

Fig. 3. Threats Taxonomy for IoT

Embedded Security threat model will span all the threats at physical and MAC layer. Security threats like device and data tampering, Side channel analysis, bus monitoring, etc will be the concerns at device level.

Storage management has crucial impact on the key management to achieve confidentiality and integrity. We must also be careful in choosing which cryptographic components to use as the building blocks since, for example, the cipher texts for some public key encryption schemes can reveal identifying information about the intended recipient .

5 Related Work

Security framework for IoT will mainly include architectures for providing and managing access control, authentication and authorization. It will provide methods for controlling the identification and authentication of users and for administering which authenticated users are granted access to protected resources. Some of the frameworks described can be used to provide several functions as shown in Table 1.

5.1 Identity Certificate Frameworks

These frameworks allow users without prior contact to authenticate to each other and digitally sign and encrypt messages. They are based on identity certificates, which are certificates that bind a public key to an identity. Examples of identity certificate frameworks include Public Key Infrastructures (PKIs), [8,14] and Pretty Good Privacy (PGP).

Table 1. State of Art Evaluation

Sr. No.	Framework	Identity Certificate Management	Single Sign-on	Federated Identity	User-centric	Device Security
1	PKI[7]	√				
2	PGP[8]	√				
3	Kerberos[9]		√			
4	Windows Live ID[10]		√		√	
5	OpenID[11]		√		√	
6	Liberty Alliance[12]		√	√	√	
7	WS-Federation[13]		√	√		

5.2 Single Sign-On

Single sign-on (SSO) allows users to be authenticated only once in a system. Users can then access all resources for which they have access permission without entering multiple passwords. Example SSO frameworks include:

Kerberos a distributed authentication service, which provides SSO within a single administrative domain.

Windows Live ID [10]: an Internet-based SSO framework used by Microsoft applications and web services such as MSN messenger.

OpenID [11]: an authentication framework that allows users to login to different web sites using a single digital identity, eliminating the need to have different usernames and passwords for each site.

Liberty Alliance [12]: a consortium that aims to establish open standards, guidelines and best practices for federated identity management.

WS-Federation [13]: a federated identity standard developed by Microsoft, IBM, VeriSign, BEA and RSA Security, which forms part of the Web Services Security framework.

5.3 Identity Federation

Federated Identity allows users of one security domain to securely access resources on another security domain, without the need for another user account. Users register with an authentication server in their own domain and other domains trust its assertions.

5.4 User-Centric Identity Management

User-centric identity management is a design principle that focuses on usability and cost-effectiveness from the user's point of view. There are three main approaches to user-centric identity management that are Managing multiple identities e.g. information cards [15], Giving users a single identity e.g. OpenID and lastly Giving users control over access to their resources.

5.5 Device Security

The Device Security Framework includes device-resident security software as well as security capabilities delivered across the network. The device-resident software is embedded into devices at the time of manufacture.

6 Proposed Security Model for IoT

Integrated and interrelated perspective on security, trust, privacy can potentially deliver an input to address protection issues in the IoT. Therefore we have chosen a cube structure as a modeling mechanism for security, trust and privacy in the IoTS, referred to as IoT. A cube has three dimensions with the ability to clearly show the intersection thereof. Therefore a cube is an ideal modeling structure for depicting the convergence of security, trust and privacy for the IoT. In IoT access information, required to grant/reject access requests, is not only complex but also composite in nature. This is a direct result of the high level of interconnectedness between things, services and people. It is clear that the type and structure of information required to grant/reject such an access request is complex and should address the following IoT issues: security (authorization), trust(reputation), privacy(respondent). This is depicted in figure 4.

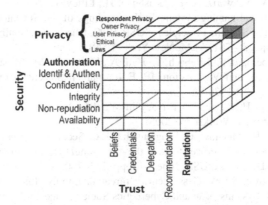

Fig. 4. Security Model for IoT

7 Conclusion

The incremental deployment of the technologies that will make up the IoT must not fail what the Internet has failed to do: provide adequate security and privacy mechanisms from the start. We must be sure that adequate security and privacy is available before the technology gets deployed and becomes part of our daily live. Security requirement and threat taxonomy insist to go for Trusted Platform Module which offers facilities for the secure generation of cryptographic keys, and limitation of their use, in addition to a hardware pseudo-random number generator. It also includes capabilities such as remote attestation and sealed storage. "Remote attestation" creates a nearly unforgeable hash key summary of the hardware and software configuration. The extent of the summary of the software is decided by the program encrypting the data. This allows a third party to verify that the software has not been changed. "Binding" encrypts data using the TPM endorsement key, a unique RSA key burned into the chip during its production, or another trusted key descended from it.

In this paper we presented a categorization of topics and technologies in the IoT with analysis of sensitivity and state in research to different security and privacy properties. We see this (1) as a basis for coming up with an integrated systems approach for security and privacy in the Internet of Things, and (2) as stimulator for discussion on the categorization and sensitivity rating in the IoT. Furthermore, we presented key challenges like identity management, embedded security and authentication in the IoT.

References

1. Silverajan, B., Harju, J.: Developing network software and communications protocols towards the internet of things. In: Proceedings of the Fourth International ICST Conference on Communication System Software and MiddlewaRE, COMSWARE 2009, Dublin, Ireland, June 16-19, pp. 1–8. ACM, New York (2009)
2. Adjie-Winoto, W., Schwartz, E., Balakrishnan, H., Lilley, J.: The design and implementation of an intentional naming system. In: Proceedings of the Seventeenth ACM Symposium on Operating Systems Principles, SOSP 1999, Charleston, South Carolina, US, December 12-15, pp. 186–201. ACM, New York (1999)
3. Beerliova, Z., Eberhard, F., Erlebach, T., Hall, A., Hoffmann, M., Mihalák, M., Ram, L.S.: Network Discovery and Verification. IEEE Journal on Selected Areas in Communications 24(12), 2168–2181 (2006)
4. Hu, Y.-C., Wang, H.J.: Location Privacy in Wireless Networks. In: Proceedings of the ACM SIGCOMM Asia Workshop (2005)
5. Kocher, P., Lee, R., McGraw, G., Raghunathan, A.: Security as a new dimension in embedded system design. In: Proceedings of the 41st Annual Design Automation Conference, DAC 2004, San Diego, CA, USA, June 7-11, pp. 753–760. ACM, New York (2004)
6. Welch, D., Lathrop, S.: Wireless security threat taxonomy. In: Information Assurance Workshop, IEEE Systems, Man and Cybernetics Society, June 18-20, pp. 76–83 (2003)
7. Public-Key Infrastructure (X.509), http://tools.ietf.org/wg/pkix/
8. Kohnfelder, L.M.: Towards a Practical Public Key System, Thesis (1978), http://dspace.mit.edu/bitstream/handle/1721.1/15993/07113748.pdf
9. Neuman, B.C., Ts'o, T.: Kerberos: an authentication service for computer networks. IEEE Communications Magazine 32(9), 33–38 (1994)
10. Introduction to Windows Live ID, download, http://msdn.microsoft.com/enus/library/bb288408.aspx/

11. OpenID, http://openid.net/specs/openid-authentication-1_1.html
12. Introduction to the Liberty Alliance Identity Architecture (2003),
    http://xml.coverpages.org/
    LibertyAllianceArchitecture200303.pdf
13. Goodner, M.: Understanding WS-Federation (2007),
    http://msdn.microsoft.com/en-us/library/bb498017.aspx
14. Shim, S.S.Y., Bhalla, P.: Federated identity management. IEEE Computer 38(12), 120–
    122 (2005)
15. Chappell, D.: Introducing Windows CardSpace,
    http://msdn.microsoft.com/en-us/library/aa480189.aspx

Identity Management Framework towards Internet of Things (IoT): Roadmap and Key Challenges

Parikshit Mahalle, Sachin Babar, Neeli R. Prasad, and Ramjee Prasad

Center for TeleInFrastruktur, Aalborg University, Aalborg, Denmark
{pnm,sdb,np,prasad}@es.aau.dk
http://www.gisfi.org

Abstract. One of the most profound changes today is the increase in mobility of portable yet powerful wireless devices capable of communicating via several different kinds of wireless radio networks of varying link-level characteristics. Requirement for identity is not adequately met in networks, especially given the emergence of ubiquitous computing devices that are mobile and use wireless communications. Addressing identity problem requires changes to the architecture for naming, addressing, and discovery. Challenges include resource discovery; ways to expose relevant privacy distinctions to users, naming and addressing that restricts precise knowledge of identity to authorized parties. This paper presents the identity management (IdM) framework for internet of things (IoT) with the study of existing systems, and addresses the key challenges.

Keywords: Identity Management, Internet of.

1 Introduction

Rapid developments in hardware and networking technology have today resulted in a diverse range of portable, yet powerful computing devices that are geared for connectivity and increased mobility over different types of networks. In 2005, the International Telecommunications Union (ITU) released a report. Outlining their vision of how networking, especially the Internet, will evolve in the face of increasing numbers of interconnected users and devices, entitled The IoT [1]. The report suggests that the number of users (both human and non-human) connected to the Internet would be counted in the billions. The vision of trillion wireless devices serving billion people reflects the increasing trend of introducing micro devices and tools in future i.e. IoT. The stakeholders in the IoT will be [2]

User – represents devices or software with the aim of utilization of services, infrastructure

Providers – of services and infrastructure with the target of business

Society – includes legal framework

Figure 1 shows the three major waves in computing. During the mainframe wave we had one machine serving a number of people. When personal computer took off, the human to machine ratio was changed to one to one e.g. almost every individual had

N. Meghanathan et al. (Eds.): CNSA 2010, CCIS 89, pp. 430–439, 2010.

their own desktop. Looking at the third wave of computing the situation comes where every individual will have several mobile devices serving him. IoT will generate more complicated privacy, authentication and access control problems with the need of interoperability, scalability and usability features. Such environments require highly secured and well defined IdM framework. Such framework has to deal with the complete life cycle of identities of users, services and devices as well as users' awareness in information is closure and privacy.

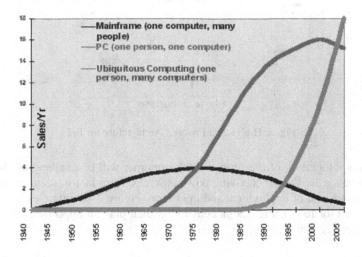

Fig. 1. Three Ways of Computing: Mainframe, PC and Ubiquitous Computing [3]

This paper is constructed according to following outline. Section 2 introduces architectural framework and design constraints for IoT. Section 3 debates about IdM in IoT. Section 4 illustrates the related work. Section 5 proposes identity modeling and requirement matrix in IoT. Section 6 focuses on key challenges and proposed IdM framework. Finally section 7 concludes this paper.

2 Architectural Framework and Design Constraints

For the IoT, it is envisioned that an incredibly high number of inexpensive pervasive devices surrounds us. Connecting them to internet will involve the integration of multiple connectivity options based on the constraints described above. In general it is envisaged that the integration will be in a hierarchical manner where sensor clusters at the lowest level connecting to a suitable access network to reach to the internet. This lowest level network is termed as edge networks depicted in figure 2.

Access gateway layer consists of a collection of network gateways providing connectivity between edge layer and internet layer. The network devices at layer will support the internet protocols and extend it further down to the access network at the edge layer as applicable. The internet layer will provide and extend the support of familiar internet protocols for networking and management.

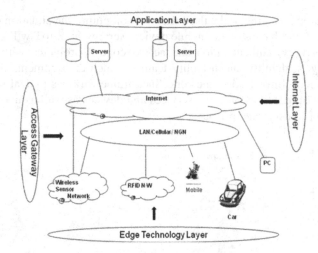

Fig. 2. High Level Layered Architecture for IoT

Seamless integration of the 'things' to the internet will be challenging. Major factors of influence are the connectivity, power sources, form factor, security, geographical factors and cost of deployment and operation. Figure 3 summarizes key factors to be considered for IoT. These design constraints shall play an important role in designing infrastructure and protocol for IoT.

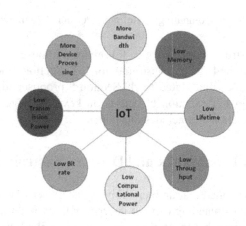

Fig. 3. Design Constraints for IoT

3   Identity Management

IdM is a combination of processes and technologies to manage and secure access to the information and resources while also protecting things' profiles. IdM can provide the capabilities to effectively manage such processes both internal and external to an IoT and, correspondingly, anyone or anything that needs to interact with it.

IdM solutions are viewed as primarily a tool for:

- Defining the identity of an entity (a person, place, or thing)
- Storing relevant information about entities, such as names and credentials
- Making that information accessible through a set of standard interfaces
- Providing a resilient, distributed, and high-performance infrastructure
- Helping to manage the relationships to resources and other entities

Figure 4 shows the schematic diagram of IdM components.

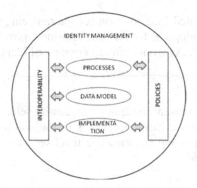

Fig. 4. IdM Component

Processes defines the set of processes require for IdM in IoT and how they should be accomplishes. Data model is a model of the identity in IoT and building data model involves determining what data we have and how to categorize exchange and structure it. Interoperability and policies are the backbone for any IdM. Implementation guidelines tell how to create systems that works with identity infrastructure. There are several network entities to be identified in the network. These network entities have a layered architecture and are used for naming, addressing and routing as follows.

Services (i.e., information related to applications/services)
End points (i.e., global unique identifier)
Location (i.e., IP address)
Path (i.e., routing)

In particular, for object to object communications, information for several kinds of object on top of end points should be identified in the network.

4 Related Work

Most of the state of the art IdM systems today are based on Service Oriented Architecture (SOA). This section discusses Identity management systems like OpenId, Liberty Alliance, Card-Space, Shibboleth and Higgins in detail.

4.1 OpenId

Basically, OpenID[4] platform is consistent with four layers- a) Identifiers, b) Discovery, c) Authentication, and d) Data Transport. The process, to be completed, involves three different entities- the end –users or the Subject, the Relying Party, and the Identity Provider, same as the Identity Metasystem. OpenID allows relying party to redirect the client to the identity provider for authentication at the identity provider site thus violating user control. The second problem with OpenID is that the URL that is used to identify the Subject is recyclable. Since OpenID permits URL based identification, it brings the issue of privacy.

4.2 Liberty Alliance

Liberty Alliance is federated IdM solution for guaranteeing interoperability, supporting privacy, promoting adoption for its specifications, providing guidelines [5] .The Liberty Alliance Project lacks from defining strength of identity.

4.3 Card-Space

Windows Card-Space is a visual metaphor for identity selector for the end-user. Windows Card-Space provides controlling power to the end-users [6]. Windows Card-Space has self issued cards and has message level security problem while communicating with identity provider.

4.4 Shibboleth

Shibboleth is a federation infrastructure based on SAML and web redirection with a Single Sign On mechanism in order to share resources. The Identity Provider is composed by the SSO service, Inter site transfer service, authentication authority, and attributes authority and artifact resolution service [7]. Shibboleth does not comply with directional identity. There are cases where it is necessary to implement uniquely identifiable identities and also directional. Shibboleth fails to offer such support. One more crucial area where Shibboleth fails to protect itself is against the susceptibility of the security of the whole system be broken down by an evil third party.

4.5 Higgins

Higgins is a software infrastructure that supports consistence user experience that works with digital identity protocols, e.g. WS-Trust, OpenID. The main objective of the Higgins project is to manage multiple contexts, interoperability, define common interfaces for an identity system [8]. The Higgins framework does not provide supports for quantitative measure identity strength and lacks the fulfillment of defining strength of identity. Higgins also has the inherent weakness of the security vulnerability.

None of these technologies conform all the requirements of IoT. Secondly, some of the technologies that are said to be strongly supportive for certain IdM feature has been shown to be also vulnerable in even in those areas. Table 1 summarizes the areas of IdM covered by various technologies [9]. Comparison is based on following five IdM technologies.

1. OpenId [4] – Distributed identities
2. Liberty Alliance [5] – Trust relations
3. Card-Space [6] - Authentication

4. Shibboleth [7] – Attribute exchange
5. Higgins [8] – User and Machine id

Table 1. Comparative summary of the state of art for IdM

Features	1	2	3	4	5
Authentication	No	No	Yes	Yes	Yes
Authentication*	No	No	No	No	No
Authorization	No	Yes	Yes	No	Yes
Single Sign On	Yes	Yes	No	Yes	No
Technologies	HTTP	SAML	XML	SAML	HTTP
Attributes Exchange	Yes	Yes	Yes	Yes	Yes
Device Identity	No	Partial	No	No	Yes
Interoperability	No	Yes	No	No	No
Federation	Yes	Yes	No	Yes	Yes
Lightweight	No	No	No	No	No
SSO with Simple	No	No	No	No	No
Scalability	Yes	No	No	No	Yes
Replay attack	Yes	Yes	Yes	Yes	Yes

*Denotes many to many authentication as in IoT multiple device communication gives need of many to many (m:n) authentication. Thus we can conclude that that there are no single technology available that suites a futuristic IoT scenario for many to many (m: n) authentication, multi device SSO, replay attack, lightweight version and device identity with privacy.

5   Identity Modeling and Requirement Matrix

IdM can be used to e.g., identify the entities responsible for designing, manufacturing, operating, maintaining, and repairing the respective embedded systems. This can improve transparency with regard to those devices. At the same time more understanding is needed with regard to the placement of identity information on physical or virtual identifiers. However the enhanced understanding of the situation can be obtained by developing combination of physical id and virtual id.Virtual identity is subset of digital information about thing. Thing may have more than one virtual identity to represent different context and aspect of its service usage. Virtual identity may contain data relevant to many parameters with the logical understanding that information may be available from any point in the architecture (distributed) with limited access to only some entities [3]. Relation between digital data and virtual identities can be shown by Venn diagram shown in figure 5.

With the VID concept a things can split its identity into several virtual identities. The concept of VIDs is in literature also known as partial identities. [2] Defines a partial identity as an identity that reflects a thing in a specific role by means of pseudonyms and attributes linked to it. In addition to benefits, IdM comes with risks and threats like loss of consumer confidence, threats like spoofing, tampering, information disclosure and authentication needs to be considered for the design of IdM [10, 11].

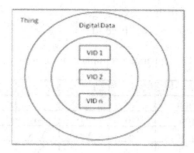

Fig. 5. Venn diagram for digital data and virtual identities

Based on the security threat model given by [12] an identity requirement matrix can be build as shown in figure 6. It shows that IdM is the framework for ensuring authentication, authorization and privacy. Identification covers determination of unique device/user/session. Authentication represents verification of user, device and extended credentials. Authorization consists of access policies and network policies. Accounting can be done for user monitoring and caching with tracking, reporting, auditing and mapping which is elaborated in later section. Provisioning takes care of managing users and devices by device importing and synchronization, integration, maintaining user details.

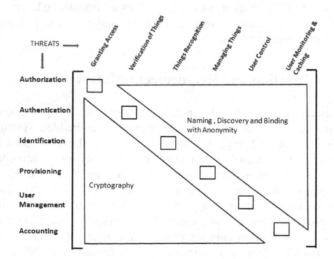

Fig. 6. Identity Requirement Matrix

6 Proposed IdM Framework

In IoT, identity information might be easily associated with location and context information read from sensors. There are five key challenges that target name and address mechanisms. Each challenge is summarized below.

- **Names and addresses that hold identity**

Rather than traditional device identifiers that reveal identity, e.g., IP addresses, MAC addresses, RFID identifiers, there is need to develop names and addresses that conceal identity by cryptographic techniques.

- **Discovery and binding**

Mechanisms that create bindings between different levels of names and addresses often reveal identity information. We seek to create binding mechanisms with cryptographic techniques so that nearby observers or service providers do not learn the identity of devices until it is necessary.

- **Management of implicit names**

Many different information leaks from a system can uniquely fingerprint a device, e.g., timers that expose clock skew [13] and responses to probes. We will develop techniques to check devices for implicit names.

- **Privacy and authentication**

Access control is an essential part of any security system. Privacy preserving attribute-based access control protects identity and enforces access control where access is based on attributes. The thing would get access granted if it possess required attributes. IoT requires a trusted identity service provider for Things. New requirements must be posted towards classic IdM extending the authentication methods, allowing identity imprinting, trust negotiation and trust revocation.

- **Multi device SSO**

Work on concepts for a multi-device sign-on to things and the services that they provide. An example would be the access to data collected from home sensor from multiple devices that a user owns.

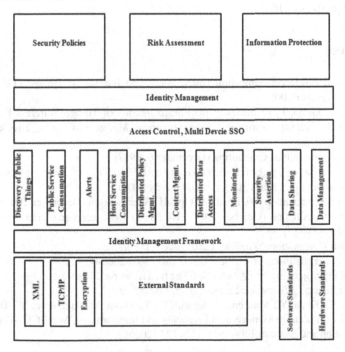

Fig. 7. IdM Framework for IoT

In IoT, interactions between device, user and a service provider should be secure, regardless of the type of device used to access or consume a service. Research aims at design of secure IdM Framework as shown in figure 7, to deliver services of devices, whilst also hiding the complexity of security management from users. Key to this framework is the device management that manages a device's security credentials and identity, and interacts with service providers on its behalf. This framework also aims at providing user with assurance that a compromised device cannot consume/provide the delivered service, and, at the same time, prevents users from illegally sharing their credentials with other users or devices. A well-deployed IdM solution at access gateway layer simplifies the creation, ongoing management and deletion of identities while eliminating oversights and errors that can compromise security. IdM provisioning allows the creation of new identities, handles the assignments and changes to rights or access, and then allows the removal or destruction of identities.

7 Conclusion

In IoT environment, service interactions between a user, device and a service provider should be secure, regardless of the type of device used to access or consume a service. Using service discovery and binding mechanisms, the framework facilitates the secure delivery of services to user devices, whilst removing the complexities of security management from the users. A user need not be worried if his/her device has been compromised. Service providers are also assured that unauthorized credential sharing is prevented. Our security analysis shows that the framework meets all the identified security objectives of IdM.

References

1. International Telecommunication Union 2005. The Internet of Things. ITU Internet Reports (November 2005)
2. Sarma, A., Girao, J.: Identities in the Future Internet of Things, Wireless Pers Commun. 49, 353–363 (2009); Springer Science+Business Media, LLC. 200, Tuesday, April 07 (2009)
3. Daniels. A Ubiquitous Computing (December 6, 1997), http://www.cc.getch.edu/class/cs6751_97_fallprojects/gacha/daniels_essay.html (last viewed on July 2008)
4. OpenID Authentication 2.0, Finalized OpenID Specification (December 2007)
5. The Liberty Alliance (October 2007), http://www.projectliberty.org/ (accessed 2008-08-15)
6. Microsoft Corporation, Windows CardSpace (2006), http://cardspace.netfx3.com/ (accessed 2008-08-15)
7. Shibboleth project, http://shibboleth.internet2.edu/
8. Higgins, http://www.eclipse.org/higgins/
9. Miyata, T., Koga, Y., Madsen, P., Adachi, S., Tsuchiya, Y., Sakamoto, Y., Takahashi, K.: A Survey on Identity Management Protocols and Standards. ACM IEICE –Transactions on Information and Systems E89-D(1), 112–123 (2006)

10. Thompson, C.W., Thompson, D.R.: Identity Management. IEEE Internet Computing, 82–85 (May/June 2007)
11. Leung, A., Mitchell, C.J.: A Device Management Framework for Secure Ubiquitous Service Delivery. In: The Fourth International Conference on Information Assurance and Security, Naples, Italy (September 2008)
12. Stango, A., Prasad, N.R., Kyriazanos, D.M.: A Threat Analysis Methodology for Security Evaluation and Enhancement Planning. In: Third International Conference on Emerging Security Information, Systems and Technologies, SECURWARE 2009, June 18-23, pp. 262–267 (2009)
13. Kohno, T., Broido, A., claffy, k.: Remote physical device fingerprinting. In: IEEE Symposium on Security and Privacy, pp. 211–225. IEEE Computer Society, Los Alamitos (May 2005)

Reputation Enhancement in a Trust Management System

Shashi Bhanwar and Seema Bawa

Centre of Excellence in Grid Computing
Computer Science and Engineering Department
Thapar University
Patiala-147004, India
{shashi,seema}@thapar.edu

Abstract. In this paper, an extended TUX-TMS: A reputation based Trust Management System is presented for enhancing reputation for enabling transaction between unknown users in grid environments. TUX-TMS evaluates trustworthiness and reputation of a domain on the basis of user feedback which is further computed using trust context factor, risk assessment, trust inheritance and trust & reputation decay. TUX-TMS is further extended by including user zones and phylogenetic tree for the users. The parameters are enhanced and redefined to secure transactions and make the information provided more trustworthy. The reputation information is also aggravated hierarchically which enables new entities to inherit domain's reputation information.

Keywords: Trust, Trust Management System, Grid Computing, Reputation, Feedback.

1 Introduction

The original vision of Grid computing aimed at having a single global infrastructure and providing users with computing power on demand [1]. In the context of grid computing the service providers and requesters may belong to various administrative domains and involve the risk of executing transactions without prior experience and knowledge about each other's reputation. In [5], two approaches are defined for handling access controls to the resources in a grid: First is the policy based approach where logical rules and verifiable properties are encoded in signed credentials; second is the reputation based approach where trust values are collected, aggregated and evaluated to disseminate reputation among the market players. Trust and reputation models play a significant role in such open markets to allow service requesters and providers to check trustworthiness, reputation and then accessing risk involved in transacting with unknown users. Reputation based models aggregate trust values and compute behavior trust of market players. Recognizing the importance of incorporating trust in such environments, there is a need for designing strategies and mechanisms to establish and evaluate trust. But, building an efficient reputation based trust management system (TMS) is a challenging task due to several intrinsic requirements of grid computing systems such as QoS(Quality of Service) and SLA(Service Level Agreement). In this paper, we extend TUX-TMS (Thapar University Extensible-Trust

N. Meghanathan et al. (Eds.): CNSA 2010, CCIS 89, pp. 440–451, 2010.

Management System) for enhancing trust in Grid Environments. The proposed extended Trust system evaluates trustworthiness of the transacting domain on the basis of number of past transactions, number of domains interacted, feedback ratings and recommendations. TUX-TMS evaluates trust on the basis of user feedback which is further computed taking metrics such as trust context factor, risk assessment, trust inheritance and trust & reputation decay into account.

The rest of the paper is organized as follows: Section 2 reviews existing trust based models in grid environments. Section 3 describes our implementation of TUX-TMS, a reputation based trust model for establishing secure grids. Section 4 describes the results of our experiments with TUX-TMS. Section 5 concludes with a brief summary and discussion of the main results and an outline of some directions for future research.

2 Related Work

Trust and reputation systems have been recognized as key factors for successful electronic commerce adoption. Review of trust and reputation based systems and security threats on these models have been discussed in [3], [4], [17], [18]. There are many trust management systems proposed in [19], [20], [21], [22], [23], [24], [25] for various computing paradigms. In grid environments, there are two different types of trust management systems: Reputation based and policy based [5]. A number of trust models have been proposed by different researchers for evaluation of trust in a grid. Some of them are discussed here:

Secure Grid Outsourcing (SeGO) system [6], [7] was developed at University of Southern California for secure scheduling of a large number of autonomous and indivisible jobs to grid. A unique feature of the work is that the authors have used a fuzzy inference approach to binding security in trusted grid computing environment. Abdul Rahman and Hailes proposed a Trust– Reputation Model [8] based on prior experiences which are based on trust characteristics from social sciences. F. Azzedin and Maheswaran proposed a Trust Model for Grid Computing Systems [9] which is extension of [8] and [10]. They have insisted on, that a direct trust value weighs more than a recommender value. The model lets a newcomer to build trust from scratch by enforcing enhanced security. Here, trust is dynamic, context specific, based on past experiences and spans over a set of values ranging from very trustworthy to very untrustworthy. Farag Azzedin and Muthucumaru proposed a Trust Model [11] for peer to peer computing systems, also. In addition to previous model [11], an accuracy measure is associated with each recommendation. Chin Li, V Varadharajan, Yan Wang and V. Pruthi proposed a Trust Management Architecture [12] for enhancing grid security that explores the three dimensional view of trust which includes belief, disbelief and uncertainty. This subjective logic based trust evaluation is based on Dempster-Shafer theory [13]. B.E. Alunkal, Laszewski et al. [14] exploits the beneficial properties of EigenTrust [31], extending the model to allow its usage in grids. They integrate the trust management system as part of the QoS management framework, proposing to probabilistically pre-select the resources based on their likelihood to deliver the requested capability and capacity. They took the basic framework of EigenTrust and adapt it for grid requirements, resulting in GridEigenTrust model. The approach of Laszewski et al. [14] is one of the few from literature to propose a reputation service as a way to improve QoS management in grids. Although they present the design of the system, they do not present experiments in order to prove the efficiency of the approach. PathTrust[15] is one of the first attempts to apply reputation methods to grids by approaching VO management phases. Authors have approached only partner selection and had not tackled organizational aspects. Their model lack dynamics, as the feedback is collected only at the dissolution of the VO. All these trust models use different mechanisms to establish trust in various environments and computing paradigms.

3   Extended TUX-TMS Model

In an extended TUX-TMS, the reputation information has been enhanced further by enhancing parameters discussed in subsequent section so as to make grid environments more secure. Section 3.1 discusses architecture of TUX-TMS.

3.1 Architecture of TUX-TMS

The architecture of the TUX-TMS is depicted in Fig.1. An end user i.e. service requestor is requested to login into the TUX-TMS using his credentials. If the user is already registered with the TUX-TMS, the Identity Management System checks and verifies authentication information provided such as security certificates or else if a user is new, he is requested to register. Firstly, the values of Trust Inheritance, Risk Assessment and Trustworthiness (TD) and Recommendation (RD) are checked and then a user is allowed a set M {D, Sp, S} where D is a set of domains {D1, D2, D3....}, and Sp is a set of service providers {Sp1, Sp2, Sp3....} and S is a set of services, a user is allowed to access {S1, S2, S3...}.

After accessing the service, the user is requested to fill in the Feedback form which is in the form of a questionnaire and the values are taken on a scale of 0-1 for trustworthiness and recommendation. The service provider is also requested to fill up the pending feedback form. Thereby, making the transaction complete. An Intrusion Detection System and audit trails checks the information provided to be from the intended players. The trust values and recommendation values are updated in their respective databases. If the values are reported from the malicious origin, the values are discarded and the malicious domains are blacklisted, by imposing a penalty. TUX-TMS DB is responsible for maintaining the database. Fig.2 presents the activity diagram of the components of TUX-TMS.

3.2 Parameters

We have considered and enhanced following parameters for our extended TUX-TMS model.

Trust: Trust is a subjective, dynamic, context dependent and non monotonic. It decays with time and can be classified into levels. Trust cannot be measured objectively but it is assumed to be a subjective degree of belief, which extends from complete distrust to complete trust. Trust is a subjective belief of a person about another person, technological solutions cannot be sufficient to resolve trust issues.

Reputation: The reputation of an entity is an expectation of its behavior based on other entities observation or information about the entity's past behavior within a specific context of a given time. Reputation of an entity is calculated by the feedback information submitted by the interacting player which consists of trustworthiness and recommendation information as well.

Identity trust: Identity trust is the trust that a subject holds on other entity without making any intermediate entity. If focuses on verifying the authenticity of an entity and determining the authorizations that the entity is entitled to access and is based on techniques including encryption, data hiding, digital signatures, authentication protocols, and access control mechanisms. We have deployed an Identity Management System to verify and validate credentials submitted by the users.

Behavior trust: Behavior trust may be considered as reputation of an entity as seen by other entities. We are calculating trustworthiness of domains and entities over a period of time on the basis of the feedback submitted by the interacting domain to determine behavior of interacting domains over a period of time.

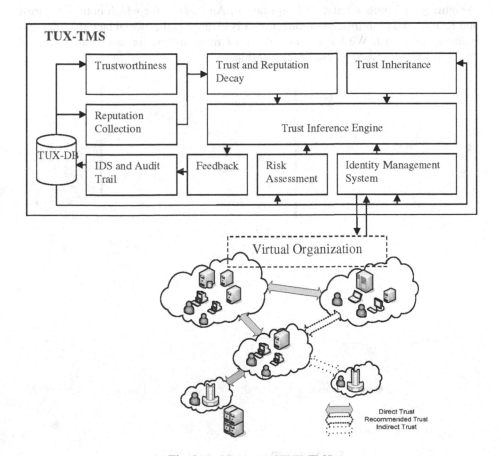

Fig. 1. Architecture of TUX-TMS

Feedback: After trust evaluation, entity decides to interact with a chosen entity. After an interaction feedback is taken, according to which trustworthiness and reputation information is updated. The feedback is submitted by the service requester as well as the provider for the interacting domain.

Trust and Reputation Updation: Trust and Reputation information is updated a successful transaction.

Trust and Reputation Decay: Trust and reputation values decays with time. The positive or negative effect of a successful interaction reduces over the time.

Trust Symmetry: If Alice trust Bob then does Bob trust Alice? The answer is not necessarily yes! This situation is called trust asymmetry problem. We have left the choice with service provider to allow only users who surpass threshold limit.

Historical accumulation of past behavior: An entity that interacts with another entity, after evaluation of trust, has to store the value for future use.

Weightage of identity trust and reputation: An identity for which both direct trust and recommendation trust exist, direct trust is given a higher weightage than the recommendation trust. We have considered trust relationships for our system such as direct, indirect and recommended relationship.

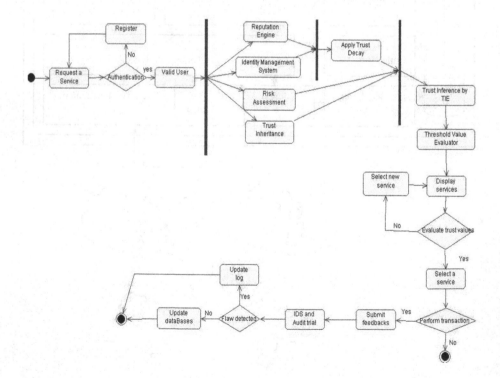

Fig. 2. TUX-TMS: An activity diagram

Trust level
Trust can be categorized into levels. Trust can range from ht to hu as shown in Table 1 where et is rarely achievable therefore, not considered for real models.

Table 1. Trust levels

Trust level	Descriptions
Et	Extremely trustworthy
Ht	Highly trustworthy
T	Trustworthy
Nu	Not trustworthy
Hu	Highly untrustworthy

Trust Inheritance
In a grid environment, entities are dynamic i.e. they can join and leave a virtual organization at any time. Hence, a trust model for such an environment should have mechanisms for managing trust for such entities. When an entity joins a domain, it inherits the Tfin from the domain, it is part of. We calculate T_i using equation 5.

Evolving trust as a newcomer
As a new entity joins a domain, it initially has no Trustworthiness and reputation values. A newcomer is allowed to interact with domain having certain threshold limit for services and it can then build its own trust values.

Trust threshold
Trust threshold may be defined as minimum trust values that are required to access the services.

False Recommendation
Reputation of an entity is calculated from recommendation of several other entities. Any entity can give fraudulent recommendation, which is taken care of by aggregating all the recommendation given by a particular entity.

Aggregation of all recommendations
All the recommendation given for a particular entity is aggregated to check any malicious of fraudulent information.

Transitive Recommendation
If A trusts B and B trusts C then A may also trust C. This is called transitivity. In open distributed environments trust information can be collected from recommenders and trust bases to check the authenticity of the users and then transaction may be committed.

Risk assessment
Risk assessment accounts for the bad behavior of the entity. Even a good known entity may also behave badly in some situations. Risk assessment checks the risk involved in transacting with a particular entity.

Intrusion detection and audit trail

Intrusion detection is a process of monitoring the events occurring in a computer system or network and analyzing them for signs of possible incidents, which are violation or imminent threats of violation of computer security policies [22]. For detecting authorized but abusive user activity, audit trails may be an appropriate means. Audit trails can establish accountability of users for their actions. They can provide evidence to establish the guilt or innocence of suspected individuals. If any malicious activity is found, trust level decreases and penalties can be imposed on the defaulters.

Interoperability

Interoperability aims at federating the use of user's credentials and providing a unique authentication and authorization framework. Users logged into disparate middleware's are allowed to log in to the system and access grid.

3.3 Partitioning of the Users

The users can be categorized according to their behaviors patterns. Table 2 shows their partitioning.

- **White zone:** The users who have always submitted honest feedback and there has been no security violation or malicious activity reported against them come under white zone users.
- **Blue zone:** The users who in spite of having good reputation and who have been submitting honest feedback in the starting have all of a sudden started submitting false feedback information come under the category of blue zone users.
- **Grey zone:** The users who have submitted some honest and some false feedback information and who have reported security violations against them come under the category of grey zone users.
- **Black zone:** The users who have only submitted false feedback and have only malicious activities come under black zone users.

Table 2. Partitioning the users

Zone	Trustworthiness	Risk involved
White	High	Low
Blue	Medium high	Medium
Grey	Medium	Medium high
Black	Negligible/Low	Very High

Further, a phylogenetic tree has been created showing the inferred evolutionary relationships among various users in these zones based upon similarities and differences in their identity and behavioral characteristics. An example is depicted in Fig.3. In a phylogenetic tree, the taxa joined together in the tree are implied to have descended from a common ancestor. In a rooted phylogenetic tree, each node with descendants represents the inferred most recent common ancestor of the descendants and the edge lengths in some trees may be interpreted as time estimates. Each node is called a taxonomic unit. Internal nodes are generally called hypothetical taxonomic units (HTUs) as they cannot be directly observed. The tree can be further, evolved for a number of users.

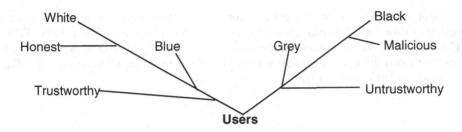

Fig. 3. A phylogenetic tree of users

4 Results and Discussion

In addition to developing a theoretical model for TUX-TMS, we also conduct a comprehensive performance analysis using various trust metrics as discussed here.

The implementation environment consists of 30 domains with users ranging from 2 to 25 in each domain. All the domains have 3-10 service providers that provide different services/resources to other domains. Users can login using different security credentials (X.509 certificate). These credentials have been generated through .NET tools. A few entities were created and the behavior of the entities evaluated over a period of time. Database is created in Microsoft SQL Server 2005. The performance of trust system is measured in terms of number of interactions that took place. We have tested the trust model using various metrics such as trust and reputation decay, trust inheritance, trust context factor and risk assessment.

A transactional database consists of sequence of transactions: t={t1........tn}. Here, transaction t is composed of a service requester requesting a service from the service provider and then providing feedback and vice versa. On the basis of the transaction taken place and feedback submitted, we have taken the trustworthiness and recommendation values and stored them for further calculations. Further, these values are used to compute reputation and trustworthiness of domain using equations 1 to 5.

$$T_{Decay} = T_w/N_t \qquad (1)$$

$$R_{Decay} = R_c/D_n \qquad (2)$$

$$T_{fin} = \alpha * T_r + \beta * R_c + \gamma \qquad (3)$$

$$R_a = R_{ank}/T_{dn} \qquad (4)$$

$$T_i = T_{fin} - R_a * 100 \qquad (5)$$

Here, T_w: Trustworthiness, T_{decay}: Trust Decay Factor, R_c= Recommendation, N_T: Number of transactions, D: Domain, R_{decay}=Reputation Decay, D_n: Total number of domains with whom transaction has taken place, T_{fin}=Total trust value, T_{dn}: Total number of domains in the system, R_a=Risk Assessment, R_{ank}=Rank of a domain, T_i=Trust Inheritance, α, β, γ=Constants used for belief, disbelief and plausibility.

Fig.4 shows the trustworthiness and recommendation values accumulated over a period of time for 30 domains, before computing the values using TUX-TMS. TUX-TMS however, due to dynamic nature and uncertainty in grid environment, uses values of trustworthiness and reputation only after decaying them with the T_{decay} and R_{decay} functions, as shown in Fig.5.

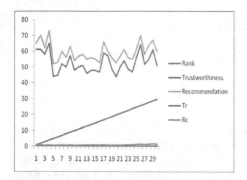
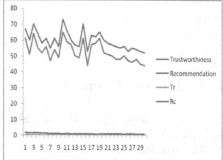

Fig. 4. Trustworthiness and Recommendation values

Fig. 5. Trust and Reputation Decay

4.1 Performance against Malicious Users

The malicious users are usually the grey zone or the black zone users where interaction with them goes at very medium high and high risk, respectively. When the user is allowed to transact with any other user on a first come first served basis, then the risk involved in transacting is increased manifold and can make system vulnerable to attacks by the malicious users. The risk may be high with some domains and low with the others. Fig. 6(a) shows hypothetical view of the risk involved in transacting with domains on first come first served basis for 30 domains.

When the user is allowed to transact with any domain with any other user on random basis, the risk can be still high. Figure 6(b) shows hypothetical view of the risk involved in transacting with any unknown domains for 30 domains.

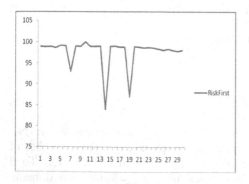
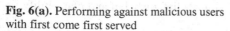
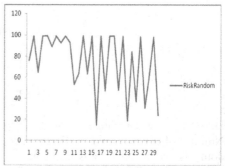

Fig. 6(a). Performing against malicious users with first come first served

Fig. 6(b). Performing against malicious users with random access

In TUX-TMS, the users have been ranked according to the trustworthiness and recommendation score in terms of context factor. In this model, we have also considered that higher the trust context factor, higher the reputation of the entity/domain.

The users are penalize for malicious activities and false feedback, where their trustworthiness and recommendation scores are discarded for such activities. The rank decreases in repository which also increases the risk involved in transacting with the domain, as shown in Fig. 6(c). Using ranking of domains and risk assessment our system promotes secure transactions.

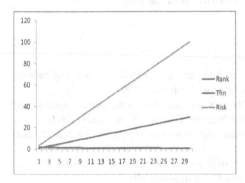
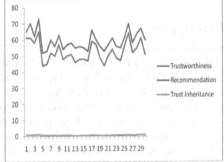

Fig. 6(c). Risk invloved in transacting with TUX-TMS

Fig. 7. Trust Inheritance

4.2 Performance in a Distributed Environment

The trustworthiness and recommendation scores are submitted and aggregated over a period of time. Only, the scores of the domains interacting are maintained, so as to avoid memory overhead.

Score of new domain remains 0 and the entity will not be able to score very well and access many services. So, registering as a new user poses threats as malicious users may try to attract the user by showing their status as trustworthy users. The trust inheritance incorporated in TUX-TMS enables users/entities with an inheritance score and allows users to access trustworthy services from other domains as services may have threshold or policies to allow users above a certain trust score or limit. Fig. 7 shows the trust inherited from the domains for the new users.

5 Conclusion

In this paper, we have extended our TUX-TMS: an extensible Reputation based Trust Management system by including definitions of parameters and their sustainability with the model. The partitioning of the users has been introduced in the paper. A phylogenetic tree is explored for the model, which may be further enhanced as the user's behavioral patterns evolutes. The activity diagram of the model shows the flow of information in the model. TUX-TMS enables user to make informed decisions about which players to trust. The grid domains are dynamic and heterogeneous in nature.

The Identity Management System incorporates authentication, authorization, confidentiality, log related and trust related functions. The trust and reputation updation ensures that the database is maintained up to date. TUX-TMS is a secure and reliable system which prohibits malicious users from submitting false feedback and penalizes them. In addition to developing a theoretical model for TUX-TMS, we also conduct a comprehensive performance analysis. Our evaluation results show that reputation can be enhanced by using various parameters. The results also show that the TUX-TMS model is flexible enough for identity and behavior trust and it also incorporates Audit trail and analysis, which keep malicious users away from harming the system.

References

[1] Assuncao, M.D.D.: Provisioning Techniques and Policies for Resource Sharing between Grids. Ph.D. Thesis. The University of Melbourne, Australia (2009)

[2] Silaghi, G.C., Arenas, A.E., Silva, L.M.: Reputation-based trust management systems and their applicability to grids. Technical Report Number TR-0064. CoreGRID (2007)

[3] Sabater, J., Sierra, C.: Review on computational trust and reputation models. Kluwer Academic Publishers 10(34), 1–28 (2005)

[4] Jøsang, A., Ismail, R., Boyd, C.: A Survey of Trust and Reputation Systems for Online Service Provision. Decision Support Systems 43(2), 618–644 (2007)

[5] Chakrabarti, A.: Grid Computing Security. Springer, Heidelberg (2007)

[6] Song, S., Hwang, K., Macwan, M.: Fuzzy Trust Integration for Security Enforcement in Grid Computing. In: Jin, H., Gao, G.R., Xu, Z., Chen, H. (eds.) NPC 2004. LNCS, vol. 3222, pp. 9–21. Springer, Heidelberg (2004)

[7] Song, S., Hwang, K., Kwok, Y.K.: Trusted Grid Computing with Security Binding and Trust Integration. Journal of Grid Computing 3(1), 24–34 (2005)

[8] Rahman, A.A., Hailes, S.: Supporting trust in virtual communities. In: Proc. of Hawaii Intl Conference on System Sciences, pp. 6007–6016. IEEE Computer Society Press, Los Alamitos (2000)

[9] Azzedin, F., Maheswaran, M.: Evolving and Managing Trust in Grid Computing Systems. In: Proc. of the 2002 IEEE Canadian Conference on Electrical & Computer Engineering, pp. 1424–1429. IEEE Press, Los Alamitos (2002)

[10] Damianou, N., Dulay, N., Lupu, E., Sloman, M.: The Ponder Policy Specification Language. In: Sloman, M., Lobo, J., Lupu, E.C. (eds.) POLICY 2001. LNCS, vol. 1995, pp. 18–38. Springer, Heidelberg (2001)

[11] Azzedin, F., Maheswaran, M.: Trust Modeling for Peer-to- Peer based Computing Systems. In: Proceedings of the International Parallel and Distributed Processing Symposium, IPDPS 2003, p. 99a (2003)

[12] Lin, C., Varadharajan, V., Wang, Y., Pruthi, V.: Enhancing Grid Security with Trust Management. In: Proc. of the 2004 IEEE International Conference on Services Computing (SCC 2004), pp. 303–310. IEEE Press, Los Alamitos (2004)

[13] Shafer, G.: Perspectives on the theory and practice of belief functions. International Journal of Approximate Reasoning 6(3), 445–480 (1992)

[14] Laszewski, G.V., Alunkal, B.E., Veljkovic, I.: Towards reputable grids. Scalable Computing: Practice and Experience 6(3), 95–106 (2005)

[15] Kerschbaum, F., Haller, J., Karabulut, Y., Robinson, P.: Pathtrust: A trust-based reputation service for virtual organization formation. In: Stølen, K., Winsborough, W.H., Martinelli, F., Massacci, F. (eds.) iTrust 2006. LNCS, vol. 3986, pp. 193–205. Springer, Heidelberg (2006)

[16] Shashi, B., Bawa, S.: TUX-TMS: Thapar University Extensible-Trust Management System. International Journal of Security, CSC Journals 4(1), 1–16 (2010)

[17] Marmol, F.L., Perez, G.M.: Security threats scenarios in trust and reputation models for distributed systems. Computers and Security 28(7), 545–556 (2009)

[18] Almenarez, F., Marın, A., Campo, C., Garcıa, C.: PTM: a pervasive trust management model for dynamic open environments. In: Privacy and Trust. First Workshop on Pervasive Security and Trust (2004)

[19] Boukerche, A., Xu, L., El-Khatib, K.: Trust-based security for wireless ad hoc and sensor networks. Computer Communications 30(11-12), 2413–2427 (2007)

[20] Carbo, J., Molina, J., Davila, J.: Trust management through fuzzy reputation. International Journal of Cooperative Information Systems 12, 135–155 (2003)

[21] Chen, H., Wu, H., Zhou, X., Gao, C.: Agent-based trust model in wireless sensor networks. In: Eighth ACIS International Conference on Software Engineering, Artificial Intelligence, Networking, and Parallel/Distributed Computing, SNPD 2003, pp. 119–124 (2007)

[22] Aberer, K.: P-Grid: A Self-Organizing Access Structure for P2P Information Systems. In: Batini, C., Giunchiglia, F., Giorgini, P., Mecella, M. (eds.) CoopIS 2001. LNCS, vol. 2172, pp. 179–194. Springer, Heidelberg (2001)

[23] Zhou, R., Hwang, K.: PowerTrust: A Robust and scalable reputation system for trusted peer-to-peer computing. IEEE Transactions on Parallel and Distributed Systems 18(4), 621–636 (2007)

[24] Marmol, F.G., Perez, G.P., Skarmeta, A.F.: TACS, A Trust Model for P2P Networks. Wireless Personal Communications 51(1), 153–164 (2008)

[25] Abrams, Z., Mcgrew, R., Plotkin, S.: A non-manipulable trust system based on Eigentrust. ACM SIGecom Exchanges 5(4), 21–30 (2005)

A-Code: A New Crypto Primitive for Securing Wireless Sensor Networks

Giovanni Schmid[1] and Francesco Rossi[2]

[1] CNR-ICAR - Sede di Napoli, Via P. Castellino n. 111, 80131 Napoli
giovanni.schmid@na.icar.cnr.it
[2] Universitá degli Studi Parthenope, Centro Direzionale Is. C4, 80143 Napoli
francesco.rossi@uniparthenope.it

Abstract. Many real-world scenarios require the effective enforcement of a common bulk of strong security services that nowadays Wireless Sensor Network (WSN) implementations are far from achieving. This paper introduces a new cryptographic primitive which seems very promising to achieve authentication of the nodes involved in a WSN in such usage scenarios. We show the feasibility of this primitive by showing some its remarkable features in the context of radio communications and by comparing its power consumption to those of Public-Key Certificates.

Keywords: wireless sensor networks, authentication, cryptographic protocols.

1 Introduction

Wireless Sensor Networks (WSN) are getting in the recent years more and more importance in applications. Industrial, agricultural, health care, environmental, security, and military users are beginning to recognize how wireless sensors can allow for better pervasiveness and easier, lower cost deployments in several physical environments, both indoor and outdoor. Actually, WSN mature deployments can revolutionize the way supervisory control and data acquisition is realized, greatly expanding their feasibility to many real-world scenarios.

However, some of such application scenarios require the effective enforcement of a common bulk of strong security services that nowadays implementations are far from achieving. The main reason of this lack roots in the circumstance that strong security is power consuming, whilst sensor devices have scarce power autonomy. For example, in order to effectively and safely employ WSN in large-scale environment monitoring, as in seismic surveillance, air/water quality controls or fire prevention, one has to meet the following two opposite requirements: (a) power autonomy of the WSN in the medium or long time-range (possibly varying from weeks to months, or also years), by using a combination of node-specific, renewable energy sources[1] and duty cycling[2], and; (b) WSN resistance to both

---

[1] e.g. solar panels.
[2] i.e., having the device wake up only occasionally to record and/or transmit sensor readings and sleeping for the most part of time.

N. Meghanathan et al. (Eds.): CNSA 2010, CCIS 89, pp. 452–462, 2010.

denial-of-service attacks and offensive actions targeted to alter data being acquired by the sensors. Requirement (a) is a direct consequence of the monitoring activity required in those application scenarios, and the fact that network deployment efforts/costs can be very high because of the high number of sensors to put in place and inhospitableness of the environment (e.g. mountain areas, forests). As for (b), it should be clear that such networks can represent valuable targets in view of vandalism, terrorism or lucrative purposes.

As a general fact, all the security services provided for a network of communicating nodes relies upon their mutual authentications. In turn, entity authentication protocols rely upon some cryptographic material (often in the form of a secret or a private key) associated by design with the genuine parties. Thus, it takes great relevance to study cryptographic primitives that can be used to establish such keys and are suitable for the WSN application scenarios previously depicted.

In this paper we introduce a new cryptographic primitive, called Authentication Code (A-Code), which allows for the establishment of authentic public keys in WSNs. A-Code is especially suited for communications over radio channels, since it has built-in protection against the most prominent radio-waves technology related ways of attack, namely *jamming* and *bit-flipping* [1]. Moreover, A-Codes give rise to key establishment protocols which seem promising for the above scenarios, where self-organization and scalability of the WSN are a must. Our experimental results show the practicality of this approach, although by just comparing power consumptions of a prototypal implementation of A-Codes with Public-Key Certificates (PKCs) on the Sun SPOT system [2]. Moreover, these results show that A-Codes outperform PKCs if used in conjunction with broadcast communications, which is often the case, for example, in routing protocols.

The paper is organized as follows. Section 2 describes the usage scenarios for which A-Codes seem a promising alternative to conventional methods. Section 3 describes the A-Code primitive, showing its dependency on Integrity Codes (I-Codes)[3] and its advantages over conventional methods. Section 4 describes our experimental platform, whilst Section 5 illustrates the power consumption experiments performed on such platform. Finally, Sections 6 and 7 discuss about related and future works, respectively.

2 Usage Scenario and Functional Requirements

The usage scenario is that of data collection - on an outdoor area, and for a period of medium to long term - through the deployment in that area of a large-scale wireless sensor network. The data collected by sensors are transmitted through the network and collected by a base station so that they can be processed by a decision-making engine. Decisions results in one or more actions, such as generating an alarm or activating an appropriate procedure.

The deployment should be possible even in areas of difficult access, which could require aerial modes for node settlement.

The network should not depend in any way by wired links or any other fixed infrastructure, including the power supply of sensors, with the exception of the base station and the communication and computing devices directly connected to it. For each sensor node, power supply is provided through the equipment of a battery and appropriate solar cells.

The WSN should be *self-organized*, meaning that it should not be necessary to determine a-priori node connections, but rather these are determined automatically depending on mutual node locations, with the goal of improving the resilience of the network. In particular, in order to optimize node energy consumption, the network must provide for adaptive behavior of node power radio transmissions in terms of a parameter-threshold, defined before the deployment of the network itself, and given the sufficient number of nodes to be considered immediate neighbors. The mesh of connections will be made wherever possible to meet the value of "sufficient adjacent nodes for each node in the network", so that only for each pair of adjacent nodes is provided a link.

The network should be *reparable*, meaning that if one or more nodes are no longer functional then they can be replaced, even without having direct physical access to the place or area location of faulty nodes, restoring the original network functionality.

The network should also be *scalable*, in that it should be possible to add one or more nodes in the same way as for the initial deployment.

The availability and integrity of data collected by sensors should be considered critical, since they result in a valuable decision. Thus, the WSN should ensure the authenticity of its nodes, the integrity of communication links among them, and their resistance to Denial of Service attacks.

3   The A-Code Primitive

In this paper we are not concerned with the specification of any WSN protocol guaranteeing in some way the security requirements indicated in the previous Section; rather, our goal is to show that the A-Code primitive is appropriate for setting up authentic cryptographic material (in particular, crypto keys) in the usage scenarios depicted therein. That cryptographic material can used later to securely route packets or establish communication (data-transfer) sessions between nodes, through suitable routing or communication protocols.

A-Code is a new security primitive that enables authentication and integrity protection of messages exchanged over a radio communication channel. Message integrity is gained through unidirectional message coding and on-off keying communication with signal anti-blocking; these are the three components which give rise to I-Codes [3].

Unidirectional message coding ensures that bit 0 cannot be changed in bit 1. Manchester code is an example of unidirectional coding scheme; it encodes each bit 1 as 10 and each bit 0 as 01. If we suppose that an adversary can only convert a bit 0 into bit 1, then the receiver will be able to detect forged messages, since such messages cannot be decoded properly.

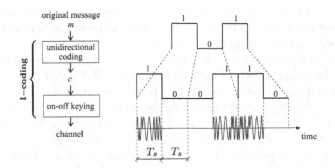

Fig. 1. Example of I-Coding using Manchester code [3]. The message m=101 is coded as c=100110.

On-off keying is a signal modulation technique such that bit 1 is transmitted as the presence of a signal, and bit 0 as the absence of a signal for a known time slice T_S. *Signal anti-blocking* uses a random energy signal, so that an adversary cannot annihilate bits 1 by jamming the signal. Considered together, on-off keying and signal anti-blocking give a good resistance against attacks based upon jamming and/or bit-flipping [1].

I-Codes can also achieve message authentication, but only through presence awareness; that is, the receiver needs to be aware of the fact that it is in the transmission range and the signal is the channel used by an authorized sender. This requires an infrastructure of authorized senders located in known positions or, alternatively, continuously signaling senders on known channels. Of course, both these two conditions cannot be satisfied in the context of the usage scenarios depicted in Section 2. Thus, we provided authentication by realizing the random energy signal that corresponds to bit 1 as the (pseudo)random payload $p(n)$ of packet n given by:

$$p(n) = H(K\|H(K\|H(....H(K\|X_{ID})....)))$$
$$= H(K\|p(n-1)) \ ,$$

where X_{ID} denotes the identifier of node X, K is a network-wide secret, H is a suitable and known cryptographic hash function, n is an integer related is some way to the number of 1 bits emitted so far by node X, and the function H is applied n times. The receiver will consider the packet authentic only if:

$$H(K\|p(n-1)) = p'(n) \ ,$$

where $p'(n)$ is the payload issued by the sender (because of the message integrity property), and the first member in the previous equality is computed by the receiver as a consequence of its knowledge of H, K and X_{ID}. This assumes that sender and receiver are somewhat synchronized. For a good efficiency , such "authenticated" 1 bits can be generated only if they represent the special 1 bit (e.g. the leftmost one) of special manchester codewords (e.g. codewords which code a meta-character plus the value of n, for a quick re sync with the receiver). This allows for great savings in computing time and power consumptions for the sender, and even more savings for the receiver.

Because of the above properties, the A-Code primitive seems particularly suitable for the usage scenario illustrated in Section 2. Conversely than conventional (both symmetric and asymmetric) primitives, it indeed allows for node authentication enforcement through neighbour discovering. This simplifies the design of power-efficient authentication protocols with the requirements of self-organization, reparability and scalability. Moreover, as we are going to show in Section 5, A-Code outperforms PKC-based authentication methods in terms of power consumption if the protocol makes large use of multicast communications, which is the case of routing protocols.

4   The Experimental Platform

In January of 2005, Sun Microsystems Labs designed a small, low-power hardware platform that could support Java language, communication of small independent devices, and networks of wireless sensors and actuators. This device was later launched on the market with the name *Sun SPOT*. Sun SPOT devices use 802.15.4 radio waves communication protocol, which allows for a maximum signal range of about 25 mt. [2]. The principal component of a Sun SPOT device is the eSPOT main board, that contains a rechargeable LI-ION battery for power consumption and the eDEMO board.

The eSPOT also contains the main processor, memory, radio transceiver and antenna, daughter board connector, battery connector and power management circuit. The eSPOT can be powered with any combination of rechargeable battery, external voltage or the USB host. Power consumption is measured by the power controller, and is managed through power conservation firmware that allows for two energy-saving modes of operation. In *shallow-sleep* mode processor clocks and radio are off, and power consumption is about 24 ma. *Deep-sleep* mode is instead a standby state which guarantees a power consumption of only 32 μA, but requires a start-up time varying from about 2 msec to 10 msec[2].

The Sun SPOT system is perhaps, at the time of writing, the most advanced platform implementing public-key cryptography for wireless transducer

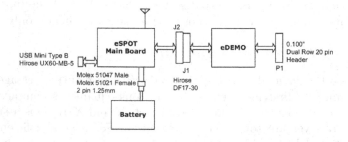

Fig. 2. The eSPOT main board [2]

application security. It implements both an highly optimized RSA cryptosystem and Elliptic Curve Cryptography (ECC). Experimental results show that ECC provides an order of magnitude performance improvement on RSA, and that public-key cryptography is very viable on small wireless devices [5].

The native Sun SPOT ECC implementation uses Public-Key Certificates (PKCs) for public-key management. In order to compare power consumptions of A-Codes with PKCs, we implemented a prototypal A-Code-based cryptosystem differing by the Sun SPOT native one just in the management of keys. Then, we designed and implemented the two following simple algorithms to set up power consumption tests through small-sized, prototypal WSNs.

Prototypal WSN - sensor node	Prototypal WSN - base station

Begin
 	
　　　Init();
 	
　　　Connection(basestation);
 	
　　While{connection is up}
 	
　　　GetData();
 	
　　　FormatData();
 	
　　　SendData();
 	
　　　ShallowSleep(time);
 	
　　End While
 	
End
	Begin
	
	　　　Init();
	
	　　　RunEngine();
	
	　　While{true}
	
	　　　Thread.NewConnection();
	
	　　End While
	
	End

The Init() function is used to initialize all instances of the java classes that implement the chosen cryptosystem. This function implements also a visual protocol based on switching on/off the sensor node led indicators to show the current values of temperature, light and residual battery charge. The GetData() function collects sensor data and battery status information, passing them to the FormatData() function. The latter is used to format data in order to send them to the base station via the SendData() function. Data are formatted as strings in which different data types are separated thanks to the special character #.

The speed at which the network reacts to the occurrence of events is an important functional requirement which depends on the application scenario. With our experiments we aimed to simulate a critical scenario, e.g. monitoring volcanic activity, thus we chose a sustained sampling rate, sending data to the basestation every 60 seconds. The base station performs the same initialization of Sun SPOT nodes via the `Init()` function, then it calls a making-decision engine implemented via function `RunEngine()`. The engine extracts data according to the data format previously described, comparing their values with reference values. If the data does not fall within expected ranges, the engine raises an alarm. The base station does a continuous polling on a given radio frequency, listening for new incoming connection requests by sensor nodes.

5   Experimental Results

Two relevant issues in experimental testing are: (a) management of measuring instruments, and (b) testing conditions.

As for (a), we used the power controller software subsystem provided by Sun SPOT system (s. Section 4) to measure the battery charge levels of a Sun SPOT device prior and after every computing task under observation.

With respect to (b), we proceeded as follows. For each test, the WSN composed of a single Sun SPOT base station and a fixed number of Sun SPOT nodes connected in a one-hop configuration to the base station (no routing). All tests were run indoor and concerned measurements of light intensities. As we told in Section 4, with our experiments we aimed to simulate critical monitoring scenarios, so for all tests we chose a sustained sampling data rate, sending data to the base station every 60 seconds. All measurements were obtained starting by the same initial values of battery power charge and environmental conditions (temperature and humidity). We started every test having a full charged battery on any node, since low charges could result in transmissive power losses of the radio signal that might compromise the test. Finally, all the test were performed at about 20 Celsius degrees and about 50% of relative humidity.

We made three kinds of tests: Survivability tests, Power consumption tests using unicast mode of communication, and Power consumption tests using multicast mode of communication. All the test were performed on Sun SPOT PKCs, I-Codes and A-Codes; except for the last kind of tests, that were performed on I-Codes and A-Codes only, since PKC-based key management does not allow for multicasting.

The goal of Survivability tests was to measure the maximum operating time for different WSN configurations (i.e. number of sensor nodes, reciprocal distance between nodes and node location) and lighting behaviors. The overall result of such tests was that all the WSN configurations under examination (whatever the crypto primitive they adopted) successfully performed their data collection activities for at least 9 hours. This is an encouraging result, since it seems to indicate that a WSN, which performs stressing data sampling and provides data security through any of the considered asymmetric cryptosystems, could be able to operate outdoor in the medium/long term by just equipping each of its sensor nodes with a low-power solar panel. It confirms, and somewhat extends to A-Codes, the results obtained in [6], where a WSN of Sun SPOT equipped with solar panels was able to operate for a period of nearly four weeks.

The purpose of the second set of tests was to verify which of the three considered crypto primitives (i.e., PKC, I-Code and A-Code) is more energy efficient in unicast communications. Each test concerned a single cryptosystem and composed of ten runs. Each run consisted in measuring the power consumption in setting up the public-keys for two communicating nodes. The average values obtained are as follows: PKC = 123.8 mA, I-Code = 126 mA, A-Code = 131.8 mA. Therefore, the more energy efficient crypto primitive for key set up using unicast communications is the PKC. These figures show an important information; namely, that differences in consumption between PKC and A-Code are very small (about 10 % more for the latter), indicating that using A-Codes for securing WSNs is a viable solution. Results for each crypto primitive are showed in Figures 3 - 4 - 5.

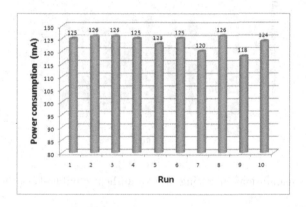

Fig. 3. Power consumptions in setting up two authentic public-keys through PKCs

Multicast mode of communication for key set up can be adopted only if the crypto primitives involved are I-Codes or A-Codes. The last set of tests were performed in order to do a comparison between unicasting and multicasting communication techniques and had as a pre-requisite that of building a prototypal WSN in which each node is capable of spreading its public key to all its neighbour nodes. The test results, depicted in Figure 6, show that - if PKCs are used - then power consumption increase quadratically with the number n of neighbour nodes involved (coherently with the fact that such approach results in $O(n^2)$ unicast communications); whilst such consumption increases linearly with n by broadcasting a public-key to the n neighbour nodes through A-Codes (or I-Codes).

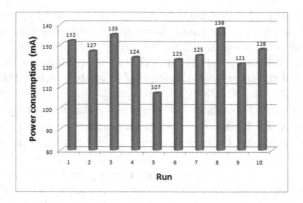

Fig. 4. Power consumptions in setting up two authentic public-keys through I-Codes

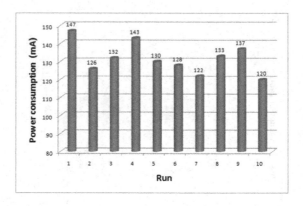

Fig. 5. Power consumptions in setting up two authentic public-keys through A-Codes

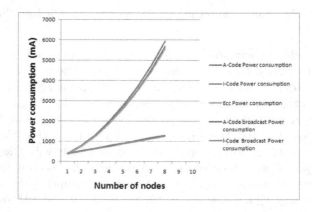

Fig. 6. PKCs versus I-Codes and A-Codes used in conjunction with multicast communications

6 Related Work

Securing WSNs has became a main research topic in the field of network security, and many contributions exist on authentication protocols for WSNs, including secure routing. A interesting survey on crypto primitives and their implementations on WSNs is given in [7]. Besides more traditional protocols based on symmetric cryptographic primitives (e.g. [9,10,12]), asymmetric protocols are getting more and more attention by the research community, now that hardware and rechargeable battery technologies allow for power-lasting node devices. And indeed, many of such protocols (e.g. [8,11]) have been proposed so far. However, to our knowledge, no other work proposes I-Code related mechanisms to achieve node authentication in WSNs. I-Codes were introduced in [3] in order to provide sender authentication in application scenarios where the receiver knows that: (1) it is in the power range of the sender, and (2) the sender has started transmitting on a special, dedicated radio-frequency (the *integrity channel*). These scenarios subsume a signaling infrastructure like in Global Positioning System, which - of course - is not the case of autonomous, self-organized WSNs. Indeed, condition (2) cannot be satisfied in such networks, because nodes act as peers; moreover, their constrained resources result in being unfeasible for them to have to continuously signal over a channel in order to get message integrity.

7 Conclusions and Future Work

The new A-Code cryptographic primitive, introduced in this paper, allows for the establishment of authentic public keys in wireless sensor networks. A-Code is especially suited for communications over radio channels, since it has built-in protection against the most prominent radio-waves technology related ways of attack. Moreover, A-Codes give rise to key establishment protocols which appear to be very effective for application scenarios where self-organization and scalability of the network are a must.

The experimental results collected so far seems to indicate that A-Codes are a viable alternative to public-key certificates, and that their usage could result in a much better power efficiency if the related cryptographic protocol can make use of multicasting. Routing protocols make large use of broadcasting, so the application of A-Codes to such protocols seems really promising.

We are indeed working to a secure routing protocol implementing A-Codes, with the aim of doing a step forward in realizing self-organized, ad-hoc and secure wireless sensor networks suited for real-word environmental monitoring scenarios.

References

1. Wireless LAN Security White Paper, Cisco Systems On-line Documentation (2009)
2. Sun Small Programmable Object Technology (Sun SPOT) - Theory of Operation, Sun Labs (2007)

3. Cagalj, M., Capkun, S., Rengaswamy, R., Tsigkogiannis, I., Srivastava, M., Hubaux, J.: Integrity (I) Codes: Message Integrity Protection and Authentication Over Insecure Channels. In: Proc. of the 2006 IEEE Symposium on Security and Privacy (2006)
4. Menezes, A., van Oorschot, P., Vanstone, S.: Hanbook of Applied Cryptography. CRC Press, Boca Raton (1997)
5. Wander, A., Gura, N., Eberle, H., Gupta, V., Shantz, S.: Energy Analysis of Public-Key Cryptography for Wireless Sensor Networks. In: Proc. of the 3rd IEEE International Conference on Pervasive Computing and Communications (2005)
6. Gupta, V.: Experiments with a Solar-powered Sun SPOT, Sun Labs (2009)
7. Roman, R., Alcaraz, C., Lopez, J.: A Survey of Cryptographic Primitives and Implementations for Hardware-Constrained Sensor Network Nodes. Mobile Netw. Appl. 12 (2007)
8. Seshadri, A., Luk, M., Perrig, A.: SAKE: Software Attestation for Key Establishment in Sensor Networks. In: Nikoletseas, S.E., Chlebus, B.S., Johnson, D.B., Krishnamachari, B. (eds.) DCOSS 2008. LNCS, vol. 5067, pp. 372–385. Springer, Heidelberg (2008)
9. Perrig, A., Canetti, R., Tygar, J., Song, D.: Efficient Authentication and Signing of Multicast Streams over Lossy Channels. In: Proceedings of the IEEE Symposium on Security and Privacy (2000)
10. Hu, Y., Perrig, A., Johnson, D.: Ariadne: A Secure On-Demand Routing Protocol for Ad Hoc Networks. Springer, Heidelberg (2005)
11. Sanzgiri, K., Dahill, B., Neil Levine, B., Shields, C., Royer, E.: A Secure Routing Protocol for Ad Hoc Networks. In: Proc. of the International Conference on Network Protocols (2002)
12. Papadimitratos, P., Haas, Z.J.: Secure Routing for Mobile Ad hoc Networks. In: Proc. of the SCS Communication Networks and Distributed Systems Modeling and Simulation Conference (2002)

Design of a Reliability-based Source Routing Protocol for Wireless Mobile Ad Hoc Networks

Natarajan Meghanathan

Jackson State University
Jackson, MS 39217, USA
natarajan.meghanathan@jsums.edu

Abstract. This paper presents a Reliability-based Source Routing (RSR) protocol for mobile ad hoc networks (MANETs). RSR works as follows: Before
sending a Route Reply (RREP) packet on a preferred path, the destination validates the discovered path by sending an encrypted Probe packet to the source. If
the source node receives the Probe packet, it sends back an Acknowledgment
back to the destination. If the Acknowledgment packet is received, the destination sends the RREP packet. Otherwise, the destination chooses the path that
has the largest Reliability Metric. The Reliability Metric of a path is the
minimum of the Reliability Metric of the constituent nodes of the path. The Reliability Metric of a node (a measure of trust) is updated based on the periodic
encrypted beacon exchange, propagation of the Route Request (RREQ), RREP
and data packets. The above procedure is repeated until a route can or cannot be
discovered.

Keywords: Trust, Reliability, Mobile Ad hoc Networks, Source Routing
Protocol, Security.

1 Introduction

Routing protocols for mobile ad hoc networks (MANETs) are of three types: Proactive (e.g. Destination Sequenced Distance Vector routing protocol – DSDV [1], Wireless Routing Protocol – WRP [2]), Reactive (e.g. Dynamic Source Routing protocol –
DSR [3], Ad hoc On-demand Distance Vector routing protocol – AODV [4]) and
hybrid (e.g. Zone Routing Protocol – ZRP [5]). A majority of the MANET literature
is available for the first two categories and in general, reactive routing is considered
more bandwidth and energy-efficient than proactive routing [6][7]. Hence, we focus
on reactive routing in this paper. In the rest of the paper, the terms 'path' and 'route',
'packet' and 'message' are used interchangeably. They mean the same.

Usually, MANET routing protocols are designed to discover the shortest path, as
swiftly as possible, between any two random nodes that anticipate communication.
The number of hops and latency is considered to be the most critical variables when
implementing these protocols. However, with the increasing awareness and use of ad
hoc networks in both governmental and industrial operations, there is a more critical
need to secure the transmission of data in a vulnerable wireless medium. As nodes in

N. Meghanathan et al. (Eds.): CNSA 2010, CCIS 89, pp. 463–472, 2010.

an ad hoc environment also function as peer routers for each other in the absence of a predefined structure, routing protocols should consider the characteristics of the nodes that route the messages. Since the nodes are wireless and are often mobile in nature, a MANET can contain an entirely different set of restrictions compared to wired networks. Uncompromised communication amongst neighboring nodes is imperative to exchange information in a confidential form.

In the past decade, several MANET routing protocols have been proposed and some of them consider strategies for secure routing. Although, there is technically no one answer to solving the security tribulations involved with passing data and network control packets among the nodes of an ad hoc network, many advancements have been made to counter specific attacks, in addition to providing robust usability to some protocols. The problem with most of the available solutions is that one configuration and technique might serve as the perfect resilience for one protocol and attack; but, may as well as be the worst for a second protocol. Without common goals to defeat the progress of distinct attacks that align to specific protocols, malicious scenarios not considered will nevertheless arise during network performance and expose many design flaws that no single routing protocol, as yet, can secure.

This paper uses a Reliability-based model to address the problem involving internal malicious attacks in reactive routing protocols during their route discovery process. The proposed solution uses source routing and hence we refer to the protocol as a Reliability-based Source Routing (RSR) protocol. Although, there are several types of attacks that may disrupt path establishment during the source-initiated route discovery process, RSR focuses on a subset of these attacks which primarily involve compromised nodes that drop every or randomly selected packets. Attacks that fall into this category are: Selfish node, failed node and Gray Hole node attacks [8]. The attacks considered in this paper models activities executed independently by each node without any counteractive dependency on other nodes in the network.

The Reliability-based approach adopted by RSR to select the best path to send the Route Reply (RREP) packets among the several paths discovered through the Route Request (RREQ) packets can also be used for other reactive source routing based protocols such as DSR and Location Prediction Based Routing (LPBR) [9]. In the near future, we will adapt the secure route discovery procedure of RSR for use with table-based reactive routing protocols such as AODV. The rest of the paper is organized as follows: Section 2 discusses related work on secure trust based routing in MANETs. Section 3 presents in detail the proposed design framework for the RSR protocol. Section 4 presents the conclusions from this paper and lists the future work.

2 Related Work

Unfortunately, no single approach is known to exist to defeat each attack or a subset of attacks for multiple MANET routing protocols. Most of the proposals available in the MANET literature focus on secure routing and intrusion detection attempts for individual attacks and protocols. Such contributions include the Secure Routing Protocol (SRP) [10] to form a countermeasure against malicious behavior that targets the discovery of topology information. As a deterrent to the wormhole attack, a packet leashing method consisting of a geographical and temporal leash was proposed in

[11]. The application of the leash is based on the ideology of authenticating either a certified location or a timestamped data so that a receiver can determine if the packet has propagated over a longer distance that does not correspond to the actual path to be taken or the network topology.

Among protocols that facilitate an evaluation of the nodes and the reliability of the paths featuring these nodes is the Security-Aware Adaptive DSR (SADSR) [12] protocol. Trust values are stored locally at each node for every other node in the network and using these values a trust value for every path is computed. To increase the probability of secure routing, paths with higher trust values are favored. Each node monitors the forwarding behavior of other nodes and also periodically transmits a probe message to neighboring nodes in the one-hop vicinity. A neighbor node responds back with an acknowledgment for a probe message. On the other hand, RSR uses encrypted beacon signals to evaluate the Reliability of the neighborhood and faraway nodes, as well as, is able to identify and probe the nodes along the route in question (not only a single-hop distant node). In addition, RSR lets each node to store a formal Reliability metric table of probed nodes for future reference and this table will be used by a node in addition to the probe results to decide on the Reliability score for a node as well as the sequence of nodes constituting a path. Another specialty of RSR is that it takes into consideration the mobility of a node while evaluating the Reliability. If two nodes are genuine (i.e. have not been compromised), but move at different mobility levels (i.e. at different velocity), then the slow moving node will be evaluated to be more reliable than the fast moving node.

3 Description of the Reliability-based Source Routing Protocol

3.1 Motivation

Fundamentally, ad hoc routing protocols often maintain the basic assumption that all of the neighboring nodes in a network interact with superior trust and do not take into account the possibility of malicious disruption during the execution of the protocol [13]. Unfortunately, promiscuous activities indeed occur and should not be disregarded, especially in an open broadcast scenario where internal active attacks can be deployed. Internal attacks through compromised nodes can be as proficient and stronger as an outside attack [13]. Malicious nodes orchestrating an internal attack have open access to the dynamically changing communication links and these nodes are able to directly emit and influence the routing decisions of their neighboring nodes. Active attacks entail the modification or deletion of transmitted packets and hence are more susceptible to detection rather than passive attacks.

3.2 Attack Model

Attacks can be categorized depending on various principles. There are specific attacks that are only hazardous in wired networks, and others concentrate on wireless environments. In this paper, we define a malicious node as a node that arbitrarily drops packets within an ad hoc network and does not forward the packets to the destined downstream nodes. Such attacks could affect the normal functionality of the routing protocols by affecting the network connectivity and increasing the packet drop ratio.

In the next paragraph, we describe several known attacks that are closely related to our attack model.

A selfish node is a node that simply does not provide any response to the network and does not cooperate to the requirements set by the routing protocol [14]. Failed or badly failed nodes occur where the node is simply not prepared to perform any required operation. Selfish node attacks involve the failure to send or forward data packets, in addition to the routing messages that may be related to the routing protocol in question. The Gray Hole attack results in selective dropping of packets. This, in turn, forces additional resource consumption in the network. Since MANET nodes are usually battery dependent, energy conservation is vital for endurance. The sleep deprivation attack on an ad hoc network is often characterized as a Denial of Service (DoS) attack [14]. By the attacker forwarding fake packets or initiating fabricated requests, battery charge is drowned until the node is considered inoperable (said to have failed).

3.3 Reliability Metric Table and Beacon Broadcasts

The RSR protocol requires each node to maintain a Reliability Metric table in its cache memory. Initially, this table is empty at each node and is updated with the periodic exchange of the encrypted beacon signals and during the propagation of the RREQ, RREP and data packets. Each node is identified with a unique ID. Nodes within the one-hop neighborhood are referred to as Neighborhood Ranged Nodes (NRNs). Each node periodically (for every one second) broadcasts beacon signals, encrypted with its private key, to its NRNs. Upon the receipt of an encrypted beacon signal from a peer node in its NRN, a node decrypts the signal using the public key of the sending node and replies back an encrypted Acknowledgment (ACK) using its private key. Upon successful decryption of the ACK using the public key of the neighbor, the Reliability Metric of the neighbor node is incremented by 1.

In addition to the one-hop broadcasts, each node periodically attempts to do a targeted broadcast to nodes that are X hops away ($X > 1$; i.e., nodes that are not 1-hop neighbors). Variable X is referred to as the 'Scope' of a broadcast. The beacon signals encrypted at the originating node are decrypted at the nodes that are 'Scope' number of hops away. These nodes then reply back through an encrypted ACK message. The time period between consecutive broadcasts of encrypted beacon signals depends on the value of the 'Scope' parameter for a broadcast and will also depend on the node density, mobility and the level of threat in the network. In general, the larger the value of the Scope for a broadcast, the larger will be the time period between consecutive broadcasts. Accordingly, the increment value of the Reliability Metric for a non-neighbor node will be half of the time period value chosen for consecutive broadcasts of encrypted beacon signals to non-neighbor nodes. Our idea of using targeted broadcast to nodes that are at a particular Scope is similar to the approach used in the proactive Fish-eye State based Routing (FSR) protocol [15].

If an ACK is not received from a neighbor node or from a distant node beyond a specific time, their Reliability Metric is decremented by 5 units and 2*(Time period between consecutive updates) units respectively. Note that in the latter case, a node I decrements the Reliability Metric value for a distant node J only if an entry already exists for the node J in the Reliability Metric table at node I, implying that node J had earlier responded with an ACK message for the beacon signal from node I. Node I will expect to receive an ACK from node J only if node J has sent such an ACK from a particular Scope (i.e., hop count) for the most recent beacon signal sent from node I. Also, once a node J ceases to exist as a 1-hop neighbor of node I, then after the first decrement update of the Reliability Metric table, node I no longer expects to receive a 1-hop ACK from node J.

3.4 Reliability Metric of a Path

The Reliability Metric of a path is the minimum of the Reliability Metrics of the constituent intermediate nodes on the path. For a particular path, the source and destination nodes of the path are assumed to have infinitely large Reliability Metric. If RSR has to choose between two or more paths that have the same Reliability Metric, RSR chooses the path that has the minimum hop count among the contending paths. If the tie cannot be still resolved, RSR arbitrarily chooses a path among the contending paths with the same Reliability Metric and minimum hop count.

3.5 Sequence of Steps for the RSR Protocol

RSR assumes that each node knows the public key of every other node in the network. This is accomplished through the transmission of public-key certificates by a sender along with the message transmitted. The sequence of steps (also illustrated in Figure 1) in the RSR protocol is as follows:

1. As in DSR and any other reactive routing protocol, the source node S floods the Route Request (RREQ) messages to the entire network.
2. The destination node D receives RREQs along several routes and chooses the path with the minimum hop count. Before sending a Route Reply (RREP) packet along this path, the destination sends an encrypted Probe packet (including the route from D to S; encrypted using the private key of D) to the source S. A forwarding node decrypts the Probe packet using the public key of the upstream node and encrypts with its own private key. This procedure is repeated along the entire path for the Probe packet. If S receives the Probe packet, it sends back an Acknowledgement (ACK) packet to D.
3. If D receives the ACK within a specified time, then D increments the Reliability Metric for all nodes on the chosen route to S by 2 units and transmits a Route Reply (RREP) packet to S, thus terminating the route discovery procedure. Each intermediate node receiving the RREP packet increments the Reliability Metric for every node on the path by 2 units.
4. If no ACK is received by D within specified time, D decrements the Reliability Metric for all the nodes on the chosen route to S by 5 units. Every intermediate node that forwarded a Probe packet from D to S waits to receive the RREP packet on the same path. If an intermediate node that forwarded a Probe packet did not receive the RREP packet within a specified time, then the intermediate node decrements the Reliability Metric for every intermediate node, excluding itself, by 5 units.

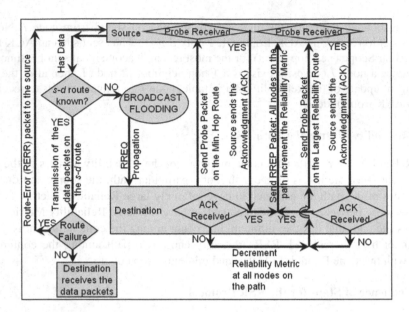

Fig. 1. Working of the Reliability-based Source Routing (RSR) Protocol

5. The destination *D* then considers all the paths through which the RREQ messages have propagated through and chooses the path with the largest Reliability Metric as the path to *S*. The Reliability Metric of a path is the minimum of the Reliability Metrics of all the constituent nodes on the path.

a. The destination *D* sends an encrypted Probe packet (as in Step 2) on the path that has the largest Reliability Metric and waits for an ACK packet from the source *S*. If the ACK packet is received within a specified time, *D* increments the Reliability Metric for all the nodes on the chosen route to *S* by 2 units and transmits the RREP packet to *S*, thus terminating the route discovery procedure. Each intermediate node receiving the RREP packet increments the Reliability Metric for all intermediate nodes on the path by 2 units.

b. If no ACK packet is received for the Probe packet, the destination node *D* decrements the Reliability Metric for every intermediate node on the chosen path for the Probe packet by 5 units. Similarly, the intermediate nodes that forwarded the Probe packet, but failed to receive a corresponding RREP packet decrement the Reliability Metric for every intermediate node on the path, excluding themselves, by 5 units.

c. The destination *D* then considers all the remaining paths traversed by the RREQ messages and chooses the path with the largest Reliability Metric, based on its updated Reliability Metric table for the nodes and a Probe packet is sent along the chosen path.

d. The above procedure is repeated until the destination *D* can successfully locate a path to the source *S* or until the discovered set of paths to the source *S* is exhausted, whichever occurs first. In the latter case (i.e., if all the discovered set of paths to the source *S* are exhausted and the destination *D* could not yet find a path to *S*), the source *S* and destination *D* are considered to be disconnected.

3.6 Logic behind the Use of the Probe Packet and the Public Key Certificate

The logic behind sending the Probe packet before notifying the best route through the RREP packet is that if the Probe packet successfully reaches the source, it is highly probable that the nodes constituting the route are not compromised. In order to make the intermediate nodes of the route to believe that they are forwarding a regular encrypted data packet, the destination stuffs the Probe packet with dummy bits such that the size of the Probe packet along with the source route appears to be a data packet sent under source routing. This would help us to effectively counter attacks in which compromised nodes are configured by the attackers not to drop any control packets, but selectively drop the data packets.

Also, if the public key certificate of a forwarding node is sent along with the Probe packet and the receiving node is able to successfully decrypt the Probe packet only using the public key extracted from the public key certificate of the forwarding node, then we are sure that the public key has not been forged. This is because the public key certificate for a node is generated by encrypting the public key of the node using the private key of the Certifying Authority (CA), which is least likely to be compromised. The public key certificate will serve as the digital signature for a node.

3.7 RSR Route Maintenance

As we use source routing, the entire route from the source S to destination D is included in the header of every data packet. With the establishment of a route that is highly likely to be secure, it may not be essential to encrypt the data packets. We leave this as an implementation issue. If an intermediate node successfully receives a data packet from its upstream node, then the Reliability Metric for the upstream node is incremented by 2 units. If an upstream node cannot successfully transmit the data packet to the immediate downstream node on the path due to a broken link with the node, the upstream node sends a Route Error (RERR) message to the source S and also decrements the Reliability Metric for the downstream node by 5 units. With this, we are also indirectly taking into consideration the mobility of a node while evaluating its Reliability. If two nodes are genuine (i.e., non-malicious), but move at different mobility levels (i.e. velocity), then the slow moving node will be evaluated to be more reliable than the fast moving node.

3.8 Increment vs. Decrement Costs

Note that the increments (refer Table 1) to the Reliability Metric are in smaller units compared to the decrements (refer Table 2). This is justifiable because the increments are done very regularly (for example the beacon signals and the data packet exchanges) and decrements are done relatively rarely (due to the movement of a node away from the transmission range of another node or dropping of packets). In other words, it takes some time to establish the Reliability, but, with one particular non-desirable event, a node can lose the hard-earned Reliability.

Table 1. RSR Table Increment Updates

No.	Message/ Event	Action	Increment Value
1	Successful receipt (decryption) of an acknowledgment (ACK) message for an encrypted beacon signal message	Increment the Reliability Metric for the node that responded with the ACK	+ 1
2	Successful receipt (decryption) of acknowledgment (ACK) message from a non-neighbor node for an encrypted beacon signal. The non-neighbor node is sent beacon signals for every time period T.	Increment the Reliability Metric for the distant non-neighbor node that responded with the ACK.	+ $T/2$
3	Successful receipt of an acknowledgment (ACK) message at the destination for a Probe packet sent to the source	Increment the Reliability Metric for all the intermediate nodes on the path to the source	+ 2
4	Successful receipt of the RREP message at the intermediate nodes of the path	An intermediate node increments the Reliability Metric for other intermediate nodes on the path	+ 2
5	Successful receipt of a data packet from an upstream node	The downstream node increments the Reliability Metric for the upstream node	+ 2

Table 2. RSR Table Decrement Updates

No.	Message/ Event	Action	Decrement Value
1	Failure to receive an acknowledgment (ACK) message for an encrypted beacon signal message	Decrement the Reliability Metric for each of the neighborhood ranged nodes that did not respond with an ACK	- 2
2	Failure to receive an acknowledgment (ACK) message from a non-neighbor node for an encrypted beacon signal. The non-neighbor node is sent beacon signals for every time period T.	Decrement the Reliability Metric for the distant non-neighbor node (for which there exists an entry in the Reliability Metric table, implying that the node had earlier responded with an ACK) that did not respond with the ACK.	- $2*T$
3	Failure to receive an acknowledgment (ACK) message at the destination for a Probe packet sent to the source	Decrement the Reliability Metric for all the intermediate nodes on the path to the source	- 5
4	Failure to receive the RREP message at the intermediate nodes of the path	An intermediate node decrements the Reliability Metric for other intermediate nodes on the path	- 5
5	Failure to be able to successfully transfer a data packet to a downstream node	The upstream node decrements the Reliability Metric for the downstream node	- 5

4 Conclusions and Future Work

The high-level contribution of this paper is the design of a Reliability-based source routing (RSR) protocol for mobile ad hoc networks. RSR primarily advocates a strong secure route discovery procedure to facilitate uninterrupted secure exchange of data packets for the reactive routing protocols. The Reliability Metric for a node is built based on the number of beacons exchanged with its neighbors, the successful propagation of the data packets, RREQ and RREP packets. The Reliability of a node is lost due to failure to respond for beacons and failure to propagate the data, RREQ and RREP packets. RSR also takes into consideration the failure of links due to node mobility and decrements the Reliability Metric of fast moving nodes more severely than that of slow moving nodes. Rather than discovering minimum hop routes that may not be stable as well as secure (like the routes discovered by DSR are not stable [16] and need not be secure too as the protocol is not security-aware), if we can afford to the discovery latency involved in validating the discovered route through a Probe packet before sending the RREP packet to the source, RSR could minimize a significant amount of route discovery overhead incurred due to frequent route discoveries. With the establishment of a route that is highly likely to be secure, it may not be even essential to encrypt the data packets. The secure route discovery procedure of RSR can be adapted for any source routing – based reactive protocol.

In continuation, we have scheduled to do the following in the immediate future: (i) Implement RSR in a discrete-event simulator, (ii) Take into account the residual energy available at a node while computing the Reliability Metric, (iii) Minimize the route acquisition delay (i.e., the discovery latency) of RSR by modifying the design such that if the Reliability Metric of all the intermediate nodes on a discovered minimum-hop route is above a certain threshold, the destination node right away responds with the RREP packet rather than validating the route through the Probe packet and (iv) Modify the design of the secure route discovery procedure of RSR so that it can be applied to table-based reactive routing protocols such as AODV.

References

1. Perkins, C.E., Bhagawat, P.: Highly Dynamic Destination Sequenced Distance Vector Routing for Mobile Computers. In: 17th International Conference of Special Interest Group on Data Communications, pp. 234–244. ACM, London (1994)
2. Murthy, S., Garcia-Luna-Aceves, J.J.: Loop-Free Internet Routing using Hierarchical Routing Trees. In: 16th International Conference on Computer Communications, pp. 101–108. IEEE, Kobe (1997)
3. Johnson, D.B., Maltz, D.A., Broch, J.: DSR: The Dynamic Source Routing Protocol for Multi-hop Wireless Ad hoc Networks. In: Perkins, C.E. (ed.) Ad hoc Networking, pp. 139–172. Addison-Wesley, New York (2001)
4. Perkins, C.E., Royer, E.M.: The Ad hoc On-demand Distance Vector Protocol. In: Perkins, C.E. (ed.) Ad hoc Networking, pp. 173–219. Addison-Wesley, New York (2000)
5. Haas, Z.J., Pearlman, M.R., Samar, P.: The Zone Routing Protocol (ZRP) for Ad hoc Networks, IETF Draft (2003)

6. Broch, J., Maltz, D.A., Johnson, D.B., Hu, Y.C., Jetcheva, J.: A Performance Comparison of Multi-hop Wireless Ad hoc Network Routing Protocols. In: 4th International Conference on Mobile Computing and Networking, pp. 85–97. ACM, Dallas (1998)
7. Johansson, P., Larson, T., Hedman, N., Mielczarek, B., DegerMark, M.: Scenario-based Performance Analysis of Routing Protocols for Mobile Ad hoc Networks. In: 5th International Conference on Mobile Computing and Networking, pp. 195–206. ACM, Seattle (1999)
8. Mishra, A., Nadkarni, J.M.: Security in Wireless Ad hoc Networks. In: The Handbook of Ad hoc Wireless Networks, pp. 499–599. CRC Press, USA (2003)
9. Meghanathan, N.: A Location Prediction Based Reactive Routing Protocol to Minimize the Number of Route Discoveries and Hop Count per Path in Mobile Ad hoc Networks. The Computer Journal 52(4), 461–482 (2002)
10. Papadimitratos, P., Haas, Z.J.: Secure Routing for Mobile Ad hoc Networks. In: Communication Networks and Distributed Systems Modeling and Simulation Conference, SCS, San Antonio, USA, pp. 27–31 (2002)
11. Hu, Y.C., Perrig, A., Johnson, D.B.: Packet Leashes: A Defense against Wormhole Attacks in Wireless Ad hoc Networks, Technical Report TR01-384, Department of Computer Science, Rice University, USA (2001)
12. Ghazizadeh, S., Ilghami, O., Sirin, E.: Security-aware Adaptive Dynamic Source Routing Protocol. In: 27th International Conference on Local Computer Networks, pp. 751–760. IEEE, Tampa (2002)
13. Papadimitratos, P., Haas, Z.J.: Secure Data Transmission in Mobile Ad hoc Networks. In: Workshop in Wireless Security. ACM, San Diego (2003)
14. Yau, P., Mitchell, C.: Security Vulnerabilities in Ad hoc Networks. In: 7th International Symposium on Communication Theory and Applications, Ambleside, UK (2003)
15. Pei, G., Gerla, M., Chen, T.-W.: Fisheye State Routing in Mobile Ad hoc Networks. In: ICDCS Workshop on Wireless Networks and Mobile Computing, Taipei, Taiwan (2000)
16. Meghanathan, N.: Exploring the Stability-Energy Consumption-Delay-Network Lifetime Tradeoff of Mobile Ad hoc Network Routing Protocols. Journal of Networks 3(2), 17–28 (2008)

Performance Evaluation and Detection of Sybil Attacks in Vehicular Ad-Hoc Networks

Jyoti Grover, Deepak Kumar, M. Sargurunathan, M.S. Gaur[*], and Vijay Laxmi

Department of Computer Engineering
Malaviya National Institute of Technology
Jaipur, India
{jgrover,gaurms,vlaxmi}@mnit.ac.in

Abstract. Vehicular Ad-hoc Networks (VANET) technology provides a fast, easy to deploy and an inexpensive solution for intelligent traffic control and traffic disaster preventive measure. In VANET, moving vehicles communicate using wireless technology. This communication can be used to divert traffic from congested or dysfunctional routes, to seek help in an emergency and to prevent accident escalation in addition to providing intelligent traffic control. However, an attacker can use the same system to spread false warning messages resulting in congestion on certain routes thereby leading to accidents or causing delay in providing help etc. One of the harmful attacks against VANET is Sybil attack, in which an attacker generates multiple identities to feign multiple nodes. In this paper, we present an implementation of simulated Sybil attack scenario in VANET and discuss its impact on network performance. A cooperative approach of Sybil attack detection, inferred through analysis of Sybil attack, is also presented.

Keywords: Sybil attack, VANET, Security, Network simulation.

1 Introduction

VANET is a specific type of Mobile Ad Hoc network (MANET) that provides communication (1) between nearby vehicles and (2) between vehicles and nearby road side equipment. It employs two communication devices - OBUs (On Board Unit) and RSUs (Road Side Unit). OBUs are installed in vehicles and RSUs are placed on roadside. Every node in VANET is also equipped with EDR (Event Data Recorder), GPS (Global Positioning system) receiver, a computing platform and Radar. Being a wireless network, VANET unfortunately inherits all the security threats associated with these networks. Sybil attack, described by Douseur [4] is a serious threat to VANET as it is the root cause of all other types of attacks in VANET. In this attack, the attacker node participates in the network by using identities of other nodes. Spoofing of identities can happen due to the broadcast nature of VANET as nodes within the communication range of sender can overhear the communication. Sybil attacker pretends to be multiple nodes simultaneously by using different addresses while transmitting.

---

[*] Corresponding Author.

N. Meghanathan et al. (Eds.): CNSA 2010, CCIS 89, pp. 473–482, 2010.

A mechanism is required for proper detection and prevention of Sybil attack. Any security mechanism designed for VANET should ensure that life critical information can neither be inserted nor be modified by any attacker. A security system used for VANET should satisfy the following constraints [1], [2] e.g. time delivery constraint, accurate location, message integrity, accountability, privacy, authenticity etc.

In this paper, we used simulation to study how the number of Sybil attackers and node mobility affects the performance of VANET. A Sybil attack can be detected by observing the behavior of nodes by their neighboring nodes in the network. These nodes exchange their observations with each other. The observations include checking a) if the number of packets received from specific nodes is greater than a threshold value and b) if most of the packets are received from same position/trajectory.

The rest of the paper is organized as follows. Section 2 describes the various types of attacks in VANET and classification of Sybil attack. Section 3 describes implementation of Sybil attack in VANET and simulation results. In section 4, we describe related work for Sybil attack detection followed by the proposed Sybil attack detection approach in section 5. Section 6 concludes the present work in progress and provides pointers for future work.

2 Attacks on Vehicular Networks

Due to a large number of autonomous network members and the presence of human factor, misbehavior of nodes in vehicular networks can not be ruled out. Several types of attacks [2], [3] have been identified and classified on the basis of layer targeted by the attacker. At physical and link layers, attacker can disturb the network by overloading the communication channel with useless messages. Attacker can inject false messages or rebroadcast an old message. Some attackers can tamper with an On-Board Unit (OBU) or destroy Road-Side Unit (RSU). At network layer, an attacker can insert false routing messages or overload the system with routing information. Privacy of drivers can be disclosed by revealing and tracking the position of drivers. Some examples of these attacks are – inserting bogus information in the network, cheating with sensor information, jamming the physical channel, replaying and dropping the packets and disclosing the ID of nodes. Attacker can also introduce worm hole and Sybil attack in VANET.

2.1 Sybil Attack and Classification

Sybil attack is a type of impersonation or spoofing attack where an attacker spoofs the identity of another node in the network and hence, all the messages directed to that victimized node are received by the attacker. There are various forms of impersonation attacks such as Stolen Identity Attack, Invisible Node Attack and Sybil Attack. In a Sybil attack, the node that spoofs the identities of other nodes is called malicious node/ Sybil attacker and the nodes whose identities get spoofed are called Sybil nodes. A typical Sybil attack is shown in figure 1. In this scenario, Sybil attacker is creating an illusion of traffic congestion on the road. In another VANET situation involving an accident on highway, the first vehicle observing the accident is sending change route/deceleration warning message to all other vehicles. Receivers may

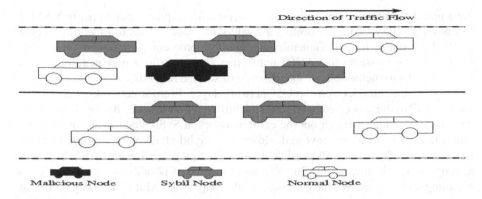

Fig. 1. Sybil Attack

forward this message to warn followers, if any. This forwarding process can be disrupted by Sybil vehicles by not forwarding the warning message. This may put the life of passengers in danger. If number of Sybil attackers increases significantly in a network, they can take over the control of the whole network. Number of Sybil nodes created by Sybil attacker depends on the communication, storage and computation resources of the attacker.

Sybil attacks can be classified into three categories based on type of communication, identity and their participation in the network [6], [7]. These categories are briefly discussed below.

- **Communication Category:** When a honest node sends a radio message to Sybil node, one of the malicious nodes listens to the message. In the same way, messages sent from Sybil nodes are actually sent from one of the malicious devices. Communication to/from Sybil nodes can be direct or indirect. In *direct* mode, all Sybil nodes created by malicious node communicate with legitimate nodes. In *indirect* communication, legitimate nodes reach the Sybil nodes through a malicious node.
- **Identity Category:** In a Sybil attack, an attacker creates a new Sybil identity. This identity can be a random 32 bit integer (*fabricated* identity) or attacker can spoof the legitimate identity of one of its neighbors (*stolen* identity).
- **Participation Category:** Multiple Sybil identities created by malicious nodes can *simultaneously* participate in an attack or the attacker can present these Sybil identities *one by one*. A particular identity may leave or join the network many times, i.e., one identity is used at a time. The number of identities used by the attacker is equal to or less than the number of physical identities. An attack through multiple Sybil nodes can adversely affect proper functioning of network.

3   Simulation of Sybil Attack in VANET

One of the major applications of VANET is to provide safety to drivers by minimizing the number of road accidents through broadcasting safety messages. Safety messages do not require any expensive encryption/decryption operations. In VANET, whenever a node receives a warning or a safety message, it tries to forward it to other nodes by broadcasting it. Generally, no routing protocol is followed for sending safety/warning messages in VANET unless there is a specific requirement for applications such as internet access, or specific type of service requests.

Sybil attack can occur on the OSI network layer. From a network layer point of view, the IP address is considered as the identifier for each node. As the IP address of each node is unique through out the entire network, a Sybil attack with simultaneous multiple identities can be prevented. However, a Sybil attack with multiple identities being used one by one is still possible because changing the IP addresses is legitimate as long as there is no conflict. But, a frequent change of IP address may in turn cause a routing table attack. We have considered the impact of Sybil attack only on the application layer as multiple identities can be shown simultaneously on the application layer unlike the network layer.

3.1 Simulation Parameters and Performance Metrics

This section describes various parameters and performance metrics used in our simulation. We conducted our experiments using NCTUns version 5.0 [8], an integrated network and traffic simulation platform. This platform provides multiple features including road network simulation, communication and network protocol simulation, vehicular traffic simulation and feedback loop among vehicles. In our simulation experiments, we used 1, 5 and 10 Sybil attackers respectively in the chosen Vehicular Network of 40 nodes.

Table 1. Simulation Parameters

Parameter	Value
Traffic type	CBR (Constant Bit Rate)
Queue size	50
Path loss model	Two ray ground
Transmitter/Receiver antenna height	1.5 meters
Transmission power	15 dBm
Simulation area	1400m × 700m
Simulation time	400 seconds
Number of total vehicles	40
Packet broadcast rate	3-10 pkt/s
Number of attackers	1,5,10
Packet size	142 bytes

These attackers randomly spoof the identities and positions of other nodes in the network. The attacker may cause harm to the network by fabricating fake safety messages, updating the messages etc. The simulation parameters used are listed in Table 1. In our setup, a Sybil attacker is implemented as follows. Whenever a malicious node is about to send a packet, it selects a random node identity and position on the field and applies it to the packet (instead of using real identity and position).

In our implementation, the Sybil attackers drop all received packets and do not forward any packets. Performance of VANET is evaluated in terms of a) average packet delivery ratio: ratio of received and transmitted packets, b) average throughput: number of packets delivered per second, c) average dropped packets and d) number of collisions: when nodes transmit at the same time on a shared channel.

3.2 Simulation Results

In our experiments, we evaluated the effect of varying the number of Sybil attackers on average throughput of the network, packet delivery ratio, dropped packets and collision packets. Figure 2 shows the experiment results.

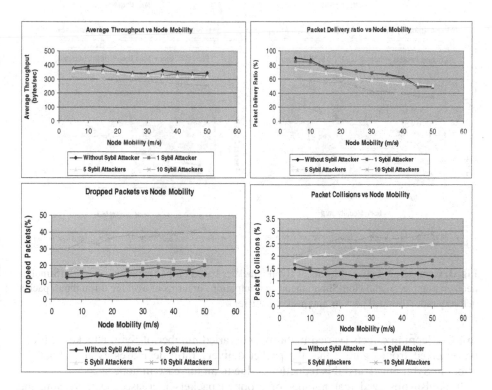

Fig. 2. Impact of Sybil attack on VANET performance in terms of average throughput, packet delivery ratio, dropped packets and packet collisions

The average throughput decreases as the number of Sybil attackers increases. Three attack scenarios are considered. In the first scenario, there is only a single Sybil attacker. In the other two scenarios, the numbers of attackers are 5 and 10 respectively.

We studied these cases with respect to varying node speed as well. Duration of links established between nodes is typically short due to high mobility of nodes. So, high speed of nodes also affects the performance of the network. This is the result of

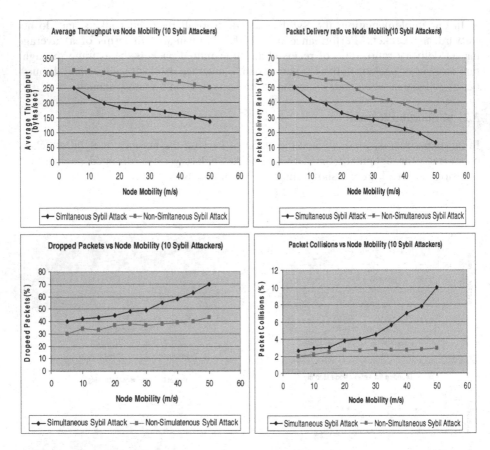

Fig. 3. Comparison between forms of Sybil attackers based on participation category (Simultaneous participation and Non-Simultaneous participation) in terms of average throughput, packet delivery ratio, dropped packets and packet collisions

two overlapping effects (varied mobility and varied number of Sybil attackers). It can be observed from figure 2 that the packet delivery ratio decreases even without the effect of Sybil attack and this reduction is due to an increase in node speed.

It is also observed that number of dropped packets increases on increasing the number of Sybil attackers. This is because a greater number of identities are captured by Sybil attackers, so all broadcast packets come from IDs of these spoofed nodes and all replies are sent back to these nodes. There is bound to be more congestion in this case. As a result, more number of packets would get dropped. Packet collision rate is also higher in case of 10 Sybil attackers as compared to the cases of 5 Sybil attackers and lone Sybil attacker due to the same reason discussed above.

In figure 3, we showed the difference in effect of a Sybil attack on VANET performance when all the Sybil identities created by attacker simultaneously participate vs. one by one participation of Sybil identities created by the Sybil attacker. We are considering 10 Sybil attackers in this case.

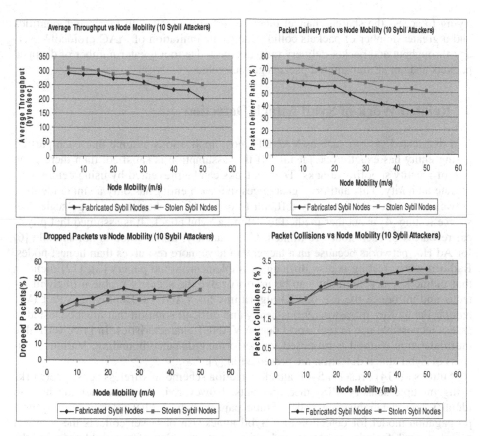

Fig. 4. Comparison between forms of Sybil attackers based on identity category (Fabricated identity and Stolen identity) in terms of average throughput, packet delivery ratio, dropped packets and packet collisions

A simultaneous Sybil attack causes a greater reduction in throughput and packet delivery ratio as compared to a one by one attack. It's because the number of packet collisions in case of a simultaneous Sybil attack is greater than in the case of one by one attack.

All identities simultaneously participate in the network and there by cause greater congestion in the network, more dropped packets and more packet collisions. Number of successful delivered packets is very low as compared to the total number of generated packets.

We also implemented a Sybil attack where the attacker fabricates multiple identities to participate in the network on behalf of these identities. In this case, the total number of nodes may increase significantly and it may lead to an illusion of traffic congestion. On the other hand, if the attacker steals the identity of an existing node, the total number of nodes will remain the same throughout the simulation. In this case as well, we considered 10 Sybil attackers. As shown in figure 4, number of packets dropped in Sybil attack with fabricated nodes is more because all packets sent to these fabricated nodes are not delivered due to their physical absence. Number of nodes trying to access the shared channel increase in Sybil attack with fabricated identities and a greater number of packets collide due to the limitation of MAC protocol. Average throughput and packet delivery ratio decrease due to a greater number of dropped packets and not all transmitted packets get delivered.

4 Related Work of Sybil Attack Detection

In a distributed system such as VANET, most applications assume that each participating entity has exactly one identity. If this assumption is satisfied, then there is no risk of identity spoofing attacks. These attacks can be prevented by using central certificate authority. This authority guarantees that each entity has only a single identity. However, in practical, it is very difficult to deploy this scheme on a large scale. Resource testing [4] is another method to defend a Sybil attack. It is assumed that physical resources of each node are limited. Unfortunately, this method is not suitable [6] for Ad Hoc networks because an attacker can have more resources than honest nodes. Radio resource testing is also difficult to implement. Some papers [2], [12] mention that public key cryptography can be used to solve the security problem of Sybil attacks and introduce the use of PKI algorithms for VANETs. Deploying VPKI (Vehicular Public Key Infrastructure) is heavy and difficult solution that must be tested to assess its possible use in real world due to VANET characteristics. In [13], verifiable multilateration method is proposed for performing distance bounding. Various solutions of Sybil attack detection are presented in [7].

Authors in [14] presents Sybil attack detection scheme in wireless sensor networks using multiple sensors RSSI measurements. However, it does not mention how to identify honest neighboring nodes. Some papers such as [10] assume a predefined propagation model for detection of a Sybil attack. An observer collects the received signal strength from its neighbors and estimates the position of its neighbors using the propagation model. This technique is not suitable due to high mobility of vehicular nodes and rapid changes in communication environment in VANET.

One method [5], [11] requires trusted monitors for observing the behavior of nodes in a network. This is not realistic in VANET because a Sybil attacker may penetrate these trusted observing nodes and these Sybil nodes will report fake data. Some methods require Global Positioning System (GPS) [9] for verifying the positions of sending nodes. GPS system has poor performance in urban scenarios and is often the cause of signal jamming and spoofing attacks.

We propose a method in which all nodes participate in observing (rather than using fixed trusted nodes) any misbehavior in VANET, and every node verifies the position of packet sender using position verification approach.

5 Proposed Sybil Attack Detection Technique for VANETs

In VANET, it is not always necessary to have the presence of fixed infrastructure i.e., road side units. At some locations, the communication between vehicles is only through Ad-Hoc network. Centralized Sybil detection technique can not be effective in a generic VANET. In such cases, Distributed Sybil attack detection technique is required instead of relying on some centralized control. Each node in the network (either a fixed road side unit or a vehicle) observes and exchanges traffic information in order to analyze the existence of a Sybil attack. All nodes in VANET keep track of each other in a distributed and cooperative manner by taking help of traffic observation proofs (refer Figure 5).

The sender incorporates its position and time-stamp within the packets. The positions are obtained from a GPS device. As a node receives a packet from neighboring node, it verifies its claimed position. The Receiver node estimates the position of sender either by measuring the received signal strength (RSS) of received packet [10, 14] or by a position verification approach based on multiple sensors as discussed in [15]. If the claimed position of sender and its position estimated by receiver match, the receiver generates the observation and forwards the packets to its neighboring nodes. Otherwise, the receiver discards the packet.

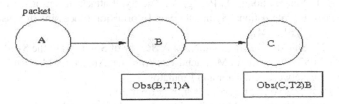

Fig. 5. Three nodes -A, B and C. A is sending a packet. Obs(B,T1)A represents the observation of node A recorded by node B at time T1. Obs(C, T2)B represents the observations of node B recorded by C at time T2.

Each node in the network broadcasts its observations and stores an observation table for its communicating nodes. In this table, observations of a given node are stored in a row sorted by time stamp. Each row describes the path of the movement of this node. If any two rows are same, it implies that one of these nodes is a Sybil attacker.

6 Conclusions

VANETs are vulnerable to different types of attacks owing to physical characteristics of environment and nodes used in wireless communication. In this paper, we analyzed the impact of Sybil attack on VANET's performance in terms of packet delivery ratio, throughput, dropped packets and collision packets with respect to varying mobility of nodes through simulation. We implemented different forms of Sybil attacks in VANET and concluded that performance of VANET degrades in presence of Sybil attack with fabricated Sybil identities and simultaneous participating Sybil identities as compared to other forms of Sybil attack. We argue that the detection of Sybil attack without using any centralized authority is difficult in VANET. Therefore, we have proposed a distributed Sybil attack detection approach. In the proposed method, nodes cooperatively exchange observations of their neighbors and assist in the detection of a Sybil attack. As a part of this work in progress, the proposed detection method would be implemented to evaluate its effectiveness in VANETs.

References

1. Raya, M., Papadimitratos, P., Hubaux, J.-P.: Secure vehicular communications. IEEE Wireless Communications Magazine, 8–15 (2006)
2. Raya, M., Hubaux, J.-P.: Securing vehicular ad hoc networks. Journal of Computer Security 15(1), 39–68 (2007)
3. Aijaz, A., Bochow, B., Dtzer, F., Festag, A., Gerlach, M., Kroh, R., Leinmuller, T.: Attacks on Inter-Vehicle Communication Systems - An Analysis. In: Proceedings of the 3rd International Workshop on Intelligent Transportation, WIT (March 2006)
4. Douceur, J.R.: The Sybil attack. In: Proceedings of the International Workshop on Peer to Peer Systems, pp. 251–260 (March 2002)
5. Piro, C., Shields, C., Levine, B.N.: Detecting the Sybil attack in mobile ad hoc network. In: International Conference on Security and Privacy in Communication Networks, pp. 1–11 (2006)
6. Newsome, J., Shi, E., Song, D., Perrig, A.: The Sybil attack in sensor networks: analysis and defences. In: International Symposium on Information Processing in Sensor Networks, pp. 259–268 (April 2004)
7. Levine, B.N., Shields, C., Margolin, N.B.: A Survey of Solutions to the Sybil Attack. Tech report 2006-052, University of Massachusetts Amherst, Amherst, MA (October 2006)
8. NCTUns 5.0, Network Simulator and Emulator, http://NSL.csie.nctu.edu.tw/nctuns.html
9. Yan, G., Olariu, S., Weigle, M.C.: Providing VANET security through active position detection. Computer Communications 31(12), 2883–2897 (2008)
10. Xiao, B., Yu, B., Gao, C.: Detection and localization of Sybil nodes in VANETs. In: Workshop on Dependability Issues in Wireless Ad Hoc Networks and Sensor Networks (DIWANS 2006), Los Angeles, Calif, USA, pp. 1–8 (September 2006)
11. Yu, H., Kaminsky, M., Schlosser, M.T., Flaxman, A.: SybilGuard: defending against Sybil attacks via social networks. In: Proc. ACM SIGCOMM (2006)
12. Golle, P., Greene, D., Staddon, J.: Detecting and correcting malicious data in VANETs. In: Proceedings of first ACM Workshop on Vehicular Ad Hoc Networks, pp. 29–37 (2004)
13. Hubaux, J.-P., Apkun, S.C., Luo, J.: The security and privacy of smart vehicles. IEEE Security and Privacy 4(3), 49–55 (2004)
14. Demirbas, M., Song, Y.: An RSSI-based Scheme for Sybil Attack Detection in Wireless Sensor Networks. In: International Symposium on World of Wireless, Mobile and Multimedia Networks, pp. 564–570. IEEE Computer Society, Washington (2006)
15. Leinmüller, T., Schoch, E., Kargl, F.: Position verification approaches for vehicular ad hoc networks. IEEE Wireless Communications Magazine (October 2006)

Clustering Approach in Speech Phoneme Recognition Based on Statistical Analysis

Gaurav Kumar Tak and Vaibhav Bhargava

ABV Indian Institute of Information Technology and Management
Gwalior (M.P.), India
gauravtakswm@gmail.com, vaibhavbhargava999@gmail.com

Abstract. In general, speech recognition is a process that is referred to convert spoken string into machine-understandable string. Speech Recognition consists of 2 processes, i) removal of background noise (background noise is generated due to the stressful noise environment) and ii) phoneme separation word by word (also involves phoneme recognition). In real time situation, sound signals consist of both noises (target noise as well as background noise).

This paper critically evaluates the currently available signal analysis techniques and the modeling of phonemes, as applied to isolated and context-independent phoneme recognition. The proposed methodology introduces the technique of determining the pure speech-signal in a noisy environment (without background noise) and phonemes-isolation word by word using some clustering approach. With the use of proposed methodology, high accuracy of background noise-isolation (obtaining clean speech-signal without background noise) and high accuracy of phoneme isolation from clean speech-signal have been achieved which can be qualitatively compared to previous research done on continuous phoneme recognition. Performance evaluation also shows the improvement to achieve the speech recognition in a stressful noise situation and better quality of phoneme separation process.

Keywords: Phoneme, g2p, TTS, ICA, CASA.

1 Introduction

Speech recognition converts spoken words into machine-readable input using some operations. The term "voice recognition" is sometimes incorrectly used to refer to speech recognition, but voice reorganization actually refers to speaker recognition, that attempts to identify the person speaking, as opposed to what is being said. A sound is an acoustic signal. In the context of a Text-to Speech (TTS) system, sounds are generated by the synthesizing component but not by the grapheme-to-phoneme conversion component. [1]

Phoneme is the smallest unit of sound that is unique (distinguishing one word from another word for a given language) or phoneme is a group of slightly different sounds which are all perceived to have the same function by speakers of the language in question. An example of a phoneme is the /k/ sound in the words *kit* and *krill*. (in transcription, phonemes are placed between slashes, as here.) [2]

N. Meghanathan et al. (Eds.): CNSA 2010, CCIS 89, pp. 483–489, 2010.

This paper focuses on the single-microphone speech source separation. Source separation has been one of the popular research topics. Now we are able to separate the background-voice from the measured sound signal .We will find here the intensity of actual sound phonemes using measured sound phonemes of a word-signal.

2 Related Work

In recent years, three major approaches, independent component analysis (ICA) and computation auditory scene analysis (CASA), trajectory regeneration have received lots of attention. ICA utilizes the statistical properties between sources and the availability of several different input mixtures; while CASA studies the perceptual organization and mimics how human listeners segregate concurrent sounds, hence CASA is always possible to have the number of microphones less than the number of source-signals. While trajectory regeneration algorithm uses the dynamic in formations (velocity and acceleration features) of the sound signal for separating the mixed speech sources. The dynamic spectral information is obtained over a time-window by linear regression. [3][12[13]

Talking of speech part on the other hand Hindi which is widely spoken in India (54%) itself has different accents spoken throughout India with change in geographical region and successful attempts have been made to recognize the words being spoken with an acceptable and very good accuracy. The place from where the speaker come also plays a role in this accuracy and also the word for which the system is performing example for some words the results a fabulous while for some not so convincing for these type of words mapping is changed of these words to get better results.

The problem of speech recognition in the noisy environment has attracted the interest of many researchers .The reason is that, though progress has been made in increasing recognition vocabulary size, reducing computational requirements, and transcending isolated-work to continuous speech system, most of the speech recognizers don't perform better in the noisy situation.

Whatever literature that is present in this field still doesn't reveal good results when sentences are said in a flow by that mean if just a word it said it might be recognized very well but same might not be the case if it occurs in a statement.

3 Proposed Methodology

The simplest sound is pure tone based sign waveform (no background noise is present). But in real situation, pure tone based sounds are rare. Most sounds, including speech phonemes, are complex waves, having a dominant or primary frequency called fundamental frequency overlaid with secondary frequencies. Fundamental frequency for speech is the rate at which the vocal cords flap against each other when producing a voiced phoneme. Multi-frequency sounds like the phonemes of speech can be represented as complex waves. Co-articulation effects: inter-phoneme influences. Neighboring phonemes, the position of a phoneme within words, and the position of the word in the sentence all influence the way a phoneme is uttered. Because of co-articulation effects, a specific utterance or instance of a phoneme is called a phone. Proposed methodology mainly follows the following steps:

[1] **Measurement of background noises:** It measures the background noises.

[2] **Compute the average mean:** It computes the average mean (statistical mean of data) using background signal values.

[3] **Statistical operation:** It finds the values of sound-signals, and then subtracts the average-mean from the measured signal values of sound wave. After this statistical operation, we will get the pure sound wave. No background noise will be present in the sound wave.

In final stage, we will be having the phonemes without background noise. Now we can further process those phonemes according to our use/application. Speech reorganization is wide research topic and currently, we use speech-signals in many applications but efficiency was poor due to presence of background noise in phonemes of sound-word.

Proposed methodology is based on the statistical analysis of received sound signals and clustering approach of those sound data. Proposed methodology follows 2 – phases, which are described below:

A.   Cleaning up the data or removal of background noise
B.   Phonemes' isolation

A. Removal of background noise

In this phase, First measure all-signal values before getting first phoneme (these all signals are generated by the background noise due to the noisy environment). If n-background signals are present and their magnitude values are $b_1, b_2, \ldots\ldots\ldots b_n$ respectively (take $b_1, b_2, \ldots\ldots b_n$ all values with positive sign).

So statistical mean of these amplitude values is

$$M_b = (b_1 + b_2 + b_3 + b_4 + \ldots\ldots\ldots + b_n)/n$$

The value of 'M_b' (statistical mean) will always be positive.

If signal value of sound wave at the i_{th}- instant is represented with S_i (this instant value also contains the background noise), then perform the following operation with

If ($S_i > 0$)
$S_i = S_i - M_b$;
Else
$S_i = S_i + M_b$;

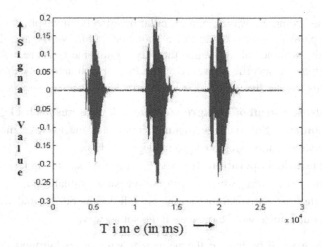

Fig. 1. Sound –wave before removal of background noise

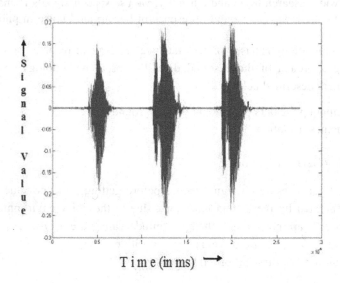

Fig. 2. Sound –wave after removal of background noise

After getting these new updated S_i-values, we will be getting sound- wave without any background noise. Signal wave with background noise is shown in figure 1 and without background noise is shown in figure2 respectively.

After getting the statistical mean (M_b), value of 'M_b' is subtracted from the sound signals. Now received sound signals are free of background noise. This approach is defined the statistical approach for remove the background noise from the actual sound signals

B. Phonemes' Isolation

Step-1
a) Divide complete sentence / statement into words then perform the following for getting the phonemes of the word.

Step-2
a) Make 3 clusters (cluster-1, cluster-2, cluster-3) having of size **k, l, m** respectively.

Cluster-1 is the collection of sound signals, which contains the reference points of the phase; in general cluster-1 is the referenced cluster.

Cluster-2 is the collection which contains the wave-points which are in higher range. Means cluster-2 stores those wave-points which can't be present in cluster-1.

Cluster-3 is the collection of those wave-points which not comes under the category of cluster2 but previous points were going in cluster-2 because at that moment we can't store those points directly into cluster-1.

b) Define 3 threshold-values (T_1, T_2, T_3)

T_1 is a real number which decides how many minimum points will exist in a cluster2 (because cluster2 is accepted as phoneme). It is divided or multiplied with mean-value of cluster1 for deciding points of cluster2.

T_2 is the threshold value which decides which wave-point will move in which cluster2 (before it is accepted as phoneme).

T_3 is the number which decide, when all points of cluster3 will be transferred to cluster1 and cluster2, cluster3 will be cleaned (because some points which lies in cluster2 (phoneme-loop) but they are not related to actual sound-signal, they are only due to noise-signals, T_3 decides which points are related to noise-signals not even actual sound-signals, and those points will be transferred to 1 from cluster2).

These 3 threshold values are used because of removing the sound-signals which are due to some noise which is not related to our actual sound-wave. These noises are not useful for our sound processing (phoneme –isolation process).

Our Algorithm uses the following steps:

(i) Initially No sound-data is present so All clusters are empty. (No sound-point in any cluster).

(ii) Using the cluster 1, 2, 3 and T1, T2, T3 sound signals will be separated into different phonemes associated with that word. In clustering operation, one cluster represents the final phoneme cluster, and the other two clusters are sample cluster and intermediate cluster respectively.

Figure 3 represents phoneme isolation process.

Here **T1, T2, T3** can be achieved using the statistical analysis of sound wave.

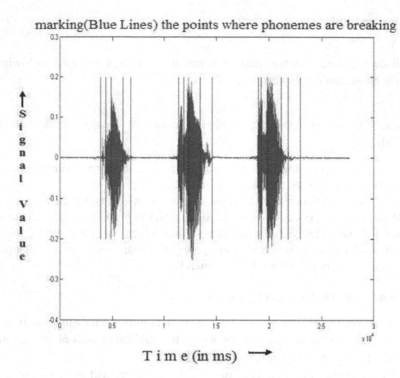

Fig. 3. Represents the separated phonemes

4   Conclusion and Limitations

In proposed methodology, if statistical mean −value (M_b) is zero(0) it implies that there is no background noise in the sound signal (means the sound wave is purely tone based sound wave and sound signals achieved in the noise free environment). The proposed methodology is more computationally efficient. Clustering approach used in phase 2 uses the dynamic allocation of sound points, so the methodology is also highly memory efficient. The above methodology works with ideal situation of the background noise (no undesirable situation with the background noise). This methodology can also be applied when more than two background noises are present in the sound wave. With the use of the proposed methodology, isolated background noise accuracies of up to 82.5% (obtaining clean speech-signal without background noise) and 83.7% for phoneme isolation of clean speech-signal have been achieved which can be qualitatively compared to previous research done on continuous phoneme recognition. Received pure sound phoneme can be used in many applications efficiently.

The above methodology is not able to handle the misbehaviour in the background noise. If any undesirable event occurs with the background noise, then that event cannot be detected with this technique. One more limitation is that if intensity of background noise is high then it is also considered as sound wave and this methodology will not be efficient. Finding *T1, T2, T3* is a difficult task in phase2.

References

[1] Furuichi, C., Aizawa, K., Inoue, K.: Speech recognition using stochastic phonemic segment model based on phoneme segmentation, Faculty of Engineering. Toin University of Yokohama, 1614 Kurogane, Midori, Yokohama, Japan

[2] Engelbrecht, H.A., du Preez, J.A.: The Interplay of Signal Analysis and Phoneme Modelling Techniques on Phoneme Recognition. Telecommunications and Digital Signal Processing Group, Department of Electronic Engineering. University of Stellenbosch, South Africa

[3] Feng, L., Hansen, L.K.: Phonemes as Short Time Cognitive Components. In: Proceedings of IEEE International Conference on Acoustics, Speech and Signal Processing, ICASSP 2006, May 14-19, vol. 5 (2006)

[4] Shirai, K., Hosaka, N., Kitagawa, E.: Speaker Adaptive Phoneme Recognition by Multilevel Clustering Based on Mutual Information Criterion, Department of Electrical Engineering. Waseda University, 3-4-1 Ohkubo, Shinjyuku - ku, Tokyo 169, Japan

[5] Hansen, John, H.L., Cairns, D.A.: Source Generator Based Real-time Recognition of Speech in Noisy stressful and Lombard Effect Environments, Robust speech processing laboratory, Department of Electrical Engineering. Duke University, Durham, North Caroline, USA

[6] Frahling, G.A., Sohler, C.: A fast k-means implementation using coresets. In: Proceedings of the Twenty-Second Annual Symposium on Computational Geometry, SCG 2006, Sedona, Arizona, USA, June 5-7, pp. 135–143. ACM, NewYork (2006), http://doi.acm.org/10.1145/1137856.1137879

[7] Johnstone, A., Altmann, G.: Automated speech recognition: a framework for research. In: Proceedings of the Second Conference on European Chapter of the Association For Computational Linguistics, European Chapter Meeting of the ACL, Geneva, Switzerland, March 27-29, pp. 239–243. Association for Computational Linguistics, Morristown (1985), http://dx.doi.org/10.3115/976931.976966

[8] Hincks, R.: Using Speech Recognition to Evaluate skills in spoken English, Department of Speech, Music and Hearing, KTH

[9] Kashima, H., Hu, J., Ray, B., Singh, M.: K-means clustering of proportional data using L1 distance. In: 19th International Conference on Pattern Recognition, ICPR 2008, December 8-11, pp. 1–4 (2008)

[10] Digalakis, V., Ostendorf, M., Rohlicek, J.R.: Improvements in the stochastic segment model for Phoneme recognition. In: Proceedings of the Workshop on Speech and Natural Language, Human Language Technology Conference, Cape Cod, Massachusetts, October 15 - 18, pp. 332–338. Association for Computational Linguistics, Morristown (1989), http://dx.doi.org/10.3115/1075434.1075491

[11] Hincks, R.: Speech technologies for pronunciation feedback and evaluation. ReCALL 15(1), 3–20 (2003), http://dx.doi.org/10.1017/S0958344003000211

[12] De Liang, W., Brown, G.J.: Computational Auditory Scene Analysis: Principles, Algorithms, and Applications. Wiley-IEEE Press (2006), ISBN: 978-0-471-74109-1

[13] Hyvärinen, A., Karhunen, J., Oja, E.: Independent Component Analysis, PG 145-164. In: Adaptive and Learning Systems for Signal Processing, Communications, and Control, Nerural Networks Research Center, Helsinki. University of Technology, Finland (2002), http://dx.doi.org/10.1002/0471221317.ch7

Knowledge Base Compound Approach towards Spam Detection

Gaurav Kumar Tak and Shashikala Tapaswi

ABV- Indian Institute of Information Technology and Management
Gwalior (M.P.), India
gauravtakswm@gmail.com, stapaswi@hotmail.com

Abstract. Currently, spam mails are the major issue over mail boxes as well as over the internet. Spam mails can be the cause of phishing attack, hacking of banking accounts, attacks on confidential data. Spamming is growing at a rapid rate since sending a flood of mails is easy and very cheap. Spam mails disturb the mind-peace, waste time and consume resources e.g., memory space and network bandwidth, so fighting against spam is a big issue in internet security.

This paper presents an approach of spam filtering which is based on mining knowledge base, analysis of the mail header, cross validation. Proposed methodology includes the several techniques of spam filtering with the higher accuracy. It works well with all kinds of spam mails (text based spam as well as image spam). Our experiments and results shows promising results, and spam's are filtered out at least 97.34 % with 0.11% false positive.

Keywords: Spam, Scam, Matching Fraction, Cross Validation.

1 Introduction

Currently, Electronic mail communication is more popular channel which is known as email. It plays a vital role in our daily life, especially in business correspondence. It has been used worldwide for years since it is practical, convenient and low cost (or free of cost) [1]. Email service is also so common and popular because of some features like Free Availability, Fast Communication, Email Marketing, Newsletters etc.

Today, Email and chat services are the most common, instantaneous and successful Internet applications, which are threatened by spam mails and spam chats. According to a report, 2003 [9], more than 50% emails are spam mails. The spam detection problem seems more serious over mailboxes today. Without a spam filter, one email user might receive over hundreds of mails daily and find that most of them are of spam category. Spam mails consume unnecessary traffic over the internet as well as email service provider. Moreover, receiving spam mails are with no use for email users.

Due to following characteristics, currently the identification process of spam mails is a difficult problem [3].

N. Meghanathan et al. (Eds.): CNSA 2010, CCIS 89, pp. 490–499, 2010.

Spam heterogeneity: Some examples of spam: chain letters; pyramid schemes (including multilevel marketing), make-money-fast schemes, phone sex lines and advertisements for pornographic web sites, and etc , these all listed by The CAUCE (Coalition against Unsolicited Commercial Email) organization. [3]

But there are many others which come in spam mail category like Nigerian scams and Lottery Fraud , etc. Scam is a whole class of sneaky behavior that is designed to transfer the money from one pocket to another under false pretenses. These spam mails also come under cyber crime category.[3]

Spam definition: There is no complete definition of spam mails. There are so many examples where one mail can be spam for one user and can be a useful mail(not a spam) for another user (e.g., notification mail of job opening or a mail from a company to its customers for advertise its products , or notification mail for any discount scheme). The mail issue of designing a system against spam filter, to define a spam mail efficiently. There are many phishing attacks which use mail notification. They should be categorized into spam mails. [3].

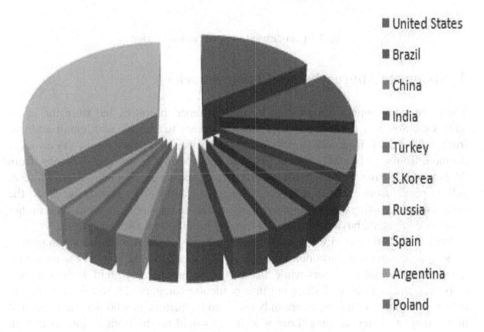

Fig. 1. Represents the spam distribution over various countries

By continent, Asia continues to dominate in spam, with more than a third of the world's unsolicited junk email relayed by the region. Asia covers 34.8% spams over all the spams . The breakdown of spam relaying by continent is as follows [6]:

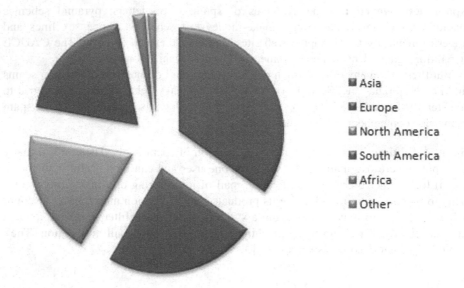

Asia
Europe
North America
South America
Africa
Other

Fig. 2. Spam distribution over various region

2   Spammer Approaches and Their Attack

There are many approaches adopted by the spammer to collect and store the email addresses. Some of those approaches are from posts to UseNet with email address, from mailing lists, from web pages, from various web and paper forms, via an Ident daemon, from a web browser, from IRC and chat rooms, from finger daemons, from AOL profiles, from domain contact points, by guessing & cleaning, from white & yellow pages, from a previous owner of the email address, by having access to the same computer, using social engineering, from the address book and emails on other people's computers, buying lists from others, by hacking into sites and etc.

With a marketing service, a person can arrange his contacts by certain demographics so that he can create custom mailing lists. This means that he can have some newsletters that go to all customers while also having some that only go to women or men or people with a history of shopping in a particular category. These tailored mailing lists ensure that your messages are only received by customers who may be interested in the subject matter, keeping those who likely would not be from feeling as though they are being spammed and unsubscribing.

With social networking sites ,when a person joins some social networking website (like shtyle.fm, yaari.com, indiarocks.com, mycantos.com, facebook.com, tagged.com etc.), then these social site use some script to approach contacts (contact mail list) of that person and sent them invitation to join the same social site. Many times they fill spam mails in peoples' inbox using this approach. There are also many several attacks which are adopted by spammers to generate the spam mails.

3 Related Work

In literature, there are many techniques described for the detection of spam and mail filtering. Some of the techniques are described as follows:

A social network is constructed based on email exchanges between various users in [11][12]. Spammers are identified by observing abnormalities in the structural properties of the network. Many times spammer uses the public social sites for increasing their mail list database. However, it is a reactive mechanism since spammers are identified after they have already sent spam. [13] creates a Bayesian network out of email exchanges to detect spam. Though Bayesian classifiers can be used for detecting spam emails, they inherently need to scan the contents of the email to compute the probability distributions for every node in the network. Since many times it is not possible, to detect spam mails for the particular inbox and its requirement for filtering the spam mails [4].

There is an effective technique to detect the spam mail that is 'Fast Effective Botnet Spam Detection'. It uses the header information of mails to detect the spam mails. It is useful for both 'Text based spam' as well as 'image based spam'. It analyzes the sender IP address, sender email address, MX records and MX hosts [1].

One approach is also described to detect the spam mails, it use the Bayesian calculation for single keyword sets and multiple keywords sets, along with its keyword contexts to improve the spam detection [5].

4 Proposed Methodology

Before proposing a new methodology for spam detection, we are aware of this fact that most of time spam mails and scams are spread out using the machine generated script. Here we propose a cross layer for the above that is based on the above facts and some other facts also.

Our system uses some knowledgebase which contains the information about previous spam mails for the particular user. Using the knowledge base, detection of spam mails is performed. It also maintains some keywords list, which can easily be pointed out as some words in the incoming mail, then perform the detection operation.

Many times when a person click a link which is available in his mailbox, (that link can be provided by the spammers) then mail address of the person is captured by the spammer and is entered in their database.

Proposed spam detection approach, follow the few steps which are as follows:

1) **Analyze the mail content:** Firstly, system analyze the mail content and sender mail address of the mail, then cross check with the previous spam list if content and sender address both are already present in any of the previous spam mails then it directly declares the mail as *"a spam"*. If the mail content partially matches with the previous spam mails then mail is filtered using the

spam threshold value (p). The spam threshold value also decides the performance and accuracy of spam detection system. It can be different for various systems.

If S_t =0.7 and matching fraction of the content of mail matches with the previous declared spam mails is greater than equal to 0.7, then the mail is declared as *"a spam"*.

Matching fraction of the content= max.(NM$_1$/N$_1$, NM$_2$/N$_2$, ..., NM$_p$/N$_p$)

NM$_p$: Number of matched words of incoming mail with the p-th spam mail.

N$_p$: Number of words in p-th spam mail.

P: The total no. of mails which are available in the spam mail list corresponding to that user.

2) **Keywords knowledge Base:** In this step, It analyzes the keywords of mails with the keywords knowledge base of spam which is prepared by the particular user for detection of spam. Using the result it declares mail as *"a spam"* or execute the next steps.

3) **Sender mail address:** System analyze the sender mail address using the mail header (check the *from* field or *reply-to* field to get the sender email address). Using the sender email address, system finds that receiver has already communicated with the same email address or not? If receiver has already communicated with that mail address, then the system declares that mail *"not a spam"*. If receiver has never communicated, then system explores the contact list of the receiver.

```
Delivered-To: vikas@decenttechnolgies.org
Return-Path: <skoost@skoost.com>
Received: from skoismta10.skoost.com (mx198.skoost.com
[80.248.17.198])
by mx.google.com with ESMTP id t10si1017262rvl.81.2010.04.14.19.41.23;
Wed, 14 Apr 2010 19:41:23 -0700 (PDT)
Received: from skoissql01 (unknown [80.248.18.51])
by skoismta10.skoost.com (Postfix) with ESMTP id AFA3B2ACDBC
for < vikas@decenttechnolgies.org >; Thu, 12 Mar 2010 02:41:22 +0000
(GMT)
MIME-Version: 1.0
From: Skoost <skoost@skoost.com>
Sender: Skoost <skoost@skoost.com>
To: "vikas@decenttechnolgies.org " < vikas@decenttechnolgies.org >
Reply-To: Skoost <skoost@skoost.com>
Date: 12 Mar 2010 02:41:22 +0000
Subject: A gift box - Skoost
Content-Type: multipart/alternative;
boundary=--boundary_6430361_eb7ef93d-fac4-4e36-bbca-0ea779a0dfbf
Message-Id: <20100415024122.AFA3B2ACDBC@skoismta10.skoost.com>


----boundary_6430361_eb7ef93d-fac4-4e36-bbca-0ea779a0dfbf
Content-Type: text/plain; charset=utf-8
Content-Transfer-Encoding: quoted-printable
```

```
Delivered-To: payal@decenttechnolgies.org
Received: by 10.141.29.11 with SMTP id g11cs495657rvj;
    Tue, 6 Apr 2010 07:07:36 -0700 (PDT)
Received: from mr.google.com ([10.141.124.15])
    by 10.141.124.15 with SMTP id b15mr1285989rvn.0.1270562856003 (num_hops = 1);
    Tue, 06 Apr 2010 07:07:36 -0700 (PDT)

MIME-Version: 1.0
Reply-To: =?UTF-8?B?4pmh4pmh0ZLimarguZPmsYnOtyTRkuKZqiAuLi4uLi4u?=
<himanshi.s@gmail.com>
Sender: 13341802658969214797@mail.orkut.com
Received: by 10.141.124.15 with SMTP id b15mr1161613rvn.0.1270562855948; Tue,
    06 Apr 2010 07:07:35 -0700 (PDT)
```

In the above example, user payal (receipt email address: payal@decenttechnologies.org) has sender user *himanshi.s@gmail.com* in her contact list. So the received mail will be marked as *"not a spam"*.

4) **Cross Validation:** During this step, system will verify the sender that sender is a genuine human user or machine generated user using some cross request.

5 Implementation and Analysis

We have implemented the proposed methodology on *"Organization Mail Server"*. We have used HTML, script languages, AJAX, XML and MySql tools for implementing the methodology . We also learnt the basic concepts of PHP, AJAX, MySQL and

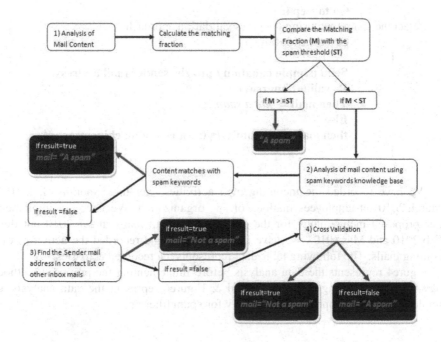

Fig. 3. Represents the steps of proposed methodology

JavaScript from the references [7] [8]. **Figure** 3   and   the following algorithm show how our system works against spam.

1) Extract Mail Content
    - Analyze the matching pattern and calculate the matching fraction with the previous spam mail and then compare the matching fraction with the spam threshold value.
>   **If (matching fraction $> = S_t$)**
>>   **then mail = *'spam'*;**
>>   **Exit;**
>   **else**
>>   **Go to step2;**

2) Analysis the mail content using 'spam keywords knowledge base (already declared by the user).
>   **If (mail content matches with the spam keywords knowledge base)**
>>   **then mail= *'spam'*;**
>>   **exit;**
>   **else**
>>   **Go to step3;**

3) Analysis the sender mail address using the contact list and previous received mails.
    -Extract mail header then Separate sender mail address.
>   **If (sender mail address is available in (contact list or previous communicated mails)**
>>   **then mail = *'not a spam'*;**
>   **else**
>>   **Go to step4;**

4) Detect the spam mail using the cross validation approach.
>>   **Cross validation ()**
>   **{**
>>   **Send (simple equation / puzzle, sender mail address)**
>>   **If (validation=true)**
>>   **Then mail = *'not a spam'*;**
>>   **Else**
>>   **then mail = 'a spam'; /* (sender is a machine user) */**
>   **}**

We have recorded the incoming mail activities over three months (Jan,2010 to March,2010) at employees mailbox of an organization. We have not implemented our proposed methodology for the detection of spam mails in Jan,2010 but during Feb,2010 and Mar,2010 , we have implemented it and recorded the activities of incoming mails. The following table data represents the recorded activities.

Figure4 represents the data analysis before implementing the proposed methodology for spam filtering and Figure5 and & Figure6 represent the data analysis after implementing the proposed methodology for spam filtering.

Table 1. Represents the data of recorded activities over mailboxes

Month	Jan,2010	Feb,2010	March,2010
Inbox	1578	1457	1546
Spam	486	679	637
False Match	4	2	3
Total mail	2068	2138	2186
% Spam Caught	23%	31%	29%
% False Match	0.19%	0.09%	0.13%

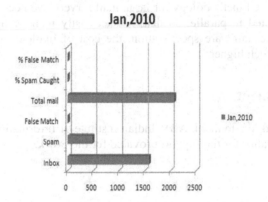

Fig. 4. Shows the mail activities of jan,2010

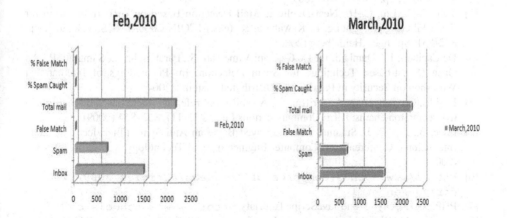

Fig. 5,6. Shows the mail activities of Feb,2010 and March,2010

6 Conclusion and Limitation

Our work is inspired by a problem with a large number of spam mails, we have encountered. We have recorded the incoming mail activities of 30 mail boxes of an organization over 3 months. From data, we have analyzed the activities over the time. The experiment results provide the complete scenario of the problem and accuracy of spam detection. Our system indicated that the spam was filtered out with 97.34 % with 0.11% false positive. Table 1 represents the recorded data over the 3 months time period.

Limitations of the proposed method is that its time complexity and space complexity is higher. So many times, it increases the workload of the mail server. So to implement the proposed methodology for large mail servers, we need more mail servers which are connected in parallel so that we can easily manage higher computation load. Due to more hardware specification, the cost of implementation of proposed methodology is much higher.

Acknowlegdement

The authors would like to thank ABV-Indian Institute of Information Technology and Management, Gwalior for the support provided for this work.

References

[1] Saraubon, K., Limthanmaphon, B.: Fast Effective Botnet Spam Detection, iccit. In: 2009 Fourth International Conference on Computer Sciences and Convergence Information Technology, pp. 1066–1070 (2009)

[2] Yeh, C.-C., Lin, C.-H.: Near-Duplicate Mail Detection Based on URL Information for Spam Filtering. In: Chong, I., Kawahara, K. (eds.) ICOIN 2006. LNCS, vol. 3961, pp. 842–851. Springer, Heidelberg (2006)

[3] De Capitani, D., Damiani, E., De Capitani Vimercati, S., Paraboschi, S., Samarati, P.: An Open Digest-based Technique for Spam Detection. In: Proceedings of International Workshop on Security in Parallel and Distributed Systems (2004)

[4] Kesidis, G., Tangpong, A., Griffin, C.: A sybil-proof referral system based on multiplicative reputation chains. IEEE Communications Letters 13(11), 862–864 (2009)

[5] Issac, B., Jap, W.J., Sutanto, J.H.: Improved Bayesian Anti-Spam Filter, iccet. In: 2009 International Conference on Computer Engineering and Technology, vol. 2, pp. 326–330 (2009)

[6] http://www.sophos.com/pressoffice/news/articles/2009/04/dirtydozen.html

[7] PHP, AJAX, MySql and JavaScript Tutorials, http://www.w3schools.com/

[8] von Ahn, L., Blum, M., Hopper, N., Langford, J.: CAPTCHA: Using Hard AI Problems for Security. In: Eurocrypt

[9] Weinstein, L.: Inside risks: Spam wars. Communication of ACM 46(8), 136 (2003)

[10] Corbato, F.J.: On computer system challenges. Journal of ACM 50(1), 30–31 (2003)

[11] O'Donnell, A.J., Mankowski, W., Abrahamson, J.: Using e-mail social network analysis for detecting nauthorized accounts. In: Third Conference on Email and Anti-Spam, Mountain View, CA (July 2006)

[12] Boykin, P.O., Roychowdhury, V.P.: Leveraging social networks to fight spam. Computer 38(4), 61–68 (2005)

[13] Sahami, M., Dumais, S., Heckerman, D., Horvitz, E.: A Bayesian approach to filtering junk E-mail. In: Learning for Text Categorization: Papers from the 1998 Workshop, Madison, Wisconsin (1998)

Trust Management Framework for Ubiquitous Applications*

N.C. Raghu, M.K. Chaithanya, P.R.L. Lakshmi, G. Jyostna, B. Manjulatha,
and N. Sarat

{raghunc,mkchaithanya,prleswari,gjyostna,bmanjulatha,sarat}@cdac.in

Abstract. With the rapid advancement in the wireless networking and mobile
technologies, devices have become tiny and are able to interact with one another seamlessly offering services which can be accessed anytime, anywhere.
Mobile devices have got the capability to dynamically form networks with other
devices and can host a variety of services which others can access. In such an
environment, security and privacy are the major barriers and addressing these
issues is vital for the penetration of ubiquitous applications. Traditional security
solutions won't suffice to the needs of ubiquitous environments formed with resource constraint devices and pose potential limitations. Context and Role
Based Access Control (CRBAC) mechanism can be used for enterprise ubiquitous applications, where as in case of peer-to-peer ubiquitous applications since
unknown entities involve in interactions, dynamic trust formation plays a vital
role. In this paper, we propose a novel approach for trust management framework using RAINBOW model which represents the human-notion of trust in
terms of computational algorithm with seven factors Peer Recommendation,
Operational Risk, Operational Cost, Reputation, Role, Privacy and Identity.

Keywords: Trust, privacy, human-notion of trust, mobile ad hoc network,
Ubiqutitous applications.

1 Introduction

In this era of computing where there is rapid progress in wireless and mobile technologies, computing environments are getting integrated to physical world and are
supporting us in our day-to-day activities, leading to ubiquitous environment. In order
to evolve seamlessly interweaved computing environment featuring multitude of heterogeneous computing devices and networking technologies there are various challenges like interface, processing, communication, security & privacy and sensing.
Security and privacy [1][2] are the major barriers and addressing these issues is very
critical for the real world deployment of ubiquitous computing technology.

Security in computing environments is mainly concerned with achieving goals like
availability, authentication, confidentiality, integrity, authorization and access control
[3]. In traditional environments, security mechanisms such as cryptography, firewalls,
intrusion detection systems, intrusion prevention systems, anti malware solutions, PKI

---

* This work is supported by Department of Information Technology, Ministry of Communications and Information Technology, Government of India.

N. Meghanathan et al. (Eds.): CNSA 2010, CCIS 89, pp. 500–508, 2010.

infrastructure and dedicated routers are used to achieve the various security goals. Static security policies are enforced from a central machine across the various machines of the network to control the access and also in defining security level for different network services. These security solutions are based on client-server architecture, requires user interaction in the form of manual logins, logouts, and security policies are context-insensitive.

Salient features of ubiquitous environment like extending computing boundaries, invisibility, creating active spaces, context awareness, mobility, adaptability etc limit the usage of traditional security solutions [4]. In fact the convenient features of ubiquitous environment make it vulnerable to new security & privacy threats [5]. Also in ubiquitous environment, information may not be complete or requests may come from unknown entities, so dynamic trust [6] [7] formation is very critical for the entities to interact or collaborate [8]. In this paper we propose a trust management framework for ubiquitous applications which is being executed as part of Ubiquitous Computing Research Centre initiative. Remaining paper is structured as follows. Second section gives security approach for typical ubiquitous applications, followed by related work of trust management in section three. Fourth section highlights the architecture of Trust Management Framework based on RAINBOW model. Fifth section gives the details of trust value calculation using Inference Engine. Paper ends with conclusions and future work.

2 Security Approach for Typical Ubiquitous Applications

In Ubiquitous environment, applications are generally categorized into two types: enterprise applications and peer-to-peer applications as shown in Fig.1. Access control to enterprise applications in these environments mainly depends on the role assigned to the user, the physical environment, time at which access is made and the task performed. Therefore Context Role Based Access Control (CRBAC) mechanism can be provided to enterprise applications which are integrated into Ubiquitous environment.

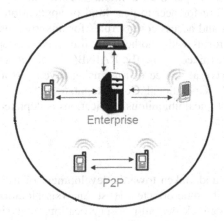

Fig. 1. Typical Ubiquitous Applications

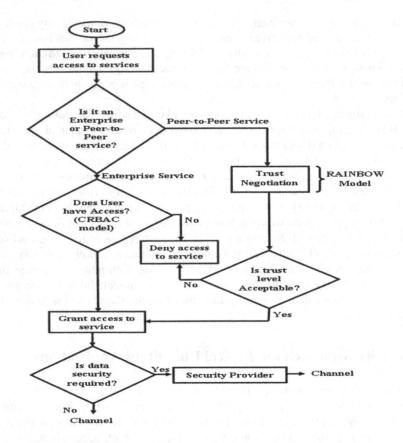

Fig. 2. Security Approach - Typical Ubiquitous Applications

In case of peer-to-peer applications there is a possibility that unknown users may involve in interactions. As per the traditional security policy, authorized users are trusted entities. Therefore for peer-to-peer kind of applications, it is not possible to maintain authorization and access control rules for unknown entities, and type of interaction an entity performs with another should depend on degree of trust. This degree of trust has to be evolved on the fly. RAINBOW model is proposed for dynamic trust negotiation to arrive at degree of trust using seven factors Peer Recommendation, Operational Risk, Operational Cost, Reputation, Role, Privacy and Identity. Security Approach for typical ubiquitous applications is depicted in Fig.2.

3 Related Work

Various projects were undertaken towards development of trust management framework. Simple Universal Logic-oriented Trust Analysis Notation (SULTAN) [9] is a trust management framework that allows specification, analysis and management of trust relationships. In this framework, all the policies are analyzed and managed at the centralized server which makes it inappropriate for decentralized Ad Hoc mobile Networks.

Policy Maker [10] is probably one of the first distributed trust management framework which makes trust decisions based on the static policies. However Trust negotiation is a dynamic process and decision need to be taken on the fly. Therefore, this approach also has limitations.

Some of the projects which are based on distributed human notion of trust management are Secure Environments for Collaboration among Ubiquitous Roaming Entities (SECURE)[11], A Human Trust Management Model and Framework (hTrust) [12], Supporting Trust in the Dynamic Establishment of peering coaLitions (STRUDEL) [13], Risk Aware Decision Framework for Trusted Mobile Interactions [14] and Trust Based on Evidence (TuBE)[15][16]. Though the above mentioned projects aimed at frameworks for dynamic trust generation, none of them tried in capturing all the important factors needed to demonstrate the human notion of trust at the same time giving equal emphasis to privacy.

4 Proposed Architecture for Trust Management Framework

Trust plays a key role in security management particularly in decentralized environments where there is lack of infrastructure. The basic idea used in this trust management framework is to represent the human-notion of trust in terms of computational algorithms for mobile ad-hoc networks. In order to arrive at the trust value seven factors Peer Recommendation, Operational Risk, Operational Cost, Reputation, Role, Privacy and Identity are considered for representing human-notion of trust and hence named it as RAINBOW model. Any kind of trust decisions between / among devices are taken solely by devices without human interference, which closely resembles the way trust is build among the individuals in the physical world.

Various components of Trust management framework are

1.   Request Handler
2.   Security Profile Manager
3.   Knowledge Base
4.   Inference Engine
5.   Decision Dispatcher & Cryptographic API

Trust Management Framework receives the request from peer-to-peer application through request handler for negotiating the trust value. Request handler forwards the request to seven modules for capturing the various factors, which in turn provides to inference engine for computing the trust value. Preferences of different ubiquitous applications as well as past interaction details are provided in knowledge base, which is maintained at clientele devices. Security profile manager helps in configuring the application preferences. These preferences are used by request handler while computing the trust value. Finally the decision is dispatched to application. Communication across the peers while calculating the trust value is secured using pre-shared key through cryptographic API.

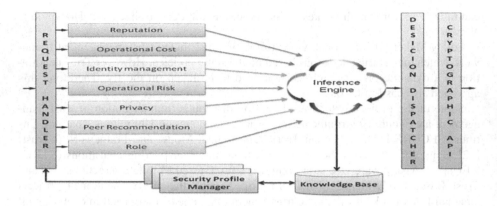

Fig. 3. Architecture of Trust Management Framework

Following are the details of the modules of RAINBOW model, which help in capturing the seven factors, to arrive at the trust value

o   **Reputation:** This module analyses and evaluates the past interaction of the entities. It maintains all the profile information in knowledge base

o   **Peer Recommendation:** This module accepts the recommendations from the peers which aids in making trust decisions

o   **Privacy:** This module looks into the privacy level defined for the application while making trust decisions

o   **Operational Cost:** This module measures the factors like battery power, bandwidth & processing required while giving access to applications

o   **Operational Risk:** This module carries out the risk-benefit analysis based on the knowledge base information.

o   **Identity Management:** This module helps the user to access the resources anonymously, by using pseudonyms thereby ensuring privacy level

o   **Role:** This module provides the required behaviour to the entity when it takes the role as a client or server in peer-to-peer application.

Role and Identity management modules help in capturing the preferences and identity of the user to maintain the session details, which inturn provides input to the other five modules. Inference engine makes decision based on the outcome of Reputation, Operational Cost, Operational Risk, Privacy and Peer Recommendation modules.

5   Trust Value Calculation Using Inference Engine

Privacy is one of the important factors to make a decision on whether to provide or deny access to application when a service request is made. For this to happen, the user needs to configure Trust / Privacy value for each application on the device. The values will be between 0 and 1 and are defined through fuzzy sets. Acceptable value for privacy is nearer to 1 if privacy is important and nearer to 0 if trust is important. The user will be provided with an interface to configure the Threshold Trust Value (**TTV**) based on the Trust-Privacy requirements of applications.

When a service request comes, Trust Value (**TV**) is calculated by considering the outcome of other four modules Operational Cost, Operational Risk, Reputation and Peer Recommendations and if this Trust Value is greater than or equals to TTV, then only the service request is accepted. This can be represented as given below.

$$\text{Provide Service} \Leftrightarrow (TV >= TTV)$$

Request processing for peer-to-peer applications is depicted through flowchart as shown in **Fig.4**.

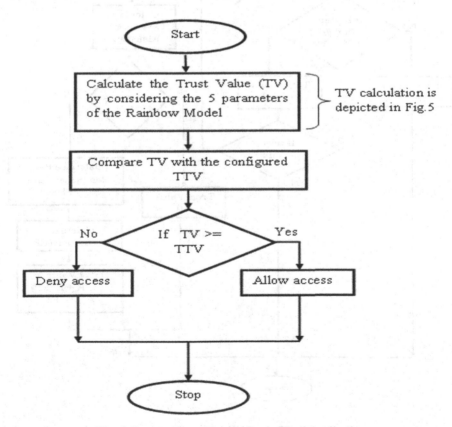

Fig. 4. Request Processing for Peer-to-Peer Application

As part of trust value calculation, first the device needs to check whether enough battery power is available for processing the request. Two levels of Threshold battery power (X and Y) can be configured for different applications by the user. In case of not having enough battery power, either the service can be denied or the user can be involved in taking a decision. Otherwise operational risk (OR) will be evaluated and in case if it is less than the threshold risk (OR_T), it is processed further. Outcome of Reputation and Recommendation modules will be considered for calculating the trust value. Trust value calculation is depicted in **Fig.5.**

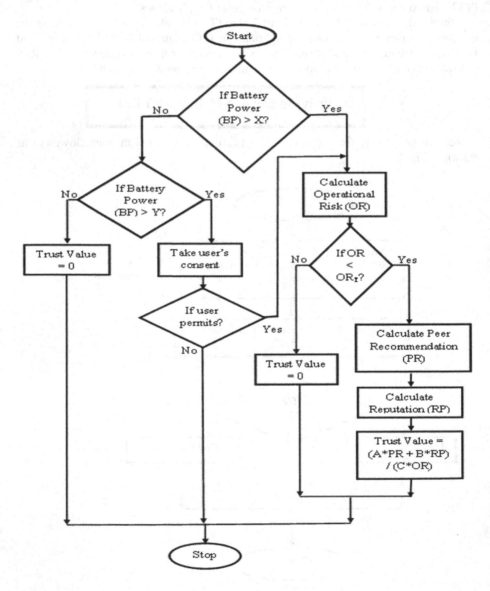

Fig. 5. Trust Value Calculation

In case if device W is providing specific services and another device X is accessing those services, their past interactions are depicted in reputation module as μ_w (X), which represents the reputation device W has on device X. μ_w (X) can be a real value in [0.0, 1.0], which is defined through fuzzy set and is considered as Reputation value (RP).

Device requests for the recommendation from the peers for calculating the trust value. For example if R_M (X), R_N (X)... R_Z (X) are the recommendations given by devices M, N .... Z on device X, then final Peer Recommendation (PR) value is a function of these recommendations.

$$PR = f (R_t (X) \forall \text{ peers t}$$

The final trust value is computed from Operational Risk (OR), Reputation (RP) and Peer Recommendation (PR). Trust Value (TV) is directly proportional to Peer Recommendations and Reputation and is inversely proportional to Operational Risk. If weightages given to PR, RP and OR are A, B and C respectively, then the final Trust Value is given by

$$\text{Trust Value} = ((A*PR) + (B*RP)) / (C*OR)$$

6 Conclusion and Future Work

In this paper we proposed a Trust Management Framework to evolve the trust value in ubiquitous environment. Efforts are made to represent the human notion of trust using computational algorithms using seven factors Role, Identity Management, Reputation, Peer Recommendation, Operational Cost, Operational Risk and Privacy to arrive at the trust value and hence named it as RAINBOW model. We presented the architecture of the Trust Management Framework as well as the design of the Inference Engine which calculates the trust value and is based on fuzzy logic. Future work includes implementation of the Trust Management Framework and testing its functionality with the identified typical applications U-Search and U-Chat.

References

[1] Kagal, L., Undercoffer, J., Perich, F., Joshi, A., Finin, T.: A security architecture based on trust management for pervasive computing systems. In: Proceedings of Grace Hopper Celebration of Women in Computing 2002 (2002)
[2] Goecks, J., Mynatt, E.: Enabling privacy Management in ubiquitous computing environment through trust and reputation Systems. In: Proceedings of the Computer-Supported Cooperative Work (2002)
[3] Lakshmi Eswari, P.R., Raghuram, N.C., Chaithanya, M.K., Manjulatha, B., Jyostna, G., Sarat Chandra Babu, N.: A comprehensive security, privacy & trust management framework for ubiquitous computing environment. In: Ubicomp India 2008 (2008)
[4] Langheinrich, M.: When trust does not compute - the role of trust in ubiquitous computing. In: Proc. of the UbiComp

[5] Al-Muhtadi, J., Ranganathan, A., Campbell, R.H., Dennis Mickunas, M.: A flexible, privacy-preserving authentication framework for ubiquitous computing environments. In: Proceedings of the 22nd International Conference on Distributed Computing Systems, July 2-5, pp. 771–776 (2002)

[6] Shankar, N., Arbaugh, W.: On trust for ubiquitous computing. In: Workshop on Security in Ubiquitous Computing (2002)

[7] English, C., Nixon, P., et al.: Dynamic trust models for ubiquitous computing environments (1996)

[8] English, C., Terzis, S., Nixon, P.: Towards self-protecting ubiquitous systems: monitoring trust-based interactions. In: Proceedings of the System Support for Ubiquitous Computing Workshop (UbiComp), Journal of Personal and Ubiquitous Computing (2004) (to appear)

[9] Grandison, T., Sloman, M.: Trust management tools for internet applications. In: Proc. of the 1st International Conference on Trust Management, Crete, Greece (May 2003)

[10] Blaze, M., Feigenbaum, J., Lacy, J.: Decentralized trust management. In: Proc. of IEEE Symposium on Security and Privacy, Oakland, Ca, pp. 164–173 (May 1996)

[11] Secure environments for collaboration among ubiquitous roaming entities. In: Proceedings of the First Internal iTrust Workshop on Trust Management in Dynamic Open Systems, Glasgow, Scotland (September 2002)

[12] Capra, L.: Engineering human trust in mobile system collaborations. In: Proceedings of the 12th International Symposium on Foundations of Software Engineering, Newport Beach, CA, USA, pp. 107–116. ACM Press, New York (November 2004)

[13] Quercia, D., Lad, M., Hailes, S., Capra, L., Bhatti, S.: STRUDEL: Supporting Trust in the Dynamic Establishment of peering coaLitions. In: Proceedings of the 21st ACM Symposium on Applied Computing, Dijon, France (April 2006)

[14] Abdul-Rahman, A., Hailes, S.: Using recommendations for managing trust in distributed systems. In: Proc. of IEEE Malaysia International Conference on Communication (MICC 1997), Kuala Lumpur, Malaysia (November 1997)

[15] Ruohomaa, S., Viljanen, L., Kutvonen, L.: Guarding enterprise collaborations with trust decisions–The TuBE approach. In: Proceedings of the First International Workshop on Interoperability Solutions to Trust, Security, Policies and QoS for Enhanced Enterprise Systems (IS-TSPQ 2006), Bordeaux, France. Springer, Heidelberg (2006)

[16] Carbone, M., Nielsen, M., Sassone, V.: A formal model for trust in dynamic networks. BRICS Report RS-03-4 (2003)

A Hybrid Address Allocation Algorithm for IPv6

Raja Kumar Murugesan and Sureswaran Ramadass

National Advanced IPv6 Centre (NAv6), Universiti Sains Malaysia,
11800 Pulau Pinang, Malaysia
{raja,sures}@nav6.usm.my

Abstract. The scalability of the Internet routing system has caught much attention in the recent years as it affects the performance of the Internet greatly. IP
address fragmentation is one main cause for routing scalability and existing address allocation practices are one major contributor to address fragmentation.
Address fragmentation increases routing table size, hence IP look-up and routing efficiency. It also constraints the processing and memory capabilities of
routers leading to failing routes if the burgeoning growth of the routing table
size is not contained. A proper address allocation algorithm coupled with appropriate address allocation policies will help to scale the existing addressing
and routing system. This research proposes a hybrid address allocation algorithm for IPv6 by combining some of the existing address allocation algorithms
leveraging on their merits. The proposed hybrid address allocation algorithm
would help in reducing address fragmentation to a greater extent compared to
the existing address allocation schemes. This would facilitate in reducing routing table size, increase scalability and hence improve the performance of the
Internet.

Keywords: IPv6, Sparse algorithm, Rate-Sparse algorithm, GAP algorithm,
aggregation, conservation, and routing scalability.

1 Introduction

IP address allocation and management are essential operational functions for the Internet. There are technical issues and implications associated with address allocation and
management policies [1]. IP address allocation policies impact the Internet infrastructure affecting the performance of the Internet. IP address fragmentation and scalability
of Internet addressing and routing are of serious concerns today with the present exponential growth of IPv6. In general, Traffic Engineering, Site Multi-homing, End Site
Renumbering, Acquisitions and Mergers, RIR address allocation policies, Dual Stack
pressures on the routing table, and Internal Customer routes put pressure on the routing
table size [2]. IP address allocation directly affects the routing table structure and
growth sizes, IP look up and hence the routing efficiency [3] – [6]. Similarly, address
fragmentation increases routing table size and therefore degrades scalability. Existing
address allocation practices are a major contributor to address fragmentation. IP address allocation and management and the scalability of the routing system are interrelated and only certain IP address allocation and management policies yield scalable
routing [7] There are two address allocation schemes namely, the sequential scheme

N. Meghanathan et al. (Eds.): CNSA 2010, CCIS 89, pp. 509–517, 2010.

and bisection or sparse scheme that are currently deployed in the real world [8]. The RIRs individually use various allocation techniques within their respective pools of address space including sparse address allocation algorithm [9]. Proper choice of address allocation algorithm could help to reduce fragmentation, reduce routing table size, and hence increase Internet addressing and routing scalability.

2   Existing IPv6 Address Allocation Algorithms

2.1   Bisection Allocation Algorithm

Bisection or sparse allocation algorithm successively halves the available address space and allocates to users allowing for their growth as illustrated below. Allocation of a new address block to a request is made by evenly splitting into two an unallocated address space where the first half would be used to accommodate growth of an existing user while the second half is made as a new allocation. This way of allocating address space accommodates potential growth of both users.

Fig. 1 illustrates a 3 bit address space and the location of the first six allocations made out of 8 locations. Initially, of an unallocated address space made available to an RIR, the total available address space is divided into two and the first half is allocated to the first requesting user and the second half is allocated to the second requesting user. When a request come from a third user the initial first half is further divided

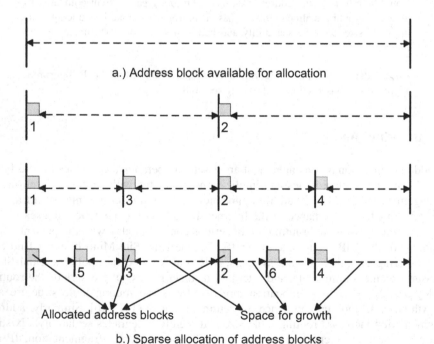

b.) Sparse allocation of address blocks

Fig. 1. Bisection address allocation algorithm

into two where the first half is left to accommodate growth of the existing allocation while the second half of the initial first half is made as a new allocation. The starting address for successive allocations can be selected according to a predefined list as shown in Table 1 that lists the first 6 start addresses within a 3 bit address space. The fourth, fifth, and sixth requesting users would have their address space allocated sequentially after the address space of second, first and third users respectively as shown in Fig. 1. Bisection of the smaller slots of the address space at the next level will be made only after the largest empty slots of the address space have been exhausted.

As address allocations are made using the bisection algorithm from the available address block, the available free space will decrease. It can be observed from the example illustrated here and Table 1 that the progressive operation of this algorithm ensures that the size of the largest free blocks is at most 1 bit longer than the smallest. This implies that a given large address space can become excessively fragmented in response to a sequence of minimal address allocation requests leading to an inability to meet a request for a large address allocation or an inability to make a subsequent address allocation to an user adjacent to a previously allocated address block [10].

Table 1. Start addresses for Bisection allocation scheme

Sequence Number	Address in binary	Decimal equivalent
1	000	0
2	100	4
3	010	2
4	110	6
5	001	1
6	101	5

2.2 Rate-Sparse Allocation Algorithm

Rate-Sparse is a variation of Sparse address allocation algorithm. Similar to sparse address allocation, each new allocation subdivides a window in half, where the selected window is the slowest growing allocation [10] [11].

In the sparse address allocation algorithm, initially, the distance between neighboring allocations is very large. So there would not be any chances for fragmentation of address space in the beginning. But with the growth in the rate of address allocation and the rate of growth of individual allocations, chances for fragmentation of address space is very high which should be avoided. So, rate-sparse follows sparse allocation by selecting successive blocks according to a predefined list as described in section 2.1 but, for a fixed number of allocations. Subsequently, before allocating a start address for any new allocation, it should be checked whether the preceding allocation has grown to occupy a certain percentage of the space potentially available to it, meaning a fast growing user. In that case the selected start address should not be allocated; instead another address should be selected [9]. In the case of the rate-sparse allocation algorithm it selects a start address where the selected window or the preceding allocation is the slowest growing allocation. This is illustrated in Fig. 2. There are also other schemes possible to select an alternative address which could be explored as future enhancement to this research.

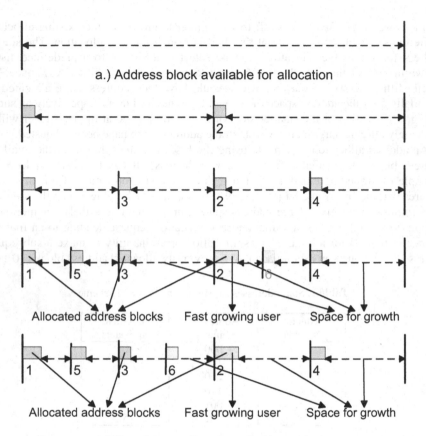

a.) Address block available for allocation

Allocated address blocks   Fast growing user   Space for growth

Allocated address blocks   Fast growing user   Space for growth

b.) Rate-Sparse allocation of address blocks

Fig. 2. Rate-Sparse address allocation algorithm

In Fig. 2, the Rate-Sparse allocation algorithm simply follows sparse allocation for the first four users. For the fifth user the space for allocation should be between 1 and 3, but before it does the allocation here it checks whether user 1 is a fast user by checking whether it has used a fixed percentage of its allocation say for e.g. 50% space potentially available to it. It is no, so this space is allocated for user 5. For user 6, the allocation space by sparse should be between user 2 and 4. But, on checking it is found that user 2 is fast and has occupied about 25% of its available space so user 6 is placed next to user 3 as it was found to be the slowest growing allocation among the rest.

3   Existing Proposals on IPv6 Address Allocation Algorithms

3.1   Growth-based Address Partitioning Algorithm (GAP)

The Growth-based Address Partitioning Algorithm (GAP) [8] [3], makes allocation based on the growth rate of each customer to reduce collisions and utilize the address space more efficiently. For n existing customers there are n possible start address locations for the $(n+1)^{th}$ customer. Unlike the bisection or sparse allocation algorithm, GAP selects a address location based on the size and growth rate of the existing and the new customers, and size of the available address space.

Fig. 3 illustrates this scheme where there are six customers to be allocated for a given address space. The order of their growth rates are assumed as $r2 > r1 > r4 = r5 \geq r3 > r6$, and the indices denote the sequence of the customers. From Fig.3 it can be observed that by the time customer 5 arrives, customer 2 has already doubled its occupied space being a fast user and hence customer 5 would find a place after 3 based on the assumed growth rate. Similar goes with customer 6, and finds a place after 3 as customers 6 and 3 have a slow growth rate compared to other existing customers.

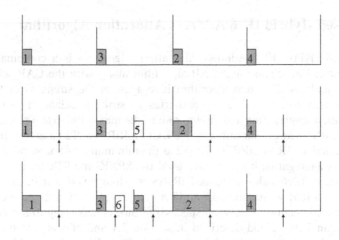

Fig. 3. GAP algorithm

3.2 Common Address Pool (CAP)

In the current system of IPv6 (IP in general) address management, The RIRs receive address space periodically from IANA, from which subsequent allocations are made to users within their regions. In an attempt to ensure that the subsequent allocations to the users are aggregated to facilitate routing scalability, the RIRs individually use various address allocation techniques within their respective allocated address space. In the present IPv6 address management system, aggregation of allocated address space is constrained by several factors. This includes, first, the HD (Host-density) ratio of 80% to be achieved by the RIRs to request for additional address space from IANA. The HD ratio is a metric for acceptable utilization of address space [12]. The HD ratio is currently used to measure IPv6 address space usage [13]. The IPv6 Address Allocation and Assignment Policy, considers a block of IPv6 address space to be 'used' when its HD ratio reaches 0.80. Second, the relatively small sizes of the IPv6 address space held by the RIRs at any one time. These constraints, over time might lead large ISPs or users to receive many discontiguous address allocations from its RIRs.

To avoid the above problem Paul Wilson et al., have proposed a scheme called Common Address Pool (CAP) [9] wherein, the RIRs collectively receive a single large IPv6 address space which can be managed as a single large IPv6 address pool, jointly by the RIRs. An RIR who wishes to make an address allocation to a user will receive the address space from the common pool instead of from a regional pool held by an RIR. From this algorithm itself it can be observed the benefits in terms of address aggregation is high if the size of the address pool allocated to the RIR is high. Hence, the authors of CAP scheme have proposed to IANA, to allocate the entire 2000::/3 for CAP to be managed by the RIRs as a single shared common address pool. Allocation from the CAP would follow sparse address allocation algorithm to achieve maximum aggregation of address blocks allocated.

4   Proposed Hybrid IPv6 Address Allocation Algorithm

The proposed Hybrid IPv6 Address Allocation Algorithm is a combination of the existing Sparse, Rate-Sparse and GAP algorithm along with the CAP scheme. This hybrid IPv6 address allocation algorithm leverages on the strengths of the address allocation schemes discussed above and tries to strike a balance between address space utilization, aggregation and growth rate to the maximum extent possible.

Currently, IPv6 address allocation by IANA to a RIR is a /12 based on sparse allocation method, and a RIR to LIR/ISP is a /32 at the minimum. As sparse allocation maximizes address aggregation it is currently used by APNIC the RIR for the Asia-Pacific region to delegate IPv6 addresses to the LIRs/ISPs, while the other RIRs don't [14].

Now, when a RIR wishes to make an IPv6 address allocation to the user, it simply follows sparse allocation, selects the successive blocks according to a predefined list as illustrated in Table 1 and described in section 2.1 and allocates to the user. This allocated block will be registered in an online Global Common Address Registry (GCAR) that could be coordinated and managed in cooperation by the RIRs possibly through the Number Resource Organization (NRO). When a subsequent address space allocation is requested by a user based on needs, to facilitate aggregation and efficient address space utilization the RIR probes the GCAR for contiguous address space and makes the requested allocation. As the CAP is very large, initially, for appreciably long time, the distance between neighboring allocations is very large and so there is no chance for fragmentation of address space. The Internet currently is facing an exponential growth in terms of IP address allocation. This is expected to burgeon further with the happening of IP convergence now and the Internet of things in the near future. So, over time depending on the rate of growth of individual allocation and rate of IPv6 address allocation, fragmentation may show up its ugly head which needs to be avoided. So, before a new address allocation is made, we have to apply both rate-sparse and GAP schemes on top of sparse allocation scheme to consider growth rate of the neighboring and the requested allocation. In reality, as it is difficult to estimate or guess how many subnets an user would need at the beginning, an initial allocations to all LIRs/ISPs are made at a minimum with a /32 address prefix. Subsequent allocations of address space are based on the HD metric requirements as defined by the RIRs.

Taking into consideration the different growth rate of the address resource requesting users the sparse algorithm is applied until 50% of the CAP is utilized. After this 50% space utilization, for any new address space allocation, an alternative address space has to be selected to accommodate the address space request which can follow different search schemes. We can either follow sequential or best fit to select the next available address space that can accommodate the requested address space. Prior to new allocation the CAP has to be checked to determine the likelihood of the preceding allocation to exhaust its available address space in the foreseeable future. Rate-sparse scheme applies here as it takes into consideration the growth rate of the existing customer. An estimate of their address space occupancy rate in a given time can be easily gauged by calculating the ratio of the address assignment to end-users made by them over that was allocated to them by the RIRs. In reality, estimating empirically based on history the number of subnets that would be needed by a user who makes a subsequent request may not be accurate. As such, it is thought here that the best alternative would be to reserve sufficient space for the user to grow gracefully so that subsequent address space allocations can be contiguous maximizing address aggregation.

5 Evaluation

If we are to allocate and reserve equal space for all the users then the allocation algorithm would basically fall back to sparse allocation scheme. Instead, to benefit the users by distinguishing between fast and slow growers so that address conservation and aggregation can be maximized and allow for subsequent allocations to be made in the same pool or pool size the growth rate of the existing and new allocations have to be considered. Hence, probing for growth rate starts with sparse once the CAP is 50% utilized. The sufficient size of the reservation window is subjective as it depends on the total CAP size and the number of LIRs/ISPs populating the CAP at any one time. IPv6 addressing scheme essentially follows a hierarchy, designed to facilitate more efficient routing and network management than efficient use of individual addresses. As such, the efficiency of the proposed hybrid IPv6 address allocation algorithm in terms of address aggregation and conservation depends on the total size of CAP and the number of LIRs/ISPs populating CAP at any given time. Given more space and/or fewer the number of LIRs/ISPs, the number of subsequent allocations that are contiguous would be more. As the numbers of LIRs/ISPs are a growing phenomenon they cannot be limited in size but the size of the common address pool can be made large. IANA has assigned the 2000::/3 address space to be allocated to RIRs for further delegation as global unicast addresses to LIRs/ISPs which is sufficiently large to be utilized in the above effort. As an example, if there are about 2048 LIRs/ISPs in a RIR, with an IANA address space allocation of a /12 currently, an RIR can allocate 512 /32 prefixes of address space contiguously to an LIR/ISP. This is equivalent to 33,554,432 /48 address prefix end-user assignments for an LIR/ISP. This research considers this big address space of /48's for a single LIR/ISP as extraordinarily large taking into considerations the number of LIRs a country may have.

Simulation results and theoretical analysis as given by Geoff Huston [10] and Mei Wang et al. [3], [8], [15] shows clearly that rate-sparse and GAP schemes demonstrate effective aggregation of address blocks. These simulations were run taking empirically the growth rate of the different RIRs based on historical date with respect to IPv4 and mapped to IPv6 in relation to allocation. This is done as the deployment of IPv6 has just started and the numbers of address space allocations are not significant enough to do the above study on IPv6 address space allocation. Moreover, the simulation were run with the RIRs regional address space of a /12 which is only 0.2% of the total address space of CAP if we consider that IANA allocates the entire 2000::/3 address space for CAP. Hence, considering the large address space of CAP and by extrapolation of the theoretical and simulation results mentioned above it can be observed that the hybrid address allocation algorithm for IPv6 would maximize address aggregation by avoiding fragmentation due to address allocation.

6 Conclusion

The sparse or binary chop address allocation algorithm maximizes the chance of aggregation of subsequent allocation. APNIC uses this scheme to allocate IPv6 addresses to its users as it is routing efficient. A variation of this sparse algorithm called rate-sparse considers the growth rate of the individual allocation and the address allocation rate before selecting a window for allocation. GAP is found to extend on this further by taking into consideration the size and growth rate of the individual user before address space is allocated. A hybrid of these algorithms has been proposed here which exploits the merits of these three techniques to allocate IPv6 addresses which will reduce fragmentation to a greater extent than the existing IPv6 address allocation algorithms. This would facilitate in enhancing routing scalability and hence improve the performance of the Internet.

Acknowledgments. This research was partially funded by e-Science grant from MOSTI (Ministry of Science, Technology and Innovation), Malaysia. 305/PNAY/613140.

References

1. Rekhter, Y., Li, T.: Implications of Various Address Allocation Policies for Internet Routing. In: RFC 2008, Internet Engineering Task Force (1996)
2. Narten, T.: Routing and Addressing Problem Statement, Network Working Group, Internet Draft (work in progress, 2009)
3. Wang, M.: A Growth-Based Address Allocation Scheme for IPv6. In: Boutaba, R., Almeroth, K.C., Puigjaner, R., Shen, S., Black, J.P. (eds.) NETWORKING 2005. LNCS, vol. 3462, pp. 671–683. Springer, Heidelberg (2005)
4. Xu, Z., Meng, X., Wittbrodt, C.J., Lu, S., Zhang, L.: IPv4 Address Allocation and the Evolution of the BGP Routing Table. In: UCLA Computer Science Department (2003)
5. Narayan, H., Govindan, R., Varghese, G.: The Impact of Address Allocation and Routing on the Structure and Implementation of Routing Tables. In: SIGCOMM 2003 (2003)
6. Bu, T., Gao, L., Towsley, D.: On Characterizing Routing table growth. In: Proceedings of Global Internet 2002. ACM SIGCOMM Computer Communication Review, vol. 32(1) (2002)

7. Rekhter, Y.: Address Ownership Considered fatal (1995)
   ftp://ftp.funet.fi/.m/mirrors1/nic.nordu.net/.../
   cidrd.rekhter.slides.ps
8. Wang, M., Dunn, L., Mao, W., Chen, T.: Reduce IP Address Fragmentation through Allocation. In: Proceedings of the 16th International Conference on Computer Communications and Networks, Hawaii, USA, pp. 371–376 (2007)
9. Wilson, P., Plzak, R., Pawlik, A.: IPv6 Address Space Management. ripe 343 (2005)
10. Huston, G.: IPv6 Address Space Management – informational (2004),
    http://submit.apnic.net/mailing-lists/sig-policy/archive/
    2004/08/msg00066.html
11. Brzozowski, J.J.: Address Allocation Methodologies & Provider Independent Addressing. In: NAv6TF/ARIN XV IPv6 Conference, Orlando, Florida (2005),
    http://www.nav6tf.org/documents/arin-nav6tf-apr05/
    3.Address_allocation_and_PIA_JJB.pdf
12. Durand, A., Huitema, C.: The Host-Density ratio for Address Assignment Efficiency: An update on the H ratio. In: RFC 3194, Internet Engineering Task Force (2001)
13. Bidron, A.: HD-ratio proposal, RIPE Policy Proposal 2005-01 (2005),
    http://www.ripe.net/ripe/policies/proposals/2005-1.html
14. Vegoda, L.: Resource management: IPv6 depletion and IPv6 registration. In: Presentation at Australian IPv6 Summit 2007, Canberra ACT (2007),
    http://www.iana.org/about/presentations/
    vegoda-canberra-ipv6-071126.pdf
15. Wang, M., Goel, A., Prabhakar, B.: Tackling IPv6 Address Scalability from the Root. In: ACM SICCOMM IPv6 workshop, Kyoto, Japan (2007)

Modeling and Performance Analysis of Efficient and Dynamic Probabilistic Broadcasting Algorithm in MANETs Routing Protocols

Deepak Dembla[1] and Yogesh Chaba[2]

[1] Associate Professor, Deptt. of CSE, AIET, Jaipur India
[2] Associate Professor-Deptt. of.CSE GJU of Science & Technology, Hisar India
dembla.deepak@gmail.com, yogeshchaba@yahoo.com

Abstract. A MANET (Mobile Adhoc network) is an autonomous system consisting of a set of mobile hosts that are free to move without the need for a wired backbone or a fixed base station. Conventional on-demand route discovery for Adhoc routing protocols extensively use simple flooding, which could potentially lead to high channel contention, causing redundant retransmissions and thus excessive packet collisions in the network. Broadcasting is an essential building block of any MANET, so it is imperative to utilize the most efficient broadcast methods possible, to ensure a reliable network. This paper proposes a new AODV-Efficient and dynamic probabilistic broadcasting approach which is quite efficient and dynamic in nature and solves the broadcast storm problem in AODV. The simulation is done on Global Mobile Simulator (GloMoSim). Routing overhead and end-to-end delays are considered as main performance evaluation metrics. The results show that at a very heavy traffic load , the normalized routing load is reduced to around 35% and 25% compared with AODV-blind flooding and AODV-fixed probability model, when used with AODV-EDPB. The data packets in proposed algorithm experience lower latency than in AODV-blind flooding and AODV-FP model. Also the results show that at higher pause times there is proportionally more decrease in normalized routing load when compared with AODV-FP and AODV-BF approaches and achieve lower overhead and improved delivery latency as compared to conventional AODV, especially in dense networks.

Keywords: MANET, AODV, broadcast, routing overhead, GloMoSim.

1 Introduction

The use of Mobile Adhoc Networks (MANETs) is critically important in situations where mobile nodes are required to communicate with each other without relying on any fixed infrastructure, such as access points. Communication between mobile or static nodes in battlefields or disaster areas cannot depend on fixed infrastructure, thus MANETs [1, 19], 20] are the only option to support network operations. In recent years, MANETs have also been considered as a vital commercial solution for road traffic management purposes, due to their fast deployment and ease of maintenance. Broadcasts form the basis of all communications in adhoc networks. The simplest

N. Meghanathan et al. (Eds.): CNSA 2010, CCIS 89, pp. 518–527, 2010.
© Springer-Verlag Berlin Heidelberg 2010

form of broadcast is referred to as blind flooding. In blind flooding, a node transmits a packet, which is received by all neighboring nodes that are within the transmission range. Upon receiving the broadcast packet, each node determines if it has transmitted the packet before.. If not, then the packet is retransmitted. This process allows for a broadcast packet to be disseminated through the adhoc network. Blind flooding terminates when all nodes have received and transmitted the packet being broadcast at least once. As all the nodes participate in the broadcast, blind flooding suffers from broadcast storm problem, which leads to redundant rebroadcasts, contention and packet collision. Broadcasting is the process in which a source node sends a message to all other nodes in MANET. Broadcasting is important in MANETs for routing information discovery, for instance, protocols such as dynamic source routing (DSR), Adhoc on demand distance vector (AODV) [2], zone routing protocol (ZRP) and location aided routing (LAR) use broadcasting to establish routes. Broadcasting in MANET poses more challenges than in wired networks due to node mobility and scarce system resources. Because of the high mobility, there is no single optimal scheme for all scenarios. Several methods have been proposed to alleviate the broadcast storm problem associated with blind flooding, such as nondeterministic or probabilistic broadcast and deterministic broadcast schemes.

In probability based schemes, the decision of rebroadcast is based on the random probability. In dense networks multiple nodes share similar transmission coverages. Thus, randomly having some nodes not rebroadcasts saves nodes and network resources without harming delivery effectiveness. In sparse networks, there is much less shared coverages, thus nodes will not receive all the broadcast packets with the probabilistic schemes unless the probability parameter is high. When the probability is 100%, this scheme is identical to flooding. The techniques for efficient broadcasting can be grouped into four families [3][4]: simple flooding method, probability-based methods, area-based methods and the neighbor knowledge-based methods. Simple flooding [5], requires each node in a MANET to rebroadcast all packets, In probability-based methods [6], each node is assigned a probability for retransmission depending upon the topology of the network. In area-based methods, a common transmission range is assumed and a node will rebroadcast if only sufficient new area can be covered with the retransmission. In neighbor knowledge based methods,[7] each node stores neighborhood state information and uses it to decide whether to retransmit or not. The objective of all these broadcasting techniques is to minimize the number of retransmitted messages and the number of nodes retransmitting the message. This formed the motivation to implement these broadcasting techniques and use them for route discovery in on-demand MANET routing protocols. This paper proposes new route discovery algorithm called Efficient and Dynamic Probabilistic Broadcasting (EDPB), which enhances probabilistic broadcast methods to propagate the RREQ packets. To evaluate the EDPB algorithm, AODV routing algorithm is used. The rest of the paper is organized as follows: Section 2 presents related work on some route discovery broadcasting techniques and focuses on brief overview of on-demand route discovery process in AODV. Section 3 describes proposed model of EDPB algorithm. Section 4 explains simulation experimentation set up and performance metrics considered in the scenario. Section 5 analyses results based on some performance metrics and finally, Section 6 concludes this work and outlines some directions of future research work.

2 Related Literature Reviews

AODV routing protocol [8][9] construct a route when it is required and does not maintain the topological information about the whole network. a source node S needs a route to some destination D, it broadcasts a RREQ packet to its immediate neighbors. Each neighboring node rebroadcasts the received RREQ packet only once if it has no valid route to the destination. Each intermediate node that forwards the RREQ packet creates a reverse route pointing towards the source node S. When the intended destination node D or an intermediate node with a valid route to the destination receives the RREQ packet, it replies by sending a route reply (RREP) packet. The RREP packet is unicast towards the source node S along the reverse path set-up by the forwarded RREQ packet. Each intermediate node that participates in forwarding the RREP packet creates a forward route pointing towards the destination D. The state created in each intermediate node along the path from S to D is a hop-by-hop state in which each node remembers only the next hop to destination nodes and not the entire route. The issue of reducing the routing overhead associated with route discovery and maintenance in on-demand routing protocols has attracted increasing attention. Probabilistic routing approaches [10] [11] have been proposed to help control the dissemination of the routing controls packets. Zhang and Agrawal [12] have described a probabilistic method for on demand route discovery, where the probability to forward an RREQ packet is determine by the number of duplicate RREQ packets received at a node. However, using the number of duplicate packets received at a node, to determine the local characteristics of the forward node is not appropriate. This is because some of the broadcast packets may be lost due to collisions. M. Bani Yassein et. al.[13], have proposed an improving on the probabilistic flooding by use multiple p, high, medium and low. These values set according to the local neighbors' information. This improving applied over the pure broadcasting, in term of reachability and saved rebroadcast. Qi.Zhang and Dharma [14] have implemented approach that uses the concept of gossip and CDS. But the construct minimal dominating set is not required. Instead of that, categorizes mobile hosts into four groups according to their neighborhood information. For each group, there is a specified value of probability so the nodes with more neighbors are given higher probability, while the nodes with fewer neighbors are given lower probability. Cartigny and Simplot [15] have proposed an algorithm which combine the advantages of both probabilistic and distance method to privilege the retransmission by nodes that are located at the radio border of the sender. The value of probability p is determined by the information collected form the nods neighbors and the constant value K which is efficiency parameters to achieve high reachability. In [16], the authors have proposed an adaptive counter based scheme in which each node dynamically adjusts its threshold value C based on local neighbors information. The fixed threshold C is computed based on a function C (n), where n is the number of neighbors of the node. In this approach the value of n can be achieved through periodic exchange of 'HELLO' packets among mobile nodes. It has been found that there is no such algorithm which can dynamically adjust the rebroadcast probability in route discovery, yet maintaining the better performance in high node mobility situations in MANETs. The proposed algorithm is an efficient solution for a reliable network.

3 Proposed Model of Efficient and Dynamic Probabilistic Broadcasting Algorithm (EDPB)

The probabilistic scheme [17][18] is one of the alternative approaches to simple flooding that aims to reduce redundancy through rebroadcast timing control in an attempt to alleviate the broadcast storm problem. In this scheme, when receiving a broadcast message for the first time, a node rebroadcasts the message with a pre-determined probability p so that every node has the same probability to rebroadcast the message, regardless of its number of neighbours. In dense networks, multiple nodes share similar transmission ranges. Therefore, these probabilities control the frequency of rebroadcasts and thus might save network resources without affecting delivery ratios. Note that in sparse networks there is much less shared coverage; thus some nodes will not receive all the broadcast packets unless the probability parameter is high. So if the rebroadcast probability p is set to a far smaller value, reachability will be poor. On the other hand, if p is set to a far larger value, many redundant rebroadcasts will be generated. The need for dynamic adjustment, thus, rises. The rebroadcast probability should be set high at the hosts in sparser areas and low at the hosts in denser areas.

This proposed simple method for density estimation requires mobile hosts to periodically exchange "HELLO" messages between neighbours to construct a 1-hop neighbour list at each host. A high number of neighbours imply that the host is in a dense area, whilst a low number of neighbors imply that the host is situated in a sparser area. Rebroadcast probability can be increased if the value of the number of neighbours is too low (or similarly if the current node is located in a sparse neighbourhood), which indirectly causes the probability at neighbouring hosts to be incremented. Similarly, the rebroadcast probabilities can be decreased, if the value of number of neighbours is too high. This kind of adaptation causes a dynamic stability between rebroadcast probabilities and the number of neighbours among neighbouring hosts.

A brief outline of the EDPB algorithm is presented in figure 1 and operates as follows. On hearing a broadcast message m at node X, the node rebroadcasts a message according to a high probability if the message is received for the first time, and the number of neighbours of node X is less than average number of neighbours typical of its surrounding environment. Hence, if node X has a low degree (in terms of the number of neighbours), retransmission should be likely. Otherwise, if X has a high degree its rebroadcast probability is set low. EDPB algorithm is a combination of the probabilistic and knowledge based approaches. It dynamically adjusts the rebroadcast probability p at each mobile host according to the value of the local number of neighbours. The value of p changes when the host moves to a different neighbourhood. In a sparser area, the rebroadcast probability is larger and in denser area, the probability is lower. Compared with the probabilistic approach where p is fixed, EDPB algorithm achieves higher saved rebroadcast. Also, the decision to rebroadcast is made immediately after receiving a packet in our algorithm without any delay.

```
On hearing a broadcast packet m at node X
Get the broadcast ID from the message: n
bar, average number of neighbor(threshold)
Get degree n of node X (no. of neighbours
of node X)
If packet m received for the first time then
If n<n bar then
Node X has a low degree
Set high rebroadcast probability p=p1;
Else Node X has a high degree
Set low rebroadcast probability=p2;
Endif
Endif
Generate a random number RN over [0,1]
If RN <= p
then rebroadcast the received message;
else drop the message
    endif
```

Fig. 1. EDPB broadcasting algorithm

4   Simulation Experimental Setup and Performance Metrics

GloMoSim is used as the simulation tool which provides substantial support for simulation of TCP, routing, and multicast protocols over wired and wireless networks. Performance evaluation of the protocols is done on parameters such as routing overhead and end-to-end delay in different network density, mobility conditions and scenarios. The simulation scenarios consist of different mobile nodes moving in different network area; each node has 250 meter transmission range and having bandwidth of 2Mbps. Each data point in the simulation results represents an average of 30

Table 1. Simulation Scenario

Parameter	Value
Transmission range	250 meters
Bandwidth	2Mbps
Simulation time	600 secs
Packet size	512 bytes
Topology size	600x600 m2
Node speed	5,10,15,20, m per sec
Pause time	0,10,25,50,75,100 sec
Number of nodes	25,50,75,100
Traffic load	5,10,15,20,25 connections
Mobility model	Random waypoint model
No. of trials	30
Data Traffic	CBR

randomly generated mobility patterns. The MAC layer protocol is IEEE 802.11.The nodes move according to the random waypoint model. This mobility model is used to simulate 30 topologies. The speed varies from 5 to 20 m/sec. The main parameters used in the simulations are summarized in Table 1.

5 Result Analysis

The traditional AODV protocol which use blind flooding during rout discovery, has been modified by replacing the blind flooding with new a efficient and dynamic probabilistic broadcasting scheme. AODV is already implemented in GloMoSim simulator. The aim is to reduce the flooding of RREQ packets during the rout discovery operation, and as a result it reduces the broadcast storm problem. The net effect is that overall network is improved by the reduced average end-to-end delay and also routing overhead. Since the decisions of the nodes are independent, the total number of possible rebroadcasts of an RREQ packet, N_b using the AODV-EDPB algorithms is

$$N_b = \sum_{i=1}^{4} p_i N_i \text{ for AODV-EDPB}$$

Where Ni is the number of nodes that chose pi . If N is the total number of nodes in the network then, the total number of rebroadcasts of an RREQ packet in AODV-EDPB, AODV-FP(fixed probability) and AODV-BF(blind flooding) are respectively related as follows :

$$\sum_{i=1}^{4} p_i N_i < p \times (N-2) < N-2$$

The value of fixed probability that used in AODV-FP is set at p= 0.8. It has been shown that this probability value enable fixed probabilistic flooding to achieve a good performance.

1. **Effect of Traffic Load:** Fig. 2 shows the performance of three protocols in terms of routing overhead vs. offered traffic load. The results in figure 3 show that at a very heavy traffic load, the normalized routing load is reduced to 45% and 25% compared with AODV-blind flooding and AODV-fixed probability model, when used with AODV-EDPB. Figure 4 shows the delays incurred by all the three protocols for different traffic loads. The number of packets transmitted on the wireless channel has a significant impact on latency. If the number of packets is high, than the number of collisions is high, and in turn leads to more retransmissions. As a result, packet experiences more latencies. And because of higher number of redundant RREQ packets of redundant rebroadcasts, AODV-EDPB experiences lower latencies than AODV-FP and AODV-FP.

2. **Effect of Network pause time load:** The results in figure 5 show the routing overhead generated by three protocols when the pause time is increased from 10 to 100 sec. Figure 6 shows the normalized routing load generated by all the three protocols with different network pause times and the number of constant bit rate is set at 30. The results reveal that when the network pause time is increased, the mobility of nodes is decreased which leads to decrease in normalized routing load. It shows that AODV-EDPB has better performance over the other two protocols. Figure 7 shows

the delays incurred by all the three protocols for different network pause time. The longer the average pause time is, the less is the node movement within the network, and this means that the nodes look like fixed rather than mobile, so the number of generated RREQ packets will be low at network with high pause time.

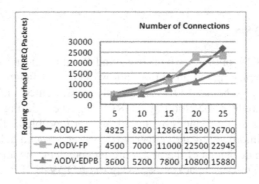

Fig. 2. Routing Overhead vs. Traffic load (No. of Connections)

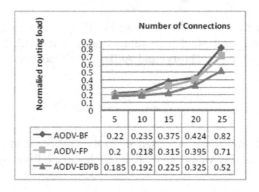

Fig. 3. Routing load vs. Traffic load (no. of connections)

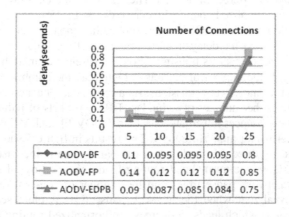

Fig. 4. Delay vs. No. of Connections

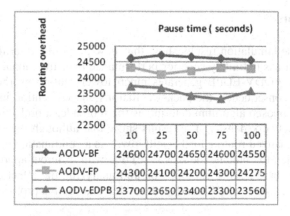

Fig. 5. Routing overhead vs. pause time

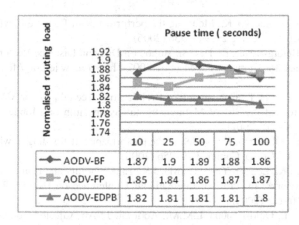

Fig. 6. Routing load vs. network traffic

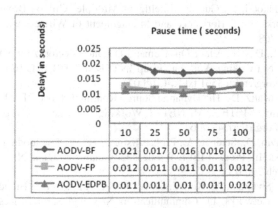

Fig. 7. Delay vs. pause time

6 Conclusions

In this paper, the simulation results show that new proposed algorithm i.e. AODV-EDPB algorithm has definitely superior performance over traditional AODV-BF and AODV-FP. The AODV-EDPB generates much lower routing overhead and end-to-end delay, as a consequence, the packet collisions and contention in the network is reduced. The proposed algorithm determines the rebroadcast probability by taking in to account the network density. The results show that although the traffic load is increased, the normalized routing load is still low. As a continuation of this research in the future, we plan to combine the AODV-EDPB with different approach which suggests solving the broadcast storm problem, and analyzing the effect of this improvement on the performance of DSR and other on demand routing protocols.

References

1. Viswanath, K., Obraczka, K.: Modeling the performance of flooding in wireless multi-hop Adhoc n/w. Comp. Comm. 29, 949–956 (2006)
2. Perkins, C., Beldig-Royer, E., Das, S.: Adhoc on Demand Distance Vector (AODV) Routing. In: Request for Comments 3561 (July 2003), http://www.ietf.org/rfc/rfc3561.txt.,RFC (2007)
3. Williams, B., Camp, T.: Comparison of Broadcasting Techniques for Mobile Adhoc Networks. In: Proc. of the 3rd ACM International Symposium on Mobile Adhoc N/W and Comp., pp. 194–205 (2002)
4. Viswanath, K., Obraczka, K.: Modeling the performance of flooding in wireless multi-hop Adhoc networks. Comp. Comm., 949–956 (2006)
5. Lim, G., Shin, K., Lee, S., Yoon, H., Ma, J.S.: Link Stability and Route Lifetime in Adhoc Wireless Networks. In: Proc. of International Conference on Parallel Processing Workshops, pp. 116–123 (2002)
6. Mohammed, M., Ould-Khaoua, L.M.M., Abdulai, J.: An Adjusted Counter-Based Broadcast Scheme for Mobile Adhoc Networks. In: Proc. of the Tenth International Conference on Computer Modeling and Simulation, pp. 441–446 (2008)
7. Barritt, J., Malakooti, B., Guo, Z.: Intelligent Multiple- Criteria Broadcasting in Mobile Ad-hoc Networks. In: Performance and Management of Wireless and Mobile Networks. LCN, pp. 761–768 (2006)
8. Perkins, E.B.-R., Das, S.: Adhoc On- Demand Distance Vector (AODV) Routing. In: IETF Mobile Adhoc Networking Working Group INTERNET DRAFT, RFC 3561 (July 2003), http://www.ietf.org/rfc/rfc3561.txt,RFC (2007)
9. Johnson, Y.H., Maltz, D.: The Dynamic Source Routing Protocol (DSR) for Mobile Adhoc Networks. In: IETF MANET Working Group INTERNET DRAFT, http://www.ietf.org/rfc/rfc4728.txt
10. Sasson, Y., Cavin, D., Schiper, A.: Probabilistic broadcast for flooding in wireless mobile Adhoc networks. In: Proc. of IEEE Wireless Communication and Networking Conference (WCNC) (March 2003)
11. Liarokapis, D., Shahrabi, A., Komninos, A.: DibA: An Adaptive Broadcasting Scheme in Mobile Adhoc Networks. In: Communication N/W and Services Research, CNSR, pp. 224–231 (2009)

12. Zhang, Q., Agrawal, D.P.: Dynamic probabilistic broadcast in MANETs. J. of Parallel and Dist. Comp. 65, 220–233 (2005)
13. Bani-Yassein, M., Ould-Khaoua, M., Mackenzei, L.M., Papanastasiou, S.: Performance analysis of adjusted probabilistic broadcasting in mobile Adhoc networks. Int. J. Wireless Inform N/W, 127–140 (2006)
14. Zhang, Q., Agrawal, D.P.: Analysis of Leveled probabilistic Routing in Mobile Adhoc Networks", OBR Center for distributed and Mobile Computing. In: ECECS, Uniy Cincinnati incinnati, OH, 45221-0030
15. Cartigny, J., Simplot, D.: Border node retransmission based probabilistic broadcast protocols in ad-hoc networks. Telecommunication Systems 22(1-4), 204 (2003)
16. Tseng, Y.-C., Ni, S.-Y., Shih, E.-Y.: Adaptive approaches to relieving broadcast vol. storm in a wireless multihop mobile Adhoc network. IEEE Transactions on Computers 52(5) (2003)
17. Yassin, M.B., Ould Khaoua, M., Mackenzie, L.M., et al.: Improving Route Discovery in on demand routing protocol using Local Topology Information in MANETs. In: ACM 2006 (2006)
18. Colagrosso, M.D.: Intelligent broadcasting in mobile Adhoc networks: Three classes of adaptive protocols. EURASIP Journal on Wireless Communication and Networking 2007, 16 (2007)
19. Perkins, C.E.: Ad Hoc networking. Addison Wesley, Reading (2001), ISBN – 0-201-30976-9
20. Toh, C.-K.: Ad Hoc Mobile Wireless Networks: Protocols and Systems. Prentice-Hall, New York (2002)

A Trust-Based Detection Algorithm of Selfish Packet Dropping Nodes in a Peer-to-Peer Wireless Mesh Network

Jaydip Sen

Innovation Lab, Tata Consultancy Services Ltd.,
Bengal Intelligent Pak, Salt Lake Electronics Complex, Kolkata - 700091, India
Jaydip.Sen@tcs.com

Abstract. Wireless mesh networks (WMNs) are evolving as a key technology for next-generation wireless networks showing rapid progress and numerous applications. These networks have the potential to provide robust and high-throughput data delivery to wireless users. In a WMN, high speed routers equipped with advanced antennas, communicate with each other in a multi-hop fashion over wireless channels and form a broadband backhaul. However, the throughput of a WMN may be severely degraded due to presence of some selfish routers that avoid forwarding packets for other nodes even as they send their own traffic through the network. This paper presents an algorithm for detection of selfish nodes in a WMN that uses statistical theory of inference for reliable clustering of the nodes based on local observations. Simulation results show that the algorithm has a high detection rate and a low false positive rate.

Keywords: Wireless mesh networks, AODV protocol, selfish nodes, clustering, node misbehavior.

1 Introduction

Wireless mesh networking has emerged as a promising concept to meet the challenges in next-generation networks such as providing flexible, adaptive, and reconfigurable architecture while offering cost-effective solutions to the service providers. Unlike traditional Wi-Fi networks, with each *access point* (AP) connected to the wired network, in WMNs only a subset of the APs are required to be connected to the wired network. The APs that are connected to the wired network are called the *Internet gateways* (IGWs), while the others are called the *mesh routers* (MRs). The MRs are connected to the IGWs using multi-hop communication. In a community-based WMN, a group of MRs managed by different operators form an access network to provide last-mile connectivity to the Internet. As with any end-user supported infrastructure, cooperative behavior in these networks cannot be assumed a priori. Preserving scarce access bandwidth and power, as well as security concerns may induce some selfish users to avoid forwarding data for other nodes. The selfish MRs degrade the routing performance in WMN by decreasing the network throughput [1].

N. Meghanathan et al. (Eds.): CNSA 2010, CCIS 89, pp. 528–537, 2010.

To enforce cooperation among nodes and detect selfish nodes in ad hoc wireless networks, various collaboration schemes have been proposed in the literature [2]. Majority of these proposals are based on trust and reputation frameworks which attempts to identify misbehaving nodes by suitable decision making algorithms. To address the issue of selfish nodes in a WMN, this paper presents a scheme that uses local observations in the nodes for detecting node misbehavior. The scheme is applicable for on-demand routing protocols like AODV, and uses statistical theory of inference and clustering techniques to make a robust and reliable classification of the nodes based on their packet forwarding activities. It also introduces some additional fields in the packet header for AODV protocol so that detection accuracy is increased.

The rest of the paper is organized as follows. Section 2 presents some related work. Section 3 gives a brief background of the AODV protocol and a finite state machine model of the local observations of a node. The proposed scheme is described in Section 4. Section 5 presents simulations results, and Section 6 concludes the paper while identifying some potential future work.

2 Related Work

The concept of neighborhood monitoring to check the activities of other nodes has been proposed by researchers in the context of wireless ad hoc networks. The idea of watchdog mechanism to monitor neighbors was first proposed by Marti et al. [3]. Buchegger et al. have proposed the CONFIDANT protocol that assigns a rating for every node in an ad hoc network based on watchdog and second-hand rating information gathered from other nodes [4]. Mahajan et al. have proposed a mechanism named CATCH [5], which consists of two modules: (i) *anonymous challenge message* (ACM) and (ii) *anonymous neighbor verification* (ANV). First, an ACM message from an unknown sender is sent to all its neighbors. In the ANV phase, a tester node sends cryptographic hash of a random token for rebroadcast and also records other hashes sent by others. The tester node releases the secret token to another node which successfully authenticates itself. Vigna et al. have proposed an approach to detect intrusions in AODV that works on stateful signature-based analysis of the observed traffic [6]. Pirzada et al. have described a model of building trust relationship between nodes in an ad hoc network [7]. Conti et al. have proposed a scheme in which a node exploits its local knowledge to estimate the reliability of a path [8]. Unlike the conventional method of denying selfish users, it provides a degraded service to these nodes by selective slow packet forwarding. Santhanam et al. have presented a mechanism to judge the behavior of a node based on observed traffic reports submitted to local sink agents dispersed throughout the network [9]. The sink nodes apply a set of forwarding rules to isolate a selfish node based on the number of times it is caught in selfish acts. Tseng et al. have applied techniques based on finite state machines to detect misbehaving nodes in the AODV routing protocol [10]. Yang et al. have described the SCAN protocol that addresses two issues: (i) routing (control packets) misbehavior, and (ii) forwarding (data packets) misbehavior [11].

The proposed mechanism in this paper relies on local observation of each node in a WMN. Based on the local information in each node and using a finite state machine model of the AODV protocol, a robust statistical theory of estimation is applied to identify selfish nodes in the network. The scheme is a modification of the protocol proposed in [12]. The objective of the proposed mechanism is to achieve higher detection efficiency by exploiting the information in some additional fields in the packet header in AODV routing. The algorithm is discussed in Section 4.

3   AODV and Modeling of the State Machine

Ad hoc on-demand distance vector (AODV) routing protocol uses an on-demand approach for finding routes to a destination node. The source node floods the *route request* (RREQ) packet in the network when a route is not available for the desired destination. It may obtain multiple routes to different destinations from a single RREQ. The RREQ carries the source identifier (*src_id*), the destination identifier (*dest_id*), the source sequence number (*src_seq_num*), the destination sequence number (*dest_seq_num*), the broadcast identifier (*bcast_id*), and the *time to live* (TTL). When an intermediate node receives a RREQ, it either forwards the request further or prepares a *route reply* (RREP) if it has a valid route to the destination. Every intermediate node, while forwarding a RREQ, enters the previous node's address and its *bcast_id*. A timer is used to delete this entry in case a RREP is not received before the timer expires. When a node receives a RREP packet, information of the previous node from which the packet was received is also stored, so that data packets may be routed to that node as the next hop towards the destination.

It is clear that AODV depends heavily on cooperation among the nodes. A selfish node can easily manipulate it to minimize its chances of being included on routes for which it is not the source or the destination. The proposed mechanism detects selfish nodes in a WMN so that they may be isolated from the network. In the following subsection, the finite state machine model of the protocol is presented.

3.1   Finite State Machine Model

In the proposed mechanism, the messages corresponding to a RREQ flooding and the unicast RREP is referred to as a *message unit*. It is clear that no node in the network can observe all the transmission in a message unit. The subset of a message unit that a node can observe is referred to as the *local message unit* (LMU). The LMU for a particular node consists of the messages transmitted by the node and its neighbors, and the messages overheard by the node. The selfish node detection is done based on data collected by each node from its observed LMUs. For each message transmission in an LMU, a node maintains a record of its sender, and the receiver, and the neighbor nodes that receive the RREQ broadcast sent by the node itself.

The finite state machine shown in Fig. 1 depicts various states in which a node may exist for each LMU [12]. The states corresponding to the numbers mentioned in Fig.1 are listed in Table 1. The final states are *shaded*. Each message sent by a node causes a transition in each of its neighbor's finite state machine. The finite state machine in one neighbor gives only a local view of the activities of that node. It does not, in any way, reflect the overall behavior of the node. The collaboration of each neighbor node makes it possible to get an accurate picture about the monitored node's behavior. In the rest of the paper, a node being monitored by its neighbors is referred to as a *monitored node*, and its neighbors are referred to as a *monitor node*. In the protocol, each node plays the dual role of a monitor node and a monitored node.

Table 1. The states of the finite state machine for a local message unit (LMU)

State	Interpretation
1: init	Initial phase; no RREQ is observed
2: unexp RREP	Receipt of a RREP without RREQ observed
3: rcvd RREQ	Receipt of a RREQ observed
4: fwd RREQ	Broadcast of a RREQ observed
5: timeout RREQ	Timeout after receipt of RREQ
6: rcvd RREP	Receipt of a RREP observed
7: LMU complete	Forwarding of a valid a RREP observed
8: timeout RREP	Timeout after receipt of a RREP

Each monitor node observes a series of interleaved LMUs for a routing session. Each LMU can be identified by the source-destination pair contained in a RREQ message. Let the kth LMU observed by a monitor node be denoted as (s_k, d_k). The pair (s_k, d_k) does not uniquely identify a LMU, because the source can issue multiple RREQs for the same destination. However, since the subsequent RREQs have some delays associated with them, it may be assumed that there is only one active LMU (s_k, d_k) at any point of time. At the start of a routing session, a monitored node is at the state 1 in its finite state machine. As the monitor node(s) observes the behavior of the monitored node based on the LMUs, it records transitions form its initial state 1 to one of its possible final states -- 5, 7 and 8.

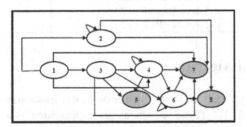

Fig. 1. Finite state machine of a monitored node

When a monitor node broadcasts a RREQ, it assumes that the monitored node has received it. The monitor node, therefore, records a state transition 1 → 3 for the monitored node's finite state machine. If a monitor node observes a monitored node to broadcast a RREQ, then a state transition of 3 → 4 is recorded if the RREQ message was previously sent by the monitor node to the monitored node; otherwise a transition of 1 → 4 is recorded since in this case, the RREQ was received by the monitored node from some other neighbor. The transition to a timeout state occurs when a monitor node finds no activity of the monitored node for the LMU before the expiry of a timer. When a monitor node observes a monitored node to forward a RREP, it records a transition to the final state – *LMU complete* (State No 7). At this state, the monitored node becomes a candidate for inclusion on a routing path. When the final state is reached, the state machine terminates and the state transitions are stored by each node for each neighbor. After sufficient number of events is collected, a statistical analysis is performed to detect the presence of any selfish nodes.

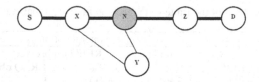

Fig. 2. An example local message unit (LMU) observed by node N

Fig. 2 depicts an example of LMU observed by the node N during the discovery of a route from the source node S to the destination node D indicated by bold lines. Table 2 shows the events observed by node N and the corresponding state transitions for each of its three neighbor nodes X, Y and Z.

Table 2. The state transitions of the neighbour nodes of node N

Neighbor	Events	State changes
X	X broadcasts RREQ	$1 \rightarrow 4$
	N broadcasts RREQ	$4 \rightarrow 4$
	N sends RREP to X	$4 \rightarrow 6$
	X sends RREP to S (overheard)	$6 \rightarrow 7$
Y	Y broadcasts RREQ	$1 \rightarrow 4$
	N broadcasts RREQ	$4 \rightarrow 4$
	Timeout	$4 \rightarrow 5$
Z	N broadcasts RREQ	$1 \rightarrow 3$
	Z broadcasts RREQ	$3 \rightarrow 4$
	Z sends RREP to N	$4 \rightarrow 7$

4   The Proposed Algorithm

A monitor node keeps track of state transitions in the finite state machine of a monitored node for each LMU. These sequences are represented as a transition matrix $T = [T_{ij}]$, where T_{ij} is the number of times the transition $i \rightarrow j$ is found. The monitor node invokes a detection algorithm every W seconds using data from the most recent $D = d * W$ seconds of observations, where d is a small integer. The parameter D, the *detection window*, is such that it allows prompt punishment of the selfish nodes with a high level of accuracy. Section 4.1 discusses the features of the algorithm.

4.1   The Features of the Algorithm

While a transition matrix summarizes the local behavior of a monitored node, it is not possible to determine the selfish behavior of a node based only on its local transition probabilities. By comparing the transition matrices of a collection of nodes, one might be able to detect selfish nodes with higher confidence. For this reason, the proposed algorithm initially clusters the neighbors of a monitor node and then classifies the clusters into selfish or cooperative nodes. The steps of the algorithm are: First, the clustering algorithm is made robust by the use of a statistical theory of inference-based approach that takes into account the pair-wise comparisons of the transition matrices of each pair of nodes. Second, for identification of the cluster that contains the selfish nodes, a measure, called *cooperation index*, for the nodes is computed. The cluster having its cooperation index less than a threshold value is assumed to contain the selfish nodes. Finally, a test is developed based on the *analysis of variance* (ANOVA) among the clusters to determine whether clustering is informative to the purpose of classification. In Section 4.2, the proposed algorithm is described.

4.2 The Detection Algorithm

In the proposed algorithm, a node is assumed to monitor the activities of its r neighbors which are identified by their respective indices 1, 2,....r. Let $T^{(r)} = [f_{ij}^{(r)}]$ denote the observed transition matrix for the rth neighbor, where $[f_{ij}^{(r)}]$ is the number of transitions from state i to state j observed in the previous detection window. If m is the number of states in the finite state machine in each node, the size of $T^{(r)}$ is m x m. Let $T_i^{(r)} = [f_{i1}^{(r)},...f_{im}^{(r)}]$ denote the ith row of the transition matrix $T^{(r)}$, which shows the transitions out of state i at the neighbor node r. If two neighbor nodes r and s have identical distributions corresponding to transitions from state i, then $T_i^{(r)} \equiv T_i^{(s)}$. To test the hypothesis $T_i^{(r)} \equiv T_i^{(s)}$ the Pearson's χ^2 test is used as follows.

$$\chi^2(i) = \frac{\sum_{l \in (r,s)} \sum_{j=1}^{m} \left[f_{ij}^{(l)} - \bar{f}_{ij}^{(l)}\right]^2}{\bar{f}_{ij}^{(l)}} \tag{1}$$

$$\bar{f}_{ij}^{(l)} = F_{ij}^{(l)} \frac{f_{ij}^{(r)} + f_{ij}^{(s)}}{F_i^{(r)} + F_i^{(s)}}$$

$F_i^{(r)}$ and $F_i^{(s)}$ denote total number of transitions for state i in $T^{(r)}$ and $T^{(s)}$ respectively. If the value of χ^2 exceeds the value of $\chi^2_{m-1,\alpha}$, then the hypothesis $T_i^{(r)} \equiv T_i^{(s)}$ is rejected at confidence interval α. If we write K_i^{rs} for the event that $\chi^2_{(i)} > \chi^2_{m-1,\alpha}$, then the conditional probability $P(T_i^{(r)} \equiv T_i^{(s)} | B_i^{rs})$ can be taken as a reasonable estimator of the similarity between r and s with respect to the state i. In absence of any prior information, it is reasonable to assume that r and s have no similarity in state i and the probability that the Pearson test rejects its hypothesis to be 0.5 [12]. In order to evaluate the similarity between r and s for all the m states, (1) is applied to all rows of $T(r)$ and $T(s)$. This yields a vector $B^{(rs)} = [B_i^{(rs)}]$, $\{i = 1,...m\}$. From the standard Markovian principle one can write:

$$L_{rs} = P(T^{(r)} \equiv T^{(s)} | B^{(rs)})$$

$$= \alpha^{S^{(rs)}} (1 - \alpha)^{m - S^{(rs)}} \approx \alpha^{S^{(rs)}} \tag{2}$$

$$\text{where } S^{(rs)} = \sum_{i=1}^{m} B_i^{(rs)} \tag{3}$$

The lower-order terms in the right hand side of (3) are ignored since $\alpha \ll 1$. For small value of α, L_{rs} monotonically decreases in $S^{(rs)}$, which, as evident from (3), represents the number of rejections of Pearson's hypothesis. Therefore, $1 - L_{rs}$ may be taken as the measure of the dissimilarity between the neighbor nodes r and s. In presence of noise, however, it is found that for two nodes r and s which have $L_{rs} \approx 1$, a third node t may cause inconsistency such that $L_{rt} \neq L_{st}$. To avoid this, clusters are not formed on the basis of pair-wise dissimilarity. To compute dissimilarity between r and s, the L values for all neighbors are computed with respect to r and s separately, and (4) is applied:

$$d_{rs} = 1 - \frac{n_{rs}^2}{n_{r/s} * n_{s/r}} \qquad (4)$$

where, $n_{rs} = \sum_{t \neq r,s} \min(L_{rt}, L_{st})$, $n_{r/s} = \sum_{t \neq r,s}^{K} L_{rt}$, and $n_{s/r} = \sum_{t \neq r,s}^{K} L_{st}$.

The computation of d_{rs} does not involve the pair-wise similarity index (L_{rs}) between nodes r and s. It measures the degree of inconsistency in similarity between r and s with all their neighbors. Since in the computation of d_{rs}, contribution of each neighbor is considered, it is a robust indicator of dissimilarity between nodes [12]. For clustering, an *agglomerative hierarchical clustering* technique is used, in which each cluster is represented by all of the objects in the cluster, and the similarity between two clusters is measured by the similarity of the closest pair of data points belonging to different clusters. After the nodes are clustered into similar sets, they are further classified into three groups: (i) a set (G) of cooperative nodes, (ii) a set (B) of selfish nodes, and (iii) a set of nodes whose behavior could not be ascertained. The *cooperation score* (C_r) of a node is computed as [12]:

$$C_r = \frac{\sum_{i,j \in G}^{m} n_{ij}^{(r)}}{|G|} - \frac{\sum_{i,j \in B}^{m} n_{ij}^{(r)}}{|B|} \qquad (5)$$

To reduce the false positives (i.e., wrongly identfiying an honest node as a selfish one), an ANOVA test is applied that computes a probability P_k of the random variation among the mean cooperation scores of k clusters [12]. A small value of P_k implies that the clusters actually represent differences in their behaviors. At each iteration, k clusters are formed and P_k is compared with a pre-defined level of significance β. If $P_k < \beta$, clusters reliably reflect the behavior of the nodes. The cluster with lowest mean cooperation score contains the selfish nodes. If $P_k > P_{k-1}$, the behavior of the nodes are not reflected in the clusters. In this case, all the nodes are classified as cooperative, and the next iteration of the algorithm is executed.

Even with the above statistical approach, there is still a possibility of misclassification. The probability of misclassification is further reduced by a new *cross-checking* mechanism that involves a minor modification in the AODV packet header. Two additional fields, *next_to_source* and *duplicate_flag* are inserted in a RREQ header to indicate respectively the next-hop address of the source, and whether the packet is a duplicate packet already broadcasted by some other nodes. In the RREP header, in addition to these two, another field called *next_to_destination* is added to indicate the node to which the packet is to be forwarded in the reverse path. With these additional fields, it is possible to detect every instance of selfish behavior in a wireless network, if the following conditions are satisfied: (i) no packet is lost due to interference, (ii) links are bi-directional, (iii) the nodes are stationary, and (iv) queuing delays are bounded [13]. The robust clustering and monitoring with additional fields substantially increase the detection as evident from the simulation results.

5 Simulation Results

The protocol is evaluated with network simulator *ns-2* [14] in order to compare it with the algorithm in [12]. The simulation parameters are listed in Table 3.

Table 3. Simulation parameters

Parameter	Value
Simulation area	900 m * 900 m
Simulation duration	1600 sec
No. of nodes in the network	50
MAC protocol	802.11b
Routing protocol	AODV
Raw channel bandwidth	11 Mbps
Traffic type	CBR UDP
Network traffic volume	60 packets/sec
Packet size	512 bytes
Time-out for RREQ broadcast	0.5 sec
Time-out for receiving RREP	3 sec
Pearson confidence (α)	0.1
Observation window (W)	100 sec
Detection window (D)	400 sec
Session arrival distribution	Poisson
Session duration distribution	Exponential

At the start of the simulation, a fraction of nodes are chosen randomly as the selfish nodes. A selfish node adopts either of the two strategies: (i) dropping RREQs (DROP_REQ) and (ii) dropping RREPs (DROP_REP). In both cases, control packets are dropped with a constant probability. For DROP_REP, a selfish node always rebroadcasts RREQs even if it has a route in its cache. To evaluate the detection efficiency and speed, the packet dropping probability is varied from 1.0 to 0.1. The value of the parameter β is chosen as 0.4 to achieve the best tradeoff between detection rate and false positive rate.

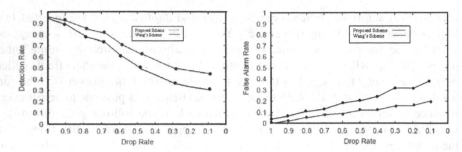

Fig. 3. The detection rate in DROP_REQ   **Fig. 4.** The false alarm rate in DROP_REQ

Fig. 3 and Fig. 4 represent respectively the detection rate and the false alarm rate when 50% nodes in the network are selfish and drop RREQs (i.e. DROP_REQ). The results are the average of 10 runs of the simulation. The algorithm performs better than Wang's algorithm since it doubly checks the detection results- from the clustering and from the routing header information to make more reliable detection.

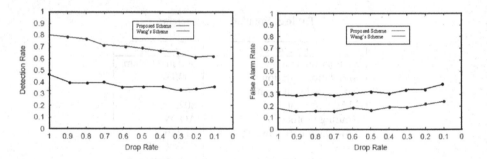

Fig. 5. The detection rate in DROP_REP   **Fig. 6.** The false alarm rate in DROP_REP

Fig. 5 and Fig. 6 show that the packet dropping (DROP_REP) has no impact on the detection rate and the false positive rate when 50% nodes in the network are selfish nodes. This difference in DROP_REQ and DROP_REP lies in the fact that while RREQ is a broadcast message sent by the source, the RREP is sent in a single path by the destination in a unicast manner. Since RREP involves only a few nodes, for majority of them the state machine will terminate in state 5, instead of states 7 and 8. It is evident that the proposed algorithm gives an average 80% increase in detection rate and 50 % reduction in false positives compared with the Wang's algorithm.

6 Conclusion and Future Work

Detection of selfish nodes is crucial in WMNs since these nodes don't forward packets for other nodes and degrade the performance of the networks. This paper has presented a statistical theory of inference-based clustering algorithm for detection of selfish nodes. Using the AODV protocol a finite state machine model is developed based on the local observations of each node. To increase the reliability of clustering, an ANOVA test and a new cross-checking mechanism are used. Simulation results show that the algorithm has high detection efficiency and reduced false alarm rates. Designing an efficient and secure routing algorithm that uses the output of the detection algorithm and avoids the selfish nodes constitutes a future plan of work.

References

1. Sen, J.: An efficient and reliable routing protocol for wireless mesh networks. In: Gervasi, O. (ed.) ICCSA 2010, Part III. LNCS, vol. 6018, pp. 246–257. Springer, Heidelberg (2010)
2. Santhanam, L., Xie, B., Agrawal, D.P.: Selfishness in Mesh Networks: Wired Multihop MANETs. IEEE Wireless Comm. Magazine 15(4), 16–23 (2008)
3. Marti, S., Giuli, T.J., Lai, K., Baker, M.: Mitigating Routing Misbehavior in Mobile Ad Hoc Networks. In: Proceeedings of MobiCom, pp. 255–265 (2000)
4. Buchegger, S., Boudec, J.-Y.L.: Performance Analysis of the CONFIDANT Protocol: Co-operation of Nodes- Fairness in Dynamic Ad-Hoc Networks. In: Proceedings of MobiHoc 2002, pp. 226–236 (2002)
5. Mahajan, R., Rodrig, M., Wetherall, D., Zahorjan, J.: Sustaining Cooperation in Multihop Wireless Networks. In: Proceedings of NSDI 2005, vol. 2, pp. 231–244 (2005)
6. Vigna, G., Gwalani, S., Srinivasan, K., Belding-Royer, E.M., Kemmerer, R.A.: An Intrusion Detection Tool for AODV-Based Ad Hoc Wireless Networks. In: Proceedings of Annual Computer Security Applications Conference (ACSAC), pp. 16–27 (2004)
7. Pirzada, A., McDonald, C.: Establishing Trust in Pure Ad Hoc Networks. In: Proceedings of the 27th Australian Conference on Computer Science, pp. 181–199 (2004)
8. Conti, M., Gregori, E., Maselli, G.: Reliable and Efficient Forwarding in MANETs. Ad Hoc Networks Journal 4(3), 398–415 (2006)
9. Santhanam, L., Nagesh, N., Yoo, Y., Agrawal, D.P.: Distributed Self-Policing Architecture for Fostering Node Cooperation in Wireless Mesh Networks. In: Cuenca, P., Orozco-Barbosa, L. (eds.) PWC 2006. LNCS, vol. 4217, pp. 147–158. Springer, Heidelberg (2006)
10. Tseng, C.Y., Balasubramanyam, P., Ko, C., Limprasittiporn, R., Rowe, J., Levitt, K.: A Specification-Based Intrusion Detection System for AODV. In: Proceedings of the First ACM Workshop on Security of Ad Hoc and Sensor Networks, pp. 125–134 (2003)
11. Yang, H., Shu, J., Meng, X., Lu, S.: SCAN: Self-Organized Network-Layer Security in Mobile Ad Hoc Networks. IEEE JSAC 24, 261–273 (2006)
12. Wang, B., Soltani, S., Shaprio, J.K., Tan, P.-N., Mutka, M.: Distributed Detection of Selfish Routing in Wireless Mesh Networks. Technical Report – MSU-CSE-06-19, Department of Computer Science and Engineering, Michigan State University (2008)
13. Kim, H.J., Peha, J.M.: Detecting Selfish Behavior in a Cooperative Commons. In: Proceedings of IEEE DySPAN, pp. 1–12 (2008)
14. Network Simulator NS-2, http://www.isi.edu/nsnam/ns

A Distributed Trust and Reputation Framework for Mobile Ad Hoc Networks

Jaydip Sen

Innovation Lab, Tata Consultancy Services Ltd.,
Bengal Intelligent Park, Salt Lake Electronics Complex, Kolkata – 700091, India
Jaydip.Sen@tcs.com

Abstract. In a multi-hop *mobile ad hoc network* (MANET), mobile nodes co-operate to form a network without using any infrastructure such as access points or base stations. The mobility of the nodes and the fundamentally limited capacity of the wireless medium, together with wireless transmission effects such as attenuation, multi-path propagation, and interference combine to create significant challenges for security in MANETs. Traditional cryptographic mechanisms such as authentication and encryption are not capable of handling some kinds of attacks such as packet dropping by malicious nodes in MANETs. This paper presents a mechanism for detecting malicious packet dropping attacks in MANETs. The mechanism depends on a trust module on each node, which is based on the reputation value computed for that node by its neighbors. The reputation value of a node is computed based on its packet forwarding behavior in the network. The reputation information is gathered, stored and exchanged between the nodes, and computed under different scenario. The proposed protocol has been simulated in a network simulator. The simulation results show the efficiency of its performance.

Keywords: Mobile ad hoc network (MANET), trust, reputation, packet dropping, node misbehavior.

1 Introduction

Although the security objectives of both ad hoc networks and traditional networks are considered the same such as availability, confidentiality, integrity, authentication, and non-repudiation, the security issues involved in ad hoc networks are quite different due to their mobile and ad hoc constraints, i.e., limited computing and communication resources, dynamic network topology as well as the mobility of the nodes. In traditional networks, most trust evidences are generated via potentially lengthy assurance processes, distributed off-line, and assumed to be valid on a long term. In contrary, few of these characteristics of trust relations and trust evidences are prevalent in MANETs. Since the security solutions developed for the wired networks are not fit for scenarios, new security solutions become essential. Cryptographic primitives such as authentication and key distribution are the usual mechanisms used for implementing security in MANETs. However, these schemes cannot provide security against some attacks such as packet dropping attack by malicious nodes.

N. Meghanathan et al. (Eds.): CNSA 2010, CCIS 89, pp. 538–547, 2010.

There are several approaches for security in MANETs [1][2]. The significant efforts done so far are mainly in the adaptation from the existing distributed trust model to ad hoc trust model. One approach of establishing trust among the nodes in a MANETs is by detecting misbehaving nodes that maliciously drop packets. These malicious nodes can be detected by utilizing the concept of *reputation*. The reputation of a node refers to the perception that another node has about its intention and activities. Reputation is a tool for motivating cooperation among nodes and so as to ensure that most of them exhibit good behavior in their activities. Each node in a network is assigned a reputation value as computed jointly by its neighbors. The higher the reputation value of a node the more trustworthy that node is. In this paper, a reputation-based distributed trust management scheme for MANETs is proposed. The nodes in a MANET collaborate to compute the reputation values of their neighbors, and identify the nodes for which reputation values fall below a pre-defined threshold value. The nodes having their reputation values below the threshold are identified as malicious.

The rest of the paper is organized as follows. Section 2 discusses some of the existing trust- and reputation-based schemes for MANETs. Section 3 describes the details of the proposed trust mechanism. Section 4 presents the results of simulation conducted on the proposed protocol. Section 5 discusses some future scope of work and concludes the paper.

2 Related Work

Different approaches exist for defining trust. Trust, in general, is a directional relationship between two entities and plays a major role in building a relationship between nodes in a network. Even though trust has been formalized as a computational model, it still means different things for different research communities such as public key authentication [3], electronic commerce [4], and P2P networks [5]. The *reputation* of an entity, on the other hand, has been defined as an expectation of its behavior based on other entities' observations or information about the entity's past behavior within a specific context at a given time [7]. In case of a MANET, the reputation of a node refers to how good the node is in terms of its contribution to routing activities in the network.

The *resurrecting duckling* security protocol proposed by Stajano et al. is particularly suited for devices without display and embedded devices that are too weak for public-key operations [8]. Eshenauer et al. have proposed a trust establishment mechanism for MANETs, in which a node in the network can generate trust evidence about any other node [9].

Among the more recent works, Repantis et al. have proposed a decentralized trust management middleware for ad hoc, peer-to-peer networks based on reputation of the nodes [10]. In the trust-based data management scheme proposed by Patwardhan et al., mobile nodes access distributed information, storage and sensory resources available in pervasive computing environment [11]. Sun et al. have presented a framework to quantitatively measure trust, model trust propagation, and defend trust evaluation system against malicious attacks [12]. Chang et al have proposed a trust-based scheme for multicast communication in a MANET [13]. Sen et al. have proposed a self-organized trust establishment scheme for nodes in a large-scale MANET in which a trust initiator is introduced during the network bootstrapping phase [14]. The authors have also proposed a distributed trust-based intrusion detection system for MANETs based on local observation and cooperation among nodes [15].

Cooperation Of Nodes-Fairness In Dynamic Ad-hoc NeTworks (CONFIDANT) is a security model for MANETs based on selective altruism and utilitarianism proposed by Buchegger et al. [6]. It is a distributed, symmetric reputation model that uses both first-hand and second-hand information for computation of reputation values. The proposed protocol in this paper has many similarities with the CONFIDANT protocol. However, the metrics for computing the reputation of a node in the proposed protocol are different from those used in CONFIDANT. The proposed protocol takes into account the historical data of the reputation of the nodes which makes the computed reputation values more robust. In contrast to the approach followed in CONFIDANT, the proposed mechanism broadcasts the reputation information to all neighbors of a node thereby making the protocol more reliable and fault-tolerant and hence more secure.

3 Trust Manager

Establishment of trust in a MANET requires successful detection of intruders and isolating them promptly so that they may not exploit any network resources. However, if one relies only on self-detecting misbehaviors, one may arrive at a wrong evaluation of trust. In fact, a node that is actually not sending any packets currently cannot detect selfish nodes in its neighborhood. As a consequence, collaboration between neighboring nodes becomes mandatory. In the proposed scheme, every node in the network monitors the behavior of its neighbors, and upon detecting any abnormal action from any of them, it broadcasts this information to other nodes in order to make them aware about its observation. The *neighbors* of a node A refer to all the nodes in the network those are one-hop distant from the node A.

The proposed mechanism builds trust through an entity, called the *trust manager* that runs on each node in the ad hoc network (Fig. 1). The Trust Manager has two main components: (i) *monitoring module* and (ii) *reputation handling module*.

3.1 The Monitoring Module

Each node in the MANET independently monitors the packet forwarding activities of its neighbors. This monitoring is related to the proportion of correctly forwarded packets with respect to the total number of packets to be forwarded during a fixed time window. Based on these statistics, if an anomaly is detected, the monitor informs the *reputation manager*, which analyses the packet loss information and take appropriate action. This is explained in Section 3.2.

3.2 The Reputation Handling Module

The main functionality of the *trust manager* is the reputation information management. This functionality involves four major activities: (i) reputation information collection, (ii) reputation information formatting, (iii) reputation information maintenance, and (iv) reputation information rating. Each of these functions is described in detail in the following sub-sections.

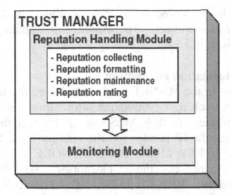

Fig. 1. The architecture of Trust Manager

3.2.1 Reputation Information Collection

This activity is the first step in the reputation information management process. In the proposed mechanism, the reputation information is collected in two ways: (a) sensing or direct monitoring, and (b) recommendations and accusations. In sensing or direct monitoring, a node A senses by itself misbehavior of one of its neighbor node say, B through its monitor module. In recommendations and accusations, the node A receives perceptions regarding a *presumed* misbehavior of a node B from its neighboring nodes. This process can be done in two ways: (i) *on-demand technique*, and (ii) *proactive technique*. In case of on-demand technique, a node A willing to compute a node B's reputation, broadcasts a reputation request to its (i.e., node A's) neighbors, and waits for reputation replies. Upon receiving the replies, it combines them in the way discussed in Section 3.2.4. In case of proactive technique, if a node A detects any misbehavior of a node B, it broadcasts the corresponding information to its neighbors even when it did not receive any reputation request related to node B from its neighborhood. The proactive technique is more suitable for protecting networks as the misbehaving information is broadcast as soon as an intrusion is detected. However, it has a high communication overhead on the network. The on-demand technique, on the other hand, has less overhead of communication. However, its security scope is limited, as all the nodes in the network do not have relevant security information all the time. For gathering reputation information, the proposed mechanism uses both the proactive and the on-demand techniques depending on the situation. To be more specific, the reputation information is exchanged as follows:

Let's first assume that two nodes A and B are present in a MANET and the node A detects that B is dropping packets. However, A will not broadcast this information to its neighbors unless B's packet dropping rate crosses a pre-defined threshold value. Packet dropping by node B may be due to some physical problems of the node or because of its malicious behavior. Use of a threshold in monitoring packet loss ensures that the number of packets being dropped is high enough, and some new routes need to be computed regardless of the reason for the packet drop.

Let us now assume that a new node D has entered into the transmission range of node A. In this case, node A sends a reputation request about node B to the node D asking for its recommendations. The node A then combines the reputation reply that it receives from D with his own observation. This combined trust metric of the node B will reflect its final trust-worthiness. The method of computing the final reputation value is discussed in Section 3.2.4.

3.2.2 Reputation Information Formatting

The neighboring nodes in the MANET need to exchange the reputation information among each other. For exchanging reputation information, the proposed mechanism uses REP_MESS messages. A REP_MESS is an IP datagram with a *reputation header* inserted between the IP Header and the data payload. The reputation header consists of three fields: (i) REP_MESS_TYPE, (ii) NODE_ID, and (iii) REP_VAL.

REP_MESS_TYPE are of three categories: (i) REP_REQUEST, (ii) REP_RESPONSE, and (iii) REP_BROADCAST. The REP_REQUEST message type is used by a node when it requests for recommendations from its neighbors about a new node that is willing to join the network. The REP_RESPONSE message type is used by a node for replying to a recommendation request. For example, let us assume that a node A has already some reputation information regarding a node B. If node A receives a recommendation request regarding node B, it needs to generate a REP_MESS message with the REP_RESPONSE type and send it to the requester. The REP_BROADCAST message type is used when a node needs to broadcast some reputation information.

NODE_ID: it represents the IP address of the malicious node or the new node that is willing to join the network.

REP_VAL: it is the reputation value that the node detecting the misbehavior has computed, and stored in its reputation table.

3.2.3 Reputation Information Maintenance

The reputation information is evaluated at each node before it is locally stored or broadcast to its neighbors. The method of evaluation of reputation is discussed in Section 3.2.4.

Each node maintains a reputation table for storing reputation information for each of its neighbors. The node gets this information by either direct monitoring or through broadcast message received from some of its neighboring nodes. The reputation table for a node is updated whenever there is any change in its reputation value. The reputation table has two fields: NODE_ID and REP_VAL. The significances of these fields have been discussed in Section 3.2.2.

3.2.4 Reputation Rating

Reputation value for a node is a number that can take values between 0 and 1. At the bootstrapping phase of the system, every node has reputation value 1. The reputation value for a node decreases if it exhibits any misbehavior. The reputation computation is done by taking into account the ratio of the correctly forwarded packets to the total number of packets that a node should forward in a given time window. The node A computes the reputation $r(A, B)$ of node B using (1).

$$r(a, B) = \frac{\# of\,packets\,forwarded}{\# of\,packets\,sent} \tag{1}$$

Let us now consider a MANET that consists of three nodes A, B, and C. Three different scenarios can be thought of as discussed below:

1. *Reputation computing during network establishment*: in this case, the nodes A, B and C meet for the first time. Each node creates an entry for the other two and assigns them reputation value of 1 to start with.

2. *Combining previous and current reputation values*: If node A detects misbehavior of node B, it needs to combine the new reputation value of node B with its previously stored reputation value. The combined reputation value is computed using (2).

$$r(A,B) = (1-\alpha)*r_{reptab}(A,B) + \alpha*r_{current}(A,B) \tag{2}$$

The factor a can take a value between 0 to 1. The value *r(A,B)* is a weighted sum of two components. The first part describes the node B's reputation value already present in the node A's reputation table. If node A have not met node B before, then the value $r_{reptab}(A,B)$ is set to 1 as mentioned earlier. The second part reflects contribution of node B's new reputation value. As a node's previous reputations are also considered, the evaluation will be more consistent and seamless. Indeed, a good node that might have met some physical problems for a short time will not be punished and discarded as its reputation will surely increase again if it is relied on for forwarding data packets. Moreover, a node's reputation should seamlessly vary. If the reputation of a node fluctuates too fast, new routing paths will be frequently invoked, and the node's energy will be quickly exhausted. However, the most recent reputation values are given higher weights by assigning higher values to the factor α (say 0.8 for example) in (2).

3. *Computing reputation when exchanging reputation information within a neighborhood*: According to the reputation collecting mechanism described in section 3.2.1, two cases need to be discussed in this scenario: (i) proactive and (ii) on-demand. These cases are presented below:

(i) *Proactive scenario*: in this case, a node A broadcasts reputation information regarding a node B to its neighborhood, in particular node to C, as soon as node B's misbehavior is detected. In this case, node C computes the reputation of node B using (3) as follows:

$$r(C,B) = r_{reptab}(C,A)*r_{broad}(A,B) + (1-r_{reptab}(C,A))*r_{reptab}(C,B) \tag{3}$$

According to (3), the reputation of node B as maintained in node C is a weighted sum taking into account the proper perception of node C regarding node B and the perception of the broadcaster. The term $r_{broad}(A, B)$ is the reputation value of node B that the node A has broadcasted. The term $r_{reptab}(C, A)$ is the node A's reputation value currently stored in node C's reputation table. The new reputation value of the node B in the node C's reputation table is computed based on the perception of the broadcasting node A. The relative weights of these two perception components will depend on the trustworthiness of the node A. If the node A is trustful, the value of $r_{broad}(A, B)$ is close to 1.

(ii) *On-demand scenario*: let us assume in this case that the MANET has n number of nodes denoted as: A, N_1, N_2, ...N_{n-1}. Let us imagine now that a new node D wants to join the network. The node A detects the presence of node D, and broadcasts a reputation request for node D in its neighborhood. If the node A receives responses from p number of neighbors, then node A computes the reputation value of node D using (4) as follows:

$$r(A,D) = \frac{\alpha * r_{reptab}(A,B)}{\alpha + \sum_{i=1}^{P} r_{reptab}(A,N_i)} + \frac{\sum_{i=1}^{P} r_{reptab}(A,N_i) * r_{reptab}(N_i,D)}{\alpha + \sum_{i=1}^{P} r_{reptab}(A,N_i)} \qquad (4)$$

In this case, the all responses from different neighbors of node A are not treated equally. Node A treats each response based on the current reputation value the sender as existing in the reputation table maintained in it. Higher the value of p, i.e., more the number of neighboring nodes of A participating in the reputation value computation of node D, more accurate will be the finally computed reputation value. In the worst case, $p = 1$, i.e., only one node from the neighbors of node A sends the response. In this case, the computed reputation value of node D will be least reliable. In this case, (4) will be effectively reduced to (3) with a multiplying factor.

4 Simulation

To test the performance of our mechanism, the 802.11 MAC layer implemented in network simulator *ns2* is used for simulation. The chosen parameters for simulation are presented in Table 1. Each node in the network is assumed to have a buffer with a capacity of 64 packets with FIFO interface queue. In the simulation, we have considered only the *Dynamic Source Routing* (DSR) protocol. However, our proposed trust model is applicable to any routing protocol for ad hoc networks.

Malicious nodes are simulated using a two-phase *Markov chain machine*. While in the *good* phase, the nodes do not drop any packets, in the *bad* phase, packets are dropped by malicious nodes based on a function. This function generates a random number between a maximum value (MAX_RATE) and a minimum value (MIN_RATE). The Markov chain machine oscillates between both phases during a period of time (t_{trans}), which may be kept fixed or varied randomly. During the simulation, t_{trans} is varied randomly between 100 sec to 200 sec. The traffic is simulated in the network by allowing 5 nodes to generate packets at the rate of 4 packets per sec.

Table 1. Simulation Parameters

Parameters	Values
Simulation duration	450 seconds
Simulation area	1000 m * 500 m
Number of mobile nodes	22
Transmission range	250 m
Movement model	Random waypoint
Maximum speed	10 m/sec
Traffic type	CBR (UDP)
Number of malicious nodes	5
Host pause time	300 sec
Max packet dropping rate	8 packets/sec
Min. packet dropping rate	1 packet/sec

Fig. 2 shows the packet-dropping pattern by a malicious node over entire period of simulation. The *good* phase of the node is during the interval 140-200 sec and 400-450 sec. On the other hand, during the intervals 0-140 sec and 240-400 sec, the node is in the *bad* phase and drops packets varying from 5 to 30. Fig. 3 depicts the performance of the protocol in computing the reputation of a malicious node as performed by one of its neighbors. Here, both the nodes are on the routing path between the source and the destination. It is noted that the reputation value decreases from 1 to 0.25 in the first 140 sec, when the malicious node is in its *bad* phase as seen in Fig. 2. For the next 100 sec (140-240), the reputation of the node increases because the node is in its *good* phase. The reason for the slow rate of growth of reputation during the *good* phase of the node may be attributed to the packet loss due to temporary interference of the channel disturbance.

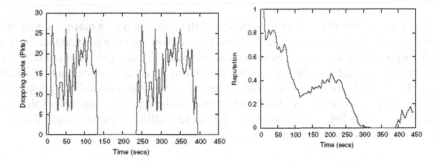

Fig. 2. Packet dropping by a malicious node   **Fig. 3.** Reputation of a malicious node

To study the performance of the protocol in a more realistic scenario, the value of t_{trans} is varied between 0 and 5 sec. Two different situations were investigated: the reputation variation of a node in a low packet dropping scenario (Fig. 4), where MAX_RATE and MIN_RATE are 5 and 0 packets respectively, and the reputation variation in presence of a high dropping configuration (Fig. 5), where MAX_RATE and MIN_RATE are 15 and 3 packets respectively. The reputation value oscillates between 0.58 and 0.78 in Fig. 4. This is because some packets are forwarded to destination; but some others are dropped during the *bad* phase.

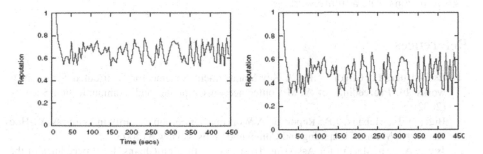

Fig. 4. Reputation in low packet drop rate   **Fig. 5.** Reputation in high packet drop rate

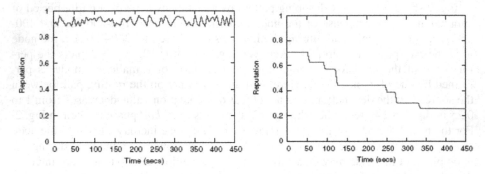

Fig. 6. Reputation of a non-malicious node   **Fig. 7.** Reputation of an accused node

Fig. 6 represents the pattern of variation of the reputation of a non-malicious node. It is observed that the highest and the lowest reputation value of the node are 0.98 and 0.85 respectively, which are quite reasonable values under the experimental setup. Finally, Fig. 7 illustrates the reputation variation of an accused node (say, Y) as computed by another node (say, X). Node X updates the reputation of Y by taking into account the trustworthiness of the broadcaster, and the previous reputation value of Y. As can be seen in Fig. 7, the reputation of Y started falling from its initial value of 0.7 after accusations were received.

5 Conclusion

In this paper, we have proposed a scheme that enables routing protocols in MANETs to detect malicious packet dropping by any node in the network. In the proposed scheme, each node in the network independently monitors the behavior of its neighbors and computes the reputation value for each of its neighboring nodes. Based on the reputation value of a node, its trustworthiness is determined. If the reputation of a node falls below a threshold value, it is no longer considered trustworthy by its neighbors and is identified as a malicious node. The results of simulation on the scheme show that it is quite effective in identifying malicious nodes in a MANET. Designing an efficient routing algorithm on top of this malicious node detection algorithm constitute a future work.

References

1. Eschenauer, L., Gligor, V.D.: A Key-Management Scheme for Distributed Sensor Networks. In: Proceedings of ACM Conference on Computer and Communication Security (2002)
2. Buttyan, L., Hubaux, J.P.: Report on A Working Session on Security in Wireless Ad-Hoc Networks. Mobile Computing and Communications Review 6 (2002)
3. Jsang, A.: An Algebra for Assessing Trust in Certification Chains. In: Proceedings of the Network and Distributed Systems Security Symposium (1999)

4. Manchala, D.W.: Trust Metrics, Models, and Protocols for Electronic Commerce Transactions. In: Proceedings of the IEEE International Conference on Distributed Computing Systems, pp. 312–321 (1998)
5. Kamvar, S.D., Schlosser, M.T., Garcia-Molina, H.: The Eigentrust Algorithm for Reputation Management in P2P Networks. In: Proceedings of the International World Wide Web Conferences (2003)
6. Bucheggar, S., Boudec, J.Y.: Performance analysis of the CONFIDANT Protocol: Cooperation of Nodes-Fairness in Dynamic Ad Hoc NeTworks. In: Proceedings of the 3rd Symposium on Mobile Ad-Hoc Networking and Computing, pp. 226–236 (2000)
7. Azzedin, F., Maheswaran, M.: Evolving and Managing Trust in Grid Computing Systems. In: Proceedings of the IEEE Canadian Conference on Electrical and Computer Engineering (2002)
8. Stajano, F., Anderson, R.: The Resurrecting Ducking: Security Issues for Ad Hoc Wireless Networks. In: Malcolm, J.A., Christianson, B., Crispo, B., Roe, M. (eds.) Security Protocols 1999. LNCS, vol. 1796, pp. 172–182. Springer, Heidelberg (2000)
9. Eshenauer, L., Gligor, V.D., Barras, J.: On Trust Establishment in Mobile Ad Hoc Networks. In: Proceedings of the Security Protocols Workshop, Cambridge (2002)
10. Repantis, T., Kalogeraki, V.: Decentralized Trust Management for Ad Hoc Peer-to-Peer Networks. International Journal of Wireless Information Networks (2006)
11. Patwardhan, A., Perich, F., Joshi, A., Finn, T., Yesha, Y.: Querying in Packs: Trustworthy Data Management in Ad Hoc Networks. International Journal of Wireless Information Networks (2006)
12. Sun, Y.L., Han, Z., Yu, W., Ray Liu, K.J.: A Trust Evaluation Framework in Distributed Frameworks: Vulnerability Analysis and Defense against Attacks. In: Proceedings of IEEE INFOCOM, pp. 23–29 (2006)
13. Chang, B.-J., Kuo, S.-L., Liang, Y.-H., Wang, D.-Y.: Markov Chain-Based Trust Model for Analyzing Trust Value in Distributed Multicasting Mobile Ad Hoc Networks. In: Proceedings of the IEEE Asia-Pacific Services Computing Conference, pp. 156–161 (2008)
14. Sen, J., Chowdhury, P.R., Sengupta, I.: A Distributed Trust Establishment Scheme for Mobile Ad Hoc Networks. In: Proceedings of the International Conference on Computing: Theory and Applications, pp. 51–58 (2007)
15. Sen, J., Ukil, A., Bera, D., Pal, A.: A Distributed Intrusion Detection System for Wireless Ad Hoc Networks. In: Proceedings of the 16th IEEE International Conference on Networking (ICON), pp. 1–6 (2008)

Towards Designing Application Specific Trust Treated Model

Farag Azzedin and Sajjad Mahmood

King Fahd University of Petroleum and Minerals,
Information and Computer Science Department, Saudi Arabia
{fazzedin,smahmood}@kfupm.edu.sa

Abstract. In this paper, we present a process based on aspect oriented methodology to treat a trust model against trust related threats. The trust services are based on a service oriented architecture. We believe that due to the crosscutting natures of concerns in trust dependent applications, concepts of aspect oriented methodology can be applied to develop specifications for trust models. The trust modeling process comprises of the trust service primary model to specify trust services and trust treated aspect model to specify threats as patterns. The primary and aspect models can be composed with application specific scenarios to develop a trust treated model. We have selected the reputation service as an example of a trust service to illustrate the trust modeling process.

Keywords: P2P, trust modeling, SOA, aspect-oriented specifications.

1 Introduction

Although traditional Peer-to-Peer (P2P) applications such as KaZaA and Bittorrent are very successful, they require each participating peer to have the application specific protocol. For example, KaZaA requires its clients to use the FastTrack protocol and BitTorrent requires its clients to use the BitTorrent protocol. Theses client protocols manage downloads and uploads. With the advances of portable devices and with the advent of wireless technology, peers can include a spectrum of appliances such as handheld devices and sensors. Such thin clients may not be capable of handling a client protocol. Unfortunately, recent P2P systems such as Distributed Hash Table (DHT) systems assume that the peers have uniform capabilities. This assumption, however, is difficult to be accepted in real dynamic systems [23]. Nodes have varying availability rate, bandwidth, storage, and computing power. Furthermore, flexibility in traditional P2P systems is needed. For example, content discovery systems supporting exact content name is cumbersome and not scalable [10].

We hypothesize that these limitations can be addressed by a service-oriented architecture (SOA) approach. A SOA approach is inherently scalable and enables custom-design options. Since the architecture is always divided into services, there can be many service providers providing the same service, improving scalability. Peers can provide and customly pick appropriate services without having

N. Meghanathan et al. (Eds.): CNSA 2010, CCIS 89, pp. 548–557, 2010.

to know internal working (e.g. overlay network structure) of other peers. Each peer does not need to implement all resource management services as it can use services of other peers to perform its tasks [5].

Since SOAs stay independent of the internal workings of the services, it needs to provide certain standards defining the services, their inputs and outputs. Anyone can provide the service as long as the standards for the service are met. This characteristic makes sure that the service-oriented architecture always provides standardization. Also, a peer can choose the best service for its needs as the peers are loosely-coupled. This can encourage service providers to improve their quality of service in order to attract more business.

Peers must make decisions regarding others who might be unknown or even malicious [16,26]. The network information system are vulnerable to threats, benign nodes can be compromised or even worse benign nodes might be lead to untrustworthy transactions [27]. Benign nodes are vulnerable to risks because of unknown, incomplete, or distorted information about each other. Therefore, nodes need to manage threats involved with interacting with outside world. Therefore, a solution is needed to nurture collaboration and encourage nodes to participate while preserving their safety.

One way to address this problem is to establish trust [1,25,17], where malicious nodes are identified and isolated from the environment. Trust is one of the most profound and irreversible changes in online systems [7]. In this paper, a trust model is decomposed of trust services in such a way that trust is modeled in a SOA fashion. We are also proposing a process to design an application specific trust model that is treated against threats. We use Aspect-Oriented Methodology (AOM) to desing our trust treated model. AOM supports separation of crosscutting features from other features during design modeling. In AOM, crosscutting features are treated as patterns described by aspect models, and other features are described by a primary model. The result of composing aspect and primary models is an integrated design model called the composed model. In this paper, we propose to use AOM to model trust for P2P systems using SOA. The trust related services such as reputation, aggregation, monitoring etc. will be designed as primary model because they describe the functionality of a trust service. The trust threats (e.g. bad mouthing) are designed as aspect models because they are not related to just one module of a trust service but impact several of them.

This paper is organized as follows. In Section 2, we outline our motivation behind writing this research paper. We describe the related work in Section 3 and explain our proposed trust treated model in Section 4. Section 4 also presents reputation service as a running example. Section 5 concludes the paper and envision future directions. Throughout this paper, we refer to the peer that wants to consume resources as a *source peer* where as the peer that provides resources as a *target peer*.

2   Motivation

Our work is motivated by the fact that peers have varying capabilities. Therefore, presenting a SOA trust as trust services is more realistic and operational.

Furthermore, we are also motivated by the need for a methodology to design trust-aware applications that mitigate trust threats prior to the implementation of an application. Recently, Georg et al. [13] have presented a methodology to develop secure applications by introducing the concepts of misuse model to represent security threats and subsequent security-treated model to design applications that are resilient to the security related attacks. Similar to security mechanisms [13], trust services are typically developed in isolation as protocols, and they provide trustworthiness at different levels depending on how they are incorporated in the design of an application. The complexity of designing trust aware application further increases as trust services can be used in isolation or they need to work together to evaluate the trustworthiness of peers in an application.

We adapt the concepts of primary model and aspect model presented in AOM to model a trust process. The primary model and aspect models are used to design trust services and trust threats, respectively. The trust modeling process provides a methodology for designing trust aware applications and provides a platform to analyze the impact of trust threats on an application. Furthermore, it will help a system analyst to analyze the effectiveness of different trust treated models for a given application.

3 Literature Review

3.1 Trust Models

Since the inception of trust systems, many researchers have tackled the notion of trustworthiness at different stages. Some trust systems assume a correlation between trustworthiness and honesty [3,24,25], i.e., they assume that trustworthy peers provides honest recommendation and untrustworthy peers provides dishonest recommendation. Such trust systems are vulnerable to badmouthing attacks. A trustworthy peer might provide dishonest recommendation to isolate other competing trustworthy peers and consequently to increase his profit.

Other trust systems [19,3] assume that the majority of the peers are honest and therefore cancel the effect of dishonest ones on the recommendation network. Others such as [2], assumed that a peer is equipped with honest recommenders, and peers are assumed to be robust and resilient to dishonest peers and risky environments. In [25], a peer's credibility is used to offset the risk of dishonest feedback. In these approaches, no mechanism is used to identify and prevent dishonest peers from polluting the recommendation network.

The trust system in [6] uses reply consistency to predict honesty. Consistent peers are assumed to be honest and vice versa. Each peer has a set of trusted allies through whom consistency check is performed. The checking is done by asking one or more of the trusted allies to send recommendation request for the target peer to the recommender. The source peer would compare the recommendation it gets directly with the one received by the trusted allies. Assuming the requests come in relatively short time, the recommender should give answers with no or little value difference. Therefore, if the difference is more than certain threshold, the recommender is being inconsistent. The recommender would be replaced from the source peer's recommender list and marked as dishonest so that it would not be included again in the list. However, this method can not detect dishonest peers that provide consistent replies.

3.2   Aspect-Oriented Methodologies

Aspect-oriented methodology allows to conceptualize and reason about multiple crosscutting concerns and weave them into a working system [8]. The concept of separating of concerns encourages good design and implementation. Aspect-oriented techniques have been applied to all phases of a software development life cycle, i.e. requirements [15], design [9] and implementation [12]. Furthermore, aspect-oriented concepts have been applied to modeling languages such as UML [20] to assist in modeling and composing crosscutting concerns. The UML has been extended based on stereotypes, tagged values and constraints to model aspect-oriented software systems. For example, Pawlack et al. [14] presents notation of group as an extension of class notation to express crosscutting concerns. Similarly, Aldawud et al. [4] models aspect, pointcut, and advice as particular classes with stereotypes.

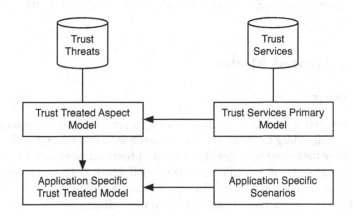

Fig. 1. Trust Modeling Process

Over the last few years, aspect oriented modeling has been applied in the area of security, trust and privacy. Recently, Geri et al. [11] have used the concepts of aspect oriented modeling to model the security mechanism in an application. The security concerns are modeled as aspects and are composed with the primary model to obtain the security related specification. Trillo et al. [22] have proposed to represent security concerns as aspect models to modularize main functionality and crosscutting security concerns. Furthermore, Tranter et al.[21] has introduced the concept of context-aware aspects where execution of an aspect depends on its context of use. The context guiding the aspect invocation can

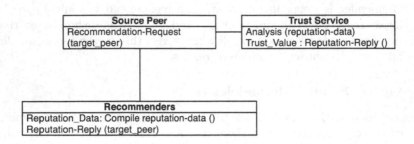

Fig. 2. Reputation Service Primary Model - Class Diagram

have a set or parameters (e.g. time and location) and that they can be combined with other contexts. They also introduce the concept of snapshot context-aware aspects to capture the behavior on a context over a time series.

We believe that due to the crosscutting nature of concerns in both traditional trust models and context-aware trust model, concepts of aspect oriented methodologies can be applied to develop specifications for trust models. However, to best of our knowledge, there is hardly any work done in applying aspect oriented concepts to specifications of both traditional and context-ware trust models.

4   Trust Treated Model

4.1   Overview

The trust treated model is a result of a design process that considerations the following: (a) Modeling the trust services regardless of trust threats, (b) modeling how to counter measure the effect of the trust threats on the trust services model, (c) compose application specific scenarios with trust treated model to enable an application to be trust-aware. In the following subsections, we discuss the trust modeling process using class and sequence diagrams. We also provide a reputation service as a running example to further illustrate primary and aspect models.

4.2   Trust Modeling Process

Trust services are represented following a SOA faction as mentioned in section 1. In any trust model, trust establishment processes should be analyzed taking into considerations trust threats that can be launched to harm and hinder the fucntionality of trust models. There are numerous trust threats as outlined in [5]. For a reputation service, recommenders can provide dishonest recommendations to distort the image of trustworthy peers. This thread is referred to as bad mouthing or slandering. On the other hand, collusion occurs when multiple dishonest recommenders team up to promote each other. This is especially true in P2P reputation

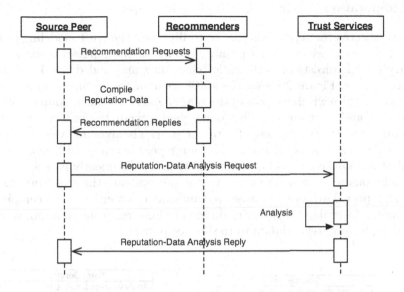

Fig. 3. Reputation Service Primary Model - Sequence Diagram

systems, where covert affiliations are untraceable and the opinions of unknown peers impacts ones decisions. A trust treated model should be designed in a way to minimize the harm caused by such threats and hence increases the confidence of peers to engage in P2P transactions.

Incorporating trust during development of an application is a complex process which needs a methodology for designing trustworthy applications. We believe that a trust modeling process needs to address three key issues: understanding the effect of trust threats to an application, how these threats can occur and what are their consequences; and mitigating these threats during the design of an application. We present a trust modeling process as shown in Figure 1.

A Trust modeling process consists of three phases, namely, trust services primary model, trust treated aspect model, and application specific trust treated model. The first phase - trust services primary model - starts with analyzing and designing trust services as a primary model. The second phase - trust treated aspect model - analyzes generic trust threats as an attack pattern and composes them with trust services primary model to develop aspect models. In this paper, we use Unified Modeling Language (UML) class diagram and sequence diagram [18] to model the primary and aspect models. The third phase - application specific trust treated model - composes application specific interaction scenarios with trust treated aspect model to generate an application specific trust treated model. An application specific trust treated model represents the design of an application incorporating resilience to the given set of known threats.

4.3 Reputation Service - A Running Example

We have selected the reputation service to illustrate the trust modeling process. In the first phase, we develop a primary model for the reputation service. The primary model consists of both static (class diagram) and dynamic (sequence diagram) views. Figure 2 shows the static view of the primary model for the reputation service which consists of three main classes, namely, source peer, recommenders and trust service. The source peer intends to use the trust service to evaluate the trustworthiness of a target peer. The dynamic view of the primary model is shown in Figure 3. The source peer interacts with reommenders to collect recommendations for a target peer and subsequently passes these recommendations to trust services to analyze and evaluate the trustworthiness of the target peer. Furthermore, every recommender can either itself compile the reputation related data or gather recommendations from other recommenders to provide reputation-related-data to the source peer.

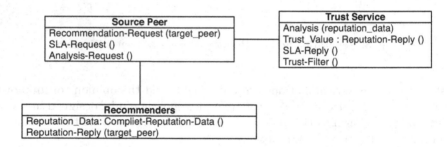

Fig. 4. Reputation Service Aspect Model - Class Diagram

Figure 4 and Figure 5 show the static and dynamic views of the trust treated aspect model, respectively. Similar to the trust service primary model, the trust treated aspect model for the reputation service consists of three classes, namely, source peer, recommenders and trust service. However, in contrast to the primary model, the source peer supports Service Level Agreement (SLA) and trust services support utilization of range of trust filters to analyze recommendations and generate trust values.

In Figure 5, the source peer sends recommendation requests to the recommenders. Once the source peer receives the recommendation replies from the recommenders, it will choose certain trust services depending on its SLA request. A SLA established between the source peer and trust services, the source peer sends an analysis request to the trust services. Based on the established SLA, an optional frame can take place where various trust filters can be applied to the compiled reputation-related-data. Trust filters are applied to manipulate the compiled reputation-related-data. For example, one trust filter might be applied to ignore reputation-related-data that is older than X number of years. Another trust filer might be applied to assign different weights to different attributes.

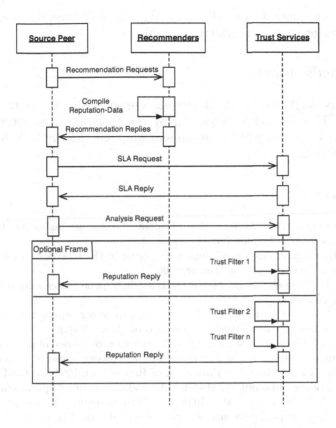

Fig. 5. Reputation Service Aspect Model - Sequence Diagram

5   Conclusions and Future Work

Traditional trust models assume that peers have uniform capabilities. Furthermore, these traditional trust models are not flexible and usually support only one resource, i.e. file sharing. With the introduction of SOA, we believe that such limitations will be solved. Representing trust models as trust services, where peers can provide and use different services without having to implement all services required by a trust model, will enable peers to perform their tasks regardless of their capabilities. In this paper, we present a process to design an application specific trust model that is treated against trust threats. Since these trust threats are crosscutting, they can be modeled as patterns. We use AOM concepts to design trust treated model as its supports separation of crosscutting features. We believe that due to the crosscutting nature of concerns in both traditional trust models and context-aware trust model, concepts of aspect oriented methodologies can be applied to develop specifications for trust models.

In future work, we plan to compose the aspect models to analyze the impact of trust threats on a trust service. Specifically, we intend to complete the trust modeling process to specify application specific scenarios and develop a prototype to generate an application specific model.

Acknowledgement

The authors would like to thank the anonymous reviewers for their valuable comments. This research is supported by the Deanship of Scientific Research at King Fahd University of Petroleum and Minerals (KFUPM) under Research Grant IN090052.

References

1. Abdul-Rahman, A.: A Framework for Decentralised Trust Reasoning. Ph.D. thesis, University College London (2005)
2. Abdul-Rahman, A., Hailes, S.: Supporting trust in virtual communities. In: Hawaii Int'l Conf. System Sciences (January 2000)
3. Aberer, K., Despotovic, Z.: Managing trust in a peer-2-peer information system (November 2001)
4. Aldawud, O., Elrad, T., Bader, A.: A UML profile for aspect oriented modeling. In: Proceedings of the OOPSLA Workshop on AOP (2001)
5. Azzedin, F., Eltoweissy, M., Khwaja, S.: Overview of service oriented architecture for resource management in p2p systems. In: Antonopoulos, N., Exarchakos, G., Li, M., Liotta, A. (eds.) The Handbook of Research on P2P and Grid Systems for Service-Oriented Computing: Models, Methodologies and Applications (2009)
6. Azzedin, F., Maheswaran, M., Mitra, A.: Trust brokering and its use for resource matchmaking in public-resource grids. Journal of Grid Computing 4(3), 247–263 (2006)
7. Clark, D.D., Wroclawski, J., Braden, R.: Tussle in cyberspace: Defining tomorrow's internet. In: Proceedings of the 2002 Conference on Applications, Technologies and Protocols for Computer Communications, pp. 347–356 (August 2002)
8. Dorina, C.P., Hui, S., Antonino, S.: Perfromance analysis of aspect-oriented UML models. Software System Model 6, 453–471 (2007)
9. Elrad, T., Aldawud, O., Bader, A.: Aspect-oriented modeling: bridging the gap between implementation and design. In: Batory, D., Consel, C., Taha, W. (eds.) GPCE 2002. LNCS, vol. 2487, pp. 189–201. Springer, Heidelberg (2002)
10. Gao, J., Steenkiste, P.: Design and evaluation of a distributed scalable content discovery system. IEEE Journal of Selected Areas in Communications 22(1) (January 2004)
11. Georg, G., Ray, I., Anastasakis, K., Bordbar, B., Toahchoodee, M., Houmb, S.H.: An aspect oriented methodology for designing secure applications. Information and Software Technology 51, 846–864 (2009)
12. Gray, J., Bapty, T., Neema, S., Schmidt, D.C., Gokhale, A., Natarajan, B.: An approach for supporting aspect-oriented domain modeling. In: Pfenning, F., Smaragdakis, Y. (eds.) GPCE 2003. LNCS, vol. 2830, pp. 151–168. Springer, Heidelberg (2003)
13. Ray, I., Georg, G., Anastasakis, K., Bordbar, B., Toahchoodee, M.: An aspect-oriented methodology for designing secure applications. Information and Software Technology 51, 846–864 (2009)

14. Pawlack, R., Duchien, L., Florin, G.: A UML notation for aspect-oriented software design. In: Proceedings of the AO Modeling with UML Workshop (2002)
15. Rashid, A., Moreira, A., Araujo, J.: Modularization and composition of aspect requirements. In: Proceedings of 2nd International Conference on Aspect-Oriented Software Development (2003)
16. Ries, S., Kangasharju, J., Mhlhuser, M.: Modeling trust for users and agents in ubiquitous computing. In: KiVS 2007, pp. 51–62 (2007)
17. Rodriguez, P., Tan, S., Gkantsidis, C.: On the feasibility of commercial, legal P2P content distribution. ACM SIGCOMM Computer Communication Review 36(1), 75–78 (2006)
18. Rumbaugh, J., Jacobson, I., Booch, G.: The Unified Modeling Language Reference Manual. Addison-Wesley, Reading (2005)
19. Sen, S., Sajja, N.: Robustness of reputation-based trust: Boolean case. In: 1st International Joint Conference on Autonomous Agents and Multi-Agent Systems (AAMAS 2002), pp. 288–293 (July 2002)
20. Straw, G., Georg, G., Song, E., Ghosh, S., France, R., Bieman, J.M.: Modeling composition directives. In: Baar, T., Strohmeier, A., Moreira, A., Mellor, S.J. (eds.) UML 2004. LNCS, vol. 3273, pp. 84–97. Springer, Heidelberg (2004)
21. Tanter, E., Gybels, K., Denker, M., Bergel, A.: Context-aware aspects. In: Löwe, W., Südholt, M. (eds.) SC 2006. LNCS, vol. 4089, pp. 227–242. Springer, Heidelberg (2006)
22. Trillo, C.P., Rocha, V.: Architectural patterns to secure applications with an aspect oriented approach. In: Proceedings of the 5th Latin American Conference on Pattern Language of Programming, pp. 89–105 (2005)
23. Wang, H., Zhu, Y., Hu, Y.: To unify structured and unstructured P2P systems. In: 19th IEEE International Parallel and Distributed Processing Symposium (April 2005)
24. Wang, Y., Vassileva, J.: Bayesian network-based trust model. In: Proceedings of IEEE/WIC International Conference on Web Intelligence, WI 2003, October 13-17, pp. 372–378 (2003)
25. Xiong, L., Liu, L.: Peertrust: Supporting reputation-based trust for peer-to-peer electronic communities. IEEE Trans. Knowledge & Data Engineering 16(7), 843–857 (2004)
26. Yan, Z., Niemi, V.: A trust model for ubiquitous systems based on vectors of trust values. In: The Seventh IEEE International Symposium on Meltimedia, ISM 2005 (December 2005)
27. Yan, Z., Niemi, V.: Towards user driven trust modeling and management. In: iTrust/PST 2008 (June 2008)

Security for Contactless Smart Cards Using Cryptography

Anuj Kundarap[1], Arpit Chhajlani[1], Rashu Singla[1], Mugdha Sawant[1],
Milind Dere[2], and Parikshit Mahalle[1]

[1] Department of Computer Engineering, Smt.Kashibai Navale College of Engineering,
Pune, India
[2] Persistent Systems Ltd., Pune, India
anuj.kundarap@gmail.com, arpitchhajlani@gmail.com,
rashu.p.singla@gmail.com, mugdha26@gmail.com,
milind_dere@persistent.co.in, parikshitmahalle@yahoo.com

Abstract. Contactless Smartcards are typically used in fields of electronic ticketing, transport and access control. More recently, they have been for electronic payment transactions. This apparent reluctance to the use of contactless smartcards in fields that involve money transactions as well as many other fields and applications is because contactless technology is erroneously believed to be less secure than contact technology. Research has shown that contactless smartcards are not fundamentally less secure than contact cards. However certain security threats are inherently facilitated by contactless smart cards and contactless technology. The various security issues in contactless technology are Eavesdropping, Denial of Service, Covert Transactions, and Man-in-the-Middle.

In this paper, we explore the possibility of using cryptography as a solution to the security issues in contactless technology. We provide the effectiveness of cryptography on these issues, the limitations we have to impose on our applications in order to use cryptography, and further enhancements that are possible to reduce, if not eliminate, the severity of security threats in contactless technology which will further enable use of contactless smart cards in more fields hitherto unexplored.

Keywords: Contactless, smart card, security, cryptography, encryption.

1 Introduction

Smart card-enabled applications are becoming more prevalent in many of today's businesses. The smart card usage predictions are up to 30 billion be the end of 2010.

Smart cards are portable, personal security devices that can securely carry sensitive information, enable secure transactions, validate an individual's identity within a secure system, and verify that an information requestor is authorized to access the information carried on the card. Smart cards not only maintain the integrity of the information stored on the card, but also make it available for secure interactions with the overall system.

N. Meghanathan et al. (Eds.): CNSA 2010, CCIS 89, pp. 558–566, 2010.
© Springer-Verlag Berlin Heidelberg 2010

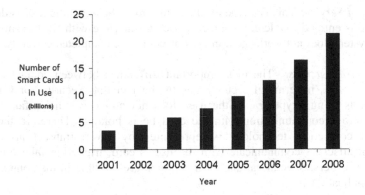

Fig. 1. Worldwide Smart Card usage [9]

There are two main differences between a contact and contactless smart card. First, there are no physical connections between the contactless card and the reader. Second, a contactless card's power to drive the secure IC is generated from energy transferred from the reader by generating an RF field and inducing an electrical current in the IC's antenna coil when it enters the reader's RF field.

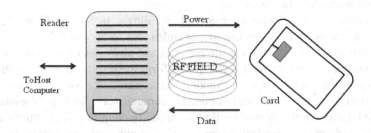

Fig. 2. Contactless smart card in RF Field

A. Security Issues

As indicated before, the main difference between a contact card and a contactless card is the fact that a user of a contactless card does not need to insert his card into the reader, a considerable convenience. However, this feature opens the door to attacks which exploit over-the-air communication channels in an unwanted manner. Various security issues that are inherently supported by contactless smart cards, which render them unsafe as compared to contact cards, are as follows[1]:

1) Eavesdropping: One of the major issues with contactless communication is the existence of easy ways to intercept and alter data being transmitted over the air. In particular, this enables local eavesdropping and provides insight into data being exchanged at a reduced cost. In the passive setting, an observer may learn useful and/or confidential information by triggering a response from the card at a distance, without the user being aware of it. This clearly implies an important privacy risk.

2) Denial of Service: This is a type of attack in which the authentic user is denied the service he is entitled to. Here, the attacker tries to interfere with RF transmissions so that the system does not work and transactions cannot be completed correctly.

3) Covert transactions: The most important difference between contact cards and contactless cards in terms of security lies in the fact that Security for Contactless Smart Cards using Cryptography the user does not notice whether a fake reader is entering into a communication with the card he is holding. Therefore the biggest threat for contactless technology is represented by covert transactions in which fraudulent attackers communicate with the user's card, triggering fake transactions using fake readers. Several variants of this attack are possible in the context of contactless applications.

4) Man-in-the-middle attacks: Man in the middle, in which a fake reader captures data by intercepting transmissions and relays the information to a fake contactless card by an alternative communication channel, such as an ultra high frequency (UHF) link, which then communicates with an alternative genuine reader.

We now explore the possibility of using cryptography as a solution to the above security threats. As a sample encryption method, we have used RSA. Hence the further discussion is based on our observations solely in our practical implementation of the system with RSA encryption.

The remainder of the paper is organised as follows. In Section II, we discuss the model architecture that we propose in our endeavour to accomplish intended results. This section shows the current workflow model and also goes on to show our changes made to current system. In Section III, we put forth the results observed on the current scenario after the application of our model. These results are based on logical reasoning and results we have practically obtained, cumulatively. Section IV evaluates our model and draws out the limitations that it implicitly conjures. These limitations are a necessary guideline for practical implementation of our proposed system. In section V we suggest future additions and enhancements that we believe will provide value-added benefits to make our model more sustainable and viable. These are not mandatory and are intended to only provide a direction of thinking for future work in this area. Section VI summarises the paper followed by references in section VII.

2 Methodology and Architecture

When we write data on a contactless smart card, the data is written into various sectors on the card. This data can be stored in Hexadecimal or ASCII format on the card. Also, for data to be stored, a number of handshaking signals are exchanged between the smart card and the reader/writer hardware. This boosts data integrity and prevents interruption errors. For data to be written onto the card, each sector must be logged in. This adds a level of security in the transaction. This makes smart card usage so convenient which makes the addressing of security issues related to smart cards all the more vital.

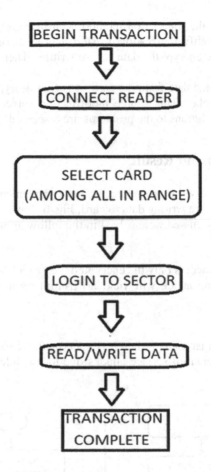

Fig. 3. Traditional method of Contactless transaction in current applications

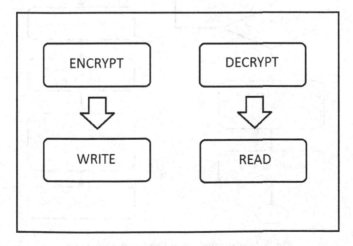

Fig. 4. Modified step of read/write

As seen in figure 3, the transaction method seen in current applications is pretty straightforward. We modify the read/write step a little in our proposal. Instead of writing data directly, we encrypt the data before writing. Then we write the encrypted data on the card.

Also, when we read the data from the card, it is first decrypted and then presented for modification or display. This simple modification solved the problems that we discussed earlier. The solutions to the problems are discussed in the next section.

3 Implementation and Result

Hence the modified card-write procedure we have implemented is shown in fig. 5. Note the steps added before writing data to card. Fig. 6 shows card-read procedure. The problems that we discussed were solved in the following way.

A. Eavesdropping

Attacker will be able to access only the encrypted data which will be of no use to him. Hence the eavesdropping attack will yield no fruitful result for any attacks on the encrypted data.

B. Denial of Service

As modification of data isn't easy when it is encrypted, we can be even more certain of the elimination of denial-of-service attacks due to fraudulent transactions on contactless smartcards.

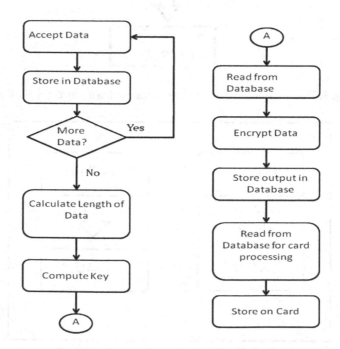

Fig. 5. Implementation of Card-Write Procedure

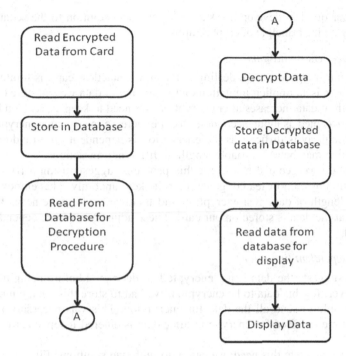

Fig. 6. Implementation of Card-Read Procedure

C. Covert Transactions

The attacker cannot enter into covert transactions with the card because encrypted data nullifies the possibility of modifying data on the card.

D. Man-in-the-Middle attacks

Cryptography also nullifies the effects of Man-in-the-Middle attacks as the encrypted data can be decrypted by the assigned user only.

It is interesting to note that these solutions are all the advantages of encryption and do not depend on the medium on which data is stored, in our case, the contactless card. This strengthens our hypothesis that the security issues are implicit properties of over-the-air communication, and not contactless smart cards, per se.

4 Evaluation and Limitations

As we have seen, cryptography provides a feasible solution to the security threats that we have discussed earlier. However, whether it provides a practical solution is a question, yet unanswered.

Further investigation reveals that even though it seems relatively straightforward, applying encryption on data isn't as bare-faced as it seems. Several limitations must be imposed on the system in order to reach a practical solution. In this section, we discuss the various hurdles faced when we intend to apply encryption as a solution to the problems discussed earlier. In the process, we proffer various limitations we impose on our system in our quest to develop a sustainable, practical solution to the security issues, based solely on the principle of cryptography.

A. Size dependent limitations

As the amount of space we are dealing with, in a contactless card, is limited (starting from 1K), there is an implicit limitation on the amount of data we can store on the card. As the length of data increases after encryption, we need to keep a check on how much data can be accepted as input, accounting for the increase in size after encryption.

This particularly is difficult as the encryption is dependent on a randomly generated key which may be of a variable length in different transactions.

The solution we decided to use for this problem suggests using a fixed-formula-key-generation method instead of generating the key randomly. That empowered us to predict the length of data post-encryption and then we could make necessary adjustments so that the data is stored on our card. These adjustments were dependent on the size of card.

B. Model dependent limitations

Our model suggests the data being encrypted or decrypted before being used in any way. However, for this data to be encrypted, we had to store this data, temporarily, in order to be able to send all the data for encryption. This was necessary in order to reduce the time required for encryption after data is entered independently, one field at a time.

In order to facilitate this need, we came up with two solutions: Files and Database. We continued our work maintaining a database table which is created and truncated at each transaction.

To evaluate our model, we consider times required for enciphering data in RSA. From the graph shown in Figure 6, we can conclude that faster algorithms will give better performance. However, the linear nature of the graph tells us that RSA provides a very stable solution, in terms of predicting time required, explaining its much celebrated nature as compared to other algorithms.

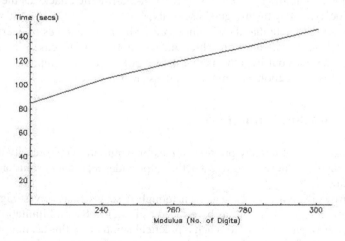

Fig. 7. Enciphering times of RSA for 1769 characters varying with size of Modulus [10]

Hence, we deduce that cryptography does indeed provide a practical solution to security issues related to contactless smart cards. We also provide the above limitations which need to be imposed on our application at the developmental stage in order to harness the feasibility of using an cryptography-based security solution.

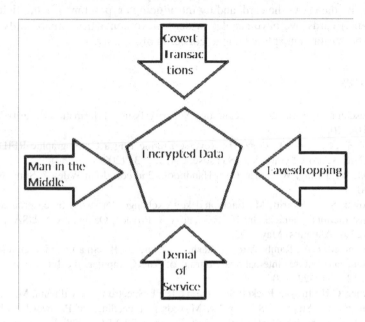

Fig. 8. Types of attacks prevented by Cryptography

5 Future Enhancements

Enhancements to this system can improve the quality of the result we see first up. Although the proposed system provides adequate security for most day-to-day applications, our hunger for the highest level of security is insatiable. Hence, we suggest the following enhancements to further improve security.

1) Mutual Authentication: The most basic and yet most significant addition to our system is mutual authentication. Here, when a reader attempts to access a card, the card must respond by authenticating it. This step directly addresses eavesdropping and covert transactions.

2) Biometrics: Adding biometric security measures to the system proves to be costlier than desired but provides a noteworthy level of security.

3) Biometric cryptography: This direct coupling of biometrics with the advantages of cryptography can multiply the security levels. This kind of innovation really provides a substantial roadblock to attackers.

6 Conclusion

Hence, we have proved that a sustainable system of security for contactless smart cards is possible through the use of cryptography. By establishing the change in the way we write data onto the card, and by introducing cryptography in the field of contactless smart cards, we have enabled wider use of contactless smart cards in fields that were heretofore unexplored due to concerns of security.

References

[1] Handschuh, H.: Contactless technology Security Issues. Information Security bulletin 9, 95–100 (2004)
[2] Nohl, S.K., Evans, D., Plötz, H.: Reverse-Engineering a Cryptographic RFID Tag. In: USENIX Security Symposium, San Jose, CA, July 31 (2008)
[3] Rankl, W., Effing, W.: Smart Card Handbook, 2nd edn. John Wiley & Sons, New York (2000)
[4] Bellovin, S.M., Merritt, M.: Encrypted key exchange: Password based protocols secure against dictionary attacks. In: IEEE Security & Privacy, Oakland, CA, USA, pp. 72–84. IEEE, Los Alamitos (May 1992)
[5] Mohammed, L.A., Ramli, A.R., Prakash, V., Daud, M.B.: Smart Card Technology: Past, Present, and Future. International Journal of The Computer, the Internet and Management 12(1), 12–22 (2004)
[6] Fancher, C.H.: In your Pocket: Smartcards, IEEE Spectrum. In: Ullmann, M., Kugler, D., Neumann, H., Stappert, S., Vogeler, M. (eds.) Proceedings of Password Authenticated Key Agreement for Contactless Smart Cards, RFIDSEC 2008, February, pp. 47–53 (1997/2008)
[7] Guillou, L.C., et al.: The smart Card: A Standardized Security Device Dedicated to Public cryptology. In: Simmons, G.J. (ed.) Contemporary Crypto-logy. The Science of Information Integrity, pp. 561–613. IEEE Press, Los Alamitos (1992)
[8] Hao, F., Anderson, R., Daugman, J.: Combining cryptography with biometrics effectively, Technical Report No.640, University of Cambridge, ISSN 1476-2986
[9] http://www.biosensorhawaii.com/possible.html
[10] http://cryptome.org/flannery-cp.htm

A Novel Approach for Compressed Video Steganography

A.P. Sherly, Sapna Sasidharan, Ashji S. Raj, and P.P. Amritha

TIFAC CORE in Cyber Security, Amrita Vishwa Vidyapeetham, Coimbatore, India
{sherlyram,sapnapv,ashjisraj,ammuviju}@gmail.com

Abstract. Steganography is the art of hiding information in ways that avert the revealing of hiding messages. This paper proposes a new Compressed Video Steganographic scheme. In this algorithm, data hiding operations are executed entirely in the compressed domain. Here data are embedded in the macro blocks of I frame with maximum scene change. To enlarge the capacity of the hidden secret information and to provide an imperceptible stego-image for human vision, a novel steganographic approach called tri-way pixel-value differencing (TPVD) is used for embedding. In this scheme all the processes are defined and executed in the compressed domain. Though decompression is not required. Experimental results demonstrate that the proposed algorithm has high imperceptibility and capacity.

Keywords: Video Steganography, MPEG-4, Tri-way PVD.

1 Introduction

The quick intensification of the Internet and communication systems in the past decade has enabled users to send digital data over network suitably. However, transmission of data in an open network is not secure, and data can be easily tampered by illegal users. Consequently, shielding data during transmission is an important task. Although cryptographic techniques can be used for this purpose, they are not secure enough because encryption can provide secure delivery of digital content, but when the content is decrypted, encryption no longer provides any security. To solve this problem, data hiding techniques were proposed and have been considered widely in various fields like covert communication, copyright protection, and broadcast monitoring and military communication.Steganography is the art of hiding information in such a way that no one can realize a hidden message in the data except the sender and the intended recipient. Steganography is also known as 'covered writing' which includes methods of transmitting secret messages through inoffensive cover mediums in such a manner that the survival of the embedded messages is undetectable. It can also be viewed as a tradeoff between detectability, robustness, and bit rate. Detectability is the apprehension of clandestine transmission and is often used in combination with encryption. It is robust to all types of processing such as transformations, filtering, truncation, and scaling. Finally, bit rate or the maximum amount of data that can be transmitted. This article considers data embedding in videos. A video can be viewed as a sequence of still images and data embedding in images seems very similar to videos. However, there are many differences between data hiding in images and videos, where the first important difference is the

N. Meghanathan et al. (Eds.): CNSA 2010, CCIS 89, pp. 567–575, 2010.

size of the host media. Since videos contain more sample number of pixels or the number of transform domain coefficients, a video has higher capacity than a still image and more data can be embedded in the video. Also, there are some characteristics in videos which cannot be found in images as perceptual redundancy in videos is due to their temporal features. Here data hiding operations are executed entirely in the compressed domain.[1][2] On the other hand, as a really higher amount of data must be embedded in the case of video sequences, there is a more demanding constraint on real-time effectiveness of the system. Furthermore, with the development of multimedia and stream media on the Internet, transmitting video on the Internet will not incur suspicion. Image-based and video-based Steganographic techniques are mainly classified into spatial domain and frequency domain based methods. The former embedding techniques are LSB, matrix, PVD embedding [5] etc. Two important parameters for evaluating the performance of a Steganographic system are capacity and imperceptibility. Capacity refers to the amount of data that can be hidden in the cover medium so that no perceptible distortion is introduced. Imperceptibility or transparency represents the invisibility of the hidden data in the cover media without degrading the perceptual quality by data embedding. Security is the other parameter in the steganographic systems, which refers to an unauthorized person's inability to detect hidden data.

In this paper, we propose a secure compressed video Steganographic architecture taking account of video statistical invisibility.This paper is organized as follows: Section 2 describes the framework of our video Steganographic system. In Section 3, the embedding and extraction mechanism is described in detail. We give the experimental results in Section 4. A conclusion is drawn finally in section 5.

2 Architecture

As shown in the Fig. 1, the architecture consists of four functions: I frame extraction, the scene change detector and the data embedder. The first section explains the extraction of I frames from MPEG video. In the second module, scene change detector analyzes the frames with maximum scene change. I frames in MPEG standard is coded in intra frame manner, we can obtain the DC picture with abstracting the DC coefficients from the DCT coefficient codes. Eq.1 describes the compare method between two conjoint I frames.

$$HD(I_i, I_{i+1}) = \sum_{k=1}^{N} (Hi(k) - Hi + 1(k))^2 / (Hi(k) + Hi + 1(k))^2 \tag{1}$$

where I_i , I_{i+1} means the ith and $i+1^{th}$ I frames, H_i and H_{i+1} are histograms of DC pictures from the ith and $i+1^{th}$ I frames.HD (I_i, I_{i+1}) is the peak value the two I frames are from different scenes, therefore the scene change point is found. Also the variances var (i) U of each DC picture from I frame will be calculated. With the third module, data embedder, secret message is hidden into the compressed video sequence without bringing perceptive distortion. To increase the capacity of the hidden secret information and to provide an imperceptible stego-image for human vision, here tri-way pixel-value differencing (TPVD) is used for embedding. To upgrade the hiding capacity of original PVD method referring to only one direction, here three different directional edges are considered and effectively adopted to design the scheme of tri-way pixel-value differencing. With these three sections, we can obtain the final stego-video.

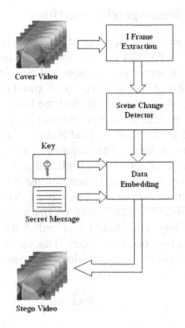

Fig. 1. Block diagram of the proposed System

3 Embedding and Extraction Mechanism

3.1 Embedding Position Selection

Compressed video sequence achieves compression through the elimination of temporal, spatial and statistical redundancies with the use of motion compensation, block quantization inside a discrete cosine transform (DCT), and Huffman run-level encoding. While selection of the embedding block calculate the maximum scene change of each block of the conjoint I frames. Select the block with which maximum scene change occurs by using threshold value. Selection of proper color channel is another issue in Video Steganography. The frames of video sequence is split into Y,Cb,Cr channels in the MPEG coding stage. According to different color resampling rules, it is possible for the ratio Y:Cb:Cr to be set to 4:2:2 or 4:2:0. Under these the only unchanged channel is the Y channel. So here Y channel is preferred as the host channel. In addition to the above selections, choosing inappropriate frame type among I-frame, P-frame or B-frame for hiding message is also a crucial issue. Usually, a conventional video consists of a number of GOPs. Each GOP is composed of one I-frame and several B-frames and P-frames. A typical I-frame adopts intra coding, which means it does not refer to any other frames. Different from an I-frame, a P-frame only refers to its nearest preceding I- or P-frame. As for a B-frame, it refers to the nearest preceding and succeeding I-frame or P-frame. In a conventional MPEG format, the content of a B- or P-frame is the so-called residual error between the current frame and the frame to which it refers. Therefore, only an I-frame can hold complete information. In this paper, we choose I-frames of an MPEG video sequence to embed the secret information.

3.2 Compressed Video Steganographic Algorithm

Here a novel steganographic approach called tri-way pixel-value differencing with pseudo-random dithering (TPVDD) is used for embedding.[3][4] TPVDD enlarges the capacity of the hidden secret information and provide an imperceptible stego-image for human vision with enhanced security. A small difference value of consecutive pixels can be located on a smooth area and the large one is located on an edged area. According to the properties of human vision, eyes can tolerate more changes in sharp-edge blocks than in smooth blocks. That is, more data can be embedded into the edge areas than into smooth areas. This capability is made used in this approach which leads to good imperceptibility with a high embedding rate. The Tri-way Differencing Scheme is explained as follows. In general, the edges in an image are roughly classified into vertical, horizontal, and two kinds of diagonal directions. Motivated from the PVD method, using two-pixel pairs on one directional edge can work efficiently for information hiding. This should accomplish more efficiency while considering four directions from four two-pixel pairs. This can be implemented by dividing the image into 2×2 blocks and one example block is shown in Figure 2

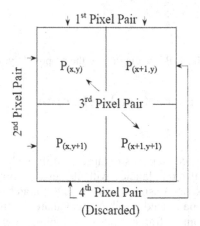

Fig. 2. An Example of four pixel pair

However, since the changing of pixel values for the fourth pixel pair affects the first and the second pairs, the fourth pair is useless and has to be discarded. Therefore, we propose that three pairs are used to embed the secret data. Before introducing the proposed algorithm, the pre-procedure is to partition the cover image into non overlapping 2×2 blocks with 4 pixels. In this scheme, each 2×2 block includes four pixels of $p(x, y)$, $p(x+1, y)$, $p(x, y+1)$, and $p(x+1, y+1)$ where x and y are the pixel location in the image. Let $p(x, y)$ be the starting point, then three pixel pairs can be found by grouping $p(x, y)$ with the right, the lower, and the lower right neighboring pixels. Those three pairs are named by P_0, P_1 and P_2 where $P_0= (p(x, y), p(x+1, y))$, $P_1= (p(x, y), p(x, y+1))$ and $P_2 = (p(x, y), p(x+1,y+1))$ respectively. When using the tri-way PVD method to embed the secret data, each pair has its modified P'_i and a new difference value d'_i for $i = 0, 1, 2$. Now, the new pixel values in each pair are different from their original ones. That is, we have three different values for the starting point $p(x, y)$ named $p'_0(x, y)$, $p'_1(x, y)$ and $p'_2(x, y)$ from P_0, P_1, and P_2 respectively. However, only one value for $p'_i(x, y)$ can exist after finishing the embedding procedures. Therefore, one of $p'_i(x, y)$ is selected as the reference point to offset the other two pixel values. That is, two pixel values of one pair are used to adjust the other two pairs and construct a new 2×2 block. Selecting different reference points results in varied distortion to the stego-image. Here, we propose an optimal selection approach to achieve minimum Mean-Square-Error (MSE). Suppose that $m_i = d'_i - d_i$, d_i and d'_i are the difference values of pixel pair i before and after embedding procedures. The rules that can exactly determine one optimal reference pair without really estimating MSE are introduced as follows.

1) If all values of m_i are great than 1 or smaller than −1, the optimal pixel pair $i_{optimal}$ is the pair with the greatest $|m|$.
2) If all m_i have the same sign and only one $m_i \in \{0,1,-1\}$, then the optimal pixel pair $i_{optimal}$ is selected from the other two pairs with the smallest $|m|$.
3) If only one m_i has a different sign from the other two pairs, the optimal pixel pair $i_{optimal}$ is selected from the other two pairs with the smallest $|m|$.
4) If only one $m_i \in \{0, 1, -1\}$ and the other two m_i has different signs, the optimal pixel pair $i_{optimal}$ is the pair with $m_i \in \{0, 1, -1\}$.
5) If there exists more than one pair with $m_i \in \{0, 1, 1\}$, the optimal pixel pair $i_{optimal}$ can be selected as any one pair with $m_i \in \{0, 1, 1\}$.

By following those selection rules described above, we can skip the calculation steps of MSE estimation to obtain the optimal reference pairs. Thus, the total computational complexity can be greatly reduced.

3.3 Adaptive Rules to Reduce Distortion

Although the proposed approach is feasible for embedding secret data, embedding large amount of bits can still cause serious image distortion easily. Since most distortion is generated from the offsetting process, the following two conditions are further designed to avoid too much offset described by

1) embed _ bit($P0$)≥5 and 1 embed _ bit($P1$)≥4
2) embed _ bit($P0$)<5 and 2 embed _ bit($P0$)≥6

Where embed_bit(Pi) represents the total embedding bits along the direction of Pi. If either one of above two conditions is satisfied, the current block being processed can probably result in higher distortion. Then we use two pixel pairs, $P0$ and $P3 = P(x,y+1)$, $P(x+1,y+1)$ and adopt the original PVD method to individually process those two pairs along one direction. If neither of the conditions is satisfied then PVD is applied to three pixel pairs $P0$, $P1$ and $P2$ in three directions. Here, we name those two conditions as "branch conditions".

3.4 Pseudo-random Dithering

This section describes how pseudo-random dithering is applied the range of pixel differences and further modification for embedding and extraction of secret message.

Step 1: pseudo-randomly select a parameter $\beta \in [0, 1]$, generated from an embedding key, for each block of two consecutive pixels, and calculate

$$l`k = lk + floor(\beta.wk) \tag{2}$$
$$u`k = lk+1 -1 \tag{3}$$

where k is a range index. Thus, instead of the fixed ranges as used in the original PVD method, the new ranges are defined by the varied $l`k$ and $u`k$. In other words, the ranges corresponding to different blocks are differently defined according to a secret key. Because $wk \leq wk+1\ u0$

$$u`k - l`k = lk+1+floor(\beta.wk+1)-1-lk-floor(\beta.wk) \geq wk-1 \tag{4}$$

Eqn. (4) indicates that the width of any varied range is no less than that of the original fixed range. If $l`k \leq |d| \leq u`k$, a total of $log2(wk)$ secret bits are embedded into the corresponding block. Convert the secret bits into a decimal value b, and calculate

$$d' = \begin{cases} |e-d| \text{ for } d{\geq}0 \text{ and mod } (e, wk) = d \\ -|e-d| \text{ for } d<0 \text{ and mod } (e, wk) =-d \end{cases}$$

Where $l`k \leq e \leq u`k$
On the extraction side, b can be restored simply by

$$b=mod(d',wk) \tag{5}$$

Note that if b values in all the blocks are 0, the proposed approach degenerates to the original PVD method and the steps in pixel difference histogram will reveal the presence of hidden data. Nonetheless occurrence of such a case is highly unlikely.

3.5 The Embedding Algorithm

The details of data hiding steps are described as follows.
1)Calculate four difference values $di,(x,y)$ for four pixel pairs in each block given by

$$d_{0, (x,y)} = P_{(x+1,y)}-P_{(x,y)}$$
$$d_{1,(x,y)} = P_{(x,y+1)}-P_{(x,y)}$$
$$d_{2,(x,y)} = P_{(x+1,y+1)}-P_{(x,y)}$$
$$d_{3,(x,y)} = P_{(x+1,y+1)}-P_{(x,y+1)}$$

2) Using $|d_{i,(x,y)}|$ ($i=0,1,2,3$) to locate a suitable $R_{k,i}$ in the range table designed ,that is to compute $j = min$ ($u_k -|d_{i,(x,y)}|$) where $u_k{\geq}d_i$ for all $1{\leq}k{\leq}n$. Then $R_{k,i}$ is the located range.
3) Compute the amount of secret data bits t_i that can be embedded in each pair by $R_{j,i}$. The value t_i can be estimated from the width $w_{j,i}$ of $R_{j,i}$, this can be defined by $t_i=log_2 w_{j,i}$.

4) If t_i of P_i (i=0,1,2,3) satisfies branch conditions, two pixel pairs P_0 and P_3 are processed using original PVD. But new difference d'_i is to calculate. Otherwise, the proposed tri-way scheme is used to process P_i.

5) Read t_i bits from the binary secret data and transform the bit sequence into a decimal value b_i.

6) Calculate the new difference value $d'_{i,(x,y)}$

7) Modify the values of p_n and p_{n+1} by the following formula:

$$(p'_n, p'_{n+1}) = (p_n - \text{ceil}(m), p_{n+1} + \text{floor}(m)) \tag{6}$$

Where (p_n, p_{n+1}) represent two pixels in P_i and $m = (d'_i - d_i)/2$

8) Using the selection rules to choose the optimal reference point $p'_{i(x,y)}$ with minimum MSE, then this selected point is used to offset the other two pixel pairs.

9) Now, the new block constructed from all pixel pairs and embedded with secret data is generated.

3.6 The Extraction Algorithm

To retrieve the embedded secret data from the stego-image, the extraction algorithm is described in the following steps.

1) Partition the stego-image into 2x2 pixel blocks, and the partition order is the same as that in the embedding stage.

2) Calculate four difference values $d^*_{i,(x,y)}$ for four pixel pairs in each block given by

$$d^*_{0,(x,y)} = P_{(x+1,y)} - P_{(x,y)}$$
$$d^*_{1,(x,y)} = P_{(x,y+1)} - P_{(x,y)}$$
$$d^*_{2,(x,y)} = P_{(x+1,y+1)} - P_{(x,y)}$$
$$d^*_{3,(x,y)} = P_{(x+1,y+1)} - P_{(x,y+1)}$$

3) Using $|d^*_{i,(x,y)}|$ (i=0,1,2,3) locate a suitable $R_{k,i}$. Also find the number of bits t_i that was embedded. If t_i satisfies the branch conditions, two independent pixel pairs are selected.Otherwise, three pixel pairs are used for further processing.

4) The secret message b^* is to calculate for stegoimage is not altered b^* is same as b. Finally b^* is converted to binary to obtain the original secret message.

4 Experimental Result

To demonstrate the accomplished performance of our proposed approach in capacity and security for hiding secret data in the stego-image, we have also conducted different experiments using different videos.According to the invisibility benchmark for the watermarked images , a minimum peak signal-to noise ratio (PSNR) value of 38 dB is adopted as the quality requirement for the stego-images

4.1 Capacity and PSNR

The secret binary data sequence S is generated by pseudo-random numbers. We set the designed range table with the width in the set of $wk \in \{8, 8, 16, 32, 64, 128\}$. Here, PSNR value is utilized to evaluate the invisibility of the stego-images. Table 1 lists the experimental results after the secret data is embedded using those two approaches. The hiding capacity (in bytes) and PSNR values achieved by the proposed scheme for I frames are shown. The listed values are the average results after embedding 100 randomly generated bit sequences into the cover frames. Two stego-frames are still hardly observed that the secret data is hidden inside. This is because of the high variance existed in the pixel values of the I frame. Therefore, this demonstrates that the proposed approach provides a promising performance in increasing the capacity of the stego-images and maintaining the imperceptible quality simultaneously. This table explains the capacity and the PSNR value after embedding.

Table 1. PSNR and Capacity of stego I frames

I Frames	Capacity	PSNR(db)
I_1	70232	40.24
I_9	70102	39.12
I_{16}	69993	42.65

Fig. 3. I frame before embedding

Fig. 4. I frame after embedding

5 Conclusion

A new Video Steganographic Scheme was proposed in this paper, operating directly in compressed domain. For data hiding tri-way pixel-value differencing (TPVD) algorithm has been used. This algorithm provides high capacity and imperceptible stego-image for human vision of the hidden secret information. Here I frame with maximum scene change blocks were used for embedding. The performance of the steganographic algorithm is studied and experimental results shows that this scheme can be applied on compressed videos with no noticeable degradation in visual quality.

References

[1] Hartung., F., Girod, B.: Watermarking of uncompressed and compressed video. Signal Processing, Special Issue on Copyright Protection and Access Control for Multimedia Services 66(3), 283–301 (1998)

[2] Liu., B., Liu., F., Yang, C., Sun, Y.: Secure Steganography in Compressed Video Bitstreams. In: The Third International Conference on Availability, Reliability and Security (2008)

[3] Chang, K.-C., Chang, C.-P., Huang, P.S., Tu, T.-M.: A Novel Image Steganographic Method Using Tri-way Pixel-Value Differencing. Journal of Multimedia 3(2) (June 2008)

[4] Lee., Y.K., Chen, L.H.: High capacity image steganographic model. IEE Proceedings on Vision, Image and Signal Processing 147(3), 288–294 (2000)

[5] Wu, D.-C., Tsai, W.-H.: A steganographic method for images by pixel-value differencing. Pattern Recognition Letters 24, 1613–1626 (2003)

[6] Dai, Y.J., Zhang, L.H., Yang, Y.X.: A New Method of MPEG VideoWatermarking Technology. In: International Conference on Communication Technology Proceedings, ICCT (2003)

[7] Langelaar, G.C., Lagendijk, R.L.: Optimal Differential Energy Watermarking of DCT Encoded Images and Video. IEEE Trans. on Image Processing 10(1), 148–158 (2001)

Privacy Preserving Data Mining by Cyptography

Anand Sharma[1] and Vibha Ojha[2]

[1] CSE Deptt., FET, MITS, Lakshmangarh, Sikar
[2] CSE Deptt., IITM, Gwalior
anand_glee@yahoo.co.in, vibha.ojha@gmail.com

Abstract. It is obvious that if a data mining algorithm is run against the union of the databases, and its output becomes known to one or more of the parties, it reveals something about the contents of the other databases. Research in secure distributed computation, which was done as part of a larger body of research in the theory of cryptography, has achieved remarkable results. These results were shown using generic constructions that can be applied to any function that has an efficient representation as a circuit. We describe these results, discuss their efficiency, and demonstrate their relevance to privacy preserving computation of data mining algorithms. Note that we consider here a distributed computing scenario, rather than a scenario where all data is gathered in a central server, which then runs the algorithm against all data. (The central server scenario introduces interesting privacy issues, too, but they are outside the scope of this paper.)

Keywords: Privacy preserving, Oblivious transfer, Cryptography.

1 Introduction

Consider a scenario in which two or more parties owning confidential databases wish to run a data mining algorithm on the union of their databases without revealing any unnecessary information. For example, consider separate medical institutions that wish to conduct a joint research while preserving the privacy of their patients. In this scenario it is required to protect privileged information, but it is also required to enable its use for research or for other purposes. In particular, although the parties realize that combining their data has some mutual benefit, none of them is willing to reveal its database to any other party.

The common definition of privacy in the cryptographic community limits the information that is leaked by the distributed computation to be the information that can be learned from the designated output of the computation. Although there are several variants of the definition of privacy, for the purpose of this discussion we use the definition that compares the result of the actual computation to that of an "ideal" computation: Consider first a party that is involved in the actual computation of a function (e.g. a data mining algorithm). Consider also an "ideal scenario", where in addition to the original parties there is also a "trusted party" who does not deviate from the behavior that we prescribe for him, and does not attempt to cheat. In the ideal scenario all parties send their inputs to the trusted party, who then computes the

N. Meghanathan et al. (Eds.): CNSA 2010, CCIS 89, pp. 576–582, 2010.
© Springer-Verlag Berlin Heidelberg 2010

function and sends the appropriate results to the other parties. Loosely speaking, a protocol is secure if anything that an adversary can learn in the actual world it can also learn in the ideal world, namely from its own input and from the output it receives from the trusted party. In essence, this means that the protocol that is run in order to compute the function does not leak any "unnecessary" information. (Of course, there are partial leaks of information that are harmless. It is hard, however, to decide which type of leakage can be tolerated. The cryptographic community therefore aims at designing protocols that do not reveal any information except for their designated output, and in many case such protocols can in fact be efficiently constructed.)

2 Privacy Preserving

Privacy preserving protocols are designed in order to preserve privacy even in the presence of adversarial participants that attempt to gather information about the inputs of their peers. There are, however, different levels of adversarial behavior. Cryptographic research typically considers two types of adversaries: A semi-honest adversary (also known as a passive, or honest but curious adversary) is a party that correctly follows the protocol specification, yet attempts to learn additional information by analyzing the messages received during the protocol execution. On the other hand, a malicious adversary may arbitrarily deviate from the protocol specification. (For example, consider a step in the protocol where one of the parties is required to choose a random number and broadcast it. If the party is semi-honest then we can assume that this number is indeed random. On the other hand, if the party is malicious, then he might choose the number in a sophisticated way that enables him to gain additional information.) It is of course easier to design a solution that is secure against semi-honest adversaries, than it is to design a solution for malicious adversaries.

A common approach is therefore to first design a secure protocol for the semi-honest case, and then transform it into a protocol that is secure against malicious adversaries. This transformation can be done by requiring each party to use zero-knowledge proofs to prove that each step that it is taking follows the specification of the protocol. More efficient transformations are often required, since this generic approach might be rather inefficient and add considerable overhead to each step of the protocol. We remark that the semi-honest adversarial model is often a realistic one. This is because deviating from a specified program which may be buried in a complex application is a non-trivial task, and because a semi-honest adversarial behavior can model a scenario in which the parties that participate in the protocol are honest, but following the protocol execution an adversary may obtain a transcript of the protocol execution by breaking into a machine used by one of the participants.

3 Cryptography: Oblivious Transfer

We describe here results of a body of cryptographic research that shows how separate parties can jointly compute any function of their inputs, without revealing any other information. As we argued above, these results achieve maximal privacy that hides all information except for the designated output of the function. This body of research attempts to model the world in a way which is both realistic and general. While there are some aspects of the "real world" that are not modeled by this research, the privacy guarantees and the generality of the results are quite remarkable.

Oblivious transfer is a basic protocol that is the main building block of secure computation. It might seem strange at first, but its role in secure computation should become clear later. (In fact, it was shown by Kilian [11] that oblivious transfer is sufficient for secure computation in the sense that given an implementation of oblivious transfer, and no other cryptographic primitive, one could construct any secure computation protocol.)

Oblivious transfer is often the most computationally intensive operation of secure protocols, and is repeated many times. Each invocation of oblivious transfer typically requires a constant number of invocations of trapdoor permutations (i.e. public-key operations, or exponentiations). It is possible to reduce the amortized overhead of oblivious transfer to one exponentiations per a logarithmic number of oblivious transfers, even for the case of malicious adversaries [15].

The problem of "oblivious polynomial evaluation" (OPE) involves a sender and a receiver. The sender's input is a polynomial Q of degree k over some finite field f and the receiver's input is an element $z \in f$ (the degree k of Q is public). The protocol is such that the receiver obtains $Q(z)$ without learning anything else about the polynomial Q, and the sender learns nothing. That is, the problem considered is the private computation of the function $(Q, z) \rightarrow (\lambda, Q(z))$. This problem was introduced in [14], where an efficient solution was also presented. The overhead of that protocol is $O(k)$ exponentiations (using methods suggested in [15]). (Note that this protocol maintains privacy in the face of a malicious adversary. In the semi-honest case a simpler OPE protocol can be designed based on any homomorphic encryption scheme, with an overhead of $O(k)$ computation and $O(k|f|)$ communication.)

The main motivation for using OPE is to utilize the fact that the output of a k degree polynomial is $(k + 1)$-wise independent. Another motivation is that polynomials can be used for approximating functions that are defined over the Real numbers.

4 Two Party Case

Yao's two-party protocol is pretty efficient, as long as the size of the inputs, and the size of the circuit computing the function, are reasonable. In fact, for many functions the efficiency of Yao's generic protocol is comparable to that of protocols that are targeted for computing the specific function. We describe here a distributed scenario of computing the ID3 algorithm, where Yao's protocol is obviously too costly. On the other hand, a specialized protocol can be designed for computing this algorithm, which uses Yao's protocol as a primitive.

We are interested in a scenario involving two parties, each one of them holding a database of different transactions, where all the transactions have the same set of attributes (this scenario is also denoted as a "horizontally partitioned" database). The parties wish to compute a decision tree by applying the ID3 algorithm to the union of their databases. An efficient privacy preserving protocol for this problem was described in [12].

A naive approach for implementing a privacy preserving solution is to apply the generic Yao protocol to the ID3 algorithm. This approach encounters two major obstacles. First, the size of the databases is typically very large. As each transaction can have many attributes, and there might be millions of transactions, the encoding of each party's input might require hundreds of millions of bits. This means that the computational overhead of running an oblivious transfer per input bit might be very high.

Most cryptographic protocols, however, compute functions over finite fields. Even if the circuit computes an approximation to the logarithm, this computation involves evaluating polynomials and therefore requires computing multiplications and exponentiations. An additional problem is that running ID3 involves many rounds. The part of the circuit computing the ith round depends on the results of the previous $i-1$ rounds. A naïve implementation could require an encoding of many copies of this step, each one of them corresponding to a specific result of the previous rounds.

A key observation is that each node of the tree can be computed separately, with the output made public, before continuing to the next node. In general, private protocols have the property that intermediate values remain hidden. However, in the case of ID3 some of these intermediate values (specifically, the assignments of attributes to nodes) are actually part of the output and may therefore be revealed. Once the attribute of a given node has been found, both parties can separately partition their remaining transactions accordingly for the coming recursive calls. This means that private distributed ID3 can be reduced to privately finding the attribute with the highest information gain. (This is a slightly simplified argument as the other steps of ID3 must also be carefully dealt with. However, the main issues arise within this step.)

5 Two Multi Party Case

The multi-party case involves three or more parties that wish to compute some function of their inputs without leaking any unnecessary information. As we have described above, there are generic constructions for this task [10; 3; 4]. Compared to the two-party case, however, it is harder to apply the generic constructions to actual scenarios. To illustrate this point we consider the case of running a secure computation for computing the result of an auction, where there is an obvious motivation for privacy and security, and also certain restrictions on the operation of the parties. The auction application, discussed in [16], is not related to data mining, but it does exemplify some of the difficulties of the multiparty case. The discussion below applies for any function that can be computed by a circuit of reasonable size.

The auction scenario is that of a "sealed bid" auction, and consists of an auctioneer and many bidders. Each bidder submits a single secret bid (i.e. the bid is sealed in an envelope). There is a known decision rule, whose inputs are the submitted bids, and whose output is the identity of the winning bidder and the amount that this bidder has to pay. For example, in an "English auction" the winning bidder is the bidder who offered the highest bid, and he has to pay the amount of his bid. In the second-price, or Vickrey, type of auction (which has some nice properties that are outside the scope of this paper) the winner is the highest bidder and he has to pay the amount of the second highest bid. Bidding is allowed until some point in time, and at that stage the decision rule is applied to the submitted bids. In the physical world bids are submitted in sealed envelopes that are kept secure until the end of the bidding period, and are then opened by the auctioneer. In the virtual world we would like to keep the bids secret during the bidding period, but we could also attempt to hide all information afterwards, except for the identity of the winning party and the amount he has to pay. For example, in the case of a Vickrey auction the auctioneer's output could be limited to the identity of the highest bidder (but not the value of his bid), and the value of the second highest bid (but not the identity of the second highest bidder). This is more privacy than can be achieved in the physical world. (In fact, some of the suggested explanations for the unpopularity of second price auctions are based on possible attacks that a malicious auctioneer can mount if he learns the bid value of the highest bidder. This phenomenon is inevitable in the real world, but can be avoided if a privacy preserving protocol is used to compute the result of the auction.)

Privacy preserving multi-party computation can be reduced to the two-party case. Namely, it is possible to use the generic two-party protocol to compute a function in the multi-party scenario. Such a reduction is described in [16]. Before describing the highlights of the reduction we first describe the advantages of this approach.

• Trust:
In order to use the two-party construction it is assumed that there are two special parties, and privacy is preserved as long as these two parties do not collude. Namely, a collusion of any number of parties (even a majority of the parties) that does not include both special parties does not affect the privacy and security of the protocol. Protocols with this security assurance might seem weaker than protocols that are secure against collusions of say, any coalition of less than one half of the parties. After all, there is a coalition of just two parties – the two special parties, is able to break the security of the system. Consider however a scenario where most of the parties are users (e.g. bidders) that have not established trust relationships between themselves, and there are one or more central parties that are more established. For example, in the auction scenario we can assume that the two special parties are the auctioneer and another party which we denote as the "issuer", and which can be, for example, an accounting firm. We know that an adversary can register many fake bidders in order to control a majority of the participating parties. It seems harder, though, for the adversary to be able to control insiders of both special parties, i.e. in the auctioneer's organization and in the accounting firm.

• Communication:
We can design the reduction such that each of the "simple" participating parties should only communicate with one of the special parties (e.g. the auctioneer), and should only send a single message to this party. This property greatly simplifies the required communication infrastructure, and enables to run the protocol without requiring all parties to be online at the same time (in fact, compared to a protocol that provides no security at all, the only new communication channel that is introduced by the secure protocol is the channel between the two special parties). When all the "simple"

parties finish sending their messages, the two special parties run a short protocol to complete the computation of the function.

• **Efficiency:**
The protocol evaluates a circuit representation of the function. The overhead per gate and per input bit is as in the two-party construction, and is lower than in the multi-party constructions.

The protocol is run with the two special parties taking the roles of the two parties in the two-party case. The issuer prepares a circuit for computing the function. This circuit might have many inputs of different parties – for example, the inputs might be the bids of the different bidders. The issuer encodes the circuit as in the two-party case, by choosing garbled values for the wires and preparing tables for every gate. The other special party (the auctioneer) is responsible for computing the result of the circuit. In order to do that it should receive the tables that were prepared by the issuer, and one garbled value for every input wire, namely the value that corresponds to the input bit associated with that wire. Once it receives the garbled values of all input wires it can compute the output of the circuit.

Given the proxy oblivious transfer protocol, the rest of the implementation is simple. Each bidder engages in a proxy oblivious transfer for each of its input bits. The input of the bidder to this protocol is the value of the input bit. The sender is the issuer, and its two inputs are the two garbled values that are associated with the corresponding input wire. The receiver is the auctioneer, and it learns the garbled value that corresponds to the input bit. This protocol consists of a single message that is sent from the bidder to the auctioneer, and then a round of communication between the auctioneer and the issuer. The auctioneer can actually wait until it receives messages from all the bidders before it runs the round of communication with the issuer in parallel for all input bits. The main computational overhead of the protocol is incurred by the proxy oblivious transfers, and is the same as in the two-party case – a proxy oblivious transfer must be executed for every input wire. Estimates in [16] show that this method can be used to securely implement Vickrey auctions that involve hundreds of bidders.

6 Conclusion

This paper was intended to demonstrate basic ideas from a large body of cryptographic research on secure distributed computation, and their applications to data mining. We described in brief the definitions of security, and the generic constructions for the two-party and multi-party scenarios. We showed that it is easier to design an implementation based on the constructions for the two-party case than it is to design one based on the multi-party constructions. The main parameter that affects the feasibility of implementing a secure protocol based on the generic constructions is the size of the best combinatorial circuit that computes the function that is evaluated. The main computational bottleneck of the constructions is the oblivious transfer protocol, and any improvement in the overhead of this protocol should directly affect the overhead of secure computation.

References

1. Beaver, D., Micali, S., Rogaway, P.: The round complexity of secure protocols. In: Proc. of 22nd ACM Symposium on Theory of Computing (STOC), pp. 503–513 (1990)
2. Bellare, M., Micali, S.: Non-Interactive Oblivious Transfer and Applications. In: Brassard, G. (ed.) CRYPTO 1989. LNCS, vol. 435, pp. 547–557. Springer, Heidelberg (1990)
3. Ben-Or, M., Goldwasser, S., Wigderson, A.: Completeness theorems for non cryptographic fault tolerant distributed computation. In: Proceedings of the 20th Annual Symposium on the Theory of Computing (STOC), pp. 1–9. ACM, New York (1988)
4. Chaum, D., Crepeau, C., Damgard, I.: Multiparty unconditionally secure protocols. In: Proceedings of the 20th Annual Symposium on the Theory of Computing (STOC), pp. 11–19. ACM, New York (1988)
5. Cramer, R.: Introduction to Secure Computation (2000), http://www.brics.dk/~cramer/papers/CRAMER_revised.ps
6. Dai, W.: The Crypto++ library, benchmark (November 3, 2002), http://www.eskimo.com/weidai/cryptlib.html
7. Even, S., Goldreich, O., Lempel, A.: A Randomized Protocol for Signing Contracts. Communications of the ACM 28, 637–647 (1985)
8. Fagin, R., Naor, M., Winkler, P.: Comparing Information Without Leaking It. Communications of the ACM 39(5), 77–85 (1996)
9. Goldreich, O.: Secure Multi-Party Computation (2002) (manuscript), http://www.wisdom.weizmann.ac.il/oded/pp.html
10. Goldreich, O., Micali, S., Wigderson, A.: How to Play any Mental Game - A Completeness Theorem for Protocols with Honest Majority. In: Proceedings of the 19th Annual Symposium on the Theory of Computing (STOC), pp. 218–229. ACM, New York (1987)
11. Kilian, J.: Founding cryptography on oblivious transfer. In: ACM STOC 1988, pp. 20–31 (1988)
12. Lindell, Y., Pinkas, B.: Privacy Preserving Data Mining. Journal of Cryptology 15(3), 177–206 (2002)
13. Luby, M.: Pseudorandomness and Cryptographic Applications. Princeton Computer Science Notes (1996)
14. Naor, M., Pinkas, B.: Oblivious Transfer and Polynomial Evaluation. In: Proceedings of the 31th Annual Symposium on the Theory of Computing (STOC), pp. 245–254. ACM, New York (1999)
15. Naor, M., Pinkas, B.: Efficient Oblivious Transfer Protocols. In: Proceedings of 12th SIAM Symposium on Discrete Algorithms (SODA), Washington DC, January 7-9, pp. 448–457 (2001)
16. Naor, M., Pinkas, B., Sumner, R.: Privacy Preserving Auctions and Mechanism Design. In: Proc. of the 1st ACM Conference on Electronic Commerce (November 1999)
17. Rabin, M.O.: How to exchange secrets by oblivious transfer, Technical Memo TR-81, Aiken Computation Laboratory (1981)
18. Savage, J.E.: Computational work and time on finite machines. Journal of the ACM 19(4), 660–674 (1972)
19. Yao, C.: How to generate and exchange secrets. In: Proceedings 27th Symposium on Foundations of Computer Science (FOCS), pp. 162–167. IEEE, Los Alamitos (1986)

A Framework for Mining Strong Positive and Negative Association Rules of Frequent Objects in Spatial Database System Using Interesting Measure

Animesh Tripathy[1], Subhalaxmi Das[1], and Prashanta Kumar Patra[2]

[1] Department of Computer Science Engineering, KIIT University, Bhubaneswar, India
[2] Department of Computer Science Engineering, CET, BPUT, Bhubaneswar, India

Abstract. Association Rule Mining (ARM) is an important problem in spatial database system. Much effort has been devoted for developing algorithms for efficiently discovering relationship between objects in space. In this paper, we propose an enhancement of existing mining algorithm for efficiently mining frequent patterns for positive and negative spatial objects for spatial objects occurring in space such as a city is located near a river. This approach reveals that the enhanced algorithm is suitable both for dense as well as sparse spatial objects when minimum support is high and it overcomes some limitations of the previous method.

Keywords: Positive Association Rule, Negative Association Rule, Lift, Frequent Pattern, Hyper-linked data structure.

1 Introduction

Spatial database is a large database system which stores complex data of objects in space [5]. Spatial dataset's integration has been widely investigated but unfortunately there exists no framework to define this process [4]. Several data mining techniques have been applied to discover knowledge from spatial databases. In particular, Association Rule Mining (ARM) discovers spatial relationships and infer valid, novel, useful and understandable patterns for generation of rules [2][3]. Extensive efforts have been devoted to developing efficient algorithms for mining frequent patterns. The main issues in frequent patterns mining are: (1) to reduce the number of database scans as spatial database is too large to fit into the main memory, and scanning data from disk is very costly; (2) to reduce the search space since every subset of can be a frequent pattern [1]. So a couple of algorithms adopting the candidate generate-and-test approach are proposed. Apriori algorithm [2] is the first algorithm which uses the Apriori property to prune the search space. A hash based algorithm [8] reduces the number of candidate patterns. The pattern growth approach [4][5] tries to avoid the above two drawbacks by constructing conditional databases for frequent patterns. The proposed algorithms differ mainly in how they represent the conditional databases that use a compact data structure [6] FP tree to represent the conditional databases, which is a combination of prefix-tree structure and node-links. FP-growth algorithm [7] is not efficient on sparse databases because prefix sharing is not common and each node still needs to maintain a couple of pointers, which incurs a huge memory space

N. Meghanathan et al. (Eds.): CNSA 2010, CCIS 89, pp. 583–592, 2010.
© Springer-Verlag Berlin Heidelberg 2010

requirement and the main memory consumption is usually hard to precisely predict. In this paper, we propose an enhancement of existing FP tree by building a FPAR/FNAR tree that has the capability of generating negative and positive association rules from dense data sets. Secondly, we use a simple memory based hyperlink data structure for mining patterns in sparse datasets that are low frequent but strongly correlated to reduce the negative influence that the disadvantageous factors bring on [6].

2 Proposed Framework

In this section we propose a framework to mine positive and negative association rules in dense and sparse dataset. These spatial objects situated close to each other for a given sample space of Indian Cities. The presence of each spatial object is recorded against each city as a transaction. We form dense and sparse data sets for the transaction list of cities based of their occurrence of higher ranked objects. Equal ranked objects are sorted in lexicographic ordering [10]. The layout of the proposed framework is given in fig. 1. The Proposed Framework can be described as a four step process. In the first step we find dense and sparse spatial data sets. Second step finds frequent dense and sparse objects. The third step constructs a FPAR/FNAR tree by finding frequent positive and negative objects in descending order of their occurrences. All possible positive and negative frequent patterns in case of sparse FPAR/FNAR tree generate complex patterns which is not useful for generation of rules. Finally we use hyper structure to mine all possible positive and negative association rules in sparse data sets.

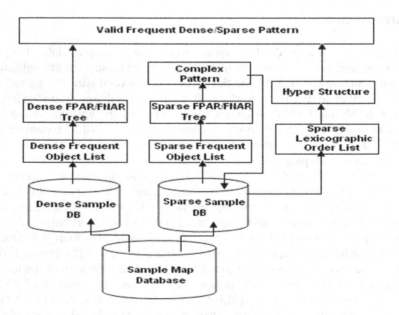

Fig. 1. Proposed Framework

2.1 Proposed Algorithm

Based on the ranking relationship we deduce a set of dense and sparse spatial objects. The proposed algorithm is used to mine valid association rules. The algorithm is divided into three phases [9].

Step 1: Call Frequent Order List procedure to find out all frequent objects.
Step 2: Call FPAR/FNAR Tree procedure to build a tree.
Step 3: Call FPAR/FNAR pattern procedure to find out all valid frequent patterns.

The first step is to generate Frequent Order List after finding all frequent objects. The positive and negative order list is generated based on occurrence of objects in descending order in each transaction. Any object that do not satisfy the minimum support count is then simply discarded. The second phase of the algorithm builds the FPAR/FNAR-Tree. For each transaction the frequent object pattern of current transaction is inserted into the tree. Then for successive transaction if any object is not found as a node in the tree, it creates a new object node and assigns one as the frequency. Otherwise the frequency of child node adds one. The FPAR/FNAR tree is mined by starting from each frequent length pattern leaf node (as an initial suffix pattern), construct its pattern base (a "sub dataset," which consists of the set of *prefix paths* in the FPAR/FNAR -tree co-occurring with the suffix pattern), then construct its (*pattern*), and perform mining recursively on such a tree. The pattern growth is achieved by the concatenation of the suffix pattern with the valid frequent patterns generated from a valid FPAR/FNAR -tree patterns. The algorithm for generation FPAR/FNAR tree is given below:

```
Input:Order List(OL)
Output:FPAR/FNAR Tree
Procedure FPAR/FNAR Tree creates as follows
Step 1:    Generate FPAR/FNAR Tree
For each positive_OL & negative_OL
Scan each transaction T in Order_list[i]
Step 2:    For each Order_list[i]
Generate Frequent Pattern[j] , such that
Pattern[j] contains object[i]>1 && !=Order_list[i]
Step 3:    Determine support count for each Pattern[j]
For each Pattern[j]
If transaction T contains Pattern[j] ==found
Count[Pattern[j]]++
Else
Consider Pattern [j++]
Step 4:  Build FPAR/FNAR Tree
For each transaction in Order_list[i]
Generate pattern_list[k]
If transaction[t] is a Frequent Pattern[j]
then insert into pattern_list[k]
select max(Pattern[k])==Root
Set counter_value==1
Generate leaf nodes for object[i] not in Pattern[j]
Set counter_value==1 for each leaf node
```

```
Step 5:   For each successive scan of Order_list[i]
If(max(Pattern[j] exists)
Increment counter_value ++
If leaf nodes exists
Increment counter_value++
Else
Generate leaf nodes for object[i] not in Pattern[j]
Set counter value==1
```

2.2 Analysis of Proposed Framework

Based on the proposed algorithm we performed the test on a sample real time data base of 250 Indian cities taken as reference to validate the proposed framework in our study of spatial database system. Table 1 shows a sample of 07 spatial objects for 12 Indian cities. The spatial objects are as Museum (Mu), Monument (Mo), Zoo (Z), Lake (L), Forest (F). We have assumed a minimum support count greater than 4. Analysis process has the following steps as per the framework discussed before.

Step 1: Find Frequent Positive and Negative objects.
Step 2: Build Ordered list of objects.
Step 3: Build a FPAR/FNAR Tree
Step 4: Generate patterns and validate it against their respective support count.
Step 5: Generate the set of positive & negative association rules.

Table 1. Spatial Dense Dataset

TID	Reference City	Positive Object	(Ordered) Positive Frequent Objects	(Oredred) Negative Frequent Objects
1	Bhubaneswar	Mu,L,Mo,Z,R,H	Mu,Z,L,Mo,R	¬F
2	Bangalore	Mu,L,Mo,Z,F	Mu,Z,L,Mo	¬H, ¬R
3	Ajmer	Mu,L,Mo,R	Mu,L,Mo,R	¬F,¬H
4	Mumbai	Mu,L,Mo,Z,R,H	Mu,Z,L,Mo,R	¬F
5	Chandigarh	Mu,L,Z,F	Mu,Z,L	¬H, ¬R
6	Trivandrum	Mu,L,Z	Mu,Z,L	¬F, ¬H, ¬R
7	Delhi	Mu,Mo,Z,F,R	Mu,Z,Mo,R	¬H
8	Ahmadabad	Mu,L,Mo,Z,R	Mu,Z,L,Mo,R	¬F,¬H
9	Pune	Mu,L,Mo,Z,R,H	Mu,Z,L,Mo,R	¬F
10	Mysore	L,Mo,Z,F,H	Z,L,Mo	¬R
11	Nagpur	Mu,L,Mo,Z	Mu,Z,L,Mo	¬F,¬H,¬R
12	Patna	Mu,Mo,Z,R	Mu,Z,Mo,R	¬F, ¬H

Each transaction is scanned once to find frequent positive & negative object. It can be viewed as being appended with the negative objects. For example, in TID (1) {Mu, L, Mo, Z, R, H} is a transaction list. So the object which is less than the minimum support is pruned. Now TID (1) can be viewed as a new transaction {Mu, Z, L, Mo, R, ¬F} if the set of negative objects is {¬F,¬H,¬R}. Then, each transaction will be used to construct the FPAR/FNAR tree as shown in fig. 2 & 3. Let's take an example TID(1) for constructing the FPAR tree then Museum(Mu) and Zoo(Z) can be combined into one node because these objects are more frequent than other in this transaction and so is inserted in to the child nodes of the sub tree. And similarly, other sub tree can be built and this procedure stops when no more transactions exists.

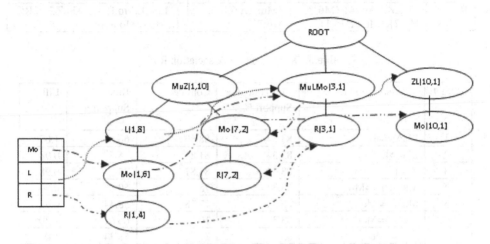

Fig. 2. Dense FPAR Tree

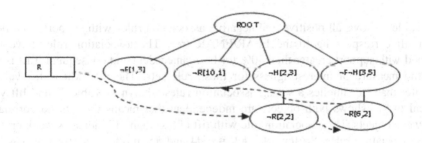

Fig. 3. Dense FNAR Tree

2.3 Mining of Association Rules for Dense Dataset

Mining of the dense FPAR tree is summarized in Table 2. Suppose we consider leaf node L. L occurs in three branches of the FPAR tree of fig. 2. The paths formed by these branches are {MuZ,L:8},{Mu,L:1} and {Z,L:1}. Therefore, considering L as a suffix, its corresponding three prefix paths for generating patterns are {Mu,Z:8},{Mu:1} and {Z:1} which generate its patterns shown in Table 2.

Table 2. Dense FPAR Pattern

Object	Generated Patterns	Valid FPAR Tree Patterns	Valid Frequent Patterns Generated
L	{Mu,Z:8},{Mu:1},{Z:1}	{Mu:10,Z:9}	{MuZ,L:8},{Mu,L:1},{Z,L:1}
Mo	{Mu,Z,L:6},{Mu,L:1}, {Mu,Z:2},{ZL:1}	{Mu:9,Z:9,L:8}	{Mu,Z,L,Mo:6},{Mu,L,Mo:1}, {Mu,Z,Mo:2},{Z,L,Mo:1}
R	{Mu,Z,L,Mo:4},{Mu,Z, Mo:2},{Mu,L,Mo:1}	{Mu:7,Z:6,L:5, Mo:7}	{Mu,Z,L,Mo,R:4},{Mu,Z,Mo,R:2 },{Mu,L,Mo,R:1}

Table 3. Dense Positive Association Rule

Rule #	Association Rule	Consequent Support %	Confidence	Rule Support %	Lift
1	Mu^Z⟹L	83.34	88.89	66.67	1.07
2	Mu⟹L	83.34	81.81	75	0.98
3	Z⟹L	83.34	81.81	75	0.98
4	Mu^Z^L⟹Mo	83.34	75	50	0.90
5	Mu^L⟹Mo	83.34	77.78	58.34	0.94
6	Mu^Z⟹Mo	83.34	100	66.67	1.20
7	Z^L⟹Mo	83.34	87.5	58.34	1.05
8	Mu^Z^ Mo⟹R	58.34	75	50	1.29
9	Mu^L^Mo⟹R	58.34	71.42	41.67	1.23

Table 3 shows all positive and negative association rules with support, confidence and lift corresponding to the FPAR/FNAR tree. The association rules have been mined with support greater than 40% for both antecedent and consequent. Lift is used as the measure of interestingness for these rule sets. The rule whose lift value is greater than "1" implies a strong association rules (shown in Table 3) and lift value equal to "1" shows both objects are independent that means there is no correlation between objects. The association rule with lift of less than "1" indicates weak or negative association rules. So for rules #2, #3, #4 and #5, further investigation has been done for possible negative association rules and the results are shown in Table 4. As the generated rules are strong rules it requires no pruning process to find invalid rules. Thus we get a set of 5 association rules for positively correlated objects and 11 association rules for negatively correlated objects. Similar approach was used to analyze the sparse dataset. This approach of building association rule is an improved approach for dense dataset as compared to sparse dataset because in dense dataset, it constructs a tree that compresses and generates a set of generalized strong positive and negative association rules for valid patterns and generated rules are higher as compared to invalid rules. But in sparse dataset, valid patterns and generated rules are much less as compared to dense data sets. The searching costs increases as the tree becomes bushy. So FPAR/FNAR tree approach is sufficient for dense dataset only.

Table 4. Examination of DENSE Negative Association Rules with Lift value

Rule #	Association Rule	Consequent Support %	Confidence	Rule Support %	Lift
1	Mu⟹¬L	16.67	18.18	17	1.09
2	¬Mu⟹L	83.34	100	8.34	1.20
3	Z⟹¬L	16.67	18.18	17	1.09
4	¬Zoo⟹Lake	83.34	100	8.34	1.20
5	Mu^Z^L⟹¬Mo	16.67	25	17	1.50
6	¬Mu^Z^L⟹Mo	83.34	100	8.34	1.20
7	Mu^¬Z^L⟹Mo	83.34	100	8.34	1.20
8	Mu^Z^¬L⟹Mo	83.34	100	8.34	1.20
9	Mu^L⟹¬Mo	16.67	20	17	1.20
10	¬Mu^L⟹Mo	83.34	100	8.34	1.20
11	Mu^¬L⟹Mo	83.34	100	8.34	1.20

3   Hyper-Linked Data Structure on Sparse Datasets

The general idea of Hyper linked mining using sparse dataset shown in Table 5. All objects in frequent-object projections are sorted according to their neighborhood relation [1]. A header table T is created, with each positive and negative frequent object entry having three fields: an object-id, a support count, and a hyperlink.

Table 5. Spatial Sparse Dataset

TID	Reference City	Positive Objects	(Order)Positive Frequent Objects	(Order)Negative Frequent Objects
1	Agra	Mu,Mo,F,R	Mu,F,Mo,R	¬Z,¬H,¬L
2	Darjeeling	Mu,Z,H	Mu,H	¬R,¬F,¬L,¬Mo
3	Ranchi	Mu,L,H	Mu,L,H	¬Z,¬R,¬F,¬Mo
4	Chennai	Mu,L,R	Mu,L,R	¬Z,¬H,¬F,¬Mo
5	Ernakulam	Mu,Mo,F,R	Mu,F,Mo,R	¬Z,¬H,¬L
6	Coimbatore	Mu,Mo,R	Mu,Mo,R	¬Z,¬H,¬F,¬L
7	Kanpur	Mu,Mo,F	Mu,F,Mo	¬Z,¬H,¬R,¬L
8	Amritsar	L,Mo,F	F,L,Mo	¬Z,¬H,¬R
9	Nashik	Mu,Mo,R	Mu,Mo,R	¬Z,¬H,¬F,¬L
10	Mussorrie	Mu,L,F,H	Mu,F,L,H	¬Z,¬R,¬Mo
11	Varanasi	Mu,Mo,R	Mu,Mo,R	¬Z,¬H,¬F,¬L
12	Ooty	Mu,L,H	Mu,L,H	¬Z,¬R,¬F,¬Mo
13	Kodaikanal	Mu,L,F,H	Mu,F,L,H	¬Z,¬R,¬Mo
14	Port blair	Mu,Mo,R	Mu,Mo,R	¬Z,¬H,¬F,¬L
15	Thekaddy	L,F,Z,H	F,L,H	¬R,¬Mo
16	Chamba	Mu,L,F,H	Mu,F,L,H	¬Z,¬R,¬Mo

The frequent-object projections are loaded into the memory, those with the same first object (in the order of the list) are linked together by the hyper-links into a queue, and the entries in header table. To mine the subsets of frequent patterns of sparse dataset, we can find the complete set of frequent patterns containing object x_2, not object x_1. To mine the F-projected database, *F-header table* is created, as shown in fig.4. In F-queue, every frequent object, except for F itself, has an entry with the same three fields as T, i.e., *object-id, support count* and *hyper-link*. The support count in TF records the support of the corresponding object in the F-projected database. Then the remaining mining can be performed without referencing any information in the original database. By traversing the F-queue once, the set of locally frequent objects, i.e., the objects those have frequency at least 6, in the F-projected database is found, which is {*H:4,L:5,Mo:4,Mu:6,R:2*}. So we only take Mu as locally frequent and consider FM: 6 as a pattern. So search along this path completes. Similarly we generate all frequent patterns. From the frequent patterns generated we mine association rules˙ as shown in Table 6. Negative association rules are also generated as per the hyper linked approach discussed above.

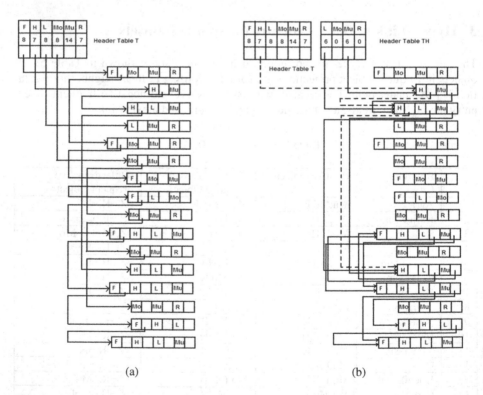

(a)   (b)

Fig. 4. (a) Hyper-structure to store Positive Frequent-Object projections. (b) Header Table TH and Mu and L queue.

Table 6. Positive & Negative Sparse object Association Rule

Rule #	Association Rule	Consequent Support %	Confidence	Rule Support %	Lift
1	F⇒Mu	87.5	75	37.5	0.88
2	H⇒Mu	87.5	85.71	37.5	0.98
3	H⇒L	50	85.71	37.5	1.71
4	L⇒Mu	87.5	75	37.5	0.88
5	Mo⇒Mu	87.5	87.5	43.75	1.00
6	Mo⇒R	43.75	75	37.5	1.71
7	Mo^Mu⇒R	43.75	85.71	37.5	1.95
8	¬ F ⇒¬Z	87.5	87.5	43.75	1.00
9	¬H⇒¬L	50	77.78	43.75	1.55
10	¬H⇒¬Z	87.5	100	56.25	1.14
11	¬Mo⇒¬R	56.25	87.5	43.75	1.56
12	¬Mo⇒¬Z	87.5	75	37.5	0.86
13	¬H^¬L⇒¬Z	87.5	100	43.75	1.14

4 Performance Study and Experimental Results

To evaluate the efficiency and scalability of FPAR/FNAR as well as H-Mine, we have performed an extensive performance study. In this section, we report our experimental results on the performance of FPAR/FNAR in comparison with *Apriori* and *FP-growth*.

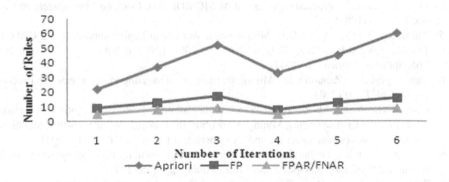

Fig. 5. No. of Iterations Vs No. of Rules generated

It shows that FPAR/FNAR outperforms *Apriori* and *FP-growth*. and is efficient and highly scalable for mining very large databases. All the experiments were performed on a 2.00 GHz Pentium PC machine with 512 Mb main memory and 40 Gb hard disk, running Microsoft Windows/NT. FPAR/FNAR and *FP-growth* were implemented by us using Visual C++6.0, while the version of *Apriori* that we used is a well-known version, available at http://fuzzy.cs.uni-magdeburg.de/~borgelt/. All reports of the iterations and number of rules generated as shown in fig. 5. We have tested various spatial data sets, with consistent results. Limited by space, only the results on some typical data sets are reported here.

5 Conclusion and Future Wok

FPAR/FNAR algorithm constructs a tree that compresses and generates a set of strong positive and negative association rules. The algorithm predicts useful negative rules with respect to existing positive rules that can assist the usefulness of rules as recommendations more accurately. So this framework will definitely enhance the process of finding spatial objects in space with respect to their correlation measure. However, some further work needs to be done on complex and sparse datasets as it was evident from experimental analysis.

References

1. Pei, J., Han, J., Lu, H., Nishio, S., Tang, S., Yang, D.: H-Mine: Fast and space-preserving frequent pattern mining in large databases. IIE Transactions 39, 593–605 (2007)
2. Wu, X., Zhang, C., Zhang, S.: Efficient mining of both positive and negative association rules. ACM Transactions on Information Systems 22(3), 381–405 (2004)
3. Dong, X., Niu, Z., Shi, X., Zhang, X., Zhu, D.: Mining both Positive and Negative Association Rules from Frequent and Infrequent Itemsets. In: Alhajj, R., Gao, H., Li, X., Li, J., Zaïane, O.R. (eds.) ADMA 2007. LNCS (LNAI), vol. 4632, pp. 122–133. Springer, Heidelberg (2007)
4. Agrawal, R., Imielinski, T., Swami, A.: Mining association rules between sets of items in large databases. In: Proceeding of the ACM SIGMOD Intl. Conf. on Management of Data, pp. 207–216 (1993)
5. Thiruvady, T.D.R., Webb, G.I.: Mining negative rules in large databases using GRD. In: Dai, H., Srikant, R., Zhang, C. (eds.) PAKDD 2004. LNCS (LNAI), vol. 3056, pp. 161–165. Springer, Heidelberg (2004)
6. Pietracaprina, A., Zandolin, D.: Mining frequent itemsets using Patricia tries. In: Proceeding of IEEE FIMI (2003)
7. Gan, M.M., Zhang, M.-Y., Wang, S.-W.: One Extended Form for Negative Association Rules and the Corresponding Mining Algorithm. In: Proceedings of the 4th International Conference on Machine Learning and Cybernetics, vol. 3, pp. 1716–1721 (2005)
8. Borgelt, C.: An Implementation of the FP-growth Algorithm. In: Proceedings of the 1st International Workshop on Open Source Data Mining, pp. 1–5 (2005)
9. Tripathy, A., Das, S., Patra, P.K.: An Improved Design Approach in Spatial Databases Using Frequent Association Rule Mining Algorithm. In: IEEE 2nd International Advance Computing Conference, pp. 410–415 (2010)
10. Vyas, R., Sharma, L.K., Tiwary, U.S.: Exploring Spatial ARM (Association Rule Mining) for Geo Decision support System. Journal of Computer Science, 882–886 (2007)

Global Search Analysis of Spatial Gene Expression Data Using Genetic Algorithm

M. Anandhavalli[1,*], M.K. Ghose[1], K. Gauthaman[2], and M. Boosha[3]

[1] Department of Computer Science Engineering, SMIT, East Sikkim, India
[2] Department of Drug Technology, Higher Institute of Medical Technology, Derna, Libya
[3] Tata Consultancy Services, Chennai, Tamil Nadu, India

Abstract. In this paper, we present a genetic algorithm to perform global searching for generating interesting association rules from Spatial Gene Expression Data. The typical approach of association rule mining is to make strong simplifying assumptions about the form of the rules, and limit the measure of rule quality to simple properties such as minimum support or minimum confidence. Minimum-support or minimum confidence means that users must specify suitable thresholds for their mining tasks though they may have no knowledge concerning their databases. The presented approach does not require users to specify thresholds. Instead of generating an unknown number of association rules, only the most interesting rules are generated according to interestingness measure as defined by the fitness function. Computational results show that applying this genetic algorithm to search for high quality association rules with their confidence and interestingness acceptably maximized leads to better results.

Keywords: Spatial Gene Expression Data, Genetic Algorithm, Association Rules, Support, Confidence, Interestingness.

1 Introduction

The main contribution here has been a great explosion of genomic data in recent years. This is due to the advances in various high-throughput biotechnologies such as spatial gene expression database. These large genomic data sets are information-rich and often contain much more information than the researchers who generated the data might have anticipated. The most popular pattern discovery method in data mining is association rule mining (ARM). Association rule mining was introduced by [1]. It aims to extract interesting correlations, frequent patterns, associations or casual structures among sets of items in transaction databases or other data repositories. The relationships are not based on inherent properties of the data themselves but rather based on the co-occurrence of the items within the database. According to Zaki [2], the mining task involves generating all association rules in the database that have a support greater than minimum support (the rules are frequent) and have a confidence greater than minimum confidence (rules are strong). So the Users have to give a suitable minimum-support for a mining task. If the minimum support value is too big, nothing is found in a database, whereas a slightly small minimum support leads to

---

*Corresponding author.

N. Meghanathan et al. (Eds.): CNSA 2010, CCIS 89, pp. 593–602, 2010.

low-performance. Although it is known that genetic algorithm is good at searching for undetermined solutions, it is still rare to see that genetic algorithm is used to mine association rules from spatial gene expression data.

In this paper, an attempt has been made to search for interesting association rules by applying genetic algorithm on the association rules generated by Fast association rule mining method in effective manner from spatial gene expression data [3].

2 Related Work

Genetic algorithm (GA) for rules discovery can be divided into two approaches, the Michigan approach and Pittsburgh approach, according to their encoding of rules in the population of chromosomes [12]. In Michigan approach, each rule is encoded into an individual. In Pittsburgh approach, a set of rules are encoded into a chromosome. For example, [7] gave a Michigan-type of genetic algorithm to discover comprehensible classification rules, having an interesting chromosome encoding and introducing a specific mutation operator. But the method is impractical when the number of attribute is large. In [10] the Michigan method is used to predict rare events. The Pittsburgh approach is used for the discovery of classes and feature patterns in [9].

A system demonstrated by GA-Nuggets to infer the values of goal attributes given the values of predicting attributes [6] which finds the first-order logic classification rules by generalizing a seed example [12]. In [11], GA is used for mining association rules for discovering changing patterns in historical data in which the entire set of rules is encoded in a single chromosome and each rule is represented by some nonbinary symbolic values. It uses a complicated fitness function and a Pittsburgh method. Association rules combined with hash tree and genetic algorithm has been proposed to mine regulated genes from yeast genome dataset by generating lots of co-regulated genes [16].

A Quant Miner algorithm by [14] works directly on a set of rule templates. A rule template is a preset format of a quantitative association rule. For each rule template, the algorithm looks for the best intervals for the numeric attributes occurring in that template, relying on a Genetic Algorithm with gain ratio as fitness function. In [13], intra Transactions, inter transactions and distributed transactions of dynamic transaction databases are considered for mining dynamic Association Rules using the principles of GA. In [15], genetic algorithm-based strategy for identifying quantitative association rules without specifying actual minimum support has been proposed for global search and it determines the intervals that form the rules without discretizing the attributes, but relative confidence is used as the fitness function.

All these recently proposed algorithms [13], [14], [15] using GA have generated the quantitative association rules in which both categorical and numeric attributes are considered and moreover the number of attributes used in those methods are very less when compared to the number attributes in spatial gene expression data and association rules.

The traditional task of mining association rules is how to find all rules $X \rightarrow Y$, such that the supports and confidences of the rules are larger than, or equal to, a minimum support, minsupp, and a minimum confidence, minconf, respectively. Both of these thresholds are user-specified. In the proposed method, we have investigated the possibility of applying genetic algorithm for mining association rules from the spatial gene expression data without using user defined thresholds.

3 Proposed Approach

The proposed ARG algorithm comprises the following steps.
1.   The set of association rules have been generated using the Fast association rule mining algorithm [3].
2.   For a given rule length k, the genetic algorithm is used to search for some interesting association k-rules, with positive confidence and interestingness as measures of fitness function.

The genetic algorithm involves the following steps:
1.   Michigan strategy is used for encoding each association rule in a single chromosome.
2.   Three genetic operators: select, crossover and mutation has been applied with thresholds on the set of rules.
    a.   The chromosome can be selected from the set of rules or population based on the fitness function which is the arithmetic weighted average of confidence and interestingness measure.
    b.   The two-point cross over method has been used to reproduce the offspring to generate a new population.
    c.   Mutation function has been applied to the genes of chromosome based on randomly generated number along with fitness function.
3.   Interesting association rules has been generated from set of association rules.

3.1 Approach Decomposition

Definition 1: The association k-rule A→C is represented by integer k+1 positive integers where antecedent $A=I_1,I_2,...,I_s$ and consequent $C=I_{s+1},...,I_k$ and s is the indicator for the separation of antecedent and consequent, $0<s<k$. The chromosome or rule is encoded as

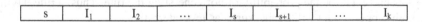

s	I_1	I_2	...	I_s	I_{s+1}	...	I_k

Fig. 1. Michigan encoding method of k-rule r_k

Definition 2: Let $I=\{i_1, i_2, ..., i_n\}$ be a set of items, where each item i_j corresponds to a value of an attribute and denoted by their indexes as $I=1,2,3,...,n$ and is a member of some transactions in database $D =\{ t_1, t_2, ..., t_n\}$, i.e. $i_j \in D$.

Definition 3: The two-point crossover method selects two positions in the rule and only the items between the two positions are swapped. It can preserve the first and the last parts of a chromosome and just swap the middle part. The method for reproducing the offspring to generate a new population is as follows.

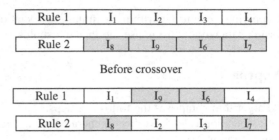

Before crossover

After two-point crossover

Fig. 2. Method of two-point crossover

Definition 4: The fitness of the rule is given as $\text{Fitness(rule)} = \dfrac{w1 * P + w2 * I}{w1 + w2}$

where w_1 and w_2 are user specified values, P is the positive confidence measure and I is the interestingness measure of the association rule.

Definition 5: The positive confidence of the rule A→C is defined as follows.

$$\text{pconf}(A \to C) = \frac{\text{supp}(A \cup C) - \text{supp}(A) \times \text{supp}(C)}{\text{supp}(A)(1 - \text{supp}(C))}$$

It is used as one of the measure for the fitness function of the corresponding association rule in genetic algorithm. supp(A) gives the support count of itemset A.

Definition 6: Interesting measure refers to finding rules that are interesting or useful to the user, not just any possible rule. It uses only the support count of the antecedent and the consequent parts of the rules A→C, and is defined as

$$I(A \to C) = \frac{\text{supp}(A \cup C)}{\text{supp}(A)} \times \frac{\text{supp}(A \cup C)}{\text{supp}(C)} \times [1 - \frac{\text{supp}(A \cup C)}{|D|}]$$

where I is interestingness and |D| is the total number of transactions in the database, supp(A ∪ C)/supp(A) gives the probability of generating the rule depending on the antecedent part, supp(A ∪ C)/supp(C) gives the probability of generating the rule depending on the consequent part, and supp(A ∪ C)/|D| gives the probability of generating the rule depending on the whole dataset. This means that the complement of this probability will be the probability of not generating the rule. Thus, a rule having a very high support count will be measured as less interesting.

3.2 Algorithm

The description of the algorithm **ARG** for generating interesting association rules are as follows.

Algorithm ARG
----

1. **Input:** Set of association rules, selection value, crossover value, mutate value.
2. **Output:** Set of strong association rules.
3. **Population ARG**(rules, select_val, crossover_val, mutate_val)

```
4.   {
              i=0;
5.            population[i] = population_initialize(rules);
6.            While not terminate(population[i]) do
7.            {
8.                     population[i+1] =0;
9.                     population_temp=0;
10.      for all rules ∈ population[i] do
11.                  If select( rule, select_val)
12.                  then population[i+1] = population[i+1] ∪ rule;
13.           population_temp = crossover ( population[i+1], crossover_val );
14.           for all rules ∈ population_temp[i] do
15.  population[i+1]=(population[i+1] - rule ) ∪ mutate(rule, mutate_val);
16.           i=i+1;
17.           }
18.  return population[i];
19.  }
20.  // To produce initial population
21.  Population_initialize(rules)
22.  {
23.           population [0] =rules;
24.           Read population size;
25.           while size(population[0]) > population_ size do
26.           {
27.                   population_temp =0
28.                   for all rules ∈ population[0] do
29.                   {
30.                   population_temp = population_temp ∪ mutate( rule,1)
31.                   }
32.           population_temp =population[ ] ∪ population_temp;
33.           }
34.  return population[0];
35.  }
36.  // To select chromosomes
37.  Select (rule, select_val)
38.  {
39.           If ( frand() * fit(rule) < select_val )
40.           return true;
41.           else return false;
42.  }
43.  // Apply two point crossover strategy
44.  Crossover(population, crossover_val)
45.  {
46.           population_new =0
47.      for all items of the rule r₁ = (A₁₁... A₁ₖ) in population
48.      {
49.           for all items of the rule r₂ = (A₂₁... A₂ₖ) in population & r₁ ≠ r₂
```

```
50.              {
51.                      If frand( ) < crossover_val
52.                      {
53.                      i=irand(k+1);
54.                      j=irand(k+1);
55.                      (i,j) =( min(i,j),max(i,j));
56.              Generate new rules r3 and r4with crossover points i and j in r1 and r2;
57.              population_new = population_new ∪ r3,r4;
58.                      }
59.              }
60.      }
61. return population_new;
62. }
63. // Apply mutate value to change items in rule rk
64. Mutate(rule, mutate_val)
65. {
66.              If (frand() * fit(rule) < mutate_val)
67.      {
68.              rule.A0 = irand(k-2) +1;
69.              i = irand(k-1) +1;
70.              rule.Ai = irand(n-1);
71.      }
72. return rule;
73. }
```

The working method of the interesting association rules generation procedure is discussed in the following steps.

1. Set of association rules generated using the Fast association rule mining algorithm has been read as input. The set of rules are considered as population, which is given in step 5 of algorithm ARG.
2. Each rule is encoded as single chromosome using Michigan's approach which is given in definition 1.
3. The population is initialized and generated. It is carried out by using two functions.
   a. Population_initialize(rules) which is given in steps 22 through 35 of the ARG algorithm. The function Population_initialize(rules) reads input parameters as set of association rules, population[0] and user defined constant value population_ size from the user and returns a population as the initial set of chromosomes. Function size(population[0]) has been used to return the number of chromosomes or rules in population[0].
   b. Mutate(rule, mutate_val) function which is given in steps 65 through 73 of the ARG algorithm. It reads a rule from the population and a mutate value to change the items in the rule at a probability of mutate_val, while also considering the fitness of rule as an additional weight and returns the mutated rule as an output. The rule has been mutated by using the randomized value and fitness of the rule. The function frand() returns a random real numbers in the range 0 to 1 and The function

        irand(k) returns a random integer numbers from 0 to k. The function
        fit(rule) is used to find the fitness of the rule using definitions 4,5,6.

4. The best offspring rules are selected for the generation of new population, which is given in steps 38 to 41 of ARG algorithm. The function *Select*(rules, select_val) selects the rules by considering their fitness value and probability select_val. It returns true if the rule is successfully selected with probability select_val, otherwise false if failed. In this function, *frand*() returns a random real numbers in the range 0 to 1, the function *fit*() is the fitness function and select_val is a population support in a range of 0 and 1.

5. Next two point crossover has been used using definition 3 to reproduce offspring chromosomes, which is given in steps 45 through 59 in ARG algorithm. The function *crossover*(population, crossover_val), randomly reproduce offspring chromosomes at a probability of crossover_val from population and returns a new population. The two cross over points are randomly generated using function *irand*(k) which returns a random integer numbers from 0 to k.

6. Finally the new population with interesting association rules has been generated using selection, crossover and mutation operators, steps 6 through 19 gives this procedure.

7. The algorithm has been terminated, which is given in step 6 of the ARG algorithm, only when the number of iterations is larger than a given maximum number of rules selected, which are generated by Fast association rule mining algorithm.

4 Results and Discussion

The proposed algorithm has been implemented in Java and tested on Linux platform. The previous study [5] related to EMAGE [4] spatial gene expression data involves the subset of data originates from the study [17] and contains 1030 gene expression patterns in a developing mouse embryo model of stages 16, 17 and 18 [8]. The ARG algorithm has been worked with all these patterns at the same time. ARG has been executed with the following values: select_value=0.9, crossover_value=0.9, mutate_value=1, population_size= 2 to 4700 rules, interesting measure weights w_1=1 and w_2=2.

For the generation association rules, Fast association rule algorithm has been executed with the minimum support ranges from 85% to 100%, and the minimum confidence is set to 90%. First ARG algorithm has been executed with only positive confidence as fitness measure and then ARG has been executed with positive confidence combined with interestingness as fitness measures. The rules generated by all algorithms for the EMAGE datasets are given in Figure 1. The execution time for generating the association rules from all algorithms are given in Figure 2.

When the minimum support increases to 90% and confidence value is set 90%, the rules generated by all the three algorithms are 1 only. When the minimum support decreases to 85% and confidence value is set 90%, the number of rules generated by Fast algorithm is 3827, ARG with positive confidence as fitness measure is 1985 and ARG with positive confidence with interestingness as fitness measure is 362 rules.

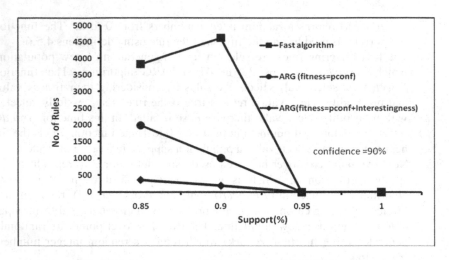

Fig. 1. Rule generation of Algorithms for EMAGE Data Set

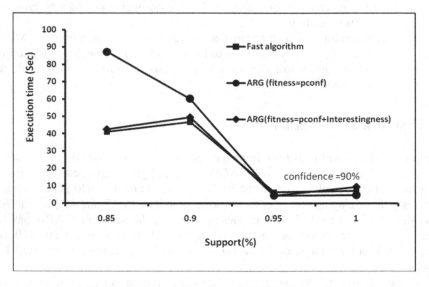

Fig. 2. Runtime of Algorithms for EMAGE Data Set

The rules generated by ARG are approximately equal to 11% of the rules generated by Fast algorithm and 5% of the rules generated by ARG with positive confidence as fitness measure. From this result, we can see that genetic algorithm ARG is able to find some interesting association rules with less execution time.

Table 1 shows the association rules found when transactions are genes that have regions of expression intersecting with the same probe pattern. Here a minimum support level of 0.06 is used, and a minimum confidence of 0.97.

Note that rule 1 and rule 2, rule 3 and rule 4 have the same genes for the antecedent and therefore reference the same spatial region in probe pattern. The genes Hmgb2,

Table 1. Some Interesting association rules based on itemsets of genes and where transaction is probe pattern, generated with ARG with positive confidence and interestingness as fitness measure with support =85% and confidence=100%

Rule	Antecedent	Consequent
1	Pax3	Etv5, Hmgb1
2	Pax3	Rara,Nr1h2,Irx5
3	Dmbx1	Hmgb1,Hmgb2,Tfam, Ubtf
4	Dmbx1	Baz2a,Baz1a,Etv5
5	Lhx1	Elk3,Buz2a,Buz1a,Otub1

mgb1 are known to be highly associated and are common to many processes [17], hence they express over much of the embryo. By considering fitness measures it has been interestingly found that genes Dmbx1, Tfam and Ubtf are also expressed along with those genes.

5 Conclusion

In this paper, a novel method of mining interesting association rules from the spatial gene expression data using genetic algorithm with positive confidence and interestingness measures as fitness function has been proposed. The proposed algorithm is good enough for generating interesting association rules without the user specified thresholds minimum support and minimum confidence from spatial gene expression data and it is very fast when compared to ARG with positive confidence as fitness measure for generating interesting association rules from spatial gene expression data.

Acknowledgments

This study has been carried out as part of Research Promotion Scheme (RPS) Project under AICTE, Govt. of India.

References

1. Agrawal, R., Imielinski, T., Swami, A.: Mining Association rules between sets of items in large databases. In: ACM SIGMOD Intl Conf. on Management of Data (ACM SIGMOD 1993), Washington, USA, pp. 207–216 (1993)
2. Zaki, M.J.: Generating non-redundant association rules. In: Sixth ACM SIGKDD International Conference on Knowledge Discovery and Data Mining, New York, pp. 34–43 (2001)
3. Anandhavalli, M., Ghose, M.K., Gauthaman, K.: Mining Spatial Gene Expression Data Using Association Rules. IJCSS 3(5), 351–357 (2009)
4. EMAGE Gene Expression Data,
   http://genex.hgu.mrc.ac.uk/Emage/database

5. van Hemert, J., Baldock, R.: Mining Spatial Gene Expression Data for Association Rules. In: Hochreiter, S., Wagner, R. (eds.) BIRD 2007. LNCS (LNBI), vol. 4414, pp. 66–76. Springer, Heidelberg (2007)
6. Freitas, A.: A genetic algorithm for generalized rule induction. In: Advances in Soft Computing Engineering Design and Manufacturing, pp. 340–353. Springer, Berlin (1999)
7. Fidelis, M., Lopes, H., Freitas, A.: Discovering comprehensible classification rules with a genetic algorithm. In: 2000 Congress on Evolutionary Computation, La Jolla, CA, USA, pp. 805–810 (2000)
8. Theiler, K.: The House Mouse Atlas of Embryonic Development. Springer, New York (1989)
9. Pei, M., Goodman, E., Punch, W.: Pattern discovery from data using genetic algorithm. In: 1st Pacific – Asia Conf. Knowledge Discovery and Data Mining, Singapore, pp. 64–276 (1997)
10. Weiss, G., Hirsh, H.: Learning to predict rare events in event sequences. In: 4th International Conference Knowledge Discovery and Data Mining, pp. 359–363. AAAI Press, Cambridge (1998)
11. Au, W., Chan, C.: An evolutionary approach for discovering changing patterns in historical data. In: Data Mining and Knowledge Discovery: Theory, Tools, and Technology IV, SPIE, vol. 4730, pp. 398–409 (2002)
12. Augier, S., Venturini, G., Kodratoff, Y.: Learning first order logic rules with a genetic algorithm. In: 1st International Conf. Knowledge Discovery and Data Mining, Montreal, Canada, pp. 21–26 (1995)
13. Venugopal, K.R., Srinivasa, K.G., Patnaik, L.M.: Dynamic association rule mining using genetic algorithms. Soft Computing for Data Mining Applications 190, 63–80 (2009)
14. Salleb-Aouissi, A., Vrain, C., Nortet, C.: QuantMiner.: A Genetic Algorithm for Mining Quantitative Association Rules. In: 20th International Conference on Artificial Intelligence (IJCAI), Hyderabad, India, pp. 1035–1040 (2007)
15. Yan, X., Zhang, C., Zhang, S.: Genetic algorithm-based strategy for identifying association rules without specifying actual minimum support. J. Expert Systems with Applications 36(2), 3066–3076 (2009)
16. Han, F., Rao, N.: Mining Co-regulated Genes using Association Rules combined with Hast-tree and Genetic algorithms. IEEE Xplore, 858–862 (2009)
17. Gray, P., et al.: Mouse brain organization revealed through direct genome-scale tf expression analysis. Science 306(5705), 2255–2257 (2004)

Design and Implementation of Pessimistic Commit Protocols in Mobile Environments

Salman Abdul Moiz[1], Lakshmi Rajamani[2], and Supriya N. Pal[3]

[1] Research Scientist, Centre for Development of Advanced Computing, Bangalore, India
[2] Professor, CSE, University College of Engineering, Osmania University, Hyderabad, India
[3] Associate Director, Centre for Development of Advanced Computing, Bangalore, India
Salman.abdul.moiz@ieee.org, drlakshmiraja@gmail.com,
supriya@ncb.ernet.in

Abstract. The Pessimistic commit protocol specifies set of rules which guarantee that every single transaction in a mobile database environment is executed to its completion or none of its operations are performed. To show the effectiveness of pessimistic commit protocols, a generic simulator is designed and implemented to demonstrate how the transactions are committed and how the data consistency is maintained when the transactions are executed concurrently. Further the constraints imposed by mobile database environments like mobility, blocking of data items etc. are effectively handled. The simulator is tested for efficiency for all timeout based strategies proposed in the literature.

Keywords: Coordinator, Participants, Mobile Host, Transaction, Offline transactions.

1 Introduction

The pessimistic approach says "No one can cause concurrency violation with my data if I don't let them at the data which I have it" [1]. A pessimistic strategy generally locks a row until the final updates are flushed to the database. As this requires the participants to be connected during the entire process, pessimistic strategies can't be successfully implemented in a disconnected mode of operations [2]. However the proposed commit protocols are implemented for mobile environment which handles mobility and disconnections effectively during the execution of transactions.

As long as the mobile clients are not involved in the concurrent access, the database consistency can be preserved even when the multiple mobile hosts are accessing the same data items. When more than one mobile host initiates the transactions requesting for the same data item, it can be locked by only one of the transaction. After committing the transaction, the data items held by the mobile host must be unlocked. When one transaction is being executed, the other transaction that needs the same data items, locked by the former has to wait for invariant time. Further there could be more delay because of disconnections for a longer time or inability of the mobile host to connect to the server due to congestion etc. To solve these problems, several concurrency control techniques are proposed.

N. Meghanathan et al. (Eds.): CNSA 2010, CCIS 89, pp. 603–612, 2010.
© Springer-Verlag Berlin Heidelberg 2010

The basic idea is that a transaction has to be executed within certain time period (Execution time). This information is maintained by fixed host. To achieve concurrency control, two phase locking protocol was   used in the traditional environment. However this protocol requires clients to communicate continuously with the server to obtain locks and detect the conflicts. Hence it is not suitable for mobile environments. In [3], A Timeout based Mobile Transaction Commitment Protocol uses timeouts to provide non-blocking protocol with restrained communication. It faces the problem of the time lag between local and global commit. In [4] the proposed Mobile 2PC protocol preserves the 2PC principle and minimizes the impact of unreliable wireless communication. This protocol assumes that all communicating partners are stationary hosts, equipped with sufficient computing resources and power supply with permanently available bandwidth.

The remaining part of this paper is organized as follows: Section 2 specifies the generic mobile database architecture. Section 3 specifies the architecture of the proposed mobile transaction management system, section 4 specifies the design and implementation of pessimistic commit protocol, section 5 specifies mobility management for the proposed pessimistic commit protocol, section 6 specifies the proposed data structures needed for implementation and section 7 concludes the paper.

2   Mobile Database System

The following figure specifies the reference model for mobile computing environments. It consists of two entities Fixed Host (FH) and Mobile Host (MH) respectively. Terminals, desktop, servers are the Fixed Host which is interconnected by means of a fixed network. Large databases can run on servers that guarantee efficient processing and reliable storage of database.

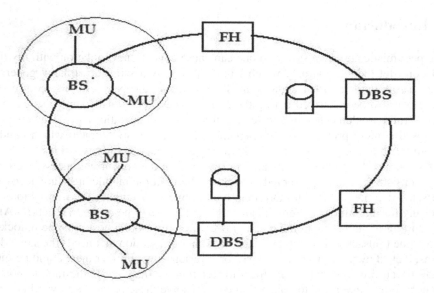

Fig. 1. Mobile Database Architecture

Mobile Hosts (MH) like Palmtops, Laptops, PDA's or Cellular phones is not always connected to the fixed network. They may be disconnected for different reasons. Mobile host may differ with respect to the computing power and storage space; however MH can run a DBMS module. Mobile host may be disconnected to save battery consumption. Hence disconnections are handled as normal situations and not as failures.

The component of the mobile transaction management system that is designed, implemented and tested is the Pessimistic commit protocol.

2.1 Pessimistic Commit Protocols

This component uses locking of data items yet enhances throughput. Four variations of this pessimistic approach are presented. The First approach uses time out mechanisms to reduce the starvation of waiting process. The second uses the dynamic timer adjustment approach to increase the overall commit rate. However two reduce the rollback operations the third strategy uses pre-emptive approach of scheduling the transactions and the fourth the predictive approach of scheduling the transaction execution. These approaches may be selected based on the business logic of the mobile application.

Mobility, disconnections and recovery issues are handled based on the strategies proposed for Mobile Transaction management Model.

3 Architecture of Mobile Transaction Management System

The generic architecture of Mobile Transaction Management System is represented in figure 2. This architecture is suitable for both online and offline transactions.

However in this paper the emphasis is on offline transactions where the transactions are executed at mobile hosts and later on the results are reconciled with the fixed host.

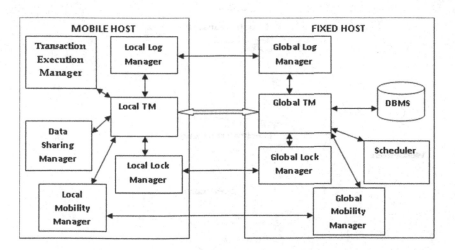

Fig. 2. Architecture of Mobile Transaction Management System

At Mobile Host, the *Local Transaction Manager* is responsible for managing the transactions at respective mobile hosts. The *Local Lock Manager*, manages the lock/unlock request initiated at mobile host. When a local transaction is committed, the *Local Log Manager* maintains log records to support Durability. The commit record in the log storage helps in reconciliation of the results onto the fixed hosts. The *Data Sharing Manager* or cache manager manages the shared data which is obtained to initiate the offline transactions. *Transaction Execution Manager* is responsible for executing offline transactions and the *Local Mobility Manager* manages the handoff information when mobile host moves from one cell to another.

At Fixed Host, the *Global Transaction Manager* is responsible for managing the transactions submitted my mobile host after the offline processing. The *Global Lock Manager* handles the lock requests initiated by Local lock Manager and makes the lock/unlock decisions. The *Global Log Manager* is responsible for making the final decision regarding the completion of a transaction and it is also responsible to maintain consistency after a failure. The *Global Mobility Manager* is responsible to manage sub-transactions to decide the final result of the transaction when the mobile host was on move during its execution. *Scheduler* is responsible for scheduling transactions for execution based on conflict resolution strategy used by the application developer.

3.1 Mapping Functionality to Architecture

Figure 3 depicts the functional requirements of Mobile Transaction Managements system captured in various use cases.

The pessimistic concurrency control supports offline transactions. Hence the mobile host initiates the request for the transaction. The Base station acts as a Global Transaction Manager. The use cases described in figure 3 are realized by following architectural elements.

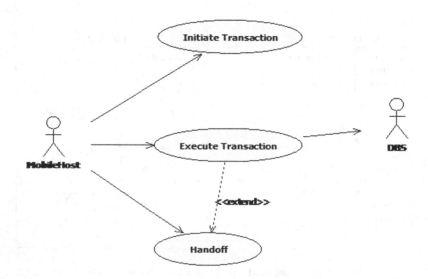

Fig. 3. Basic functionality of MTMS

- *Initiate Transaction*: The Local TM initiates the request for a transaction and the Global Transaction Manager along with Global Lock Manager locks the required data items. Scheduler is used to schedule a transaction for execution by maintaining a job queue. The required data items are copied to the mobile host for execution. The optimistic approach doesn't involve lock manager at both sites.

- *Execute transaction*: The transactions are locally committed by transaction execution manager; the results are logged by Local Log Manager. The results are reconciled with the database at fixed host using Global Log Manager and Global Transaction Manger.   In Pessimistic protocols, after successful completion of a transaction, Global Lock Manager is invoked for unlocking the data items.

- *Handoff*: When mobile host moves from one cell to another, the local mobility manager is used for registering to new Base station. The Global Mobility Manager is used to integrate the results of sub-transactions executed in various cells.

In Pessimistic Commit Protocols and Optimistic protocols, the base station acts as the coordinator and the Mobile hosts and the Database System as participants. In figure 2 the architectural elements specified at fixed host i.e. Global Transaction Manager, Global Lock Manager, Global Log Manager, Scheduler & Global Mobility Manager are logical components of the coordinator i.e. the base station.

4 Design and Implementation of Pessimistic Commit Protocols

The Pessimistic Commit Protocols uses Locking mechanism to lock the data items needed to execute an offline transaction. The transactions are then executed at mobile hosts and later results are integrated with the fixed host. To avoid blocking of data items, timeout based strategy is used in this approach where the transaction is supposed to be executed within the timer value "t".

Each transaction is executed in two phases. In the first phase request for the transaction is issued and in the second phase the execution of the requested transaction is performed.

Figure 4 depicts the behavior of Initiate Transactions for Pessimistic Protocols. An application specific user interface is provided at mobile host, where the mobile user request for execution of a transaction (1: fillform()). The request is sent to the base station (2: Submit ()), where the authorization for executing a transaction is checked (3: isTransValid()).

Then the data items needed to execute the transactions are locked if they are available (4: DataItemsAvlbl()). The information regarding the new transaction request is entered into current Transaction relations maintained at the base station and the data items are read by the mobile host (5: ReadDataItems()). After sending the data items to the mobile host, the base station starts the timer (6: StartTimer()).

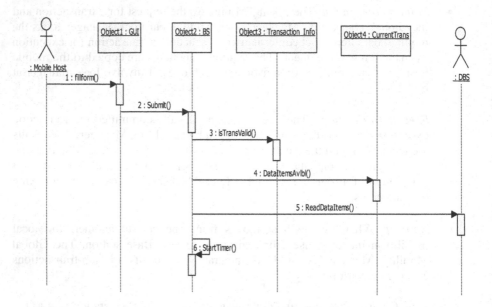

Fig. 4. Behavior of initiating a transaction for Pessimistic Protocols

These design considerations are applicable to Algorithmic approach [8], dynamic timer adjustment strategy [5] and preemptive approaches [6] of pessimistic commit protocols. However for the predictive approach [7], the data items are locked only when time for execution of a transaction is less than the timer value or partially more than the timer value "t". This business logic is implemented in isTrasValid() routine.

Figure 5 depicts the behavior of executing a transaction. If the transaction is successfully executed at mobile host before the expiry of the timer, the results are logged and are sent to fixed host for integration (2: commit()). The base station upon receiving the results updates the database system (3: Updatedata()) and unlocks the data items (4: unlockdataitems()). After successful execution of the transaction, the respective entry is removed from CurrentTrans Class.

If the timer expires before the completion of transaction, then the base station may rollback the transaction, if no other transaction is requesting for the data items which are currently locked.

A transaction which is under execution and its timer expires (1: isTimerExpired()); it has to be rolled back (2: rollback()) (Algorithmic Approach). However the transaction which was rolled back may not again execute within the same time period, it is suggested to increase the timer at the time of rollback (3: updateTimer()) (Dynamic Timer Adjustment Strategy). In case of Preemptive approach, when the timer expires the remaining time of execution is compared with the transaction if any waiting in a queue. If the remaining time of the current transaction is less it will proceed its execution. Otherwise it may be rolled back. This logic is implemented in isTimerExpired() routine. When the base station decides to rollback a transaction, the execution of the transaction may no longer continue at mobile host as such the thread at mobile host is destroyed (4. <<destroy>>).

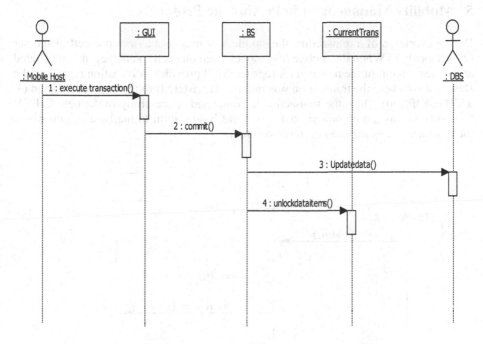

Fig. 5. Behavior of executing a transaction for Pessimistic Protocols

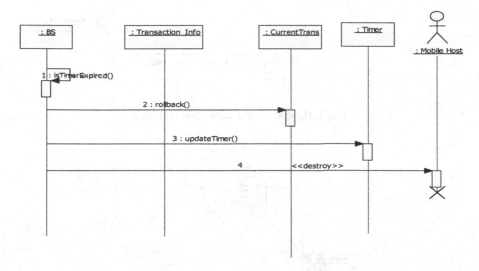

Fig. 6. Timeout behavior of Base Station

5 Mobility Management in Pessimistic Protocols

During execution of a transaction, the mobile host may move from one cell to another (2: isHandOff) . When the mobile host moves from one cell to another, it is registered at the base station in the new cell (3: register ()). It provides information regarding the Base station where the transaction was initiated (registered) to the new base station (4: addHandOffInfo). Once the transaction is completed successfully in the new Cell (5: Commit), results are communicated by current base station to the base station where the transaction was initiated (6: returnresult()).

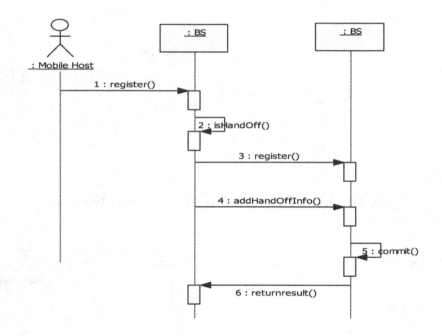

Fig. 7. Handoff during transaction execution

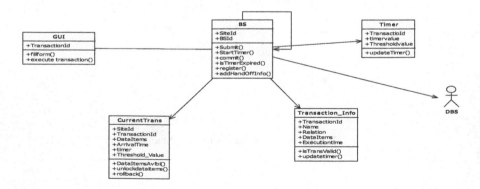

Fig. 8. Class diagram for the implementation of Pessimistic Protocols

As described in figure 8, the Current Trans, Transactio_Info, Timer and BS are modeled as persistent classes. The Current Trans class acts as Home Location Register.

6 Data Structures

(a) The Transaction_Info relation stores the list of possible transactions which can be executed on mobile host. This information is stored at base station

Table 1. Structure of Transaction_Info relation

TransactionId	Name	Relation	Data Item(s)	Execution Time

Each transaction is identified by Transactionid or Name. The transaction uses the data items of the relation for execution of transaction. The execution time specifies expected time for execution of a transaction.

The advantage of using this relation is to reduce the lookup operation needed to know the data items for execution of a transaction.

(b) The Current Transactions relation contains the list of current transactions executed at site i

Table 2. Structure of Current Transactions Relation

Site_Id	TransactionId	Data_Items	Arrival Time

The Site_Id represents a particular mobile host that requested for execution of a transaction identified by TransactionId which needs Data_Items . TheArrival Time specifies the time at which the data items are copied onto mobile host for offline execution of transaction. This relation is used keep track of all sites, which are executing a particular transaction. This relation helps in managing the row locking.

(c) Timer relation maintains the timer information needed for executing a transaction

Table 3. Structure of Timer Relation

TransactionId	Timer Value	Threshold Value

For each transaction, the timer value which represents the expected time in which the transaction must completed and the Threshold value which represents the time in which the transaction must complete otherwise it may be aborted. This attribute is used in dynamic timer adjustment strategy, pre-emptive strategy and predictive strategy.

(d) Base Station relation maintains the information of mobile host during handoffs

Table 4. Structure of Base Station Relation

Site Id	Base Station Id

The base station id represents the base station to which a mobile host is identified by SiteId is registered.

7 Conclusion

The Pessimistic commit protocols were verified using the simulated environment. The conceptual and logical design for the simulator was presented. The simulator works effectively for all timeout based pessimistic commit protocols. It was implemented using the Model view controller architecture. The functionality of base station corresponds to controller component and the model represents the Database system and the view corresponds to the user interface provided by mobile application. The future work may present the simulator for the implementation of optimistic commit protocols.

References

1. Plourede, S.W.: Handling Concurrency Issues in .NET (2005), http://www.15seconds.com/issue/030604.htm (Web retreieve February 19, 2005)
2. Basu, S., Rahman, S.M.: Improving Optimistic Concurrency Control using Hybrid Techniques of Snapshot Isolation & ROCC. In: Kumar, V., Prabhu, N., Dunham, M., Seydim, A.Y. (eds.) Proceedings of Mid-west Instruction & Computing Symposium 2006, TCOT - A Timeout based Mobile Transaction Commitment Protocol, IIS 9979453 (2004)
3. Nouali, N., Doucet, A., Drias, H.: A Two-Phase Commit Protocol for Mobile Wireless Environment. In: 16th Australasian Database Conference, vol. 39 (2005)
4. Moiz, S.A., Rajamani, L.: Single Lock Manager Approach for achieving Concurrency in Mobile Environments. In: Aluru, S., Parashar, M., Badrinath, R., Prasanna, V.K. (eds.) HiPC 2007. LNCS, vol. 4873, pp. 650–660. Springer, Heidelberg (2007)
5. Moiz, S.A., Rajamani, L.: Concurrency Control Strategy to Reduce frequent rollbacks in Mobile Environments. In: 2009 IEEE/IFIP International Symposium on Trusted Computing (TrustCom 2009), vol. 2, pp. 709–714 (2009), ISBN# 978-0-7695-3823-5
6. Moiz, S.A., Rajamani, L.: An Efficient Strategy for achieving Concurrency Control in Mobile Environments. In: Hong, C.S., Tonouchi, T., Ma, Y., Chao, C.-S. (eds.) APNOMS 2009. LNCS, vol. 5787, pp. 519–522. Springer, Heidelberg (2009)
7. Moiz, S.A., Rajamani, L.: An Algorithmic approach for achieving concurrency in Mobile Environments. In: 1st National Conference on Computing for Nation Development, INDIACom (2007), ISBN #978-81-094526-0-1, ISSN # 0973-7529

On Analyzing the Degree of Coldness in Iowa, a North Central Region, United States: An XML Exploitation in Spatial Databases

Sugam Sharma and Shashi K. Gadia

226 Atanasoff Hall,
Department of Computer Science
Iowa State University, Ames, Iowa,
USA 50011
sugam.k.sharma@gmail.com, gadia@cs.iastate.edu

Abstract. State of Iowa is an agricultural rich state in north central region and is divided into 99 counties. NCRA in the United States maintains agricultural databases to facilitate crop and risk analysis, pest management and forecasting. NC94 is one such dataset which is intensively used and is available for public use through many sources to process and analyze to get future predictions about agriculture. In this work we calculate the cumulative degree of coldness in Iowa with spatial granularity as county in last 30 years. To demonstrate the degree of coldness, we choose blue as the base color and counties are rendered with different shades of blue color based on the degree of coldness. Higher intensity of the color reflects the higher coldness whereas the lower intensity corresponds to lower coldness. We expect that the results of this research provide direct benefits to farmers and will attract the attention of agricultural/ computational scientific community.

Keywords: NC94, XML, Coldness, County, Iowa.

1 Introduction

Spatial databases are exploited vastly in different applications of diversified areas such as geography, geology, city planning, agriculture, environmental study, traffic navigation, aerospace industries, and so on. We focus on spatio-temporal database arising in agriculture.

The North Central region is one of the most intensely cultivated areas for row crop production. Iowa is one such state in north central region of United States. For last 50 year, The North Central Regional Association of Agricultural Experiment Station (NCRA) in the United States is verifying, developing and validating agricultural databases. The association has collected an important, internally consistent dataset called the *NC94*. The *NC94* dataset is used intensively to facilitate crop and risk analysis, pest management and forecasting. In addition, it is publicly accessed through the internet, allowing the public to ask ad-hoc queries [1].

N. Meghanathan et al. (Eds.): CNSA 2010, CCIS 89, pp. 613–624, 2010.
© Springer-Verlag Berlin Heidelberg 2010

NC94 is a compilation of 30 years county-level crop-climate-soil database, focused on producing a continuous high quality county-level data of commonly measured quantities of air temperature, precipitation, crop yield and soils data. It is an important resource in the agricultural community and analyzing the dataset would yield invaluable understanding for scientists, public, farmers, planners, and policy makers to improve crop practices and yields, undertake scientific studies, and develop policy.

In this research, only the climatic data of *NC94* dataset has been used. Climate data is in Geographical Markup Language (GML) format. It has been developed by the OpenGIS as a medium for uniform geographic data storage and exchange among diverse applications and is being exploited enormously in geospatial databases. The climate data is loaded in a local storage called CanStoreX before any executable query is applied.

CanStoreX is an XML storage technology known as a Canonical Storage for XML [2]. It paginates a large XML document and stores it in the storage. Thus CanStoreX is used as a back-end for storing NC-94 data hiding the heterogeneity in climate, crop, and soil data in order to allow the user a simple view of counties as objects where geographical and time dimensions are implicit and taken for granted. Currently, binary pagination algorithm has been tested for XML documents up to 1 terabytes in size. An XML document in CanStoreX remains in a ready state for access. All the related commands are run from an integrated GUI based framework.

This integrated GUI framework, an in-house development, provides a common platform to run the parametric query of different subsystems. To make GUI aware about a subsystem, a suffix is assigned before the command of that subsystem is issued e.g. NC94 :> loadnc94data climate where NC94 is the name of target subsystem. Once the data is uploaded (use LoadNC94Data) in local CanStoreX, it needs to be opened (use OpenNC94Database command) before any parametric query is run.

The GUI also provides button-based following features to execute certain commands and a single click event on any button fires the respective command.

- Load Command
- Clear Command
- Save Command
- Run Command
- Run Selected Command

The execution of a parametric climate query on the common GUI framework returns the desired data of *NC94* data set which is used as the input for further processing. The output returned by parametric query is in text format and consists of many attributes. Some of the attributes are of our great interest and help to get the degree of coldness in an individual county when applied to a model to calculate the coldness.

The rest of the paper is organized as follows:

Section 2 describes our approach toward this research work. In section 3 we discuss the formulation view of our approaches. In section 4 analyze the results. In section 5 the related work has been discussed. Section 6 discusses the future work and concludes the paper.

2 Approach

The motivation behind the research work is to analyze the coldness in all counties in Iowa in 30 years period. Figure 1 shows object oriented complete architecture of our research methodology and this section elaborates each and every object as follows.

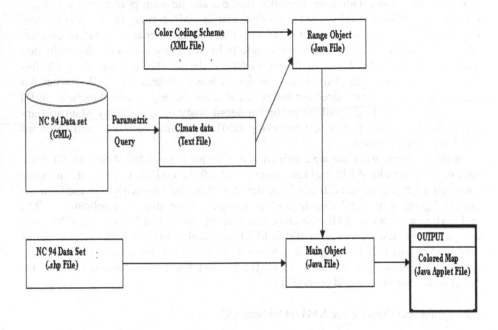

Fig. 1. Architecture of research methodology

2.1 NC94 Dataset

The North Central region is one of the most intensely cultivated areas for row crop production. Iowa is one such state in north central region of United States. It is also known as the "Food Capital of the World." For last 50 year, The North Central Regional Association of Agricultural Experiment Station (NCRA) in the United States is verifying, developing and validating agricultural databases. The association has collected an important, internally consistent dataset called the *NC94*. The NC94 dataset is used intensively to facilitate crop and risk analysis, pest management and forecasting. In addition, it is publicly accessed through the internet, allowing the public to ask ad-hoc queries [1]. In order to use the *NC94* dataset for scientific purpose, many scientific data formats are used with software packages to store and process it for environmental development. Despite the advantages of the scientific data formats, it is not easy for the public to directly access the rich dataset stored in scientific data formats because they are not database management systems which directly support ad-hoc queries.

NC94 dataset contains the important spatial data of north central region of United States. It is a compilation of 30 years crop-climate-soil database, focused on producing a continuous high quality county-level data of commonly measured quantities of air temperature, precipitation, crop yield and soils data. It is an important resource in the agricultural community and analyzing the dataset would yield invaluable understanding for scientists, public, farmers, planners, and policy makers to improve crop practices and yields, undertake scientific studies, and develop policy. We use *NC94* data set in two formats; 1) shape file format, and 2) GML format. In [4] authors mention that IEM (Iowa Environmental Mesonet) has collected many important datasets of evolving atmospheric, soil and hydrologic fields for analysis and for dissemination and have provided the shape file format of *NC94* dataset. We use the shape file format for the graphical display of all counties in Iowa whereas the GML format has been used to fetch the required attributes to calculate the degree of coldness in all 99 counties of Iowa. In [5] authors present a detail study on Geography Markup Language (GML), issues that arise from using GML for spatial databases and solutions that have been proposed.

In this research, work we are confined with climatic data of *NC94* dataset. Climatic data is in Geographical Markup Language (GML) format. GML is an XML encoding for storing geographic data. It has been developed by the OpenGIS as a medium for uniform geographic data storage and exchange among diverse applications. The underlying concepts of XML therefore can also be applied to GML data. GML is a comparatively new language in the field of geographic information systems but is exploited enormously in geospatial databases. Though there is a need to develop few more data processing techniques for GML, but today it is an efficient medium for geographic data storage and processing.

2.2 Canonical Storage for XML (CanStoreX)

CanStoreX is an in-house developed XML storage technology known as Canonical Storage for XML [2]. It ramifies an XML document into pages and stores them in the paginated form in the storage. The initial implementation of CanStoreX for storing XML document and DOM API, called DiskDOM for their access was undertaken by Shihe Ma [3], and used textual representation for pages, and a common Java based DOM API for navigation within pages. Thus every page is seen as a java based Node object by its DiskDOM. Due to heap-based management of memory for the objects in Java, the system would choke when paginating or accessing XML documents beyond 1 gigabyte range. Currently, binary pagination algorithm has been tested for XML documents up to 1 terabytes in size.

Pages within the storage are interconnected using special nodes called storage facilitating nodes (*sfn*). Currently there are two types of *sfn* available to facilitate: f-node, and c-node. The f-node is used to group one or more siblings having the same parent. A c-node contains a pointer to a child page where a subtree rooted at an f-node resides. Each page itself is organized as a self contained legal XML document. Thus the whole XML document becomes a tree of pages where each page, and XML document on its own right, is stored as a tree in a binary format. An XML document in CanStoreX remains in a ready state for access.

Previously only climate data was available and was stored in an older version of CanStoreX where XML was stored in text form. The newer binary version of CanStoreX allows a readily available tree-like navigation in the paginated XML document. Addition of crop and soil data requires different internal representation in order to achieve a uniform view for users that is at par with the climate data. Further, the internals were conformed to use the version of CanStoreX where pages are stored in binary, rather than text form.

Thus CanStoreX is used as a back-end for storing *NC94* data hiding the heterogeneity in climate, crop, and soil data in order to allow the user a simple view of counties as objects where geographical and time dimensions are implicit and taken for granted. Following lines of XML tags show XML representation of a fractional part of *NC94* dataset. Attributes with name as StFIPS and CoFIps are correspond to state and county FIPS (Federal Information Processing Standards) code which make a county as a unique location with respect to that spatial *NC94* database.

```
<?xml version="1.0" encoding="UTF-8" standalone="no" ?>
<Database Name="NC-94" homogeniety="false">
<RelationList number="3">
<Relationame="climate"StorageFragment         Key="FIPS"         ctype="hybrid"
spatialGranularity="county"
SpatialRepresentation="FIPS"TemporalGranularity="day"TemporalRepresentation="
                        integer" rtype="spatiotemporal">
<Key> <Attribute>FIPS</Attribute> </Key>
  <AttributeList number="9">
      <Attribute length="32" name="FIPS" pos="0" type="string" />
      <Attribute length="4" name="StFIPS" pos="1" type="integer" />
      <Attribute length="4" name="CoFIPS" partition="true" pos="2"
      type="integer" />
      <Attribute length="4" name="Year" pos="3" type="integer" />
      <Attribute length="4" name="Day" pos="4" type="integer" />
      <Attribute length="4" name="Radiation" pos="5" type="float" />
      <Attribute length="4" name="MaxTemp" pos="6" type="float" />
      <Attribute length="4" name="MinTemp" pos="7" type="float" />
      <Attribute length="4" name="Precipitation" pos="8" type="float" />
  </AttributeList>
  <SpatialRelation name="county_gml" />
  </Relation>
...
</RelationList>
</Database>
```

Following is the curtailed XML catalog of Climate relation. Each tuple has a key attribute as *FIPS* which differentiates it from rests of the tuples. As we are dealing with spatial data, the first left most bits of FIPS value show the state FIPS (FIPs value is 19 for Iowa State) and right most three bits represent the county in that state. Rests of the tags are self descriptive.

```
<Relation name="climate" homogeneity="true" TupleSize="64 bytes">
 <Tuple pageID="833">
  <KeyAttributes>
  <Attribute name="FIPS" value="19001" />
 </KeyAttributes>
   <ParametricElement domain="temporal">
    <Interval start="0" end="10958" />
   </ParametricElement>
   <Info totalPages="43" totalItems="10958" />
 </Tuple>
<Tuple pageID="876">
  <KeyAttributes>
   <Attribute name="FIPS" value="19003" />
  </KeyAttributes>
  <ParametricElement domain="temporal">
   <Interval start="0" end="10958" />
  </ParametricElement>
  <Info totalPages="43" totalItems="10958" />
 </Tuple>
 ...
</Relation>
```

2.3 Common GUI

In this research work we use an in-house graphical user interface (GUI) to run the parametric commands [4]. This interface provides a common platform to run the query of different subsystems. To make GUI aware about a subsystem, a suffix is assigned before the command of that subsystem is issued. Figure 2 shows a snapshot of common GUI and a sample command is shown below:

$$NC94 :> loadnc94data \; climate;$$

GUI parser parses this above string in two substrings with :> as a separator. The left side of :> is the suffix which represents the target subsystem and the first part in the right side is the command and second part separated by a single space is the relation name on which query is applied.

As figure 2 shows, GUI has four text areas: 1) the left top text area is used to write the command prefixed by the subsystem, 2) the bottom left reflects the status of the command just fired, 3) top right text area displays the results of execution of the command just got executed, and 4) the bottom right area gives the performance statistics such as disk accesses are displayed, and a flags area where status of several flags can be indicated. In addition there are radio buttons to load, and execute same command files.

Buttons to clear input and output panes, find & replace, and to reset certain counters are included. The functionalities of buttons from left to right in GUI are as follows.

- Load Command - It allows the user to load a text file containing a batch of commands into the command editor pane.

- Clear Command - It clears the contents of the command editor pane.

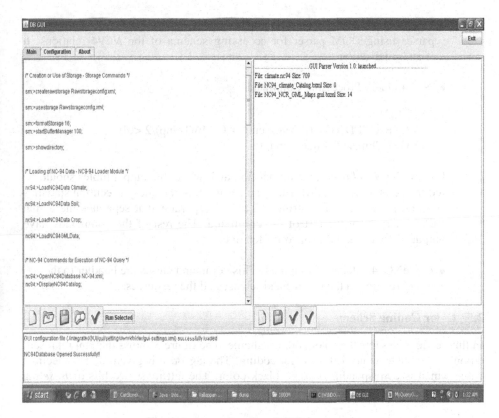

Fig. 2. In-house developed GUI framework

- Save Command -It allows the user to save the batch of commands from the command editor pane into a text file.

- Run Command - It executes all the command in the command editor pane. Two different commands are separated by a character ";".

- Run Selected Command - It gives the flexibility to the user to execute only the highlighted command in the command editor pane.

2.4 ParaSQL Query

In our research work we use the below sets of commands for loading the *NC94* dataset to the storage, parsing the client query and creating a parse tree, building a expression tree, executing a query, and redirecting the resultant tuples to the output text file.

- LoadNC94Data -This command is used for invoking the loader module for loading the NC94 data set into the common storage. Out of 'climate' or 'soil' or 'crop', this command takes any one of he relations as input parameter and loads the specific relation into the common storage.

- OpenNC94Database -This command opens the *NC94* XML catalog and parses using DOM parser for accessing schema of the *NC94* relations. It is an initialization step.

- NC94 Query Processing Command

  SELECT *
  RESTRICTED TO [[(C.MaxTemp + C.MinTemp)/2 <0]]
  FROM Climate C ‖ queryop.txt;

It takes the *NC94* query, the output filename where the output tuples should be redirected and the log XML filename for logging the query execution statistics as input parameters. The string "‖" acts a separator that separates the actual *NC94* query from the rest of the command. The rest of the commands have output file name and the log xml filename.

- CloseNC94Database Command -This command closes the handler to the *NC94* relation in the storage and releases all the resources.

2.5 Color Coding Scheme

In this section we show the color coding scheme. The figure 3 shows the xml representation of the contents needed for color coding. The tag *Base* is given the hexadecimal value which is corresponding to dark black color. The left most two bits of *Base* tag value are correspond to red color, the middle two bits are corresponded to green color

```
<Color_Coding_Scheme>

    <Base>000000</Base>

    <Number_of_Range>5</Number_of_Range>

    <Lowest_Value> 100</Lowest_Value>

    <Highest_Value> 500</Highest_Value>

</Color_Coding_Scheme>
```

Fig. 3. XML representation of color coding scheme

whereas the last two right most bits are used to manipulate the blue color. Tag *Number_of_Ranges* shows the range of shades of a base color we use in the rendition of the map. The tag *Lowest_Value* and *Highest_Value* are the highest and lowest boundaries of degree of coldness, one can expect. These values have substantial marginal difference from the actual value of the degree of coldness in any county.

Range and *Main* are two user defined java objects. *Range* generates a map (java Collection interface) which consists of the set of county FIPs and the corresponding degree of coldness as the key-value pairs and injects this map to Main object. Based on the degree of coldness, *Main* object helps to paint the county with a shade of blue color.

3 Formulation

This section describes the mathematical formulation of the model we use in our research work to calculate the degree of coldness and color coding scheme to render the coldness on the map.

3.1 Algorithm to Calculate the Degree of Coldness

The below is the pseudocode to calculate the degree of coldness in a county.

Line 1 helps to store the set of states extracted from *NC94* dataset into an array. As for this research purpose we are interested to confine within Iowa only so the array in line 1 is iterated to extract the spatial data in Iowa only and variable S in line 4 temporarily holds the state name. Line 5 helps to check whether the stored state in variable S is Iowa. Once line 5 returns true, all counties of Iowa are extracted and stored in another array CC as shown in line 7.

ALGORITHM 1. To calculate the degree of coldness in a county

---

1. Array SS ← {set of all states in North Central Region in NC-94 dataset }
2. WHILE (SS. length >=0)
3. BEGIN
4.   S ← Extracted state from array
5.   IF (S equals Iowa)
6.   BEGIN
7.   Array CC ← set of counties of Iowa
8.   for(int i=0; i <=CC.length; i++)
9.   BEGIN
10.   Number of cold days: $n \leftarrow \left\{ \left(\dfrac{Temp.MAX + Temp.MIN}{2} \right) \leq 0 \right\}$
11.   Number of day in 30 years: N
12.   Degree of coldness = n/N
13.   END
14.   END
15. END

This array is iterated to calculate the number of days in which the average of maximum temperature and minimum temperature is less than zero and line 10 in this pseudocode is corresponding to that operation. Once the numbers of cold days are calculated, then it is extremely straight forward to calculate the degree of coldness over a 30 years period and line 12 in pseudocode helps to return the degree of coldness of a particular county at a time, thus finally when the *for* loop in line 8 is exhausted, we obtain the calculated degree of coldness for all counties in Iowa.

3.2 Model to Calculate the Darkness

Let us assume that *Highest_Value* is the highest limit and *Lowest_Value* is the lowest limit of the degree of coldness expected in any county. We supply these values in XML file. We further assume that *Current_Value* represents the actual degree of coldness for a particular county calculated using Algorithm 1. Then the degree of darkness is obtained as follows.

$$\text{Degree of darkness} = \frac{\text{Highest\_Value} - \text{Current\_Value}}{\text{Highest\_Value} - \text{Lowest\_Value}}$$

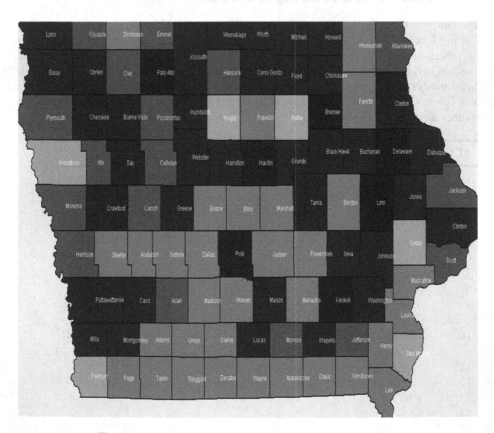

Fig. 4. The display of degree of coldness in all counties of Iow

4 Results

Figure 4 is a map showing all 99 counties of Iowa State. Each and every county is painted with a shade of blue color. The shade with higher intensity reflects the higher degree of coldness and the shade with lower intensity reflects the lower degree of coldness in a particular county for duration of 30 years.

In the map we see that most of the counties at up north in Iowa have more intensified shades whereas the counties at the down south in Iowa have lighter shades of blue color. From this we can infer that the upper side (north) counties of Iowa have higher degree of coldness than that of down side (south).

County Palo Alto is one of the counties consisting of highest degree of coldness whereas Cedar belongs to that set of counties which has lowest degree of coldness.

5 Related Work

In [6] author has compiled the detailed discussion about the common GUI and its command execution. He has discussed each and every features of GUI and talked about all parametric commands useful to process *NC94* dataset. In paper [7] authors have given a broad description of XML language with additional features. Authors in paper [8] give a tour of a database management system designed from scratch for storing and processing XML data, called Natix. This motivated Ma [3] for the development of CanStoreX technology. The paper [9] describes the overall design and architecture of the Timber XML database system, based upon bulk algebra for manipulating trees, and natively stores XML. This also worked as a strong motivation behind the development of CanStoreX technology. In the paper [10] authors present an XML-based implementation methodology for the parametric temporal data model and in the implementation, they develop a new XML storage called CanStoreX (Canonical Storage for XML) and build the temporal database system on top of the CanStoreX. In [11] North Central Regional Association of State Agricultural Experiment Station Directors (NCRA) develops a strategy for data collection that helps in study, efficient crop management and to reduce the risk factors associated with agriculture practices, which depends on various factors. The collection and organization of data based on the states in the north-central region of the United States is mentioned as the primary goal of the Association and climate, crop and soil data is collected for these states. The result of data collection and organization efforts is the *NC94* dataset which we use extensively in our research work.

6 Conclusion and Future Work

Iowa State is an agricultural rich state in north central region of United States. Entire Iowa State is divided into 99 counties. In this paper, we have calculated and analyzed the cumulative degree of coldness in all counties over last 30 years duration and the calculation of the degree of coldness is based on the precipitation. The degree of coldness has been depicted using blue as the base color. The increase and decrease in degree of coldness is analogous to the higher and lower intensity of the base color respectively. We expect that the obtained results will provide direct benefits to farmers and help agricultural/ computational scientific community in future research.

The future task involves the calculation of monthly precipitation, cumulative high temperature, monthly high temperature, heat precipitation ratio, and growing degree Days (GDD), a measure of heat accumulation used by horticulturists and gardeners to predict the date about a flower to bloom or a crop to reach maturity.

References

1. Seo-Young, N.: Hybrid Storage Design for NC-94 Database within the Parametric Data Model Framework. In: Proceedings of the International Conference on Computational Science and Its Applications, Part II, Glasgow, UK, May 8-11, pp. 145–154 (2006)
2. Patanroi, D.: Binary Page Implementation of a Canonical Native Storage for XML. Master's thesis, Department of Computer Science, Iowa State University, Ames, Iowa (August 2005)
3. Ma, S.: Implementation of a canonical native storage for XML. Master's Thesis, Department of Computer Science, Iowa State University (2004)
4. Gadia, S.K., Gutowski, W.J., Al-Kaisi, M., Taylor, S.E., Herzmann, D.: Database tools promoting extensive, user-friendly access to the iowa environmental mesonet. Baker Proposal (2004)
5. Sripada, L.N., Lu, C.-T., Wu, W.: Evaluating GML Support for Spatial Databases. In: 28th Annual International Computer Software and Applications Conference - Workshops and Fast Abstracts - (COMPSAC 2004) compsac, vol. 2, pp. 74–77 (2004)
6. Narayanan, V.: A Workbench for Advanced Database Implementation and Benchmarking. Master's thesis, Department of Computer Science, Iowa State University, Ames, Iowa (2009)
7. Bray, T., Paoli, J., Sperberg-McQueen, C.M., Maler, E., Yergeau, F.: Extensible- Markup Language (XML) 1.0., W3C recommendation, 4th edn., August 16 (2006)
8. Fiebig, T., Helmer, S., Kanne, C.-C., Moerkotte, G., Neumann, J., Schiele, R., Westmann, T.: Anatomy of a native XML base management system. Springer, Heidelberg (2002)
9. Jagadish, H.V., Al-Khalifa, S., Chapman, A., Lakshmanan, L.V.S., Nierman, A., Paparizos, S., Patel, J.M., Srivastava, D., Wiwatwattana, N., Wu, Y., Yu, C.: TIMBER: A native XML database. VLDB Journal 11(4), 274–291 (2002)
10. Noh, S.-Y., Gadia, S.K., Ma, S.: An XML-based methodology for parametric temporal database model implementation. Journal of Systems and Software 81(6) (June 2008)
11. North Central Regional Association of State Agricultural Experiment Station Directors. Expected Outcomes. NC094: Impact of Climate and Soils on Crop Selection and Management (September 2004)

Implementation of MPEG-7 Document Management System Based on Native Database

Byeong-Tae Ahn

Information & Communication Center, Catholic University, Songsim Campus Yeouido
P.O. BOX 960, Yeongdeungpo-gu, Seoul, 150-010, Korea
ahnbt@catholic.ac.kr

Abstract. Embedded database technology can be used to manage MPEG-7 data with limited resources. In that case, we need a clustering method for the efficient storage of MPEG-7 documents. The present study designed and implemented a MPEG-7 document management system that can store MPEG-7 documents efficiently in mobile terminals such as PDA. The system used Berkeley DB XML, an embedded XML database system based on MPEG-7 data clustering.

Keywords: MPEG-7, Embedded Database, XML.

1 Introduction

In order to manage large-capacity multimedia contents efficiently in mobile environment, it is essential to manage metadata about multimedia contents under limited resources.

Recently, MPEG-7 has been adopted as an international standard of multimedia contents description method for the effective handling of multimedia. MPEG-7 is a standard method of describing multimedia contents, namely, a standard that defines the metadata of multimedia in the form of XML[1]. The object of MPEG-7 is how to express the contents of multimedia data. Accordingly, it enables the extraction of characteristics from multimedia data or the use of multimedia data through a search engine. MPEG-7 defines characteristics extracted from multimedia using descriptors and description schemes in the form of XML, and makes it possible to handle multimedia data in various forms[2].

For the effective management of MPEG-7 documents in mobile terminals, native embedded XML database technology can be used as an efficient method of storing MPEG-7 documents in such terminals[3]. Here, we need the support of a clustering method suitable for the characteristic of MPEG-7 data.

The present study designed and implemented a MPEG-7 document management system (MDMS) based on Berkeley DB XML[4], a native embedded XML database system, using a MPEG-7 data clustering method. The developed MDMS stores MPEG-7 documents, clustering them based on MPEG-7 schema.

This paper is composed as follows. First, Section 2 reviews related works, and Section 3 explain the proposed clustering method. Section 4 designs MDMS, and Section 5

N. Meghanathan et al. (Eds.): CNSA 2010, CCIS 89, pp. 625–634, 2010.
© Springer-Verlag Berlin Heidelberg 2010

implements the system. Lastly, Section 6 draws conclusions and suggests tasks for future research.

2 Related Works

MPEG-7 database management can utilize XML document database management technology. For this reason, recent researches on MPEG-7 database management are mainly focused on how to apply XML document database management technology[5]. In this trend, researches on MPEG-7 database management system are performed in two directions. One is to expand existing database management systems (mainly relational and object-oriented relational database systems) with the functions of XML document management so that they can support MPEG-7, and the other is to expand native XML database management systems. Representative systems for the former are DB2 XML Extender of IBM[6], Web DataBlade of Informix[7], XML for SQL Server 2000 of Microsoft[8], Oracle 9i of Oracle[9], etc. These database systems expand existing XML document management functions, and are used mainly in data-centered applications. Representative systems for the latter are Tamino of Software AG[10], X-Hive/DB of X-Hive[11], XIS of eXcelon[12], Ipedo of Ipedo[13], etc. These database systems store XML documents in the form of parsed XML, and are used mainly in document-centered applications.

In general, native XML database systems define a logical model of XML documents and use the model in storing and retrieving XML documents according to the model, and are used mainly in document-centered applications. Thus, native XML database systems are divided into text-based ones and model-based ones according to the model storing XML documents[14]. Text-based native XML database systems store the whole of an XML document in text, and provide several database functions to access the document, and model-based native XML database systems stores a binary model of XML documents like a DOM tree. However, few of them are applied to an embedded system in consideration of mobile environment.

In general, an embedded system has very limited hardware resources. Thus, in consideration of limited hardware resources of the embedded system for handling multimedia, mobile devices like PDA must use a method that retrieves only necessary multimedia and metadata information from the server and manages them.

Recently with increasing necessity of XML document database management in mobile devices, researches are being made actively on embedded XML DBMS and, as a result, various types of embedded XML DBMS are being developed. Representative embedded XML DBMSs are InfonyteDB[15], etc. They enable the update of XML document data on the level of element, the smallest data unit. However, they do not provide key functions of traditional DBMS such as transaction management, parallel control and recovery management. Recently, however, Sleepycat developed an embedded database system called Berkeley DB XML that supports XML[4]. This is open software built on Berkeley DB[12], which is a product for industrial use and contains approved basic functions of database systems. Most of all, in order to supports various types of devices, the software allow users to choose functions and build up embedded DBMS freely. In addition, as it is provided as a library directly connected to client applications, it enhances performance through reducing transactions between processes or systems. We developed MDMS adopting the MPEG-7 data clustering technique in order to utilize Berkeley DB XML in MPEG-7 database management.

3 MPEG-7 Data Clustering

Berkeley DB XML mentioned above was developed as a database system managing ordinary XML documents. Accordingly, we need a management method that reflect characteristics specific to MPEG-7 although MPEG-7 is one of XML document forms. In the article[13] we proposed a new data clustering method applicable to MPEG-7 documents. In this research, we adopted the method to develop MDMS, and this chapter gives a brief explanation about the method.

Because MPEG-7 documents are a type of XML, they use an XML database system. Here, various XML document clustering methods proposed in[13] can be applied. Different from ordinary XML documents, however, MPEG-7 documents deal with the characteristics of multimedia, so the clustering policy must consider this aspect thoroughly.

The MPEG-7 data clustering method indicates relevancies among elements using a number between 0 and 99. This is called R-CT (Relationship-ClusTer) attribute, which was added to the existing MPEG-7 schema. In order to extract the level of the R-CT attribute, various MPEG-7 applications were analyzed and, based on the results of the analysis, three rules were formulated. First, if the parent element was the same, the same level was given and the R-CT attribute was set at 1. If the parent element was different, different levels were given, and the R-CT attribute was set at a number between 2 and 9. Lastly, in case definition was made separately when the user generated a MPEG-7 schema, the user-defined level was given and the R-CT attribute was set at a number between 10 and 99. The redefined MPEG-7 schema was analyzed by the system, and semantic blocks were formed, which clustered elements considered to be handled together semantically. There are two rules of forming semantic blocks: (Rule S1) if elements have a value for the R-CT attributes and have child nodes, they are clustered into the same semantic block; and (Rule 2) if elements have cardinality and have child nodes, they are clustered into the same semantic block.

First, each element is analyzed by applying Rule S1. For the example above, the R-CT attribute has a value from 1 to 3. Next, elements with cardinality are searched according to Rule S2. We can see that S2 was applied to those with cardinality among elements, to which Rule S1 was applied. Fig. 1 is the final form resulting from dividing an actual MPEG-7 schema tree into semantic blocks using the semantic block composition rules. Largely eight semantic blocks were formed. The tree of these semantic blocks is simplified further. That is, nodes belonging to the same semantic block are merged into a node.

Lastly, the simplified semantic block tree is stored in the way that document instances generated from the same semantic block are positioned closely to one another within a physical block based on depth-first search (DFS). First, the root node is visited, and then its child nodes are visited one by one through DFS to check if the corresponding child node can be stored within the designated block. Instances generated based on the simplified semantic block tree are stored within the same block as much as possible. Fig. 2 shows how instances were stored by block applied to the example above.

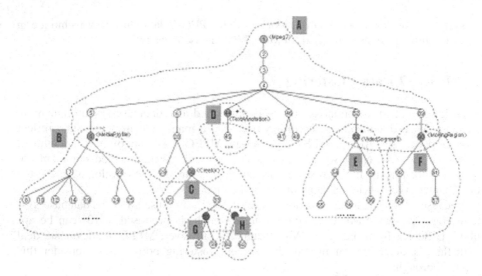

Fig. 1. Semantic Block Schema Graph

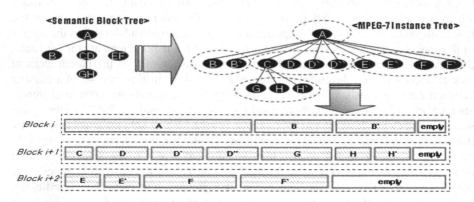

Fig. 2. Classified by Group Storage Type

Because the MPEG-7 data clustering storage method consider the relationships among MPEG-7 elements, it reduces the storage space in the limited system in comparison with that before the application of clustering, and forms the semantic block most optimal for a specific application. However, it requires the preliminary work of analyzing various applications and setting their R-CT. For more details, see[13].

4   Design of MDMS

Adopting the MPEG-7 clustering method presented in the previous chapter, we developed a MPEG-7 document management system (MDMS). This chapter examines the design of the MDMS.

4.1 General Structure of MDMS

Fig. 3 is the general structure of the MDMS.

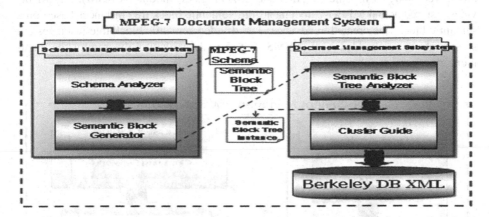

Fig. 3. Architecture of MDMS

The MDMS consists largely of two subsystems: schema management subsystem (SMS) generating semantic block trees based on redefined MPEG-7 schema documents and document management subsystem that divides a generated semantic block tree into semantic block instances based on actual MPEG-7 documents and stores them into Berkeley DB XML in the clustering method.

4.2 Schema Management Subsystem

The schema management subsystem (SMS) is composed of two modules: schema analysis module (SAM) that analyzes a schema and the R-CT attribute of each element, and semantic block generation module (SGM) that generates semantic blocks based on the analyzed schema and express them in a tree. Fig. 4 is the structural diagram of SMS.

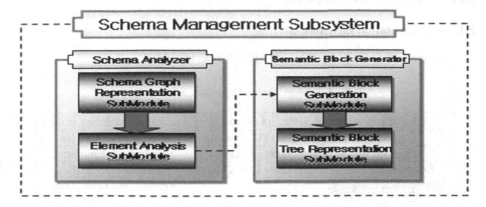

Fig. 4. Schema Management Subsystem

4.3 Document Management Subsystem

The document management subsystem is largely composed of two modules: semantic block tree analysis module (STAM) and cluster guide module (CSGM). STAM divides a stored actual MPEG-7 document into semantic block tree instances based on a semantic block tree created in advance. The divided semantic block tree instances are stored into the embedded XML DBMS. Fig. 5 is the structural diagram of the document management subsystem.

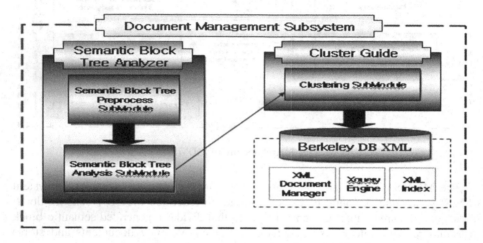

Fig. 5. Document Management Subsystem

5   Implementation of MDMS

This chapter examines the result of implementing the MDSM designed in the previous chapter. First, we explain implementation environment and then the package components of the MDMS. In addition, we describe the detailed class diagram of the packages and how to use the packages.

5.1 Implementation Environment

The environment for implementing the MDMS is as in Table 1.

Table 1. Implementation Environment of MDMS

Classification	Main Environment	Test Emulator Environment
Computer	Pentium IV, 2.8GHz	Pentium IV. 2.8GHz
Operation	Window XP	Window CE Emulator
Database System	Berkeley DB XML	Berkeley DB XML
Development Language	Java	Visual Studio.Net, Java

In the desktop computer for main environment was used Berkeley DB XML 2.0 to store MPEG-7 documents, and Java was used as a system development language. APIs for connection to the embedded XML database were designed using APIs provided by Berkeley DB XML 2.0 used for implementation. In addition, index queries to be used in the embedded XML database were processed using the index processing functions of Berkeley DB XML. Moreover, because MDSS should be executed in the real embedded system, we tested using a window CE emulator.

5.2 MDMS Packages

Fig. 6 is the package diagram of the MDMS. The MDMS is composed of six packages. In the diagram, rectangles indicate packages. Among the packages, bdbxml is a package for Berkeley DB XML, which adapted open APIs for the MDMS.

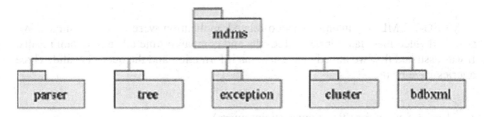

Fig. 6. Packages of MDMS

The mdms package is composed of four interfaces and five classes describing the structure of the MDMS. The DocumentManager interface is composed of objects for managing MPEG-7 documents. The SchemaManager interface is composed of objects for managing MPEG-7 schemas. The SemanticBlock interface provides functions for generating semantic blocks through schema analysis and for managing generated semantic blocks. The DbManager interface is composed of functions to communicate with Berkeley DB XML.

5.3 Storage Structure

Fig. 7 shows the structure of how MPEG-7 documents are actually stored in embedded Berkeley DB XML. Berkeley DB XML is composed of a number of containers. Each container is composed of blocks, the size of which is limited for storage, and XML documents fitting the size of the blocks are stored. MPEG-7 instance sub-trees generated with semantic blocks are clustered and stored in blocks within each container.

5.4 Comparison of MPEG-7 Document Clustering Method

This section compares the proposed MPEG-7 document clustering method with existing methods: for which we chose the Berkeley DB XML storage method and the OrientX clustering storage method that do not use a separate clustering policy.

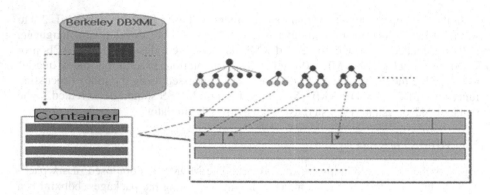

Fig. 7. Storage structure of Berkeley DB XML

MPEG-7 XML documents of video-related application were used as samples. We searched video metadata for desired results and compared time taken to obtain results. It was assumed that we already have schema information and the query is valid. Three queries were made.

1) Q1 case: Search for title of video (point query)
for $a in doc("video@MPEG7_Video.xml")//Title
  return <Video_Title> {$a}   </Video_Title>

2) Q2 case: Search for abstract information of video (join)
for $a in
doc("video@MPEG7_Video.xml")//SpatioTemporalDecomposition/MovingRegion/Te mporalDecomposition/StillRegion
 return <summary>
         {$a/MediaTimePoint}
         {for $b in $a/TextAnnotation
          return <KeyImage> $b} </KeyImage>} </summary>

3) Q3 case: Search for desired video segment meta information based on searched abstract information (ordered access query)
for $b in
doc("video@MPEG7_Video.xml")//SpatioTemporalDecomposition/MovingRegion/Te mporalDecomposition/StillRegion/
return <Summary> <title> {$b/TextAnnotation} </title>
        {for $a in
doc("video@MPEG7_Video.xml")//VideoSegment/MediaTime[MediaTimePoint = $b/MediaTimePoint] return <SegmentInfo> {$a/price}
         </SegmentInfo>} </Summary>

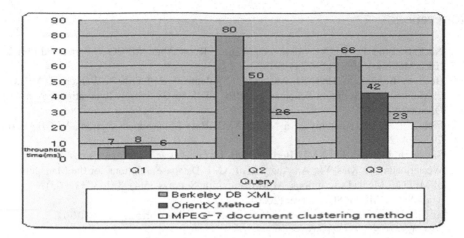

Fig. 8. Comparison of query processing time

Fig. 8 below compares the mean processing time of the methods in processing the three queries. The mean processing time was similar when retrieving specific records (Q1) but showed large differences when getting summarized information (joint operation) on videos (Q2) and finding video segments based on the summarized information (Q3).

The proposed MPEG-7 document clustering storage method expresses redefined schema in graph and forms it into a semantic block tree with relevant elements. Thus, in initial storage, it needs additional processing time for forming the semantic block tree and the time is longer when documents are complex. After storage, however, MPEG-7 document search for the corresponding media files can be done fast. In addition, frequent queries for the same media files can be processed fast.

6 Conclusions and Future Work

The present study designed and implemented a MPEG-7 document management system (MDMS) based on embedded XML DB, adopting the MPEG-7 data clustering method that can store MPEG-7 document efficiently in mobile devices.

The advantages of the proposed MDMS are as follows. First, it improves the speed of query processing by supporting clustering based on MPEG-7 schemas. Second, it is applicable to various applications by generating optimal semantic blocks for MPEG-2 applications. Third, it can manage MPEG-7 documents efficiently in mobile terminals with limited resources using the embedded XML database system.

The proposed MDMS defines the rules of generating semantic blocks in advance based on various MPEG-7 applications. However, we need generation rules more automatic and more optimal for real meanings. Thus, in order to support the generation of perfect semantic blocks, additional development is necessary for setting various R-CT attributes. That is, through research on more efficient clustering algorithms, we need to meet the needs of MPEG-7 applications that are getting more complicated and diversified.

References

1. Nack, F., Lindsay, A.: Everything You Want to Know About MPEG-7: Part 1 and Part 2. IEEE Multimedia 6(3), 65–77 (1999)
2. Beek, P., Benitez, A., Heuer, J., Martinez, J., Salembier, P., Smith, J., Walker, T.: MPEG-7: Multimedia Description Schemes, ISO/IEC FDIS 15938-5:2001. International Standard Document (2001)
3. Fiebig, T., et al.: Anatomy of a Native XML Base Management System. VLDB 11(4), 292–314 (2002)
4. Sleepycat, Berkeley DB XML, Berkeley DB, http://www.sleepycat.com
5. Westermann, U., Klas, W.: An Analysis of XML Database Solutions for the Management of MPEG-7 Media Descriptions. ACM Computing Surveys 35(4), 331–373 (2003)
6. MicroSoft, XML for SQL Server (2000),
   http://www.microsoft.com/technet/prodtechnol/sql/2000/evaluate/xmlsql.mspx
7. Oracle, Oracle 9i, http://www.oracle.com
8. Software AG, Tamino,
   http://www1.softwareag.com/corporate/products/tamino/
9. X-Hive, X-Hive/DB, http://www.x-hive.com/products/db/index.html
10. Eunjung, K.: The Design of Effective Storage Structure and Index Model in XML Document. KISC 29(2), 110–118 (2001)
11. Infonyte, Infonyte DB 3.0, http://www.infonyte.com/
12. Sleepycat, Berkeley DB, http://www.sleepycat.com/products/bdb.html
13. Kang, B.S., et al.: Design of MPEG-7 Document Storage System Based on Embedded XML DB. KMMS 8(2), 11 (2005)
14. Guillaume, A., Murtagh, F.: Clustering of XML Document. Computer Physics Communications 127, 215–227 (2000)
15. AlphaWorks, IBM MPEG-7 Annotation Tool,
   http://www.alphaworks.ibm.com/tech/videoannex

Author Index